CONTEMPORARY
AMERICAN POETRY

CONTEMPORARY AMERICAN POETRY

FIFTH EDITION

Edited by A. Poulin, Jr.

State University of New York,
College at Brockport

HOUGHTON MIFFLIN COMPANY   BOSTON
Dallas   Geneva, Illinois
Palo Alto   Princeton, New Jersey

Acknowledgments begin on page 753.

Printed in the U.S.A.

Library of Congress Catalog Card Number: 90-83001

ISBN: 0-395-43231-6

CDEFGHIJ-B-998765432

AMERICAN POETRY

Whatever it is, it must have
A stomach that can digest
Rubber, coal, uranium, moons, poems.

Like the shark, it contains a shoe.
It must swim for miles through the desert
Uttering cries that are almost human.

— Louis Simpson

Left to right: Daphne Poulin, Peter Hunzek, A. Poulin, Jr., and Basilike Poulin.

for Basilike and Daphne

Contents

A chronological listing of the poets in *Contemporary American Poetry* immediately follows this table of contents on page xxix.

CONTENTS

CONTENTS

Contemporary American Poetry: A Chronology

The following is a listing of the poets in *Contemporary American Poetry* by year of birth. Information about each poet's life and work is found in the Notes on the Poets (page 671), and the wider literary, social, and cultural context of American poetry since World War II is discussed in the essay "Contemporary American Poetry: The Radical Tradition" (page 651).

1905	Stanley Kunitz	326	1926	Robert Creeley	90
1908	Theodore Roethke	492	1926	Allen Ginsberg	174
1910	Charles Olson	438	1926	James Merrill	396
1911	Elizabeth Bishop	42	1926	Frank O'Hara	418
1913	Robert Hayden	236	1926	W. D. Snodgrass	538
1914	John Berryman	32	1927	John Ashbery	12
1914	David Ignatow	256	1927	Galway Kinnell	290
1914	Randall Jarrell	268	1927	W. S. Merwin	406
1914	William Stafford	566	1927	James Wright	640
1915	Isabella Gardner	164	1928	Donald Hall	202
1917	Gwendolyn Brooks	66	1928	Philip Levine	352
1917	Robert Lowell	376	1928	Anne Sexton	502
1919	Robert Duncan	140	1929	Adrienne Rich	476
1919	Lawrence Ferlinghetti	152	1930	Gary Snyder	554
1921	Richard Wilbur	606	1932	Sylvia Plath	462
1923	Robert Bly	56	1934	Mark Strand	586
1923	James Dickey	102	1935	Mary Oliver	428
1923	Alan Dugan	128	1935	Charles Wright	630
1923	Richard Hugo	246	1936	Lucille Clifton	78
1923	Denise Levertov	340	1936	Marge Piercy	450
1923	John Logan	362	1936	C. K. Williams	618
1923	Louis Simpson	526	1937	Marvin Bell	22
1924	Lucien Stryk	596	1938	Michael Harper	214
1925	Donald Justice	278	1938	Charles Simic	514
1925	Carolyn Kizer	304	1941	Robert Hass	224
1925	Maxine Kumin	316	1942	William Matthews	386
1925	Gerald Stern	576	1943	Louise Glück	190
1926	A. R. Ammons	2	1952	Rita Dove	116

Preface

For this Fifth Edition of *Contemporary American Poetry*, which also marks its twentieth anniversary, I have added five poets not previously included. In an effort to keep the anthology "contemporary," the new poets represent a younger generation of writers whose reputations were established from the late 1960s into the 1980s. In this edition I have also revised a few selections of poems with which I was not entirely satisfied, and added as much recent poetry as possible. Several of the poems published here have not yet been collected in individual volumes.

I have also updated and revised my general essay, "Contemporary American Poetry: The Radical Tradition" (page 651), as well as the Notes on the Poets (page 671). Because of the importance of technology in our culture and the widening availability of audiotape and videotape recordings, I have introduced selected discographies and videographies to the Notes on the Poets. The selected bibliography of postwar criticism of American poetry has been revised to reflect recent scholarship.

* * *

The fifty-six poets presented here are among those who have shaped the contours and direction of the mainstream of American poetry from World War II to the present. While achieving an individual and collective distinction all their own, they also have contributed to and expanded American poetic traditions.

Some critics may still be honing or inventing sharper tools with which to evaluate American poetry since 1945; eventually literary history may arrive at its own harsher, retrospective conclusions. However, today, for us, these poets clearly are among the major voices in contemporary American poetry. I hope this book reflects the quality of our communal experiences for almost half a century as much as it testifies to the vitality of our own American imagination and of our poetry.

My primary concern while preparing this edition was to offer an anthology at once discriminatingly representative and generously selective. Keeping that balance as the number of fine poets multiplies means, regrettably, excluding a number of distinguished writers. I've tried to select poets whose work is representative of the rich vitality and diversity of contemporary American poetry. And I've attempted to represent each poet as fully and equitably as possible, selecting works that reflect each poet's characteristic subjects, themes, and styles.

Various poets in this book share a number of characteristics, and they might have been grouped accordingly. However, I have chosen to arrange them in a simple alphabetical order. No contemporary poet belongs to one "school" exclusively; some belong to no school at all. And attempts to categorize poets in such a fashion often simply convince the discriminating

reader that so-and-so isn't just a confessional, Beat, New York, or Projecti-
vist poet. Besides, such an approach also may lead the reader to a given
set of anticipations, thereby violating the integrity of the individual poem,
the uniqueness of the individual poet, and the spontaneity of the reader's
own response. For much the same reasons, I've placed all critical appara-
tus at the back of the book, where readers may turn should they feel
uncontrollably compelled to do so.

In my essay on "The Radical Tradition," I've attempted to delineate
the major characteristics of contemporary poetry and to view it from a
critical and historical perspective, in the hope of providing readers with a
sense of how and why today's poetry is both new and a continuation of
various American literary traditions. For each poet, I've supplied a selected
bibliography of primary and secondary works (including audio and video
recordings) and a biographical and critical note sketching some of the
prominent features of the writer's work. In these notes, I've taken schools
into account now and then, but primarily I've let the poet's work — and
not any set of critical assumptions — serve as my point of departure.

Regardless of how representative and generous it may be, an anthology
is necessarily no more than an *introduction*. Indeed, the genuine measure
of this anthology's success will be the extent to which it encourages readers
to buy and read individual books by the poets represented. Thus, at the
turn of the millennium, I offer *Contemporary American Poetry* as a gathering of our communal imagination, an invitation, a door.

With each edition of this anthology I have tried to be sensitive to the
responsibility I bear as editor. I hope I have lived up to that responsibility
by offering teachers and students an intelligent and justifiable selection of
the best poetry published in this country during the past five decades.

This edition of *Contemporary American Poetry* would have been impossible without the generous cooperation of many of the poets, their
agents, and their publishers, especially in the intricate negotiations for
permission to reprint poems. I am grateful to all involved. I trust readers
will agree that the full-page photographs of the poets add a personal and
human dimension too often lacking in anthologies, and I want to thank
the photographers for supplying so many stunning photographs.

For useful reviews of the fourth edition, I want to thank Neil Berman,
United States Naval Academy; David Citino, The Ohio State University;
Toi Derricotte, University of Pittsburgh; Alan Golding, University of Lou-
isville; John Hardaway, Phoenix College (AZ); Kurt Heinzelman, The
University of Texas at Austin; John N. Miller, Denison University (OH);
Fred Moramarco, San Diego State University; Eric Pankey, Washington
University (MO); Frank Steele, Western Kentucky University; and Peter
Wood, Trenton State College (NJ).

I continue to be indebted to a long list of other individuals for their
presence, assistance, and suggestions, but in trying to name them all I

would risk overlooking too many. They should know that the absence of their names does not reflect an absence from my thoughts. However, I would be most remiss if I did not acknowledge the encouragement and suggestions I've received from Michael Waters (Salisbury State College, Maryland) over the many years of working on the last four editions of this anthology. The presence of several poets and poems in *Contemporary American Poetry* is the direct result of his judicious exhortations. I also must acknowledge the invaluable help I've received from my assistants, Rachel Piccione and Michelle Simel, and the sensitive suggestions and inestimable support I received from my editor at Houghton Mifflin . . .

. . . and you, Basilike, Daphne, Peter — spouse, daughter, son, friends, all.

A. Poulin, Jr.
December 9, 1990
Brockport, New York

CONTEMPORARY
AMERICAN POETRY

A. R. Ammons

APOLOGIA PRO VITA SUA

I started picking up the stones
throwing them into one place
and by sunrise I was going far away
for the large ones
always turning to see never lost
the cairn's height
lengthening my radial reach:

the sun watched with deep concentration
and the heap through the hours grew
and became by nightfall
distinguishable from all the miles around
of slate and sand:

during the night the wind falling
turned earthward its lofty freedom and speed
and the sharp blistering sound muffled
toward dawn and the blanket was
drawn up over a breathless face:

even so you can see in full dawn
the ground there lifts
a foreign thing desertless in origin.

HE HELD RADICAL LIGHT

He held radical light
as music in his skull: music
turned, as
over ridges immanences of evening light
rise, turned
back over the furrows of his brain
into the dark, shuddered,
shot out again
in long swaying swirls of sound:

reality had little weight in his transcendence
so he
had trouble keeping
his feet on the ground, was
terrified by that
and liked himself, and others, mostly
under roofs:
nevertheless, when the
light churned and changed

his head to music, nothing could keep him
off the mountains, his
head back, mouth working,
wrestling to say, to cut loose
from the high, unimaginable hook:
released, hidden from stars, he ate,
burped, said he was like any one
of us: demanded he
was like any one of us.

WORKING WITH TOOLS

I make a simple assertion
like a nice piece of stone
and you
alert to presence and entrance
man your pick and hammer

and by chip and deflection
distract simplicity
and cut my assertion
back to mangles, little heaps:

well, baby, that's the way
you get along: it's all right,
I understand such
ways of being afraid:
sometimes you want my come-on

hard, something to
take in and be around:

sometimes you want
a vaguer touch: I understand
and won't give assertion up.

THE UNIFYING PRINCIPLE

Ramshackles, archipelagoes, loose constellations
are less fierce, subsidiary centers, with the
attenuations of interstices, roughing the salience,

jarring the outbreak of too insistent commonalty:
a board, for example, not surrendering the rectitude
of its corners, the island of the oaks an

admonishment to pines, underfigurings (as of the Bear)
that take identity on: this motion is against
the grinding oneness of seas, hallows distinction

into the specific: but less lovely, too, for how
is the mass to be amassed, by what sanction
neighbor touch neighbor, island bear resemblance,

how are distinction's hard lines to be dissolved
(and preserved): what may all the people turn to,
the old letters, the shaped, characteristic peak

generations of minds have deflected and kept:
a particular tread that sometimes unweaves, taking
more shape on, into dance: much must be

tolerated as out of timbre, out of step, as being not
in its time or mood (the hiatus of the unconcerned)
and much room provided for the wretched to find caves

to ponder way off in: what then can lift the people
and only when they choose to rise or what can make
them want to rise, though business prevents: the

unifying principle will be a
phrase shared, an old cedar long known, general
wind-shapes in a usual sand: those objects single,

single enough to be uninterfering, multiple by
the piling on of shared sight, touch, saying:
when it's found the people live the small wraths of ease.

CUT THE GRASS

The wonderful workings of the world: wonderful,
wonderful: I'm surprised half the time:
ground up fine, I puff if a pebble stirs:

I'm nervous: my morality's intricate: if
a squash blossom dies, I feel withered as a stained
zucchini and blame my nature: and

when grassblades flop to the little red-ant
queens burring around trying to get aloft, I blame
my not keeping the grass short, stubble

firm: well, I learn a lot of useless stuff, meant
to be ignored: like when the sun sinking in the
west glares a plane invisible, I think how much

revelation concealment necessitates: and then I
think of the ocean, multiple to a blinding
oneness and realize that only total expression

expresses hiding: I'll have to say everything
to take on the roundness and withdrawal of the deep dark:
less than total is a bucketful of radiant toys.

THE CITY LIMITS

When you consider the radiance, that it does not withhold
itself but pours its abundance without selection into every
nook and cranny not overhung or hidden; when you consider

that birds' bones make no awful noise against the light but
lie low in the light as in a high testimony; when you consider
the radiance, that it will look into the guiltiest

swervings of the weaving heart and bear itself upon them,
not flinching into disguise or darkening; when you consider
the abundance of such resource as illuminates the glow-blue

bodies and gold-skeined wings of flies swarming the dumped
guts of a natural slaughter or the coil of shit and in no
way winces from its storms of generosity; when you consider

that air or vacuum, snow or shale, squid or wolf, rose or lichen,
each is accepted into as much light as it will take, then
the heart moves roomier, the man stands and looks about, the

leaf does not increase itself above the grass, and the dark
work of the deepest cells is of a tune with May bushes
and fear lit by the breadth of such calmly turns to praise.

THE ETERNAL CITY

After the explosion or cataclysm, that big
display that does its work but then fails
out with destructions, one is left with the

pieces: at first, they don't look very valuable,
but nothing sizable remnant around for
gathering the senses on, one begins to take

an interest, to sort out, to consider closely
what will do and won't, matters having become
not only small but critical: bulbs may have been

uprooted: they should be eaten, if edible, or
got back in the ground: what used to be garages,
even the splinters, should be collected for

fires: some unusually deep holes or cleared
woods may be turned to water supplies or
sudden fields: ruinage is hardly ever a

pretty sight but it must when splendor goes
accept into itself piece by piece all the old
perfect human visions, all the old perfect loves.

WHITE DWARF

As I grow older
arcs swollen inside
now and then fall
back, collapsing, into
forming walls:
the temperature shoots
up with what I am not
and am: from
multiplicities, dark
knots, twanging twists,
structures come into sight,
chief of these
a blade of fire only now
so late, so sharp and standing,
burning confusion up.

DISTRACTION

During my glorious,
crazy years, I
went about the business of
the universe relentlessly,
inquired of goat
and zygote,
frill and floss,
touched, tasted,
prodded, and tested and as
it were kept the
whole thing going
by
central attention's
central node:

now my anklebones hurt
when I stand up
or the mail truck
drops by to bury

me under two
small obligations: I
can't quite remember
what call I went to find
or why so much
fell to me: in fact,
sometimes
a whole green sunset
will wash dark
as if it could go
right by without me.

BREAKING OUT

I have let all my balloons aloose
what will become of them now
pricked they will show some weight
or caught under a cloud lack
ebullience to feel through

but they are all let loose
yellow, red, blue, thin-skinned, tough
and let go they have put me down
I was an earth thing all along
my feet are catching in the brush

EXTRICATION

I tangled with
the world to
let it go
but couldn't free

it: so I made
words
to wrestle in my
stead and went

off silent to
the quick flow
of brooks, the
slow flow of stone

VOLITIONS

The wind turned
me round and
round all day, so
cold it planed
me, quick it

polished me
down: a spindle
by dusk,
too lean to
bear the open dark,

I said, sky,
drive me
into the
ground here,
still me with the ground.

CHISELED CLOUDS

A single
cemetery
wipes out
most
of my
people,
skinny old
slabs
leaning this
way
and that

as
in stray
winds,
holding names:

still, enough
silver
cathedrals fill
this
afternoon sky
to
house everyone
ever
lost from
the
light's returning.

LOFT

A sheet of shale chips
loose on my porch stoop
and its three hundred

million years, disrupted,
rise like plain ice-air
around me, thinning

the present time:
I spin the sheet
sheer in a long arc

to the yard's shrub bank:
the grain splinters and,
reentering,

sinks toward the foundation
of its next three
hundred million years.

John Ashbery

SOME TREES

These are amazing: each
Joining a neighbor, as though speech
Were a still performance.
Arranging by chance

To meet as far this morning
From the world as agreeing
With it, you and I
Are suddenly what the trees try

To tell us we are:
That their merely being there
Means something; that soon
We may touch, love, explain.

And glad not to have invented
Such comeliness, we are surrounded:
A silence already filled with noises,
A canvas on which emerges

A chorus of smiles, a winter morning.
Placed in a puzzling light, and moving,
Our days put on such reticence
These accents seem their own defense.

"THEY DREAM ONLY OF AMERICA"

They dream only of America
To be lost among the thirteen million pillars of grass:
"This honey is delicious
Though it burns the throat."

And hiding from darkness in barns
They can be grownups now
And the murderer's ash tray is more easily —
The lake a lilac cube.

He holds a key in his right hand.
"Please," he asked willingly.
He is thirty years old.
That was before

We could drive hundreds of miles
At night through dandelions.
When his headache grew worse we
Stopped at a wire filling station.

Now he cared only about signs.
Was the cigar a sign?
And what about the key?
He went slowly into the bedroom.

"I would not have broken my leg if I had not fallen
Against the living room table. What is it to be back
Beside the bed? There is nothing to do
For our liberation, except wait in the horror of it.

And I am lost without you."

LEAVING THE ATOCHA STATION

The arctic honey blabbed over the report causing darkness
And pulling us out of there experiencing it
he meanwhile . . .   And the fried bats they sell there
dropping from sticks, so that the menace of your prayer folds . . .
Other people . . .   flash
the garden are you boning
and defunct covering . . .   Blind dog expressed royalties . . .
comfort of your perfect tar grams nuclear world bank tulip
Favorable to   near the night pin
loading formaldehyde.   the table torn from you
Suddenly   and we are close
Mouthing the root   when you think
generator   homes enjoy leered

The worn stool blazing   pigeons from the roof
                driving tractor to squash
Leaving the Atocha Station   steel

infected bumps the screws
    everywhere   wells
abolished top ill-lit
scarecrow falls   Time, progress and good sense
strike of shopkeepers dark blood
no forest you can name drunk scrolls
the completely new Italian hair . . .
Baby . . .   ice falling off the port
The centennial   Before we can

           old   eat
members with their chins
         so high up   rats
   relaxing the cruel discussion
  suds   the painted corners
white   most aerial
     garment crow
              and when the region took us back
the person left us like birds
  it was fuzz on the passing light
over disgusted heads, far into amnesiac
permanent house depot   amounts he can
       decrepit mayor . . .   exalting flea
for that we turn around
experiencing it is not to go into
the epileptic prank forcing bar
to borrow out onto tide-exposed fells
over her morsel, she chasing you
and the revenge he'd get
establishing the vultural over
rural area cough protection
murdering quintet. Air pollution terminal
the clean fart genital enthusiastic toe prick album serious evening flames
the lake over your hold   personality
     lightened . . .   roar
You are freed
    including barrels
head of the swan   forestry
the night and stars fork
That is, he said
   and rushing under the hoops of
equations probable
    absolute mush   the right
entity   chain store   sewer opened their books

The flood dragged you
    I coughed to the window
last month: juice, earlier
like the slacks   to be declining
    the peaches   more
  fist
sprung expecting the cattle
false loam   imports
          next time around

DEFINITION OF BLUE

The rise of capitalism parallels the advance of romanticism
And the individual is dominant until the close of the nineteenth century.
In our own time, mass practices have sought to submerge the personality
By ignoring it, which has caused it instead to branch out in all directions
Far from the permanent tug that used to be its notion of "home."
These different impetuses are received from everywhere
And are as instantly snapped back, hitting through the cold atmosphere
In one steady, intense line.

There is no remedy for this "packaging" which has supplanted the old
    sensations.
Formerly there would have been architectural screens at the point where
    the action became most difficult
As a path trails off into shrubbery — confusing, forgotten, yet continuing
    to exist.
But today there is no point in looking to imaginative new methods
Since all of them are in constant use. The most that can be said for them
    further
Is that erosion produces a kind of dust or exaggerated pumice
Which fills space and transforms it, becoming a medium
In which it is possible to recognize oneself.

Each new diversion adds its accurate touch to the ensemble, and so
A portrait, smooth as glass, is built up out of multiple corrections
And it has no relation to the space or time in which it was lived.
Only its existence is a part of all being, and is therefore, I suppose, to be
    prized
Beyond chasms of night that fight us
By being hidden and present.
And yet it results in a downward motion, or rather a floating one

JOHN ASHBERY

In which the blue surroundings drift slowly up and past you
To realize themselves some day, while, you, in this nether world that
    could not be better
Waken each morning to the exact value of what you did and said, which
    remains.

AS YOU CAME FROM THE HOLY LAND

of western New York state
were the graves all right in their bushings
was there a note of panic in the late August air
because the old man had peed in his pants again
was there turning away from the late afternoon glare
as though it too could be wished away
was any of this present
and how could this be
the magic solution to what you are in now
whatever has held you motionless
like this so long through the dark season
until now the women come out in navy blue
and the worms come out of the compost to die
it is the end of any season

you reading there so accurately
sitting not wanting to be disturbed
as you came from that holy land
what other signs of earth's dependency were upon you
what fixed sign at the crossroads
what lethargy in the avenues
where all is said in a whisper
what tone of voice among the hedges
what tone under the apple trees
the numbered land stretches away
and your house is built in tomorrow
but surely not before the examination
of what is right and will befall
not before the census
and the writing down of names

remember you are free to wander away
as from other times other scenes that were taking place

the history of someone who came too late
the time is ripe now and the adage
is hatching as the seasons change and tremble
it is finally as though that thing of monstrous interest
were happening in the sky
but the sun is setting and prevents you from seeing it

out of night the token emerges
its leaves like birds alighting all at once under a tree
taken up and shaken again
put down in weak rage
knowing as the brain does it can never come about
not here not yesterday in the past
only in the gap of today filling itself
as emptiness is distributed
in the idea of what time it is
when that time is already past

STREET MUSICIANS

One died, and the soul was wrenched out
Of the other in life, who, walking the streets
Wrapped in an identity like a coat, sees on and on
The same corners, volumetrics, shadows
Under trees. Farther than anyone was ever
Called, through increasingly suburban airs
And ways, with autumn falling over everything:
The plush leaves the chattels in barrels
Of an obscure family being evicted
Into the way it was, and is. The other beached
Glimpses of what the other was up to:
Revelations at last. So they grew to hate and forget each other.

So I cradle this average violin that knows
Only forgotten showtunes, but argues
The possibility of free declamation anchored
To a dull refrain, the year turning over on itself
In November, with the spaces among the days
More literal, the meat more visible on the bone.
Our question of a place of origin hangs
Like smoke: how we picnicked in pine forests,

JOHN ASHBERY

In coves with the water always seeping up, and left
Our trash, sperm and excrement everywhere, smeared
On the landscape, to make of us what we could.

PARADOXES AND OXYMORONS

This poem is concerned with language on a very plain level.
Look at it talking to you. You look out a window
Or pretend to fidget. You have it but you don't have it.
You miss it, it misses you. You miss each other.

The poem is sad because it wants to be yours, and cannot.
What's a plain level? It is that and other things,
Bringing a system of them into play. Play?
Well, actually, yes, but I consider play to be

A deeper outside thing, a dreamed role-pattern,
As in the division of grace these long August days
Without proof. Open-ended. And before you know
It gets lost in the stream and chatter of typewriters.

It has been played once more. I think you exist only
To tease me into doing it, on your level, and then you aren't there
Or have adopted a different attitude. And the poem
Has set me softly down beside you. The poem is you.

ONE COAT OF PAINT

We will all have to just hang on for a while,
It seems, now. This could mean "early retirement"
For some, if only for an afternoon of pottering around
Buying shoelaces and the like. Or it could mean a spell
In some enchanter's cave, after several centuries of which
You wake up curiously refreshed, eager to get back
To the crossword puzzle, only no one knows your name
Or who you are, really, or cares much either. To seduce
A fact into becoming an object, a pleasing one, with some
Kind of esthetic quality, which would also add to the store

Of knowledge and even extend through several strata
Of history, like a pin through a cracked wrist bone,
Connecting these in such a dynamic way that one would be forced
To acknowledge a new kind of superiority without which the world
Could no longer conduct its business, even simple stuff like bringing
Water home from wells, coals to hearths, would of course be
An optimal form of it but in any case the thing's got to
Come into being, something has to happen, or all
We'll have left is disagreements, *désagréments*, to name a few.
O don't you see how necessary it is to be around,
To be ferried from here to that near, smiling shore
And back again into the arms of those that love us,
Not many, but of such infinite, superior sweetness
That their lie is for us and it becomes stained, encrusted,
Finally gilded in some exasperating way that turns it
To a truth plus something, delicate and dismal as a star,
Cautious as a drop of milk, so that they let us
Get away with it, some do at any rate?

VETIVER

Ages passed slowly, like a load of hay,
As the flowers recited their lines
And pike stirred at the bottom of the pond.
The pen was cool to the touch.
The staircase swept upward
Through fragmented garlands, keeping the melancholy
Already distilled in letters of the alphabet.

It would be time for winter now, its spun-sugar
Palaces and also lines of care
At the mouth, pink smudges on the forehead and cheeks,
The color once known as "ashes of roses."
How many snakes and lizards shed their skins
For time to be passing on like this,
Sinking deeper in the sand as it wound toward
The conclusion. It had all been working so well and now,
Well, it just kind of came apart in the hand
As a change is voiced, sharp
As a fishhook in the throat, and decorative tears flowed
Past us into a basin called infinity.

There was no charge for anything, the gates
Had been left open intentionally.
Don't follow, you can have whatever it is.
And in some room someone examines his youth,
Finds it dry and hollow, porous to the touch.
O keep me with you, unless the outdoors
Embraces both of us, unites us, unless
The birdcatchers put away their twigs,
The fishermen haul in their sleek empty nets
And others become part of the immense crowd
Around this bonfire, a situation
That has come to mean us to us, and the crying
In the leaves is saved, the last silver drops.

POSTURE OF UNEASE

It all seems like dirt now.
There is a film of dust on the lucid morning
Of an autumn landscape, that must be worse
Where it's tightening up,
Where not everything has its own two feet to stand on.

It gets more and more simplistic:
Good and bad, evil and bad; what else do we know?
Flavors that keep us from caring too long.

But there was that train of thought
That satisfied one nicely: how one was going to climb down
Out of here, hopefully
To arrive on a perfectly flat spit of sand
Level with the water.

And everything would look new and worn again.
Suddenly, a shout, a convincing one.
People in twos and threes turn up, and
There's more to it than that.

But for all you I
Have neglected, ignored,
Left to stew in your own juices,
Not been that friend that is approaching,
I ask forgiveness, a song new like rain.
Please sing it to me.

Marvin Bell

WHITE CLOVER

Once when the moon was out about three-quarters
and the fireflies who are the stars
of backyards
were out about three-quarters
and about three-fourths of all the lights
in the neighborhood
were on because people can be at home,
I took a not so innocent walk
out among the lawns,
navigating by the light of lights,
and there there were many hundreds of moons
on the lawns
where before there was only polite grass.
These were moons on long stems,
their long stems giving their greenness
to the center of each flower
and the light giving its whiteness to the tops
of the petals. I could say
it was light from stars
touched the tops of flowers and no doubt
something heavenly reaches what grows outdoors
and the heads of men who go hatless,
but I like to think we have a world
right here, and a life
that isn't death. So I don't say it's better
to be right here. I say this is where
many hundreds of core-green moons
gigantic to my eye
rose because men and women had sown green grass,
and flowered to my eye in man-made light,
and to some would be as fire in the body
and to others a light in the mind
over all their property.

THE EXTERMINATION OF THE JEWS

to Donald Justice

A thousand years from now
they will be remembered as heroes.
A thousand years from now
they will still be promised their past.

Objects of beauty notwithstanding,
once more they will appear
for their ruin, seeking a purse,
hard bread or a heavy weapon

for those who must survive,
but no one shall survive.
We who have not forgotten,
our children shall outremember:

their victims' pious chanting —
last wishes, last Yiddish, last dreaming —
were defeats with which the Gestapo
continues ceasing and ceasing.

from THE ESCAPE INTO YOU

Homage to the Runner

The form of this "sport" is pain,
riding up into it, he hurts to win.
These are the moments when death is really
possible, when a man can fit into
his enlarged heart all that is known
or was or shall be pumping fulfills.

The love of form is a black occasion
through which some light must show
in a hundred years of commitment.
By the time the body aches to end it,
the poem begins, at first in darkness,
surrounded by counterfeits of leisure.

Run away. Leave them to ease.
What does it matter you wind up alone?
There is no finish; you can stop for no one.
When your wife cries, you pass a kiss.
When your sons worry, you flash a smile.
When your women wave, you ignore them.

TO DOROTHY

You are not beautiful, exactly.
You are beautiful, inexactly.
You let a weed grow by the mulberry
and a mulberry grow by the house.
So close, in the personal quiet
of a windy night, it brushes the wall
and sweeps away the day till we sleep.

A child said it, and it seemed true:
"Things that are lost are all equal."
But it isn't true. If I lost you,
the air wouldn't move, nor the tree grow.
Someone would pull the weed, my flower.
The quiet wouldn't be yours. If I lost you,
I'd have to ask the grass to let me sleep.

DURING THE WAR

I was one of those who sees something cross the moon
and is never again the same person.
I was one of those who fought for an envelope, for a stamp.
I was one who felt the pain of the potted plant
and the loneliness of the tree.

It was all in my mind. It was an idea I had!
Was it such a bad idea?
Did it hurt anyone? Did it even delay for a minute
a father thousands of miles from me
fleeing a tank from my own beloved country?

Did it hasten the deaths by bombing?
Did it quicken the suffering of the homeless?

Certainly not. Absolutely, unequivocally, the answer is No.
My love for the tree did not interfere
with one decision of a committee, one staff meeting.
My joining forces with the mysterious
did not blot a single marching order, nor break a rifle.

The world went on without me. To its mind,
I was no part of it, but to my mind I was too much a part.
I put it all down on paper but in code.
Even at night, I watched the skies like a spy
for the intersection of a planet and the future.

THE LAST THING I SAY

to a thirteen-year-old sleeping,
tone of an angel, breath of a soft wing,
I say through an upright dark space
as I narrow it pulling the door
sleepily to let the words go surely into
the bedroom until I close them in
for good, a nightwatchman's-worth
of grace and a promise for morning
not so far from some God's first notion
that the world be an image by first light
so much better than pictures of hope
drawn by firelight in ashes,
so much clearer too, a young person
wanting to be a man might draw one finger
along an edge of this world and it
would slice a mouth there
to speak blood and then should he put that wound
into the mouth of his face,
he will be kissed there and taste
the salt of his father as he lowers
himself from his son's high bedroom
in the heaven of his image of
a small part of himself and sweet dreams.

DRAWN BY STONES, BY EARTH,
BY THINGS THAT HAVE BEEN IN THE FIRE

I can tell you about this because I have held in my hand
the little potter's sponge called an "elephant ear."
Naturally, it's only a tiny version of an ear,
but it's the thing you want to pick up out of the toolbox
when you wander into the deserted ceramics shop
down the street from the cave where the fortune-teller works.
Drawn by stones, by earth, by things that have been in the fire.

The elephant ear listens to the side of the vase
as it is pulled upwards from a dome of muddy clay.
The ear listens to the outside wall of the pot
and the hand listens to the inside wall of the pot,
and between them a city rises out of dirt and water.
Inside this city live the remains of animals,
animals who prepared for two hundred years to be clay.

Rodents make clay, and men wearing spectacles make clay,
though the papers they were signing go up in flames
and nothing more is known of these long documents
except by those angels who divine in our ashes.
Kings and queens of the jungle make clay
and royalty and politicians make clay although
their innocence stays with their clothes until unravelled.

There is a lost soldier in every ceramic bowl.
The face on the dinner plate breaks when the dish does
and lies for centuries unassembled in the soil.
These things that have the right substance to begin with,
put into the fire at temperatures that melt glass,
keep their fingerprints forever, it is said,
like inky sponges that walk away in the deep water.

THEY

My destiny has been to prune one tree
to make it look more and more common.
Friends, I am still at it.

MARVIN BELL

It has been suggested
that I permit myself to be tattooed all over
and become, myself, a tree. Stick my arms out.

But that wouldn't be me. Nor would there be,
afterwards, as there is now,
the object of my desire

in the form of my desire unveiling.
What do they think this is all about?
Nothing was known before I came to know it.

The purpose of a tree is that I have given it:
to be the same result of chaos,
to be so completely known it may be overlooked.

LONG ISLAND

The things I did, I did because of trees,
wildflowers and weeds, because of ocean and sand,
because the dunes move about under houses built on stilts,
and the wet fish slip between your hands back into the sea,
because during the War we heard strafing across the Bay
and after the War we found shell casings with our feet.
Because old tires ringed the boat docks,
and sandbags hung from the prows of speedboats,
and every road in every country ends at the water,
and because a child thinks each room in his house big,
and if the truth be admitted, his first art galleries
were the wallpaper in his bedroom and the carlights
warming the night air as he lay in bed counting.

The things I did, I counted in wattage and ohms,
in the twelve zones that go from pure black to pure white,
in the length of the trumpet and the curves of the cornet,
in the cup of the mouthpiece. In the compass and protractor,
in the perfect bevelled ruler, in abstract geometry,
and if the truth be known, in the bowing of cattails
he first read his Heraclitus and in the stretching box turtle
he found his theory of relativity and the gist of knowledge.

He did what he did. The action of his knee in walking
was not different from the over-stretching of an ocean wave,
and the proofs of triangles, cones and parallelograms
were neither more nor less than the beauty of a fast horse
which runs through the numbers of the stopwatch and past the finish.

The things I counted, I counted beyond the finish,
beyond rolling tar roadways that squared the fields,
where I spun on the ice, wavered in fog, sped up or idled,
and, like Perry, like Marco Polo, a young man I saw
alone walk unlit paths, encircled by rushes
and angry dogs, to the indentations of his island.
And if the truth be told, he learned of Columbus,
of Einstein, of Michelangelo, on such low roads and local waters.
Weakfish hauled weakening from the waters at night,
and the crab rowing into the light, told him in their way
that the earth moved around the sun in the same way,
with the branched mud-print of a duck's foot to read,
and life in the upturned bellies of the fishkill in the creek.

HOW HE GREW UP

He found the corner of town where the last street
bent, and outdoor lights went down a block
or so and no more. In the long list of states
and their products, there was bauxite, rope,
fire engines, shoes, even a prison, but not one
was famous for purposeless streets and late
walks. Often he missed the truth of lists
while gone for a walk, with most lights out
all over town, and no one told him, when he
returned, the ten things it was best to, or
the dozen it was better not to. He knew
the window would be lit most of the night
down at the camera shop, and the gentle
librarian would keep the house of books open
if he stopped by at closing. Up the street he went,
leaving the lamps, each night until he met
the smell of the bay, a fact to be borne home
to sleep, certain of another day. The houses of

friends were dark. He never told, in those days.
Something was missing from the lists of
best and how to and whose town did what.
He figured, when no other was mentioned,
it might be his town at the top of some list:
but it was hard to read things on paper
in the bony moonlight. So he never knew.
People ask him all the time to have been
where what happened happened, that made
the news, but usually the big things happened
while he was out walking: the War, the War, etc.

IF I HAD ONE THING TO SAY

I see words effaced in the footprints of the conquered,
slowly sinking into the earth in a round sort
of way, indirect, like sunlight at night, and I see
the speeches of the conquerors preserved on paper,
hurried to a lead mine in the mountains and buried
deeper than atomic mushrooms, insulated
from firestorm and radiation and residue even if
the world has to wait ten thousand years for Adam.

I see grass growing rapidly in those footprints,
and the earth curving in space, and the lean of all
that holds on, from the laughter of the lone coyote
high up in the night to the wishbone of the kill,
hung head down to drain and every part used
and remembered as long as song, deep as prayer,
with the words handed down through centuries
of naming and telling and there's always another Adam.

I see dust made of the fibers of grass, of paper,
from the rubbings of the dirt, the pumice of dead bone,
from the cells of our skin migrating to the surface,
and I see that the dust will never settle, neither
in time nor space, but in the rain of a thousand centuries
many things clear now to us — impulses at the core —
may come to rest in the form of a thought, and this
may be the way it is already: the way it was for Adam.

ENDING WITH A LINE FROM LEAR

I will try to remember. It was light.
It was also dark, in the grave. I could feel
how dark it was, how black it would be
without my father. When he was gone.
But he was not gone, not yet. He was only
a corpse, and I could still touch him
that afternoon. Earlier the same afternoon.
This is the one thing that scares me:
losing my father. I don't want him to go.
I am a young man. I will never be older.
I am wearing a tie and a watch. The sky,
gray, hangs over everything. Today
the sky has no curve to it, and no end.
He is deep into his mission. He has business
to attend to. He wears a tie but no watch.
I will skip a lot of what happens next.
Then the moment comes. Everything, everything
has been said, and the wheels start to turn.
They roll, the straps unwind, and the coffin
begins to descend. Into the awful damp.
Into the black center of the earth. I
am being left behind. The center of my body
sinks down into the cold fire of the grave.
But still my feet stand on top of the dirt.
My father's grave. I will never again.
Never. Never. Never. Never. Never.

John Berryman

THE SONG OF THE TORTURED GIRL

After a little I could not have told —
But no one asked me this — why I was there.
I asked. The ceiling of that place was high
And there were sudden noises, which I made.
I must have stayed there a long time today:
My cup of soup was gone when they brought me back.

Often "Nothing worse now can come to us"
I thought, the winter the young men stayed away,
My uncle died, and mother broke her crutch.
And then the strange room where the brightest light
Does not shine on the strange men: shines on me.
I feel them stretch my youth and throw a switch.

Through leafless branches the sweet wind blows
Making a mild sound, softer than a moan;
High in a pass once where we put our tent,
Minutes I lay awake to hear my joy.
— I no longer remember what they want.
Minutes I lay awake to hear my joy.

from THE DREAM SONGS

1

Huffy Henry hid   the day,
unappeasable Henry sulked.
I see his point, — a trying to put things over.
It was the thought that they thought
they could *do* it made Henry wicked & away.
But he should have come out and talked.

All the world like a woolen lover
once did seem on Henry's side.
Then came a departure.
Thereafter nothing fell out as it might or ought.

I don't see how Henry, pried
open for all the world to see, survived.

What he has now to say is a long
wonder the world can bear & be.
Once in a sycamore I was glad
all at the top, and I sang.
Hard on the land wears the strong sea
and empty grows every bed.

4

Filling her compact & delicious body
with chicken páprika, she glanced at me
twice.
Fainting with interest, I hungered back
and only the fact of her husband & four other people
kept me from springing on her

or falling at her little feet and crying
'You are the hottest one for years of night
Henry's dazed eyes
have enjoyed, Brilliance.' I advanced upon
(despairing) my spumoni. — Sir Bones: is stuffed,
de world, wif feeding girls.

— Black hair, complexion Latin, jewelled eyes
downcast . . . The slob beside her   feasts . . . What wonders is
she sitting on, over there?
The restaurant buzzes. She might as well be on Mars.
Where did it all go wrong? There ought to be a law against Henry.
— Mr. Bones: there is.

8

The weather was fine. They took away his teeth,
white & helpful; bothered his backhand;
halved his green hair.
They blew out his loves, his interests. 'Underneath,'
(they called in iron voices) 'understand,
is nothing. So there.'

The weather was very fine. They lifted off
his covers till he showed, and cringed & pled
to see himself less.
They installed mirrors till he flowed. 'Enough'
(murmured they) 'if you will watch Us instead,
yet you may saved be. Yes.'

The weather fleured. They weakened all his eyes,
and burning thumbs into his ears, and shook
his hand like a notch.
They flung long silent speeches. (Off the hook!)
They sandpapered his plumpest hope. (So capsize.)
They took away his crotch.

9

Deprived of his enemy, shrugged to a standstill
horrible Henry, foaming. Fan their way
toward him who will
in the high wood: the officers, their rest,
with p.a. echoing: his girl comes, say,
conned in to test

if he's still human, see: she love him, see,
therefore she get on the Sheriff's mike & howl
'Come down, come down'.
Therefore he un-budge, furious. He'd flee
but only Heaven hangs over him foul.
At the crossways, downtown,

he dreams the folks are buying parsnips & suds
and paying rent to foes. He slipt & fell.
It's golden here in the snow.
A mild crack: a far rifle. Bogart's duds
truck back to Wardrobe. Fancy the brain from hell
held out so long. Let go.

13

God bless Henry. He lived like a rat,
with a thatch of hair on his head
in the beginning.

Henry was not a coward. Much.
He never deserted anything; instead
he stuck, when things like pity were thinning.

So may be Henry was a human being.
Let's investigate that.
. . . We did; okay.
He is a human American man.
That's true. My lass is braking.
My brass is aching. Come & diminish me, & map my way.

God's Henry's enemy. We're in business . . . Why,
what business must be clear.
A cornering.
I couldn't feel more like it. — Mr Bones,
as I look on the saffron sky,
you strikes me as ornery.

14

Life, friends, is boring. We must not say so.
After all, the sky flashes, the great sea yearns,
we ourselves flash and yearn,
and moreover my mother told me as a boy
(repeatingly) 'Ever to confess you're bored
means you have no

Inner Resources.' I conclude now I have no
inner resources, because I am heavy bored.
Peoples bore me,
literature bores me, especially great literature,
Henry bores me, with his plights & gripes
as bad as achilles,

who loves people and valiant art, which bores me.
And the tranquil hills, & gin, look like a drag
and somehow a dog
has taken itself & its tail considerably away
into mountains or sea or sky, leaving
behind: me, wag.

29

There sat down, once, a thing on Henry's heart
só heavy, if he had a hundred years
& more, & weeping, sleepless, in all them time
Henry could not make good.
Starts again always in Henry's ears
the little cough somewhere, an odour, a chime.

And there is another thing he has in mind
like a grave Sienese face a thousand years
would fail to blur the still profiled reproach of. Ghastly,
with open eyes, he attends, blind.
All the bells say: too late. This is not for tears;
thinking.

But never did Henry, as he thought he did,
end anyone and hacks her body up
and hide the pieces, where they may be found.
He knows: he went over everyone, & nobody's missing.
Often he reckons, in the dawn, them up.
Nobody is ever missing.

45

He stared at ruin. Ruin stared straight back.
He thought they was old friends. He felt on the stair
where her papa found them bare
they became familiar. When the papers were lost
rich with pals' secrets, he thought he had the knack
of ruin. Their paths crossed

and once they crossed in jail; they crossed in bed;
and over an unsigned letter their eyes met,
and in an Asian city
directionless & lurchy at two & three,
or trembling to a telephone's fresh threat,
and when some wired his head

to reach a wrong opinion, 'Epileptic'.
But he noted now that: they were not old friends.

He did not know this one.
This one was a stranger, come to make amends
for all the imposters, and to make it stick.
Henry nodded, un-.

46

I am, outside. Incredible panic rules.
People are blowing and beating each other without mercy.
Drinks are boiling. Iced
drinks are boiling. The worse anyone feels, the worse
treated he is. Fools elect fools.
A harmless man at an intersection said, under his breath: "Christ!"

That word, so spoken, affected the vision
of, when they trod to work next day, shopkeepers
who went & were fitted for glasses.
Enjoyed they then an appearance of love & law.
Millenia whift & waft — one, one — er, er . . .
Their glasses were taken from them, & they saw.

Man has undertaken the top job of all,
son fin. Good luck.
I myself walked at the funeral of tenderness.
Followed other deaths. Among the last,
like the memory of a lovely fuck,
was: *Do, ut des.*

55

Peter's not friendly. He gives me sideways looks.
The architecture is far from reassuring.
I feel uneasy.
A pity, — the interview began so well:
I mentioned fiendish things, he waved them away
and sloshed out a martini

strangely needed. We spoke of indifferent matters —
God's health, the vague hell of the Congo,
John's energy,

anti-matter matter. I felt fine.
Then a change came backward. A chill fell.
Talk slackened,

died, and he began to give me sideways looks.
'Christ,' I thought 'what now?' and would have askt for another
but didn't dare.
I feel my application   failing. It's growing dark,
some other sound is overcoming. His last words are:
'We betrayed me.'

230

There are voices, voices. Light's dying. Birds have quit.
He lied about me, months ago. His friendly wit
now slid to apology.
I am sorry that senior genius remembered it.
I am nothing, to occupy his thought
one moment. We

went at his bidding to his cabin, three,
in two bodies; and he spoke like Jove.
I sat there full of love,
salt with attention, while his jokes like nods
pierced for us our most strange history. He
seemed to be in charge of the odds:

hurrah. Three. Three. I must remember that.
I love great men I love. Nobody's great.
I must remember that.
We all fight. Having fought better than the rest,
he sings, & mutters & prophesies in the West
and is our flunked test.

I always come in prostrate; Yeats & Frost.

384

The marker slants, flowerless, day's almost done,
I stand above my father's grave with rage,

often, often before
I've made this awful pilgrimage to one
who cannot visit me, who tore his page
out: I come back for more,

I spit upon this dreadful banker's grave
who shot his heart out in a Florida dawn
O ho alas alas
When will indifference come, I moan & rave
I'd like to scrabble till I got right down
away down under the grass

and ax the casket open ha to see
just how he's taking it, which he sought so hard
we'll tear apart
the mouldering grave clothes ha & then Henry
will heft the ax once more, his final card,
and fell it on the start.

from ELEVEN ADDRESSES TO THE LORD

1

Master of beauty, craftsman of the snowflake,
inimitable contriver,
endower of Earth so gorgeous & different from the boring Moon,
thank you for such as it is my gift.

I have made up a morning prayer to you
containing with precision everything that most matters.
'According to Thy will' the thing begins.
It took me off & on two days. It does not aim at eloquence.

You have come to my rescue again & again
in my impassable, sometimes despairing years.
You have allowed my brilliant friends to destroy themselves
and I am still here, severely damaged, but functioning.

Unknowable, as I am unknown to my guinea pigs:
how can I 'love' you?
I only as far as gratitude & awe
confidently & absolutely go.

I have no idea whether we live again.
It doesn't seem likely
from either the scientific or the philosophical point of view
but certainly all things are possible to you,

and I believe as fixedly in the Resurrection-appearances to Peter & to Paul
as I believe I sit in this blue chair.
Only that may have been a special case
to establish their initiatory faith.

Whatever your end may be, accept my amazement.
May I stand until death forever at attention
for any your least instruction or enlightenment.
I even feel sure you will assist me again, Master of insight & beauty.

HENRY'S UNDERSTANDING

He was reading late, at Richard's, down in Maine,
aged 32? Richard & Helen long in bed,
my good wife long in bed.
All I had to do was strip & get into my bed,
putting the marker in the book, & sleep,
& wake to a hot breakfast.

Off the coast was an island, P'tit Manaan,
the bluff from Richard's lawn was almost sheer.
A chill at four o'clock.
It only takes a few minutes to make a man.
A concentration upon now & here.
Suddenly, unlike Bach,

& horribly, unlike Bach, it occurred to me
that *one* night, instead of warm pajamas,
I'd take off all my clothes
& cross the damp cold lawn & down the bluff
into the terrible water & walk forever
under it out toward the island.

Elizabeth Bishop

THE MAN-MOTH*

Here, above,
cracks in the buildings are filled with battered moonlight.
The whole shadow of Man is only as big as his hat.
It lies at his feet like a circle for a doll to stand on,
and he makes an inverted pin, the point magnetized to the moon.
He does not see the moon; he observes only her vast properties,
feeling the queer light on his hands, neither warm nor cold,
of a temperature impossible to record in thermometers.

But when the Man-Moth
pays his rare, although occasional, visits to the surface,
the moon looks rather different to him. He emerges
from an opening under the edge of one of the sidewalks
and nervously begins to scale the faces of the buildings.
He thinks the moon is a small hole at the top of the sky,
proving the sky quite useless for protection.
He trembles, but must investigate as high as he can climb.

Up the façades,
his shadow dragging like a photographer's cloth behind him,
he climbs fearfully, thinking that this time he will manage
to push his small head through that round clean opening
and be forced through, as from a tube, in black scrolls on the light.
(Man, standing below him, has no such illusions.)
But what the Man-Moth fears most he must do, although
he fails, of course, and falls back scared but quite unhurt.

Then he returns
to the pale subways of cement he calls his home. He flits,
he flutters, and cannot get aboard the silent trains
fast enough to suit him. The doors close swiftly.
The Man-Moth always seats himself facing the wrong way
and the train starts at once at its full, terrible speed,
without a shift in gears or a gradation of any sort.
He cannot tell the rate at which he travels backwards.

* Newspaper misprint for "mammoth."

43

Each night he must
be carried through artificial tunnels and dream recurrent dreams.
Just as the ties recur beneath his train, these underlie
his rushing brain. He does not dare look out the window,
for the third rail, the unbroken draught of poison,
runs there beside him. He regards it as a disease
he has inherited the susceptibility to. He has to keep
his hands in his pockets, as others must wear mufflers.

If you catch him,
hold up a flashlight to his eye. It's all dark pupil,
an entire night itself, whose haired horizon tightens
as he stares back, and closes up the eye. Then from the lids
one tear, his only possession, like the bee's sting, slips.
Slyly he palms it, and if you're not paying attention
he'll swallow it. However, if you watch, he'll hand it over,
cool as from underground springs and pure enough to drink.

THE FISH

I caught a tremendous fish
and held him beside the boat
half out of water, with my hook
fast in a corner of his mouth.
He didn't fight.
He hadn't fought at all.
He hung a grunting weight,
battered and venerable
and homely. Here and there
his brown skin hung in strips
like ancient wallpaper,
and its pattern of darker brown
was like wallpaper:
shapes like full-blown roses
stained and lost through age.
He was speckled with barnacles,
fine rosettes of lime,
and infested
with tiny white sea-lice,
and underneath two or three
rags of green weed hung down.
While his gills were breathing in

the terrible oxygen
— the frightening gills,
fresh and crisp with blood,
that can cut so badly —
I thought of the coarse white flesh
packed in like feathers,
the big bones and the little bones,
the dramatic reds and blacks
of his shiny entrails,
and the pink swim-bladder
like a pig peony.
I looked into his eyes
which were far larger than mine
but shallower, and yellowed,
the irises backed and packed
with tarnished tinfoil
seen through the lenses
of old scratched isinglass.
They shifted a little, but not
to return my stare.
— It was more like the tipping
of an object toward the light.
I admired his sullen face,
the mechanism of his jaw,
and then I saw
that from his lower lip
— if you could call it a lip —
grim, wet, and weaponlike,
hung five old pieces of fish-line,
or four and a wire leader
with the swivel still attached,
with all their five big hooks
grown firmly in his mouth.
A green line, frayed at the end
where he broke it, two heavier lines,
and a fine black thread
still crimped from the strain and snap
when it broke and he got away.
Like medals with their ribbons
frayed and wavering,
a five-haired beard of wisdom
trailing from his aching jaw.
I stared and stared
and victory filled up
the little rented boat,

from the pool of bilge
where oil had spread a rainbow
around the rusted engine
to the bailer rusted orange,
the sun-cracked thwarts,
the oarlocks on their strings,
the gunnels — until everything
was rainbow, rainbow, rainbow!
And I let the fish go.

THE ARMADILLO

for Robert Lowell

This is the time of year
when almost every night
the frail, illegal fire balloons appear.
Climbing the mountain height,

rising toward a saint
still honored in these parts,
the paper chambers flush and fill with light
that comes and goes, like hearts.

Once up against the sky it's hard
to tell them from the stars —
planets, that is — the tinted ones:
Venus going down, or Mars,

or the pale green one. With a wind,
they flare and falter, wobble and toss;
but if it's still they steer between
the kite sticks of the Southern Cross,

receding, dwindling, solemnly
and steadily forsaking us,
or, in the downdraft from a peak,
suddenly turning dangerous.

Last night another big one fell.
It splattered like an egg of fire
against the cliff behind the house.
The flame ran down. We saw the pair

of owls who nest there flying up
and up, their whirling black-and-white
stained bright pink underneath, until
they shrieked up out of sight.

The ancient owl's nest must have burned.
Hastily, all alone,
a glistening armadillo left the scene,
rose-flecked, head down, tail down,

and then a baby rabbit jumped out,
short-eared, to our surprise.
So soft! — a handful of intangible ash
with fixed, ignited eyes.

Too pretty, dreamlike mimicry!
O falling fire and piercing cry
and panic, and a weak mailed fist
clenched ignorant against the sky!

NORTH HAVEN

In memoriam: Robert Lowell

I can make out the rigging of a schooner
a mile off; I can count
the new cones on the spruce. It is so still
the pale bay wears a milky skin, the sky
no clouds, except for one long, carded horse's-tail.

The islands haven't shifted since last summer,
even if I like to pretend they have
— drifting, in a dreamy sort of way,
a little north, a little south or sidewise,
and that they're free within the blue frontiers of bay.

This month, our favorite one is full of flowers:
Buttercups, Red Clover, Purple Vetch,
Hawkweed still burning, Daisies pied, Eyebright,
the Fragrant Bedstraw's incandescent stars,
and more, returned, to paint the meadows with delight.

The Goldfinches are back, or others like them,
and the White-throated Sparrow's five-note song,
pleading and pleading, brings tears to the eyes.
Nature repeats herself, or almost does:
repeat, repeat, repeat; revise, revise, revise.

Years ago, you told me it was here
(in 1932?) you first "discovered *girls*"
and learned to sail, and learned to kiss.
You had "such fun," you said, that classic summer.
("Fun" — it always seemed to leave you at a loss . . .)

You left North Haven, anchored in its rock,
afloat in mystic blue . . . And now — you've left
for good. You can't derange, or re-arrange,
your poems again. (But the Sparrows can their song.)
The words won't change again. Sad friend, you cannot change.

IN THE WAITING ROOM

In Worcester, Massachusetts,
I went with Aunt Consuelo
to keep her dentist's appointment
and sat and waited for her
in the dentist's waiting room.
It was winter. It got dark
early. The waiting room
was full of grown-up people,
arctics and overcoats,
lamps and magazines.
My aunt was inside
what seemed like a long time
and while I waited I read
the *National Geographic*
(I could read) and carefully
studied the photographs:
the inside of a volcano,
black, and full of ashes;
then it was spilling over
in rivulets of fire.
Osa and Martin Johnson

dressed in riding breeches,
laced boots, and pith helmets.
A dead man slung on a pole
— "Long Pig," the caption said.
Babies with pointed heads
wound round and round with string;
black, naked women with necks
wound round and round with wire
like the necks of light bulbs.
Their breasts were horrifying.
I read it right straight through.
I was too shy to stop.
And then I looked at the cover:
the yellow margins, the date.

Suddenly, from inside,
came an *oh!* of pain
— Aunt Consuelo's voice —
not very loud or long.
I wasn't at all surprised;
even then I knew she was
a foolish, timid woman.
I might have been embarrassed,
but wasn't. What took me
completely by surprise
was that it was *me*:

my voice, in my mouth.
Without thinking at all
I was my foolish aunt,
I — we — were falling, falling,
our eyes glued to the cover
of the *National Geographic*,
February, 1918.

I said to myself: three days
and you'll be seven years old.
I was saying it to stop
the sensation of falling off
the round, turning world
into cold, blue-black space.
But I felt: you are an *I*,
you are an *Elizabeth*,
you are one of *them*.
Why should you be one, too?

I scarcely dared to look
to see what it was I was.
I gave a sidelong glance
— I couldn't look any higher —
at shadowy gray knees,
trousers and skirts and boots
and different pairs of hands
lying under the lamps.
I knew that nothing stranger
had ever happened, that nothing
stranger could ever happen.

Why should I be my aunt,
or me, or anyone?
What similarities —
boots, hands, the family voice
I felt in my throat, or even
the *National Geographic*
and those awful hanging breasts —
held us all together
or made us all just one?
How — I didn't know any
word for it — how "unlikely" . . .
How had I come to be here,
like them, and overhear
a cry of pain that could have
got loud and worse but hadn't?

The waiting room was bright
and too hot. It was sliding
beneath a big black wave,
another, and another.

Then I was back in it.
The War was on. Outside,
in Worcester, Massachusetts,
were night and slush and cold,
and it was still the fifth
of February, 1918.

THE MOOSE

For Grace Bulmer Bowers

From narrow provinces
of fish and bread and tea,
home of the long tides
where the bay leaves the sea
twice a day and takes
the herrings long rides,

where if the river
enters or retreats
in a wall of brown foam
depends on if it meets
the bay coming in,
the bay not at home;

where, silted red,
sometimes the sun sets
facing a red sea,
and others, veins the flats'
lavender, rich mud
in burning rivulets;

on red, gravelly roads,
down rows of sugar maples,
past clapboard farmhouses
and neat, clapboard churches,
bleached, ridged as clamshells,
past twin silver birches,

through late afternoon
a bus journeys west,
the windshield flashing pink,
pink glancing off of metal,
brushing the dented flank
of blue, beat-up enamel;

down hollows, up rises,
and waits, patient, while
a lone traveller gives
kisses and embraces
to seven relatives
and a collie supervises.

Goodbye to the elms,
to the farm, to the dog.
The bus starts. The light
grows richer; the fog,
shifting, salty, thin,
comes closing in.

Its cold, round crystals
form and slide and settle
in the white hens' feathers,
in gray glazed cabbages,
on the cabbage roses
and lupins like apostles;

the sweet peas cling
to their wet white string
on the whitewashed fences;
bumblebees creep
inside the foxgloves,
and evening commences.

One stop at Bass River.
Then the Economies —
Lower, Middle, Upper;
Five Islands, Five Houses,
where a woman shakes a tablecloth
out after supper.

A pale flickering. Gone.
The Tantramar marshes
and the smell of salt hay.
An iron bridge trembles
and a loose plank rattles
but doesn't give way.

On the left, a red light
swims through the dark:
a ship's port lantern.
Two rubber boots show,
illuminated, solemn.
A dog gives one bark.

A woman climbs in
with two market bags,
brisk, freckled, elderly.

"A grand night. Yes, sir,
all the way to Boston."
She regards us amicably.

Moonlight as we enter
the New Brunswick woods,
hairy, scratchy, splintery;
moonlight and mist
caught in them like lamb's wool
on bushes in a pasture.

The passengers lie back.
Snores. Some long sighs.
A dreamy divagation
begins in the night,
a gentle, auditory,
slow hallucination. . . .

In the creakings and noises,
an old conversation
— not concerning us,
but recognizable, somewhere,
back in the bus:
Grandparents' voices

uninterruptedly
talking, in Eternity:
names being mentioned,
things cleared up finally;
what he said, what she said,
who got pensioned;

deaths, deaths and sicknesses;
the year he remarried;
the year (something) happened.
She died in childbirth.
That was the son lost
when the schooner foundered.

He took to drink. Yes.
She went to the bad.
When Amos began to pray
even in the store and
finally the family had
to put him away.

"Yes . . ." that peculiar
affirmative. "Yes . . ."
A sharp, indrawn breath,
half groan, half acceptance,
that means "Life's like that.
We know *it* (also death)."

Talking the way they talked
in the old featherbed,
peacefully, on and on,
dim lamplight in the hall,
down in the kitchen, the dog
tucked in her shawl.

Now, it's all right now
even to fall asleep
just as on all those nights.
— Suddenly the bus driver
stops with a jolt,
turns off his lights.

A moose has come out of
the impenetrable wood
and stands there, looms, rather,
in the middle of the road.
It approaches; it sniffs at
the bus's hot hood.

Towering, antlerless,
high as a church,
homely as a house
(or, safe as houses).
A man's voice assures us
"Perfectly harmless. . . ."

Some of the passengers
exclaim in whispers,
childishly, softly,
"Sure are big creatures."
"It's awful plain."
"Look! It's a she!"

Taking her time,
she looks the bus over,
grand, otherworldly.

Why, why do we feel
(we all feel) this sweet
sensation of joy?

"Curious creatures,"
says our quiet driver,
rolling his *r*'s.
"Look at that, would you."
Then he shifts gears.
For a moment longer,

by craning backward,
the moose can be seen
on the moonlit macadam;
then there's a dim
smell of moose, an acrid
smell of gasoline.

ONE ART

The art of losing isn't hard to master;
so many things seem filled with the intent
to be lost that their loss is no disaster.

Lose something every day. Accept the fluster
of lost door keys, the hour badly spent.
The art of losing isn't hard to master.

Then practice losing farther, losing faster:
places, and names, and where it was you meant
to travel. None of these will bring disaster.

I lost my mother's watch. And look! my last, or
next-to-last, of three loved houses went.
The art of losing isn't hard to master.

I lost two cities, lovely ones. And, vaster,
some realms I owned, two rivers, a continent.
I miss them, but it wasn't a disaster.

— Even losing you (the joking voice, a gesture
I love) I shan't have lied. It's evident
the art of losing's not too hard to master
though it may look like (*Write* it!) like disaster.

Robert Bly

SURPRISED BY EVENING

There is unknown dust that is near us,
Waves breaking on shores just over the hill,
Trees full of birds that we have never seen,
Nets drawn down with dark fish.

The evening arrives; we look up and it is there,
It has come through the nets of the stars,
Through the tissues of the grass,
Walking quietly over the asylums of the waters.

The day shall never end, we think:
We have hair that seems born for the daylight;
But, at last, the quiet waters of the night will rise,
And our skin shall see far off, as it does under water.

WAKING FROM SLEEP

Inside the veins there are navies setting forth,
Tiny explosions at the water lines,
And seagulls weaving in the wind of the salty blood.

It is the morning. The country has slept the whole winter.
Window seats were covered with fur skins, the yard was full
Of stiff dogs, and hands that clumsily held heavy books.

Now we wake, and rise from bed, and eat breakfast! —
Shouts rise from the harbor of the blood,
Mist, and masts rising, the knock of wooden tackle in the sunlight.

Now we sing, and do tiny dances on the kitchen floor.
Our whole body is like a harbor at dawn;
We know that our master has left us for the day.

POEM IN THREE PARTS

I

Oh, on an early morning I think I shall live forever!
I am wrapped in my joyful flesh,
As the grass is wrapped in its clouds of green.

II

Rising from a bed, where I dreamt
Of long rides past castles and hot coals,
The sun lies happily on my knees;
I have suffered and survived the night
Bathed in dark water, like any blade of grass.

III

The strong leaves of the box-elder tree,
Plunging in the wind, call us to disappear
Into the wilds of the universe,
Where we shall sit at the foot of a plant,
And live forever, like the dust.

SNOWFALL IN THE AFTERNOON

I

The grass is half-covered with snow.
It was the sort of snowfall that starts in late afternoon,
And now the little houses of the grass are growing dark.

II

If I reached my hands down, near the earth,
I could take handfuls of darkness!
A darkness was always there, which we never noticed.

ROBERT BLY

III

As the snow grows heavier, the cornstalks fade farther away,
And the barn moves nearer to the house.
The barn moves all alone in the growing storm.

IV

The barn is full of corn, and moving toward us now,
Like a hulk blown toward us in a storm at sea;
All the sailors on deck have been blind for many years.

IN A TRAIN

There has been a light snow.
Dark car tracks move in out of the darkness.
I stare at the train window marked with soft dust.
I have awakened at Missoula, Montana, utterly happy.

DRIVING TO TOWN LATE TO MAIL A LETTER

It is a cold and snowy night. The main street is deserted.
The only things moving are swirls of snow.
As I lift the mailbox door, I feel its cold iron.
There is a privacy I love in this snowy night.
Driving around, I will waste more time.

WATERING THE HORSE

How strange to think of giving up all ambition!
Suddenly I see with such clear eyes
The white flake of snow
That has just fallen in the horse's mane!

ROBERT BLY

AFTER LONG BUSYNESS

I start out for a walk at last after weeks at the desk.
Moon gone, plowing underfoot, no stars; not a trace of light!
Suppose a horse were galloping toward me in this open field?
Every day I did not spend in solitude was wasted.

COUNTING SMALL-BONED BODIES

Let's count the bodies over again.

If we could only make the bodies smaller,
The size of skulls,
We could make a whole plain white with skulls in the moonlight!

If we could only make the bodies smaller,
Maybe we could get
A whole year's kill in front of us on a desk!

If we could only make the bodies smaller,
We could fit
A body into a finger-ring, for a keepsake forever.

LOOKING INTO A FACE

Conversation brings us so close! Opening
The surfs of the body,
Bringing fish up near the sun,
And stiffening the backbones of the sea!

I have wandered in a face, for hours,
Passing through dark fires.
I have risen to a body
Not yet born,
Existing like a light around the body,
Through which the body moves like a sliding moon.

THE HERMIT

Darkness is falling through darkness,
Falling from ledge
To ledge.
There is a man whose body is perfectly whole.
He stands, the storm behind him,
And the grass blades are leaping in the wind.
Darkness is gathered in folds
About his feet.
He is no one. When we see
Him, we grow calm,
And sail on into the tunnels of joyful death.

SHACK POEM

1

I don't even know these roads I walk on,
I see the backs of white birds.
Whales rush by, their teeth ivory.

2

Far out at the edge of the heron's wing,
where the air is disturbed by the last feather,
there is the Kingdom. . . .

3

Hurrying to brush between the Two Fish,
the wild woman flies on . . .
blue glass stones a path on earth mark her going.

4

I sit down and fold my legs. . . .
The half dark in the room is delicious.
How marvelous to be a thought entirely surrounded by brains!

ROBERT BLY

LOOKING INTO A TIDE POOL

It is a tide pool, shallow, water coming in, clear, tiny white shell-people on the bottom, asking nothing, not even directions! On the surface the noduled seaweed, lying like hands, slowly drawing back and returning, hands laid on fevered bodies, moving back and forth, as the healer sings wildly, shouting to Jesus and his dead mother.

OPENING THE DOOR OF A BARN I THOUGHT WAS EMPTY ON NEW YEAR'S EVE

I got there by dusk. I open the double barn doors and go in. Sounds of breathing! Thirty steers are wandering around, the partitions gone. Creatures heavy, shaggy, slowly moving in the dying light. Bodies with no St. Teresas look straight at me. The floor is cheerful with clean straw. Snow gleams in the feeding lot through the other door. The bony legs of the steers look frail in the pale light from the snow, like uncles who live in the city.

The windowpanes are clotted with dust and cobwebs. The dog stands up on his hind legs to look over the worn wooden gate. Large shoulders watch him, and he suddenly puts his paws down, frightened. After a while, he puts them up again. A steer's head swings to look at him, and stares for three or four minutes, unable to get a clear picture from the instinct reservoir, then suddenly the steer bolts. . . .

But their enemies are asleep; everyone is asleep. These breathing ones do not demand eternal life; they ask only to eat the crushed corn and the hay, coarse as rivers, and cross the rivers, and sometimes feel an affection run along the heavy nerves. Each of them has the wonder and bewilderment of the large animal, a body with a lamp lit inside, fluttering on a windy night.

INSECT HEADS

These insects, golden
and Arabic, sailing in the husks of galleons,
their octagonal heads also
hold sand paintings of the next life.

PASSING AN ORCHARD BY TRAIN

Grass high under apple trees.
The bark of the trees rough and sexual,
the grass growing heavy and uneven.

We cannot bear disaster, like
the rocks —
swaying nakedly
in open fields.

One slight bruise and we die!
I know no one on this train.
A man comes walking down the aisle.
I want to tell him
that I forgive him, that I want him
to forgive me.

DRIVING MY PARENTS HOME AT CHRISTMAS

As I drive my parents home through the snow,
their frailty hesitates on the edge of a mountainside.
I call over the cliff,
only snow answers.
They talk quietly
of hauling water, of eating an orange,
of a grandchild's photograph left behind last night.
When they open the door of their house, they disappear.
And the oak when it falls in the forest who hears it through miles and
    miles of silence?
They sit so close to each other . . . as if pressed together by the snow.

FOR MY SON NOAH, TEN YEARS OLD

Night and day arrive, and day after day goes by,
and what is old remains old, and what is young remains young, and grows
    old.

The lumber pile does not grow younger, nor the two-by-fours lose their
    darkness,
but the old tree goes on, the barn stands without help so many years;
    the advocate of darkness and night is not lost.

The horse steps up, swings on one leg, turns its body,
the chicken flapping claws onto the roost, its wings whelping and wal-
    loping,
but what is primitive is not to be shot out into the night and the dark.
And slowly the kind man comes closer, loses his rage, sits down at table.

So I am proud only of those days that pass in undivided tenderness,
when you sit drawing, or making books, stapled, with messages to the
    world,
or coloring a man with fire coming out of his hair.
Or we sit at a table, with small tea carefully poured.
So we pass our time together, calm and delighted.

AT MIDOCEAN

All day I loved you in a fever, holding on to the tail of the horse.
I overflowed whenever I reached out to touch you.
My hand moved over your body, covered with its dress,
burning, rough, an animal's hand or foot moving over leaves.
The rainstorm retires, clouds open, sunlight
sliding over ocean water a thousand miles from land.

IN RAINY SEPTEMBER

In rainy September, when leaves grow down to the dark,
I put my forehead down to the damp, seaweed-smelling sand.
What can we do but choose? The only way for human beings
is to choose. The fern has no choice but to live;
for this crime it receives earth, water, and night.

We close the door. "I have no claim on you."
Dusk comes. "The love I have had with you is enough."
We know we could live apart from one another.

The sheldrake floats apart from the flock.
The oaktree puts out leaves alone on the lonely hillside.

Men and women before us have accomplished this.
I would see you, and you me, once a year.
We would be two kernels and not be planted.
We stay in the room, door closed, lights out.
I weep with you without shame and without honor.

A MAN WRITES TO A PART OF HIMSELF

What cave are you in, hiding, rained on?
Like a wife, starving, without care,
Water dripping from your head, bent
Over ground corn . . .

You raise your face into the rain
That drives over the valley —
Forgive me, your husband,
On the streets of a distant city, laughing,
With many appointments,
Though at night going also
To a bare room, a room of poverty,
To sleep beside a bare pitcher and basin
In a room with no heat —

Which of us two then is the worse off?
And how did this separation come about?

Gwendolyn Brooks

from **A STREET IN BRONZEVILLE**

to David and Keziah Brooks

the mother

Abortions will not let you forget.
You remember the children you got that you did not get,
The damp small pulps with a little or with no hair,
The singers and workers that never handled the air.
You will never neglect or beat
Them, or silence or buy with a sweet.
You will never wind up the sucking-thumb
Or scuttle off ghosts that come.
You will never leave them, controlling your luscious sigh,
Return for a snack of them, with gobbling mother-eye.

I have heard in the voices of the wind the voices of my dim killed children.
I have contracted. I have eased
My dim dears at the breasts they could never suck.
I have said, Sweets, if I sinned, if I seized
Your luck
And your lives from your unfinished reach,
If I stole your births and your names,
Your straight baby tears and your games,
Your stilted or lovely loves, your tumults, your marriages, aches, and your
    deaths,
If I poisoned the beginnings of your breaths,
Believe that even in my deliberateness I was not deliberate.
Though why should I whine,
Whine that the crime was other than mine? —
Since anyhow you are dead.
Or rather, or instead,
You were never made.
But that too, I am afraid,
Is faulty: oh, what shall I say, how is the truth to be said?
You were born, you had body, you died.
It is just that you never giggled or planned or cried.

Believe me, I loved you all.
Believe me, I knew you, though faintly, and I loved, I loved you
All.

a song in the front yard

I've stayed in the front yard all my life.
I want a peek at the back
Where it's rough and untended and hungry weed grows.
A girl gets sick of a rose.

I want to go in the back yard now
And maybe down the alley,
To where the charity children play.
I want a good time today.

They do some wonderful things.
They have some wonderful fun.
My mother sneers, but I say it's fine
How they don't have to go in at quarter to nine.
My mother, she tells me that Johnnie Mae
Will grow up to be a bad woman.
That George'll be taken to Jail soon or late
(On account of last winter he sold our back gate).

But I say it's fine. Honest, I do.
And I'd like to be a bad woman, too,
And wear the brave stockings of night-black lace
And strut down the streets with paint on my face.

of De Witt Williams on his way to Lincoln Cemetery

He was born in Alabama.
He was bred in Illinois.
He was nothing but a
Plain black boy.

Swing low swing low sweet sweet chariot.
Nothing but a plain black boy.

Drive him past the Pool Hall.
Drive him past the Show.
Blind within his casket,
But maybe he will know.

Down through Forty-seventh Street:
Underneath the L,
And Northwest Corner, Prairie,
That he loved so well.

Don't forget the Dance Halls —
Warwick and Savoy,
Where he picked his women, where
He drank his liquid joy.

Born in Alabama.
Bred in Illinois.
He was nothing but a
Plain black boy.

Swing low swing low sweet sweet chariot.
Nothing but a plain black boy.

THE LOVERS OF THE POOR

      arrive. The Ladies from the Ladies' Betterment
        League
Arrive in the afternoon, the late light slanting
In diluted gold bars across the boulevard brag
Of proud, seamed faces with mercy and murder hinting
Here, there, interrupting, all deep and debonair,
The pink paint on the innocence of fear;
Walk in a gingerly manner up the hall.
Cutting with knives served by their softest care,
Served by their love, so barbarously fair.
Whose mothers taught: You'd better not be cruel!
You had better not throw stones upon the wrens!
Herein they kiss and coddle and assault
Anew and dearly in the innocence
With which they baffle nature. Who are full,
Sleek, tender-clad, fit, fiftyish, a-glow, all
Sweetly abortive, hinting at fat fruit,
Judge it high time that fiftyish fingers felt
Beneath the lovelier planes of enterprise.
To resurrect. To moisten with milky chill.

To be a random hitching-post or plush.
To be, for wet eyes, random and handy hem.
                    Their guild is giving money to the poor.
The worthy poor. The very very worthy
And beautiful poor. Perhaps just not too swarthy?
Perhaps just not too dirty nor too dim
Nor — passionate. In truth, what they could wish
Is — something less than derelict or dull.
Not staunch enough to stab, though, gaze for gaze!
God shield them sharply from the beggar-bold!
The noxious needy ones whose battle's bald
Nonetheless for being voiceless, hits one down.
            But it's all so bad! and entirely too much for
                them.
The stench; the urine, cabbage, and dead beans,
Dead porridges of assorted dusty grains,
The old smoke, *heavy* diapers, and, they're told,
Something called chitterlings. The darkness. Drawn
Darkness, or dirty light. The soil that stirs.
The soil that looks the soil of centuries.
And for that matter the *general* oldness. Old
Wood. Old marble. Old tile. Old old old.
Not homekind Oldness! Not Lake Forest, Glencoe.
Nothing is sturdy, nothing is majestic,
There is no quiet drama, no rubbed glaze, no
Unkillable infirmity of such
A tasteful turn as lately they have left,
Glencoe, Lake Forest, and to which their cars
Must presently restore them. When they're done
With dullards and distortions of this fistic
Patience of the poor and put-upon.
            They've never seen such a make-do-ness as
Newspaper rugs before! In this, this "flat,"
Their hostess is gathering up the oozed, the rich
Rugs of the morning (tattered! the bespattered. . . .)
Readies to spread clean rugs for afternoon.
Here is a scene for you. The Ladies look,
In horror, behind a substantial citizeness
Whose trains clank out across her swollen heart.
Who, arms akimbo, almost fills a door.
All tumbling children, quilts dragged to the floor
And tortured thereover, potato peelings, soft-
Eyed kitten, hunched-up, haggard, to-be-hurt.
            Their League is alloting largesse to the Lost.

But to put their clean, their pretty money, to put
Their money collected from delicate rose-fingers
Tipped with their hundred flawless rose-nails seems . . .
      They own Spode, Lowestoft, candelabra,
Mantels, and hostess gowns, and sunburst clocks,
Turtle soup, Chippendale, red satin "hangings,"
Aubussons and Hattie Carnegie. They Winter
In Palm Beach; cross the Water in June; attend,
When suitable, the nice Art Institute;
Buy the right books in the best bindings; saunter
On Michigan, Easter mornings, in sun or wind.
Oh Squalor! This sick four-story hulk, this fibre
With fissures everywhere! Why, what are bringings
Of loathe-love largesse? What shall peril hungers
So old old, what shall flatter the desolate?
Tin can, blocked fire escape and chitterling
And swaggering seeking youth and the puzzled wreckage
Of the middle-passage, and urine and stale shames
And, again, the porridges of the underslung
And children children children. Heavens! That
Was a rat, surely, off there, in the shadows? Long
And long-tailed? Gray? The Ladies from the Ladies'
Betterment League agree it will be better
To achieve the outer air that rights and steadies,
To hie to a house that does not holler, to ring
Bells elsetime, better presently to cater
To no more Possibilities, to get
Away. Perhaps the money can be posted.
Perhaps they two may choose another Slum!
Some serious sooty half-unhappy home! —
Where loathe-love likelier may be invested.
      Keeping their scented bodies in the center
Of the hall as they walk down the hysterical hall,
They allow their lovely skirts to graze no wall,
Are off at what they manage of a canter,
And, resuming all the clues of what they were,
Try to avoid inhaling the laden air.

WE REAL COOL

> The Pool Players.
> Seven at the Golden Shovel.

We real cool. We
Left school. We

Lurk late. We
Strike straight. We

Sing sin. We
Thin gin. We

Jazz June. We
Die soon.

AN ASPECT OF LOVE,
ALIVE IN THE ICE AND FIRE

LaBohem Brown

It is the morning of our love.

In a package of minutes there is this We.
How beautiful.
Merry foreigners in our morning,
we laugh, we touch each other,
are responsible props and posts.

A physical light is in the room.

Because the world is at the window
we cannot wonder very long.

You rise. Although
genial, you are in yourself again.
I observe
your direct and respectable stride.
You are direct and self-accepting as a lion

in African velvet. You are level, lean,
remote.

There is a moment in Camaraderie
when interruption is not to be understood.
I cannot bear an interruption.
This is the shining joy;
the time of not-to-end.

On the street we smile.
We go
in different directions
down the imperturbable street.

TO DON AT SALAAM

I like to see you lean back in your chair
so far you have to fall but do not —
your arms back, your fine hands
in your print pockets.

Beautiful. Impudent.
Ready for life.
A tied storm.

I like to see you wearing your boy smile
whose tribute is for two of us or three.

Sometimes in life
things seem to be moving
and they are not
and they are not
there.
You are there.

Your voice is the listened-for music.
Your act is the consolidation.

I like to see you living in the world.

THE NEAR-JOHANNESBURG BOY

*In South Africa the Black children ask each other: "Have you been detained yet?
How many times have you been detained?"*

———

*The herein boy does not live in Johannesburg. He is not allowed to live there.
Perhaps he lives in Soweto.*

My way is from woe to wonder.
A Black boy near Johannesburg, hot
in the Hot Time.

Those people
do not like Black among the colors.
They do not like our
calling our country ours.
They say our country is not ours.

Those people.
Visiting the world as I visit the world.
Those people.
Their bleach is puckered and cruel.

It is work to speak of my Father. My Father.
His body was whole till they Stopped it.
Suddenly.
With a short shot.
But, before that, physically tall and among us,
he died every day. Every moment.
My Father . . . .
First was the crumpling.
No. First was the Fist-and-the-Fury.
Last was the crumpling. It is
a little used rag that is Under, it is not,
it is not my Father gone down.

About my Mother. My Mother
was this loud laugher
below the sunshine, below the starlight at festival.
My Mother is still this loud laugher!
Still moving straight in the Getting-It-Done (as she names it.)

Oh a strong eye is my Mother.
Except when it seems we are lax in our looking.

Well, enough of slump, enough of Old Story.
Like a clean spear of fire
I am moving. I am not still. I am ready
to be ready.
I shall flail
in the Hot Time.

Tonight I walk with
a hundred of playmates to where
the hurt Black of our skin is forbidden.
There, in the dark that is our dark, there,
a-pulse across earth that is our earth, there,
there exulting, there Exactly, there redeeming, there Roaring Up
(oh my Father)
we shall forge with the Fist-and-the-Fury:
we shall flail in the Hot Time:
we shall
we shall

TORNADO AT TALLADEGA

Who is that bird
reporting the storm? —
after What came through
to do some landscaping.

Certain trees
stick across the road.
They are unimportant now.
They cannot sass anymore.
Not a one of these, the bewildered,
can announce anymore "How fine I am!"
Here, roots, ire, origins exposed,
across this twig-strewn, leaf-strewn road they lie,
mute, and ashamed, and through.

It happened all of a sudden.

Certain women and men and children
come out to stare.

TELEPHONE CONVERSATIONS

After discussing William Faulkner with George Kent. September, 1980.

Telephone conversations
are little lives.
Their tempers and temperatures
fall and get up and fall.

Each one is New.
There is the birth —
easy or difficult.
The little baby prospers or declines.
Sings. Sobs.
Limps. Lulls.

But suddenly
(sometimes)
an imminence of light.
Ribbons of fire and music.
A democratic transportation.

TO THE YOUNG WHO WANT TO DIE

Sit down. Inhale. Exhale.
The gun will wait. The lake will wait.
The tall gall in the small seductive vial
will wait will wait:
will wait a week: will wait through April.
You do not have to die this certain day.
Death will abide, will pamper your postponement.
I assure you death will wait. Death has
a lot of time. Death can
attend to you tomorrow. Or next week. Death is
just down the street; is most obliging neighbor;
can meet you any moment.

You need not die today.
Stay here — through pout or pain or peskyness.
Stay here. See what the news is going to be tomorrow.

Graves grow no green that you can use.
Remember, green's your color. You are Spring.

TO BLACK WOMEN

Sisters,
where there is cold silence —
no hallelujahs, no hurrahs at all, no handshakes,
no neon red or blue, no smiling faces —
prevail.
Prevail across the editors of the world!
who are obsessed, self-honeying and self-crowned
in the seduced arena.

      It has been a
hard trudge, with fainting, bandaging and death.
There have been startling confrontations.
There have been tramplings. Tramplings
of monarchs and of other men.

But there remain large countries in your eyes.
Shrewd sun.
The civil balance.
The listening secrets.

And you create and train your flowers still.

Lucille Clifton

ADMONITIONS

boys
i don't promise you nothing
but this
what you pawn
i will redeem
what you steal
i will conceal
my private silence to
your public guilt
is all i got

girls
first time a white man
opens his fly
like a good thing
we'll just laugh
laugh real loud my
black women

children
when they ask you
why is your mama so funny
say
she is a poet
she don't have no sense

MISS ROSIE

when i watch you
wrapped up like garbage
sitting, surrounded by the smell
of too old potato peels
or
when i watch you
in your old man's shoes
with the little toe cut out
sitting, waiting for your mind

like next week's grocery
i say
when i watch you
you wet brown bag of a woman
who used to be the best looking gal in georgia
used to be called the Georgia Rose
i stand up
through your destruction
i stand up

[IF I STAND IN MY WINDOW]

if i stand in my window
naked in my own house
and press my breasts
against my windowpane
like black birds pushing against glass
because i am somebody
in a New Thing

and if the man come to stop me
in my own house
naked in my own window
saying i have offended him
i have offended his

Gods

let him watch my black body
push against my own glass
let him discover self
let him run naked through the streets
crying
praying in tongues

THE LOST BABY POEM

the time i dropped your almost body down
down to meet the waters under the city
and run one with the sewage to the sea

what did i know about waters rushing back
what did i know about drowning
or being drowned

you would have been born into winter
in the year of the disconnected gas
and no car   we would have made the thin
walk over genesee hill into the canada wind
to watch you slip like ice into strangers' hands
you would have fallen naked as snow into winter
if you were here i could tell you these
and some other things

if i am ever less than a mountain
for your definite brothers and sisters
let the rivers pour over my head
let the sea take me for a spiller
of seas   let black men call me stranger
always   for your never named sake

GOD'S MOOD

these daughters are bone,
they break.
he wanted stone girls
and boys with branches for arms
that he could lift his life with
and be lifted by.
these sons are bone.

he is tired of years that keep turning into age
and flesh that keeps widening.
he is tired of waiting for his teeth to
bite him and walk away.

he is tired of bone,
it breaks.
he is tired of eve's fancy and
adam's whining ways.

LUCILLE CLIFTON

ROOTS

call it our craziness even,
call it anything.
it is the life thing in us
that will not let us die.
even in death's hand
we fold the fingers up
and call them greens and
grow on them,
we hum them and make music.
call it our wildness then,
we are lost from the field
of flowers, we become
a field of flowers.
call it our craziness
our wildness
call it our roots,
it is the light in us
it is the light of us
it is the light, call it
whatever you have to,
call it anything.

[COME HOME FROM THE MOVIES]

come home from the movies,
black girls and boys,
the picture be over and the screen
be cold as our neighborhood.
come home from the show,
don't be the show.
take off some flowers and plant them,
pick us some papers and read them,
stop making some babies and raise them.
come home from the movies
black girls and boys,
show our fathers how to walk like men,
they already know how to dance.

TO A DARK MOSES

you are the one
i am lit for.
come with your rod
that twists
and is a serpent.
i am the bush.
i am burning.
i am not consumed.

SHE UNDERSTANDS ME

it is all blood and breaking,
blood and breaking. the thing
drops out of its box squalling
into the light. they are both squalling,
animal and cage. her bars lie wet, open
and empty and she has made herself again
out of flesh out of dictionaries,
she is always emptying and it is all
the same wound the same blood the same breaking.

CUTTING GREENS

curling them around
i hold their bodies in obscene embrace
thinking of everything but kinship.
collards and kale
strain against each strange other
away from my kissmaking hand and
the iron bedpot.
the pot is black,
the cutting board is black,
my hand,
and just for a minute
the greens roll black under the knife,

and the kitchen twists dark on its spine
and i taste in my natural appetite
the bond of live things everywhere.

[AT LAST WE KILLED THE ROACHES]

relief

childlike

at last we killed the roaches.
mama and me. she sprayed,
i swept the ceiling and they fell

ugh

dying onto our shoulders, in our hair *yuck*

?

covering us with red. the tribe was broken,
the cooking pots were ours again *?*
and we were glad, such cleanliness was grace *!*

Biblical

when i was twelve. only for a few nights,
and then not much, my dreams were blood

grace vs. turmoil of dreams

my hands were blades and it was murder murder
all over the place.

exaggeration of dreams

→ defensiveness

BREAKLIGHT

light keeps on breaking.
i keep knowing
the language of other nations.
i keep hearing
tree talk
water words
and i keep knowing what they mean.
and light just keeps on breaking.
last night
the fears of my mother came
knocking and when i
opened the door
they tried to explain themselves
and i understood
everything they said.

THE CARVER

for fred

sees the man
in the wood and
calls his name and
the man in the wood
breaks through the bark and
the nations of wood call
the carver
Brother

HOMAGE TO MY HIPS

these hips are big hips
they need space to
move around in.
they don't fit into little
petty places. these hips
are free hips.
they don't like to be held back.
these hips have never been enslaved,
they go where they want to go
they do what they want to do.
these hips are mighty hips.
these hips are magic hips.
i have known them
to put a spell on a man and
spin him like a top!

[THERE IS A GIRL INSIDE]

there is a girl inside.
she is randy as a wolf.
she will not walk away
and leave these bones
to an old woman.

she is a green tree
in a forest of kindling.
she is a green girl
in a used poet.

she has waited
patient as a nun
for the second coming,
when she can break through gray hairs
into blossom

and her lovers will harvest
honey and thyme
and the woods will be wild
with the damn wonder of it.

FORGIVING MY FATHER

it is friday. we have come
to the paying of the bills.
all week you have stood in my dreams
like a ghost, asking for more time
but today is payday, payday old man;
my mother's hand opens in her early grave
and i hold it out like a good daughter.

there is no more time for you. there will
never be time enough daddy daddy old lecher
old liar. i wish you were rich so i could take it all
and give the lady what she was due
but you were the son of a needy father,
the father of a needy son;
you gave her all you had
which was nothing. you have already given her
all you had.

you are the pocket that was going to open
and come up empty any friday.
you were each other's bad bargain, not mine.
daddy old pauper   old prisoner,   old dead man
what am i doing here collecting?

you lie side by side in debtors' boxes
and no accounting will open them up.

I ONCE KNEW A MAN

i once knew a man who had wild horses killed.
when he told about it
the words came galloping out of his mouth
and shook themselves and headed off in
every damn direction. his tongue
was wild and wide and spinning when he talked
and the people he looked at closed their eyes
and tore the skins off their backs as they walked away
and stopped eating meat.
there was no holding him once he got started;
he had had wild horses killed one time and
they rode him to his grave.

SPEAKING OF LOSS

i began with everything;
parents, two extra fingers
a brother to ruin. i was
a rich girl with no money
in a red dress. how did i come
to sit in this house
wearing a name i never heard
until i was a woman? someone has stolen
my parents and hidden my brother.
my extra fingers are cut away.
i am left with plain hands and
nothing to give you but poems.

[HERE IS ANOTHER BONE TO PICK WITH YOU]

here is another bone to pick with you
o mother whose bones i worry for scraps,
nobody warned me about daughters;

how they bewitch you into believing
you have thrown off a pot that is yourself
then one night you creep into their rooms and
their faces have hardened into odd flowers
their voices are choosing in foreign elections and
their legs are open to strange unwieldy men.

THE LOST WOMEN

i need to know their names
those women i would have walked with
jauntily the way men go in groups
swinging their arms, and the ones
those sweating women whom i would have joined
after a hard game to chew the fat
what would we have called each other laughing
joking into our beer? where are my gangs,
my teams, my mislaid sisters?
all the women who could have known me,
where in the world are their names?

from TREE OF LIFE

adam thinking

she
stolen from my bone
is it any wonder
i hunger to tunnel back
inside   desperate
to reconnect the rib and clay
and to be whole again

some need is in me
struggling to roar through my
mouth into a name
this creation is so fierce
i would rather have been born

eve thinking

it is wild country here
brothers and sisters coupling
claw and wing
groping one another

i wait
while the clay two-foot
rumbles in his chest
searching for language to

call me
but he is slow
tonight as he sleeps
i will whisper into his mouth
our names

lucifer understanding at last

thy servant lord

bearer of lightning
and of lust

thrust between the
legs of the earth
into this garden

phallus and father
doing holy work

oh sweet delight
oh eden

if the angels
hear of this

there will be no peace
in heaven

Robert Creeley

THE BUSINESS

To be in love is like going outside to see what kind of day

it is. Do not
mistake me. If you love

her how prove she
loves also, except that it

occurs, a remote chance on
which you stake

yourself? But barter for
the Indian was a means of sustenance.

There are records.

I KNOW A MAN

As I sd to my
friend, because I am
always talking, — John, I

sd, which was not his
name, the darkness sur-
rounds us, what

can we do against
it, or else, shall we &
why not, buy a goddamn big car,

drive, he sd, for
christ's sake, look
out where yr going.

ROBERT CREELEY

A FORM OF WOMEN

I have come far enough
from where I was not before
to have seen the things
looking in at me through the open door

and have walked tonite
by myself
to see the moonlight
and see it as trees

and shapes more fearful
because I feared
what I did not know
but have wanted to know.

My face is my own, I thought.
But you have seen it
turn into a thousand years.
I watched you cry.

I could not touch you.
I wanted very much to
touch you
but could not.

If it is dark
when this is given to you,
have care for its content,
when the moon shines.

My face is my own.
My hands are my own.
My mouth is my own
but I am not.

Moon, moon,
when you leave me alone
all the darkness is
an utter blackness,

a pit of fear,
a stench,

hands unreasonable
never to touch.

But I love you.
Do you love me.
What to say
when you see me.

A WICKER BASKET

Comes the time when it's later
and onto your table the headwaiter
puts the bill, and very soon after
rings out the sound of lively laughter —

Picking up change, hands like a walrus,
and a face like a barndoor's,
and a head without any apparent size,
nothing but two eyes —

So that's you, man,
or me. I make it as I can,
I pick up, I go
faster than they know —

Out the door, the street like a night,
any night, and no one in sight,
but then, well, there she is,
old friend Liz —

And she opens the door of her cadillac,
I step in back,
and we're gone.
She turns me on —

There are very huge stars, man, in the sky,
and from somewhere very far off someone hands me a slice of
    apple pie,
with a gob of white, white ice cream on top of it,
and I eat it —

Slowly. And while certainly
they are laughing at me, and all around me is racket
of these cats not making it, I make it

in my wicker basket.

THE FLOWER

I think I grow tensions
like flowers
in a wood where
nobody goes.

Each wound is perfect,
encloses itself in a tiny
imperceptible blossom,
making pain.

Pain is a flower like that one,
like this one,
like that one,
like this one.

THE RAIN

All night the sound had
come back again,
and again falls
this quiet, persistent rain.

What am I to myself
that must be remembered,
insisted upon
so often? Is it

that never the ease,
even the hardness,
of rain falling
will have for me

something other than this,
something not so insistent —
am I to be locked in this
final uneasiness.

Love, if you love me,
lie next to me.
Be for me, like rain,
the getting out

of the tiredness, the fatuousness, the semi-
lust of intentional indifference.
Be wet
with a decent happiness.

THE MEMORY

Like a river she was,
huge roily mass of water
carrying tree trunks
and divers drunks.

Like a Priscilla, a feminine Benjamin,
a whore gone right over
the falls,
she was.

Did you know her.
Did you love her, brother.
Did wonder pour down
on the whole goddamn town.

THE RESCUE

The man sits in a timelessness
with the horse under him in time
to a movement of legs and hooves
upon a timeless sand.

Distance comes in from the foreground
present in the picture as time
he reads outward from
and comes from that beginning.

A wind blows in
and out and all about the man
as the horse ran
and runs to come in time.

A house is burning in the sand.
A man and horse are burning.
The wind is burning.
They are running to arrive.

THE LANGUAGE

Locate *I*
love you some-
where in

teeth and
eyes, bite
it but

take care not
to hurt, you
want so

much so
little. Words
say everything,

I
love you
again,

then what
is emptiness
for. To

fill, fill.
I heard words
and words full

of holes
aching. Speech
is a mouth.

THE WINDOW

Position is where you
put it, where it is,
did you, for example, that

large tank there, silvered,
with the white church along-
side, lift

all that, to what
purpose? How
heavy the slow

world is with
everything put
in place. Some

man walks by, a
car beside him on
the dropped

road, a leaf of
yellow color is
going to

fall. It
all drops into
place. My

face is heavy
with the sight. I can
feel my eye breaking.

ROBERT CREELEY

ON VACATION

Things seem empty
on vacation if the labors
have not been physical,

if tedium was rather
a daily knot, a continuum,
if satisfaction was almost

placid. On Sundays the restlessness
grows, on weekends, on
months of vacation myself grows

vacuous. Taking walks, swimming,
drinking, I am always afraid
of having more. Hence a true

Puritan, I shall never rest from my labors
until all rest with me, until I am
driven by that density home.

MOMENT

Whether to *use* time, or to *kill* time, either
still preys on my mind.

One's come now to the graveyard,
where the bones of the dead are.

All rods *have* come
here, truly common —

except the body is moved,
still, to some other use.

FIRST RAIN

These retroactive small
instances of feeling

reach out for a common
ground in the wet

first rain of a faded
winter. Along the grey

iced sidewalk revealed
piles of dogshit, papers,

bits of old clothing, are
the human pledges,

call them, "We are here and
have been all the time." I

walk quickly. The wind
drives the rain, drenching

my coat, pants, blurs
my glasses, as I pass.

MOTHER'S VOICE

In these few years
since her death I hear
mother's voice say
under my own, I won't

want any more of that.
My cheekbones resonate
with her emphasis. Nothing
of not wanting only

but the distance there from
common fact of others
frightens me. I look out
at all this demanding world

and try to put it quietly back,
from me, say, thank you,
I've already had some
though I haven't

and would like to
but I've said no, she has,
it's not my own voice anymore.
It's higher as hers was

and accommodates too simply
its frustrations when
I at least think I want more
and must have it.

LOST

One could reach up into
the air, to see if it was

still there, shoved back
through the hole, the little

purpose, hidden it was,
the small, persisting agencies,

arms and legs, the ears
of wonder covered with area,

all eyes, the echoes, the aches
and pains of patience, the

inimitable here and now of all,
ever again to be one and only one,

to look back to see the long distance
or to go forward, having only lost.

ROBERT CREELEY

FIRST LOVE

Oh your face is there a mirror days
weeks we lived those other places in
all that ridiculous waste the young we
wanted not to be walked endless streets
in novels read about life went home at
night to sleep in tentative houses left
one another somewhere now unclear no persons really left but for paper a child or
two or three and whatever physical events
were carved then on that tree like initials
a heart a face of quiet blood and somehow
you kept saying and saying an unending pain.

James Dickey

THE HEAVEN OF ANIMALS

Here they are. The soft eyes open.
If they have lived in a wood
It is a wood.
If they have lived on plains
It is grass rolling
Under their feet forever.

Having no souls, they have come,
Anyway, beyond their knowing.
Their instincts wholly bloom
And they rise.
The soft eyes open.

To match them, the landscape flowers,
Outdoing, desperately
Outdoing what is required:
The richest wood,
The deepest field.

For some of these,
It could not be the place
It is, without blood.
These hunt, as they have done,
But with claws and teeth grown perfect,

More deadly than they can believe.
They stalk more silently,
And crouch on the limbs of trees,
And their descent
Upon the bright backs of their prey

May take years
In a sovereign floating of joy.
And those that are hunted
Know this as their life,
Their reward: to walk

Under such trees in full knowledge
Of what is in glory above them,

And to feel no fear,
But acceptance, compliance.
Fulfilling themselves without pain

At the cycle's center,
They tremble, they walk
Under the tree,
They fall, they are torn,
They rise, they walk again.

THE PERFORMANCE

The last time I saw Donald Armstrong
He was staggering oddly off into the sun,
Going down, off the Philippine Islands.
I let my shovel fall, and put that hand
Above my eyes, and moved some way to one side
That his body might pass through the sun,

And I saw how well he was not
Standing there on his hands,
On his spindle-shanked forearms balanced,
Unbalanced, with his big feet looming and waving
In the great, untrustworthy air
He flew in each night, when it darkened.

Dust fanned in scraped puffs from the earth
Between his arms, and blood turned his face inside out,
To demonstrate its suppleness
Of veins, as he perfected his role.
Next day, he toppled his head off
On an island beach to the south,

And the enemy's two-handed sword
Did not fall from anyone's hands
At that miraculous sight,
As the head rolled over upon
Its wide-eyed face, and fell
Into the inadequate grave

JAMES DICKEY

He had dug for himself, under pressure.
Yet I put my flat hand to my eyebrows
Months later, to see him again
In the sun, when I learned how he died,
And imagined him, there,
Come, judged, before his small captors,

Doing all his lean tricks to amaze them —
The back somersault, the kip-up —
And at last, the stand on his hands,
Perfect, with his feet together,
His head down, evenly breathing,
As the sun poured up from the sea

And the headsman broke down
In a blaze of tears, in that light
Of the thin, long human frame
Upside down in its own strange joy,
And, if some other one had not told him,
Would have cut off the feet

Instead of the head,
And if Armstrong had not presently risen
In kingly, round-shouldered attendance,
And then knelt down in himself
Beside his hacked, glittering grave, having done
All things in this life that he could.

THE HOSPITAL WINDOW

I have just come down from my father.
Higher and higher he lies
Above me in a blue light
Shed by a tinted window.
I drop through six white floors
And then step out onto pavement.

Still feeling my father ascend,
I start to cross the firm street,

JAMES DICKEY

My shoulder blades shining with all
The glass the huge building can raise.
Now I must turn round and face it,
And know his one pane from the others.

Each window possesses the sun
As though it burned there on a wick.
I wave, like a man catching fire.
All the deep-dyed windowpanes flash,
And, behind them, all the white rooms
They turn to the color of Heaven.

Ceremoniously, gravely, and weakly,
Dozens of pale hands are waving
Back, from inside their flames.
Yet one pure pane among these
Is the bright, erased blankness of nothing.
I know that my father is there,

In the shape of his death still living.
The traffic increases around me
Like a madness called down on my head.
The horns blast at me like shotguns,
And drivers lean out, driven crazy —
But now my propped-up father

Lifts his arm out of stillness at last.
The light from the window strikes me
And I turn as blue as a soul,
As the moment when I was born.
I am not afraid for my father —
Look! He is grinning; he is not

Afraid for my life, either,
As the wild engines stand at my knees
Shredding their gears and roaring,
And I hold each car in its place
For miles, inciting its horn
To blow down the walls of the world

That the dying may float without fear
In the bold blue gaze of my father.
Slowly I move to the sidewalk

With my pin-tingling hand half dead
At the end of my bloodless arm.
I carry it off in amazement,

High, still higher, still waving,
My recognized face fully mortal,
Yet not; not at all, in the pale,
Drained, otherworldly, stricken,
Created hue of stained glass.
I have just come down from my father.

IN THE MOUNTAIN TENT

I am hearing the shape of the rain
Take the shape of the tent and believe it,
Laying down all around where I lie
A profound, unspeakable law.
I obey, and am free-falling slowly

Through the thought-out leaves of the wood
Into the minds of animals.
I am there in the shining of water
Like dark, like light, out of Heaven.

I am there like the dead, or the beast
Itself, which thinks of a poem —
Green, plausible, living, and holy —
And cannot speak, but hears,
Called forth from the waiting of things,

A vast, proper, reinforced crying
With the sifted, harmonious pause,
The sustained intake of all breath
Before the first word of the Bible.

At midnight water dawns
Upon the held skulls of the foxes
And weasels and tousled hares
On the eastern side of the mountain.
Their light is the image I make

As I wait as if recently killed,
Receptive, fragile, half-smiling,
My brow watermarked with the mark
On the wing of a moth

And the tent taking shape on my body
Like ill-fitting, Heavenly clothes.
From holes in the ground comes my voice
In the God-silenced tongue of the beasts.
"I shall rise from the dead," I am saying.

SLED BURIAL, DREAM CEREMONY

While the south rains, the north
Is snowing, and the dead southerner
Is taken there. He lies with the top of his casket
Open, his hair combed, the particles in the air
Changing to other things. The train stops

In a small furry village, and men in flap-eared caps
And others with women's scarves tied around their heads
And business hats over those, unload him,
And one of them reaches inside the coffin and places
The southerner's hand at the center

Of his dead breast. They load him onto a sled,
An old-fashioned sled with high-curled runners,
Drawn by horses with bells, and begin
To walk out of town, past dull red barns
Inching closer to the road as it snows

Harder, past an army of gunny-sacked bushes,
Past horses with flakes in the hollows of their sway-backs,
Past round faces drawn by children
On kitchen windows, all shedding basic-shaped tears.
The coffin top still is wide open;

His dead eyes stare through his lids,
Not fooled that the snow is cotton. The woods fall
Slowly off all of them, until they are walking

JAMES DICKEY

Between rigid little houses of ice-fishers
On a plain which is a great plain of water

Until the last rabbit track fails, and they are
At the center. They take axes, shovels, mattocks,
Dig the snow away, and saw the ice in the form
Of his coffin, lifting the slab like a door
Without hinges. The snow creaks under the sled

As they unload him like hay, holding his weight by ropes.
Sensing an unwanted freedom, a fish
Slides by, under the hole leading up through the snow
To nothing, and is gone. The coffin's shadow
Is white, and they stand there, gunny-sacked bushes,

Summoned from village sleep into someone else's dream
Of death, and let him down, still seeing the flakes in the air
At the place they are born of pure shadow
Like his dead eyelids, rocking for a moment like a boat
On utter foreignness, before he fills and sails down.

THE SHEEP CHILD

Farm boys wild to couple
With anything   with soft-wooded trees
With mounds of earth   mounds
Of pinestraw   will keep themselves off
Animals by legends of their own:
In the hay-tunnel dark
And dung of barns, they will
Say   I have heard tell

That in a museum in Atlanta
Way back in a corner somewhere
There's this thing that's only half
Sheep   like a woolly baby
Pickled in alcohol   because
Those things can't live   his eyes
Are open   but you can't stand to look
I heard from somebody who . . .

But this is now almost all
Gone. The boys have taken
Their own true wives in the city,
The sheep are safe in the west hill
Pasture   but we who were born there
Still are not sure. Are we,
Because we remember, remembered
In the terrible dust of museums?

Merely with his eyes, the sheep-child may

Be saying   saying

   I am here, in my father's house.
   I who am half of your world, came deeply
   To my mother in the long grass
   Of the west pasture, where she stood like moonlight
   Listening for foxes. It was something like love
   From another world that seized her
   From behind, and she gave, not lifting her head
   Out of dew, without ever looking, her best
   Self to that great need. Turned loose, she dipped her face
   Farther into the chill of the earth, and in a sound
   Of sobbing   of something stumbling
   Away, began, as she must do,
   To carry me. I woke, dying,

   In the summer sun of the hillside, with my eyes
   Far more than human. I saw for a blazing moment
   The great grassy world from both sides,
   Man and beast in the round of their need,
   And the hill wind stirred in my wool,
   My hoof and my hand clasped each other,
   I ate my one meal
   Of milk, and died
   Staring. From dark grass I came straight

   To my father's house, whose dust
   Whirls up in the halls for no reason
   When no one comes   piling deep in a hellish mild corner,
   And, through my immortal waters,
   I meet the sun's grains eye
   To eye, and they fail at my closet of glass.
   Dead, I am most surely living

In the minds of farm boys: I am he who drives
Them like wolves from the hound bitch and calf
And from the chaste ewe in the wind.
They go into woods   into bean fields   they go
Deep into their known right hands. Dreaming of me,
They groan   they wait   they suffer
Themselves, they marry, they raise their kind.

ADULTERY

We have all been in rooms
We cannot die in, and they are odd places, and sad.
Often Indians are standing eagle-armed on hills

In the sunrise   open wide to the Great Spirit
Or gliding in canoes   or cattle are browsing on the walls
Far away   gazing down with the eyes of our children

Not far away   or there are men driving
The last railspike, which has turned
Gold in their hands. Gigantic forepleasure lives

Among such scenes, and we are alone with it
At last. There is always some weeping
Between us   and someone is always checking

A wrist watch by the bed to see how much
Longer we have left. Nothing can come
Of this   nothing can come

Of us: of me with my grim techniques
Or you who have sealed your womb
With a ring of convulsive rubber:

Although we come together,
Nothing will come of us. But we would not give
It up, for death is beaten

By praying Indians   by distant cows   historical
Hammers   by hazardous meetings that bridge
A continent. One could never die here

JAMES DICKEY

Never die   never die
While crying. My lover, my dear one
I will see you next week

When I'm in town. I will call you
If I can. Please get hold of   please don't
Oh God, Please don't any more I can't bear . . . Listen:

We have done it again   we are
Still living. Sit up and smile,
God bless you. Guilt is magical.

DEER AMONG CATTLE

Here and there in the searing beam
Of my hand going through the night meadow
They all are grazing

With pins of human light in their eyes.
A wild one also is eating
The human grass,

Slender, graceful, domesticated
By darkness, among the bred-
for-slaughter,

Having bounded their paralyzed fence
And inclined his branched forehead onto
Their green frosted table,

The only live thing in this flashlight
Who can leave whenever he wishes,
Turn grass into forest,

Foreclose inhuman brightness from his eyes
But stands here still, unperturbed,
In their wide-open country,

The sparks from my hand in his pupils
Unmatched anywhere among cattle,

Grazing with them the night of the hammer
As one of their own who shall rise.

FALSE YOUTH: AUTUMN: CLOTHES OF THE AGE

— for Susan Tuckerman Dickey —

Three red foxes on my head, come down
There last Christmas from Brooks Brothers
As a joke, I wander down Harden Street
In Columbia, South Carolina, fur-haired and bald,
Looking for impulse in camera stores and redneck greeting cards.
A pole is spinning
Colors I have little use for, but I go in
Anyway, and take off my fox hat and jacket
They have not seen from behind yet. The barber does what he can
With what I have left, and I hear the end man say, as my own
Hair-cutter turns my face
To the floor, Jesus, if there's anything I hate
It's a middle-aged hippie. Well, so do I, I swallow
Back: so do I   so do I
And to hell. I get up, and somebody else says
When're you gonna put on that hat,
Buddy? Right now. Another says softly,
Goodbye, Fox. I arm my denim jacket
On and walk to the door, stopping for the murmur of chairs,
And there it is
hand-stitched by the needles of the mother
Of my grandson   eagle riding on his claws with a banner
Outstretched as the wings of my shoulders,
Coming after me with his flag
Disintegrating, his one eye raveling
Out, filthy strings flying
From the white feathers, one wing nearly gone:
Blind eagle but flying
Where I walk, where I stop with my fox
Head at the glass to let the row of chairs spell it out
And get a lifetime look at my bird's

One word, raggedly blazing with extinction and soaring loose
In red threads burning up white until I am shot in the back
Through my wings   or ripped apart
For rags:

Poetry.

PURGATION

homage, Po Chü-yi

Before and after the eye, grasses go over the long fields.
Every season they walk on
by us, as though I — no; I and you,
Dear friend — decreed it. One time or another

They are here. Grass   season . . .   yet we are no longer the best
Of us.
Lie stiller, closer; in the April I love

For its juices, there is too much green for your grave.
I feel that the Spring should ignite with what is
Unnatural as we; ours, but God-suspected. It should come in one furious
step, and leave
Some — a little — green for us; never quite get every one of the
hummocks tremoring vaguely

Tall in the passed-through air. They'd make the old road *be*
The road for old men, where you and I used to wander toward
The beetle-eaten city gate, as the year leaned into us.
Oh fire, come *on!* I trust you!

My ancient human friend, you are dead, as we both know.

But I remember, and I call for something serious, uncalled-for
By anyone else, to sweep, to *use*
the dryness we've caused to become us! Like the grasshopper

I speak, nearly covered with dust, from the footprint   and ask
Not for the line-squall   lightning:
the cloud's faking veins — Yes! I
catch myself:

JAMES DICKEY

No; not the ripped cloud's open touch   the fireball hay
     Of August
                but for flame too old to live
   Or die, to travel like a wide wild contrary
 Single-minded brow over the year's right growing
In April
         over us   *for us*   as we sway stubbornly near death
     From both sides   age-gazing

    Both sighing like grass and fire.

Rita Dove

NEXUS

I wrote stubbornly into the evening.
At the window, a giant praying mantis
rubbed his monkey wrench head against the glass,
begging vacantly with pale eyes;

and the commas leapt at me like worms
or miniature scythes blackened with age.
The praying mantis screeched louder,
his ragged jaws opening onto formlessness.

I walked outside;
the grass hissed at my heels.
Up ahead in the lapping darkness
he wobbled, magnified and absurdly green,
a brontosaurus, a poet.

"TEACH US TO NUMBER OUR DAYS"

In the old neighborhood, each funeral parlor
is more elaborate than the last.
The alleys smell of cops, pistols bumping their thighs,
each chamber steeled with a slim blue bullet.

Low-rent balconies stacked to the sky.
A boy plays tic-tac-toe on a moon
crossed by TV antennae, dreams

he has swallowed a blue bean.
It takes root in his gut, sprouts
and twines upward, the vines curling
around the sockets and locking them shut.

And this sky, knotting like a dark tie?
The patroller, disinterested, holds all the beans.

August. The mums nod past, each a prickly heart on a sleeve.

RITA DOVE

ADOLESCENCE — III

With Dad gone, Mom and I worked
The dusky rows of tomatoes.
As they glowed orange in sunlight
And rotted in shadow, I too
Grew orange and softer, swelling out
Starched cotton slips.

The texture of twilight made me think of
Lengths of Dotted Swiss. In my room
I wrapped scarred knees in dresses
That once went to big-band dances;
I baptized my earlobes with rosewater.
Along the window-sill, the lipstick stubs
Glittered in their steel shells.

Looking out at the rows of clay
And chicken manure, I dreamed how it would happen:
He would meet me by the blue spruce,
A carnation over his heart, saying,
"I have come for you, Madam;
I have loved you in my dreams."
At his touch, the scabs would fall away.
Over his shoulder, I see my father coming toward us:
He carries his tears in a bowl,
And blood hangs in the pine-soaked air.

THEN CAME FLOWERS

I should have known if you gave me flowers
They would be chrysanthemums.
The white spikes singed my fingers.
I cried out; they spilled from the green tissue
And spread at my feet in a pool of soft fire.

If I begged you to stay, what good would it do me?
In the bed, you would lay the flowers between us.

I will pick them up later, arrange them with pincers.
All night from the bureau they'll watch me, their
Plumage as proud, as cocky as firecrackers.

IN THE BULRUSH

Cut a cane that once
grew in the river.
Lean on it. Weigh

a stone in your hands
and put it down again.
Watch it moss over.

Strike the stone
to see if it's thinking
of water.

READING HÖLDERLIN ON THE PATIO
WITH THE AID OF A DICTIONARY

One by one, the words
give themselves
up, white flags dispatched
from a silent camp.

When had my shyness returned?

This evening, the sky refused
to lie down. The sun crouched
behind leaves, but the trees
had long since walked away.
The meaning that surfaces

comes to me aslant and
I go to meet it, stepping
out of my body
word for word, until I am

everything at once: the perfume
of the world in which
I go under,
a skindiver
remembering air.

A FATHER OUT WALKING ON THE LAWN

Five rings light your approach across
the dark. You're lonely, anyone

can tell — so many of you
trembling, at the center the thick

dark root. Out here on a lawn
twenty-one years
gone under the haunches of a neighbor's

house, American Beauties
lining a driveway the mirror image of your own,

you wander, waiting to be
discovered. What
can I say to a body
that merely looks

like you? The willow, infatuated with its
surroundings, quakes; not that violent
orgasm not the vain promise of

a rose relinquishing
its famous scent all for you, no,

not even the single
brilliant feather

a blue jay loses in flight
which dangles momentarily, azure scimitar,
above the warm eaves of your house —
nothing can change
this travesty, this

magician's skew of scarves
issuing from an opaque heart.

Who sees you anyway, except
at night, and with a fantastic eye?

If only you were bright enough to touch!

from THOMAS AND BEULAH

Variation on Pain

Two strings, one pierced cry.
So many ways to imitate
The ringing in his ears.

He lay on the bunk, mandolin
In his arms. Two strings
For each note and seventeen
Frets; ridged sound
Humming beneath calloused
Fingertips.

There was a needle
In his head but nothing
Fit through it. Sound quivered
Like a rope stretched clear
To land, tensed and brimming,
A man gurgling air.

Two greased strings
For each pierced lobe:
So is the past forgiven.

Compendium

He gave up fine cordials and
his hounds-tooth vest.

He became a sweet tenor
in the gospel choir.

Canary, usurper
of his wife's affections.

Girl girl
girl girl.

In the parlor, with streamers,
a bug on a nail.

The canary courting its effigy.
The girls fragrant in their beds.

Daystar

She wanted a little room for thinking:
but she saw diapers steaming on the line,
a doll slumped behind the door.

So she lugged a chair behind the garage
to sit out the children's naps.

Sometimes there were things to watch —
the pinched armor of a vanished cricket,
a floating maple leaf. Other days
she stared until she was assured
when she closed her eyes
she'd see only her own vivid blood.

She had an hour, at best, before Liza appeared
pouting from the top of the stairs.
And just *what* was mother doing
out back with the field mice? Why,

building a palace. Later
that night when Thomas rolled over and
lurched into her, she would open her eyes
and think of the place that was hers
for an hour — where
she was nothing,
pure nothing, in the middle of the day.

RITA DOVE

Sunday Greens

She wants to hear
wine pouring.
She wants to taste
change. She wants
pride to roar through
the kitchen till it shines
like straw, she wants

lean to replace
tradition. Ham knocks
in the pot, nothing
but bones, each
with its bracelet
of flesh.

The house stinks
like a zoo in summer,
while upstairs
her man sleeps on.
Robe slung over
her arm and
the cradled hymnal,

she pauses, remembers
her mother in a slip
lost in blues,
and those collards,
wild-eared,
singing.

Company

No one can help him anymore.
Not the young thing next door
in the red pedal pushers,
not the canary he drove distracted

with his mandolin. There'll be
no more trees to wake him in moonlight,
nor a single dry spring morning
when the fish are lonely for company.

She's standing there telling him: give it up.
She is weary of sirens and his face
worn with salt. *If this is code,*

she tells him, *listen: we were good,*
though we never believed it.
And now he can't even touch her feet.

MISSISSIPPI

In the beginning was the dark
moan and creak, a sidewheel
moving through. Thicker
then, scent of lilac,
scent of thyme; slight hairs
on a wrist lying down in sweat.
We were falling down
river, carnal
slippage and shadow melt.
We were standing on the deck
of the New World, before maps:
tepid seizure of a breeze
and the spirit hissing away . . .

SILOS

Like martial swans in spring paraded against the city sky's
shabby blue, they were always too white and
suddenly there.

They were never fingers, never xylophones, although once
a stranger said they put him in mind of Pan's pipes
and all the lost songs of Greece. But to the townspeople
they were like cigarettes, the smell chewy and bitter
like a field shorn of milkweed, or beer brewing, or
a fingernail scorched over a flame.

No, no, exclaimed the children. They're a fresh packet of chalk,
dreading math work.

They were masculine toys. They were tall wishes. They
were the ribs of the modern world.

THE BREATHING, THE ENDLESS NEWS

Every god is lonely, an exile
composed of parts: elk horn,
cloven hoof. Receptacle

for wishes, each god is empty
without us, penitent,
raking our yards into windblown piles. . . .

Children know this: they are
the trailings of gods. Their eyes
hold nothing at birth then fill slowly

with the myth of ourselves. Not so the dolls,
out for the count, each toe pouting from
the slumped-over toddler clothes:

no blossoming there. So we
give our children dolls, and
they know just what to do —

line them up and shoot them.
With every execution
doll and god grow stronger.

AFTER READING *MICKEY IN THE NIGHT KITCHEN*
FOR THE THIRD TIME BEFORE BED

I'm in the milk and the milk's in me! . . . I'm Mickey!

My daughter spreads her legs
to find her vagina:
hairless, this mistaken
bit of nomenclature
is what a stranger cannot touch
without her yelling. She demands
to see mine and momentarily
we're a lopsided star
among the spilled toys,
my prodigious scallops
exposed to her neat cameo.

And yet the same glazed
tunnel, layered sequences.
She is three; that makes this
innocent. *We're pink!*
she shrieks, and bounds off.

Every month she wants
to know where it hurts
and what the wrinkled string means
between my legs. *This is good blood*
I say, but that's wrong, too.
How to tell her that it's what makes us —
black mother, cream child.
That we're in the pink
and the pink's in us.

THE ISLAND WOMEN OF PARIS

skim from curb to curb like regatta,
from Pont Neuf to the Quai de la Rappe
in cool negotiation with traffic,

each a country to herself
transposed to this city
by a fluke called "imperial courtesy."

The island women glide past held aloft
by a wire running straight to heaven.
Who can ignore their ornamental bearing,
turbans haughty as parrots,
or deft braids carved into airy cages
transfixed on their manifest brows?

The island women move through Paris
as if they had just finished inventing
their destinations. It's better
not to get in their way. And better
not look an island woman in the eye —
unless you like feeling unnecessary.

Alan Dugan

LOVE SONG: I AND THOU

Nothing is plumb, level, or square:
  the studs are bowed, the joists
are shaky by nature, no piece fits
  any other piece without a gap
or pinch, and bent nails
  dance all over the surfacing
like maggots. By Christ
  I am no carpenter. I built
the roof for myself, the walls
  for myself, the floors
for myself, and got
  hung up in it myself. I
danced with a purple thumb
  at this house-warming, drunk
with my prime whiskey: rage.
  Oh I spat rage's nails
into the frame-up of my work:
  it held. It settled plumb,
level, solid, square and true
  for that great moment. Then
it screamed and went on through,
  skewing as wrong the other way.
God damned it. This is hell,
  but I planned it, I sawed it,
I nailed it, and I
  will live in it until it kills me.
I can nail my left palm
  to the left-hand crosspiece but
I can't do everything myself.
  I need a hand to nail the right,
a help, a love, a you, a wife.

TRIBUTE TO KAFKA
FOR SOMEONE TAKEN

The party is going strong.
The doorbell rings. It's
for someone named me.
I'm coming. I take
a last drink, a last
puff on a cigarette,
a last kiss at a girl,
and step into the hall,
                              bang,
shutting out the laughter. "Is
your name you?" "Yes."
"Well come along then."
"See here. See here. See here."

GENERAL PROTHALAMION
FOR WARTIMES

Marry. Sweets, tarts and sweets,
come among soots and sherds.
The dairy of the breasts
and warehouse of the balls
will out-last granaries
when grains and futures fall,

granted a lasting. Lust
that lasts a bloodshot night
protected from the air
will breakfast in wrecked day,
excused because it must,
and find its scavenge there.

Given a harvest of wives
and lopping-off of males,
granted that some survive,

the warden of the weak
is number, blood's variety
marauding in the streets.

So, penis, guide the flesh
to shelter in the womb
when sirens and the police
lament all other homes,
and if born, suckling mouths
grow privily with fangs,

well, fangs are promises
to live on what is left,
granted some leavings, and
monsters are replies.
So, marry. Sours and sweets
come among shots and cries.

TO A RED-HEADED DO-GOOD WAITRESS

Every morning I went to her charity and learned
to face the music of her white smile so well
that it infected my black teeth as I escaped,
and those who saw me smiled too and went in
the White Castle, where she is the inviolable lady.

There cripples must be bright, and starvers noble:
no tears, no stomach-cries, but pain made art
to move her powerful red pity toward philanthropy.
So I must wear my objectively stinking poverty
like a millionaire clown's rags and sing, "Oh I

got plenty o' nuttin'," as if I made
a hundred grand a year like Gershwin, while
I get a breakfast every day from her for two
weeks and nothing else but truth: she has
a policeman and a wrong sonnet in fifteen lines.

FOR MASTURBATION

I have allowed myself
this corner and am God.
Here in the must
beneath their stoop
I will do as I will,
either as act as act,
or dream for the sake of dreams,
and if they find me out
in rocket ships or jets
working to get away,

then let my left great-toe-
nail grow into the inside knob
of my right ankle bone and let
my fingernails make eight new moons
temporarily in the cold salt marshes of my palms!
THIS IS THE WAY IT IS, and if
it is "a terrible disgrace"
it is as I must will,
because I am not them
though I am theirs to kill.

FABRICATION OF ANCESTORS

For old Billy Dugan, shot in the ass in the Civil War, my father said.

The old wound in my ass
has opened up again, but I
am past the prodigies
of youth's campaigns, and weep
where I used to laugh
in war's red humors, half
in love with silly-assed pains
and half not feeling them.
I have to sit up with
an indoor unsittable itch

ALAN DUGAN

before I go down late
and weeping to the storm-
cellar on a dirty night
and go to bed with the worms.
So pull the dirt up over me
and make a family joke
for Old Billy Blue Balls,
the oldest private in the world
with two ass-holes and no
place more to go to for a laugh
except the last one. Say:
The North won the Civil War
without much help from me
although I wear a proof
of the war's obscenity.

POEM

What's the balm
for a dying life,
dope, drink, or Christ,
is there one?

I puke and choke
with it and find
no peace of mind
in flesh, and no hope.

It flows away
in mucous juice.
Nothing I can do
can make it stay,

so I give out
and water the garden: it
is all shit
for the flowers anyhow.

ALAN DUGAN

ELEGY FOR A PURITAN CONSCIENCE

I closed my ears with stinging bugs
and sewed my eyelids shut
but heard a sucking at the dugs
and saw my parents rut.

I locked my jaw with rusty nails
and cured my tongue in lime
but ate and drank in garbage pails
and said these words of crime.

I crushed my scrotum with two stones
and drew my penis in
but felt your wound expect its own
and fell in love with sin.

PRAYER

God, I need a job because I need money.
Here the world is, enjoyable with whiskey,
women, ultimate weapons, and class!
But if I have no money, then my wife
gets mad at me, I can't drink well,
the armed oppress me, and no boss
pays me money. But when I work,
Oh I get paid!, the police are courteous,
and I can have a drink and breathe air.

I feel classy. I am where the arms are.
The wife is wife in deed. The world
is interesting!, except I have to be
indoors all day and take shit, and make
weapons to kill outsiders with. I miss
the air and smell that paid work stinks
when done for someone else's profit, so I quit,

enjoy a few flush days in air, drunk, then
I need a job again. I'm caught in a steel cycle.

ON LEAVING TOWN

This must be a bad dream. We will wake up
tomorrow naked in the prior garden, each
entwined in his particular love. We will
get up to natural water, fruits, and what?,
a gambol with the lions? Nonsense. This
is petrified obsession, perfect in tautology,
visible in the smoke, the layout of the streets,
and prison buildings. The city has put on
glass armor in rock war against its death,
which is internal. It rides out radiate
on country roads to ride down enemy foliage.
Why? There's nothing left in it to kill
except its people, and they look thoroughly every way —
left, right, front, back, up, down, and in —
before they cross another, or its streets. Such animals,
joyful of desolate beauties, they are so tough, the live ones,
that they stand around like Easter Island statues of survival won
by casual struggle, proud of their tension or their craft.
Oh I reject the dream but not the city. I
have loved its life and left it and I am
a better animal for having learned its ways;
but it is not enough to be a captive animal,
social in town. Escaped emotions: boredom and fear.

UNTITLED POEM

Once, one of my students read a book we had.
She was doing a history assignment on
the decline and fall of the Roman Empire

and crying. When I asked her why
she said Because. All those people died.
I said that if you start to cry for the dead
you won't have much time for anything else.
Besides, after all the city people were killed
or died off, because their cultures got too high,
the barbarians kept some peasants alive
for their food value. Some barbarian raped
some peasant woman who produced
a child who ultimately produced you
and me, so there is this family continuity,
so don't cry, it's obvious, look around!
This is the reason why we Americans
are a nation of peasants and barbarians.

ON FINDING THE TREE OF LIFE

After Genesis 3: 22–23

If there is an outside out there
one should go out to try to find it.
This I did. There is a garden world
out there, with birds, trees, and the tree
they call The Tree of Life. The birds
avoid it, naturally. The bunches of red
berries are intact except for one bunch. It's
partly eaten. The spoor around the tree
is old, but it would indicate that some
stupid godforsaken human or beast
had staggered around and crawled away
in the first agonies of immortality.
It's too bad for it, whoever it is
and will be: our own deaths are bad enough.

ALAN DUGAN

LAST STATEMENT FOR A LAST ORACLE

After this oracle there will be no more oracles.
The precinct is hereby desanctified. You wanted it,
you have it. From now on everything I say
will be a lie said for cash. Now, for the last time,
here's the truth: You have won with your horse power
and numbers from the north. You will go on
winning forever — this is your damnation —
until your conquests and the insides of your heads
are alike, and you and I know what it's like
in there, so if some dirty beast remembers,
on some future dirty night, what it was like
once to have been a human being and pleasing to me
in a fair exchange of pure sacrifice for pure prophecy
he will throw himself into a fire and howl to death.
I will now drop back into the fire you are
so curious about. When you get drunk tonight
and pee on it, it, you and I will go out like the light
and an acid yellow smoke will take the place of our souls.
We will have to go on living a lie for a while, however,
in the unspeakable condition I have referred to in passing.

SURVIVING THE HURRICANE

When the neighbor's outhouse went by
and landed upside down on my property,
unoccupied, I laughed and yelled, "It's mine,"
but what's so funny? the TV says
that many, many will get blown away
in the hurricane's uproarious humors,
and now the horizontal rain comes through
my wall, the wallpaper heaves and cries
and runs down to the floor as pulp
as the windows go out with the wind,
poof!, and the wind picks off the roof
two shingles at a time in love-me-nots,

and there is no difference inside or out:
Leaning against the wall or the wind
is the same. This wet is that wet.
There is no protection anywhere except
I go stand in the upside-down outhouse
with the crapper over my stinking head,
once it has dripped dry of its storm-borne shit,
and be the dry mummy of its sarcophagus
under the whole hurricane of the universe.
That's what's so funny: Egypt.

CLOSING TIME AT THE SECOND AVENUE DELI

This is the time of night of the delicatessen
when the manager is balancing
a nearly empty ketchup bottle
upside-down on a nearly full ketchup bottle
and spreading his hands slowly away
from the perfect balance like shall I say
a priest blessing the balance, the achievement
of perfect emptiness, of perfect fullness? No,
this is a kosher delicatessen. The manager
is not like. He is not like a priest,
he is not even like a rabbi, he
is not like anyone else except the manager
as he turns to watch the waitress
discussing the lamb stew with my wife,
how most people eat the whole thing,
they don't take it home in a container,
as she mops up the tables, as the
cashier shall I say balances out?
No. The computer does all that. This
is not the time for metaphors. This is the time
to turn out the lights, and yes,
imagine it, those two ketchup bottles
will stand there all night long
as acrobatic metaphors of balance,
of emptiness, of fullness perfectly contained,
of any metaphor you wish unless

the manager snaps his fingers at the door,
goes back, and separates them for the night
from that unnatural balance, and the store goes dark
as my wife says should we take a cab
or walk, the stew is starting to drip already.
Shall I say that the container can not
contain the thing contained anymore? No.
Just that the lamb stew is leaking all across town
in one place: it is leaking on the floor of the taxi-cab,
and that somebody is going to pay for this ride.

Robert Duncan

OFTEN I AM PERMITTED TO RETURN
TO A MEADOW

as if it were a scene made-up by the mind,
that is not mine, but is a made place,

that is mine, it is so near to the heart,
an eternal pasture folded in all thought
so that there is a hall therein

that is a made place, created by light
wherefrom the shadows that are forms fall.

Wherefrom fall all architectures I am
I say are likenesses of the First Beloved
whose flowers are flames lit to the Lady.

She it is Queen Under The Hill
whose hosts are a disturbance of words within words
that is a field folded.

It is only a dream of the grass blowing
east against the source of the sun
in an hour before the sun's going down

whose secret we see in a children's game
of ring a round of roses told.

Often I am permitted to return to a meadow
as if it were a given property of the mind
that certain bounds hold against chaos,

that is a place of first permission,
everlasting omen of what is.

ROBERT DUNCAN

POETRY, A NATURAL THING

    Neither our vices nor our virtues
further the poem. "They came up
    and died
just like they do every year
    on the rocks."

    The poem
feeds upon thought, feeling, impulse,
    to breed   itself,
a spiritual urgency at the dark ladders leaping.

This beauty is an inner persistence
    toward the source
striving against (within) down-rushet of the river,
    a call we heard and answer
in the lateness of the world
    primordial bellowings
from which the youngest world might spring,

salmon not in the well where the
    hazelnut falls
but at the falls battling, inarticulate,
    blindly making it.

This is one picture apt for the mind.

A second: a moose painted by Stubbs,
where last year's extravagant antlers
    lie on the ground.
The forlorn moosey-faced poem wears
    new antler-buds,
    the same,

"a little heavy, a little contrived",

his only beauty to be
    all moose.

ROBERT DUNCAN

INGMAR BERGMAN'S *SEVENTH SEAL*

This is the way it is. We see
three ages in one: the child Jesus
innocent of Jerusalem and Rome
— magically at home in joy —
that's the year from which
our inner persistence has its force.

The second, Bergman shows us,
carries forward image after image
of anguish, of the Christ crossd
and sends up from open sores of the plague
(shown as wounds upon His corpse)
from lacerations in the course of love
(the crown of whose kingdom tears the flesh)

. . . There is so much suffering!
What possibly protects us
from the emptiness, the forsaken cry,
the utter dependence, the vertigo?
Why do so many come to love's edge
only to be stranded there?

The second face of Christ, his
evil, his Other, emaciated, pain and sin.
Christ, what a contagion!
What a stink it spreads round

our age! It's our age!
and the rage of the storm is abroad.
The malignant stupidity of statesmen rules.
The old riders thru the forests race
        shouting: the wind! the wind!
Now the black horror cometh again.

And I'll throw myself down
as the clown does in Bergman's *Seventh Seal*
to cower as if asleep with his wife and child,
hid in the caravan under the storm.

Let the Angel of Wrath pass over.
Let the end come.

War, stupidity and fear are powerful.
We are only children. To bed! to bed!
    To play safe!

To throw ourselves down
helplessly, into happiness,
      into an age of our own, into
      our own days.
There where the Pestilence roars,
where the empty riders of the horror go.

SUCH IS THE SICKNESS OF MANY A GOOD THING

Was he then Adam of the Burning Way?
hid away in the heat like wrath
    conceald in Love's face,
or the seed, Eris in Eros,
    key and lock
of what I was?   I could not speak
    the releasing
word.   For into a dark
    matter he came
and askt me to say what
    I could not say.   "I . ."

All the flame in me stopt
    against my tongue.
My heart was a stone, a dumb
    unmanageable thing in me,
a darkness that stood athwart
    his need
for the enlightening, the
    "I love you" that has
only this one quick in time,
    this one start
when its moment is true.

Such is the sickness of many a good thing
that now into my life from long ago this
refusing to say I love you has bound
the weeping, the yielding, the
    yearning to be taken again,
into a knot, a waiting, a string

> so taut it taunts the song,
> it resists the touch. It grows dark
> to draw down the lover's hand
> from its lightness to what's
>   underground.

BENDING THE BOW

We've our business to attend Day's duties,
bend back the bow in dreams as we may
til the end rimes in the taut string
with the sending. Reveries are rivers and flow
where the cold light gleams reflecting the window upon the
    surface of the table,
the presst-glass creamer, the pewter sugar bowl, the litter
    of coffee cups and saucers,
carnations painted growing upon whose surfaces. The whole
composition of surfaces leads into the other
                current disturbing
what I would take hold of. I'd been

in the course of a letter — I am still
in the course of a letter — to a friend,
who comes close in to my thought so that
the day is hers. My hand writing here
there shakes in the currents of . . . of air?
of an inner anticipation of . . . ?   reaching to touch
ghostly exhilarations in the thought of her.

             At the extremity of this
                design
"there is a connexion working in both directions, as in
            the bow and the lyre" —
only in that swift fulfillment of the wish
                that sleep
            can illustrate my hand
            sweeps the string.

You stand behind the where-I-am.
The deep tones and shadows I will call a woman.
The quick high notes . . . You are a girl there too,
    having something of sister and of wife,
                inconsolate,
and I would play Orpheus for you again,

recall the arrow or song
to the trembling daylight
from which it sprang.

from the Emperor Julian, *Hymn to the Mother of the Gods:*

*And Attis encircles the heavens like a tiara, and thence
sets out as though to descend to earth.*

*For the even is bounded, but the uneven is without bounds
and there is no way through or out of it.*

MY MOTHER WOULD BE A FALCONRESS

My mother would be a falconress,
And I, her gay falcon treading her wrist,
would fly to bring back
from the blue of the sky to her, bleeding, a prize,
where I dream in my little hood with many bells
jangling when I'd turn my head.

My mother would be a falconress,
and she sends me as far as her will goes.
She lets me ride to the end of her curb
where I fall back in anguish.
I dread that she will cast me away,
for I fall, I mis-take, I fail in her mission.

She would bring down the little birds.
And I would bring down the little birds.
When will she let me bring down the little birds,
pierced from their flight with their necks broken,
their heads like flowers limp from the stem?

I tread my mother's wrist and would draw blood.
Behind the little hood my eyes are hooded.
I have gone back into my hooded silence,
talking to myself and dropping off to sleep.

For she has muffled my dreams in the hood she has made me,
sewn round with bells, jangling when I move.
She rides with her little falcon upon her wrist.
She uses a barb that brings me to cower.

ROBERT DUNCAN

She sends me abroad to try my wings
and I come back to her.   I would bring down
the little birds to her
I may not tear into, I must bring back perfectly.

I tear at her wrist with my beak to draw blood,
and her eye holds me, anguisht, terrifying.
She draws a limit to my flight.
Never beyond my sight, she says.

She trains me to fetch and to limit myself in fetching.
She rewards me with meat for my dinner.
But I must never eat what she sends me to bring her.

Yet it would have been beautiful, if she would have carried me,
always, in a little hood with the bells ringing,
at her wrist, and her riding
to the great falcon hunt, and me
flying up to the curb of my heart from her heart
to bring down the skylark from the blue to her feet,
straining, and then released for the flight.

My mother would be a falconress,
and I her gerfalcon, raised at her will,
from her wrist sent flying, as if I were her own
pride, as if her pride
knew no limits, as if her mind
sought in me flight beyond the horizon.

Ah, but high, high in the air I flew.
And far, far beyond the curb of her will,
were the blue hills where the falcons nest.
And then I saw west to the dying sun —
it seemd my human soul went down in flames.

I tore at her wrist, at the hold she had for me,
until the blood ran hot and I heard her cry out,
far, far beyond the curb of her will

to horizons of stars beyond the ringing hills of the world where
     the falcons nest
I saw, and I tore at her wrist with my savage beak.
I flew, as if sight flew from the anguish in her eye beyond her sight,
sent from my striking loose, from the cruel strike at her wrist,
striking out from the blood to be free of her.

My mother would be a falconress,
and even now, years after this,
when the wounds I left her had surely heald,
and the woman is dead,
her fierce eyes closed, and if her heart
were broken, it is stilld

I would be a falcon and go free.
I tread her wrist and wear the hood,
talking to myself, and would draw blood.

THE TORSO   **PASSAGES 18**

Most beautiful!   the red-flowering eucalyptus,
the madrone, the yew

Is he . . .

So thou wouldst smile, and take me in thine arms
The sight of London to my exiled eyes
Is as Elysium to a new-come soul

If he be Truth
I would dwell in the illusion of him

His hands unlocking from chambers of my male body

such an idea in man's image

rising tides that sweep me towards him

. . . *homosexual?*

and at the treasure of his mouth

pour forth my soul

his soul   commingling

I thought a Being more than vast, His body leading
into Paradise,   his eyes
quickening a fire in me,   a trembling

ROBERT DUNCAN

hieroglyph: At the root of the neck

the clavicle, for the neck is the stem of the great artery
   upward into his head that is beautiful

               At the rise of the pectoral muscles

the nipples, for the breasts are like sleeping fountains
   of feeling in man, waiting above the beat of his heart,
   shielding the rise and fall of his breath, to be
   awakend

                  At the axis of his mid hriff

the navel, for in the pit of his stomach the chord from
   which first he was fed has its temple

                  At the root of the groin

the pubic hair, for the torso is the stem in which the man
   flowers forth and leads to the stamen of flesh in which
   his seed rises

a wave of need and desire over   taking me

                  cried out my name

(This was long ago.   It was another life)

                  and said,

         What do you want of me?

I do not know, I said.   I have fallen in love.   He
      has brought me into heights and depths my heart
            would fear   without him.   His look

      pierces my side   •   fire eyes   •

I have been waiting for you, he said:
            I know what you desire

         you do not yet know   but through me   •

And I am with you everywhere.   In your falling

I have fallen from a high place.   I have raised myself

      from darkness in your   rising

             wherever you are

   my hand in your hand   seeking   the locks, the keys

I am there.   Gathering me, you gather

      your Self   •

For my Other is not a woman but a man

the King upon whose bosom let me lie.

from DANTE ÉTUDES

The Work

                    [De Monarchia, I, IV]

"The work proper to the human race,   taken as a whole,   is to keep the whole capacity of the potential intellect constantly actualized,   primarily for speculation,   and secondarily (by extension, and for the sake of the other) for action."

      I enact my being here

     for the sake of

     a speculation in the nature of Man,

        needs time and space   (a stage)
        that only peace of mind provides.

  Hence: that the human attain
    its proper work,   right ratio
    and the equilibrations
    Imagination demands

      to take its spring

     from the hidden

not yet among us

pivot of what   we are doing

sing.

"not riches, not pleasures, not honors, not length of life, not
health, not strength"   — what do we know of from where Life is
ever moving us? —   "not beauty, but peace"

leisure (time without anxiety for time)

for furor   toward

Justice — not the requital of grievances,
     not retribution for wrongs,   not paying back,

but for that   freeing the grievance in us,

the fit of the work

to the requirement recognized

volunteered   an emotional

distribution:

thus exact riming
and the timing of syllables
that the idea "count"
and custom enter the poem

and that there be heart,

a harmony

large enough to account for

conflict

in the adequate concept seen to provide

contrast

the Artist   rejoices in.

Lawrence Ferlinghetti

[CONSTANTLY RISKING ABSURDITY]

Constantly risking absurdity
                and death
      whenever he performs
            above the heads
                  of his audience
    the poet like an acrobat
          climbs on rime
             to a high wire of his own making
and balancing on eyebeams
            above a sea of faces
     paces his way
         to the other side of day
   performing entrechats
         and sleight-of-foot tricks
and other high theatrics
         and all without mistaking
     any thing
       for what it may not be

   For he's the super realist
           who must perforce perceive
     taut truth
         before the taking of each stance or step
in his supposed advance
         toward that still higher perch
where Beauty stands and waits
        with gravity
          to start her death-defying leap

   And he
     a little charleychaplin man
           who may or may not catch
     her fair eternal form
         spreadeagled in the empty air
    of existence

LAWRENCE FERLINGHETTI

[SOMETIME DURING ETERNITY]

Sometime during eternity
                        some guys show up
    and one of them
                who shows up real late
                                is a kind of carpenter
            from some square-type place
                            like Galilee
            and he starts wailing
                        and claiming he is hep
            to who made heaven
                            and earth
                                    and that the cat
                who really laid it on us
                            is his Dad

        And moreover
            he adds
                    It's all writ down
                        on some scroll-type parchments
            which some henchmen
                            leave lying around the Dead Sea somewheres
                a long time ago
                            and which you won't even find
    for a coupla thousand years or so
                            or at least for
        nineteen hundred and fortyseven
                                of them
                to be exact
                            and even then
        nobody really believes them
                            or me
                                for that matter

    You're hot
                they tell him

    And they cool him

    They stretch him on the Tree to cool

And everybody after that
                              is always making models
              of this Tree
                        with Him hung up
and always crooning His name
                              and calling Him to come down
              and sit in
                        on their combo
              as if he is the king cat
                              who's got to blow
or they can't quite make it

Only he don't come down
                              from His Tree

Him just hang there
              on His Tree
                        looking real Petered out
              and real cool
                        and also
              according to a roundup
                        of late world news
from the usual unreliable sources
                        real dead

[THE PENNYCANDYSTORE BEYOND THE EL]

The pennycandystore beyond the El
is where I first
              fell in love
                        with unreality
Jellybeans glowed in the semi-gloom
of that september afternoon
A cat upon the counter moved among
                        the licorice sticks
              and tootsie rolls
        and Oh Boy Gum

Outside the leaves were falling as they died
A wind had blown away the sun
A girl ran in

Her hair was rainy
Her breasts were breathless in the little room

Outside the leaves were falling
                        and they cried
                                    Too soon! too soon!

I AM WAITING

        I am waiting for my case to come up
        and I am waiting
        for a rebirth of wonder
        and I am waiting for someone
        to really discover America
        and wail
        and I am waiting
        for the discovery
        of a new symbolic western frontier
        and I am waiting
        for the American Eagle
        to really spread its wings
        and straighten up and fly right
        and I am waiting
        for the Age of Anxiety
        to drop dead
        and I am waiting
        for the war to be fought
        which will make the world safe
        for anarchy
        and I am waiting
        for the final withering away
        of all governments
        and I am perpetually awaiting
        a rebirth of wonder

        I am waiting for the Second Coming
        and I am waiting
        for a religious revival
        to sweep thru the state of Arizona
        and I am waiting
        for the Grapes of Wrath to be stored
        and I am waiting
        for them to prove

that God is really American
and I am seriously waiting
for Billy Graham and Elvis Presley
to exchange roles seriously
and I am waiting
to see God on television
piped onto church altars
if only they can find
the right channel
to tune in on
and I am waiting
for the Last Supper to be served again
with a strange new appetizer
and I am perpetually awaiting
a rebirth of wonder

I am waiting for my number to be called
and I am waiting
for the living end
and I am waiting
for dad to come home
his pockets full
of irradiated silver dollars
and I am waiting
for the atomic tests to end
and I am waiting happily
for things to get much worse
before they improve
and I am waiting
for the Salvation Army to take over
and I am waiting
for the human crowd
to wander off a cliff somewhere
clutching its atomic umbrella
and I am waiting
for Ike to act
and I am waiting
for the meek to be blessed
and inherit the earth
without taxes
and I am waiting
for forests and animals
to reclaim the earth as theirs
and I am waiting
for a way to be devised

to destroy all nationalisms
without killing anybody
and I am waiting
for linnets and planets to fall like rain
and I am waiting for lovers and weepers
to lie down together again
in a new rebirth of wonder

I am waiting for the Great Divide to be crossed
and I am anxiously waiting
for the secret of eternal life to be discovered
by an obscure general practitioner
and save me forever from certain death
and I am waiting
for life to begin
and I am waiting
for the storms of life
to be over
and I am waiting
to set sail for happiness
and I am waiting
for a reconstructed Mayflower
to reach America
with its picture story and tv rights
sold in advance to the natives
and I am waiting
for the lost music to sound again
in the Lost Continent
in a new rebirth of wonder

I am waiting for the day
that maketh all things clear
and I am waiting
for Ole Man River
to just stop rolling along
past the country club
and I am waiting
for the deepest South
to just stop Reconstructing itself
in its own image
and I am waiting
for a sweet desegregated chariot
to swing low
and carry me back to Ole Virginie
and I am waiting

for Ole Virginie to discover
just why Darkies are born
and I am waiting
for God to lookout
from Lookout Mountain
and see the Ode to the Confederate Dead
as a real farce
and I am awaiting retribution
for what America did
to Tom Sawyer
and I am perpetually awaiting
a rebirth of wonder

I am waiting for Tom Swift to grow up
and I am waiting
for the American Boy
to take off Beauty's clothes
and get on top of her
and I am waiting
for Alice in Wonderland
to retransmit to me
her total dream of innocence
and I am waiting
for Childe Roland to come
to the final darkest tower
and I am waiting
for Aphrodite
to grow live arms
at a final disarmament conference
in a new rebirth of wonder

I am waiting
to get some intimations
of immortality
by recollecting my early childhood
and I am waiting
for the green mornings to come again
youth's dumb green fields come back again
and I am waiting
for some strains of unpremeditated art
to shake my typewriter
and I am waiting to write
the great indelible poem
and I am waiting
for the last long careless rapture

and I am perpetually waiting
for the fleeing lovers on the Grecian Urn
to catch each other up at last
and embrace
and I am waiting
perpetually and forever
a renaissance of wonder

MONET'S LILIES SHUDDERING

Monet never knew
             he was painting his 'Lilies' for
a lady from the Chicago Art Institute
     who went to France and filmed
         today's lilies
           by the 'Bridge at Giverny'
               a leaf afloat among them
the film of which now flickers
    at the entrance to his framed visions
      with a Debussy piano soundtrack
flooding with a new fluorescence (fleur-essence?)
  the rooms and rooms
         of waterlilies

Monet caught a Cloud in a Pond
              in 1903
    and got a first glimpse
            of its lilies
and for twenty years returned
    again and again to paint them
       which now gives us the impression
         that he floated thru life on them
               and their reflections
    which he also didn't know
      we would have occasion
          to reflect upon

Anymore than he could know
    that John Cage would be playing a
      'Cello with Melody-driven Electronics'
        tonight at the University of Chicago
And making those Lilies shudder and shed
             black light

MAKING LOVE IN POETRY

(After Breton)

In a war where every second counts
Time drops to the ground
like a shadow from a tree
under which we lie
in a wood boat built from it
by an unknown carpenter beyond the sea
upon which peach pits float
fired by a gunner who has run out of ammunition
for a cannon whose muzzle bites heartshaped holes
out of the horizon of our flesh
stunned in sun and baffled into silence
between the act of sex
and the act of poetry
blissed-out in the darkening air
at the moment of loving and coming
there is no glimpsing of
the misery of the world

ASCENDING OVER OHIO

The angels coming down the aisles
have their wings on backwards
They are not wings for flying
but gossamer illusions
in my TV mind
making these airline ladies
the ministers of my madness
even though each one wears
the same airline uniform
with a spare set of wings on lapels
each is also my ministering angel
my *belle dame sans merci*
come down to earth to fetch me
for the final flight to the heavens
where fly back and forth
the transworld spirits
of all the greatest gods

Buddha floats by holding the Christchild
in a Chinese scroll of sky
unrolling before us
as we ascend
over Warren Ohio
where fiftythousand lost bodies look up
as I release a shower of golden parachutes
with fiftythousand re-inflatable balloons
and fiftythousand valid passports
to the rest of the imaginary universe
where live and love and sing
the most ravenously beautiful bodies & souls
in all eternity
As one comes down the aisle now
spreading her gossamer wings
over me
and offering me
the sweet pneumatic ecstasy
of her airborne breasts

USES OF POETRY

So what is the use of poetry these days
What use is it What good is it
these days and nights in the Age of Autogeddon
in which poetry is what has been paved over
to make a freeway for armies of the night
as in that palm paradiso just north of Nicaragua
where promises made in the plazas
will be betrayed in the back country
or in the so-green fields
of the Concord Naval Weapons Station
where armed trains run over green protesters
where poetry is made important by its absence
the absence of birds in a summer landscape
the lack of love in a bed at midnight
or lack of light at High Noon
in the not-so-White House
For even bad poetry has relevance
for what it does not say
for what it leaves out
Yes what of the sun streaming down

in the meshes of morning
what of white nights and mouths of desire
lips saying Lulu over and over
and all things born with wings that sing
and far far cries upon a beach at nightfall
and light that never was on land and sea
and caverns measured-out by man
where once the sacred rivers ran
near cities by the sea
through which we walk and wander absently
astounded constantly
by the mad spectacle of existence
and all these talking animals on wheels
heroes and heroines with a thousand eyes
with bent hearts and hidden oversouls
with no more myths to call their own
constantly astounded as I am still
by these bare-face bipeds in clothes
these stand-up tragedians
pale idols in the night streets
trance-dancers in the dust of the Last Waltz
in this time of gridlock Autogeddon
where the voice of the poet still sounds distantly
the voice of the Fourth Person Singular
the voice within the voice of the turtle
the face behind the face of the race
a book of light at night
the very voice of life as Whitman heard it
a wild soft laughter
(ah but to free it still
from the word-processor of the mind!)
And I am a reporter for a newspaper
on another planet
come to file a down-to-earth story
of the What When Where How and Why
of this astounding life down here
and of the strange clowns in control of it
the curious clowns in control of it
with hands upon the windowsills
of dread demonic mills
casting their own dark shadows
into the earth's great shadow
in the end of time unseen
in the supreme hashish of our dream

Isabella Gardner

SUMMERS AGO

For Edith Sitwell

> *The Ferryman fairied us out to sea*
> *Gold gold gold sang the apple-tree*

Children I told you I tell you our sun was a hail of gold!
I say that sun stoned, that sun stormed our tranquil, our blue bay
bellsweet saltfresh water (bluer than tongue-can-tell, daughter)
and dazed us, darlings, and dazzled us, I say that sun crazed
(that sun clove) our serene as ceramic selves and our noon glazed cove,
and children all that grew wild by the wonderful water shot tall
as tomorrow, reeds suddenly shockingly green had sprouted like sorrow
and crimson explosions of roses arose in that flurry of Danaean glory
while at night we did swoon ah we swanned to a silverer moonlight than
    listen or lute,
we trysted in gondolas blown from glass and kissed in fluted Venetian
    bliss.

> Sister and brother I your mother
> Once was a girl in skirling weather
> Though summer and swan must alter, falter,
> I waltzed on the water once, son and daughter.

LINES TO A SEAGREEN LOVER

For Maurice English

My lover never danced with me
Not minuet nor sarabande
We walked (embracing) on the sand

My lover never swam with me
We waded to our ankle bones
And winced and shivered on the stones

My lover never flew with me
We stared at sea birds slicing space
And cried What freedom Look what grace

I wish my love had lain with me
Not on the sand beside the sea
But under my ailanthus tree

IN THE MUSEUM

Small and emptied woman you lie here a thousand years dead
your hands on your diminished loins flat in this final bed
teeth jutting from your unwound head your spiced bones black and dried,
who knew you and kissed you and kept you and wept when you died;
died you young had you grace? Risus sardonicus replied.
Then quick I seized my husband's hand while he stared at his bride.

THE WIDOW'S YARD

For Myra

"Snails lead slow idyllic lives . . ."
The rose and the laurel leaves
in the raw young widow's yard
were littered with silver. Hardly a leaf lacked the decimal scale
of the self of a snail. Frail
in friendship I observed with care
these creatures (meaning to spare
the widow's vulnerable eyes
the hurting pity in my gaze).

Snails, I said, are tender skinned.
Excess in nature . . . sun rain wind
are killers. To save themselves
snails shrink to shelter in their shells
where they wait safe and patient
until the elements are gent-
ler. And do they not have other foes?

the widow asked. Turtles crows
foxes rats, I replied, and canned
heat that picnickers abandon. Also parasites invade
their flesh and alien eggs are laid
inside their skins. Their mating
too is perilous. The meeting
turns their faces blue with bliss
and consummation of this
absolute embrace is so
extravagantly slow
in coming that love begun
at dawn may end in fatal sun.

The widow told me that her
husband knew snails' ways and his garden had been Eden for them. He
said the timid snail could lift three
times his weight straight up and haul
a wagon toy loaded with a whole
two hundred times his body's burden.
Then as we left the garden
she said that at the first faint chill
the first premonition of fall
the snails go straight to earth . . . excrete
the lime with which they then secrete
the openings in their shells . . . and wait for spring.
It is those little doors which sing,
she said, when they are boiled.
She smiled at me when I recoiled.

THE MILKMAN

The door was bolted and the windows of my porch
were screened to keep invaders out, the mesh of rust-
proof wire sieved the elements. Did my throat parch
then sat I at my table there and ate with lust
most chaste, the raw red apples; juice, flesh, rind and core.
One still and summer noon while dining in the sun
I was poulticing my thirst with apples, slaking care,
when suddenly I felt a whir of dread. Soon, soon,

stiff as bone, I listened for the Milkman's tread.
I heard him softly bang the door of the huge truck
and then his boots besieged my private yard. I tried
to keep my eyes speared to the table, but the suck
of apprehension milked my force. At last he mounted
my backstairs, climbed to the top, and there he stood still
outside the bolted door. The sun's color fainted.
I felt the horror of his quiet melt me, steal
into my sockets, and seduce me to him from
my dinner. His hand clung round the latch like rubber.
I felt him ooze against the screen and shake the frame.
I had to slide the bolt; and thus I was the robber
of my porch. Breathing smiling shape of fright,
the Milkman made his entrance; insistent donor,
he held in soft bleached hands the bottled sterile fruit,
and gave me this fatal, this apostate dinner.
Now in winter I have retreated from the porch
into the house and the once red apples rot where
I left them on the table. Now if my throat parch
for fruit the Milkman brings a quart for my despair.

LETTER FROM SLOUGH POND

Here where you left me alone
the soft wind sighs through my wishbone
the sun is lapping at my flesh
I couple with the ripples of the fresh
pond water I am rolled by the roiling sea.
Love, in our wide bed, do you lie lonely?
The spoon of longing stirs my marrow
and I thank God this bed is narrow.

PART OF THE DARKNESS

I had thought of the bear in his lair as fiercely free, feasting on honey and
   wildwood fruits;

I had imagined a forest lunge, regretting the circus shuffle and the zoo's
   prescribed pursuits.

Last summer I took books and children to Wisconsin's Great North woods.
   We drove

one night through miles of pines and rainy darkness to a garbage grove

that burgeoned broken crates and bulging paper bags and emptied cans of
   beer,

to watch for native bears, who local guides had told us, scavenged there.

After parking behind three other cars (leaving our headlights on but dim)

We stumbled over soggy moss to join the families blinking on the rim

of mounded refuse bounded east north and west by the forest.

The parents hushed and warned their pushing children each of whom
   struggled to stand nearest

the arena, and presently part of the darkness humped away from the foliage
   and lumbered bear-shaped

toward the heaping spoilage. It trundled into the litter while we gaped,

and for an instant it gaped too, bear-faced, but not a tooth was bared. It
   grovelled

carefully while tin cans clattered and tense tourists tittered. Painstakingly
   it nosed and ravelled

rinds and husks and parings, the used and the refused; bear-skinned and
   doggedly explored

the second-hand remains while headlights glared and flashlights stared
   and shamed bored

children booed, wishing aloud that it would trudge away so they might
   read its tracks.

They hoped to find an as yet unclassified spoor, certain that no authentic
   bear would turn his back

upon the delicacies of his own domain to flounder where mere house-
   wives' leavings rot.

I also was reluctant to concede that there is no wild honey in the forest
and no forest in the bear.

Bereaved, we started home, leaving that animal there.

ON LOOKING IN THE LOOKING GLASS

Your small embattled eyes dispute a face
that middle-aging sags and creases.
Besieged, your eyes protest and plead,
your wild little eyes are bright, and bleed.

And now in an instant's blink my stare
seizes in your beleaguered glare
the pristine gaze the blown-glass stance
of your once
total innocence.
I see and dare the child you were.

And for a wink's lasting, There
Now in your blistered eyes dazzles the flare
of Youth with years and love to swear
the kindling enkindled fire
heedless and sheer . . .
I see and fear the girl you were.

And now for a tic's lending, Now for the stint
of a second's fission I light to the glint
of your Daemon, that familiar whom you stint
so prodigally. Shunting, shan't-
ing, wincing fabricant
I see the maker that you want
and aren't.

And now just now I closed your eyes
your infant ancient naked eyes.
Gaze glare and flare and glint are buried by
my neutral eye-
lids. These island citadels are now surrendered
and with imagination's eye I see you dead.

THE ACCOMPLICES

Must now accomplish the division of remains.
Assassins they will now be scrupulous
take pains to be exact in the division of each part
(Let not the question of the genitals impede
the disposition of their singular dead.)
Each must be left with half a
head and half a heart a hand
for him a hand for her a lung apiece
and an iambic foot for each and then surcease.
As to the disposal of the parts his portion
will rot in the attic carried there
and then forgot. His half the heart
plopped in an Etruscan jar they bought in Tuscany
the rest of his share he will lock in a trunk
her half a heart she will pound in a mortar
and eat. The rest of her share
will be burned until charred black.

THAT WAS THEN

for Riva Blevitsky

Union Pier Michigan. We called it Shapiro
Shangri La. People said I needed a passport.
I was the only Shicksa there Kolya Shura
Manya Tanya and Sonya, Sulya Myra and
Vera they were there. And Riva a young girl then.
Soda pop and ice cream parlors, no bars,
Delicatessens but no liquor stores.
They spoke fractured English fractured Yiddish
and fractured Russian when they did not want
their children to understand. Most husbands
drove down from Chicago fridays but mine
came to me thursdays bringing the squat green
bottles of Chilean white wine I drank
(he was angry if I forgot to buy
cucumbers). My daughter then five, now in
Bedlam, chased butterflies and thirty years

ago my infant son, now for some years
lost, was happy too. I washed his diapers
in a tub and hung them up in the sun.
Instead of a play-pen, my husband, Seymour,
called Simcha which means joy, made a paddock
for him. Dan did not like to be cooped up
(nor did Rose, my daughter Rosy; nor did she)
not then, not later, never. Dan was last
seen in Colombia, South America.
Simcha little Rosy littler Daniel
and the Shicksa we were all of us joy-
full then in Shapiro Shangri La when
we were young and laughing. On the lake beach
the women waded and gossiped. The men,
supine on the hot sand sucked in the sun
through every work and city tired pore
and on the blithe beach played chess needling each
other, "singing" they called it. The Shicksa
swam and her daughter, round pink Rosy made
castles out of sand and when the big rough
boy's unseeing feet crushed her battlements
she cried. (As she would later, as she did
later, as she does now and must again
in inexorable time.) Ah but then
it was different. The first summer at our
Michigan Shangri La we shared one half
a cottage with Seymour's sister Molly
Molly the matriarch and my mother
too Molly ample Yiddish mama
bountiful heart bountiful flesh married
to tender Ben Blevitsky book-binder
and Bolshevik, not Communist though he
thought he was and paid his Party dues.
He pressed on me, a bemused fellow traveller
The Daily Worker which I occasionally
scanned. Aside from Ben's misguided fealty
to a party that betrayed his each, his
every dream, he taught the Shicksa wisdom,
ancient, Hebraic, of the heart and pulse.
This Shicksa loved him all his life. He died
attacking Zionists. In the debate
the heckling hit his heart and aged eighty-two
gentle Ben Blevitsky fell down and died.

That first summer the Shicksa shared the stove
with Molly who wouldn't let her cook
a meal but did teach her to cook kugel
and fix gefilte fish. (It was only
the Shicksa's second marriage and so she
had not yet lost her appetite for cooking,
that came after the fourth marriage when
she recklessly played house with a fifth man.)
Political not pious there was not
kept, a kosher kitchen. Molly and Ben
once took the bus to Chicago saying
they'd be back saturday night for supper
saying Be well Bellotchka but don't cook!
Later Molly's cheeks streaming with laughter
crowed to cronies "The Shicksa cooked a haser
for the Shabbas!" Stuck with cloves it was,
the scored cuts thumbed full of dark brown sugar
hot powdered mustard and the fresh squeezed juice
of sweet oranges and the whole ham smeared
with that luscious mixture and therewith glazed
and all ate that haser with high delight
the Blevitskys, Molly, Ben, and their Bob and Riva
Rose, Simcha and his Bellotchka — the cook
ate and ate while the infant Daniel slept.

That was then. That was then.

THIS NEIGHBORHOOD

"Now I am on the wing."

I have migrated to another place.
This neighborhood is not familiar. I
Walk safely down these streets without the face
That can be recognized, without the sly
And swaggering pretense of kindred heart
With which I wooed so desperately the bold
And myriad tenants of my life. Apart
At last and yet a part afire a-cold
Unfeathered but impassioned in the bone
Like dying Ivan I am on the wing
Articulate alight aloud alone.
Plucked clean and raw the skeleton will sing.

Allen Ginsberg

HOWL

for Carl Solomon

I

I saw the best minds of my generation destroyed by madness, starving
hysterical naked,
dragging themselves through the negro streets at dawn looking for an angry
fix,
angelheaded hipsters burning for the ancient heavenly connection to the
starry dynamo in the machinery of night,
who poverty and tatters and hollow-eyed and high sat up smoking in the
supernatural darkness of cold-water flats floating across the tops of
cities contemplating jazz,
who bared their brains to Heaven under the El and saw Mohammedan
angels staggering on tenement roofs illuminated,
who passed through universities with radiant cool eyes hallucinating Arkansas and Blake-light tragedy among the scholars of war,
who were expelled from the academies for crazy & publishing obscene
odes on the windows of the skull,
who cowered in unshaven rooms in underwear, burning their money in
wastebaskets and listening to the Terror through the wall,
who got busted in their pubic beards returning through Laredo with a belt
of marijuana for New York,
who ate fire in paint hotels or drank turpentine in Paradise Alley, death,
or purgatoried their torsos night after night
with dreams, with drugs, with waking nightmares, alcohol and cock and
endless balls,
incomparable blind streets of shuddering cloud and lightning in the mind
leaping toward poles of Canada & Paterson, illuminating all the motionless world of Time between,
Peyote solidities of halls, backyard green tree cemetery dawns, wine drunk-
enness over the rooftops, storefront boroughs of teahead joyride neon
blinking traffic light, sun and moon and tree vibrations in the roaring
winter dusks of Brooklyn, ashcan rantings and kind king light of mind,
who chained themselves to subways for the endless ride from Battery to
holy Bronx on benzedrine until the noise of wheels and children
brought them down shuddering mouth-wracked and battered bleak of
brain all drained of brilliance in the drear light of Zoo,
who sank all night in submarine light of Bickford's floated out and sat

175

through the stale beer afternoon in desolate Fugazzi's, listening to the
crack of doom on the hydrogen jukebox,
who talked continuously seventy hours from park to pad to bar to Bellevue
to museum to the Brooklyn Bridge,
a lost battalion of platonic conversationalists jumping down the stoops off
fire escapes off windowsills off Empire State out of the moon,
yacketayakking screaming vomiting whispering facts and memories and
anecdotes and eyeball kicks and shocks of hospitals and jails and wars,
whose intellects disgorged in total recall for seven days and nights with
brilliant eyes, meat for the Synagogue cast on the pavement,
who vanished into nowhere Zen New Jersey leaving a trail of ambiguous
picture postcards of Atlantic City Hall,
suffering Eastern sweats and Tangerian bone-grindings and migraines of
China under junk-withdrawal in Newark's bleak furnished room,
who wandered around and around at midnight in the railroad yard wondering where to go, and went, leaving no broken hearts,
who lit cigarettes in boxcars boxcars boxcars racketing through snow toward lonesome farms in grandfather night,
who studied Plotinus Poe St. John of the Cross telepathy and bop kaballa
because the cosmos instinctively vibrated at their feet in Kansas,
who loned it through the streets of Idaho seeking visionary indian angels
who were visionary indian angels,
who thought they were only mad when Baltimore gleamed in supernatural
ecstasy,
who jumped in limousines with the Chinaman of Oklahoma on the impulse of winter midnight streetlight smalltown rain,
who lounged hungry and lonesome through Houston seeking jazz or sex
or soup, and followed the brilliant Spaniard to converse about America
and Eternity, a hopeless task, and so took ship to Africa,
who disappeared into the volcanoes of Mexico leaving behind nothing but
the shadow of dungarees and the lava and ash of poetry scattered in
fireplace Chicago,
who reappeared on the West Coast investigating the F.B.I. in beards
and shorts with big pacifist eyes sexy in their dark skin passing out
incomprehensible leaflets,
who burned cigarette holes in their arms protesting the narcotic tobacco
haze of Capitalism,
who distributed Supercommunist pamphlets in Union Square weeping
and undressing while the sirens of Los Alamos wailed them down,
and wailed down Wall, and the Staten Island ferry also wailed,
who broke down crying in white gymnasiums naked and trembling before
the machinery of other skeletons,
who bit detectives in the neck and shrieked with delight in policecars
for committing no crime but their own wild cooking pederasty and
intoxication,

who howled on their knees in the subway and were dragged off the roof
    waving genitals and manuscripts,
who let themselves be fucked in the ass by saintly motorcyclists, and
    screamed with joy,
who blew and were blown by those human seraphim, the sailors, caresses
    of Atlantic and Caribbean love,
who balled in the morning in the evenings in rosegardens and the grass
    of public parks and cemeteries scattering their semen freely to whom-
    ever come who may,
who hiccupped endlessly trying to giggle but wound up with a sob behind
    a partition in a Turkish Bath when the blonde & naked angel came
    to pierce them with a sword,
who lost their loveboys to the three old shrews of fate the one eyed shrew
    of the heterosexual dollar the one eyed shrew that winks out of the
    womb and the one eyed shrew that does nothing but sit on her ass
    and snip the intellectual golden threads of the craftsman's loom,
who copulated ecstatic and insatiate with a bottle of beer a sweetheart a
    package of cigarettes a candle and fell off the bed, and continued along
    the floor and down the hall and ended fainting on the wall with a
    vision of ultimate cunt and come eluding the last gyzym of con-
    sciousness,
who sweetened the snatches of a million girls trembling in the sunset, and
    were red eyed in the morning but prepared to sweeten the snatch of
    the sunrise, flashing buttocks under barns and naked in the lake,
who went out whoring through Colorado in myriad stolen night-cars,
    N.C., secret hero of these poems, cocksman and Adonis of Denver —
    joy to the memory of his innumerable lays of girls in empty lots &
    diner backyards, moviehouses' rickety rows, on mountaintops in caves
    or with gaunt waitresses in familiar roadside lonely petticoat upliftings
    & especially secret gas-station solipsisms of johns, & hometown alleys
    too,
who faded out in vast sordid movies, were shifted in dreams, woke on a
    sudden Manhattan, and picked themselves up out of basements hung-
    over with heartless Tokay and horrors of Third Avenue iron dreams
    & stumbled to unemployment offices,
who walked all night with their shoes full of blood on the snowbank docks
    waiting for a door in the East River to open to a room full of steamheat
    and opium,
who created great suicidal dramas on the apartment cliff-banks of the
    Hudson under the wartime blue floodlight of the moon & their heads
    shall be crowned with laurel in oblivion,
who ate the lamb stew of the imagination or digested the crab at the
    muddy bottom of the rivers of Bowery,
who wept at the romance of the streets with their pushcarts full of onions
    and bad music,

who sat in boxes breathing in the darkness under the bridge, and rose up
to build harpsichords in their lofts,

who coughed on the sixth floor of Harlem crowned with flame under the
tubercular sky surrounded by orange crates of theology,

who scribbled all night rocking and rolling over lofty incantations which
in the yellow morning were stanzas of gibberish,

who cooked rotten animals lung heart feet tail borsht & tortillas dreaming
of the pure vegetable kingdom,

who plunged themselves under meat trucks looking for an egg,

who threw their watches off the roof to cast their ballot for Eternity outside
of Time, & alarm clocks fell on their heads every day for the next
decade,

who cut their wrists three times successively unsuccessfully, gave up and
were forced to open antique stores where they thought they were growing old and cried,

who were burned alive in their innocent flannel suits on Madison Avenue
amid blasts of leaden verse & the tanked-up clatter of the iron regiments of fashion & the nitroglycerine shrieks of the fairies of advertising & the mustard gas of sinister intelligent editors, or were run down
by the drunken taxicabs of Absolute Reality,

who jumped off the Brooklyn Bridge this actually happened and walked
away unknown and forgotten into the ghostly daze of Chinatown soup
alleyways & firetrucks, not even one free beer,

who sang out of their windows in despair, fell out of the subway window,
jumped in the filthy Passaic, leaped on negroes, cried all over the
street, danced on broken wineglasses barefoot smashed phonograph
records of nostalgic European 1930's German jazz finished the whiskey
and threw up groaning into the bloody toilet, moans in their ears and
the blast of colossal steamwhistles,

who barreled down the highways of the past journeying to each other's
hotrod-Golgotha jail-solitude watch or Birmingham jazz incarnation,

who drove crosscountry seventytwo hours to find out if I had a vision or
you had a vision or he had a vision to find out Eternity,

who journeyed to Denver, who died in Denver, who came back to Denver
& waited in vain, who watched over Denver & brooded & loned in
Denver and finally went away to find out the Time, & now Denver
is lonesome for her heroes,

who fell on their knees in hopeless cathedrals praying for each other's
salvation and light and breasts, until the soul illuminated its hair for
a second,

who crashed through their minds in jail waiting for impossible criminals
with golden heads and the charm of reality in their hearts who sang
sweet blues to Alcatraz,

who retired to Mexico to cultivate a habit, or Rocky Mount to tender

Buddha or Tangiers to boys or Southern Pacific to the black locomo-
tive or Harvard to Narcissus to Woodlawn to the daisychain or grave,

who demanded sanity trials accusing the radio of hypnotism & were left
with their insanity & their hands & a hung jury,

who threw potato salad at CCNY lectures on Dadaism and subsequently
presented themselves on the granite steps of the madhouse with shaven
heads and harlequin speech of suicide, demanding instantaneous
lobotomy,

and who were given instead the concrete void of insulin metrasol electricity hydrotherapy psychotherapy occupational therapy pingpong &
amnesia,

who in humorless protest overturned only one symbolic pingpong table,
resting briefly in catatonia,

returning years later truly bald except for a wig of blood, and tears and
fingers, to the visible madman doom of the wards of the madtowns of
the East,

Pilgrim State's Rockland's and Greystone's foetid halls, bickering with the
echoes of the soul, rocking and rolling in the midnight solitude-bench
dolmen-realms of love, dream of life a nightmare, bodies turned to
stone as heavy as the moon,

with mother finally ******, and the last fantastic book flung out of the
tenement window, and the last door closed at 4 AM and the last telephone slammed at the wall in reply and the last furnished room emptied down to the last piece of mental furniture, a yellow paper rose
twisted on a wire hanger in the closet, and even that imaginary, nothing but a hopeful little bit of hallucination —

ah, Carl, while you are not safe I am not safe, and now you're really in
the total animal soup of time —

and who therefore ran through the icy streets obsessed with a sudden flash
of the alchemy of the use of the ellipse the catalog the meter & the
vibrating plane,

who dreamt and made incarnate gaps in Time & Space through images
juxtaposed, and trapped the archangel of the soul between 2 visual
images and joined the elemental verbs and set the noun and dash of
consciousness together jumping with sensation of Pater Omnipotens
Aeterna Deus

to recreate the syntax and measure of poor human prose and stand before
you speechless and intelligent and shaking with shame, rejected yet
confessing out the soul to conform to the rhythm of thought in his
naked and endless head,

the madman bum and angel beat in Time, unknown, yet putting down
here what might be left to say in time come after death,

and rose reincarnate in the ghostly clothes of jazz in the goldhorn shadow
of the band and blew the suffering of America's naked mind for love

into an eli eli lamma lamma sabacthani saxophone cry that shivered
the cities down to the last radio
with the absolute heart of the poem of life butchered out of their own
bodies good to eat a thousand years.

II

What sphinx of cement and aluminum bashed open their skulls and ate
up their brains and imagination?
Moloch! Solitude! Filth! Ugliness! Ashcans and unobtainable dollars!
Children screaming under the stairways! Boys sobbing in armies! Old
men weeping in the parks!
Moloch! Moloch! Nightmare of Moloch! Moloch the loveless! Mental
Moloch! Moloch the heavy judger of men!
Moloch the incomprehensible prison! Moloch the crossbone soulless jail-
house and Congress of sorrows! Moloch whose buildings are judge-
ment! Moloch the vast stone of war! Moloch the stunned governments!
Moloch whose mind is pure machinery! Moloch whose blood is running
money! Moloch whose fingers are ten armies! Moloch whose breast is
a cannibal dynamo! Moloch whose ear is a smoking tomb!
Moloch whose eyes are a thousand blind windows! Moloch whose skyscrapers stand in the long streets like endless Jehovahs! Moloch whose
factories dream and croak in the fog! Moloch whose smokestacks and
antennae crown the cities!
Moloch whose love is endless oil and stone! Moloch whose soul is electricity and banks! Moloch whose poverty is the specter of genius! Moloch
whose fate is a cloud of sexless hydrogen! Moloch whose name is the
Mind!
Moloch in whom I sit lonely! Moloch in whom I dream Angels! Crazy
in Moloch! Cocksucker in Moloch! Lacklove and manless in Moloch!
Moloch who entered my soul early! Moloch in whom I am a consciousness without a body! Moloch who frightened me out of my natural
ecstasy! Moloch whom I abandon! Wake up in Moloch! Light streaming out of the sky!
Moloch! Moloch! Robot apartments! invisible suburbs! skeleton treasuries!
blind capitals! demonic industries! spectral nations! invincible mad-
houses! granite cocks! monstrous bombs!
They broke their backs lifting Moloch to Heaven! Pavements, trees, radios,
tons! lifting the city to Heaven which exists and is everywhere about
us!
Visions! omens! hallucinations! miracles! ecstasies! gone down the American river!
Dreams! adorations! illuminations! religions! the whole boatload of sensitive bullshit!

Breakthroughs! over the river! flips and crucifixions! gone down the flood!
  Highs! Epiphanies! Despairs! Ten years' animal screams and suicides!
  Minds! New loves! Mad generation! down on the rocks of Time!
Real holy laughter in the river! They saw it all! the wild eyes! the holy
  yells! They bade farewell! They jumped off the roof! to solitude! wav-
  ing! carrying flowers! Down to the river! into the street!

III

Carl Solomon! I'm with you in Rockland
    where you're madder than I am
I'm with you in Rockland
    where you must feel very strange
I'm with you in Rockland
    where you imitate the shade of my mother
I'm with you in Rockland
    where you've murdered your twelve secretaries
I'm with you in Rockland
    where you laugh at this invisible humor
I'm with you in Rockland
    where we are great writers on the same dreadful typewriter
I'm with you in Rockland
    where your condition has become serious and is reported on the radio
I'm with you in Rockland
    where the faculties of the skull no longer admit the worms of the
    senses
I'm with you in Rockland
    where you drink the tea of the breasts of the spinsters of Utica
I'm with you in Rockland
    where you pun on the bodies of your nurses the harpies of the Bronx
I'm with you in Rockland
    where you scream in a straightjacket that you're losing the game of
    the actual pingpong of the abyss
I'm with you in Rockland
    where you bang on the catatonic piano the soul is innocent and im-
    mortal it should never die ungodly in an armed madhouse
I'm with you in Rockland
    where fifty more shocks will never return your soul to its body again
    from its pilgrimage to a cross in the void
I'm with you in Rockland
    where you accuse your doctors of insanity and plot the Hebrew socialist
    revolution against the fascist national Golgotha
I'm with you in Rockland

where you will split the heavens of Long Island and resurrect your
living human Jesus from the superhuman tomb
I'm with you in Rockland
where there are twentyfive-thousand mad comrades all together singing
the final stanzas of the Internationale
I'm with you in Rockland
where we hug and kiss the United States under our bedsheets the
United States that coughs all night and won't let us sleep
I'm with you in Rockland
where we wake up electrified out of the coma by our own souls'
airplanes roaring over the roof they've come to drop angelic bombs
the hospital illuminates itself imaginary walls collapse   O skinny le-
gions run outside   O starry spangled shock of mercy the eternal war
is here   O victory forget your underwear we're free
I'm with you in Rockland
in my dreams you walk dripping from a sea-journey on the highway
across America in tears to the door of my cottage in the Western night

San Francisco 1955–56

AMERICA

America I've given you all and now I'm nothing.
America two dollars and twentyseven cents January 17, 1956.
I can't stand my own mind.
America when will we end the human war?
Go fuck yourself with your atom bomb.
I don't feel good don't bother me.
I won't write my poem till I'm in my right mind.
America when will you be angelic?
When will you take off your clothes?
When will you look at yourself through the grave?
When will you be worthy of your million Trotskyites?
America why are your libraries full of tears?
America when will you send your eggs to India?
I'm sick of your insane demands.
When can I go into the supermarket and buy what I need with my good
looks?
America after all it is you and I who are perfect not the next world.
Your machinery is too much for me.

You made me want to be a saint.
There must be some other way to settle this argument.
Burroughs is in Tangiers I don't think he'll come back it's sinister.
Are you being sinister or is this some form of practical joke?
I'm trying to come to the point.
I refuse to give up my obsession.
America stop pushing I know what I'm doing.
America the plum blossoms are falling.
I haven't read the newspapers for months, everyday somebody goes on
    trial for murder.
America I feel sentimental about the Wobblies.
America I used to be a communist when I was a kid I'm not sorry.
I smoke marijuana every chance I get.
I sit in my house for days on end and stare at the roses in the closet.
When I got to Chinatown I get drunk and never get laid.
My mind is made up there's going to be trouble.
You should have seen me reading Marx.
My psychoanalyst thinks I'm perfectly right.
I won't say the Lord's Prayer.
I have mystical visions and cosmic vibrations.
America I still haven't told you what you did to Uncle Max after he came
    over from Russia.

I'm addressing you.
Are you going to let your emotional life be run by Time Magazine?
I'm obsessed by Time Magazine.
I read it every week.
Its cover stares at me every time I slink past the corner candystore.
I read it in the basement of the Berkeley Public Library.
It's always telling me about responsibility. Businessmen are serious. Movie
    producers are serious. Everybody's serious but me.
It occurs to me that I am America.
I am talking to myself again.

Asia is rising against me.
I haven't got a chinaman's chance.
I'd better consider my national resources.
My national resources consist of two joints of marijuana millions of geni-
    tals an unpublishable private literature that goes 1400 miles an hour
    and twentyfive-thousand mental institutions.
I say nothing about my prisons nor the millions of underprivileged who
    live in my flowerpots under the light of five hundred suns.
I have abolished the whorehouses of France, Tangiers is the next to go.
My ambition is to be President despite the fact that I'm a Catholic.

America how can I write a holy litany in your silly mood?
I will continue like Henry Ford my strophes are as individual as his
    automobiles more so they're all different sexes.
America I will sell you strophes $2500 apiece $500 down on your old
    strophe
America free Tom Mooney
America save the Spanish Loyalists
America Sacco & Vanzetti must not die
America I am the Scottsboro boys.
America when I was seven momma took me to Communist Cell meetings
    they sold us garbanzos a handful per ticket a ticket costs a nickel and
    the speeches were free everybody was angelic and sentimental about
    the workers it was all so sincere you have no idea what a good thing
    the party was in 1935 Scott Nearing was a grand old man a real mensch
    Mother Bloor made me cry I once saw Israel Amter plain. Everybody
    must have been a spy.
America you don't really want to go to war.
America it's them bad Russians.
Them Russians them Russians and them Chinamen. And them Russians.
The Russia wants to eat us alive. The Russia's power mad. She wants to
    take our cars from out our garages.
Her wants to grab Chicago. Her needs a Red Readers' Digest. Her wants
    our auto plants in Siberia. Him big bureaucracy running our filling-
    stations.
That no good. Ugh. Him make Indians learn read. Him need big black
    niggers. Hah. Her make us all work sixteen hours a day. Help.
America this is quite serious.
America this is the impression I get from looking in the television set.
America is this correct?
I'd better get right down to the job.
It's true I don't want to join the Army or turn lathes in precision parts
    factories, I'm nearsighted and psychopathic anyway.
America I'm putting my queer shoulder to the wheel.

LOVE POEM ON THEME BY WHITMAN

I'll go into the bedroom silently and lie down between the bridegroom
    and the bride,
those bodies fallen from heaven stretched out waiting naked and restless,
arms resting over their eyes in the darkness,
bury my face in their shoulders and breasts, breathing their skin,

and stroke and kiss neck and mouth and make back be open and known,
legs raised up crook'd to receive, cock in the darkness driven tormented
    and attacking
roused up from hole to itching head,
bodies locked shuddering naked, hot lips and buttocks screwed into each
    other
and eyes, eyes glinting and charming, widening into looks and abandon,
and moans of movement, voices, hands in air, hands between thighs,
hands in moisture on softened hips, throbbing contraction of bellies
till the white come flow in the swirling sheets,
and the bride cry for forgiveness, and the groom be covered with tears of
    passion and compassion,
and I rise up from the bed replenished with last intimate gestures and
    kisses of farewell —
all before the mind wakes, behind shades and closed doors in a darkened
    house
where the inhabitants roam unsatisfied in the night,
nude ghosts seeking each other out in the silence.

PSALM III

    To God: to illuminate all men. Beginning with Skid Road.
    Let Occidental and Washington be transformed into a
higher place, the plaza of eternity.
    Illuminate the welders in shipyards with the brilliance of
their torches.
    Let the crane operator lift up his arm for joy.
    Let elevators creak and speak, ascending and descending in
awe.
    Let the mercy of the flower's direction beckon in the eye.
    Let the straight flower bespeak its purpose in straightness —
to seek the light.
    Let the crooked flower bespeak its purpose in crookedness —
to seek the light.
    Let the crookedness and straightness bespeak the light.
    Let Puget Sound be a blast of light.
    I feed on your Name like a cockroach on a crumb — this
cockroach is holy.

Seattle 1956

WALES VISITATION

White fog lifting & falling on mountain-brow
        Trees moving in rivers of wind
                The clouds arise
    as on a wave, gigantic eddy lifting mist
        above teeming ferns exquisitely swayed
                    along a green crag
        glimpsed thru mullioned glass in valley raine —
Bardic, O Self, Visitacione, tell naught
      but what seen by one man in a vale in Albion,
        of the folk, whose physical sciences end in Ecology,
              the wisdom of earthly relations,
      of mouths & eyes interknit ten centuries visible
        orchards of mind language manifest human,
    of the satanic thistle that raises its horned symmetry
    flowering above sister grass-daisies' pink tiny
              bloomlets angelic as lightbulbs —

Remember 160 miles from London's symmetrical thorned tower
      & network of TV pictures flashing bearded your Self
    the lambs on the tree-nooked hillside this day bleating
    heard in Blake's old ear, & the silent thought of Wordsworth in
              eld Stillness
    clouds passing through skeleton arches of Tintern Abbey —
        Bard Nameless as the Vast, babble to Vastness!
All the Valley quivered, one extended motion, wind
              undulating on mossy hills
    a giant wash that sank white fog delicately down red runnels
             on the mountainside
    whose leaf-branch tendrils moved asway
            in granitic undertow down —
and lifted the floating Nebulous upward, and lifted the arms of the
                              trees
        and lifted the grasses an instant in balance
        and lifted the lambs to hold still
    and lifted the green of the hill, in one solemn wave
A solid mass of Heaven, mist-infused, ebbs thru the vale,
     a wavelet of Immensity, lapping gigantic through Llanthony
                    Valley,
    the length of all England, valley upon valley under Heaven's ocean
              tonned with cloud-hang,
        Heaven balanced on a grassblade —
Roar of the mountain wind slow, sigh of the body,

One Being on the mountainside stirring gently
          Exquisite scales trembling everywhere in balance,
one motion thru the cloudy sky-floor shifting on the million
                    feet of daisies,
one Majesty the motion that stirred wet grass quivering
    to the farthest tendril of white fog poured down
        through shivering flowers on the mountain's
                head —
No imperfection in the budded mountain,
    Valleys breathe, heaven and earth move together,
daisies push inches of yellow air, vegetables tremble
        green atoms shimmer in grassy mandalas,
sheep speckle the mountainside, revolving their jaws with empty
                  eyes,

        horses dance in the warm rain,
    tree-lined canals network through live farmland,
        blueberries fringe stone walls
    on hill breasts nippled with hawthorn,
pheasants croak up meadow-bellies haired with fern —
Out, out on the hillside, into the ocean sound, into delicate
        gusts of wet air,
Fall on the ground, O great Wetness, O Mother, No harm on
              thy body!
Stare close, no imperfection in the grass,
      each flower Buddha-eye, repeating the story,
      the myriad-formed soul
Kneel before the foxglove raising green buds, mauve bells drooped
    doubled down the stem trembling antennae,
    & look in the eyes of the branded lambs that stare
    breathing stockstill under dripping hawthorn —
I lay down mixing my beard with the wet hair of the mountainside,
    smelling the brown vagina-moist ground, harmless,
    tasting the violet thistle-hair, sweetness —
One being so balanced, so vast, that its softest breath
    moves every floweret in the stillness on the valley floor,
    trembles lamb-hair hung gossamer rain-beaded in the grass,
    lifts trees on their roots, birds in the great draught
    hiding their strength in the rain, bearing same weight,

    Groan thru breast and neck, a great Oh! to earth heart
        Calling our Presence together
    The great secret is no secret
      Senses fit the winds,
        Visible is visible,

rain-mist curtains wave through the bearded vale,
grey atoms wet the wind's Kaballah
Crosslegged on a rock in dusk rain,
rubber booted in soft grass, mind moveless,
breath trembles in white daisies by the roadside,
Heaven breath and my own symmetric
Airs wavering thru antlered green fern
drawn in my navel, same breath as breathes thru Capel-Y-Ffn,
Sounds of Aleph and Aum
through forests of gristle,
my skull and Lord Hereford's Knob equal,
All Albion one.
What did I notice? Particulars! The
vision of the great One is myriad —
smoke curls upward from ash tray,
house fire burned low,
The night, still wet & moody black heaven
starless
upward in motion with wet wind.

July 29, 1967 (LSD) — August 3, 1967 (London)

ON NEAL'S ASHES

Delicate eyes that blinked blue Rockies all ash
nipples, Ribs I touched w/ my thumb are ash
mouth my tongue touched once or twice all ash
bony cheeks soft on my belly are cinder, ash
earlobes & eyelids, youthful cock tip, curly pubis
breast warmth, man palm, high school thigh,
baseball bicept arm, asshole anneal'd to silken skin
all ashes, all ashes again.

August 1968

FOURTH FLOOR, DAWN, UP ALL NIGHT WRITING LETTERS

Pigeons shake their wings on the copper church roof
out my window across the street, a bird perched on the cross
surveys the city's blue-grey clouds. Larry Rivers

'll come at 10 AM and take my picture. I'm taking
your picture, pigeons. I'm writing you down, Dawn.
I'm immortalizing your exhaust, Avenue A bus.
O Thought, now you'll have to think the same thing forever!

New York, June 7, 1980, 6:48 AM

ODE TO FAILURE

Many prophets have failed, their voices silent
ghost-shouts in basements nobody heard dusty laughter in family attics
nor glanced them on park benches weeping with relief under empty sky
Walt Whitman viva'd local losers — courage to Fat Ladies in the Freak
    Show! nervous prisoners whose mustached lips dripped sweat on chow
    lines —
Mayakovsky cried, Then die! my verse, die like the workers' rank & file
    fusilladed in Petersburg!
Prospero burned his Power books & plummeted his magic wand to the
    bottom of dragon seas
Alexander the Great failed to find more worlds to conquer!
O Failure I chant your terrifying name, accept me your 54 year old
    Prophet
epicking Eternal Flop! I join your Pantheon of mortal bards, & hasten
    this ode with high blood pressure
rushing to the top of my skull as if I wouldn't last another minute, like
    the Dying Gaul! to
You, Lord of blind Monet, deaf Beethoven, armless Venus de Milo,
    headless Winged Victory!
I failed to sleep with every bearded rosy-cheeked boy I jacked off over
My tirades destroyed no Intellectual Unions of KGB & CIA in turtlenecks
    & underpants, their woolen suits and tweeds
I never dissolved Plutonium or dismantled the nuclear Bomb before my
    skull lost hair
I have not yet stopped the Armies of entire Mankind in their march toward
    World War III
I never got to Heaven, Nirvana, X, Whatchamacallit, I never left Earth,
I never learned to die.

Boulder, March 7/October 10, 1980

Louise Glück

COTTONMOUTH COUNTRY

Fish bones walked the waves off Hatteras.
And there were other signs
That Death wooed us, by water, wooed us
By land: among the pines
An uncurled cottonmouth that rolled on moss
Reared in the polluted air.
Birth, not death, is the hard loss.
I know. I also left a skin there.

LOVE POEM

There is always something to be made of pain.
Your mother knits.
She turns out scarves in every shade of red.
They were for Christmas, and they kept you warm
while she married over and over, taking you
along. How could it work,
when all those years she stored her widowed heart
as though the dead come back.
No wonder you are the way you are,
afraid of blood, your women
like one brick wall after another.

MESSENGERS

You have only to wait, they will find you.
The geese flying low over the marsh,
glittering in black water.
They find you.

And the deer —
how beautiful they are,
as though their bodies did not impede them.

Slowly they drift into the open
through bronze panels of sunlight.

Why would they stand so still
if they were not waiting?
Almost motionless, until their cages rust,
the shrubs shiver in the wind,
squat and leafless.

You have only to let it happen:
that cry — *release, release* — like the moon
wrenched out of earth and rising
full in its circle of arrows

until they come before you
like dead things, saddled with flesh,
and you above them, wounded and dominant.

THANKSGIVING

They have come again to graze the orchard,
knowing they will be denied.
The leaves have fallen; on the dry ground
the wind makes piles of them, sorting
all it destroys.

What doesn't move, the snow will cover.
It will give them away; their hooves
make patterns which the snow remembers.
In the cleared field, they linger
as the summoned prey whose part
is not to forgive. They can afford to die.
They have their place in the dying order.

THE DROWNED CHILDREN

You see, they have no judgment.
So it is natural that they should drown,
first the ice taking them in

and then, all winter, their wool scarves
floating behind them as they sink
until at last they are quiet.
And the pond lifts them in its manifold dark arms.

But death must come to them differently,
so close to the beginning.
As though they had always been
blind and weightless. Therefore
the rest is dreamed, the lamp,
the good white cloth that covered the table,
their bodies.

And yet they hear the names they used
like lures slipping over the pond:
What are you waiting for
come home, come home, lost
in the waters, blue and permanent.

THE GARDEN

1 The Fear of Birth

One sound. Then the hiss and whir
of houses gliding into their places.
And the wind
leafs through the bodies of animals —

But my body that could not content itself
with health — why should it be sprung back
into the chord of sunlight?

It will be the same again.
This fear, this inwardness,
until I am forced into a field
without immunity
even to the least shrub that walks
stiffly out of the dirt, trailing
the twisted signature of its root,
even to a tulip, a red claw.

And then the losses,
one after another,
all supportable.

2 The Garden

The garden admires you.
For your sake it smears itself with green pigment,
the ecstatic reds of the roses,
so that you will come to it with your lovers.

And the willows —
see how it has shaped these green
tents of silence. Yet
there is still something you need,
your body so soft, so alive, among the stone animals.

Admit that it is terrible to be like them,
beyond harm.

3 The Fear of Love

That body lying beside me like obedient stone —
once its eyes seemed to be opening,
we could have spoken.

At that time it was winter already.
By day the sun rose in its helmet of fire
and at night also, mirrored in the moon.
Its light passed over us freely,
as though we had lain down
in order to leave no shadows,
only these two shallow dents in the snow.
And the past, as always, stretched before us,
still, complex, impenetrable.

How long did we lie there
as, arm in arm in their cloaks of feathers,
the gods walked down
from the mountain we built for them?

4 Origins

As though a voice were saying
You should be asleep by now —
But there was no one. Nor
had the air darkened,
though the moon was there,
already filled in with marble.

As though, in a garden crowded with flowers,
a voice had said
How dull they are, these golds,
so sonorous, so repetitious
until you closed your eyes,
lying among them, all
stammering flame:

And yet you could not sleep,
poor body, the earth
still clinging to you —

5   The Fear of Burial

In the empty field, in the morning,
the body waits to be claimed.
The spirit sits beside it, on a small rock —
nothing comes to give it form again.

Think of the body's loneliness.
At night pacing the sheared field,
its shadow buckled tightly around.
Such a long journey.
And already the remote, trembling lights of the village
not pausing for it as they scan the rows.
How far away they seem,
the wooden doors, the bread and milk
laid like weights on the table.

PALAIS DES ARTS

Love long dormant showing itself:
the large expected gods
caged really, the columns
sitting on the lawn, as though perfection
were not timeless but stationary — that
is the comedy, she thinks,
that they are paralyzed. Or like the matching swans,
insular, circling the pond: restraint so passionate
implies possession. They hardly speak.
On the other bank, a small boy throws bits of bread
into the water. The reflected monument

is stirred, briefly, stricken with light —
She can't touch his arm in innocence again.
They have to give that up and begin
as male and female, thrust and ache.

THE MIRROR

Watching you in the mirror I wonder
what it is like to be so beautiful
and why you do not love
but cut yourself, shaving
like a blind man. I think you let me stare
so you can turn against yourself
with greater violence,
needing to show me how you scrape the flesh away
scornfully and without hesitation
until I see you correctly,
as a man bleeding, not
the reflection I desire.

MOCK ORANGE

It is not the moon, I tell you.
It is these flowers
lighting the yard.

I hate them.
I hate them as I hate sex,
the man's mouth
sealing my mouth, the man's
paralyzing body —

and the cry that always escapes,
the low, humiliating
premise of union —

In my mind tonight
I hear the question and pursuing answer

fused in one sound
that mounts and mounts and then
is split into the old selves,
the tired antagonisms. Do you see?
We were made fools of.
And the scent of mock orange
drifts through the window.

How can I rest?
How can I be content
when there is still
that odor in the world?

HYACINTH

1

Is that an attitude for a flower, to stand
like a club at the walk; poor slain boy,
is that a way to show
gratitude to the gods? White
with colored hearts, the tall flowers
sway around you, all the other boys,
in the cold spring, as the violets open.

2

There were no flowers in antiquity
but boys' bodies, pale, perfectly imagined.
So the gods sank to human shape with longing.
In the field, in the willow grove,
Apollo sent the courtiers away.

3

And from the blood of the wound
a flower sprang, lilylike, more brilliant
than the purples of Tyre.
Then the god wept: his vital grief
flooded the earth.

4

Beauty dies: that is the source
of creation. Outside the ring of trees
the courtiers could hear
the dove's call transmit
its uniform, its inborn sorrow —
They stood listening, among the rustling willows.
Was this the god's lament?
They listened carefully. And for a short time
all sound was sad.

5

There is no other immortality:
in the cold spring, the purple violets open.
And yet, the heart is black,
there is its violence frankly exposed.
Or is it not the heart at the center
but some other word?
And now someone is bending over them,
meaning to gather them —

6

They could not wait
in exile forever.
Through the glittering grove
the courtiers ran
calling the name
of their companion
over the birds' noise,
over the willows' aimless sadness.
Well into the night they wept,
their clear tears
altering no earthly color.

LOUISE GLÜCK

THE TRIUMPH OF ACHILLES

In the story of Patroclus
no one survives, not even Achilles
who was nearly a god.
Patroclus resembled him; they wore
the same armor.

Always in these friendships
one serves the other, one is less than the other:
the hierarchy
is always apparent, though the legends
cannot be trusted —
their source is the survivor,
the one who has been abandoned.

What were the Greek ships on fire
compared to this loss?

In his tent, Achilles
grieved with his whole being
and the gods saw

he was a man already dead, a victim
of the part that loved,
the part that was mortal.

CELESTIAL MUSIC

I have a friend who still believes in heaven.
Not a stupid person, yet with all she knows, she literally talks to god,
she thinks someone listens in heaven.
On earth, she's unusually competent.
Brave, too, able to face unpleasantness.

We found a caterpillar dying in the dirt, greedy ants crawling over it.
I'm always moved by weakness, by disaster, always eager to oppose vitality.
But timid, also, quick to shut my eyes.
Whereas my friend was able to watch, to let events play out
according to nature. For my sake, she intervened,
brushing a few ants off the torn thing, and set it down across the road.

My friend says I shut my eyes to god, that nothing else explains
my aversion to reality. She says I'm like the child who buries her head in
    the pillow
so as not to see, the child who tells herself
that light causes sadness —
My friend is like the mother. Patient, urging me
to wake up an adult like herself, a courageous person —
In my dreams, my friend reproaches me. We're walking
on the same road, except it's winter now;
she's telling me that when you love the world you hear celestial music:
look up, she says. When I look up, nothing.
Only clouds, snow, a white business in the trees
like brides leaping to a great height —
Then I'm afraid for her; I see her
caught in a net deliberately cast over the earth —

In reality, we sit by the side of the road, watching the sun set;
from time to time, the silence pierced by a birdcall.
It's this moment we're both trying to explain, the fact
that we're at ease with death, with solitude.
My friend draws a circle in the dirt; inside, the caterpillar doesn't move.
She's always trying to make something whole, something beautiful, an
    image
capable of life apart from her.
We're very quiet. It's peaceful sitting here, not speaking, the composition
fixed, the road turning suddenly dark, the air
going cool, here and there the rocks shining and glittering —
it's this stillness that we both love.
The love of form is a love of endings.

THE UNTRUSTWORTHY SPEAKER

Don't listen to me; my heart's been broken.
I don't see anything objectively.

I know myself; I've learned to hear like a psychiatrist.
When I speak passionately,
that's when I'm least to be trusted.

It's very sad, really: all my life, I've been praised
for my intelligence, my powers of language, of insight.
In the end, they're wasted —

I never see myself,
standing on the front steps, holding my sister's hand.
That's why I can't account
for the bruises on her arm, where the sleeve ends.

In my own mind, I'm invisible: that's why I'm dangerous.
People like me, who seem selfless,
we're the cripples, the liars;
we're the ones who should be factored out
in the interest of truth.

When I'm quiet, that's when the truth emerges.
A clear sky, the clouds like white fibers.
Underneath, a little gray house, the azaleas
red and bright pink.

If you want the truth, you have to close yourself
to the older daughter, block her out:
when a living thing is hurt like that,
in its deepest workings,
all function is altered.

That's why I'm not to be trusted.
Because a wound to the heart
is also a wound to the mind.

Donald Hall

CHRISTMAS EVE IN WHITNEYVILLE

December, and the closing of the year;
The momentary carolers complete
Their Christmas Eves, and quickly disappear
Into their houses on each lighted street.

Each car is put away in each garage;
Each husband home from work, to celebrate,
Has closed his house around him like a cage,
And wedged the tree until the tree stood straight.

Tonight you lie in Whitneyville again,
Near where you lived, and near the woods or farms
Which Eli Whitney settled with the men
Who worked at mass-producing firearms.

The main street, which was nothing after all
Except a school, a stable, and two stores,
Was improvised and individual,
Picking its way alone, among the wars.

Now Whitneyville is like the other places,
Ranch houses stretching flat beyond the square,
Same stores and movie, same composite faces
Speaking the language of the public air.

Old houses of brown shingle still surround
This graveyard where you wept when you were ten
And helped to set a coffin in the ground.
You left a friend from school behind you then,

And now return, a man of fifty-two.
Talk to the boy. Tell him about the years
When Whitneyville quadrupled, and how you
And all his friends went on to make careers,

Had cars as long as hayracks; boarded planes
For Rome or Paris where the pace was slow
And took the time to think how yearly gains,
Profit and volume made the business grow.

"The things I had to miss," you said last week,
"Or thought I had to, take my breath away."
You propped yourself on pillows, where your cheek
Was hollow, stubbled lightly with new gray.

This love is jail; another sets us free.
Tonight the houses and their noise distort
The thin rewards of solidarity.
The houses lean together for support.

The noises fail, and lights go on upstairs.
The men and women are undressing now
To go to sleep. They put their clothes on chairs
To take them up again. I think of how,

All over Whitneyville, when midnight comes,
They lie together and are quieted,
To sleep as children sleep, who suck their thumbs,
Cramped in the narrow rumple of each bed.

They will not have unpleasant thoughts tonight.
They make their houses jails, and they will take
No risk of freedom for the appetite,
Or knowledge of it, when they are awake.

The lights go out and it is Christmas Day.
The stones are white, the grass is black and deep.
I will go back and leave you here to stay
Where the dark houses harden into sleep.

MAPLE SYRUP

August, goldenrod blowing. We walk
into the graveyard, to find
my grandfather's grave. Ten years ago
I came here last, bringing
marigolds from the round garden
outside the kitchen.
I didn't know you then.
                    We walk
among carved names that go with photographs

on top of the piano at the farm:
Keneston, Wells, Fowler, Batchelder, Buck.
We pause at the new grave
of Grace Fenton, my grandfather's
sister. Last summer
we called on her at the nursing home,
eighty-seven, and nodding
in a blue housedress. We cannot find
my grandfather's grave.
       Back at the house
where no one lives, we potter
and explore the back chamber
where everything comes to rest: spinning wheels,
pretty boxes, quilts,
bottles, books, albums of postcards.
Then with a flashlight we descend
firm steps to the root cellar — black,
cobwebby, huge,
with dirt floors and fieldstone walls,
and above the walls, holding the hewn
sills of the house, enormous
granite foundation stones.
Past the empty bins
for squash, apples, carrots, and potatoes,
we discover the shelves for canning, a few
pale pints
of tomato left, and — what
is this? — syrup, maple syrup
in a quart jar, syrup
my grandfather made twenty-five
years ago
for the last time.
     I remember
coming to the farm in March
in sugaring time, as a small boy.
He carried the pails of sap, sixteen-quart
buckets, dangling from each end
of a wooden yoke
that lay across his shoulders, and emptied them
into a vat in the saphouse
where fire burned day and night
for a week.
     Now the saphouse
tilts, nearly to the ground,

like someone exhausted
to the point of death, and next winter
when snow piles three feet thick
on the roofs of the cold farm,
the saphouse will shudder and slide
with the snow to the ground.
                              Today
we take my grandfather's last
quart of syrup
upstairs, holding it gingerly,
and we wash off twenty-five years
of dirt, and we pull
and pry the lid up, cutting the stiff,
dried rubber gasket, and dip our fingers
in, you and I both, and taste
the sweetness, you for the first time,

the sweetness preserved, of a dead man
in the kitchen he left
when his body slid
like anyone's into the ground.

KICKING THE LEAVES

1

Kicking the leaves, October, as we walk home together
from the game, in Ann Arbor,
on a day the color of soot, rain in the air;
I kick at the leaves of maples,
reds of seventy different shades, yellow
like old paper; and poplar leaves, fragile and pale;
and elm leaves, flags of a doomed race.
I kick at the leaves, making a sound I remember
as the leaves swirl upward from my boot,
and flutter; and I remember
Octobers walking to school in Connecticut,
wearing corduroy knickers that swished
with a sound like leaves; and a Sunday buying
a cup of cider at a roadside stand

on a dirt road in New Hampshire; and kicking the leaves,
autumn 1955 in Massachusetts, knowing
my father would die when the leaves were gone.

2

Each fall in New Hampshire, on the farm
where my mother grew up, a girl in the country,
my grandfather and grandmother
finished the autumn work, taking the last vegetables in
from the cold fields, canning, storing roots and apples
in the cellar under the kitchen. Then my grandfather

raked leaves against the house
as the final chore of autumn.
One November I drove up from college to see them.
We pulled big rakes, as we did when we hayed in summer,
pulling the leaves against the granite foundations
around the house, on every side of the house,
and then, to keep them in place, we cut spruce boughs
and laid them across the leaves,
green on red, until the house
was tucked up, ready for snow
that would freeze the leaves in tight, like a stiff skirt.
Then we puffed through the shed door,
taking off boots and overcoats, slapping our hands,
and sat in the kitchen, rocking, and drank
black coffee my grandmother made,
three of us sitting together, silent, in gray November.

3

One Saturday when I was little, before the war,
my father came home at noon from his half day at the office
and wore his Bates sweater, black on red,
with the crossed hockey sticks on it, and raked beside me
in the back yard, and tumbled in the leaves with me,
laughing, and carried me, laughing, my hair full of leaves,
to the kitchen window
where my mother could see us, and smile; and motion
to set me down, afraid I would fall and be hurt.

4

Kicking the leaves today, as we walk home together
from the game, among crowds of people
with their bright pennants, as many and bright as leaves,
my daughter's hair is the red-yellow color
of birch leaves, and she is tall like a birch,
growing up, fifteen, growing older; and my son
flamboyant as maple, twenty,
visits from college, and walks ahead of us, his step

springing, impatient to travel
the woods of the earth. Now I watch them
from a pile of leaves beside this clapboard house
in Ann Arbor, across from the school
where they learned to read,
as their shapes grow small with distance, waving,
and I know that I
diminish, not them, as I go first
into the leaves, taking
the way they will follow, Octobers and years from now.

5

This year the poems came back, when the leaves fell.
Kicking the leaves, I heard the leaves tell stories,
remembering, and therefore looking ahead, and building
the house of dying. I looked up into the maples
and found them, the vowels of bright desire.
I thought they had gone forever
while the bird sang *I love you, I love you*
and shook its black head
from side to side, and its red eye with no lid,
through years of winter, cold
as the taste of chickenwire, the music of cinderblock.

6

Kicking the leaves, I uncover the lids of graves.
My grandfather died at seventy-seven, in March
when the sap was running; and I remember my father
twenty years ago,

coughing himself to death at fifty-two in the house
in the suburbs. Oh, how we flung
leaves in the air! How they tumbled and fluttered around us,
like slowly cascading water, when we walked together
in Hamden, before the war, when Johnson's Pond
had not surrendered to houses, the two of us
hand in hand, and in the wet air the smell of leaves
burning;
and in six years I will be fifty-two.

7

Now I fall, now I leap and fall
to feel the leaves crush under my body, to feel my body
buoyant in the ocean of leaves, the night of them,
night heaving with death and leaves, rocking like the ocean.
Oh, this delicious falling into the arms of leaves,
into the soft laps of leaves!
Face down, I swim into the leaves, feathery,
breathing the acrid odor of maple, swooping
in long glides to the bottom of October —
where the farm lies curled against winter, and soup steams
its breath of onion and carrot
onto damp curtains and windows; and past the windows
I see the tall bare maple trunks and branches, the oak
with its few brown weathery remnant leaves,
and the spruce trees, holding their green.
Now I leap and fall, exultant, recovering
from death, on account of death, in accord with the dead,
the smell and taste of leaves again,
and the pleasure, the only long pleasure, of taking a place
in the story of leaves.

OX CART MAN

In October of the year,
he counts potatoes dug from the brown field,
counting the seed, counting
the cellar's portion out,
and bags the rest on the cart's floor.

He packs wool sheared in April, honey
in combs, linen, leather
tanned from deerhide,
and vinegar in a barrel
hooped by hand at the forge's fire.

He walks by his ox's head, ten days
to Portsmouth Market, and sells potatoes,
and the bag that carried potatoes,
flaxseed, birch brooms, maple sugar, goose
feathers, yarn.

When the cart is empty he sells the cart.
When the cart is sold he sells the ox,
harness and yoke, and walks
home, his pockets heavy
with the year's coin for salt and taxes,

and at home by fire's light in November cold
stitches new harness
for next year's ox in the barn,
and carves the yoke, and saws planks
building the cart again.

GREAT DAY IN THE COWS' HOUSE

In the dark tie-up seven huge Holsteins
lower their heads to feed, chained loosely to old saplings
with whitewashed bark still on them.
They are long dead; they survive, in the great day
that cancels the successiveness of creatures.
Now she stretches her wrinkly neck, her turnip-eye
rolls in her skull, she sucks up breath,
and stretching her long mouth mid-chew she expels:
mm-mmm-mmmmm-mmmmmmmm-ugghwanchhh . . .
— Sweet bellowers enormous and interchangeable,
your dolorous ululations
swell out barnsides, fill spaces inside haymows,
resound down valleys. Moos of revenant cattle
shake ancient timbers and timbers still damp with sap.
*

Now it is warm, late June. The old man strokes
white braids of milk, *strp strp*, from ruminant beasts
with hipbones like tentpoles, the rough
black-and-white hanging crudely upon them.
Now he tilts back his head to recite a poem
about an old bachelor who loves a chicken named Susan.
His voice grows loud with laughter and emphasis
in the silent tie-up where old noises gather.

*

Now a tail lifts to waterfall huge and yellow
or an enormous flop presses out. Done milking, he lifts
with his hoe a leather-hinged board
to scrape manure onto the pile underneath, in April
carted for garden and fieldcorn.
                              The cows in their house
decree the seasons; spring seeds corn,
summer hays, autumn fences, and winter saws ice
from Eagle Pond, sledging it up hill to pack it away
in sawdust; through August's parch and Indian summer
great chunks of the pond float in the milkshed tank.

*

Pull down the spiderwebs! Whitewash the tie-up!
In the great day there is also the odor of poverty
and anxiety over the Agricultural Inspector's visit.

*

They are long dead; they survive, in the great day
of August, to convene afternoon and morning
for milking. Now they graze Ragged Mountain: —
steep sugarbush, little mountain valleys and brooks,
high clovery meadows, slate-colored lowbush blueberries.
When grass is sweetest they are slow to leave it;
late afternoons he spends hours searching . . .
He knows their secret places; he listens for one peal
of a cowbell carried on a breeze; he calls:
"Ke-bosh, ke-bo-o-sh, ke-bosh, ke-bosh . . ."
He climbs dry creekbeds and old logging roads
or struggles up needle-banks pulling on fir branches.
He hacks with his jackknife a chunk of sprucegum
oozing from bark and softens it in his cheek-pouch
for chewing.
               Then he pushes through hemlock's gate
to join the society of Holsteins; they look up from grass
as if mildly surprised, and file immediately downward.

*

Late in October after the grass freezes
the cattle remain in their stalls, twice a day loosed
to walk stiff-legged to the watering trough
from which the old man lifts a white lid of ice.
Twice a day he shovels ensilage into their stalls
and shakes hay down from the loft, stuffing a forkful
under each steaming nose.
                In late winter,
one after one, the pink-white udders
dry out as new calves swell their mothers' bellies.
Now these vessels of hugeness bear, one after one,
skinny-limbed small Holsteins eager to suck
the bounty of freshening. Now he climbs to the barn
in boots and overalls, two sweaters,
a cloth cap, and somebody's old woolen coat;
now he parts the calf from its mother after feeding,
and strips the udder clean,
to rejoice in the sweet frothing tonnage of milk.
*
Now in April, when snow remains on the north side
of boulders and sugar maples, and green
starts from wet earth in open places the sun touches,
he unchains the cows one morning after milking
and lopes past them to open the pasture gate.
Now he returns whooping and slapping their buttocks
to set them to pasture again, and they are free
to wander eating all day long. Now these wallowing
big-eyed calf-makers, bone-rafters for leather,
awkward arks, cud-chewing lethargic mooers
roll their enormous heads, trot, gallop, bounce,
cavort, stretch, leap, and bellow —
as if everything heavy and cold vanished at once
and cow spirits floated
weightless as clouds in the great day's windy April.
*
When his neighbor discovers him at eighty-seven, his head
leans into the side of his last Holstein;
she has kicked the milkpail over, and blue milk drains
through floorboards onto the manure pile in the great day.

DONALD HALL

from THE DAY I WAS OLDER

The Pond

We lie by the pond on a late August afternoon
as a breeze from low hills in the west stiffens water
and agitates birch leaves yellowing above us.
You set down your book
and lift your eyes to white trunks tilting from shore.
A mink scuds through ferns; an acorn tumbles.
Soon we will turn to our daily business.
You do not know that I am watching, taking pleasure
in your breasts that rise and fall as you breathe.
Then I see mourners gathered by an open grave.

The Day

Last night at suppertime I outlived my father, enduring
the year, month, day, hour, and moment
when he lay back on a hospital bed in the guest room
among cylinders of oxygen — mouth open, nostrils and pale
blue lips fixed unquivering. Father of my name,
father of long fingers, I remember your dark hair
and your face almost unwrinkled. Now I have waked
more mornings to frost whitening the grass,
read the newspaper more times, and stood more times,
my hand on a doorknob without opening the door.

The Cup

From the Studebaker's backseat, on our Sunday drives,
I watched her earrings sway. Then I walked uphill
beside an old man carrying buckets
under birches on an August day. Striding at noontime,
I looked at wheat and at river cities. In the crib
my daughter sighed opening her eyes. I kissed the cheek
of my father dying. By the pond an acorn fell.
You listening here, you reading these words as I write them,
I offer this cup to you: Though we drink
from this cup every day, we will never drink it dry.

Michael S. Harper

NEW SEASON

My woman has picked
all the leaves,
rolled her hands into locks,
gone into the woods
where I have taught her
the language of these wood leaves,
and the red sand plum trees.
It is a digest
of my taking these leaves with hunger;
it is love she understands.
From my own wooden smell
she has shed her raisin skin
and come back
sweetened into brilliant music:
Her song is our new season.

BLACK STUDY

No one's been told
that black men
went first to the moon
the dark side
for dark brothers
without space ship
gravity complex
in our computer centers
government campuses
instant play and replay
white mice and pig-guineas
in concentric digital rows.

Someone has been
pulling brother's curls
into fancy barbed wire,
measuring his forelegs,
caressing his dense innards

into formaldehyde
pruning the jellied marrow:
a certain formula is appearing:
someone has been studying you.

HERE WHERE COLTRANE IS

Soul and race
are private dominions,
memories and modal
songs, a tenor blossoming,
which would paint suffering
a clear color but is not in
this Victorian house
without oil in zero degree
weather and a forty-mile-an-hour wind;
it is all a well-knit family:
a love supreme.
Oak leaves pile up on walkway
and steps, catholic as apples
in a special mist of clear white
children who love my children.
I play "Alabama"
on a warped record player
skipping the scratches
on your faces over the fibrous
conical hairs of plastic
under the wooden floors.

Dreaming on a train from New York
to Philly, you hand out six
notes which become an anthem
to our memories of you:
oak, birch, maple,
apple, cocoa, rubber.
For this reason Martin is dead;
for this reason Malcolm is dead;
for this reason Coltrane is dead;
in the eyes of my first son are the browns
of these men and their music.

MICHAEL S. HARPER

THE BORNING ROOM

I stand in moonlight
in our borning room,
now a room of closets
changed by the owners.
Once only the old
and newborn slept
on this first floor,
this boarded door
closed now to the hearth
of our wood burning.

I look over the large bed
at the shape of my woman;
there is no image
for her, no place
for the spring child.
Her cornered shape dreams
a green robed daughter
warmed in a bent room
close to fireplace oven,
warmed by an apple tree:
the old tried to make it new,
the new old; we will not die here.

SONG: *I WANT A WITNESS*

Blacks in frame houses
call to the helicopters,
their antlered arms
spinning; jeeps pad
these glass-studded streets;
on this hill are tanks painted gold.
Our children sing
spirituals of *Motown*,
idioms these streets suckled
on a southern road.
This scene is about power,

terror, producing
love and pain and pathology;
in an army of white dust,
blacks here to *testify*
and *testify*, and *testify*,
and *redeem*, and *redeem*,
in black smoke coming,
as they wave their arms,
as they wave their tongues.

NIGHTMARE BEGINS RESPONSIBILITY

I place these numbed wrists to the pane
watching white uniforms whisk over
him in the tube-kept
prison
fear what they will do in experiment
watch my gloved stickshifting gasolined hands
breathe *boxcar-information-please* infirmary tubes
distrusting white-pink mending paperthin
silkened end hairs, distrusting tubes
shrunk in his *trunk-skincapped*
shaven head, in thighs
distrusting-white-hands-picking-baboon-light
on this son who will not make his second night
of this ward strewn intensive airpocket
where his father's asthmatic
hymns of *night-train*, train done gone
his mother can only know that he has flown
up into essential calm unseen corridor
going boxscarred home, *mamaborn, sweetsonchild*
gonedowntown into *researchtestingwarehousebatteryacid*
mam-son-done-gone/me telling her 'nother
train tonight, no music, no breathstroked
heartbeat in my infinite distrust of them:
and of my distrusting self
white-doctor-who-breathed-for-him-all-night
say it for two sons gone,
say nightmare, say it loud
panebreaking heartmadness:
nightmare begins responsibility.

MICHAEL S. HARPER

GRANDFATHER

In 1915 my grandfather's
neighbors surrounded his house
near the dayline he ran
on the Hudson
in Catskill, NY
and thought they'd burn
his family out
in a movie they'd just seen
and be rid of his kind:
the death of a lone black
family is *the Birth
of a Nation*,
or so they thought.
His 5'4" waiter gait
quenched the white jacket smile
he'd brought back from watered
polish of my father
on the turning seats,
and he asked his neighbors
up on his thatched porch
for the first blossom of fire
that would burn him down.

They went away, his nation,
spittooning their torched necks
in the shadows of the riverboat
they'd seen, posse decomposing;
and I see him on Sutter
with white bag from your
restaurant, challenged by his first
grandson to a foot-race
he will win in white clothes.

I see him as he buys galoshes
for his railed yard near Mineo's
metal shop, where roses jump
as the el circles his house
toward Brooklyn, where his rain fell;
and I see cigar smoke in his eyes,
chocolate Madison Square Garden chews
he breaks on his set teeth,

stitched up after cancer,
the great white nation immovable
as his weight wilts
and he is on a porch
that won't hold my arms,
or the legs of the race run
forwards, or the film
played backwards on his grandson's eyes.

HEALING SONG

He stoops down eating sunflowers
snowballed at his prayer-rugged
table, 'message/solution/masses'
his ghetto-blues-plantation,
driven into inner/outer realities
as buffers drawn from his eyes.

Penned in that magnificent voice
where *victorola* mutters 'Koppin' songs,
his sedge burning night-trains,
this serape-man found wanting
only in that 'God Don't Like Ugly'
phrase; he draws his own lightning,
believing differently,
an angel surrendering angles of desire:
his masked heart-centered soul reveals.

Rused in dance steps of jubilo,
atavisms of worship shutting out sound,
his full essential flowering
balances in the 4 a.m. traduction,
his Emancipation Tree.

Hidden in ancient tetters
of autobiography,
he tropes of 1863 *moverings*,
his Osceolas already sacrificed
as Lincoln's mass production lines
funnel bodies to the Crater;
his Easter families agonize
at blue doors of transformation.

Self-accused in venial sins, his gorgeous
offerings lift blind pigs to Bessie's
witchdoctoring, her blue-black tongue
singing down Jesus,
'watch your goin' be like comin' back,'
he witnesses flesh pull down in anger,
killing calves of hunger to no higher law.

Ragboned Bob Hayden, shingled in slime,
reaches for his cereus ladder of midnight flight,
his seismographic heartbeats
sphinctered in rhiney polygraphs of light;
Dee-troit born and half-blind
in diction of arena and paradise,
his ambient nightmare-dreams streak his tongue;
mementos of his mother, of Erma, he image-makes
peopling the human family of God's mirror,
mingling realities, this creature of transcendence
a love-filled shadow, congealed and clarified.

MOTEL ROOM

Nobody comes in in this dream;
nobody comes into steam heat either
because it burns,
but it could be cold:
extremes are what we need
so that the excess
of balancing haves
and have nots
collect somewhere:

right now it is this bed,
kingsized, a crack
in the middle,
no space necessary
to hold your own
so you hold each other.

This is the room number of change,
the self at bay with itself.

PROTÉGÉ: 1962

In the front row
and big as a house
the kid sits there
waiting for the word;

he gets it from a crow,
a broken-winged woman
who needs a drink,
and he comes to her aid

because she can't talk —
too frightened to speak.
He goes up to put his arm,
the tight shirt of his bicep

like rings of a telephone
booth where he gets her to speak.
She comes alive
in the Algonquin,

which is no place
for any lady
without text in Los Angeles
should be found out in class.

She takes the waning
light of a sunset
on the wrong side of the field,
an earthquake

on the continent of gone Indians:
"God aint always there
when you call on him;
but he's always on time."

Next class session
she's dead;
the bulging boy in his team
shirt begins to read

MICHAEL S. HARPER

her few books
to herd the braves
who never talked
to any selves but horses.

Robert Hass

LETTER

I had wanted to begin
by telling you I saw another
tanager below the pond
where I had sat for half an hour
feeding on wild berries
in the little clearing near the pines
that hide the lower field
and then looked up from red berries
to the quick red bird brilliant
in the light. I have seen
more yarrow and swaying
Queen Anne's lace around the woods
as hawkweed and nightshade
wither and drop seed. A new blue flower,
sweet, yellow-stamened, ovary inferior,
has recently sprung up.
                              But I had the odd
feeling, walking to the house
to write this down, that I had left
the birds and flowers in the field,
rooted or feeding. They are not in my
head, are not now on this page.
It was very strange to me, but I think
their loss was your absence. I wanted
to be walking up with Leif, the sun
behind us skipping off the pond,
the windy maple sheltering the house,
and find you there and say
here! a new blue flower (ovary inferior)
and busy Leif and Kris with naming
in a world I love. You even have
my field guide. It's you I love.
I have believed so long
in the magic of names and poems.
I hadn't thought them bodiless
at all. Tall Buttercup. Wild Vetch.
"Often I am permitted to return
to a meadow." It all seemed real to me

225

last week. Words. You are the body
of my world, root and flower, the
brightness and surprise of birds.
I miss you, love. Tell Leif
you're the names of things.

BOOKBUYING IN THE TENDERLOIN

A statuary Christ bleeds sweating grief
in the Gethsemane garden of St. Boniface Church
where empurpled Irish winos lurch
to their salvation. When incense and belief
will not suffice: ruby port in the storm
of muscatel-made images of hell
the city spews at their shuffling feet.
In the Longshoremen's Hall across the street,
three decades have unloaded since the fight
to oust the manic Trotskyite
screwballs from the brotherhood. All goes well
since the unions closed their ranks,
boosted their pensions, and hired the banks
to manage funds for the workingman's cartel.
Christ in plaster, the unions minting coin,
old hopes converge upon the Tenderloin
where Comte, Considerant, Fourier
are thick with dust in the two-bit tray
of cavernous secondhand bookstores
and the streets suffuse the ten-cent howl
of jukebox violence, just this side of blues.
Negro boy-whores in black tennis shoes
prowl in front of noisy hustler bars.
Like Samuel Gompers, they want more
on this street where every other whore
is painfully skinny, wears a bouffant,
and looks like a brown slow-blooming annual flower.
In the places that I haunt, no power
to transform the universal squalor
nor wisdom to withstand the thin wrists

of the girls who sell their bodies for a dollar
or two, the price of a Collected Maeterlinck.
The sky glowers. My God, it is a test,
this riding out the dying of the West.

THE FAILURE OF BUFFALO TO LEVITATE

Millard Fillmore died here.
His round body is weighted by marble angels.
He lies among the great orators of the Iroquois.

Paint does not arrest the tradebook houses
in their elegant decay. They peel like lizards
in the dying avenues of elm.

Gentle enough, night drifts
above the yellow bursts of aspen in the park.
Something innocent and reptilian

suffers here, cumbrously.
The souls of the wives of robber barons
are imprisoned in the chandeliers.

MEDITATION AT LAGUNITAS

All the new thinking is about loss.
In this it resembles all the old thinking.
The idea, for example, that each particular erases
the luminous clarity of a general idea. That the clown-
faced woodpecker probing the dead sculpted trunk
of that black birch is, by his presence,
some tragic falling off from a first world
of undivided light. Or the other notion that,
because there is in this world no one thing
to which the bramble of *blackberry* corresponds,
a word is elegy to what it signifies.

ROBERT HASS

We talked about it late last night and in the voice
of my friend, there was a thin wire of grief, a tone
almost querulous. After a while I understood that,
talking this way, everything dissolves: *justice,*
pine, hair, woman, you and *I.* There was a woman
I made love to and I remembered how, holding
her small shoulders in my hands sometimes,
I felt a violent wonder at her presence
like a thirst for salt, for my childhood river
with its island willows, silly music from the pleasure boat,
muddy places where we caught the little orange-silver fish
called *pumpkinseed.* It hardly had to do with her.
Longing, we say, because desire is full
of endless distances. I must have been the same to her.
But I remember so much, the way her hands dismantled bread,
the thing her father said that hurt her, what
she dreamed. There are moments when the body is as numinous
as words, days that are the good flesh continuing.
Such tenderness, those afternoons and evenings,
saying *blackberry, blackberry, blackberry.*

LIKE THREE FAIR BRANCHES
FROM ONE ROOT DERIV'D

I am outside a door and inside
the words do not fumble
as I fumble saying this.
It is the same in the dream
where I touch you. Notice
in this poem the thinning out
of particulars. The gate
with the three snakes is burning,
symbolically, which doesn't mean
the flames can't hurt you.
Now it is the pubic arch instead
and smells of oils and driftwood,
of our bodies working very hard
at pleasure but they are not
thinking about us. Bless them,
it is not a small thing to be

happily occupied, go by them
on tiptoe. Now the gate is marble
and the snakes are graces.
You are the figure in the center.
On the left you are going away
from yourself. On the right
you are coming back. Meanwhile
we are passing through the gate
with everything we love. We go
as fire, as flesh, as marble.
Sometimes it is good and sometimes
it is dangerous like the ignorance
of particulars, but our words are clear
and our movements give off light.

THE PURE ONES

Roads to the north of here are dry.
First red buds prick out the lethal spring
and corncrakes, swarming, lower in clouds
above the fields from Paris to Béziers.
This is God's harvest: the village boy
whose tongue was sliced in two,
the village crones slashing cartilage
at the knees to crawl to Carcassonne.
— If the world were not evil in itself,
the blessed one said, then every choice
would not constitute a loss.
This sickness of this age is flesh,
he said. Therefore we build with stone.
The dead with their black lips are heaped
on one another, intimate as lovers.

THE ORIGIN OF CITIES

She is first seen dancing which is a figure
not for art or prayer or the arousal of desire
but for action simply; her breastband is copper,

her crown imitates the city walls. Though she draws us
to her, like a harbor or a rivermouth she sends us away.
A figure of the outward. So the old men grown lazy
in patrician ways lay out cash for adventures.
Imagining a rich return, they buy futures
and their slaves haunt the waterfront for news of ships.
The young come from the villages dreaming.
Pleasure and power draw them. They are employed
to make inventories and grow very clever,
multiplying in their heads, deft at the use of letters.
When they are bored, they write down old songs from the villages,
and the cleverest make new songs in the old forms
describing the pleasures of the city, their mistresses,
old shepherds and simpler times. And the temple
where the farmer grandfathers of the great merchants worshipped,
the dim temple across from the marketplace
which was once a stone altar in a clearing in the forest,
where the nightwatch pisses now against a column in the moonlight,
is holy to them; the wheat mother their goddess of sweaty sheets,
of what is left in the air when that glimpsed beauty
turns the corner, of love's punishment and the wracking
of desire. They make songs about that. They tell
stories of heroes and brilliant lust among the gods.
These are amusements. She dances, the ships go forth,
slaves and peasants labor in the fields, maimed soldiers
ape monkeys for coins outside the wineshops,
the craftsmen work in bronze and gold, accounts
are kept carefully, what goes out, what returns.

PICKING BLACKBERRIES WITH A FRIEND
WHO HAS BEEN READING JACQUES LACAN

August is dust here. Drought
stuns the road,
but juice gathers in the berries.

We pick them in the hot
slow-motion of midmorning.
Charlie is exclaiming:

for him it is twenty years ago
and raspberries and Vermont.
We have stopped talking

about *L'Histoire de la vérité*,
about subject and object
and the mediation of desire.

Our ears are stoppered
in the bee-hum. And Charlie,
laughing wonderfully,

beard stained purple
by the word *juice*,
goes to get a bigger pot.

LATE SPRING

And then in mid-May the first morning of steady heat,

the morning, Leif says, when you wake up, put on shorts, and that's it for the day,

when you pour coffee and walk outside, blinking in the sun.

Strawberries have appeared in the markets, and peaches will soon;

squid is so cheap in the fishstores you begin to consult Japanese and Italian cookbooks for the various and ingenious ways of preparing *ika* and *calamari*;

and because the light will enlarge your days, your dreams at night will be as strange as the jars of octopus you saw once in a fisherman's boat under the summer moon;

and after swimming, white wine; and the sharing of stories before dinner is prolonged because the relations of the children in the neighborhood have acquired village intensity and the stories take longer telling;

and there are the nights when the fog rolls in that nobody likes — hey, fog, the Miwok sang, who lived here first, you better go home, pelican is beating your wife —

and after dark in the first cool hour, your children sleep so heavily in their beds exhausted from play, it is a pleasure to watch them,

Leif does not move a muscle as he lies there; no, wait; it is Luke who lies there in his eight-year-old body,

Leif is taller than you are and he isn't home; when he is, his feet will extend past the end of the mattress, and Kristin is at the corner in the dark, talking to neighborhood boys;

things change; there is no need for this dream-compelled narration; the rhythm will keep me awake, changing.

SPRING DRAWING 2

A man says *lilacs against white houses, two sparrows, one streaked, in a thinning birch*, and can't find his way to a sentence.

In order to be respectable, Thorstein Veblen said, desperate in Palo Alto, a thing must be wasteful, i.e., "a selective adaptation of forms to the end of conspicuous waste."

So we try to throw nothing away, as Keith, making dinner for us as his grandmother had done in Jamaica, left nothing; the kitchen was as clean at the end as when he started; even the shrimp shells and carrot fronds were part of the process,

and he said, when we tried to admire him, "Listen, I should send you into the chickenyard to look for a rusty nail to add to the soup for iron."

The first temptation of Sakyamuni was desire, but he saw that it led to fulfillment and then to desire, so that one was easy.

Because I have pruned it badly in successive years, the climbing rose has sent out, among the pale pink floribunda, a few wild white roses from the rootstalk.

Suppose, before they said *silver* or *moonlight* or *wet grass*, each poet had to agree to be responsible for the innocence of all the suffering on earth,

because they learned in arithmetic, during the long school days, that if there was anything left over,

you had to carry it. The wild rose looks weightless, the floribunda are heavy with the richness and sadness of Europe

as they imitate the dying, petal by petal, of the people who bred them.

You hear pain singing in the nerves of things; it is not a song.

The gazelle's head turned; three jackals are eating his entrails and he is watching.

A STORY ABOUT THE BODY

The young composer, working that summer at an artist's colony, had watched her for a week. She was Japanese, a painter, almost sixty, and he thought he was in love with her. He loved her work, and her work was like the way she moved her body, used her hands, looked at him directly when she made amused and considered answers to his questions. One night, walking back from a concert, they came to her door and she turned to him and said, "I think you would like to have me. I would like that too, but I must tell you that I have had a double mastectomy," and when he didn't understand, "I've lost both my breasts." The radiance that he had carried around in his belly and chest cavity — like music — withered very quickly, and he made himself look at her when he said, "I'm sorry. I don't think I could." He walked back to his own cabin through the pines, and in the morning he found a small blue bowl on the porch outside his door. It looked to be full of rose petals, but he found when he picked it up that the rose petals were on top; the rest of the bowl — she must have swept them from the corners of her studio — was full of dead bees.

PRIVILEGE OF BEING

Many are making love. Up above, the angels
in the unshaken ether and crystal of human longing
are braiding one another's hair, which is strawberry blond
and the texture of cold rivers. They glance
down from time to time at the awkward ecstasy —
it must look to them like featherless birds
splashing in the spring puddle of a bed —
and then one woman, she is about to come,
peels back the man's shut eyelids and says,
look at me, and he does. Or is it the man
tugging the curtain rope in that dark theater?
Anyway, they do, they look at each other;
two beings with evolved eyes, rapacious,
startled, connected at the belly in an unbelievably sweet
lubricious glue, stare at each other,
and the angels are desolate. They hate it. They shudder pathetically
like lithographs of Victorian beggars
with perfect features and alabaster skin hawking rags
in the lewd alleys of the novel.
All of creation is offended by this distress.
It is like the keening sound the moon makes sometimes,
rising. The lovers especially cannot bear it,
it fills them with unspeakable sadness, so that
they close their eyes again and hold each other, each
feeling the mortal singularity of the body
they have enchanted out of death for an hour or so,
and one day, running at sunset, the woman says to the man,
I woke up feeling so sad this morning because I realized
that you could not, as much as I love you,
dear heart, cure my loneliness,
wherewith she touched his cheek to reassure him
that she did not mean to hurt him with this truth.
And the man is not hurt exactly,
he understands that life has limits, that people
die young, fail at love,
fail of their ambitions. He runs beside her, he thinks
of the sadness they have gasped and crooned their way out of
coming, clutching each other with old, invented
forms of grace and clumsy gratitude, ready

to be alone again, or dissatisfied, or merely
companionable like the couples on the summer beach
reading magazine articles about intimacy between the sexes
to themselves, and to each other,
and to the immense, illiterate, consoling angels.

Robert Hayden

FREDERICK DOUGLASS

When it is finally ours, this freedom, this liberty, this beautiful
and terrible thing, needful to man as air,
usable as earth; when it belongs at last to all,
when it is truly instinct, brain matter, diastole, systole,
reflex action; when it is finally won; when it is more
than the gaudy mumbo jumbo of politicians:
this man, this Douglass, this former slave, this Negro
beaten to his knees, exiled, visioning a world
where none is lonely, none hunted, alien,
this man, superb in love and logic, this man
shall be remembered. Oh, not with statues' rhetoric,
not with legends and poems and wreaths of bronze alone,
but with the lives grown out of his life, the lives
fleshing his dream of the beautiful, needful thing.

"FROM THE CORPSE WOODPILES, FROM THE ASHES"

From the corpse woodpiles, from the ashes
and staring pits of Dachau,
Buchenwald they come —

O David, Hirschel, Eva,
cops and robbers with me once,
their faces are like yours —

From Johannesburg, from Seoul.
Their struggles are all horizons.
Their deaths encircle me.

Through target streets I run,
in light part nightmare
and part vision fleeing

What I cannot flee, and reach
that cold cloacal cell
where He, who is man beatified

And Godly mystery,
lies chained, His pain
our anguish and our anodyne.

THOSE WINTER SUNDAYS

Sundays too my father got up early
and put his clothes on in the blueblack cold,
then with cracked hands that ached
from labor in the weekday weather made
banked fires blaze. No one ever thanked him.

I'd wake and hear the cold splintering, breaking.
When the rooms were warm, he'd call,
and slowly I would rise and dress,
fearing the chronic angers of that house,

Speaking indifferently to him,
who had driven out the cold
and polished my good shoes as well.
What did I know, what did I know
of love's austere and lonely offices?

NIGHT, DEATH, MISSISSIPPI

I

A quavering cry. Screech-owl?
Or one of them?
The old man in his reek
and gauntness laughs —

One of them, I bet —
and turns out the kitchen lamp,
limping to the porch to listen
in the windowless night.

Be there with Boy and the rest
if I was well again.
Time was. Time was.
White robes like moonlight

In the sweetgum dark.
Unbucked that one then
and him squealing bloody Jesus
as we cut it off.

Time was. A cry?
A cry all right.
He hawks and spits,
fevered as by groinfire.

Have us a bottle,
Boy and me —
he's earned him a bottle —
when he gets home.

II

Then we beat them, he said,
beat them till our arms was tired
and the big old chains
messy and red.

O Jesus burning on the lily cross

Christ, it was better
than hunting bear
which don't know why
you want him dead.

O night, rawhead and bloodybones night

You kids fetch Paw
some water now so's he
can wash that blood
off him, she said.

O night betrayed by darkness not its own

MONET'S "WATERLILIES"

(for Bill and Sonja)

Today as the news from Selma and Saigon
poisons the air like fallout,
    I come again to see
the serene great picture that I love.

Here space and time exist in light
the eye like the eye of faith believes.
    The seen, the known
dissolve in iridescence, become
illusive flesh of light
    that was not, was, forever is.

O light beheld as through refracting tears.
Here is the aura of that world
    each of us has lost.
Here is the shadow of its joy.

SOLEDAD

(And I, I am no longer of that world)

Naked, he lies in the blinded room
chainsmoking, cradled by drugs, by jazz
as never by any lover's cradling flesh.

Miles Davis coolly blows for him:
O *pena negra*, sensual Flamenco blues;
the red clay foxfire voice of Lady Day

(lady of the pure black magnolias)
sobsings her sorrow and loss and fare you well,
dryweeps the pain his treacherous jailers

have released him from for awhile.
His fears and his unfinished self
await him down in the anywhere streets.

He hides on the dark side of the moon,
takes refuge in a stained-glass cell,
flies to a clockless country of crystal.

Only the ghost of Lady Day knows where
he is. Only the music. And he swings
oh swings: beyond complete immortal now.

THE NIGHT-BLOOMING CEREUS

    And so for nights
we waited, hoping to see
the heavy bud
    break into flower.

    On its neck-like tube
hooking down from the edge
of the leaf-branch
    nearly to the floor,

    the bud packed
tight with its miracle swayed
stiffly on breaths
    of air, moved

    as though impelled
by stirrings within itself.
It repelled as much
    as it fascinated me

    sometimes — snake,
eyeless bird head,
beak that would gape
    with grotesque life-squawk.

    But you, my dear,
conceded less to the bizarre
than to the imminence
    of bloom. Yet we agreed

we ought
to celebrate the blossom,
paint ourselves, dance
in honor of

archaic mysteries
when it appeared. Meanwhile
we waited, aware
of rigorous design.

Backster's
polygraph, I thought,
would have shown
(as clearly as it had

a philodendron's
fear) tribal sentience
in the cactus, focused
energy of will.

That belling of
tropic perfume — that
signalling
not meant for us;

the darkness
cloyed with summoning
fragrance. We dropped
trivial tasks

and marvelling
beheld at last the achieved
flower. Its moonlight
petals were

still unfold-
ing, the spike fringe of the outer
perianth recessing
as we watched.

Lunar presence,
foredoomed, already dying,
it charged the room
with plangency

ROBERT HAYDEN

older than human
cries, ancient as prayers
invoking Osiris, Krishna,
Tezcátlipóca.

We spoke
in whispers when
we spoke
at all . . .

THE PRISONERS

Steel doors — guillotine gates —
of the doorless house closed massively.
We were locked in with loss.

Guards frisked us, marked our wrists,
then let us into the drab Rec Hall —
splotched green walls, high windows barred —

where the dispossessed awaited us.
Hands intimate with knife and pistol,
hands that had cruelly grasped and throttled

clasped ours in welcome. I sensed the plea
of men denied: Believe us human
like yourselves, who but for Grace. . . .

We shared reprieving Hidden Words
revealed by the Godlike imprisoned
One, whose crime was truth.

And I read poems I hoped were true.
It's like you been there, brother, been there,
the scarred young lifer said.

ROBERT HAYDEN

THE TATTOOED MAN

I gaze at you,
longing longing,
as from a gilt
and scarlet cage;
silent, speak
your name, cry —
Love me.
To touch you, once
to hold you close —
My jungle arms,
their prized chimeras,
appall. You fear
the birds-of-paradise
perched on my thighs.
Oh to break through,
to free myself —
lifer in The Hole —
from servitude
I willed. Or was
it evil circumstance
that drove me to seek
in strangeness strange
abiding-place?
Born alien,
homeless everywhere,
did I, then, choose
bizarrity,
having no other choice?

Hundreds have paid
to gawk at me —
grotesque outsider whose
unnaturalness
assures them they
are natural, they indeed
belong.
But you but you,
for whom I would
endure caustic acids,
keenest knives —
you look at me with pain,

avert your face,
love's own,
ineffable and pure
and not for gargoyle
kisses such as mine.
Da Vinci's Last Supper —
a masterpiece
in jewel colors
on my breast
(I clenched my teeth in pain;
all art is pain
suffered and outlived);
gryphons, naked Adam
embracing naked Eve,
a gaiety of imps
in cinnabar;
the Black Widow
peering from the web
she spun, belly to groin —
These that were my pride
repel the union of
your flesh with mine.
I yearn I yearn.
And if I dared
the agonies
of metamorphosis,
would I not find
you altered then?
I do not want
you other than you are.
And I — I cannot
(will not?) change.
It is too late
for any change
but death.
I am I.

Richard Hugo

DEATH OF THE KAPOWSIN TAVERN

I can't ridge it back again from char.
Not one board left. Only ash a cat explores
and shattered glass smoked black and strung
about from the explosion I believe
in the reports. The white school up for sale
for years, most homes abandoned to the rocks
of passing boys — the fire, helped by wind
that blew the neon out six years before,
simply ended lots of ending.

A damn shame. Now, when the night chill
of the lake gets in a troller's bones
where can the troller go for bad wine
washed down frantically with beer?
And when wise men are in style again
will one recount the two-mile glide of cranes
from dead pines or the nameless yellow
flowers thriving in the useless logs,
or dots of light all night about the far end
of the lake, the dawn arrival of the idiot
with catfish — most of all, above the lake
the temple and our sanctuary there?

Nothing dies as slowly as a scene.
The dusty jukebox cracking through
the cackle of a beered-up crone —
wagered wine — sudden need to dance —
these remain in the black debris.
Although I know in time the lake will send
wind black enough to blow it all away.

G.I. GRAVES IN TUSCANY

They still seem G.I., the uniform lines
of white crosses, the gleam that rolls
white drums over the lawn. Machines

247

that cut the grass left their maneuvers plain.
Our flag doesn't seem silly though plainly
it flies only because there is wind.

Let them go by. I don't want to turn in.
After ten minutes I'd be sick of their names
or the names of their towns. Then
some guide would offer a tour
for two thousand lire, smiling the places
of battle, feigning hate for the Krauts.
I guess visitors come. A cross here and there
is rooted in flowers. Maybe in Scranton
a woman is saving. Maybe in books
what happened and why is worked out.

The loss is so damn gross. I remember
a washtub of salad in basic, blacktop acres
of men waiting to march, passing three hours
of bombers, en route to Vienna, and bombing
and passing two hours of planes, coming back.
Numbers are vulgar. If I stayed
I'd count the men in years of probable loss.

I'm a liar. I'm frightened to stop.
Afraid of a speech I might make,
corny over some stone with a name
that indicates Slavic descent — you there,
you must be first generation,
I'm third. The farm, I'm told, was hard
but it all means something. Think
of Jefferson, of the Constitution,
not of these children
beside me, bumming a smoke and laughing.

DEGREES OF GRAY IN PHILIPSBURG

You might come here Sunday on a whim.
Say your life broke down. The last good kiss
you had was years ago. You walk these streets

laid out by the insane, past hotels
that didn't last, bars that did, the tortured try
of local drivers to accelerate their lives.
Only churches are kept up. The jail
turned 70 this year. The only prisoner
is always in, not knowing what he's done.

The principal supporting business now
is rage. Hatred of the various grays
the mountain sends, hatred of the mill,
The Silver Bill repeal, the best liked girls
who leave each year for Butte. One good
restaurant and bars can't wipe the boredom out.
The 1907 boom, eight going silver mines,
a dance floor built on springs —
all memory resolves itself in gaze,
in panoramic green you know the cattle eat
or two stacks high above the town,
two dead kilns, the huge mill in collapse
for fifty years that won't fall finally down.

Isn't this your life? That ancient kiss
still burning out your eyes? Isn't this defeat
so accurate, the church bell simply seems
a pure announcement: ring and no one comes?
Don't empty houses ring? Are magnesium
and scorn sufficient to support a town,
not just Philipsburg, but towns
of towering blondes, good jazz and booze
the world will never let you have
until the town you came from dies inside?

Say no to yourself. The old man, twenty
when the jail was built, still laughs
although his lips collapse. Someday soon,
he says, I'll go to sleep and not wake up.
You tell him no. You're talking to yourself.
The car that brought you here still runs.
The money you buy lunch with,
no matter where it's mined, is silver
and the girl who serves you food
is slender and her red hair lights the wall.

MONTGOMERY HOLLOW

Birds here should have names so hard to say
you name them over. They finally found
the farmer hanging near the stream.
Only insect hum today and the purple odor
of thyme. You'd bet your throat against
the way a mind goes bad. You conquer loss
by going to the place it happened
and replaying it, saying the name
of the face in the open casket right.

People die in cities. Unless it's war
you never see the bodies. They die in print,
over phones in paramouric flats.
Here, you find them staring down the sun,
flies crawling them like bacon. Wives
scream two days running and the pain is gone.
Here, you find them living.

To know a road you own it, every bend
and pebble and the weeds along it,
dust that itches when the August hayrake
rambles home. You own the home.
You own the death of every bird you name.
To live good, keep your life and the scene.
Cow, brook, hay: these are names of coins.

for Stanley Kauffmann

MONTANA RANCH ABANDONED

Cracks in eight log buildings, counting sheds
and outhouse, widen and a ghost peeks out.
Nothing, tree or mountain, weakens wind
coming for the throat. Even wind must work
when land gets old. The rotting wagon tongue
makes fun of girls who begged to go to town.
Broken brakerods dangle in the dirt.

Alternatives were madness or a calloused moon.
Wood they carved the plowblade from
turned stone as nameless gray. Indifferent flies
left dung intact. One boy had to leave
when horses pounded night, and miles away
a neighbor's daughter puked. Mother's cry
to dinner changed to caw in later years.

Maybe raiding bears or eelworms made them quit,
or daddy died, or when they planted wheat
dead Flatheads killed the plant. That stove
without a grate can't warm the ghost.
Tools would still be good if cleaned, but mortar
flakes and log walls sag. Even if you shored,
cars would still boom by beyond the fence, no glance
from drivers as you till the lunar dust.

THE HOUSE ON 15TH S.W.

Cruelty and rain could be expected.
Any season. The talk was often German
and we cried at the death of strangers.
Potatoes mattered and neighbors who came
to marvel at our garden. I never helped
with the planting. I hid in woods these houses
built on either side replaced. Ponds
duplicated sky. I watched my face
play out dreams of going north with clouds.

North surely was soft. North was death
and women and the women soft. The tongue
there was American and kind. Acres of women
would applaud me as I danced, and acres
of graves would dance when sun announced
another cloud was dead. No grating scream
to meals or gratuitous beatings,
no crying, raging fists against closed doors,
twisted years I knew were coming at me,
hours alone in bars with honest mirrors,
being fun with strangers, being liked

so much the chance of jail was weak
from laughter, and my certainty of failure
mined by a tyrant for its pale perverted ore.

My pride in a few poems, my shame
of a wasted life, no wife, no children,
cancel out. I'm left neutral as this house,
not caring to go in. Light would be soft
and full, not harsh and dim remembered.
The children, if there are children inside,
would be normal, clean, not at all
the soiled freaks I had counted on.

FARMER, DYING

Seven thousand acres of grass have faded yellow
from his cough. These limp days, his anger,
legend forty years from moon to Stevensville,
lives on, just barely, in a Great Falls whore.
Cruel times, he cries, cruel winds. His geese roam
unattended in the meadow. The gold last leaves
of cottonwoods ride Burnt Fork creek away.
His geese grow fat without him. Same old insult.
Same indifferent rise of mountains south,
hunters drunk around the fire ten feet from his fence.

What's killing us is something autumn. Call it
war or fever. You know it when you see it: flare.
Vine and fire and the morning deer come half
a century to sip his spring, there, at the far end
of his land, wrapped in cellophane by light.
What lives is what he left in air, definite,
unseen, hanging where he stood the day he roared.
A bear prowls closer to his barn each day.
Farmers come to watch him die. They bring crude offerings
of wine. Burnt Fork creek is caroling. He dies white
in final anger. The bear taps on his pane.

And we die silent, our last days loaded with the scream
of Burnt Fork creek, the last cry of that raging farmer.
We have aged ourselves to stone trying to summon

mercy for ungrateful daughters. Let's live him
in ourselves, stand deranged on the meadow rim
and curse the Baltic back, moon, bear and blast.
And let him shout from his grave for us.

for Hank and Nancy

THE HILLTOP

I like bars close to home and home run down,
a signal to the world, I'm weak. I like a bar
to be a home. Take this one. Same men every night.
Same jokes. Traffic going by
fifteen feet away and punchboards never paying off.
Churn of memory and ulcer. Most of all
the stale anticipation of the girl
sure to walk in someday fresh from '39,
not one day older, holding out her arms.

Soon, I say to no one late each night,
I'll be all right. I put five dollars
in the jukebox and never hear a tune.
I take pride drinking alone and being kind.
When I walk in, people say my name.
By ten, the loveliest girl in Vegas
swims about the room, curving in and counter
to the flow of smoke. Her evil sister
swings her legs and giggles in my drink.

When I'm at home, the kitchen light stays on.
Help me, friend. By dawn, a hundred dogs
are gnawing at my throat. My gnarled phlegm
chokes up yellow. My empty room
revolves tornado and my relatives
are still unnamed. A dozen practiced gestures
get me through the day. By five, I'm crawling
up the hill, certain I'll live, my Hilltop smile
perfected and my coin naïve.

for Susan Zwinger

RICHARD HUGO

HERE, BUT UNABLE TO ANSWER

in memory, Herbert Hugo

A small dawn, sailor. First light glints
off water and it rays across your face
some ill-defined religion. I see you
always on the bridge alone, vigorous
and handsome. Eight bells. You bellow orders.
Your voice rolls back the wind.
Your eyes light numbers on the compass green.

Had I found you lost, I swear
I would have torn the clouds apart right
beneath the north star long enough
for you to fix position, and we'd have gone
sailing, sailing down our boyhood rivers
out to open sea, you proud of my power
over uncooperative sky. What a team
and never to be. You gone to China. I alone
with two old people and in nightmare earth
becoming drier. No new crop. No growth.

Even in war we lived a war apart.
You who desperately wanted combat
stuck piloting new ships from Pittsburgh
to the gulf. Me and my unwanted self
praying the final bomb run out, praying me alone
home safe, then all the others I forgot.
Forgive the bad nerves I brought home,
these hands still trembling with sky, that deafening
dream exploding me awake. Books will call
that war the last one worth the toll.

Father, now you're buried much too close for me
to a busy highway. I still see you up there
on the bridge, night sky wide open and you naming
wisely every star again, your voice enormous
with the power of moon, of tide. I seldom
sail off course. I swim a silent green.
When I dream, the compass lights stay on.

RICHARD HUGO

DISTANCES

Driving a prairie, we see a mill far off
and though clouds climbing out of the stack
pollute the air we find the sight lovely.
Horses on the rim of a distant rise
move faintly. We barely see them move
though they run wild. Or when a mile offshore
whales romp and spout, we admire
fountains in Rome, and the distant cathedral
that makes all daylit hours dawn. Artillery
lights a glorious horizon too far for us
to hear the thundering guns. We remain
out of earshot of scream.

Clouds bring rivers closer, bring closer
the homesteader's cabin, the antelope herd.
Clouds move on and the day opens to distance.
Animals are dots. They could be cattle or sheep.
Whatever, they no doubt graze safely and sky
drums wide. Whole symphonies live between
here and a distant whatever-we-look-at.
At night, what we can't see advances
fast and armed over the quaking plain.

All things came close and harmless
first thing this morning, a new trick of light.
Let's learn that trick. If we can, it will mean
we live in this world, neighbor to goat,
neighbor to trout, and we can take comfort
in low birds that hang long enough for us
to read markings and look up names
we'll whisper to them from now on.

David Ignatow

COMMUNION

Let us be friends, said Walt,
and buildings sprang up
quick as corn and people
were born into them, stock
brokers, admen, lawyers and doctors
and they contended
                    among themselves
that they might know
                    each other.

Let us be friends, said Walt.
We are one and occasionally two
of which the one is made
and cemeteries were laid out
miles in all directions
to fill the plots with the old
and young, dead of murder, disease,
rape, hatred, heartbreak and insanity
to make way for the new
and the cemeteries spread over the land
their white scab monuments.

Let us be friends, said Walt, and the graves
were opened and coffins laid on top
of one another for lack of space.
It was then the gravediggers slit
their throats, being alone in the world,
not a friend to bury.

SUNDAY AT THE STATE HOSPITAL

I am sitting across the table
eating my visit sandwich.
The one I brought him stays suspended
near his mouth; his eyes focus
on the table and seem to think,

his shoulders hunched forward.
I chew methodically,
pretending to take him
as a matter of course.
The sandwich tastes mad
and I keep chewing.
My past is sitting in front of me
filled with itself
and trying with almost no success
to bring the present to its mouth.

MY PLACE

I have a place to come to.
It's my place. I come to it
morning, noon and night
and it is there. I expect it
to be there whether or not
it expects me — my place
where I start from and go
towards so that I know
where I am going and what
I am going from, making me
firm in my direction.

I am good to talk to,
you feel in my speech
a location, an expectation
and all said to me in reply
is to reinforce this feeling
because all said is towards
my place and the speaker
too grows his
from which he speaks to mine
having located himself
through my place.

DAVID IGNATOW

EPITAPH

There were no hidden motives to his life,
he is remembered for his meanness.
Beyond that we may look into the sky
and lose ourselves in the blue air.

Reason with me,
I'll believe in reason
though my father is dead,
and when I die
remember of me
I sought for a reason.

In the mirror the face I see
before me is my father's face,
as if I were thinking his thoughts
about me, in love
and disapproval.
I turn my face away.

Forgive me, father,
as I have forgiven you
my sins.

THE BAGEL

I stopped to pick up the bagel
rolling away in the wind,
annoyed with myself
for having dropped it
as it were a portent.
Faster and faster it rolled,
with me running after it
bent low, gritting my teeth,
and I found myself doubled over
and rolling down the street
head over heels, one complete somersault
after another like a bagel
and strangely happy with myself.

DAVID IGNATOW

RESCUE THE DEAD

Finally, to forgo love is to kiss a leaf,
is to let rain fall nakedly upon your head,
is to respect fire,
is to study man's eyes and his gestures
as he talks,
is to set bread upon the table
and a knife discreetly by,
is to pass through crowds
like a crowd of oneself.
Not to love is to live.

To love is to be led away
into a forest where the secret grave
is dug, singing, praising darkness
under the trees.

To live is to sign your name,
is to ignore the dead,
is to carry a wallet
and shake hands.

To love is to be a fish.
My boat wallows in the sea.
You who are free,
rescue the dead.

AGAINST THE EVIDENCE

As I reach to close each book
lying open on my desk, it leaps up
to snap at my fingers. My legs
won't hold me, I must sit down.
My fingers pain me
where the thick leaves snapped together
at my touch.

DAVID IGNATOW

All my life
I've held books in my hands
like children, carefully turning
their pages and straightening out
their creases. I use books
almost apologetically. I believe
I often think their thoughts for them.
Reading, I never know where theirs leave off
and mine begin. I am so much alone
in the world, I can observe the stars
or study the breeze, I can count the steps
on a stair on the way up or down,
and I can look at another human being
and get a smile, knowing
it is for the sake of politeness.
Nothing must be said of estrangement
among the human race and yet
nothing is said at all
because of that.
But no book will help either.
I stroke my desk,
its wood so smooth, so patient and still.
I set a typewriter on its surface
and begin to type
to tell myself my troubles.
Against the evidence, I live by choice.

FIRST COFFIN POEM

I love you, my plain pine box,
because you also are a bench,
with the lid down. Can you see
my friends in a row seated
at ease with themselves?
I am in a coffin
and it has been set against the wall
of a living room. It is just before
dinner and several friends are standing
about with glasses in their hands,

drinking to the possibilities
that life offers.
                    The coffin also
could be placed as a table
in front of a grand sofa, with food
and drinks served on it, and an ashtray.

It would be so much simpler, less gruesome
to use an actual coffee table, you say,
or a real bench, but ah, that would prove
how rigid we must be about ourselves
and cause us to languish, caught
in a limitation. We must make one thing
do for another.
                    I am hope, in urging you
to use my pine box. Take me to your home
when I die imperceptibly. Without fuss
place me against the wall in my coffin,
a conversation piece, an affirmation of change.
I am, sincerely, yours.

WAITING INSIDE

I protest my isolation
but protest is a mark of my defeat,
even as I write.
                    Being a victim,
I am an accuser. Being human,
others feel my fallen weight
upon their thoughts and are oppressed —
as I am, their guilt unlike mine
and unrelated and without hope in it
of change for me.
                    Guilty, my oppressor
and I go separate ways
though we could relieve each other
by going together, as Whitman wrote,
with our arms around each other's waists,
in support.

DAVID IGNATOW

from SHADOWING THE GROUND

1

The world is so difficult to give up,
tied to it by small things,
my eyes noting movement,
color and form. I am watching,
unable to leave, for something
is happening, and so I stand
in a shower of rain
or under a hot sun, wornout
with looking.

7

This is the solution: to be happy with slaughter;
to be confident in theft; to be warm and loving
in deception; to be aesthetically pleased
with unhappiness and, in agreement,
to lie down in the blood of our innocence.

9

Old men spend their days farting
in private to entertain themselves
in the absence of friends
long since gone.

Old men take long walks by themselves
at a slow pace, in rhythm with their hearts,
watching themselves, death
in their trembling steps,
in mediation with their lives.

25

Here I am
at the toilet bowl
overlooking the cemetery

and as I gaze down
at my own foregone conclusion
calmly piss.

33

White-haired, I walk in on my parents
and they, in their twenties, dark-haired
and with fresh complexions, are stunned.
I have stepped out of my crib
in the room set apart from theirs
to show myself an old man
in their youth.

I cannot spare them;
I tell them grief is pure
in what there is to know
between birth and death.

I take their hands
and lead them in a circle,
locking eyes, hands, bodies
with the past in our future.

38

I would be buried beside my parents
to be told, Yes, our darling son,
it could have been better,
but we loved you. Lie down
beside us, face up to the sky.

42

We are an aging couple
in a house surrounded
by silence, left
to ourselves to do with
our lives as we wish
in the security of our persons,
to act as we had wanted to

DAVID IGNATOW

since youth — freely
and spontaneously
towards one another,
given our lives'
long wish in old age,
lying in separate beds
in separate rooms.

43

I don't know which to mourn. Both have died on me, my wife and my car. I feel strongly about my car, but I am also affected by my wife. Without my car, I can't leave the house to keep myself from being alone. My wife gave me two children, both of whom, of course, no longer live with us, as was to be expected, as we in our youth left our parents behind. With my car, I could visit my children, when they are not too busy.

Before she died, my wife urged me to find another woman. It's advice I'd like to take up but not without a car. Without a car, I cannot find myself another woman. That's the sum of it.

47

We are here to make each other die
with perfect willingness,
like flagellants who
when they are done
lying in blood upon the floor
have reached the climax
they were seeking:
to be destroyed
and delighted
at the same time
and from the same source.

55

How lonely it is to live.
What am I waiting for by living,
in the morning especially,

as I awaken to the silence
of the trees?

Do I think I can write myself
out of this to form an other
who will keep me company?
That other is nothing else
but the thought of dying
to save myself from further loneliness.

59

I just know I am growing near to death,
with nothing done to remake the world
a paradise. This is my deep frustration.

Smell the grass.

61

About death, I have no compunctions.
It belongs to me.
We speak with the same voice
and shake hands; we are so alike
no one yet has told us apart.

About death, I would have no compunctions,
if it should tire of me at some moment.
I would know we had borne each other
equally, our burdens equal
with our pleasures. Death leaving
shall deprive me of my life
but then death too shall be deprived
of being.

66

Ignatow is dying
and so is the sun.

DAVID IGNATOW

67

I live with my contradictions
intact, seeking transcendence
but loving bread. I shrug
at both and from behind
the summer screen I look
out upon the dark, knowing
death as one form
of transcendence, but
so is life.

Randall Jarrell

THE BLACK SWAN

When the swans turned my sister into a swan
    I would go to the lake, at night, from milking:
The sun would look out through the reeds like a swan,
    A swan's red beak; and the beak would open
And inside there was darkness, the stars and the moon.

Out on the lake a girl would laugh.
    "Sister, here is your porridge, sister,"
I would call; and the reeds would whisper,
    "Go to sleep, go to sleep, little swan."
My legs were all hard and webbed, and the silky

Hairs of my wings sank away like stars
    In the ripples that ran in and out of the reeds:
I heard through the lap and hiss of water
    Someone's "Sister . . . sister," far away on the shore,
And then as I opened my beak to answer

I heard my harsh laugh go out to the shore
    And saw — saw at last, swimming up from the green
Low mounds of the lake, the white stone swans:
    The white, named swans . . . "It is all a dream,"
I whispered, and reached from the down of the pallet

To the lap and hiss of the floor.
    And "Sleep, little sister," the swans all sang
From the moon and stars and frogs of the floor.
    But the swan my sister called, "Sleep at last, little sister,"
And stroked all night, with a black wing, my wings.

TO THE NEW WORLD

(For an emigrant of 1939)

In that bad year and city of your birth
They traded bread for bank-notes weight for weight,
And nothing but the statues kept the smile

The waltzers wore once: excluding, innocent,
The face of old and comfortable injustice.
And if you wept,
Dropped red into a city where the husbandless
And fatherless were weeping too, who cared
For one more cry or one more child? You grew,

Time put words into your mouth, and you put sugar
Upon your windowsill and waited for a brother —
The stork was greedy, ate, brought nothing in return.
But your life was thinking of you, took you back to Prague,
At school there, timid, boisterous, you spoke
The unaccustomed Czech —
The children laughed at you. For you were learning
New words and a new life, the old
City and its new country too were learning
An old wish: to be just; yes, to be free.

"I saw summer in my time." Summer is ending.
The storms plunge from the tree of winter, death
Moves like an impulse over Europe. Child,
What man is just or free? — but fortunate,
Warm in time's hand, turning and trusting to his face;
And that face changes.
Time is a man for men, and He is willing
For many a new life, for others death. Already
He buys His trench-coat, falls, writes His big book;

Points here, points here: to Jews, to wicked friends —
His words are the moments of a man's life . . .
And now the men march. One morning you awoke
And found Vienna gone, your father said:
"Us next!" And you were next.
Us next!
Cried map and mouth, oppressors and oppressed,
The appeasers as they gave you — but you were gone.
"I had a speech, a city." *What is your name?*
"My name is what my name was." *You have no name.*

So the dream spoke to you: in Zurich, Paris,
In London on a lawn. The unbefriending sea
Cried to you, "Stranger!" Superb, inhospitable,
The towers of the island turned their gaze
Past the girl who looked to the great statue:

So green, so gay . . .
That is how you came. Your face shows white
Against the dark time, your words are indistinct,
One cry among so many, lost in the sound

Of degradation and of agony, the peoples dying.
The net was laid for you, and you are free.
Past the statue there is summer, and the summer smiles
The smile of justice or injustice: blind,
Comfortable, including. Here are the lives
And their old world;
Far off, inside you, a conclusive face
Watches in accusation, in acceptance. It is He.
You escaped from nothing: the westering soul
Finds Europe waiting for it over every sea.

90 NORTH

At home, in my flannel gown, like a bear to its floe,
I clambered to bed; up the globe's impossible sides
I sailed all night — till at last, with my black beard,
My furs and my dogs, I stood at the northern pole.

There in the childish night my companions lay frozen,
The stiff furs knocked at my starveling throat,
And I gave my great sigh: the flakes came huddling,
Were they really my end? In the darkness I turned to my rest.

— Here, the flag snaps in the glare and silence
Of the unbroken ice. I stand here,
The dogs bark, my beard is black, and I stare
At the North Pole . . .
                                    And now what? Why, go back.

Turn as I please, my step is to the south.
The world — my world spins on this final point
Of cold and wretchedness: all lines, all winds
End in this whirlpool I at last discover.

And it is meaningless. In the child's bed
After the night's voyage, in that warm world

Where people work and suffer for the end
That crowns the pain — in that Cloud-Cuckoo-Land

I reached my North and it had meaning.
Here at the actual pole of my existence,
Where all that I have done is meaningless,
Where I die or live by accident alone —

Where, living or dying, I am still alone;
Here where North, the night, the berg of death
Crowd me out of the ignorant darkness,
I see at last that all the knowledge

I wrung from the darkness — that the darkness flung me —
Is worthless as ignorance: nothing comes from nothing,
The darkness from the darkness. Pain comes from the darkness
And we call it wisdom. It is pain.

THE SNOW-LEOPARD

His pads furring the scarp's rime,
Weightless in greys and ecru, gliding
Invisibly, incuriously
As the crystals of the cirri wandering
A mile below his absent eyes,
The leopard gazes at the caravan.
The yaks groaning with tea, the burlaps
Lapping and lapping each stunned universe
That gasps like a kettle for its thinning life
Are pools in the interminable abyss
That ranges up through ice, through air, to night.
Raiders of the unminding element,
The last cold capillaries of their kind,
They move so slowly they are motionless
To any eye less stubborn than a man's. . . .
From the implacable jumble of the blocks
The grains dance icily, a scouring plume,
Into the breath, sustaining, unsustainable,
They trade to that last stillness for their death.
They sense with misunderstanding horror, with desire,
Behind the world their blood sets up in mist

The brute and geometrical necessity:
The leopard waving with a grating purr
His six-foot tail; the leopard, who looks sleepily —
Cold, fugitive, secure — at all that he knows,
At all that he is: the heart of heartlessness.

THE DEATH OF THE BALL TURRET GUNNER

From my mother's sleep I fell into the State,
And I hunched in its belly till my wet fur froze.
Six miles from earth, loosed from its dream of life,
I woke to black flak and the nightmare fighters.
When I died they washed me out of the turret with a hose.

EIGHTH AIR FORCE

If, in an odd angle of the hutment,
A puppy laps the water from a can
Of flowers, and the drunk sergeant shaving
Whistles O *Paradiso!* — shall I say that man
Is not as men have said: a wolf to man?

The other murderers troop in yawning;
Three of them play Pitch, one sleeps, and one
Lies counting missions, lies there sweating
Till even his heart beats: One; One; One.
O *murderers!* . . . Still, this is how it's done:

This is a war. . . . But since these play, before they die,
Like puppies with their puppy; since, a man,
I did as these have done, but did not die —
I will content the people as I can
And give up these to them: Behold the man!

I have suffered, in a dream, because of him,
Many things; for this last saviour, man,
I have lied as I lie now. But what is lying?
Men wash their hands, in blood, as best they can:
I find no fault in this just man.

A CAMP IN THE PRUSSIAN FOREST

I walk beside the prisoners to the road.
Load on puffed load,
Their corpses, stacked like sodden wood,
Lie barred or galled with blood

By the charred warehouse. No one comes today
In the old way
To knock the fillings from their teeth;
The dark, coned, common wreath

Is plaited for their grave — a kind of grief.
The living leaf
Clings to the planted profitable
Pine if it is able;

The boughs sigh, mile on green, calm, breathing mile,
From this dead file
The planners ruled for them. . . . One year
They sent a million here:

Here men were drunk like water, burnt like wood.
The fat of good
And evil, the breast's star of hope
Were rendered into soap.

I paint the star I sawed from yellow pine —
And plant the sign
In soil that does not yet refuse
Its usual Jews

Their first asylum. But the white, dwarfed star —
This dead white star —
Hides nothing, pays for nothing; smoke
Fouls it, a yellow joke,

The needles of the wreath are chalked with ash,
A filmy trash
Litters the black woods with the death
Of men; and one last breath

Curls from the monstrous chimney. . . . I laugh aloud
Again and again;
The star laughs from its rotting shroud
Of flesh. O star of men!

THE WOMAN AT THE WASHINGTON ZOO

The saris go by me from the embassies.

Cloth from the moon. Cloth from another planet.
They look back at the leopard like the leopard.

And I. . . .
        this print of mine, that has kept its color
Alive through so many cleanings; this dull null
Navy I wear to work, and wear from work, and so
To my bed, so to my grave, with no
Complaints, no comment: neither from my chief,
The Deputy Chief Assistant, nor his chief —
Only I complain. . . . this serviceable
Body that no sunlight dyes, no hand suffuses
But, dome-shadowed, withering among columns,
Wavy beneath fountains — small, far-off, shining
In the eyes of animals, these beings trapped
As I am trapped but not, themselves, the trap,
Aging, but without knowledge of their age,
Kept safe here, knowing not of death, for death —
Oh, bars of my own body, open, open!

The world goes by my cage and never sees me.
And there come not to me, as come to these,
The wild beasts, sparrows pecking the llamas' grain,
Pigeons settling on the bears' bread, buzzards
Tearing the meat the flies have clouded. . . .
                        Vulture,
When you come for the white rat that the foxes left,
Take off the red helmet of your head, the black
Wings that have shadowed me, and step to me as man:
The wild brother at whose feet the white wolves fawn,

To whose hand of power the great lioness
Stalks, purring. . . .
                              You know what I was,
You see what I am: change me, change me!

THE PLAYER PIANO

I ate pancakes one night in a Pancake House
Run by a lady my age. She was gay.
When I told her that I came from Pasadena
She laughed and said, "I lived in Pasadena
When Fatty Arbuckle drove the El Molino bus."

I felt that I had met someone from home.
No, not Pasadena, Fatty Arbuckle.
Who's that? Oh, something that we had in common
Like — like — the false armistice. Piano rolls.
She told me her house was the first Pancake House

East of the Mississippi, and I showed her
A picture of my grandson. Going home —
Home to the hotel — I began to hum,
"Smile a while, I bid you sad adieu,
When the clouds roll back I'll come to you."

Let's brush our hair before we go to bed,
I say to the old friend who lives in my mirror.
I remember how I'd brush my mother's hair
Before she bobbed it. How long has it been
Since I hit my funnybone? had a scab on my knee?

Here are Mother and Father in a photograph,
Father's holding me. . . . They both look so *young*.
I'm so much older than they are. Look at them,
Two babies with their baby. I don't blame you,
You weren't old enough to know any better;

If I could I'd go back, sit down by you both,
And sign our true armistice: you weren't to blame.
I shut my eyes and there's our living room.

The piano's playing something by Chopin,
And Mother and Father and their little girl

Listen. Look, the keys go down by themselves!
I go over, hold my hands out, play I play —
If only, somehow, I had learned to live!
The three of us sit watching, as my waltz
Plays itself out a half-inch from my fingers.

Donald Justice

LANDSCAPE WITH LITTLE FIGURES

There were some pines, a canal, a piece of sky.
The pines are the houses now of the very poor,
Huddled together, in a blue, ragged wind.
Children go whistling their dogs, down by the mudflats,
Once the canal. There's a red ball lost in the weeds.
It's winter, it's after supper, it's goodbye.
O goodbye to the houses, the children, the little red ball,
And the pieces of sky that will go on falling for days.

COUNTING THE MAD

This one was put in a jacket,
This one was sent home,
This one was given bread and meat
But would eat none,
And this one cried No No No No
All day long.

This one looked at the window
As though it were a wall,
This one saw things that were not there,
This one things that were,
And this one cried No No No No
All day long.

This one thought himself a bird,
This one a dog,
And this one thought himself a man,
An ordinary man,
And cried and cried No No No No
All day long.

VARIATIONS FOR TWO PIANOS

There is no music now in all Arkansas.
Higgins is gone, taking both his pianos.

Movers dismantled the instruments, away
Sped the vans. The first detour untuned the strings.
There is no music now in all Arkansas.

Up Main Street, past the cold shopfronts of Conway,
The brash, self-important brick of the college,
Higgins is gone, taking both his pianos.

Warm evenings, the windows open, he would play
Something of Mozart's for his pupils, the birds.
There is no music now in all Arkansas.

How shall the mockingbird mend her trill, the jay
His eccentric attack, lacking a teacher?
Higgins is gone, taking both his pianos.

There is no music now in all Arkansas.

for Thomas Higgins, pianist

BUS STOP

Lights are burning
In quiet rooms
Where lives go on
Resembling ours.

The quiet lives
That follow us —
These lives we lead
But do not own —

Stand in the rain
So quietly
When we are gone,
So quietly . . .

And the last bus
Comes letting dark
Umbrellas out —
Black flowers, black flowers.

And lives go on.
And lives go on
Like sudden lights
At street corners

Or like the lights
In quiet rooms
Left on for hours,
Burning, burning.

MEN AT FORTY

Men at forty
Learn to close softly
The doors to rooms they will not be
Coming back to.

At rest on a stair landing,
They feel it
Moving beneath them now like the deck of a ship,
Though the swell is gentle.

And deep in mirrors
They rediscover
The face of the boy as he practices tying
His father's tie there in secret

And the face of that father,
Still warm with the mystery of lather.
They are more fathers than sons themselves now.
Something is filling them, something

That is like the twilight sound
Of the crickets, immense,
Filling the woods at the foot of the slope
Behind their mortgaged houses.

DONALD JUSTICE

THE MISSING PERSON

He has come to report himself
A missing person.

The authorities
Hand him the forms.

He knows how they have waited
With the learned patience of barbers

In small shops, idle,
Stropping their razors.

But now that these spaces in his life
Stare up at him blankly,

Waiting to be filled in,
He does not know how to begin.

Afraid that he may not answer
To his description of himself,

He asks for a mirror.
They reassure him

That he can be nowhere
But wherever he finds himself

From moment to moment
Which, for the moment, is here.

And he might like to believe them.
But in the mirror

He sees what is missing.
It is himself

He sees there emerging
Slowly, as from the dark

Of a furnished room
Only by darkness,

One who receives no mail
And is known to the landlady only

For keeping himself to himself,
And for whom it will be years yet

Before he can trust to the light
This last disguise, himself.

HANDS

> Les mains ne trouvaient plus
> De bonheur dans les poches.
>
> Guillevic

No longer do the hands know
The happiness of pockets.

Sometimes they hang at the sides
Like the dead weights of a clock.

Sometimes they clench into fists
Around the neck of anger.

Formerly there were brothers
To clasp, shoulders to rest on.

If now they unfold like maps,
All their countries seem foreign.

They dream of returning to
The dark home of the pockets.

They want to wash themselves clean
Of the blood of old salutes,

To scrub away the perfumes
Of the flesh they have tasted.

And all that they grasp is air.
Think of the hands as breathing,

DONALD JUSTICE

Opening, closing. Think of
The emptiness of the hands.

POEM

This poem is not addressed to you.
You may come into it briefly,
But no one will find you here, no one.
You will have changed before the poem will.

Even while you sit there, unmovable,
You have begun to vanish. And it does not matter.
The poem will go on without you.
It has the spurious glamor of certain voids.

It is not sad, really, only empty.
Once perhaps it was sad, no one knows why.
It prefers to remember nothing.
Nostalgias were peeled from it long ago.

Your type of beauty has no place here.
Night is the sky over this poem.
It is too black for stars.
And do not look for any illumination.

You neither can nor should understand what it means.
Listen, it comes without guitar,
Neither in rags nor any purple fashion.
And there is nothing in it to comfort you.

Close your eyes, yawn. It will be over soon.
You will forget the poem, but not before
It has forgotten you. And it does not matter.
It has been most beautiful in its erasures.

O bleached mirrors! Oceans of the drowned!
Nor is one silence equal to another.
And it does not matter what you think.
This poem is not addressed to you.

VARIATIONS ON A TEXT BY VALLEJO

Me moriré en Paris con aguacero . . .

I will die in Miami in the sun,
On a day when the sun is very bright,
A day like the days I remember, a day like other days,
A day that nobody knows or remembers yet,
And the sun will be bright then on the dark glasses of strangers
And in the eyes of a few friends from my childhood
And of the surviving cousins by the graveside,
While the diggers, standing apart, in the still shade of the palms,
Rest on their shovels, and smoke,
Speaking in Spanish softly, out of respect.

I think it will be on a Sunday like today,
Except that the sun will be out, the rain will have stopped,
And the wind that today made all the little shrubs kneel down;
And I think it will be a Sunday because today,
When I took out this paper and began to write,
Never before had anything looked so blank,
My life, these words, the paper, the gray Sunday;
And my dog, quivering under a table because of the storm,
Looked up at me, not understanding,
And my son read on without speaking, and my wife slept.

Donald Justice is dead. One Sunday the sun came out,
It shone on the bay, it shone on the white buildings,
The cars moved down the street slowly as always, so many,
Some with their headlights on in spite of the sun,
And after a while the diggers with their shovels
Walked back to the graveside through the sunlight,
And one of them put his blade into the earth
To lift a few clods of dirt, the black marl of Miami,
And scattered the dirt, and spat,
Turning away abruptly, out of respect.

DONALD JUSTICE

SONATINA IN YELLOW

Du schnell vergehendes Daguerrotyp
In meinen langsamer vergehenden Händen.

Rilke

The pages of the album,
As they are turned, turn yellow; a word,
Once spoken, obsolete,
No longer what was meant. Say it.
The meanings come, or come back later,
Unobtrusive, taking their places.

Think of the past. Think of forgetting the past.
It was an exercise requiring further practice;
A difficult exercise, played through by someone else.
Overheard from another room, now,
It seems full of mistakes.
                         So the voice of your father,
Rising as from the next room still
With all the remote but true affection of the dead,
Repeats itself, insists,
Insisting you must listen, rises
In the familiar pattern of reproof
For some childish error, a nap disturbed,
Or vase, broken or overturned;
Rises and subsides. And you do listen.
Listen and forget. Practice forgetting.

Forgotten sunlight still
Blinds the eyes of faces in the album.
The faces fade, and there is only
A sort of meaning that comes back,
Or for the first time comes, but comes too late
To take the places of the faces.

                                    Remember
The dead air of summer. Remember
The trees drawn up to their full height like fathers,
The underworld of shade you entered at their feet.
Enter the next room. Enter it quietly now,
Not to disturb your father sleeping there. *He stirs.*
Notice his clothes, how scrupulously clean,
Unwrinkled from the nap; his face, freckled with work,

Smoothed by a passing dream. The vase
Is not yet broken, still young roses
Drink there from perpetual waters. *He rises, speaks . . .*

Repeat it now, no one was listening.
So your hand moves, moving across the keys,
And slowly the keys grow darker to the touch.

PRESENCES

Everyone, everyone went away today.
They left without a word, and I think
I did not hear a single goodbye today.

And all that I saw was someone's hand, I think,
Thrown up out there like the hand of someone drowning,
But far away, too far to be sure what it was or meant.

No, but I saw how everything had changed
Later, just as the light had; and at night
I saw that from dream to dream everything changed.

And those who might have come to me in the night,
The ones who did come back but without a word,
All those I remembered passed through my hands like clouds —

Clouds out of the south, familiar clouds —
But I could not hold onto them, they were drifting away,
Everything going away in the night again and again.

TWO SMALL VICES BEGINNING
WITH THE LETTER "L"

Lethargy

It smiles to see me
Still in my bathrobe.

It sits in my lap
And will not let me rise.

Now it is kissing my eyes.
Arms enfold me, arms

Pale with a thick down.
It seems I am falling asleep

To the sound of a story
Being read me.

This is the story.
Weeks have passed

Since first I lifted my hand
To set it down.

Luxury

You are like a sun of the tropics
Peering through blinds

Drawn for siesta.
Already you teach me

The Spanish for sunflower.
Such iridescence!

You, alone on the clean sheet,
Unadorned.

You, like the spilt moon.
You, like a star

Hidden by sun-goggles.
You shall have a thousand lovers.

You, spread here like butter,
Like doubloons, like flowers.

CHILDREN WALKING HOME FROM SCHOOL
THROUGH GOOD NEIGHBORHOOD

They are like figures held in some glass ball,
One of those in which, when shaken, snowstorms occur;
But this one is not yet shaken.

And they go unaccompanied still,
Out along this walkway between two worlds,
This almost swaying bridge.
      October sunlight checkers their path;
It frets their cheeks and bare arms now with shadow
Almost too pure to signify itself.
And they progress slowly, somewhat lingeringly,
Independent, yet moving all together,
Like polyphonic voices that crisscross
In short-lived harmonies.

      Today, a few stragglers.
One, a girl, stands there with hands spaced out, so —
A gesture in a story. Someone's school notebook spills,
And they bend down to gather up the loose pages.
(Bright sweaters knotted at the waist; solemn expressions.)
Not that they would shrink or hold back from what may come,
For now they all at once run to meet it, a little swirl of colors,
Like the leaves already blazing and falling farther north.

DANCE LESSONS OF THE THIRTIES

Wafts of old incense mixed with Cuban coffee
Hung on the air; a fan turned; it was summer.
And (of the buried life) some last aroma
Still clung to the tumbled cushions of the sofa.

At lesson time, pushed back, it used to be
The thing we managed always just to miss
With our last-second dips and twirls — all this
While the Victrola wound down gradually.

And this was their exile, those brave ladies who taught us
So much of art, and stepped off to their doom
Demonstrating the foxtrot with their daughters
Endlessly around a sad and makeshift ballroom —

O little lost Bohemias of the suburbs!

Galway Kinnell

FIRST SONG

Then it was dusk in Illinois, the small boy
After an afternoon of carting dung
Hung on the rail fence, a sapped thing
Weary to crying. Dark was growing tall
And he began to hear the pond frogs all
Calling on his ear with what seemed their joy.

Soon their sound was pleasant for a boy
Listening in the smoky dusk and the nightfall
Of Illinois, and from the fields two small
Boys came bearing cornstalk violins
And they rubbed the cornstalk bows with resins
And the three sat there scraping of their joy.

It was now fine music the frogs and the boys
Did in the towering Illinois twilight make
And into dark in spite of a shoulder's ache
A boy's hunched body loved out of a stalk
The first song of his happiness, and the song woke
His heart to the darkness and into the sadness of joy.

ON FROZEN FIELDS

1

We walk across the snow,
The stars can be faint,
The moon can be eating itself out,
There can be meteors flaring to death on earth,
The Northern Lights can be blooming and seething
And tearing themselves apart all night,
We walk arm in arm, and we are happy.

2

You in whose ultimate madness we live,
You flinging yourself out into the emptiness,
You — like us — great an instant,

O only universe we know, forgive us.

VAPOR TRAIL REFLECTED IN THE FROG POND

1

The old watch: their
thick eyes
puff and foreclose by the moon. The young, heads
trailed by the beginnings of necks,
shiver,
in the guarantee they shall be bodies.

In the frog pond
the vapor trail of a SAC bomber creeps,

I hear its drone, drifting, high up
in immaculate ozone.

2

And I hear,
coming over the hills, America singing,
her varied carols I hear:
crack of deputies' rifles practicing their aim on stray dogs at night,
sput of cattleprod,
TV groaning at the smells of the human body,
curses of the soldier as he poisons, burns, grinds, and stabs
the rice of the world,
with open mouth, crying strong, hysterical curses.

3

And by rice paddies in Asia
bones

wearing a few shadows
walk down a dirt road, smashed
bloodsuckers on their heel, knowing
the flesh a man throws down in the sunshine
dogs shall eat
and the flesh that is upthrown in the air
shall be seized by birds,
shoulder blades smooth, unmarked by old feather-holes,
hands rivered
by blue, erratic wanderings of the blood,
eyes crinkled up
as they gave up at the drifting sun that gives us our lives,
seed dazzled over the footbattered blaze of the earth.

THE BEAR

1

In late winter
I sometimes glimpse bits of steam
coming up from
some fault in the old snow
and bend close and see it is lung-colored
and put down my nose
and know
the chilly, enduring odor of bear.

2

I take a wolf's rib and whittle
it sharp at both ends
and coil it up
and freeze it in blubber and place it out
on the fairway of the bears.

And when it has vanished
I move out on the bear tracks,
roaming in circles
until I come to the first, tentative, dark
splash on the earth.

And I set out
running, following the splashes
of blood wandering over the world.
At the cut, gashed resting places
I stop and rest,
at the crawl-marks
where he lay out on his belly
to overpass some stretch of bauchy ice
I lie out
dragging myself forward with bear-knives in my fists.

3

On the third day I begin to starve,
at nightfall I bend down as I knew I would
at a turd sopped in blood,
and hesitate, and pick it up,
and thrust it in my mouth, and gnash it down,
and rise
and go on running.

4

On the seventh day,
living by now on bear blood alone,
I can see his upturned carcass far out ahead, a scraggled,
steamy hulk,
the heavy fur riffling in the wind.

I come up to him
and stare at the narrow-spaced, petty eyes,
the dismayed
face laid back on the shoulder, the nostrils
flared, catching
perhaps the first taint of me as he
died.

I hack
a ravine in his thigh, and eat and drink,
and tear him down his whole length
and open him and climb in
and close him up after me, against the wind,
and sleep.

5

And dream
of lumbering flatfooted
over the tundra,
stabbed twice from within,
splattering a trail behind me,
splattering it out no matter which way I lurch,
no matter which parabola of bear-transcendence,
which dance of solitude I attempt,
which gravity-clutched leap,
which trudge, which groan.

6

Until one day I totter and fall —
fall on this
stomach that has tried so hard to keep up,
to digest the blood as it leaked in,
to break up
and digest the bone itself: and now the breeze
blows over me, blows off
the hideous belches of ill-digested bear blood
and rotted stomach
and the ordinary, wretched odor of bear,

blows across
my sore, lolled tongue a song
or screech, until I think I must rise up
and dance. And I lie still.

7

I awaken I think. Marshlights
reappear, geese
come trailing again up the flyway.
In her ravine under old snow the dam-bear
lies, licking
lumps of smeared fur
and drizzly eyes into shapes
with her tongue. And one
hairy-soled trudge stuck out before me,
the next groaned out,
the next,

the next,
the rest of my days I spend
wandering: wondering
what, anyway,
was that sticky infusion, that rank flavor of blood, that poetry, by which
    I lived?

from THE BOOK OF NIGHTMARES

Under the Maud Moon

1

On the path,
by this wet site
of old fires —
black ashes, black stones, where tramps
must have squatted down,
gnawing on stream water,
unhouseling themselves on cursed bread,
failing to get warm at a twigfire —

I stop,
gather wet wood,
cut dry shavings, and for her,
whose face
I held in my hands
a few hours, whom I gave back
only to keep holding the space where she was,

I light
a small fire in the rain.

The black
wood reddens, the deathwatches inside
begin running out of time, I can see
the dead, crossed limbs
longing again for the universe, I can hear
in the wet wood the snap
and re-snap of the same embrace being torn.

The raindrops trying
to put the fire out

fall into it and are
changed: the oath broken,
the oath sworn between earth and water, flesh and spirit, broken,
to be sworn again,
over and over, in the clouds, and to be broken again,
over and over, on earth.

2

I sit a moment
by the fire, in the rain, speak
a few words into its warmth —
stone   saint   smooth stone — and sing
one of the songs I used to croak
for my daughter, in her nightmares.

Somewhere out ahead of me
a black bear sits alone
on his hillside, nodding from side
to side. He sniffs
the blossom-smells, the rained earth,
finally he gets up,
eats a few flowers, trudges away,
his fur glistening
in the rain.

The singed grease streams
out of the words, the one
held note
remains — a love-note
twisting under my tongue, like the coyote's bark,
curving off, into a
howl.

3

A round-
cheeked girlchild comes awake
in her crib. The green
swaddlings tear open,
a filament or vestment
tears, the blue
flower opens.

And she who is born,
she who sings and cries,
she who begins the passage, her hair
sprouting out,
her gums budding for her first spring on earth,
the mist still clinging about
her face, puts
her hand
into her father's mouth, to take hold of
his song.

4

It is all over,
little one, the flipping
and overleaping, the watery
somersaulting alone in the oneness
under the hill, under
the old, lonely bellybutton
pushing forth again
in remembrance,
the drifting there furled in the dark,
pressing a knee or elbow
along a slippery wall, sculpting
the world with each thrash — the stream
of omphalos blood humming all about you.

5

Her head
enters the headhold
which starts sucking her forth: being itself
closes down all over her, gives her
into the shuddering
grip of departure, the slow,
agonized clenches making
the last molds of her life in the dark.

6

The black eye
opens, the pupil

droozed with black hairs
stops, the chakra
on top of the brain throbs a long moment in world light,

and she skids out on her face into light,
this peck
of stunned flesh
clotted with celestial cheesiness, glowing
with the astral violet
of the underlife. And as they cut

her tie to the darkness
she dies
a moment, turns blue as a coal,
the limbs shaking
as the memories rush out of them. When

they hang her up
by the feet, she sucks
air, screams
her first song — and turns rose,
the slow,
beating, featherless arms
already clutching at the emptiness.

7

When it was cold
on our hillside, and you cried
in the crib rocking
through the darkness, on wood
knifed down to the curve of the smile, a sadness
stranger than ours, all of it
flowing from the other world,
I used to come to you
and sit by you
and sing to you. You did not know,
and yet you will remember,
in the silent zones
of the brain, a specter, descendant
of the ghostly forefathers, singing
to you in the nighttime —
not the songs
of light said to wave

through the bright hair of angels,
but a blacker
rasping flowering on that tongue.

For when the Maud moon
glimmered in those first nights,
and the Archer lay
sucking the icy biestings of the cosmos,
in his crib of stars,

I had crept down
to riverbanks, their long rustle
of being and perishing, down to marshes
where the earth oozes up
in cold streaks, touching the world
with the underglimmer
of the beginning,
and there learned my only song.

And in the days
when you find yourself orphaned,
emptied
of all wind-singing, of light,
the pieces of cursed bread on your tongue,

may there come back to you
a voice,
spectral, calling you
sister!
from everything that dies.

And then
you shall open
this book, even if it is in the book of nightmares.

LAST SONGS

What do they sing, the last birds
coasting down the twilight,
banking
across woods filled with darkness, their

frayed wings
curved on the world like a lover's arms
which form, night after night, in sleep,
an irremediable absence?

2

Silence. Ashes
in the grate. Whatever it is
that keeps us from heaven,
sloth, wrath, greed, fear, could we only
reinvent it on earth
as song.

SAINT FRANCIS AND THE SOW

The bud
stands for all things,
even for those things that don't flower,
because everything flowers from within, of self-blessing.
Though sometimes it's necessary
to reteach a thing its loveliness,
to put a hand on its brow
of the flower
and retell it in words and in touch
it is lovely
until it flowers again from within, of self-blessing.
As Saint Francis
put his hand on the creased forehead
of the sow, and told her in words and in touch
blessings of earth on the sow, and the sow
began remembering all down her thick length,
from the earthen snout all the way through the fodder and slops
to the spiritual curl of the tail,
from the hard spininess spiked out from the spine
down through the great, unbreakable heart
to the sheer blue milken dreaminess shuddering and squirting
from the fourteen teats into the fourteen mouths sucking and blowing
     beneath them:
the long, perfect loveliness of sow.

from WHEN ONE HAS LIVED A LONG TIME ALONE

3

When one has lived a long time alone,
among regrets so immense the past occupies
nearly all the room there is in consciousness,
one notices in the snake's eyes, which look back
without giving any less attention to the future,
the first coating of the opaque, milky-blue
leucoma snakes get when about to throw their skins
and become new — meanwhile continuing,
of course, to grow old — the same *bleu passé*
that bleaches the corneas of the blue-eyed
when they lie back at the end and look for heaven,
a fading one knows means they will never find it
when one has lived a long time alone.

4

When one has lived a long time alone,
one holds the snake near the loudspeaker disgorging
gorgeous sound and watches him crook
his forepart into four right angles,
as though trying to slow down the music
flowing through him, in order to absorb it
like milk of paradise into the flesh,
until a glimmering appears at his mouth,
such a drop of intense fluid as, among humans,
could form after long exciting at the tip
of the penis, and as he straightens himself out
he has the pathos one finds in the penis,
when one has lived a long time alone.

8

When one has lived a long time alone,
one likes alike the pig, who brooks no deferment
of gratification, and the porcupine, or thorned pig,
who enters the cellar but not the house itself
because of eating down the cellar stairs on the way up,

and one likes the worm, who by bunching herself together
and expanding works her way through the ground,
no less than the butterfly, who totters full of worry
among the day lilies, as they darken,
and more and more one finds one likes
any other species better than one's own,
which has gone amok, making one self-estranged,
when one has lived a long time alone.

10

When one has lived a long time alone,
and the hermit thrush calls and there is an answer,
and the bullfrog head half out of water repeats
the sexual cantillations of his first spring,
and the snake lowers himself over the threshold
and disappears among the stones, one sees
they all live to mate with their kind, and one knows,
after a long time of solitude, after the many steps taken
away from one's kind, toward the kingdom of strangers,
the hard prayer inside one's own singing
is to come back, if one can, to one's own,
a world almost lost, in the exile that deepens,
when one has lived a long time alone.

11

When one has lived a long time alone,
one wants to live again among men and women,
to return to that place where one's ties with the human
broke, where the disquiet of death and now also
of history glimmers its firelight on faces,
where the gaze of the new baby looks past the gaze
of the great granny, and where lovers speak,
on lips blowsy from kissing, that language
the same in each mouth, and like birds at daybreak
blether the song that is both earth's and heaven's,
until the sun has risen, and they stand
in the halo of being made one: kingdom come,
when one has lived a long time alone.

Carolyn Kizer

from PRO FEMINA

Three

I will speak about women of letters, for I'm in the racket.
Our biggest successes to date? Old maids to a woman.
And our saddest conspicuous failures? The married spinsters
On loan to the husbands they treated like surrogate fathers.
Think of that crew of self-pitiers, not-very-distant,
Who carried the torch for themselves and got first-degree burns.
Or the sad sonneteers, toast-and-teasdales we loved at thirteen;
Middle-aged virgins seducing the puerile anthologists
Through lust-of-the-mind; barbiturate-drenched Camilles
With continuous periods, murmuring softly on sofas
When poetry wasn't a craft but a sickly effluvium,
The air thick with incense, musk, and emotional blackmail.

I suppose they reacted from an earlier womanly modesty
When too many girls were scabs to their stricken sisterhood,
Impugning our sex to stay in good with the men,
Commencing their insecure bluster. How they must have swaggered
When women themselves endorsed their own inferiority!
Vestals, vassals and vessels, rolled into several,
They took notes in rolling syllabics, in careful journals,
Aiming to please a posterity that despises them.
But we'll always have traitors who swear that a woman surrenders
Her Supreme Function, by equating Art with aggression
And failure with Femininity. Still it's just as unfair
To equate Art with Femininity, like a prettily-packaged commodity
When we are the custodians of the world's best-kept secret:
Merely the private lives of one-half of humanity.

But even with masculine dominance, we mares and mistresses
Produced some sleek saboteuses, making their cracks
Which the porridge-brained males of the day were too thick to perceive,
Mistaking young hornets for perfectly harmless bumblebees.
Being thought innocuous rouses some women to frenzy;
They try to be ugly by aping the ways of the men
And succeed. Swearing, sucking cigars and scorching the bedspread,
Slopping straight shots, eyes blotted, vanity-blown
In the expectation of glory: *she writes like a man!*
This drives other women mad in a mist of chiffon
(one poetess draped her gauze over red flannels, a practical feminist).

But we're emerging from all that, more or less,
Except for some lady-like laggards and Quarterly priestesses
Who flog men for fun, and kick women to maim competition.
Now, if we struggle abnormally, we may almost seem normal;
If we submerge our self-pity in disciplined industry;
If we stand up and be hated, and swear not to sleep with editors;
If we regard ourselves formally, respecting our true limitations
Without making an unseemly show of trying to unfreeze our assets;
Keeping our heads and our pride while remaining unmarried;
And if wedded, kill guilt in its tracks when we stack up the dishes
And defect to the typewriter. And if mothers, believe in the luck of our
    children,
Whom we forbid to devour us, whom we shall not devour,
And the luck of our husbands and lovers, who keep free women.

THE UNGRATEFUL GARDEN

Midas watched the golden crust
That formed over his streaming sores,
Hugged his agues, loved his lust,
But damned to hell the out-of-doors

Where blazing motes of sun impaled
The serried roses, metal-bright.
"Those famous flowers," Midas wailed,
"Have scorched my retina with light."

This gift, he'd thought, would gild his joys,
Silt up the waters of his grief;
His lawns a wilderness of noise,
The heavy clang of leaf on leaf.

Within, the golden cup is good
To heft, to sip the yellow mead.
Outside, in summer's rage, the rude
Gold thorn has made his fingers bleed.

"I strolled my halls in golden shift,
As ruddy as a lion's meat.
Then I rushed out to share my gift,
And golden stubble cut my feet."

Dazzled with wounds, he limped away
To climb into his golden bed.
Roses, roses can betray.
"Nature is evil," Midas said.

A WIDOW IN WINTERTIME

Last night a baby gargled in the throes
Of a fatal spasm. My children are all grown
Past infant strangles; so, reassured, I knew
Some other baby perished in the snow.
But no. The cat was making love again.

Later, I went down and let her in.
She hung her tail, flagging from her sins.
Though she'd eaten, I forked out another dinner,
Being myself hungry all ways, and thin
From metaphysic famines she knows nothing of,

The feckless beast! Even so, resemblances
Were on my mind: female and feline, though
She preens herself from satisfaction, and does
Not mind lying even in snow. She is
Lofty and bedraggled, without need to choose.

As an ex-animal, I look fondly on
Her excesses and simplicities, and would not return
To them; taking no marks for what I have become,
Merely that my nine lives peal in my ears again
And again, ring in these austerities.

These arbitrary disciplines of mine,
Most of them trivial: like covering
The children on my way to bed, and trying
To live well enough alone, and not to dream
Of grappling in the snow, claws plunged in fur,

Or waken in a caterwaul of dying.

CAROLYN KIZER

THE COPULATING GODS

Brushing back the curls from your famous brow,
Lingering over the prominent temple vein
Purple as Aegean columns in the dawn,
Calm now, I ponder how self-consciously
The gods must fornicate.
It is that sense of unseen witness:
Those mortals with whom we couple or have coupled,
Clinging to our swan-suits, our bull-skins,
Our masquerades in coin and shrubbery.

We were their religion before they were born.
The spectacle of our carnality
Confused them into spiritual lust.
The headboard of our bed became their altar;
Rare nectar, shared, a common sacrament.
The wet drapery of our sheets, molded
To noble thighs, is made the basis
For a whole new aesthetic:
God is revealed as the first genius.

Men continue to invent our histories,
Deny our equal pleasure in each other.
Club-foot, nymphomaniac, they dub us,
Then fabricate the net that God will cast
Over our raptures: we, trussed up like goats,
Paraded past the searchlights of the sky
By God himself, the ringmaster and cuckold,
Amidst a thunderous laughter and applause.

Tracing again the bones of your famous face,
I know we are not their history but our myth.
Heaven prevents time; and our astral raptures
Float buoyant in the universe. Come, kiss!
Come, swoon again, we who invented dying
And the whole alchemy of resurrection.
They will concoct a scripture explaining this.

SEMELE RECYCLED

After you left me forever,
I was broken into pieces,
and all the pieces flung into the river.
Then the legs crawled ashore
and aimlessly wandered the dusty cow-track.
They became, for a while, a simple roadside shrine:
A tiny table set up between the thighs
held a dusty candle, weed, and fieldflower chains
placed reverently there by children and old women.
My knees were hung with tin triangular medals
to cure all forms of hysterical disease.

After I died forever in the river,
my torso floated, bloated in the stream,
catching on logs or stones among the eddies.
White water foamed around it, then dislodged it;
after a whirlwind trip, it bumped ashore.
A grizzled old man who scavenged along the banks
had already rescued my arms and put them by,
knowing everything has its uses, sooner or later.

When he found my torso, he called it his canoe,
and, using my arms as paddles,
he rowed me up and down the scummy river.
When catfish nibbled my fingers, he scooped them up
and blessed his re-usable bait.
Clumsy but serviceable, that canoe!
The trail of blood that was its wake
attracted the carp and eels, and the river turtle,
easily landed, dazed by my tasty red.

A young lad found my head among the rushes
and placed it on a dry stone.
He carefully combed my hair with a bit of shell
and set small offerings before it
which the birds and rats obligingly stole at night,
so it seemed I ate.
And the breeze wound through my mouth and empty sockets
so my lungs would sigh and my dead tongue mutter.

Attached to my throat like a sacred necklace
was a circlet of small snails.
Soon the villagers came to consult my oracular head
with its waterweed crown.
Seers found occupation, interpreting sighs,
and their papyrus rolls accumulated.

Meanwhile, young boys retrieved my eyes
they used for marbles in a simple game
— till somebody's pretty sister snatched at them
and set them, for luck, in her bridal diadem.
Poor girl! When her future groom caught sight of her,
all eyes, he crossed himself in horror,
and stumbled away in haste
through her dowered meadows.

What then of my heart and organs,
my sacred slit
which loved you best of all?
They were caught in a fisherman's net
and tossed at night into a pen for swine.
But they shone so by moonlight that the sows stampeded,
trampled each other in fear, to get away.
And the fisherman's wife, who had 13 living children
and was contemptuous of holy love,
raked the rest of me onto the compost heap.

Then in their various places and helpful functions,
the altar, oracle, offal, canoe, and oars
learned the wild rumor of your return.
The altar leapt up and ran to the canoe,
scattering candle grease and wilted grasses.
Arms sprang to their sockets, blind hands with nibbled nails
groped their way, aided by loud lamentation,
to the bed of the bride, snatched up those unlucky eyes
from her discarded veil and diadem,
and rammed them home. O what a bright day it was!
This empty body danced on the river bank.
Hollow, it called and searched among the fields
for those parts that steamed and simmered in the sun,
and never would have found them.

But then your great voice rang out under the skies
my name! — and all those private names

for the parts and places that had loved you best.
And they stirred in their nest of hay and dung.
The distraught old ladies chasing their lost altar,
and the seers pursuing my skull, their lost employment,
and the tumbling boys, who wanted the magic marbles,
and the runaway groom, and the fisherman's 13 children
set up such a clamor, with their cries of "Miracle!"
that our two bodies met like a thunderclap
in mid-day — right at the corner of that wretched field
with its broken fenceposts and startled, skinny cattle.
We fell in a heap on the compost heap
and all our loving parts made love at once,
while the bystanders cheered and prayed and hid their eyes
and then went decently about their business.

And here it is, moonlight again; we've bathed in the river
and are sweet and wholesome once more.
We kneel side by side in the sand;
we worship each other in whispers.
But the inner parts remember fermenting hay,
the comfortable odor of dung, the animal incense,
and passion, its bloody labor,
its birth and rebirth and decay.

from THE BLESSING

I

Daughter-my-mother,
you have observed my worst.
Holding me together at your expense
has made you burn cool.

So did I in childhood:
nursed her old hurts and doubts,
myself made cool to shallowness.
She grew out as I grew in.
At mid-point our furies met.

My mother's dust has rested
for fifteen years

in the front hall closet
because we couldn't bear to bury it.
Her dust-lined, dust-coated urn
squats among the size-eleven overshoes.
My father, who never forgets
his overshoes,
has forgotten that.

Hysterical-tongued daughter
of a dead marriage,
you shed hot tears in the bed
of that benign old woman
whose fierce joy you were:
tantrums in the closet
taking upon yourself the guilt
the split parents never felt.

Child and old woman
soothing each other,
sharing the same face
in a span of seventy years
the same mother wit.

III

Daughter, you lived through
my difficult affairs
as I tried to console
your burnt-out childhood.
We coped with our fathers,
compared notes
on the old one and the cold one,
learned to moderate our hates.
Risible in suffering,
we grew up together.

Mother-my-daughter,
I have been blessed
on both sides of my life.
Forgive me if sometimes
like my fading father
I see you as one.

Not that I confuse
your two identities
as he does, taking off
or putting on his overshoes
but my own role:

I lean on the bosom
of that double mother,
the ghost by night, the girl by day;
I between my
two mild furies,
alone but comforted.

And I will whisper blithely
in your dreams
when you are as old as I,
my hard time over.

Meanwhile, keep warm
your love, your bed,
and your wise heart and head,
my good daughter.

for Ashley

BITCH

Now, when he and I meet, after all these years,
I say to the bitch inside me, don't start growling.
He isn't a trespasser anymore,
Just an old acquaintance tipping his hat.
My voice says, "Nice to see you,"
As the bitch starts to bark hysterically.
He isn't an enemy now,
Where are your manners, I say, as I say,
"How are the children? They must be growing up."
At a kind word from him, a look like the old days,
The bitch changes her tone: she begins to whimper.
She wants to snuggle up to him, to cringe.
Down, girl! Keep your distance
Or I'll give you a taste of the choke-chain.

"Fine, I'm just fine," I tell him.
She slobbers and grovels.
After all, I am her mistress. She is basically loyal.
It's just that she remembers how she came running
Each evening, when she heard his step;
How she lay at his feet and looked up adoringly
Though he was absorbed in his paper;
Or, bored with her devotion, ordered her to the kitchen
Until he was ready to play.
But the small careless kindnesses
When he'd had a good day, or a couple of drinks,
Come back to her now, seem more important
Than the casual cruelties, the ultimate dismissal.
"It's nice to know you are doing so well," I say.
He couldn't have taken you with him;
You were too demonstrative, too clumsy,
Not like the well-groomed pets of his new friends.
"Give my regards to your wife," I say. You gag
As I drag you off by the scruff,
Saying, "Goodbye! Goodbye! Nice to have seen you again."

AFTERNOON HAPPINESS

At a party I spy a handsome psychiatrist,
And wish, as we all do, to get her advice for free.
Doctor, I'll say, I'm supposed to be a poet.
All life's awfulness has been grist to me.
We learn that happiness is a Chinese meal,
While sorrow is a nourishment forever.
My new environment is California Dreamer.
I'm fearful I'm forgetting how to brood.
And, Doctor, another thing has got me worried:
I'm not drinking as much as I should . . .

At home, I want to write a happy poem
On love, or a love poem of happiness.
But they won't do, the tensions of everyday,
The rub, the minor abrasions of any two
Who share one space. Ah, there's no substitute for tragedy!
But in this chapter, tragedy belongs
To that other life, the old life before *us*.

CAROLYN KIZER

Here is my aphorism of the day:
Happy people are monogamous,
Even in California. So how does the poem play

Without the paraphernalia of betrayal and loss?
I don't have a jealous eye or fear
And neither do you. In truth, I'm fond
Of your ex-mate, whom I name, "my wife-in-law."
My former husband, that old disaster, is now just funny,
So laugh we do, in what Cyril Connolly
Has called the endless, nocturnal conversation
Of marriage. Which may be the best part.
Darling, must I love you in light verse
Without the tribute of profoundest art?

Of course it won't last. You will break my heart
Or I yours, by dying. I could weep over that.
But now it seems forced, here in these heaven hills,
The mourning doves mourning, the squirrels mating,
My old cat warm in my lap, here on our terrace

As from below comes a musical cursing
As you mend my favorite plate. Later of course
I could pick a fight; there is always material in that.
But we don't come from fighting people, those
Who scream out red-hot iambs in their hate.

No, love, the heavy poem will have to come
From *temps perdu*, fertile with pain, or perhaps
Detonated by terrors far beyond this place
Where the world rends itself, and its tainted waters
Rise in the east to erode our safety here.
Much as I want to gather a lifetime thrift
And craft, my cunning skills tied in a knot for you,
There is only this useless happiness as gift.

© Kelly Wise

Maxine Kumin

MORNING SWIM

Into my empty head there come
a cotton beach, a dock wherefrom

I set out, oily and nude
through mist, in chilly solitude.

There was no line, no roof or floor
to tell the water from the air.

Night fog thick as terry cloth
closed me in its fuzzy growth.

I hung my bathrobe on two pegs.
I took the lake between my legs.

Invaded and invader, I
went overhand on that flat sky.

Fish twitched beneath me, quick and tame.
In their green zone they sang my name

and in the rhythm of the swim
I hummed a two-four-time slow hymn.

I hummed *Abide with Me*. The beat
rose in the fine thrash of my feet,

rose in the bubbles I put out
slantwise, trailing through my mouth.

My bones drank water; water fell
through all my doors. I was the well

that fed the lake that met my sea
in which I sang *Abide with Me*.

STONES

The moving of stones, that sly jockeying thrust
takes place at night underground, shoulders first.

They bud in their bunkers like hydras. They puff
up head after head and allow them to drop off

on their own making quahogs, cow flops, eggs and knee
caps. In this way one stone can infuse a colony.

Eyeless and unsurprised they behave
in the manner of stones: swallow turnips, heave graves

rise up openmouthed into walls and from time
to time imitate oysters or mushrooms.

The doors of my house are held open by stones
and to see the tame herd of them hump their backbones

as cumbrous as bears across the pasture in
an allday rain is to believe for an afternoon

of objects that waver and blur
in some dark obedient order.

WOODCHUCKS

Gassing the woodchucks didn't turn out right.
The knockout bomb from the Feed and Grain Exchange
was featured as merciful, quick at the bone
and the case we had against them was airtight,
both exits shoehorned shut with puddingstone,
but they had a sub-sub-basement out of range.

Next morning they turned up again, no worse
for the cyanide than we for our cigarettes
and state-store Scotch, all of us up to scratch.
They brought down the marigolds as a matter of course
and then took over the vegetable patch
nipping the broccoli shoots, beheading the carrots.

The food from our mouths, I said, righteously thrilling
to the feel of the .22, the bullets' neat noses.
I, a lapsed pacifist fallen from grace
puffed with Darwinian pieties for killing,
now drew a bead on the littlest woodchuck's face.
He died down in the everbearing roses.

Ten minutes later I dropped the mother. She
flipflopped in the air and fell, her needle teeth
still hooked in a leaf of early Swiss chard.
Another baby next. O one-two-three
the murderer inside me rose up hard,
the hawkeye killer came on stage forthwith.

There's one chuck left. Old wily fellow, he keeps
me cocked and ready day after day after day.
All night I hunt his humped-up form. I dream
I sight along the barrel in my sleep.
If only they'd all consented to die unseen
gassed underground the quiet Nazi way.

HOW IT IS

Shall I say how it is in your clothes?
A month after your death I wear your blue jacket.
The dog at the center of my life recognizes
you've come to visit, he's ecstatic.
In the left pocket, a hole.
In the right, a parking ticket
delivered up last August on Bay State Road.
In my heart, a scatter like milkweed,
a flinging from the pods of the soul.
My skin presses your old outline.
It is hot and dry inside.

I think of the last day of your life,
old friend, how I would unwind it, paste
it together in a different collage,
back from the death car idling in the garage,
back up the stairs, your praying hands unlaced,
reassembling the bites of bread and tuna fish
into a ceremony of sandwich,

running the home movie backward to a space
we could be easy in, a kitchen place
with vodka and ice, our words like living meat.

Dear friend, you have excited crowds
with your example. They swell
like wine bags, straining at your seams.
I will be years gathering up our words,
fishing out letters, snapshots, stains,
leaning my ribs against this durable cloth
to put on the dumb blue blazer of your death.

THE LONGING TO BE SAVED

When the barn catches fire
I am wearing the wrong negligee.
It hangs on me like a gunny sack.
I get the horses out, but they
wrench free, wheel, dash back
and three or four trips are required.
Much whinnying and rearing as well.
This happens whenever I travel.

At the next stopover, the children take off
their doctor and lawyer disguises
and turn back into little lambs.
They cower at windows from which flames
shoot like the tattered red cloth
of dimestore devil suits. They refuse
to jump into my waiting arms, although
I drilled them in this technique, years ago.

Finally they come to their senses and leap
but each time, the hoop holds my mother.
Her skin is as dry and papery
as a late onion. I take her
into my bed, an enormous baby
I do not especially want to keep.
Three nights of such disquiet
in and out of dreams as thin as acetate

until, last of all, it's you
trapped in the blazing fortress.

I hold the rope as you slide from danger.
It's tricky in high winds and drifting snow.
Your body swaying in space
grows heavier, older, stranger

and me in the same gunny sack
and the slamming sounds as the gutted building burns.
Now the family's out, there's no holding back.
I go in to get my turn.

THE EXCREMENT POEM

It is done by us all, as God disposes, from
the least cast of worm to what must have been
in the case of the brontosaur, say, spoor
of considerable heft, something awesome.

We eat, we evacuate, survivors that we are.
I think these things each morning with shovel
and rake, drawing the risen brown buns
toward me, fresh from the horse oven, as it were,

or culling the alfalfa-green ones, expelled
in a state of ooze, through the sawdust bed
to take a serviceable form, as putty does,
so as to lift out entire from the stall.

And wheeling to it, storming up the slope,
I think of the angle of repose the manure
pile assumes, how sparrows come to pick
the redelivered grain, how inky-cap

coprinus mushrooms spring up in a downpour.
I think of what drops from us and must then
be moved to make way for the next and next.
However much we stain the world, spatter

it with our leavings, make stenches, defile
the great formal oceans with what leaks down,
trundling off today's last barrowful,
I honor shit for saying: We go on.

THE GRACE OF GELDINGS IN RIPE PASTURES

Glutted, half asleep, browsing in
timothy grown so tall I see them
as though a pale-green stage scrim

they circle, nose to rump,
a trio of trained elephants.
It begins to rain, as promised.

Bit by bit they soak up drops
like laundry dampened to be ironed.
Runnels bedeck them. Their sides

drip like the ribs of very broad
umbrellas. And still they graze
and grazing, one by one let down

their immense, indolent penises
to drench the everlasting grass
with the rich nitrogen

then repeats them.

IN THE PEA PATCH

These as they clack in the wind
saying castanets, saying dance with me,
saying do me, dangle their intricate
nuggety scrota

and these with the light shining through
call up a woman in a gauzy dress
young, with tendrils of hair at her neck,
leaning in a summer doorway

and as the bloom of the lime-green pod
rubs away under the polishing thumb
in the interior
sweet for the taking, nine little fetuses
nod their cloned heads.

MAXINE KUMIN

FAMILY REUNION

The week in August you come home,
adult, professional, aloof,
we roast and carve the fatted calf
— in our case home-grown pig, the chine
garlicked and crisped, the applesauce
hand-pressed. Hand-pressed the greengage wine.

Nothing is cost-effective here.
The peas, the beets, the lettuces
hand sown, are raised to stand apart.
The electric fence ticks like the slow heart
of something we fed and bedded for a year,
then killed with kindness's one bullet
and paid Jake Mott to do the butchering.

In winter we lure the birds with suet,
thaw lungs and kidneys for the cat.
Darlings, it's all a circle from the ring
of wire that keeps the raccoons from the corn
to the gouged pine table that we lounge around,
distressed before any of you was born.

Benign and dozy from our gluttonies,
the candles down to stubs, defenses down,
love leaking out unguarded the way
juice dribbles from the fence when grounded
by grass stalks or a forgotten hoe,
how eloquent, how beautiful you seem!

Wearing our gestures, how wise you grow,
ballooning to overfill our space,
the almost-parents of your parents now.
So briefly having you back to measure us
is harder than having let you go.

IN THE PARK

You have forty-nine days between
death and rebirth if you're a Buddhist.
Even the smallest soul could swim

the English Channel in that time
or climb, like a ten-month-old child,
every step of the Washington Monument
to travel across, up, down, over or through
— you won't know till you get there which to do.

He laid on me for a few seconds
said Roscoe Black, who lived to tell
about his skirmish with a grizzly bear
in Glacier Park. *He laid on me*
not doing anything. I could feel
his heart beating against my heart.
Never mind *lie* and *lay*, the whole world
confuses them. For Roscoe Black you might say
all forty-nine days flew by.

I was raised on the Old Testament.
In it God talks to Moses, Noah,
Samuel, and they answer.
People confer with angels. Certain
animals converse with humans.
It's a simple world, full of crossovers.
Heaven's an airy Somewhere, and God
has a nasty temper when provoked,
but if there's a Hell, little is made of it.
No longtailed Devil, no eternal fire,
and no choosing what to come back as.
When the grizzly bear appears, he lies/lays down
on atheist and zealot. In the pitch-dark
each of us waits for him in Glacier Park.

NURTURE

From a documentary on marsupials I learn
that a pillowcase makes a fine
substitute pouch for an orphaned kangaroo.

I am drawn to such dramas of animal rescue.
They are warm in the throat. I suffer, the critic proclaims,
from an overabundance of maternal genes.

Bring me your fallen fledgling, your bummer lamb,
lead the abused, the starvelings, into my barn.
Advise the hunted deer to leap into my corn.

And had there been a wild child —
filthy and fierce as a ferret, he is called
in one nineteenth-century account —

a wild child to love, it is safe to assume,
given my fireside inked with paw prints,
there would have been room.

Think of the language we two, same and not-same,
might have constructed from sign,
scratch, grimace, grunt, vowel:

Laughter our first noun, and our long verb, howl.

Stanley Kunitz

SINGLE VISION

Before I am completely shriven
I shall reject my inch of heaven.

Cancel my eyes, and, standing, sink
Into my deepest self; there drink

Memory down. The banner of
My blood, unfurled, will not be love,

Only the pity and the pride
Of it, pinned to my open side.

When I have utterly refined
The composition of my mind,

Shaped language of my marrow till
Its forms are instant to my will,

Suffered the leaf of my heart to fall
Under the wind, and, stripping all

The tender blanket from my bone,
Rise like a skeleton in the sun,

I shall have risen to disown
The good mortality I won.

Directly risen with the stain
Of life upon my crested brain,

Which I shall shake against my ghost
To frighten him, when I am lost.

Gladly, as any poison, yield
My halved conscience, brightly peeled;

Infect him, since we live but once,
With the unused evil in my bones.

I'll shed the tear of souls, the true
Sweat, Blake's intellectual dew,

Before I am resigned to slip
A dusty finger on my lip.

FATHER AND SON

Now in the suburbs and the falling light
I followed him, and now down sandy road
Whiter than bone-dust, through the sweet
Curdle of fields, where the plums
Dropped with their load of ripeness, one by one.
Mile after mile I followed, with skimming feet,
After the secret master of my blood,
Him, steeped in the odor of ponds, whose indomitable love
Kept me in chains. Strode years; stretched into bird;
Raced through the sleeping country where I was young,
The silence unrolling before me as I came,
The night nailed like an orange to my brow.

How should I tell him my fable and the fears,
How bridge the chasm in a casual tone,
Saying, "The house, the stucco one you built,
We lost. Sister married and went from home,
And nothing comes back, it's strange, from where she goes.
I lived on a hill that had too many rooms:
Light we could make, but not enough of warmth,
And when the light failed, I climbed under the hill.
The papers are delivered every day;
I am alone and never shed a tear."

At the water's edge, where the smothering ferns lifted
Their arms, "Father!" I cried, "Return! You know
The way. I'll wipe the mudstains from your clothes;
No trace, I promise, will remain. Instruct
Your son, whirling between two wars,
In the Gemara of your gentleness,
For I would be a child to those who mourn

And brother to the foundlings of the field
And friend of innocence and all bright eyes.
O teach me how to work and keep me kind."

Among the turtles and the lilies he turned to me
The white ignorant hollow of his face.

eek

END OF SUMMER

An agitation of the air,
A perturbation of the light
Admonished me the unloved year
Would turn on its hinge that night.

I stood in the disenchanted field
Amid the stubble and the stones,
Amazed, while a small worm lisped to me
The song of my marrow-bones.

Blue poured into summer blue,
A hawk broke from his cloudless tower,
The roof of the silo blazed, and I knew
That part of my life was over.

Already the iron doors of the north
Clangs open: birds, leaves, snows
Order their populations forth,
And a cruel wind blows.

THE WAR AGAINST THE TREES

The man who sold his lawn to standard oil
Joked with his neighbors come to watch the show
While the bulldozers, drunk with gasoline,
Tested the virtue of the soil
Under the branchy sky
By overthrowing first the privet-row.

Forsythia-forays and hydrangea-raids
Were but preliminaries to a war
Against the great-grandfathers of the town,
So freshly lopped and maimed.
They struck and struck again,
And with each elm a century went down. *powerful line*

All day the hireling engines charged the trees,
Subverting them by hacking underground
In grub-dominions, where dark summer's mole
Rampages through his halls,
Till a northern seizure shook
Those crowns, forcing the giants to their knees. ✓

I saw the ghosts of children at their games
Racing beyond their childhood in the shade,
And while the green world turned its death-foxed page
And a red wagon wheeled,
I watched them disappear
Into the suburbs of their grievous age. ✓

Ripped from the craters much too big for hearts
The club-roots bared their amputated coils,
Raw gorgons matted blind, whose pocks and scars
Cried Moon! on a corner lot
One witness-moment, caught
In the rear-view mirrors of the passing cars.

INDIAN SUMMER AT LAND'S END

The season stalls, unseasonably fair,
blue-fair, serene, a stack of golden discs,
each disc a day, and the addition slow.
I wish you were here with me to walk the flats,
towards dusk especially when the tide is out
and the bay turns opal, filled with rolling fire

that washes on the mouldering wreck offshore,
our mussel-vineyard, strung with bearded grapes.
Last night I reached for you and shaped you there
lying beside me as we drifted past
the farthest seamarks and the watchdog bells,
and round Long Point throbbing its frosty light,
until we streamed into the open sea.
What did I know of voyaging till now?
Meanwhile I tend my flock, strange golden puffs
diminutive as wrens, with snipped-off tails,
who bounce down from the trees. High overhead,
on the trackless roads, skywriting V and yet
another V, the southbound Canada express
hoots of horizons and distances. . . .

THE ARTIST

His paintings grew darker every year.
They filled the walls, they filled the room;
eventually they filled his world —
all but the ravishment.
When voices faded, he would rush to hear
the scratched soul of Mozart
endlessly in gyre.
Back and forth, back and forth,
he paced the paint-smeared floor,
diminishing in size each time he turned,
trapped in his monumental void,
raving against his adversaries.
At last he took a knife in his hand
and slashed an exit for himself
between the frames of his tall scenery.
Through the holes of his tattered universe
the first innocence and the light
came pouring in.

STANLEY KUNITZ

THE PORTRAIT

My mother never forgave my father
for killing himself,
especially at such an awkward time
and in a public park,
that spring
when I was waiting to be born.
She locked his name
in her deepest cabinet
and would not let him out,
though I could hear him thumping.
When I came down from the attic
with the pastel portrait in my hand
of a long-lipped stranger
with a brave moustache
and deep brown level eyes,
she ripped it into shreds
without a single word
and slapped me hard.
In my sixty-fourth year
I can feel my cheek
still burning.

THE UNQUIET ONES

Years ago I lost
both my parents' addresses.
Father and mother lie
in their neglected cribs,
obscure as moles,
unvisited.
I do not need to summon them.
When I put out the light
I hear them stir, dissatisfied,
in their separate places,

in death as in life
remote from each other,
having no conversation
except in the common ground
of their son's mind.
They slip through narrow crevices
and, suddenly blown tall,
glide into my cave of phantoms,
unwelcome guests, but not
unloved, dark emissaries
of the two-faced god.

THE KNOT

I've tried to seal it in,
that cross-grained knot
on the opposite wall,
scored in the lintel of my door,
but it keeps bleeding through
into the world we share.
Mornings when I wake,
curled in my web,
I hear it come
with a rush of resin
out of the trauma
of its lopping-off.
Obstinate bud,
sticky with life,
mad for the rain again,
it racks itself with shoots
that crackle overhead,
dividing as they grow.
Let be! Let be!
I shake my wings
and fly into its boughs.

THE WELLFLEET WHALE

1

You have your language too,
    an eerie medley of clicks
        and hoots and trills,
location-notes and love calls,
    whistles and grunts. Occasionally,
        it's like furniture being smashed,
or the creaking of a mossy door,
    sounds that all melt into a liquid
        song with endless variations,
as if to compensate
    for the vast loneliness of the sea.
        Sometimes a disembodied voice
breaks in, as if from distant reefs,
    and it's as much as one can bear
        to listen to its long mournful cry,
a sorrow without name, both more
    and less than human. It drags
        across the ear like a record
running down.

2

No wind. No waves. No clouds.
    Only the whisper of the tide,
        as it withdrew, stroking the shore,
a lazy drift of gulls overhead,
    and tiny points of light
        bubbling in the channel.
It was the tag-end of summer.
    From the harbor's mouth
        you coasted into sight,
flashing news of your advent,
    the crescent of your dorsal fin
        clipping the diamonded surface.

We cheered at the sign of your greatness
   when the black barrel of your head
      erupted, ramming the water,
and you flowered for us
   in the jet of your spouting.

3

All afternoon you swam
   tirelessly round the bay,
      with such an easy motion,
the slightest downbeat of your tail,
   an almost imperceptible
      undulation of your flippers,
you seemed like something poured,
   not driven; you seemed
      to marry grace with power.
And when you bounded into air,
   slapping your flukes,
      we thrilled to look upon
pure energy incarnate
   as nobility of form.
      You seemed to ask of us
not sympathy, or love,
   or understanding,
      but awe and wonder.

That night we watched you
   swimming in the moon.
      Your back was molten silver.
We guessed your silent passage
   by the phosphorescence in your wake.
      At dawn we found you stranded on the rocks.

4

There came a boy and a man
   and yet other men running, and two
      schoolgirls in yellow halters

and a housewife bedecked
    with curlers, and whole families in beach
        buggies with assorted yelping dogs.
The tide was almost out.
    We could walk around you,
        as you heaved deeper into the shoal,
crushed by your own weight,
    collapsing into yourself,
        your flippers and your flukes
quivering, your blowhole
    spasmodically bubbling, roaring.
        In the pit of your gaping mouth
you bared your fringework of baleen,
    a thicket of horned bristles.
        When the Curator of Mammals
arrived from Boston
    to take samples of your blood
        you were already oozing from below.
Somebody had carved his initials
    in your flank. Hunters of souvenirs
        had peeled off strips of your skin,
a membrane thin as paper.
    You were blistered and cracked by the sun.
    The gulls had been pecking at you.
The sound you made was a hoarse and fitful bleating.

What drew us to the magnet of your dying?
    You made a bond between us,
        the keepers of the nightfall watch,
who gathered in a ring around you,
    boozing in the bonfire light.
        Toward dawn we shared with you
your hour of desolation,
    the huge lingering passion
        of your unearthly outcry,
as you swung your blind head
    toward us and laboriously opened
        a bloodshot, glistening eye,
in which we swam with terror and recognition.

5

Voyager, chief of the pelagic world,
    you brought with you the myth
        of another country, dimly remembered,
where flying reptiles
    lumbered over the steaming marshes
        and trumpeting thunder lizards
wallowed in the reeds.
    While empires rose and fell on land,
        your nation breasted the open main,
rocked in the consoling rhythm
    of the tides. Which ancestor first plunged
        head-down through zones of colored twilight
to scour the bottom of the dark?
    You ranged the North Atlantic track
        from Port-of-Spain to Baffin Bay,
edging between the ice-floes
    through the fat of summer,
        lob-tailing, breaching, sounding,
grazing in the pastures of the sea
    on krill-rich orange plankton
        crackling with life.
You prowled down the continental shelf,
    guided by the sun and stars
        and the taste of alluvial silt
on your way southward
    to the warm lagoons,
        the tropic of desire,
where the lovers lie belly to belly
    in the rub and nuzzle of their sporting;
        and you turned, like a god in exile,
out of your wide primeval element,
    delivered to the mercy of time.
        Master of the whale-roads,
let the white wings of the gulls
    spread out their cover.
        You have become like us,
disgraced and mortal.

THE ABDUCTION

Some things I do not profess
to understand, perhaps
not wanting to, including
whatever it was they did
with you or you with them
that timeless summer day
when you stumbled out of the wood,
distracted, with your white blouse torn
and a bloodstain on your skirt.
"Do you believe?" you asked.
Between us, through the years,
from bits, from broken clues,
we pieced enough together
to make the story real:
how you encountered on the path
a pack of sleek, grey hounds,
trailed by a dumbshow retinue
in leather shrouds; and how
you were led, through leafy ways,
into the presence of a royal stag,
flaming in his chestnut coat,
who kneeled on a swale of moss
before you; and how you were borne
aloft in triumph through the green,
stretched on his rack of budding horn,
till suddenly you found yourself alone
in a trampled clearing.

That was a long time ago,
almost another age, but even now,
when I hold you in my arms,
I wonder where you are.
Sometimes I wake to hear
the engines of the night thrumming
outside the east bay window
on the lawn spreading to the rose garden.
You lie beside me in elegant repose,
a hint of transport hovering on your lips,
indifferent to the harsh green flares
that swivel through the room,
searchlights controlled by unseen hands.

STANLEY KUNITZ

Out there is childhood country,
bleached faces peering in
with coals for eyes.
Our lives are spinning out
from world to world;
the shapes of things
are shifting in the wind.
What do we know
beyond the rapture and the dread?

© David Geier

Denise Levertov

THE JACOB'S LADDER

The stairway is not
a thing of gleaming strands
a radiant evanescence
for angels' feet that only glance in their tread, and need not
touch the stone.

It is of stone.
A rosy stone that takes
a glowing tone of softness
only because behind it the sky is a doubtful, a doubting
night gray.

A stairway of sharp
angles, solidly built.
One sees that the angels must spring
down from one step to the next, giving a little
lift of the wings:

and a man climbing
must scrape his knees, and bring
the grip of his hands into play. The cut stone
consoles his groping feet. Wings brush past him.
The poem ascends.

HYPOCRITE WOMEN

Hypocrite women, how seldom we speak
of our own doubts, while dubiously
we mother man in his doubt!

And if at Mill Valley perched in the trees
the sweet rain drifting through western air
a white sweating bull of a poet told us

our cunts are ugly — why didn't we
admit we have thought so too? (And
what shame? They are not for the eye!)

No, they are dark and wrinkled and hairy,
caves of the Moon . . .   And when a
dark humming fills us, a

coldness towards life,
we are too much women to
own to such unwomanliness.

Whorishly with the psychopomp
we play and plead — and say
nothing of this later.   And our dreams,

with what frivolity we have pared them
like toenails, clipped them like ends of
split hair.

A PSALM PRAISING THE HAIR OF MAN'S BODY

My great brother
          Lord of the Song
wears the ruff of
          forest bear.

Husband, thy fleece of silk is black,
          a black adornment;
lies so close to the turns of the flesh,
burns my palm-stroke.

My great brother
          Lord of the Song
wears the ruff of
          forest bear.

Strong legs of our son are dusted dark with hair.
Told of long roads,
we know his stride.

My great brother
          Lord of the Song
wears the ruff of
          forest bear.

Hair of man, man-hair, hair of
breast and groin, marking contour as
    silverpoint marks in cross-
    hatching, as river-
    grass on the woven current
    indicates ripple,
praise.

THE WINGS

Something hangs in back of me,
I can't see it, can't move it.

I know it's black,
a hump on my back.

It's heavy. You
can't see it.

What's in it? Don't tell me
you don't know. It's

what you told me about —
black

inimical power, cold
whirling out of it and

around me and
sweeping you flat.

But what if,
like a camel, it's

pure energy I store,
and carry humped and heavy?

Not black, not
that terror, stupidity

of cold rage; or black
only for being pent there?

What if released in air
it became a white

source of light, a fountain
of light? Could all that weight

be the power of flight?
Look inward: see me

with embryo wings, one
feathered in soot, the other

blazing ciliations of ember, pale
flare-pinions. Well —

could I go
on one wing,

the white one?

THE ALTARS IN THE STREET

On June 17th, 1966, The New York Times reported that, as part of the Buddhist campaign of non-violent resistance, Viet-Namese children were building altars in the streets of Saigon and Hue, effectively jamming traffic.

Children begin at green dawn nimbly to build
topheavy altars, overweighted with prayers,
thronged each instant more densely

with almost-visible ancestors.
Where tanks have cracked the roadway
the frail altars shake; here a boy

with red stumps for hands steadies a corner,
here one adjusts with his crutch the holy base.
The vast silence of Buddha overtakes

and overrules the oncoming roar
of tragic life that fills alleys and avenues;
it blocks the way of pedicabs, police, convoys.

The hale and maimed together
hurry to construct for the Buddha
a dwelling at each intersection. Each altar

made from whatever stones, sticks, dreams, are at hand,
is a facet of one altar; by noon
the whole city in all its corruption,

all its shed blood the monsoon cannot wash away,
has become a temple,
fragile, insolent, absolute.

THE POEM UNWRITTEN

For weeks the poem of your body,
of my hands upon your body
　　　stroking, sweeping, in the rite of
　　　worship, going
　　　their way of wonder down
　　　from neck-pulse to breast-hair to level
　　　belly to cock —
for weeks that poem, that prayer,
unwritten.

　　　The poem unwritten, the act
left in the mind, undone. The years
a forest of giant stones, of fossil stumps,
blocking the altar.

1970

WAYS OF CONQUEST

You invaded my country by accident,
not knowing you had crossed the border.
Vines that grew there touched you.
　　　　　　　You ran past them,
shaking raindrops off the leaves — you or the wind.
It was toward the hills you ran,
inland —

DENISE LEVERTOV

I invaded your country with all my
'passionate intensity,'
pontoons and parachutes of my blindness.
But living now in the suburbs of the capital
incognito,
       my will to take the heart of the city
       has dwindled. I love
its unsuspecting life,
its adolescents who come to tell me their dreams in the dusty park
among the rocks and benches,
I the stranger who will listen.
I love
the wild herons who return each year to the marshy outskirts.
What I invaded has
invaded me.

WEDDING-RING

My wedding-ring lies in a basket
as if at the bottom of a well.
Nothing will come to fish it back up
and onto my finger again.
          It lies
among keys to abandoned houses,
nails waiting to be needed and hammered
into some wall,
telephone numbers with no names attached,
idle paperclips.
          It can't be given away
for fear of bringing ill-luck.
          It can't be sold
for the marriage was good in its own
time, though that time is gone.
          Could some artificer
beat into it bright stones, transform it
into a dazzling circlet no one could take
for solemn betrothal or to make promises
living will not let them keep? Change it
into a simple gift I could give in friendship?

PASSAGE

The spirit that walked upon the face of the waters
walks the meadow of long grass;
green shines to silver where the spirit passes.

Wind from the compass points, sun at meridian,
these are forms the spirit enters,
breath, *ruach*, light that is witness and by which we witness.

The grasses numberless, bowing and rising, silently
cry hosanna as the spirit
moves them and moves burnishing

over and again upon mountain pastures
a day of spring, a needle's eye
space and time are passing through like a swathe of silk.

THE WELL

At sixteen I believed the moonlight
could change me if it would.
                    I moved my head
on the pillow, even moved my bed
as the moon slowly
crossed the open lattice.

I wanted beauty, a dangerous
gleam of steel, my body thinner,
my pale face paler.
                    I moonbathed
diligently, as others sunbathe.
But the moon's unsmiling stare
kept me awake. Mornings,
I was flushed and cross.

It was on dark nights of deep sleep
that I dreamed the most, sunk in the well,
and woke rested, and if not beautiful,
filled with some other power.

DENISE LEVERTOV

STANDOFF

Assail God's hearing with gull-screech knifeblades.

Cozen the saints to plead our cause, claiming
grace abounding.

God crucified on the resolve not to displume
our unused wings

hears: nailed palms
cannot beat off the flames of insistent sound,

strident or plaintive,
nor reach to annul freedom —

nor would God renege.

Our shoulders ache. The abyss
gapes at us.

When shall we
dare to fly?

INTIMATION

I am impatient with these branches, this light.
The sky, however blue, intrudes.
Because I've begun to see
there is something else I must do,
I can't quite catch the rhythm
of days I moved well to in other winters.
The steeple tree
was cut down, the one that daybreak
used to gild — that fervor of birds and cherubim
subdued. Drought has dulled
many a green blade.
                    Because
I know a different need has begun
to cast its lines out from me into

DENISE LEVERTOV

a place unknown, I reach
for a silence almost present,
elusive among my heartbeats.

THE BLIND MAN'S HOUSE
AT THE EDGE OF THE CLIFF

At the jutting rim of the land he lives,
but not from ignorance,
not from despair.
He knows one extra step from his seaward
wide-open door would be
a step into salt air,
and he has no longing to shatter himself
far below, where the breakers
grind granite to sand.
No, he has chosen a life
pitched at the brink, a nest on the swaying
tip of a branch, for good reason:

dazzling within his darkness
is the elusive deep horizon. Here
nothing intrudes, palpable shade,
between his eager
inward gaze
and the vast enigma.
If he could fly he would drift forever
into that veil, soft and receding.

He knows that if he could see
he would be no wiser.
High on the windy cliff he breathes
face to face with desire.

STELE (I–II c. B.C.)

They part at the edge of substance.
Henceforth, he will be shadow
in a land of shadow.

And she — she too will be going
slowly down a road of cloud,
weightless, untouched, untouching.
This is the last crossroad.
Her right hand and his left
are clasped, but already,
muffled in his acceptance of fate,
his attention recedes from her.
Her left hand rises, fingertips trace
the curve of his warm face
as it cools and fades.
He has looked down his road,
he is ready to go, not willingly
yet without useless resistance.
She too accepts the truth, there is no way back,
but she has not looked, yet, at the path
accorded to her. She has not given herself,
not yet, to her shadowhood.

WHERE IS THE ANGEL?

Where is the angel for me to wrestle?
No driving snow in the glass bubble,
but mild September.

Outside, the stark shadows
menace, and fling their huge arms about
unheard. I breathe

a tepid air, the blur
of asters, of brown fern and gold-dust
seems to murmur,

and that's what I hear, only that.
Such clear walls of curved glass:
I see the violent gesticulations

and feel — no, not nothing. But in this
gentle haze, nothing commensurate.
It is pleasant in here. History

mouths, volume turned off. A band of iron,
like they put round a split tree,
circles my heart. In here

it is pleasant, but when I open
my mouth to speak, I too
am soundless. Where is the angel

to wrestle with me and wound
not my thigh but my throat,
so curses and blessings flow storming out

and the glass shatters, and the iron sunders?

Philip Levine

ANIMALS ARE PASSING FROM OUR LIVES

It's wonderful how I jog
on four honed-down ivory toes
my massive buttocks slipping
like oiled parts with each light step.

I'm to market. I can smell
the sour, grooved block, I can smell
the blade that opens the hole
and the pudgy white fingers

that shake out the intestines
like a hankie. In my dreams
the snouts drool on the marble,
suffering children, suffering flies,

suffering the consumers
who won't meet their steady eyes
for fear they could see. The boy
who drives me along believes

that any moment I'll fall
on my side and drum my toes
like a typewriter or squeal
and shit like a new housewife

discovering television,
or that I'll turn like a beast
cleverly to hook his teeth
with my teeth. No. Not this pig.

TO A CHILD TRAPPED IN A BARBER SHOP

You've gotten in through the transom
    and you can't get out
till Monday morning or, worse,
    till the cops come.

That six-year-old red face
            calling for mama
is yours; it won't help you
            because your case

is closed forever, hopeless.
        So don't drink
the Lucky Tiger, don't
            fill up on grease

because that makes it a lot worse,
            that makes it a crime
against property and the state
            and that costs time.

We've all been here before,
            we took our turn
under the electric storm
            of the vibrator

and stiffened our wills to meet
            the close clippers
and heard the true blade mowing
            back and forth

on a strip of dead skin,
            and we stopped crying.
You think your life is over?
            It's just begun.

COMING HOME

Detroit, 1968

A winter Tuesday, the city pouring fire,
Ford Rouge sulfurs the sun, Cadillac, Lincoln,
Chevy gray. The fat stacks
of breweries hold their tongues. Rags,
papers, hands, the stems of birches
dirtied with words.
                    Near the freeway
you stop and wonder what came off,

recall the snowstorm where you lost it all,
the wolverine, the northern bear, the wolf
caught out, ice and steel raining
from the foundries in a shower
of human breath. On sleds in the false sun
the new material rests. One brown child
stares and stares into your frozen eyes
until the lights change and you go
forward to work. The charred faces, the eyes
boarded up, the rubble of innards, the cry
of wet smoke hanging in your throat,
the twisted river stopped at the color of iron.
We burn this city every day.

STARLIGHT

My father stands in the warm evening
on the porch of my first house.
I am four years old and growing tired.
I see his head among the stars,
the glow of his cigarette, redder
than the summer moon riding
low over the old neighborhood. We
are alone, and he asks me if I am happy.
"Are you happy?" I cannot answer.
I do not really understand the word,
and the voice, my father's voice, is not
his voice, but somehow thick and choked,
a voice I have not heard before, but
heard often since. He bends and passes
a thumb beneath each of my eyes.
The cigarette is gone, but I can smell
the tiredness that hangs on his breath.
He has found nothing, and he smiles
and holds my head with both his hands.
Then he lifts me to his shoulder,
and now I too am there among the stars,
as tall as he. Are you happy? I say.
He nods in answer, Yes! oh yes! oh yes!
And in that new voice he says nothing,
holding my head tight against his head,

his eyes closed up against the starlight,
as though those tiny blinking eyes
of light might find a tall, gaunt child
holding his child against the promises
of autumn, until the boy slept
never to waken in that world again.

Fleeting moment of
Communion
- loneliness
- isolation
- insight

YOU CAN HAVE IT

My brother comes home from work
and climbs the stairs to our room.
I can hear the bed groan and his shoes drop
one by one. You can have it, he says.

The moonlight streams in the window
and his unshaven face is whitened
like the face of the moon. He will sleep
long after noon and waken to find me gone.

Thirty years will pass before I remember
that moment when suddenly I knew each man
has one brother who dies when he sleeps
and sleeps when he rises to face this life,

and that together they are only one man
sharing a heart that always labors, hands
yellowed and cracked, a mouth that gasps
for breath and asks, Am I gonna make it?

All night at the ice plant he had fed
the chute its silvery blocks, and then I
stacked cases of orange soda for the children
of Kentucky, one gray box-car at a time

with always two more waiting. We were twenty
for such a short time and always in
the wrong clothes, crusted with dirt
and sweat. I think now we were never twenty.

In 1948 in the city of Detroit, founded
by de la Mothe Cadillac for the distant purposes

PHILIP LEVINE

of Henry Ford, no one wakened or died,
no one walked the streets or stoked a furnace,

for there was no such year, and now
that year has fallen off all the old newspapers,
calendars, doctors' appointments, bonds,
wedding certificates, drivers licenses.

The city slept. The snow turned to ice.
The ice to standing pools or rivers
racing in the gutters. Then bright grass rose
between the thousands of cracked squares,

and that grass died. I give you back 1948.
I give you all the years from then
to the coming one. Give me back the moon
with its frail light falling across a face.

Give me back my young brother, hard
and furious, with wide shoulders and a curse
for God and burning eyes that look upon
all creation and say, You can have it.

LET ME BEGIN AGAIN

Let me begin again as a speck
of dust caught in the night winds
sweeping out to sea. Let me begin
this time knowing the world is
salt water and dark clouds, the world
is grinding and sighing all night, and dawn
comes slowly and changes nothing. Let
me go back to land after a lifetime
of going nowhere. This time lodged
in the feathers of some scavenging gull
white above the black ship that docks
and broods upon the oily waters of
your harbor. This leaking freighter
has brought a hold full of hayforks
from Spain, great jeroboams of dark
Algerian wine and quill pens that can't

write English. The sailors have stumbled
off toward the bars or the bright houses.
The captain closes his log and falls asleep.
1/10'28. Tonight I shall enter my life
after being at sea for ages, quietly,
in a hospital named for an automobile.
The one child of millions of children
who has flown alone by the stars
above the black wastes of moonless waters
that stretched forever, who has turned
golden in the full sun of a new day.
A tiny wise child who this time will love
his life because it is like no other.

THE HOUSE

This poem has a door, a locked door,
and windows drawn against the day,
but at night the lights come on, one
in each room, and the neighbors swear
they hear music and the sound of dancing.
These days the neighbors will swear
to anything. That is not why
the house is locked and no one goes
in or out all day long. That is because
this is a poem first and a house only
at night when everyone should be asleep.
The milkman tries to stop at dawn,
for he has three frosty white bottles
to place by the back door, but his horse
shakes his head back and forth, and so
he passes on his way. The papers pile
up on the front porch until the rain
turns them into gray earth, and they run
down the stairs and say nothing
to anyone. Who ever made this house
had no idea of beauty — it's all gray —
and no idea of what a happy family
needs on a day in spring when tulips
shout from their brown beds in the yard.
Back there the rows are thick with weeds,

stickers, choke grass, the place has gone
to soggy mulch, and the tools are hanging
unused from their hooks in the tool room.
Think of a marriage taking place at one
in the afternoon on a Sunday in June
in the stuffy front room. The dining table
is set for twenty, and the tall glasses
filled with red wine, the silver sparkling.
But no one is going in or out, not even
a priest in his long white skirt, or a boy
in pressed shorts, or a plumber with a fat bag.

WHAT WORK IS

We stand in the rain in a long line
waiting at Ford Highland Park. For work.
You know what work is — if you're
old enough to read this you know what
work is, although you may not do it.
Forget you. This is about waiting,
shifting from one foot to another.
Feeling the light rain falling like mist
into your hair, blurring your vision
until you think you see your own brother
ahead of you, maybe ten places.
You rub your glasses with your fingers,
and of course it's someone else's brother,
narrower across the shoulders than
yours but with the same sad slouch, the grin
that does not hide the stubbornness,
the sad refusal to give in to
rain, to the hours wasted waiting,
to the knowledge that somewhere ahead
a man is waiting who will say, "No,
we're not hiring today," for any
reason he wants. You love your brother,
now suddenly you can hardly stand
the love flooding you for your brother,
who's not beside you or behind or
ahead because he's home trying to
sleep off a miserable night shift

at Cadillac so he can get up
before noon to study his German.
Works eight hours a night so he can sing
Wagner, the opera you hate most,
the worst music ever invented.
How long has it been since you told him
you loved him, held his wide shoulders,
opened your eyes wide and said those words,
and maybe kissed his cheek? You've never
done something so simple, so obvious,
not because you're too young or too dumb,
not because you're jealous or even mean
or incapable of crying in
the presence of another man, no,
just because you don't know what work is.

AMONG CHILDREN

I walk among the rows of bowed heads —
the children are sleeping through fourth grade
so as to be ready for what is ahead,
the monumental boredom of junior high
and the rush forward tearing their wings
loose and turning their eyes forever inward.
These are the children of Flint, their fathers
work at the spark plug factory or truck
bottled water in 5 gallon sea-blue jugs
to the widows of the suburbs. You can see
already how their backs have thickened,
how their small hands, soiled by pig iron,
leap and stutter even in dreams. I would like
to sit down among them and read slowly
from *The Book of Job* until the windows
pale and the teacher rises out of a milky sea
of industrial scum, her gowns streaming
with light, her foolish words transformed
into song, I would like to arm each one
with a quiver of arrows so that they might
rush like wind there where no battle rages
shouting among the trumpets, Ha! Ha!
How dear the gift of laughter in the face

PHILIP LEVINE

of the 8 hour day, the cold winter mornings
without coffee and oranges, the long lines
of mothers in old coats waiting silently
where the gates have closed. Ten years ago
I went among these same children, just born,
in the bright ward of the Sacred Heart and leaned
down to hear their breaths delivered that day,
burning with joy. There was such wonder
in their sleep, such purpose in their eyes
closed against autumn, in their damp heads
blurred with the hair of ponds, and not one
turned against me or the light, not one
said, I am sick, I am tired, I will go home,
not one complained or drifted alone,
unloved, on the hardest day of their lives.
Eleven years from now they will become
the men and women of Flint or Paradise,
the majors of a minor town, and I
will be gone into smoke or memory,
so I bow to them here and whisper
all I know, all I will never know.

John Logan

THREE MOVES

Three moves in six months and I remain
the same.
Two homes made two friends.
The third leaves me with myself again.
(We hardly speak.)
Here I am with tame ducks
and my neighbors' boats,
only this electric heat
against the April damp.
I have a friend named Frank —
The only one who ever dares to call
and ask me, "How's your soul?"
I hadn't thought about it for a while,
and was ashamed to say I didn't know.
I have no priest for now.
Who
will forgive me then. Will you?
Tame birds and my neighbors' boats.
The ducks honk about the floats . . .
They walk dead drunk onto the land and grounds,
iridescent blue and black and green and brown.
They live on swill
our aged houseboats spill.
But still they are beautiful.
Look! The duck with its unlikely beak
has stopped to pick
and pull
at the potted daffodil.
Then again they sway home
to dream
bright gardens of fish in the early night.
Oh these ducks are all right.
They will survive.
But I am sorry I do not often see them climb.
Poor sons-a-bitching ducks.
You're all fucked up.
What do you do that for?
Why don't you hover near the sun anymore?
Afraid you'll melt?

These foolish ducks lack a sense of guilt,
and so all their multi-thousand-mile range
is too short for the hope of change.

Seattle, April 1965

TO A YOUNG POET WHO FLED

Your cries make us afraid, but we love your delicious music!
— *Kierkegaard*

So you said you'd go home to work on your father's farm.
We've talked of how it is the poet alone can touch
with words, but I would touch you with my hand, my lost son,
to say good-bye again. You left some work, and have gone.
You don't know what you mean. Oh, not to me as a son,
for I have others. Perhaps too many. I cannot
answer all the letters. If I seem to brag, I add
I know how to shatter an image of the father
(twice have tried to end the yearning of an orphan son,
but opened up in him, and in me, another wound).
No — I say this: you don't know the reason of your gift.
It's not the suffering. Others have that. The gift of tears
is the hope of saints, Monica again and Austin.
I mean the gift of the structure of a poet's jaw,
which makes the mask that's cut out of the flesh of his face
a megaphone — as with the goat clad Greeks — to ampli-
fy the light gestures of his soul toward the high stone seats.
The magic of the mouth that can melt to tears the rock
of hearts. I mean the wand of tongues that charms the exile
of listeners into a bond of brothers, breaking
down the lines of lead that separate a man from a
man, and the husbands from their wives, in these old, burned glass
panels of our lives. The poet's jaw has its tongue ripped
as Philomel, its lips split (and kissed beside the grave),
the jawbone patched and cracked with fists and then with the salve
of his fellows. If they make him bellow, like a slave
cooked inside the ancient, brass bull, still that small machine
inside its throat makes music for an emperor's guest
out of his cries. Thus his curse: the poet cannot weep
but with a public and musical grief, and he laughs

with the joys of others. Yet, when the lean blessings come,
they are sweet, and great. My son, I could not make your choice.
Let me take your hand. I am too old or young to say,
"I'd rather be a swineherd in the hut, understood
by swine, than be a poet misunderstood by men."

SPRING OF THE THIEF

But if I look the ice is gone from the lake
and the altered air
no longer fills with the small
terrible bodies of the snow.
Only once these late winter weeks
the dying flakes
fell instead as manna or as wedding rice
blooming in the light
about the bronze Christ
and the thieves. There these three
still hang, more than man-
sized and heavier than life
on a hill over the lake
where I walk
this Third Sunday of Lent.
I come from Mass
melancholy at its ancient story
of the unclean ghost
a man thought he'd lost.
It came back into his well-swept house
and at the final state that man
was worse than he began.
Yet again today
there is the faintest edge of green
to trees about St. Joseph's Lake.
Ah God if our confessions show contempt
because we let them free us of our guilt
to sin again
forgive us still . . . before the leaves . . .
before the leaves have formed
you can glimpse the Christ and Thieves
on top of the hill. One of them was saved.
That day the snow had seemed to drop like grace

upon the four of us,
or like the peace of intercourse,
suddenly I wanted to confess —
or simply talk.
I paid a visit to the mammoth Sacred Heart
Church, and found it shut.
Who locked him out or in?
The name of God is changing in our time.
What is his winter name?
Where was his winter home?
Oh I've kept my love to myself before.
Even those ducks weave down the shore
together, drunk with hope
for the April water. One spring festival
near here I stripped and strolled
through a rain filled field.
Spread eagled on the soaking earth
I let the rain
move its audible little hands
gently on my skin . . . let the dark rain
raise up my love.
But why? I was alone
and no one saw how ardent I grew.
And when I rolled naked in the snow one night
as St. Francis with his Brother Ass
or a hard bodied Finn
I was alone. Underneath
the howling January moon
I knelt and dug my fist
full of the cold winter sand
and rubbed and
hid my manhood under it.
Washed up at some ancient or half-heroic shore
I was ashamed that I was naked there.
Before Nausicaä and the saints. Before myself.
But who took off my coat? Who put it on?
Who drove me home?
Blessed be sin if it teaches men shame.
Yet because of it we cannot talk
and I am separated from myself.
So what is all this reveling in snow and rain?
Or in the summer sun when the heavy gold
body weeps with joy or grief or love?
When we speak of God, is it God we speak of?

JOHN LOGAN

Perhaps his winter home
is in that field where I rolled or ran . . .
this hill where once the snow
fell serene as rain.
Oh I have walked around the lake
when I was not alone —
sometimes with my wife have seen these swans
dip down their necks
graceful as a girl, showering white and wet!
I've seen their heads delicately turn.
Have gone sailing with my quiet, older son.
And once on a morning walk
a student who had just come back
in fall found a perfect hickory shell
among the bronze and red
leaves and purple flowers of the time
and put its white bread into my hand.
Ekelöf said there is a freshness
nothing can destroy in us —
not even we ourselves.
Perhaps that
Freshness is the changed name of God.
Where all the monsters also hide
I bear him in the ocean of my blood
and in the pulp of my enormous head.
He lives beneath the unkempt potter's grass
of my belly and chest.
I feel his terrible, aged heart
moving under mine . . . can see the shadows
of the gorgeous light
that plays at the edges of his giant eye . . .
or tell the faint press and hum
of his eternal pool of sperm.
Like sandalwood! *Like sandalwood*
the righteous man
perfumes the axe that falls on him.
The cords of elm, of cedar oak and pine
will pile again in fall.
The ribs and pockets of the barns will swell.
Winds and fires in the field rage
and again burn out each
of the ancient roots.
Again at last the late November snow
will fill those fields, change this hill,

throw these figures in relief
and raining on them
will transform
the bronze Christ's brow and cheek,
the white face and thigh of the thief.

March–April, 1962

SUZANNE

You make us want to stay alive, Suzanne,
the way you turn

your blonde head.
The way you curve your slim hand

toward your breast.
When you drew your legs

up, sitting by the fire,
and let your bronze hair

stream about your knees
I could see the grief

of the girl in your eyes.
It touched the high,

formal bones of your face.
Once I heard it in your lovely voice

when you sang —
the terrible time of being young.

Yet you bring us joy with your
self, Suzanne, wherever you are.

And once, although I wasn't here,
you left three roses on my stair.

One party night when you were high
you fled barefoot down the hall,

the fountain of your laughter
showering through the air.

"Chartreuse," you chanted
(the liqueur you always wanted),

"I have yellow chartreuse hair!"
Oh it was a great affair.

You were the most exciting person there.
Yesterday when I wasn't here

again,
you brought a blue, porcelain

egg to me —
colored beautifully

for the Russian Easter.
Since then, I have wanted to be your lover,

but I have only touched your shoulder
and let my fingers brush your hair,

because you left three roses on my stair.

LOVE POEM

Last night you would not come,
and you have been gone so long.
I yearn to find you in my aging, earthen arms
again (your alchemy can change my clay to skin).
I long to turn and watch again
from my half-hidden place
the lost, beautiful slopes and fallings of your face,
the black, rich leaf of each eyelash,
fresh, beach-brightened stones of your teeth.
I want to listen as you breathe yourself to sleep
(for by our human art we mime
the sleeper till we dream).
I want to smell the dark

herb gardens of your hair — touch the thin shock
that drifts over your high brow when
you rinse it clean,
for it is so fine.
I want to hear the light,
long wind of your sigh.
But again tonight I know you will not come.
I will never feel again
your gentle, sleeping calm
from which I took
so much strength, so much of my human heart.
Because the last time
I reached to you
as you sat upon the bed
and talked, you caught both my hands
in yours and crossed them gently on my breast.
I died mimicking the dead.

from POEM IN PROGRESS

Second Prelude. Reality in Albuquerque: The Son

Passing through Albuquerque where I'd read poetry,
I find myself beside a quite young drinking buddy.
Black-haired and bright-eyed Chicano kid, he wants a coke
with three cherries in it. He gets that and then asks me,
as folks next to each other in bars are apt to talk,
why there are no cherries in *my* glass.
"Because," I say, knowing I sound absolutely
absurd, "Screwdrivers just never *have* cherries in them."
Surreal, I think. What's this kid doing in here at ten
o'clock A.M. anyway. "No school today," he says.
"Teacher's convention." He is
only seven and his father is tending the bar.
He asks me where all my kids are.
"In New York where I live," I lie.
Then tell the truth, that I am flying back there tonight.
"And your wife?" Third degree, I think. Well, part of bar talk.
"Why, New York too," I lie again.
How the hell can I tell this kid
I hardly ever see my sons
because they are three thousand miles

away from me (and then some). Perhaps *you* understand
what I mean — but him? Both of us
in the bar at ten A.M. He walks to the juke box
with a quarter given by his father, then looks back,
admits he cannot read well. So
we select together, and agree on two pieces,
playing first that morning song, "Bridge Over Troubled Water."

POEM FOR MY BROTHER

Blue's my older brother's color. Mine is brown, you see.
So today I bought this ring
of gold and lapis lazuli flecked with a bright bronze.
His blue is the light hue of his eyes. Brown's the color
of our dead mother's long hair,
which fell so beautifully about her young shoulders
in the picture, and of my own eyes (I can't tell hers).
I loved my brother, but never quite knew what to think.
For example, he would beat
me up as soon as the folks
left the house, and I would cry big, loud feminine tears.
He was good at sports and played football, and so instead
I was in the marching band.
My brother stole rubbers from the store and smoked cigars
and pipes, which made me sick. But
once we swam together in
the Nishnabotna river
near home, naked, our blue overalls piled together
by the water, their copper
buttons like the bronze glints in my ring. I remember
once when I was very young
I looked deep into a pool
of blue water — we had no mirror — and I was so
amazed I looked over my shoulder, for I did not
imagine it was me, caught
in that cerulean sky.
Thinking it was someone other, I tell you I confused myself with my brother!
Nothing goes with gold, but I can see in this rich blue
stone the meeting of our clothes like the touching of hands
when he taught me to hold my fishing pole well and wound

up the reel for me. You know
blue's the last of the primary colors to be named.
Why, some primitive societies still have no word
for it except "dark." It's associated with black:
in the night brother and I
would play at games that neither of us could understand.
But this is not a confession; it is a question.
We've moved apart and don't write,
and our children don't even know their own cousin!
So, I would have you know I
want this ring to *engage* us
in reconciliation.
Blue's the color of the heart.
I won't live forever. Is it too late now to be
a brother to my brother?
Let the golden snake bend round
again to touch itself and
all at once burst into azure!

AVOCADO

for Robert Bly

It is a green globe like a vegetable light bulb
with a stem to meet either soil or small living tree;
it is mottled like an old man's face or is wizened
like the enormous head of a fetus. Now the stem
has come away from a navel.
It has the stolid heft of a stone. The smell seeps up
and leads the mind far away to the earth's ancient cave.
Its taste is also pungent dirt with a kind of bark
that is quite difficult to chew:
here is the small tomb of woman.
Mother smells its fresh soil even with her dead sense. She feels
its husk. Her body inside is the soft flesh of fruit,
and her heart this oval green core.
Her grief, her anger is that she
no longer has life, but the stuff of her breathes a residue that has remained in earth
and in the minds of the children.
Oh, now I know her skin sighs green

as this fluted fruit: her spirit
is the taste of it, transmuted.

Honolulu
January 30, 1981

HAPPENING ON AEGINA

The beach on Aegina is a bit tawdry, although
the island lies gorgeous beyond.
Rusted cans, a blue abandoned bic and overturned
boats, paint peeling, lying dead on the beach in the sun.
My small friend Al wades gingerly
among the rocks, legs half cut off
by water. His black socks look despairing in their shoes
left behind. What brings this scene alive is a sailboat
quite far out and glowing with a strange brightness in the light
and the goddess on the beach — Daphne, Al's fifteen year old
daughter lying in the sun
in a blue bikini, her luminescent body
oiled, narrow hips, narrow bosom.
Her slim body brings to mind the one pillar still standing
in the temple to Apollo
on this ancient isle of Aegina.
Except for long black hair and eyebrows, unmistakably
a girl's, she's androgynous. Suddenly I feel she has been left behind
by that mysterious boat, its diaphanous sail
like wings just disappearing in the long twilight sun.

June 22–23 1982
Aegina, Greece

BELIEVE IT

There is a two-headed goat, a four-winged chicken
and a sad lamb with seven legs
whose complicated little life was spent in Hopland,
California. I saw the man with doubled eyes

who seemed to watch in me my doubts about my spirit.
Will it snag upon this aging flesh?

There is a strawberry that grew
out of a carrot plant, a blade
of grass that lanced through a thick rock,
a cornstalk nineteen-feet-two-inches tall grown by George
Osborne of Silome, Arkansas.
There is something grotesque growing in me I cannot tell.

It has been waxing, burgeoning, for a long time.
It weighs me down like the chains of the man of Lahore
who began collecting links on his naked body
until he crawled around the town carrying the last
thirteen years of his life six-hundred-seventy pounds.
Each link or each lump in me is an offense against love.

I want my own lit candle lamp buried in my skull
like the Lighthouse Man of Chungking,
who could lead the travelers home.
Well, I am still a traveler and I don't know where
I live. If my home is here, inside my breast,
light it up! And I will invite you in as my first guest.

for Tina Logan
After visiting the Believe It or Not Museum
with her in San Francisco
— 1980

THE GIFT

Your gift to me was like a girl
dressed in white (beautiful!) bringing
me a glass of cold fresh water from the lucid spring.
Your gift was like the quick vision
of a pair of swift roan ponies
galloping together along a wild, white sand beach.
Like the sight of two young people
making love with tenderness in a field of flowers,
whose blossoms are of a deep rich indigo and wine.
Your gift was like a small pillar
covered with lapis lazuli.

JOHN LOGAN

A girl shaking out her long hair.
Like the naked back of a man
washing, the view caught just as he bends to the bronze pan.
Like the taut neck of a guitar
trembling with the music it gives.
The hand of a friend extended.
I felt it was the green burst of light after the sun
goes down so slowly out at sea.
Your present was of the flesh and so much more beside.
All that I will give back again.
This is my testament of love.

Robert Lowell

COLLOQUY IN BLACK ROCK

Here the jack-hammer jabs into the ocean;
My heart, you race and stagger and demand
More blood-gangs for your nigger-brass percussions,
Till I, the stunned machine of your devotion,
Clanging upon this cymbal of a hand,
Am rattled screw and footloose. All discussions

End in the mud-flat detritus of death.
My heart, beat faster, faster. In Black Mud
Hungarian workmen give their blood
For the martyre Stephen, who was stoned to death.

Black Mud, a name to conjure with: O mud
For watermelons gutted to the crust,
Mud for the mole-tide harbor, mud for mouse,
Mud for the armored Diesel fishing tubs that thud
A year and a day to wind and tide; the dust
Is on this skipping heart that shakes my house,

House of our Savior who was hanged till death.
My heart, beat faster, faster. In Black Mud
Stephen the martyre was broken down to blood:
Our ransom is the rubble of his death.

Christ walks on the black water. In Black Mud
Darts the kingfisher. On Corpus Christi, heart,
Over the drum-beat of St. Stephen's choir
I hear him, *Stupor Mundi,* and the mud
Flies from his hunching wings and beak — my heart,
The blue kingfisher dives on you in fire.

CHRISTMAS EVE UNDER HOOKER'S STATUE

Tonight a blackout. Twenty years ago
I hung my stocking on the tree, and hell's
Serpent entwined the apple in the toe

To sting the child with knowledge. Hooker's heels
Kicking at nothing in the shifting snow,
A cannon and a cairn of cannon balls
Rusting before the blackened Statehouse, know
How the long horn of plenty broke like glass
In Hooker's gauntlets. Once I came from Mass;

Now storm-clouds shelter Christmas, once again
Mars meets his fruitless star with open arms,
His heavy saber flashes with the rime,
The war-god's bronzed and empty forehead forms
Anonymous machinery from raw men;
The cannon on the Common cannot stun
The blundering butcher as he rides on Time —
The barrel clinks with holly. I am cold:
I ask for bread, my father gives me mould;

His stocking is full of stones. Santa in red
Is crowned with wizened berries. Man of war,
Where is the summer's garden? In its bed
The ancient speckled serpent will appear,
And black-eyed susan with her frizzled head.
When Chancellorsville mowed down the volunteer,
"All wars are boyish," Herman Melville said;
But we are old, our fields are running wild:
Till Christ again turn wanderer and child.

MEMORIES OF WEST STREET AND LEPKE

Only teaching on Tuesdays, book-worming
in pajamas fresh from the washer each morning,
I hog a whole house on Boston's
"hardly passionate Marlborough Street,"
where even the man
scavenging filth in the back alley trash cans,
has two children, a beach wagon, a helpmate,
and is a "young Republican."
I have a nine months' daughter,
young enough to be my granddaughter.
Like the sun she rises in her flame-flamingo infants' wear.

These are the tranquillized *Fifties*,
and I am forty. Ought I to regret my seedtime?
I was a fire-breathing Catholic C.O.,
and made my manic statement,
telling off the state and president, and then
sat waiting sentence in the bull pen
beside a Negro boy with curlicues
of marijuana in his hair.

Given a year,
I walked on the roof of the West Street Jail, a short
enclosure like my school soccer court,
and saw the Hudson River once a day
through sooty clothesline entanglements
and bleaching khaki tenements.
Strolling, I yammered metaphysics with Abramowitz,
a jaundice-yellow ("it's really tan")
and fly-weight pacifist,
so vegetarian,
he wore rope shoes and preferred fallen fruit.
He tried to convert Bioff and Brown,
the Hollywood pimps, to his diet.
Hairy, muscular, suburban,
wearing chocolate double-breasted suits,
they blew their tops and beat him black and blue.

I was so out of things, I'd never heard
of the Jehovah's Witnesses.
"Are you a C.O.?" I asked a fellow jailbird.
"No," he answered, "I'm a J.W."
He taught me the "hospital tuck,"
and pointed out the T-shirted back
of *Murder Incorporated's* Czar Lepke,
there piling towels on a rack,
or dawdling off to his little segregated cell full
of things forbidden the common man:
a portable radio, a dresser, two toy American
flags tied together with a ribbon of Easter palm.
Flabby, bald, lobotomized,
he drifted in a sheepish calm,
where no agonizing reappraisal
jarred his concentration on the electric chair —
hanging like an oasis in his air
of lost connections. . . .

ROBERT LOWELL

MAN AND WIFE

Tamed by *Miltown*, we lie on Mother's bed;
the rising sun in war paint dyes us red;
in broad daylight her gilded bed-posts shine,
abandoned, almost Dionysian.
At last the trees are green on Marlborough Street,
blossoms on our magnolia ignite
the morning with their murderous five days' white.
All night I've held your hand,
as if you had
a fourth time faced the kingdom of the mad —
its hackneyed speech, its homicidal eye —
and dragged me home alive. . . . Oh my *Petite*,
clearest of all God's creatures, still all air and nerve:
you were in your twenties, and I,
once hand on glass
and heart in mouth,
outdrank the Rahvs in the heat
of Greenwich Village, fainting at your feet —
too boiled and shy
and poker-faced to make a pass,
while the shrill verve
of your invective scorched the traditional South.

Now twelve years later, you turn your back.
Sleepless, you hold
your pillow to your hollows like a child;
your old-fashioned tirade —
loving, rapid, merciless —
breaks like the Atlantic Ocean on my head.

"TO SPEAK OF WOE THAT IS IN MARRIAGE"

"It is the future generation that presses into being by means of these exuberant feelings and supersensible soap bubbles of ours."

— *Schopenhauer*

"The hot night makes us keep our bedroom windows open.
Our magnolia blossoms. Life begins to happen.

My hopped up husband drops his home disputes,
and hits the streets to cruise for prostitutes,
free-lancing out along the razor's edge.
This screwball might kill his wife, then take the pledge.
Oh the monotonous meanness of his lust. . . .
It's the injustice . . . he is so unjust —
whiskey-blind, swaggering home at five.
My only thought is how to keep alive.
What makes him tick? Each night now I tie
ten dollars and his car key to my thigh. . . .
Gored by the climacteric of his want,
he stalls above me like an elephant."

SKUNK HOUR

(for Elizabeth Bishop)

Nautilus Island's hermit
heiress still lives through winter in her Spartan cottage;
her sheep still graze above the sea.
Her son's a bishop. Her farmer
is first selectman in our village;
she's in her dotage.

Thirsting for
the hierarchic privacy
of Queen Victoria's century,
she buys up all
the eyesores facing her shore,
and lets them fall.

The season's ill —
we've lost our summer millionaire,
who seemed to leap from an L. L. Bean
catalogue. His nine-knot yawl
was auctioned off to lobstermen.
A red fox stain covers Blue Hill.

And now our fairy
decorator brightens his shop for fall;
his fishnet's filled with orange cork,
orange, his cobbler's bench and awl;

there is no money in his work,
he'd rather marry.

One dark night,
my Tudor Ford climbed the hill's skull;
I watched for love-cars. Lights turned down,
they lay together, hull to hull,
where the graveyard shelves on the town. . . .
My mind's not right.

A car radio bleats,
"Love, O careless Love. . . ." I hear
my ill-spirit sob in each blood cell,
as if my hand were at its throat. . . .
I myself am hell;
nobody's here —

only skunks, that search
in the moonlight for a bite to eat.
They march on their soles up Main Street:
white stripes, moonstruck eyes' red fire
under the chalk-dry and spar spire
of the Trinitarian Church.

I stand on top
of our back steps and breathe the rich air —
a mother skunk with her column of kittens swills the garbage pail.
She jabs her wedge-head in a cup
of sour cream, drops her ostrich tail,
and will not scare.

EYE AND TOOTH

My whole eye was sunset red,
the old cut cornea throbbed,
I saw things darkly,
as through an unwashed goldfish globe.

I lay all day on my bed.
I chain-smoked through the night,
learning to flinch
at the flash of the matchlight.

Outside, the summer rain,
a simmer of rot and renewal,
fell in pinpricks.
Even new life is fuel.

My eyes throb.
Nothing can dislodge
the house with my first tooth
noosed in a knot to the doorknob.

Nothing can dislodge
the triangular blotch
of rot on the red roof,
a cedar hedge, or the shade of a hedge.

No ease from the eye
of the sharp-skinned hawk in the birdbook there,
with reddish-brown buffalo hair
on its shanks, one ascetic talon

clasping the abstract imperial sky.
It says:
an eye for an eye,
a tooth for a tooth.

No ease for the boy at the keyhole,
his telescope,
when the women's white bodies flashed
in the bathroom. Young, my eyes began to fail.

Nothing! No oil
for the eye, nothing to pour
on those waters or flames.
I am tired. Everyone's tired of my turmoil.

HISTORY

History has to live with what was here,
clutching and close to fumbling all we had —
it is so dull and gruesome how we die,
unlike writing, life never finishes.

Abel was finished; death is not remote,
a flash-in-the-pan electrifies the skeptic,
his cows crowding like skulls against high-voltage wire,
his baby crying all night like a new machine.
As in our Bibles, white-faced, predatory,
the beautiful, mist-drunken hunter's moon ascends —
a child could give it a face: two holes, two holes,
my eyes, my mouth, between them a skull's no-nose —
O there's a terrifying innocence in my face
drenched with the silver salvage of the mornfrost.

HOMECOMING

What was is . . . since 1930;
the boys in my old gang
are senior partners. They start up
bald like baby birds
to embrace retirement.

At the altar of surrender,
I met you
in the hour of credulity.
How your misfortune came out clearly
to us at twenty.

At the gingerbread casino,
how innocent the nights we made it
on our *Vesuvio* martinis
with no vermouth but vodka
to sweeten the dry gin —

the lash across my face
that night we adored . . .
soon every night and all,
when your sweet, amorous
repetition changed.

ROBERT LOWELL

EPILOGUE

Those blessèd structures, plot and rhyme —
why are they no help to me now
I want to make
something imagined, not recalled?
I hear the noise of my own voice:
The painter's vision is not a lens,
it trembles to caress the light.
But sometimes everything I write
with the threadbare art of my eye
seems a snapshot,
lurid, rapid, garish, grouped,
heightened from life,
yet paralyzed by fact.
All's misalliance.
Yet why not say what happened?
Pray for the grace of accuracy
Vermeer gave to the sun's illumination
stealing like the tide across a map
to his girl solid with yearning.
We are poor passing facts,
warned by that to give
each figure in the photograph
his living name.

William Matthews

THE SEARCH PARTY

I wondered if the others felt
as heroic
and as safe: *my* unmangled family
slept while I slid uncertain feet ahead
behind my flashlight's beam.
Stones, thick roots as twisted as
a ruined body,
what did I fear?
I hoped my batteries
had eight more lives
than the lost child.
I feared I'd find something.

Reader, by now you must be sure
you know just where we are,
deep in symbolic woods.
Irony, self-accusation,
someone else's suffering.
The search is that of art.

You're wrong, though it's
an intelligent mistake.
There was a real lost child.
I don't want to swaddle it
in metaphor.
I'm just a journalist
who can't believe in objectivity.
I'm in these poems
because I'm in my life.
But I digress.

A man four volunteers
to the left of me
made the discovery.

We circled in like waves
returning to the parent shock.

You've read this far, you might as well
have been there too. Your eyes accuse
me of false chase. Come off it,
you're the one who thought it wouldn't
matter what we found.
Though we came with lights
and tongues thick in our heads,
the issue was a human life.
The child was still
alive. Admit you're glad.

BLUES FOR JOHN COLTRANE, DEAD AT 41

Although my house floats on a lawn
as plush as a starlet's body
and my sons sleep easily,
I think of death's salmon breath
leaping back up the saxophone
with its wet kiss.

Hearing him dead,
I feel it in my feet
as if the house were rocked
by waves from a soundless speedboat
planing by, full throttle.

SWIMMING OFF CAPE HATTERAS

After an inland winter
my flesh falls off
like the glad lover's underwear.

Safely among the netting bones
my blood swims with the sea.

WILLIAM MATTHEWS

GOOD NIGHT

I sneak into my sons' room
to hear them breathe,
the hum of their intricate
bodies using air.

In her sleep my wife
has pushed away the covers.
Her nightgown is above her waist.
She has burrowed up
like a worm sensing rain.

None of these things is mine!
If I left them out overnight
I would not rust. Now I can lock
the door, turn out lights,
go to bed.
When I calm down and sleep
I dream that the earth beneath the house
is an old ship,
creaking spars and swollen hullgrain,
drifting in new waters.

PISSING OFF THE BACK OF THE BOAT
INTO THE NIVERNAIS CANAL

It's so cold my cock is furled
like a nutmeat and cold,
for all its warm aspirations
and traffic of urine. 37
years old and it takes me a second
to find it, the poor pink slug,
so far from the brash volunteer
of the boudoir. I arc a few
finishing stutters into the water.
Already they're converted,
opaque and chill. How com-
modious the dark universe is,

and companionable the stars.
How drunk I am. I shake
my shriveled nozzle and three
drops lurk out like syllables
from before there were languages. Snug
in my pants it would leak a whole sentence
in Latin. How like a lock-keeper's
life a penis biography would be,
bucolic and dull. What the penis
knows of sex is only arithmetic.
The tongue can kiss and tell.
But the imagination has,
as usual, most of the fun.
It makes discriminations,
bad jokes. It knows itself
to be tragic and thereby silly.
And it can tell a dull story well,
drop by reluctant drop.
What it can't do is be a body
nor survive time's acid work
on the body it enlivens,
I think as I try not to pitch
my wine-dulled body and wary
imagination with it into the inky
canal by a small force
of tugging my zipper up.
How much damage to themselves
the body and imagination
can absorb, I think as I drizzle
to sleep, and how much
the imagination makes
of its body of work
a place to recover itself.

MASTERFUL

They say you can't think and hit at the same time,
but they're wrong: you think with your body, and the whole

wave of impact surges patiently through you
into your wrists, into your bat, and meets the ball

as if this exact and violent tryst had been a fevered
secret for a week. The wrists "break," as the batting

coaches like to say, but what they do is give away
their power, spend themselves, and the ball benefits.

When Ted Williams took — we should say "gave" —
batting practice, he'd stand in and chant to himself

"My name is Ted Fucking Ballgame and I'm the best
fucking hitter in baseball," and he was, jubilantly

grim, lining them out pitch after pitch, crouching
and uncoiling from the sweet ferocity of excellence.

PUBERTY

Remember the way we bore our bodies to the pond
like raccoons with food to wash? Onto the blue,
smooth foil of the gift-wrapped water I slid

my embarrassing self. All the water I knew
was from books. I had read of the surfless Adriatic
and read how the North Atlantic erected by night

its wavering cliffs of fog and cul-de-sacs of ice,
only to turn to the dawn its chill, placid cheek.
But twitch and thrash in my chair as I might,

it was true what the swimming teacher told me:
once you learn how to float, it's almost impossible
to go under. I tried and tried, and so I can tell you

how we greet the news by which we survive: with rage.
A bucolic boy adrift on a Xenia, Ohio, pond?
Not on your life. Like you, I gulped and learned to swim.

BLUE NOTES

How often the blues begin early morning.
In the net of waking, on the mesh: bitter dew.
It's as if we'd been watered with nightmares

and these last squibs were the residue,
a few splatters from an evaporated eloquence
we can't reconstruct for all the cocaine

in Bogotá or winter wheat in Montana.
The blues tick in the wrist, even as the body
trudges its earnest portage to the shower.

Fight fire with fire and water with water.
You know that smirk in the blues? It turns out
the joke's on us. Each emotion lusts for its opposite —

which is to say, for itself. Our water music
every morning rains death's old sweet song,
but relentless joy infests the blues all day.

SMOKE GETS IN YOUR EYES

I love the smoky libidinal murmur
of a jazz crowd, and the smoke coiling
and lithely uncoiling like a choir
of vaporous cats. I like to slouch back
with that I'll-be-here-a-while tilt
and sip a little Scotch and listen,
keeping time and remembering the changes,
and now and then light up a cigarette.

It's the reverse of music: only a small
blue slur comes out — parody and rehearsal,
both, for giving up the ghost. There's a nostril-
billowing, sulphurous blossom from the match,
a dismissive waggle of the wrist,
and the match is out. What would I look like

in that thumb-sucking, torpid, eyes-glazed
and happy instant if I could snare myself

suddenly in a mirror, unprepared by vanity
for self-regard? I'd loose a cumulus of smoke,
like a speech balloon in the comic strips,
though I'd be talking mutely to myself,
and I'd look like I love the fuss of smoking:
hands like these, I should be dealing blackjack
for a living. And doesn't habit make us
predictable to ourselves? The stubs pile up
and ashes drift against the ashtray rims
like snow against a snow fence. The boy
who held his breath till he turned blue
has caught a writhing wisp of time itself
in his long-suffering lungs. It'll take years —
he'll tap his feet to music, check his watch
(you can't fire him; he quits), shun fatty foods —
but he'll have his revenge; he's killing time.

ONIONS

How easily happiness begins by
dicing onions. A lump of sweet butter
slithers and swirls across the floor
of the sauté pan, especially if its
errant path crosses a tiny slick
of olive oil. Then a tumble of onions.

This could mean soup or risotto
or chutney (from the Sanskrit
chatni, to lick). Slowly the onions
go limp and then nacreous
and then what cookbooks call clear,
though if they were eyes you could see

clearly the cataracts in them.
It's true it can make you weep
to peel them, to unfurl and to tease
from the taut ball first the brittle,

caramel-colored and decrepit
papery outside layer, the least

recent the reticent onion
wrapped around its growing body,
for there's nothing to an onion
but skin, and it's true you can go on
weeping as you go on in, through
the moist middle skins, the sweetest

and thickest, and you can go on
in to the core, to the bud-like,
acrid, fibrous skins densely
clustered there, stalky and incomplete, and these are the most
pungent, like the nuggets of nightmare

and rage and murmury animal
comfort that infant humans secrete.
This is the best domestic perfume.
You sit down to eat with a rumor
of onions still on your twice-washed
hands and lift to your mouth a hint

of a story about loam and usual
endurance. It's there when you clean up
and rinse the wine glasses and make
a joke, and you leave the minutest
whiff of it on the light switch,
later, when you climb the stairs.

MOOD INDIGO

From the porch; from the hayrick where her prickled
brothers hid and chortled and slurped into their young pink
lungs the ash-blond dusty air that lay above the bales

like low clouds; and from the squeak and suck
of the well-pump and from the glove of rust it implied
on her hand; from the dress parade of clothes

in her mothproofed closet; from her tiny Philco
with its cracked speaker and Sunday litany
(*Nick Carter, The Shadow, The Green Hornet, Sky King*);

from the loosening bud of her body; from hunger,
as they say, and from reading; from the finger
she used to dial her own number; from the dark

loam of the harrowed fields and from the very sky;
it came from everywhere. Which is to say it was
always there, and that it came from nowhere.

It evaporated with the dew, and at dusk when dark
spread in the sky like water in a blotter, it spread, too,
but it came back and curdled with milk and stung

with nettles. It was in the bleat of the lamb, the way
a clapper is in a bell, and in the raucous, scratchy
gossip of the crows. It walked with her to school and lay

with her to sleep and at last she was well pleased.
If she were to sew, she would prick her finger with it.
If she were to bake, it would linger in the kitchen

like an odor snarled in the deepest folds of childhood.
It became her dead pet, her lost love, the baby sister
blue and dead at birth, the chill headwaters of the river

that purled and meandered and ran and ran until
it issued into her, as into a sea, and then she was its
and it was wholly hers. She kept to her room, as we

learned to say, but now and then she'd come down
and pass through the kitchen, and the screen door
would close behind her with no more sound than

an envelope being sealed, and she'd walk for hours
in the fields like a lithe blue rain, and end up
in the barn, and one of us would go and bring her in.

James Merrill

ANGEL

Above my desk, whirring and self-important
(Though not much larger than a hummingbird)
In finely woven robes, school of Van Eyck,
Hovers an evidently angelic visitor.
He points one index finger out the window
At winter snatching to its heart,
To crystal vacancy, the misty
Exhalations of houses and of people running home
From the cold sun pounding on the sea;
While with the other hand
He indicates the piano
Where the Sarabande No. 1 lies open
At a passage I shall never master
But which has already, and effortlessly mastered me.
He drops his jaw as if to say, or sing,
'Between the world God made
And this music of Satie,
Each glimpsed through veils, but whole,
Radiant and willed,
Demanding praise, demanding surrender,
How can you sit there with your notebook?
What do you think you are doing?'
However he says nothing — wisely: I could mention
Flaws in God's world, or Satie's; and for that matter
How did he come by *his* taste for Satie?
Half to tease him, I turn back to my page,
Its phrases thus far clotted, unconnected.
The tiny angel shakes his head.
There is no smile on his round, hairless face.
He does not want even these few lines written.

AFTER GREECE

Light into the olive entered
And was oil. Rain made the huge pale stones
Shine from within. The moon turned his hair white

397

JAMES MERRILL

Who next stepped from between the columns,
Shielding his eyes. All through
The countryside were old ideas
Found lying open to the elements.
Of the gods' houses only
A minor premise here and there
Would be balancing the heaven of fixed stars
Upon a Doric capital. The rest
Lay spilled, their fluted drums half sunk in cyclamen
Or deep in water's biting clarity
Which just barely upheld me
The next week, when I sailed for home.
But where is home — these walls?
These limbs? The very spaniel underfoot
Races in sleep, toward what?
It is autumn. I did not invite
Those guests, windy and brittle, who drink my liquor.
Returning from a walk I find
The bottles filled with spleen, my room itself
Smeared by reflection on to the far hemlocks.
I some days flee in dream
Back to the exposed porch of the maidens
Only to find my great-great-grandmothers
Erect there, peering
Into a globe of red Bohemian glass.
As it swells and sinks, I call up
Graces, Furies, Fates, removed
To my country's warm, lit halls, with rivets forced
Through draper, and nothing left to bear.
They seem anxious to know
What holds up heaven nowadays.
I start explaining how in that vast fire
Were other irons — well, Art, Public Spirit,
Ignorance, Economics, Love of Self,
Hatred of Self, a hundred more,
Each burning to be felt, each dedicated
To sparing us the worst; how I distrust them
As I should have done those ladies; how I want
Essentials: salt, wine, olive, the light, the scream —
No! I have scarcely named you,
And look, in a flash you stand full-grown before me,
Row upon row, Essentials,
Dressed like your sister caryatids
Or tombstone angels jealous of their dead,

With undulant coiffures, lips weathered, cracked by grime,
And faultless eyes gone blank beneath the immense
Zinc and gunmetal northern sky. . . .
Stay then. Perhaps the system
Calls for spirits. This first glass I down
To the last time
I ate and drank in that old world. May I
Also survive its meanings, and my own.

A DEDICATION

Hans, there are moments when the whole mind
Resolves into a pair of brimming eyes, or lips
Parting to drink from the deep spring of a death
That freshness they do not yet need to understand.
These are the moments, if ever, an angel steps
Into the mind, as kings into the dress
Of a poor goatherd, for their acts of charity.
There are moments when speech is but a mouth pressed
Lightly and humbly against the angel's hand.

THE OCTOPUS

There are many monsters that a glassen surface
Restrains. And none more sinister
Than vision asleep in the eye's tight translucence.
Rarely it seeks now to unloose
Its diamonds. Having divined how drab a prison
The purest mortal tissue is,
Rarely it wakes. Unless, coaxed out by lusters
Extraordinary, like the octopus
From the gloom of its tank half-swimming half-drifting
Toward anything fair, a handkerchief
Or child's face dreaming near the glass, the writher
Advances in a godlike wreath
Of its own wrath. Chilled by such fragile reeling
A hundred blows of a boot-heel
Shall not quell, the dreamer wakes and hungers.

Percussive pulses, drum or gong,
Build in his skull their loud entrancement,
Volutions of a Hindu dance.
His hands move clumsily in the first conventional
Gestures of assent.
He is willing to undergo the volition and fervor
Of many fleshlike arms, observe
These in their holiness of indirection
Destroy, adore, evolve, reject —
Till on glass rigid with his own seizure
At length the sucking jewels freeze.

LABORATORY POEM

Charles used to watch Naomi, taking heart
And a steel saw, open up turtles, live.
While she swore they felt nothing, he would gag
At blood, at the blind twitching, even after
The murky dawn of entrails cleared, revealing
Contours he knew, egg-yellows like lamps paling.

Well then. She carried off the beating heart
To the kymograph and rigged it there, a rag
In fitful wind, now made to strain, now stopped
By her solutions tonic or malign
Alternately in which it would be steeped.
What the heart bore, she noted on a chart,

For work did not stop only with the heart.
He thought of certain human hearts, their climb
Through violence into exquisite disciplines
Of which, as it now appeared, they all expired.
Soon she would fetch another and start over,
Easy in the presence of her lover.

CHARLES ON FIRE

Another evening we sprawled about discussing
Appearances. And it was the consensus
That while uncommon physical good looks

Continued to launch one, as before, in life
(Among its vaporous eddies and false calms),
Still, as one of us said into his beard,
"Without your intellectual and spiritual
Values, man, you are sunk." No one but squared
The shoulders of his own unloveliness.
Long-suffering Charles, having cooked and served the meal,
Now brought out little tumblers finely etched
He filled with amber liquor and then passed.
"Say," said the same young man, "in Paris, France,
They do it this way" — bounding to his feet
And touching a lit match to our host's full glass.
A blue flame, gentle, beautiful, came, went
Above the surface. In a hush that fell
We heard the vessel crack. The contents drained
As who should step down from a crystal coach.
Steward of spirits, Charles's glistening hand
All at once gloved itself in eeriness.
The moment passed. He made two quick sweeps and
Was flesh again. "It couldn't matter less,"
He said, but with a shocked, unconscious glance
Into the mirror. Finding nothing changed,
He filled a fresh glass and sank down among us.

from UP AND DOWN

The Emerald

Hearing that on Sunday I would leave,
My mother asked if we might drive downtown.
Why certainly — off with my dressing gown!
The weather had turned fair. *We* were alive.

Only the gentle General she married
Late, for both an old way out of harm's,
Fought for breath, surrendered in her arms,
With military honors now lay buried.

That week the arcana of his medicine chest
Had been disposed of, and his clothes. Gold belt
Buckle and the letter from President Roosevelt
Went to an unknown grandchild in the West.

Downtown, his widow raised her parasol
Against the Lenten sun's not yet detectable
Malignant atomies which an electric needle
Unfreckles from her soft white skin each fall.

Hence too her chiffon scarf, pale violet,
And spangle-paste dark glasses. Each spring we number
The new dead. Above ground, who can remember
Her as she once was? Even I forget,

Fail to attend her, seem impervious . . .
Meanwhile we have made through a dense shimmy
Of parked cars burnished by the midday chamois
For Mutual Trust. Here cool gloom welcomes us,

And all, director, guard, quite palpably
Adore her. Spinster tellers one by one
Darting from cages, sniffing to meet her son,
Think of her having a son — ! She holds the key

Whereby palatial bronze gates shut like jaws
On our descent into this inmost vault.
The keeper bends his baldness to consult,
Brings a tin box painted mud-brown, withdraws.

She opens it. Security. Will. Deed.
Rummages further. Rustle of tissue, a sprung
Lid. Her face gone queerly lit, fair, young,
Like faces of our dear ones who have died.

No rhinestone now, no dilute amethyst,
But of the first water, linking star to pang,
Teardrop to fire, my father's kisses hang
In lipless concentration round her wrist.

Gray are these temple-drummers who once more
Would rouse her, girl-bride jeweled in his grave.
Instead, she next picks out a ring. "He gave
Me this when you were born. Here, take it for —

For when you marry. For your bride. It's yours."
A den of greenest light, it grows, shrinks, glows,
Hermetic stanza bedded in the prose
Of the last thirty semiprecious years.

I do not tell her, it would sound theatrical,
Indeed this green room's mine, my very life.
We are each other's; there will be no wife;
The little feet that patter here are metrical.

But onto her worn knuckle slip the ring.
Wear it for me. I silently entreat,
Until — until the time comes. Our eyes meet.
The world beneath the world is brightening.

THE VICTOR DOG

for Elizabeth Bishop

Bix to Buxtehude to Boulez,
The little white dog on the Victor label
Listens long and hard as he is able.
It's all in a day's work, whatever plays.

From judgment, it would seem, he has refrained.
He even listens earnestly to Bloch,
Then builds a church upon our acid rock.
He's man's — no — he's the Leiermann's best friend,

Or would be if hearing and listening were the same.
Does he hear? I fancy he rather smells
Those lemon-gold arpeggios in Ravel's
'Les jets d'eau du palais de ceux qui s'aiment.'

He ponders the Schumann Concerto's tall willow hit
By lightning, and stays put. When he surmises
Through one of Bach's eternal boxwood mazes
The oboe pungent as a bitch in heat,

Or when the calypso decants its raw bay rum
Or the moon in *Wozzeck* reddens ripe for murder,
He doesn't sneeze or howl; just listens harder.
Adamant needles bear down on him from

Whirling of outer space, too black, too near —
But he was taught as a puppy not to flinch,
Much less to imitate his bête noire Blanche
Who barked, fat foolish creature, at King Lear.

Still others fought in the road's filth over Jezebel,
Slavered on hearths of horned and pelted barons.
His forebears lacked, to say the least, forbearance.
Can nature change in him? Nothing's impossible.

The last chord fades. The night is cold and fine.
His master's voice rasps through the grooves' bare groves.
Obediently, in silence like the grave's
He sleeps there on the still-warm gramophone

Only to dream he is at the première of a Handel
Opera long thought lost — *Il Cane Minore.*
Its allegorical subject is his story!
A little dog revolving round a spindle

Gives rise to harmonies beyond belief,
A cast of stars. . . . Is there in Victor's heart
No honey for the vanquished? Art is art.
The life it asks of us is a dog's life.

WATERSPOUT

Where foam-white openwork
Rumples over slate,
Flash of a fork, the first
Wild syllables in flight,
The massive misty forces
Here to be faced are not
Of wind or water quite
So much as thought uptwisted
Helplessly by thought,
A fullblown argument
Sucked racing through whose veins
Whitebait and jellyfish
Repeat the lacy helices
Threaded into the stem
Of a Murano — wait:
Spirits intoxicate
The drinker, not the glass;
Yet *goblets* — three of them —

JAMES MERRILL

Weave up to be counted
Like drunks in the stormlight.
Poor crazy scene, poor brain
That cries and reels and clouds . . .
From somewhere above clouds,
Above thunder and levin
And the herring gull's high scream
(At which one glass may seem
To shatter), from this heaven
Slaked by the spinal fluid,
A bright-eyed reveller
Looks down on cloth outspread,
Strewn silver, fruits de mer,
The lighthouse salt-cellar —
A world exhausted, drained
But, like his word, unbroken;
Looks down and keeps his head.

W. S. Merwin

THE DRUNK IN THE FURNACE

For a good decade
The furnace stood in the naked gully, fireless
And vacant as any hat. Then when it was
No more to them than a hulking black fossil
To erode unnoticed with the rest of the junk-hill
By the poisonous creek, and rapidly to be added
To their ignorance,

They were afterwards astonished
To confirm, one morning, a twist of smoke like a pale
Resurrection, staggering out of its chewed hole,
And to remark then other tokens that someone,
Cosily bolted behind the eye-holed iron
Door of the drafty burner, had there established
His bad castle.

Where he gets his spirits
It's a mystery. But the stuff keeps him musical:
Hammer-and-anvilling with poker and bottle
To his jugged bellowings, till the last groaning clang
As he collapses onto the rioting
Springs of a litter of car-seats ranged on the grates,
To sleep like an iron pig.

In their tar-paper church
On a text about stoke-holes that are sated never
Their Reverend lingers. They nod and hate trespassers.
When the furnace wakes, though, all afternoon
Their witless offspring flock like piped rats to its siren
Crescendo, and agape on the crumbling ridge
Stand in a row and learn.

DEAD HAND

Temptations still nest in it like basilisks.
Hang it up till the rings fall.

AIR

Naturally it is night.
Under the overturned lute with its
One string I am going my way
Which has a strange sound.

This way the dust, that way the dust.
I listen to both sides
But I keep right on.
I remember the leaves sitting in judgment
And then winter.

I remember the rain with its bundle of roads.
The rain taking all its roads.
Nowhere.

Young as I am, old as I am,

I forget tomorrow, the blind man.
I forget the life among the buried windows.
The eyes in the curtains.
The wall
Growing through the immortelles.
I forget silence
The owner of the smile.

This must be what I wanted to be doing,
Walking at night between the two deserts,
Singing.

WE CONTINUE

for Galway Kinnell

The rust, a little pile of western color, lies
At the end of its travels,
Our instrument no longer.

Those who believe
In death have their worship cut out for them.
As for myself, we
Continue,

An old
Scar of light our trumpet,

Pilgrims with thorns
To the eye of the cold
Under flags made by the blind,
In one fist

This letter that vanishes
If the hand opens:

Charity, come home,
Begin.

SOME LAST QUESTIONS

What is the head
      A. Ash
What are the eyes
      A. The wells have fallen in and have
         Inhabitants
What are the feet
      A. Thumbs left after the auction
No what are the feet
      A. Under them the impossible road is moving
         Down which the broken necked mice push
         Balls of blood with their noses
What is the tongue
      A. The black coat that fell off the wall
         With sleeves trying to say something
What are the hands
      A. Paid
No what are the hands
      A. Climbing back down the museum wall
         To their ancestors the extinct shrews that will
         Have left a message
What is the silence
      A. As though it had a right to more
Who are the compatriots
      A. They make the stars of bone

W. S. MERWIN

DECEMBER NIGHT

The cold slope is standing in darkness
But the south of the trees is dry to the touch

The heavy limbs climb into the moonlight bearing feathers
I came to watch these
White plants older at night
The oldest
Come first to the ruins

And I hear magpies kept awake by the moon
The water flows through its
Own fingers without end

Tonight once more
I find a single prayer and it is not for men

FOR THE ANNIVERSARY OF MY DEATH

Every year without knowing it I have passed the day
When the last fires will wave to me
And the silence will set out
Tireless traveller
Like the beam of a lightless star
Then I will no longer
Find myself in life as in a strange garment
Surprised at the earth
And the love of one woman
And then shamelessness of men
As today writing after three days of rain
Hearing the wren sing and the falling cease
And bowing not knowing to what

TERGVINDER'S STONE

One time my friend Tergvinder brought a large round boulder into his
living room. He rolled it up the steps with the help of some two-by-fours,
and when he got it out into the middle of the room, where some people

have coffee tables (though he had never had one there himself) he left it. He said that was where it belonged.

It is really a plain-looking stone. Not as large as Plymouth Rock by a great deal, but then it does not have all the claims of a big shaky promotion campaign to support. That was one of the things Tergvinder said about it. He made no claims at all for it, he said. It was other people who called it Tergvinder's Stone. All he said was that according to him it belonged there.

His dog took to peeing on it, which created a problem (Tergvinder had not moved the carpet before he got the stone to where he said it belonged). Their tomcat took to squirting it, too. His wife fell over it quite often at first and it did not help their already strained marriage. Tergvinder said there was nothing to be done about it. It was in the order of things. That was a phrase he seldom employed, and never when he conceived that there was any room left for doubt.

He confided in me that he often woke in the middle of the night, troubled by the ancient, nameless ills of the planet, and got up quietly not to wake his wife, and walked through the house naked, without turning on any lights. He said that at such times he found himself listening, listening, aware of how some shapes in the darkness emitted low sounds like breathing, as they never did by day. He said he had become aware of a hole in the darkness in the middle of the living room, and out of that hole a breathing, a mournful dissatisfied sound of an absence waiting for what belonged to it, for something it had never seen and could not conceive of, but without which it could not rest. It was a sound, Tergvinder said, that touched him with fellow-feeling, and he had undertaken — oh, without saying anything to anybody — to assuage, if he could, that wordless longing that seemed always on the verge of despair. How to do it was another matter, and for months he had circled the problem, night and day, without apparently coming any closer to a solution. Then one day he had seen the stone. It had been there all the time at the bottom of his drive, he said, and he had never really seen it. Never recognized it for what it was. The nearer to the house he had got it, the more certain he had become. The stone had rolled into its present place like a lost loved one falling into arms that had long ached for it.

Tergvinder says that now on nights when he walks through the dark house he comes and stands in the living room doorway and listens to the peace in the middle of the floor. He knows its size, its weight, the touch of it, something of what is thought of it. He knows that it is peace. As he listens, some hint of that peace touches him too. Often, after a while, he steps down into the living room and goes and kneels beside the stone and they converse for hours in silence — a silence broken only by the sound of his own breathing.

W. S. MERWIN

DO NOT DIE

In each world they may put us
farther apart
do not die
as this world is made I might
live forever

ANIMULA

Look soul
soul
barefoot presence
through whom blood falls as through
a water clock
and tears rise before they wake
I will take you

at last to
where the wind stops
by the river we
know
by that same water
and the nights are not separate
remember

A DOOR

This is a place where a door might be
here where I am standing
in the light outside all the walls

there would be a shadow here
all day long
and a door into it
where now there is me

and somebody would come and knock
on this air
long after I have gone

and there in front of me a life
would open

THE BLACK JEWEL

In the dark
there is only the sound of the cricket

south wind in the leaves
is the cricket
so is the surf on the shore
and the barking across the valley

the cricket never sleeps
the whole cricket is the pupil of one eye
it can run it can leap it can fly
in its back the moon
crosses the night

there is only one cricket
when I listen

the cricket lives in the unlit ground
in the roots
out of the wind
it has only the one sound

before I could talk
I heard the cricket
under the house
then I remembered summer

mice too and the blind lightning
are born hearing the cricket
dying they hear it
bodies of light turn listening to the cricket
the cricket is neither alive nor dead
the death of the cricket
is still the cricket
in the bare room the luck of the cricket
echoes

A FAMILY

Would you believe me
if I told you the name of the farmers
at the end of the lake
where it grew shallow over the mossy rocks

and if you came in the morning the grass was blue
the fur of the rocks was wet the small frogs jumped
and the lake was silent behind you
except for echoes

you tied your boat carefully to a tree
before setting out across the cool pasture
watching for the bull
all the way to the barn

or if you came in the afternoon
the pasture glared and hummed the dark leaves smelled
from beside the water and the barn was drunk
by the time you got to it

to climb on the beams
to dive into the distant hay
will you believe
the names of the farmer's children

SON

As the shadow closed   on the face once my father's
three times leaning forward   far off she called
Good night in a whisper   from before I was born
later through the burial   a wren went on singing

then it was that I left   for the coast to live
a single long mountain   close to the shore
from it the sun rose   and everyone there asked me
who I was   I asked them who they were

at that time I found the cave   under the mountain
drawings still on the walls   carved fragments in the dirt
all my days I spent there   groping in the floor
but some who came from nearby   were wrecking the place for a game

garbage through holes overhead   broken cars dead animals
in the evenings they rolled huge rocks   down to smash the roof
nothing that I could do   kept them from it for long

the old story   the old story

and in the mornings the cave   full of new daylight

TO THE INSECTS

Elders

we have been here so short a time
and we pretend that we have invented memory

we have forgotten what it is like to be you
who do not remember us

we remember imagining that what survived us
would be like us

and would remember the world as it appears to us
but it will be your eyes that will fill with light

we kill you again and again
and we turn into you

eating the forests
eating the earth and the water

and dying of them
departing from ourselves

leaving you the morning
in its antiquity

AFTER THE ALPHABETS

I am trying to decipher the language of insects
they are the tongues of the future
their vocabularies describe buildings as food
they can depict dark water and the veins of trees

they can convey what they do not know
and what is known at a distance
and what nobody knows
they have terms for making music with the legs
they can recount changing in a sleep like death
they can sing with wings
the speakers are their own meaning in a grammar without horizons
they are wholly articulate
they are never important they are everything

CHORD

While Keats wrote they were cutting down the sandalwood forests
while he listened to the nightingale they heard their own axes echoing
    through the forests
while he sat in the walled garden on the hill outside the city they thought
    of their gardens dying far away on the mountain
while the sound of the words clawed at him they thought of their wives
while the tip of his pen travelled the iron they had coveted was hateful to
    them
while he thought of the Grecian woods they bled under red flowers
while he dreamed of wine the trees were falling from the trees
while he felt his heart they were hungry and their faith was sick
while the song broke over him they were in a secret place and they were
    cutting it forever
while he coughed they carried the trunks to the hole in the forest the size
    of a foreign ship
while he groaned on the voyage to Italy they fell on the trails and were
    broken
when he lay with the odes behind him the wood was sold for cannons
when he lay watching the window they came home and lay down
and an age arrived when everything was explained in another language

LOSING A LANGUAGE

A breath leaves the sentences and does not come back
yet the old still remember something that they could say

but they know now that such things are no longer believed
and the young have fewer words

many of the things the words were about
no longer exist

the noun for standing in mist by a haunted tree
the verb for I

the children will not repeat
the phrases their parents speak

somebody has persuaded them
that it is better to say everything differently

so that they can be admired somewhere
farther and farther away

where nothing that is here is known
we have little to say to each other

we are wrong and dark
in the eyes of the new owners

the radio is incomprehensible
the day is glass

when there is a voice at the door it is foreign
everywhere instead of a name there is a lie

nobody has seen it happening
nobody remembers

this is what the words were made
to prophesy

here are the extinct feathers
here is the rain we saw

WITNESS

I want to tell what the forests
were like

I will have to speak
in a forgotten language

Frank O'Hara

AUTOBIOGRAPHIA LITERARIA

When I was a child
I played by myself in a
corner of the schoolyard
all alone.

I hated dolls and I
hated games, animals were
not friendly and birds
flew away.

If anyone was looking
for me I hid behind a
tree and cried out "I am
an orphan."

And here I am, the
center of all beauty!
writing these poems!
Imagine!

POEM

The eager note on my door said "Call me,
call when you get in!" so I quickly threw
a few tangerines into my overnight bag,
straightened my eyelids and shoulders, and

headed straight for the door. It was autumn
by the time I got around the corner, oh all
unwilling to be either pertinent or bemused, but
the leaves were brighter than grass on the sidewalk!

Funny, I thought, that the lights are on this late
and the hall door open; still up at this hour, a
champion jai-alai player like himself? Oh fie!
for shame! What a host, so zealous! And he was

there in the hall, flat on a sheet of blood that
ran down the stairs. I did appreciate it. There are few
hosts who so thoroughly prepare to greet a guest
only casually invited, and that several months ago.

POEM

All the mirrors in the world
don't help, nor am I moved

by the calm emergence of my
image in the rain, it is not

I who appears or imagines. See,
if you can, if you can make

the unpleasant trip, the
house where shadows of my own

childhood are watered and forced
like overgrown bludgeons, you

must look, for I cannot. I
cannot face that fearful usage,

and my eyes in, say, the glass
of a public bar, become a

depraved hunt for other reflections. And what a blessed

relief! when it is some
disgusting sight, anything

but the old shadowy bruising,
anything but my private haunts.

When I am fifty shall my
face drift into those elongations

of innocence and confront me?
Oh rain, melt me! mirror, kill!

TO MY DEAD FATHER

Don't call to me father
wherever you are I'm
still your little son
running through the dark

I couldn't do what you
say even if I could hear
your roses no longer grow
my heart's black as their

bed their dainty thorns
have become my face's
troublesome stubble you
must not think of flowers

And do not frighten my
blue eyes with hazel flecks
or thicken my lips when
I face my mirror don't ask

that I be other than your
strange son understanding
minor miracles not death
father I am alive! father

forgive the roses and me

MEDITATIONS IN AN EMERGENCY

Am I to become profligate as if I were a blonde? Or religious as if I
were French?

Each time my heart is broken it makes me feel more adventurous (and
how the same names keep recurring on that interminable list!), but one
of these days there'll be nothing left with which to venture forth.

Why should I share you? Why don't you get rid of someone else for
a change?

I am the least difficult of men. All I want is boundless love.

Even trees understand me! Good heavens, I lie under them, too, don't I? I'm just like a pile of leaves.

However, I have never clogged myself with the praises of pastoral life, nor with nostalgia for an innocent past of perverted acts in pastures. No. One need never leave the confines of New York to get all the greenery one wishes — I can't even enjoy a blade of grass unless I know there's a subway handy, or a record store or some other sign that people do not totally *regret* life. It is more important to affirm the least sincere; the clouds get enough attention as it is and even they continue to pass. Do they know what they're missing? Uh huh.

My eyes are vague blue, like the sky, and change all the time; they are indiscriminate but fleeting, entirely specific and disloyal, so that no one trusts me. I am always looking away. Or again at something after it has given me up. It makes me restless and that makes me unhappy, but I cannot keep them still. If only I had grey, green, black, brown, yellow eyes; I would stay at home and do something. It's not that I'm curious. On the contrary, I am bored but it's my duty to be attentive, I am needed by things as the sky must be above the earth. And lately, so great has *their* anxiety become, I can spare myself little sleep.

Now there is only one man I love to kiss when he is unshaven. Heterosexuality! you are inexorably approaching. (How discourage her?)

St. Serapion, I wrap myself in the robes of your whiteness which is like midnight in Dostoevsky. How am I to become a legend, my dear? I've tried love, but that hides you in the bosom of another and I am always springing forth from it like the lotus — the ecstasy of always bursting forth! (but one must not be distracted by it!) or like a hyacinth, "to keep the filth of life away," yes, there, even in the heart, where the filth is pumped in and slanders and pollutes and determines. I will my will, though I may become famous for a mysterious vacancy in that department, that greenhouse.

Destroy yourself, if you don't know!

It is easy to be beautiful; it is difficult to appear so. I admire you, beloved, for the trap you've set. It's like a final chapter no one reads because the plot is over.

"Fanny Brown is run away — scampered off with a Cornet of Horse; I do love that little Minx, & hope She may be happy, tho' She has vexed me by this Exploit a little too. — Poor silly Cecchina! or F:B: as we used to call her. — I wish She had a good Whipping and 10,000 pounds." — Mrs. Thrale.

I've got to get out of here. I choose a piece of shawl and my dirtiest suntans. I'll be back, I'll re-emerge, defeated, from the valley; you don't want me to go where you go, so I go where you don't want me to. It's only afternoon, there's a lot ahead. There won't be any mail downstairs. Turning, I spit in the lock and the knob turns.

TO JOHN ASHBERY

I can't believe there's not
another world where we will sit
and read new poems to each other
high on a mountain in the wind.
You can be Tu Fu, I'll be Po Chü-i
and the Monkey Lady'll be in the moon,
smiling at our ill-fitting heads
as we watch snow settle on a twig.
Or shall we be really gone? this
is not the grass I saw in my youth!
and if the moon, when it rises
tonight, is empty — a bad sign,
meaning "You go, like the blossoms."

WHY I AM NOT A PAINTER

I am not a painter, I am a poet.
Why? I think I would rather be
a painter, but I am not. Well,

for instance, Mike Goldberg
is starting a painting. I drop in.
"Sit down and have a drink" he
says. I drink; we drink. I look
up. "You have SARDINES in it."
"Yes, it needed something there."

"Oh." I go and the days go by
and I drop in again. The painting
is going on, and I go, and the days
go by. I drop in. The painting is
finished. "Where's SARDINES?"
All that's left is just
letters, "It was too much," Mike says.

But me? One day I am thinking of
a color: orange. I write a line
about orange. Pretty soon it is a
whole page of words, not lines.
Then another page. There should be
so much more, not of orange, of
words, of how terrible orange is
and life. Days go by. It is even in
prose, I am a real poet. My poem
is finished and I haven't mentioned
orange yet. It's twelve poems, I call
it ORANGES. And one day in a gallery
I see Mike's painting, called SARDINES.

THE DAY LADY DIED

It is 12:20 in New York a Friday
three days after Bastille day, yes
it is 1959 and I go get a shoeshine
because I will get off the 4:19 in Easthampton
at 7:15 and then go straight to dinner
and I don't know the people who will feed me

I walk up the muggy street beginning to sun
and have a hamburger and a malted and buy
an ugly NEW WORLD WRITING to see what the poets
in Ghana are doing these days
                            I go on to the bank
and Miss Stillwagon (first name Linda I once heard)
doesn't even look up my balance for once in her life
and in the GOLDEN GRIFFIN I get a little Verlaine
for Patsy with drawings by Bonnard although I do
think of Hesiod, trans. Richmond Lattimore or

Brendan Behan's new play or *Le Balcon* or *Les Nègres*
of Genet, but I don't, I stick with Verlaine
after practically going to sleep with quandariness

and for Mike I just stroll into the PARK LANE
Liquor Store and ask for a bottle of Strega and
then I go back where I came from to 6th Avenue
and the tobacconist in the Ziegfeld Theatre and
casually ask for a carton of Gauloises and a carton
of Picayunes, and a NEW YORK POST with her face on it

and I am sweating a lot by now and thinking of
leaning on the john door in the 5 SPOT
while she whispered a song along the keyboard
to Mal Waldron and everyone and I stopped breathing

STEPS

How funny you are today New York
like Ginger Rogers in *Swingtime*
and St. Bridget's steeple leaning a little to the left

here I have just jumped out of a bed full of V-days
(I got tired of D-days) and blue you there still
accepts me foolish and free
all I want is a room up there
and you in it
and even the traffic halt so thick is a way
for people to rub up against each other
and when their surgical appliances lock
they stay together
for the rest of the day (what a day)
I go by to check a slide and I say
that painting's not so blue

where's Lana Turner
she's out eating
and Garbo's backstage at the Met
everyone's taking their coat off
so they can show a rib-cage to the rib-watchers
and the park's full of dancers with their tights and shoes
in little bags

who are often mistaken for worker-outers at the West Side Y
why not
the Pittsburgh Pirates shout because they won
and in a sense we're all winning
we're alive

the apartment was vacated by a gay couple
who moved to the country for fun
they moved a day too soon
even the stabbings are helping the population explosion
though in the wrong country
and all those liars have left the UN
the Seagram Building's no longer rivalled in interest
not that we need liquor (we just like it)

and the little box is out on the sidewalk
next to the delicatessen
so the old man can sit on it and drink beer
and get knocked off it by his wife later in the day
while the sun is still shining

oh god it's wonderful
to get out of bed
and drink too much coffee
and smoke too many cigarettes
and love you so much

YESTERDAY DOWN AT THE CANAL

You say that everything is very simple and interesting
it makes me feel very wistful, like reading a great Russian novel does
I am terribly bored
sometimes it is like seeing a bad movie
other days, more often, it's like having an acute disease of the kidney
god knows it has nothing to do with the heart
nothing to do with people more interesting than myself
yak yak
that's an amusing thought
how can anyone be more amusing than oneself
how can anyone fail to be
can I borrow your forty-five

FRANK O'HARA

I only need one bullet preferably silver
if you can't be interesting at least you can be a legend
(but I hate all that crap)

POEM

Lana Turner has collapsed!
I was trotting along and suddenly
it started raining and snowing
and you said it was hailing
but hailing hits you on the head
hard so it was really snowing and
raining and I was in such a hurry
to meet you but the traffic
was acting exactly like the sky
and suddenly I see a headline
LANA TURNER HAS COLLAPSED!
there is no snow in Hollywood
there is no rain in California
I have been to lots of parties
and acted perfectly disgraceful
but I never actually collapsed
oh Lana Turner we love you get up

Mary Oliver

THE SWIMMING LESSON

Feeling the icy kick, the endless waves
Reaching around my life, I moved my arms
And coughed, and in the end saw land.

Somebody, I suppose,
Remembering the medieval maxim,
Had tossed me in,
Had wanted me to learn to swim,

Not knowing that none of us, who ever came back
From that long lonely fall and frenzied rising,
Ever learned anything at all
About swimming, but only
How to put off, one by one,
Dreams and pity, love and grace, —
How to survive in any place.

SLEEPING IN THE FOREST

I thought the earth
remembered me, she
took me back so tenderly, arranging
her dark skirts, her pockets
full of lichens and seeds. I slept
as never before, a stone
on the riverbed, nothing
between me and the white fire of the stars
but my thoughts, and they floated
light as moths among the branches
of the perfect trees. All night
I heard the small kingdoms breathing
around me, the insects, and the birds
who do their work in the darkness. All night
I rose and fell, as if in water, grappling
with a luminous doom. By morning
I had vanished at least a dozen times
into something better.

MARY OLIVER

THE FISH

She climbs from the sea; moonlight
    blazes the black rocks,
        the surface razzle-dazzle
        of sweet water
threading out of the tide. She
    moves upstream, the flow
        pressing against her;
            she feels it, lets the hot
blade of her body pause,
    drifts backward, whips awake. She
        moves upstream; she is heavy;
            deep in her belly
life that is to be
    stirs like a million planets; she
        moves upstream; when the waters
            divide she follows
the fragrance spilling
    from her old birth pond; she
        sees the waterfalls — gleaming
            stairways of stone,
water ripped and boiling
    like white logs — and knows beyond
        lies the green pond
            rich with the shadows
of last year's swimmers where she
    will nest her eggs and the fierce prince
        quicken them; she flies
            upstream — she arcs
in the long gown of her body, she leaps
    into the walls of water,
        she falls through like the torn
            silvery half-drowned body
of any woman come to term, caught
    as mortality drives triumphantly toward
        immortality, the shaken bones like
            cages of fire.

MARY OLIVER

MUSIC LESSONS

Sometimes, in the middle of the lesson,
we exchanged places. She would gaze a moment at her hands
spread over the keys; then the small house with its knickknacks,
its shut windows,

its photographs of her sons and the serious husband,
vanished as new shapes formed. Sound
became music, and music a white
scarp for the listener to climb

alone. I leaped rock over rock to the top
and found myself waiting, transformed,
and still she played, her eyes luminous and willful,
her pinned hair falling down —

forgetting me, the house, the neat green yard,
she fled in that lick of flame all tedious bonds:
supper, the duties of flesh and home,
the knife at the throat, the death in the metronome.

THE BLACK WALNUT TREE

My mother and I debate:
we could sell
the black walnut tree
to the lumberman,
and pay off the mortgage.
Likely some storm anyway
will churn down its dark boughs,
smashing the house. We talk
slowly, two women trying
in a difficult time to be wise.
Roots in the cellar drains,
I say, and she replies
that the leaves are getting heavier
every year, and the fruit
harder to gather away.

But something brighter than money
moves in our blood — an edge
sharp and quick as a trowel
that wants us to dig and sow.
So we talk, but we don't do
anything. That night I dream
of my fathers out of Bohemia
filling the blue fields
of fresh and generous Ohio
with leaves and vines and orchards.
What my mother and I both know
is that we'd crawl with shame
in the emptiness we'd made
in our own and our fathers' backyard.
So the black walnut tree
swings through another year
of sun and leaping winds,
of leaves and bounding fruit,
and, month after month, the whip-
crack of the mortgage.

THE KITTEN

More amazed than anything
I took the perfectly black
stillborn kitten
with the one large eye
in the center of its small forehead
from the house cat's bed
and buried it in a field
behind the house.

I suppose I could have given it
to a museum,
I could have called the local
newspaper.

But instead I took it out into the field
and opened the earth
and put it back
saying, it was real,

saying, life is infinitely inventive,
saying, what other amazements
lie in the dark seed of the earth, yes,

I think I did right to go out alone
and give it back peacefully, and cover the place
with the reckless blossoms of weeds.

TASTING THE WILD GRAPES

The red beast
who lives in the side of these hills
won't come out for anything you have:
money or music. Still, there are moments
heavy with light and good luck. Walk
quietly under these tangled vines
and pay attention, and one morning
something will explode underfoot
like a branch of fire; one afternoon
something will flow down the hill
in plain view, a muscled sleeve the color
of all October! And forgetting
everything you will leap to name it
as though for the first time, your lit blood
rushing not to a word but a sound
small-boned, thin-faced, in a hurry,
lively as the dark thorns of the wild grapes
on the unsuspecting tongue!
The fox! The fox!

AN OLD WHOREHOUSE

We climbed through a broken window,
walked through every room.

Out of business for years,
the mattresses held only

rainwater, and one
woman's black shoe. Downstairs

spiders had wrapped up
the crystal chandelier.

A cracked cup lay in the sink.
But we were fourteen,   → edge of sexual Knowledge

and no way dust could hide
the expected glamour from us,

or teach us anything. → teach what?
We whispered, we imagined. reverence power

It would be years before
we'd learn how effortlessly

sin blooms, then softens,
like any bed of flowers.

IN BLACKWATER WOODS

Look, the trees
are turning
their own bodies
into pillars

of light,
are giving off the rich
fragrance of cinnamon
and fulfillment,

the long tapers
of cattails
are bursting and floating away over
the blue shoulders

of the ponds,
and every pond,
no matter what its
name is, is

nameless now.
Every year
everything
I have ever learned

in my lifetime
leads back to this: the fires
and the black river of loss
whose other side

is salvation,
whose meaning
none of us will ever know.
To live in this world

you must be able
to do three things:
to love what is mortal;
to hold it

against your bones knowing
your own life depends on it;
and, when the time comes to let it go,
to let it go.

A VISITOR

My father, for example,
who was young once
and blue-eyed,
returns
on the darkest of nights
to the porch and knocks
wildly at the door,
and if I answer
I must be prepared
for his waxy face,
for his lower lip
swollen with bitterness.
And so, for a long time,
I did not answer,
but slept fitfully

between his hours of rapping.
But finally there came the night
when I rose out of my sheets
and stumbled down the hall.
The door fell open

and I knew I was saved
and could bear him,
pathetic and hollow,
with even the least of his dreams
frozen inside him,
and the meanness gone.
And I greeted him and asked him
into the house,

and lit the lamp,
and looked into his blank eyes
in which at last
I saw what a child must love,
I saw what love might have done
had we loved in time.

SINGAPORE

In Singapore, in the airport,
a darkness was ripped from my eyes.
In the women's restroom, one compartment stood open.
A woman knelt there, washing something in the white bowl.

Disgust argued in my stomach
and I felt, in my pocket, for my ticket.

A poem should always have birds in it.
Kingfishers, say, with their bold eyes and gaudy wings.
Rivers are pleasant, and of course trees.
A waterfall, or if that's not possible, a fountain rising and falling.
A person wants to stand in a happy place, in a poem.

When the woman turned I could not answer her face.
Her beauty and her embarrassment struggled together, and neither
    could win.

She smiled and I smiled. What kind of nonsense is this?
Everybody needs a job.

Yes, a person wants to stand in a happy place, in a poem.
But first we must watch her as she stares down at her labor, which is
    dull enough.
She is washing the tops of the airport ashtrays, as big as hubcaps, with
    a blue rag.
Her small hands turn the metal, scrubbing and rinsing.
She does not work slowly, nor quickly, but like a river.
Her dark hair is like the wing of a bird.

I don't doubt for a moment that she loves her life.
And I want her to rise up from the crust and the slop and fly down to
    the river.
This probably won't happen.
But maybe it will.
If the world were only pain and logic, who would want it?

Of course, it isn't.
Neither do I mean anything miraculous, but only
the light that can shine out of a life. I mean
the way she unfolded and refolded the blue cloth,
the way her smile was only for my sake; I mean
the way this poem is filled with trees, and birds.

Charles Olson

MAXIMUS, TO HIMSELF

I have had to learn the simplest things
last. Which made for difficulties.
Even at sea I was slow, to get the hand out, or to cross
a wet deck.
       The sea was not, finally, my trade.
But even my trade, at it, I stood estranged
from that which was most familiar. Was delayed,
and not content with the man's argument
that such postponement
is now the nature of
obedience,

       that we are all late
       in a slow time,
       that we grow up many
       And the single
       is not easily
       known

It could be, though the sharpness (the *achiote*)
I note in others,
makes more sense
than my own distances. The agilities

       they show daily
       who do the world's
       businesses
       And who do nature's
       as I have no sense
       I have done either

I have made dialogues,
have discussed ancient texts,
have thrown what light I could, offered
what pleasures
doceat allows

       But the known?
This, I have had to be given,
a life, love, and from one man
the world.

Tokens.
But sitting here
I look out as a wind
and water man, testing
And missing
some proof

I know the quarters
of the weather, where it comes from,
where it goes. But the stem of me,
this I took from their welcome,
or their rejection, of me

And my arrogance
was neither diminished
nor increased,
by the communication

2

It is undone business
I speak of, this morning,
with the sea
stretching out
from my feet

I, MAXIMUS OF GLOUCESTER, TO YOU

Off-shore, by islands hidden in the blood
jewels & miracles, I, Maximus
a metal hot from boiling water, tell you
what is a lance, who obeys the figures of
the present dance

1

the thing you're after
may lie around the bend
of the nest (second, time slain, the bird! the bird!

And there! (strong) thrust, the mast! flight

> (of the bird
> o kylix, o
> Antony of Padua
> sweep low, o bless

the roofs, the old ones, the gentle steep ones
on whose ridge-poles the gulls sit, from which they depart,

> And the flake-racks

of my city!

2

love is form, and cannot be without
important substance (the weight
say, 58 carats each one of us, perforce
our goldsmith's scale

> feather to feather added
> (and what is mineral, what
> is curling hair, the string
> you carry in your nervous beak, these

> make bulk, these, in the end, are
> the sum

> (o my lady of good voyage
> in whose arm, whose left arm rests

no boy but a carefully carved wood, a painted face, a schooner!
a delicate mast, as bow-sprit for

> forwarding

3

the underpart is, though stemmed, uncertain
is, as sex is, as moneys are, facts!
facts, to be dealt with, as the sea is, the demand
that they be played by, that they only can be, that they must
be played by, said he, coldly, the
ear!

By ear, he sd.
But that which matters, that which insists, that which will last,
that! o my people, where shall you find it, how, where, where shall you
     listen
when all is become billboards, when, all, even silence, is spray-gunned?

when even our bird, my roofs,
cannot be heard

when even you, when sound itself is neoned in?

when, on the hill, over the water
where she who used to sing,
when the water glowed,
black, gold, the tide
outward, at evening

when bells came like boats
over the oil-slicks, milkweed
hulls

And a man slumped,
attentionless,
against pink shingles

o sea city)

                              4

one loves only form,
and form only comes
into existence when
the thing is born

                    born of yourself, born
                    of hay and cotton struts,
                    of street-pickings, wharves, weeds
                    you carry in, my bird

                              of a bone of a fish
                              of a straw, or will
                              of a color, of a bell
                              of yourself, torn

5

love is not easy
but how shall you know,
New England, now
that pejorocracy is here, how
that street-cars, o Oregon, twitter
in the afternoon, offend
a black-gold loin?

how shall you strike,
o swordsman, the blue-red back
when, last night, your aim
was mu-sick, mu-sick, mu-sick
And not the cribbage game?

(o Gloucester-man,
weave
your birds and fingers
new, your roof-tops,
clean shit upon racks
sunned on
American
braid
with others like you, such
extricable surface
as faun and oral,
satyr lesbos vase

o kill kill kill kill kill
those
who advertise you
out)

6

in! in! the bow-sprit, bird, the beak
in, the bend is, in, goes in, the form
that which you make, what holds, which is
the law of object, strut after strut, what you are, what you must be, what
the force can throw up, can, right now hereinafter erect,
the mast, the mast, the tender
mast!

The nest, I say, to you, I Maximus, say
under the hand, as I see it, over the waters
from this place where I am, where I hear,
can still hear

from where I carry you a feather
as though, sharp, I picked up,
in the afternoon delivered you
a jewel,
           it flashing more than a wing,
than any old romantic thing,
than memory, than place,
than anything other than that which you carry

than that which is,
call it a nest, around the head of, call it
the next second

than that which you
can do!

THE LIBRARIAN

The landscape (the landscape!) again: Gloucester,
the shore one of me is (duplicates), and from which
(from offshore, I, Maximus) am removed, observe.

In this night I moved on the territory with combinations
(new mixtures) of old and known personages: the leader,
my father, in an old guise, here selling books and manuscripts.
My thought was, as I looked in the window of his shop,
there should be materials here for Maximus, when, then,
I saw he was the young musician has been there (been before me)

before. It turned out it wasn't a shop, it was a loft (wharf-
house) in which, as he walked me around, a year ago
came back (I had been there before, with my wife and son,

I didn't remember, he presented me insinuations via
himself and his girl) both of whom I had known for years.
But never in Gloucester. I had moved them in, to my country.

His previous appearance had been in my parents' bedroom where I
found him intimate with my former wife: this boy
was now the Librarian of Gloucester, Massachusetts!

> Black space,
> old fish-house.
> Motions
> of ghosts.
> I,
> dogging
> his steps.

> He
> (not my father,
> by name himself
> with his face
> twisted
> at birth)
> possessed of knowledge
> pretentious
> giving me
> what in the instant
> I knew better of.

> But the somber
> place, the flooring
> crude like a wharf's
> and a barn's
> space

I was struck by the fact I was in Gloucester, and that my daughter
was there — that I would see her! She was over the Cut. I
hadn't even connected her with my being there, that she was

here. That she was there (in the Promised Land — the Cut!
But there was this business, of poets, that all my Jews
were in the fish-house too, that the Librarian had made a party

I was to read. They were. There were many of them, slumped
around. It was not for me. I was outside. It was the Fort.
The Fort was in East Gloucester — old Gorton's Wharf, where the
    Library

was. It was a region of coal houses, bins. In one a gang
was beating someone to death, in a corner of the labyrinth
of fences. I could see their arms and shoulders whacking

down. But not the victim. I got out of there. But cops
tailed me along the Fort beach toward the Tavern

The places still
half-dark, mud,
coal-dust.

There is no light
east
of the Bridge

Only on the headland
toward the harbor
from Cressy's

have I seen it (once
when my daughter ran
out on a spit of sand

isn't even there.) Where
is Bristow? when does I-A
get me home? I am caught

in Gloucester. (What's buried
behind Lufkin's
Diner? Who is

Frank Moore?

MAXIMUS TO GLOUCESTER, LETTER 27 [WITHHELD]

I come back to the geography of it,
the land falling off to the left
where my father shot his scabby golf
and the rest of us played baseball
into the summer darkness until no flies
could be seen and we came home

to our various piazzas where the women
buzzed

To the left the land fell to the city,
to the right, it fell to the sea

I was so young my first memory
is of a tent spread to feed lobsters
to Rexall conventioneers, and my father,
a man for kicks, came out of the tent roaring
with a bread-knife in his teeth to take care of
a druggist they'd told him had made a pass at
my mother, she laughing, so sure, as round
as her face, Hines pink and apple,
under one of those frame hats women then

This, is no bare incoming
of novel abstract form, this

is no welter or the forms
of those events, this,

Greeks, is the stopping
of the battle

        It is the imposing
of all those antecedent predecessions, the precessions

of me, the generation of those facts
which are my words, it is coming

from all that I no longer am, yet am,
the slow westward motion of

more than I am

There is no strict personal order

for my inheritance.

        No Greek will be able

to discriminate my body.

CHARLES OLSON

An American

is a complex of occasions,

themselves a geometry

of spatial nature.

I have this sense,

that I am one

with my skin

Plus this — plus this:

that forever the geography

which leans in

on me I compell

backwards I compell Gloucester

to yield, to

change

Polis

is this

A LATER NOTE ON LETTER #15

In English the poetics became meubles — furniture —
thereafter (after 1630

& Descartes was the value

until Whitehead, who cleared out the gunk
by getting the universe in (as against man alone

& that concept of history (not Herodotus's,
which was a verb, to find out for yourself:
'istorin, which makes any one's acts a finding out for him or her
self, in other words restores the traum: that we act somewhere

at least by seizure, that the objective (example Thucidides, or
the latest finest tape-recorder, or any form of record on the spot

— live television or what — is a lie

as against what we know went on, the dream: the dream being
self-action with Whitehead's important corollary: that no event

is not penetrated, in intersection or collision with, an eternal
event

The poetics of such a situation
are yet to be found out

January 15, 1962

MOONSET, GLOUCESTER, DECEMBER 1, 1957, 1:58 AM

Goodbye red moon
In that color you set
west of the Cut I should imagine
forever Mother

After 47 years this month
a Monday at 9 AM
you set I rise I hope
a free thing as probably
what you more were Not
the suffering one you sold
sowed me on Rise
Mother from off me
God damn you God damn me my
misunderstanding of you

I can die now I just begun to live

Marge Piercy

A WORK OF ARTIFICE

The bonsai tree
in the attractive pot
could have grown eighty feet tall
on the side of a mountain
till split by lightning.
But a gardener
carefully pruned it.
It is nine inches high.
Every day as he
whittles back the branches
the gardener croons,
It is your nature
to be small and cozy,
domestic and weak;
how lucky, little tree,
to have a pot to grow in.
With living creatures
one must begin very early
to dwarf their growth:
the bound feet,
the crippled brain,
the hair in curlers,
the hands you
love to touch.

THE SKYSCRAPERS OF THE FINANCIAL DISTRICT
DANCE WITH GASMAN

The skyscrapers are dancing by the river,
they are leaping over their reflections
their lightning bright zigzag and beady reflections
jagged and shattered on East River.
With voices shrill as children's whistles they hop
while the safes pop open like corn
and the files come whizzing through the air
to snow on the streets that lie throbbing,
eels copulating in heaps.

Ticker tape hangs in garlands from the wagging streetlamps.
Standard Oil and General Foods have amalgamated
and Dupont, Schenley and AT&T lie down together.
It does not matter, don't hope, it does not matter.
In the morning the buildings stand smooth and shaven and straight
and all goes on whirring and ticking.
Money is reticulated and stronger than steel or stone or vision,
though sometimes at night
the skyscrapers bow and lean and leap under no moon.

THE FRIEND

We sat across the table.
he said, cut off your hands.
they are always poking at things.
they might touch me.
I said yes.

Food grew cold on the table.
he said, burn your body.
it is not clean and smells like sex.
it rubs my mind sore.
I said yes.

I love you, I said.
That's very nice, he said
I like to be loved,
that makes me happy.
Have you cut off your hands yet?

BARBIE DOLL

This girlchild was born as usual
and presented dolls that did pee-pee
and miniature GE stoves and irons
and wee lipsticks the color of cherry candy.
Then in the magic of puberty, a classmate said:
You have a great big nose and fat legs.

She was healthy, tested intelligent,
possessed strong arms and back,
abundant sexual drive and manual dexterity.
She went to and fro apologizing.
Everyone saw a fat nose on thick legs.

She was advised to play coy,
exhorted to come on hearty,
exercise, diet, smile and wheedle.
Her good nature wore out
like a fan belt.
So she cut off her nose and her legs
and offered them up.

In the casket displayed on satin she lay
with the undertaker's cosmetics painted on,
a turned-up putty nose,
dressed in a pink and white nightie.
Doesn't she look pretty? everyone said.
Consummation at last.
To every woman a happy ending.

TO BE OF USE

The people I love the best
jump into work head first
without dallying in the shallows
and swim off with sure strokes almost out of sight.
They seem to become natives of that element,
the black sleek heads of seals
bouncing like half-submerged balls.

I love people who harness themselves, an ox to a heavy cart,
who pull like water buffalo, with massive patience,
who strain in the mud and the muck to move things forward,
who do what has to be done, again and again.

I want to be with people who submerge
in the task, who go into the fields to harvest
and work in a row and pass the bags along,
who are not parlor generals and field deserters

but move in a common rhythm
when the food must come in or the fire be put out.

The work of the world is common as mud.
Botched, it smears the hands, crumbles to dust.
But the thing worth doing well done
has a shape that satisfies, clean and evident.
Greek amphoras for wine or oil,
Hopi vases that held corn, are put in museums
but you know they were made to be used.
The pitcher cries for water to carry
and a person for work that is real.

YOU ASK WHY SOMETIMES I SAY STOP

You ask why sometimes I say stop
why sometimes I cry no
while I shake with pleasure.
What do I fear, you ask,
why don't I always want to come
and come again to that molten
deep sea center where the nerves
fuse open and the brain
and body shine with a black wordless light
fluorescent and heaving like plankton.

If you turn over the old refuse
of sexual slang, the worn buttons
of language, you find men
talk of spending and women
of dying.

You come in a torrent and ease
into limpness. Pleasure takes me
farther and farther from shore
in a series of breakers, each
towering higher before it
crashes and spills flat.

I am open then as a palm held out,
open as a sunflower, without

crust, without shelter, without
skin, hideless and unhidden.
How can I let you ride
so far into me and not fear?

Helpless as a burning city,
how can I ignore that the extremes
of pleasure are fire storms
that leave a vacuum into which
dangerous feelings (tenderness,
affection, l o v e) may rush
like gale force winds.

DIGGING IN

This fall you will taste carrots
you planted, you thinned, you mulched,
you weeded and watered. You don't
know yet they will taste like yours,
not others, not mine.
This earth is yours as you love it.

We drink the water of this hill
and give our garbage to its soil.
We haul thatch for it and seaweed.
Out of it rise supper and roses
for the bedroom and herbs
for your next cold.

Your flesh grows out of this hill
like the maple trees. Its sweetness
is baked by this sun. Your eyes
have taken in sea and the light leaves
of the locust and the dark bristles
of the pine.

When we work in the garden you say
that now it feels sexual, the plants
pushing through us, the shivering
of the leaves. As we make love
later the oaks bend over us,
the hill listens.

The cats come and sit on the foot
of the bed to watch us.
Afterwards they purr.
The tomatoes grow faster and the beans.
You are learning to live in circles
as well as straight lines.

TOUCH TONES

We learn each other in braille,
what the tongue and teeth taste,
what the fingers trace, translate
into arias of knowledge and delight
of silk and stubble, of bark
and velvet and wet roses,
warbling colors that splash through
bronze, violet, dragonfly jade,
the red of raspberries, lacquer, odor
of resin, the voice that later
comes unbidden as a Mozart horn
concerto circling in the ears.

You are translated from label,
politic mask, accomplished patter,
to the hands round hefting,
to a weight, a thrust, a scent
sharp as walking in early
morning a path through a meadow
where a fox has been last night
and something in the genes saying
FOX to that rich ruddy smell.
The texture of lambswool, of broadcloth
can speak a name in runes. Absent,
your presence carols in the blood.

MY MOTHER'S BODY

1

The dark socket of the year
the pit, the cave where the sun lies down
and threatens never to rise,
when despair descends softly as the snow
covering all paths and choking roads:

then hawk-faced pain seized you
threw you so you fell with a sharp
cry, a knife tearing a bolt of silk.
My father heard the crash but paid
no mind, napping after lunch,

yet fifteen hundred miles north
I heard and dropped a dish.
Your pain sunk talons in my skull
and crouched there cawing, heavy
as a great vessel filled with water,

oil or blood, till suddenly next day
the weight lifted and I knew your mind
had guttered out like the Chanukah
candles that burn so fast, weeping
veils of wax down the chanukiyot.

Those candles were laid out,
friends invited, ingredients bought
for latkes and apple pancakes,
that holiday for liberation
and the winter solstice

when tops turn like little planets.
Shall you have all or nothing
take half or pass by untouched?
Nothing you got, Nun said the dreidl
as the room stopped spinning.

The angel folded you up like laundry
your body thin as an empty dress.
Your clothes were curtains

hanging on the window of what had
been your flesh and now was glass.

Outside in Florida shopping plazas
loudspeakers blared Christmas carols
and palm trees were decked with blinking
lights. Except by the tourist
hotels, the beaches were empty.

Pelicans with pregnant pouches
flapped overhead like pterodactyls.
In my mind I felt you die.
First the pain lifted and then
you flickered and went out.

2

I walk through the rooms of memory.
Sometimes everything is shrouded in dropcloths,
every chair ghostly and muted.

Other times memory lights up from within
bustling scenes acted just the other side
of a scrim through which surely I could reach

my fingers tearing at the flimsy curtain
of time which is and isn't and will be
the stuff of which we're made and unmade.

In sleep the other night I met you, seventeen,
your first nasty marriage just annulled,
thin from your abortion, clutching a book

against your cheek and trying to look
older, trying to look middle class,
trying for a job at Wanamaker's,

dressing for parties in cast-off
stage costumes of your sisters'. Your eyes
were hazy with dreams. You did not

notice me waving as you wandered
past and I saw your slip was showing.
You stood still while I fixed your clothes,

as if I were your mother. Remember me
combing your springy black hair, ringlets
that seemed metallic, glittering;

remember me dressing you, my seventy-year-
old mother who was my last doll baby,
giving you too late what your youth had wanted.

3

What is this mask of skin we wear,
what is this dress of flesh,
this coat of few colors and little hair?

This voluptuous seething heap of desires
and fears, squeaking mice turned up
in a steaming haystack with their babies?

This coat has been handed down, an heirloom,
this coat of black hair and ample flesh,
this coat of pale slightly ruddy skin.

This set of hips and thighs, these buttocks,
they provided cushioning for my grandmother
Hannah, for my mother Bert and for me

and we all sat on them in turn, those major
muscles on which we walk and walk and walk
over the earth in search of peace and plenty.

My mother is my mirror and I am hers.
What do we see? Our face grown young again,
our breasts grown firm, legs lean and elegant.

Our arms quivering with fat, eyes
set in the bark of wrinkles, hands puffy,
our belly seamed with childbearing.

Give me your dress so I can try it on.
Oh it will not fit you, Mother, you are too fat.
I will not fit you, Mother.

I will not be the bride you can dress,
the obedient dutiful daughter you would chew,
a dog's leather bone to sharpen your teeth.

You strike me sometimes just to hear the sound.
Loneliness turns your fingers into hooks
barbed and drawing blood with their caress.

My twin, my sister, my lost love,
I carry you in me like an embryo
as once you carried me.

4

What is it we turn from, what is it we fear?
Did I truly think you could put me back inside?
Did I think I would fall into you as into a molten
furnace and be recast, that I would become you?

What did you fear in me, the child who wore
your hair, the woman who let that black hair
grow long as a banner of darkness, when you
a proper flapper wore yours cropped?

You pushed and you pulled on my rubbery
flesh, you kneaded me like a ball of dough.
Rise, rise, and then you pounded me flat.
Secretly the bones formed in the bread.

I became willful, private as a cat.
You never knew what alleys I had wandered.
You called me bad and I posed like a gutter
queen in a dress sewn of knives.

All I feared was being stuck in a box
with a lid. A good woman appeared to me
indistinguishable from a dead one
except that she worked all the time.

Your payday never came. Your dreams ran
with bright colors like Mexican cottons
that bled onto the drab sheets of the day
and would not bleach with scrubbing.

MARGE PIERCY

My dear, what you said was one thing
but what you sang was another, sweetly
subversive and dark as blackberries,
and I became the daughter of your dream.

This body is your body, ashes now
and roses, but alive in my eyes, my breasts,
my throat, my thighs. You run in me
a tang of salt in the creek waters of my blood,

you sing in my mind like wine. What you
did not dare in your life you dare in mine.

© Rollie McKenna

Sylvia Plath

THE COLOSSUS

I shall never get you put together entirely,
Pieced, glued, and properly jointed.
Mule-bray, pig-grunt and bawdy cackles
Proceed from your great lips.
It's worse than a barnyard.

Perhaps you consider yourself an oracle,
Mouthpiece of the dead, or of some god or other.
Thirty years now I have labored
To dredge the silt from your throat.
I am none the wiser.

Scaling little ladders with gluepots and pails of lysol
I crawl like an ant in mourning
Over the weedy acres of your brow
To mend the immense skull plates and clear
The bald, white tumuli of your eyes.

A blue sky out of the Oresteia
Arches above us. O father, all by yourself
You are pithy and historical as the Roman Forum.
I open my lunch on a hill of black cypress.
Your fluted bones and acanthine hair are littered

In their old anarchy to the horizon-line.
It would take more than a lightning-stroke
To create such a ruin.
Nights, I squat in the cornucopia
Of your left ear, out of the wind,

Counting the red stars and those of plum-color.
The sun rises under the pillar of your tongue.
My hours are married to shadow.
No longer do I listen for the scrape of a keel
On the blank stones of the landing.

DADDY

You do not do, you do not do
Any more, black shoe
In which I have lived like a foot
For thirty years, poor and white,
Barely daring to breathe or Achoo.

Daddy, I have had to kill you.
You died before I had time ——
Marble-heavy, a bag full of God,
Ghastly statue with one grey toe
Big as a Frisco seal

And a head in the freakish Atlantic
Where it pours bean green over blue
In the waters off beautiful Nauset.
I used to pray to recover you.
Ach, du.

In the German tongue, in the Polish town
Scraped flat by the roller
Of wars, wars, wars.
But the name of the town is common.
My Polack friend

Says there are a dozen or two.
So I never could tell where you
Put your foot, your root,
I never could talk to you.
The tongue stuck in my jaw.

It stuck in a barb wire snare.
Ich, ich, ich, ich,
I could hardly speak.
I thought every German was you.
And the language obscene

An engine, an engine
Chuffing me off like a Jew.
A Jew to Dachau, Auschwitz, Belsen.
I began to talk like a Jew.
I think I may well be a Jew.

The snows of the Tyrol, the clear beer of Vienna
Are not very pure or true.
With my gypsy ancestress and my weird luck
And my Taroc pack and my Taroc pack
I may be a bit of a Jew.

I have always been scared of *you*,
With your Luftwaffe, your gobbledygoo.
And your neat moustache
And your Aryan eye, bright blue.
Panzer-man, panzer-man, O You ——

Not God but a swastika
So black no sky could squeak through.
Every woman adores a Fascist,
The boot in the face, the brute
Brute heart of a brute like you.

You stand at the blackboard, daddy,
In the picture I have of you,
A cleft in your chin instead of your foot
But no less a devil for that, no not
Any less the black man who

Bit my pretty red heart in two.
I was ten when they buried you.
At twenty I tried to die
And get back, back, back to you.
I thought even the bones would do.

But they pulled me out of the sack,
And they stuck me together with glue.
And then I knew what to do.
I made a model of you,
A man in black with a Meinkampf look

And a love of the rack and the screw.
And I said I do, I do.
So daddy, I'm finally through.
The black telephone's off at the root,
The voices just can't worm through.

If I've killed one man, I've killed two ——
The vampire who said he was you

And drank my blood for a year,
Seven years, if you want to know.
Daddy, you can lie back now.

There's a stake in your fat black heart
And the villagers never liked you.
They are dancing and stamping on you.
They always *knew* it was you.
Daddy, daddy, you bastard, I'm through.

MARY'S SONG

The Sunday lamb cracks in its fat.
The fat
Sacrifices its opacity. . . .

A window, holy gold.
The fire makes it precious,
The same fire

Melting the tallow heretics,
Ousting the Jews.
Their thick palls float

Over the cicatrix of Poland, burnt-out
Germany.
They do not die.

Grey birds obsess my heart,
Mouth-ash, ash of eye.
They settle. On the high

Precipice
That emptied one man into space
The ovens glowed like heavens, incandescent.

It is a heart,
This holocaust I walk in,
O golden child the world will kill and eat.

NICK AND THE CANDLESTICK

I am a miner. The light burns blue.
Waxy stalactites
Drip and thicken, tears

The earthen womb
Exudes from its dead boredom.
Black bat airs

Wrap me, raggy shawls,
Cold homicides.
They weld to me like plums.

Old cave of calcium
Icicles, old echoer.
Even the newts are white,

Those holy Joes.
And the fish, the fish ———
Christ! They are panes of ice,

A vice of knives,
A piranha
Religion, drinking

Its first communion out of my live toes.
The candle
Gulps and recovers its small altitude,

Its yellows hearten.
O love, how did you get here?
O embryo

Remembering, even in sleep,
Your crossed position.
The blood blooms clean

In you, ruby.
The pain
You wake to is not yours.

Love, love,
I have hung our cave with roses.
With soft rugs ——

The last of Victoriana.
Let the stars
Plummet to their dark address,

Let the mercuric
Atoms that cripple drip
Into the terrible well,

You are the one
Solid the spaces lean on, envious.
You are the baby in the barn.

LADY LAZARUS

I have done it again.
One year in every ten
I manage it ——

A sort of walking miracle, my skin
Bright as a Nazi lampshade,
My right foot

A paperweight,
My face a featureless, fine
Jew linen.

Peel off the napkin
O my enemy.
Do I terrify? ——

The nose, the eye pits, the full set of teeth?
The sour breath
Will vanish in a day.

Soon, soon the flesh
The grave cave ate will be
At home on me

And I a smiling woman.
I am only thirty.
And like the cat I have nine times to die.

This is Number Three.
What a trash
To annihilate each decade.

What a million filaments.
The peanut-crunching crowd
Shoves in to see

Them unwrap me hand and foot ——
The big strip tease.
Gentleman, ladies,

These are my hands,
My knees.
I may be skin and bone,

Nevertheless, I am the same, identical woman.
The first time it happened I was ten.
It was an accident.

The second time I meant
To last it out and not come back at all.
I rocked shut

As a seashell.
They had to call and call
And pick the worms off me like sticky pearls.

Dying
Is an art, like everything else.
I do it exceptionally well.

I do it so it feels like hell.
I do it so it feels real.
I guess you could say I've a call.

It's easy enough to do it in a cell.
It's easy enough to do it and stay put.
It's the theatrical

Comeback in broad day
To the same place, the same face, the same brute
Amused shout:

"A miracle!"
That knocks me out.
There is a charge

For the eyeing of my scars, there is a charge
For the hearing of my heart ——
It really goes.

And there is a charge, a very large charge,
For a word or a touch
Or a bit of blood

Or a piece of my hair or my clothes.
So, so, Herr Doktor.
So, Herr Enemy.

I am your opus,
I am your valuable,
The pure gold baby

That melts to a shriek.
I turn and burn.
Do not think I underestimate your great concern.

Ash, ash —
You poke and stir.
Flesh, bone, there is nothing there ——

A cake of soap,
A wedding ring,
A gold filling.

Herr God, Herr Lucifer,
Beware
Beware.

Out of the ash
I rise with my red hair
And I eat men like air.

CUT

for Susan O'Neill Roe

What a thrill ——
My thumb instead of an onion.
The top quite gone
Except for a sort of a hinge

Of skin,
A flap like a hat,
Dead white.
Then that red plush.

Little pilgrim,
The Indian's axed your scalp.
Your turkey wattle
Carpet rolls

Straight from the heart.
I step on it,
Clutching my bottle
Of pink fizz.

A celebration, this is.
Out of a gap
A million soldiers run,
Redcoats, every one.

Whose side are they on?
O my
Homunculus, I am ill.
I have taken a pill to kill

The thin
Papery feeling.
Saboteur,
Kamikaze man ——

The stain on your
Gauze Ku Klux Klan
Babushka
Darkens and tarnishes and when

The balled
Pulp of your heart
Confronts its small
Mill of silence

How you jump ——
Trepanned veteran,
Dirty girl,
Thumb stump.

ARIEL

Stasis in darkness.
Then the substanceless blue
Pour of tor and distances.

God's lioness,
How one we grow,
Pivot of heels and knees! — The furrow

Splits and passes, sister to
The brown arc
Of the neck I cannot catch,

Nigger-eye
Berries cast dark
Hooks ——

Black sweet blood mouthfuls,
Shadows.
Something else

Hauls me through air ——
Thighs, hair;
Flakes from my heels.

White
Godiva, I unpeel ——
Dead hands, dead stringencies.

And now I
Foam to wheat, a glitter of seas.
The child's cry

Melts in the wall.
And I
Am the arrow,

The dew that flies
Suicidal, at one with the drive
Into the red

Eye, the cauldron of morning.

WINTER TREES

The wet dawn inks are doing their blue dissolve.
On their blotter of fog the trees
Seem a botanical drawing.
Memories growing, ring on ring,
A series of weddings.

Knowing neither abortions nor bitchery,
Truer than women,
They seed so effortlessly!
Tasting the winds, that are footless,
Waist-deep in history.

Full of wings, otherworldliness.
In this, they are Ledas.
O mother of leaves and sweetness
Who are these pietas?
The shadows of ringdoves chanting, but easing nothing.

CROSSING THE WATER

Black lake, black boat, two black, cut-paper people.
Where do the black trees go that drink here?
Their shadows must cover Canada.

A little light is filtering from the water flowers.
Their leaves do not wish us to hurry:
They are round and flat and full of dark advice.

Cold worlds shake from the oar.
The spirit of blackness is in us, it is in the fishes.
A snag is lifting a valedictory, pale hand;

Stars open among the lilies.
Are you not blinded by such expressionless sirens?
This is the silence of astounded souls.

WITCH BURNING

In the marketplace they are piling the dry sticks.
A thicket of shadows is a poor coat. I inhabit
The wax image of myself, a doll's body.
Sickness begins here: I am a dartboard for witches.
Only the devil can eat the devil out.
In the month of red leaves I climb to a bed of fire.

It is easy to blame the dark: the mouth of a door,
The cellar's belly. They've blown my sparkler out.
A black-sharded lady keeps me in a parrot cage.
What large eyes the dead have!
I am intimate with a hairy spirit.
Smoke wheels from the beak of this empty jar.

If I am a little one, I can do no harm.
If I don't move about, I'll knock nothing over. So I said,
Sitting under a potlid, tiny and inert as a rice grain.
They are turning the burners up, ring after ring.
We are full of starch, my small white fellows. We grow.
It hurts at first. The red tongues will teach the truth.

Mother of beetles, only unclench your hand:
I'll fly through the candle's mouth like a singeless moth.
Give me back my shape. I am ready to construe the days
I coupled with dust in the shadow of a stone.
My ankles brighten. Brightness ascends my thighs.
I am lost, I am lost, in the robes of all this light.

BRASÍLIA

Will they occur,
These people with torsos of steel
Winged elbows and eyeholes

Awaiting masses
Of cloud to give them expression,
These super-people! —

And my baby a nail
Driven in, driven in.
He shrieks in his grease,

Bones nosing for distances.
And I, nearly extinct,
His three teeth cutting

Themselves on my thumb —
And the star,
The old story.

In the lane I meet sheep and wagons,
Red earth, motherly blood.
O You who eat

People like light rays, leave
This one
Mirror safe, unredeemed

By the dove's annihilation,
The glory
The power, the glory.

© Diana Rivera

Adrienne Rich

AUNT JENNIFER'S TIGERS

Aunt Jennifer's tigers prance across a screen,
Bright topaz denizens of a world of green.
They do not fear the men beneath the tree;
They pace in sleek chivalric certainty.

Aunt Jennifer's fingers fluttering through her wool
Find even the ivory needle hard to pull.
The massive weight of Uncle's wedding band
Sits heavily upon Aunt Jennifer's hand.

When Aunt is dead, her terrified hands will lie
Still ringed with ordeals she was mastered by.
The tigers in the panel that she made
Will go on prancing, proud and unafraid.

PLANETARIUM

Thinking of Caroline Herschel (1750–1848)
astronomer, sister of William; and others.

A woman in the shape of a monster
a monster in the shape of a woman
the skies are full of them

a woman   'in the snow
among the Clocks and instruments
or measuring the ground with poles'

in her 98 years to discover
8 comets

she whom the moon ruled
like us
levitating into the night sky
riding the polished lenses

Galaxies of women, there
doing penance for impetuousness

477

ribs chilled
in those spaces   of the mind

An eye,

   'virile, precise and absolutely certain'
   from the mad webs of Uranusborg

         encountering the NOVA

every impulse of light exploding
from the core
as life flies out of us

   Tycho whispering at last
   'Let me not seem to have lived in vain'

What we see, we see
and seeing is changing

the light that shrivels a mountain
and leaves a man alive

Heartbeat of the pulsar
heart sweating through my body

The radio impulse
pouring in from Taurus

   I am bombarded yet   I stand

I have been standing all my life in the
direct path of a battery of signals
the most accurately transmitted most
untranslatable language in the universe
I am a galactic cloud so deep   so invo-
luted that a light wave could take 15
years to travel through me   And has
taken   I am an instrument in the shape
of a woman trying to translate pulsations
into images   for the relief of the body
and the reconstruction of the mind.

1968

ADRIENNE RICH

DIVING INTO THE WRECK

First having read the book of myths,
and loaded the camera,
and checked the edge of the knife-blade,
I put on
the body-armor of black rubber
the absurd flippers
the grave and awkward mask.
I am having to do this
not like Cousteau with his
assiduous team
aboard the sun-flooded schooner
but here alone.

There is a ladder.
The ladder is always there
hanging innocently
close to the side of the schooner.
We know what it is for,
we who have used it.
Otherwise
it's a piece of maritime floss
some sundry equipment.

I go down.
Rung after rung and still
the oxygen immerses me
the blue light
the clear atoms
of our human air.
I go down.
My flippers cripple me,
I crawl like an insect down the ladder
and there is no one
to tell me when the ocean
will begin.

First the air is blue and then
it is bluer and then green and then
black I am blacking out and yet
my mask is powerful
it pumps my blood with power

ADRIENNE RICH

the sea is another story
the sea is not a question of power
I have to learn alone
to turn my body without force
in the deep element.

And now: it is easy to forget
what I came for
among so many who have always
lived here
swaying their crenellated fans
between the reefs
and besides
you breathe differently down here. ✓

I came to explore the wreck.
The words are purposes.   the poet
The words are maps.   the historian
I came to see the damage that was done
and the treasures that prevail.
I stroke the beam of my lamp
slowly along the flank
of something more permanent
than fish or weed

the thing I came for: how do we get
the wreck and not the story of the wreck   at the essence
the thing itself and not the myth   of things?
the drowned face always staring
toward the sun
the evidence of damage
beauty +   worn by salt and sway into this threadbare beauty
destruction/   (the ribs of the disaster
terror   curving their assertion)
among the tentative haunters.

This is the place.
And I am here, the mermaid whose dark hair
streams black, the merman in his armored body
We circle silently
about the wreck
we dive into the hold.
I am she: I am he

whose drowned face sleeps with open eyes
whose breasts still bear the stress
whose silver, copper, vermeil cargo lies
obscurely inside barrels
half-wedged and left to rot
we are the half-destroyed instruments
that once held to a course
the water-eaten log
the fouled compass

We are, I am, you are
by cowardice or courage
the one who find our way
back to this scene
carrying a knife, a camera
a book of myths √
in which
our names do not appear.

1972

SPLITTINGS

1

My body opens over San Francisco like the daylight raining down   each pore crying the change of light
I am not with her   I have been waking off and on
all night to that pain   not simply absence but
the presence of the past   destructive
to living here and now   Yet if I could instruct
myself, if we could learn to learn from pain
even as it grasps us   if the mind, the mind that lives
in this body could refuse   to let itself be crushed
in that grasp   it would loosen   Pain would have to stand
off from me and listen   its dark breath still on me
but the mind could begin to speak to pain
and pain would have to answer:

We are older now
we have met before   these are my hands before your eyes
my figure blotting out   all that is not mine

I am the pain of division   creator of divisions
it is I who blot your lover from you
and not the time-zones nor the miles
It is not separation calls me forth   but I
who am separation   And remember
I have no existence   apart from you

2

I believe I am choosing something new
not to suffer uselessly   yet still to feel
Does the infant memorize the body of the mother
and create her in absence?   or simply cry
primordial loneliness?   does the bed of the stream
once diverted   mourning   remember wetness?

But we, we live so much in these
configurations of the past   I choose
to separate her   from my past we have not shared
I choose not to suffer uselessly
to detect primordial pain as it stalks toward me
flashing its bleak torch in my eyes   blotting out
her particular being   the details of her love
I will not be divided   from her or from myself
by myths of separation
while her mind and body in Manhattan are more with me
than the smell of eucalyptus coolly burning   on these hills

3

The world tells me I am its creature
I am raked by eyes   brushed by hands
I want to crawl into her for refuge   lay my head
in the space   between her breast and shoulder
abnegating power for love
as women have done   or hiding
from power in her love   like a man
I refuse these givens   the splitting
between love and action   I am choosing
not to suffer uselessly   and not to use her
I choose to love   this time   for once
with all my intelligence

1974

ADRIENNE RICH

from TWENTY-ONE LOVE POEMS

I

Wherever in this city, screens flicker
with pornography, with science-fiction vampires,
victimized hirelings bending to the lash,
we also have to walk . . . if simply as we walk
through the rainsoaked garbage, the tabloid cruelties
of our own neighborhoods.
We need to grasp our lives inseparable
from those rancid dreams, that blurt of metal, those disgraces,
and the red begonia perilously flashing
from a tenement sill six stories high,
or the long-legged young girls playing ball
in the junior highschool playground.
No one has imagined us. We want to live like trees,
sycamores blazing through the sulfuric air,
dappled with scars, still exuberantly budding,
our animal passion rooted in the city.

II

I wake up in your bed. I know I have been dreaming.
Much earlier, the alarm broke us from each other,
you've been at your desk for hours. I know what I dreamed:
our friend the poet comes into my room
where I've been writing for days,
drafts, carbons, poems are scattered everywhere,
and I want to show her one poem
which is the poem of my life. But I hesitate,
and wake. You've kissed my hair
to wake me. *I dreamed you were a poem,*
I say, *a poem I wanted to show someone . . .*
and I laugh and fall dreaming again
of the desire to show you to everyone I love,
to move openly together
in the pull of gravity, which is not simple,
which carries the feathered grass a long way down the upbreathing air.

XII

Sleeping, turning in turn like planets
rotating in their midnight meadow:
a touch is enough to let us know

we're not alone in the universe, even in sleep:
the dream-ghosts of two worlds
walking their ghost-towns, almost address each other.
I've wakened to your muttered words
spoken light- or dark-years away
as if my own voice had spoken.
But we have different voices, even in sleep,
and our bodies, so alike, are yet so different
and the past echoing through our bloodstreams
is freighted with different language, different meanings —
though in any chronicle of the world we share
it could be written with new meaning
we were two lovers of one gender,
we were two women of one generation.

XXI

The dark lintels, the blue and foreign stones
of the great round rippled by stone implements
the midsummer night light rising from beneath
the horizon — when I said "a cleft of light"
I meant this. And this is not Stonehenge
simply nor any place but the mind
casting back to where her solitude,
shared, could be chosen without loneliness,
not easily nor without pains to stake out
the circle, the heavy shadows, the great light.
I choose to be a figure in that light,
half-blotted by darkness, something moving
across that space, the color of stone
greeting the moon, yet more than stone:
a woman. I choose to walk here. And to draw this circle.

INTEGRITY

the quality or state of being complete; unbroken condition; entirety
— *Webster*

A wild patience has taken me this far

as if I had to bring to shore
a boat with a spasmodic outboard motor

old sweaters, nets, spray-mottled books
tossed in the prow
some kind of sun burning my shoulder-blades.
Splashing the oarlocks. Burning through.
Your fore-arms can get scalded, licked with pain
in a sun blotted like unspoken anger
behind a casual mist.

The length of daylight
this far north, in this
forty-ninth year of my life
is critical.

The light is critical: of me, of this
long-dreamed, involuntary landing
on the arm of an inland sea.
The glitter of the shoal
depleting into shadow
I recognize: the stand of pines
violet-black really, green in the old postcard
but really I have nothing but myself
to go by; nothing
stands in the realm of pure necessity
except what my hands can hold.

Nothing but myself? . . . My selves.
After so long, this answer.
As if I had always known
I steer the boat in, simply.
The motor dying on the pebbles
cicadas taking up the hum
dropped in the silence.

Anger and tenderness: my selves.
And now I can believe they breathe in me
as angels, not polarities.
Anger and tenderness: the spider's genius
to spin and weave in the same action
from her own body, anywhere —
even from a broken web.

The cabin in the stand of pines
is still for sale. I know this. Know the print
of the last foot, the hand that slammed and locked that door,
then stopped to wreathe the rain-smashed clematis

back on the trellis
for no one's sake except its own.
I know the chart nailed to the wallboards
the icy kettle squatting on the burner.
The hands that hammered in those nails
emptied that kettle one last time
are these two hands
and they have caught the baby leaping
from between trembling legs
and they have worked the vacuum aspirator
and stroked the sweated temples
and steered the boat here through this hot
misblotted sunlight, critical light
imperceptibly scalding
the skin these hands will also salve.

1978

NORTH AMERICAN TIME

I

When my dreams showed signs
of becoming
politically correct
no unruly images
escaping beyond borders
when walking in the street I found my
themes cut out for me
knew what I would not report
for fear of enemies' usage
then I began to wonder

II

Everything we write
will be used against us
or against those we love.
These are the terms,
take them or leave them.

Poetry never stood a chance
of standing outside history.

One line typed twenty years ago
can be blazed on a wall in spraypaint
to glorify art as detachment
or torture of those we
did not love but also
did not want to kill

We move   but our words stand
become responsible
for more than we intended

and this is verbal privilege

III

Try sitting at a typewriter
one calm summer evening
at a table by a window
in the country, try pretending
your time does not exist
that you are simply you
that the imagination simply strays
like a great moth, unintentional
try telling yourself
you are not accountable
to the life of your tribe
the breath of your planet

IV

It doesn't matter what you think.
Words are found responsible
all you can do is choose them
or choose
to remain silent.   Or, you never had a choice,
which is why the words that do stand
are responsible

and this is verbal privilege

V

Suppose you want to write
of a woman braiding
another woman's hair —

straight down, or with beads and shells
in three-strand plaits or corn-rows —
you had better know the thickness
the length   the pattern
why she decides to braid her hair
how it is done to her
what country it happens in
what else happens in that country

You have to know these things

VI

Poet, sister: words —
whether we like it or not —
stand in a time of their own.
No use protesting   *I wrote that*
before Kollontai was exiled
Rosa Luxembourg, Malcolm,
Anna Mae Aquash, murdered,
before Treblinka, Birkenau,
Hiroshima, before Sharpeville,
Biafra, Bangla Desh, Boston,
Atlanta, Soweto, Beirut, Assam
— those faces, names of places
sheared from the almanac
of North American time

VII

I am thinking this in a country
where words are stolen out of mouths
as bread is stolen out of mouths
where poets don't go to jail
for being poets, but for being
dark-skinned, female, poor.
I am writing this in a time
when anything we write
can be used against those we love
where the context is never given
though we try to explain, over and over
For the sake of poetry at least
I need to know these things

VIII

Sometimes, gliding at night
in a plane over New York City
I have felt like some messenger
called to enter, called to engage
this field of light and darkness.
A grandiose idea, born of flying.
But underneath the grandiose idea
is the thought that what I must engage
after the plane has raged into the tarmac
after climbing my old stairs, sitting down
at my old window
is meant to break my heart and reduce me to silence.

IX

In North America time stumbles on
without moving, only releasing
a certain North American pain.
Julia de Burgos wrote:
That my grandfather was a slave
is my grief; had he been a master
that would have been my shame.
A poet's words, hung over a door
in North America, in the year
nineteen-eighty-three.
The almost-full moon rises
timelessly speaking of change
out of the Bronx, the Harlem River
the drowned towns of the Quabbin
the pilfered burial mounds
the toxic swamps, the testing-grounds

and I start to speak again.

FOR AN OCCUPANT

Did the fox speak to you?
Did the small brush-fires on the hillside
smoke her out?

Were you standing on the porch
not the kitchen porch   the front
one of poured concrete   full in the rising moon
and did she appear   wholly on her own
asking no quarter   wandering by
on impulse   up the drive   and on
into the pine-woods
but were you standing there
at the moment of moon and burnished light
leading your own life   till she caught your eye
asking no charity
but did she speak to you?

1983

from TURNING

5

Whatever you are that has tracked us this far,
I never thought you were on our side,
I only thought you did not judge us.

Yet as a cell might hallucinate
the eye — intent, impassioned —
behind the lens of the microscope

so I have thought of you,
whatever you are — a mindfulness —
whatever you are: the place beyond all places,

beyond boundaries, green lines,
wire-netted walls
the place beyond documents.

Unnameable by choice.
So why am I out here, trying
to read your name in the illegible air?

— vowel washed from a stone,
solitude of no absence,
forbidden face-to-face

— trying to hang these wraiths
of syllables, breath
without echo, why?

FOR A FRIEND IN TRAVAIL

*The love of a fellow-creature in all its fullness consists simply in the ability to say
to him, "What are you going through?"*

— *Simone Weil*

Waking from violence: the surgeon's probe left in the foot
paralyzing the body from the neck down.
Dark before dawn: wrapped in a shawl, to walk the house
the Drinking Horn slung in the northwest,
half-slice of moon to the south
through dark panes.   A time to speak to you.

What are you going through? she said, is love's great question.
Philosopher of oppression, theorist
of the victories of force.

We write from the marrow of our bones.   What she did not
ask, or tell: how victims save their own lives.

That crawl along the ledge, then the ravelling span of fibre strung
from one side to the other, I've dreamed that too.
Waking, not sure we made it.   Relief, appallment, of waking.
Consciousness.   O, no.   To sleep again.
O to sleep without dreaming.

How day breaks, when it breaks, how clear and light the moon
melting into the moon-colored air
moist and sweet, here on the western edge.
Love for the world, and we are part of it.
How the poppies break from their sealed envelopes
she did not tell.

What are you going through, there on the other edge?

Theodore Roethke

THE PREMONITION

Walking this field I remember
Days of another summer.
Oh that was long ago! I kept
Close to the heels of my father,
Matching his stride with half-steps
Until we came to a river.
He dipped his hand in the shallow:
Water ran over and under
Hair on a narrow wrist bone;
His image kept following after, —
Flashed with the sun in the ripple.
But when he stood up, that face
Was lost in a maze of water.

CUTTINGS

(later)

This urge, wrestle, resurrection of dry sticks,
Cut stems struggling to put down feet,
What saint strained so much,
Rose on such lopped limbs to a new life?

I can hear, underground, that sucking and sobbing,
In my veins, in my bones I feel it, —
The small waters seeping upward,
The tight grains parting at last.
When sprouts break out,
Slippery as fish,
I quail, lean to beginnings, sheath-wet.

FORCING HOUSE

Vines tougher than wrists
And rubbery shoots,
Scums, mildews, smuts along stems,

Great cannas or delicate cyclamen tips, —
All pulse with the knocking pipes
That drip and sweat,
Sweat and drip,
Swelling the roots with steam and stench,
Shooting up lime and dung and ground bones, —
Fifty summers in motion at once,
As the live heat billows from pipes and pots.

WEED PULLER

Under the concrete benches,
Hacking at black hairy roots, —
Those lewd monkey-tails hanging from drainholes, —
Digging into the soft rubble underneath,
Webs and weeds,
Grubs and snails and sharp sticks,
Or yanking tough fern-shapes,
Coiled green and thick, like dripping smilax,
Tugging all day at perverse life:
The indignity of it! —
With everything blooming above me,
Lilies, pale-pink cyclamen, roses,
Whole fields lovely and inviolate, —
Me down in that fetor of weeds,
Crawling on all fours,
Alive, in a slippery grave.

MY PAPA'S WALTZ

Why a waltz?

The whiskey on your breath
Could make a small boy dizzy;
But I hung on like death:
Such waltzing was not easy.

tenacious love for father

incongruous

We romped until the pans
Slid from the kitchen shelf;

disruption

domestic life upset

love/violence out of control

My mother's countenance
Could not unfrown itself.

The hand that held my wrist
Was battered on one knuckle;
At every step you missed
My right ear scraped a buckle.

You beat time on my head
With a palm caked hard by dirt,
Then waltzed me off to bed
Still clinging to your shirt.

ELEGY FOR JANE

My Student, Thrown by a Horse

I remember the neckcurls, limp and damp as tendrils;
And her quick look, a sidelong pickerel smile;
And how, once startled into talk, the light syllables leaped for her,
And she balanced in the delight of her thought,
A wren, happy, tail into the wind,
Her song trembling the twigs and small branches.
The shade sang with her;
The leaves, their whispers turned to kissing;
And the mold sang in the bleached valleys under the rose.

Oh, when she was sad, she cast herself down into such a pure depth,
Even a father could not find her:
Scraping her cheek against straw;
Stirring the clearest water.

My sparrow, you are not here,
Waiting like a fern, making a spiny shadow.
The sides of wet stones cannot console me,
Nor the moss, wound with the last light.

If only I could nudge you from this sleep,
My maimed darling, my skittery pigeon.
Over this damp grave I speak the words of my love:
I, with no rights in this matter,
Neither father nor lover.

THE WAKING

I wake to sleep, and take my waking slow.
I feel my fate in what I cannot fear.
I learn by going where I have to go.

We think by feeling. What is there to know?
I hear my being dance from ear to ear.
I wake to sleep, and take my waking slow.

Of those so close beside me, which are you?
God bless the Ground! I shall walk softly there,
And learn by going where I have to go.

Light takes the Tree; but who can tell us how?
The lowly worm climbs up a winding stair;
I wake to sleep, and take my waking slow.

Great Nature has another thing to do
To you and me; so take the lively air,
And, lovely, learn by going where to go.

This shaking keeps me steady. I should know.
What falls away is always. And is near.
I wake to sleep, and take my waking slow.
I learn by going where I have to go.

I KNEW A WOMAN

I knew a woman, lovely in her bones,
When small birds sighed, she would sigh back at them;
Ah, when she moved, she moved more ways than one:
The shapes a bright container can contain!
Of her choice virtues only gods should speak,
Or English poets who grew up on Greek
(I'd have them sing in chorus, cheek to cheek).

How well her wishes went! She stroked my chin,
She taught me Turn, and Counter-turn, and Stand;
She taught me Touch, that undulant white skin;

I nibbled meekly from her proffered hand;
She was the sickle; I, poor I, the rake,
Coming behind her for her pretty sake
(But what prodigious mowing we did make).

Love likes a gander, and adores a goose:
Her full lips pursed, the errant note to seize;
She played it quick, she played it light and loose;
My eyes, they dazzled at her flowing knees;
Her several parts could keep a pure repose,
Or one hip quiver with a mobile nose
(She moved in circles, and those circles moved).

Let seed be grass, and grass turn into hay:
I'm martyr to a motion not my own;
What's freedom for? To know eternity.
I swear she cast a shadow white as stone.
But who would count eternity in days?
These old bones live to learn her wanton ways:
(I measure time by how a body sways).

MEDITATION AT OYSTER RIVER

1

Over the low, barnacled, elephant-colored rocks,
Come the first tide-ripples, moving, almost without sound, toward me,
Running along the narrow furrows of the shore, the rows of dead clam
    shells;
Then a runnel behind me, creeping closer,
Alive with tiny striped fish, and young crabs climbing in and out of the
    water.

No sound from the bay. No violence.
Even the gulls quiet on the far rocks,
Silent, in the deepening light,
Their cat-mewing over,
Their child-whimpering.

At last one long undulant ripple,
Blue-black from where I am sitting,

Makes almost a wave over a barrier of small stones,
Slapping lightly against a sunken log.
I dabble my toes in the brackish foam sliding forward,
Then retire to a rock higher up on the cliff-side.
The wind slackens, light as a moth fanning a stone:
A twilight wind, light as a child's breath
Turning not a leaf, not a ripple.
The dew revives on the beach-grass;
The salt-soaked wood of a fire crackles;
A fish raven turns on its perch (a dead tree in the rivermouth),
Its wings catching a last glint of the reflected sunlight.

2

The self persists like a dying star,
In sleep, afraid. Death's face rises afresh,
Among the shy beasts, the deer at the salt-lick,
The doe with its sloped shoulders loping across the highway,
The young snake, poised in green leaves, waiting for its fly,
The hummingbird, whirring from quince-blossom to morning-glory —
With these I would be.
And with water: the waves coming forward, without cessation,
The waves, altered by sand-bars, beds of kelp, miscellaneous driftwood,
Topped by cross-winds, tugged at by sinuous undercurrents
The tide rustling in, sliding between the ridges of stone,
The tongues of water, creeping in, quietly.

3

In this hour,
In this first heaven of knowing,
The flesh takes on the pure poise of the spirit,
Acquires, for a time, the sandpiper's insouciance,
The hummingbird's surety, the kingfisher's cunning —
I shift on my rock, and I think:
Of the first trembling of a Michigan brook in April,
Over a lip of stone, the tiny rivulet;
And that wrist-thick cascade tumbling from a cleft rock,
Its spray holding a double rain-bow in early morning,
Small enough to be taken in, embraced, by two arms, —
Or the Tittebawasee, in the time between winter and spring,
When the ice melts along the edges in early afternoon.

And the midchannel begins cracking and heaving from the pressure
    beneath,
The ice piling high against the iron-bound spiles,
Gleaming, freezing hard again, creaking at midnight —
And I long for the blast of dynamite,
The sudden sucking roar as the culvert loosens its debris of branches and
    sticks,
Welter of tin cans, pails, old bird nests, a child's shoe riding a log,
As the piled ice breaks away from the battered spiles,
And the whole river begins to move forward, its bridges shaking.

4

Now, in this waning of light,
I rock with the motion of morning;
In the cradle of all that is,
I'm lulled into half-sleep
By the lapping of water,
Cries of the sandpiper.
Water's my will, and my way,
And the spirit runs, intermittently,
In and out of the small waves,
Runs with the intrepid shorebirds —
How graceful the small before danger!

In the first of the moon,
All's a scattering,
A shining.

IN A DARK TIME

In a dark time, the eye begins to see,
I meet my shadow in the deepening shade;
I hear my echo in the echoing wood —
A lord of nature weeping to a tree.
I live between the heron and the wren,
Beasts of the hill and serpents of the den.

What's madness but nobility of soul
At odds with circumstance? The day's on fire!

I know the purity of pure despair,
My shadow pinned against a sweating wall.
That place among the rocks — is it a cave,
Or winding path? The edge is what I have.

A steady storm of correspondences!
A night flowing with birds, a ragged moon,
And in broad day the midnight come again!
A man goes far to find out what he is —
Death of the self in a long, tearless night,
All natural shapes blazing unnatural light.

Dark, dark my light, and darker my desire.
My soul, like some heat-maddened summer fly,
Keeps buzzing at the sill. Which I is *I*?
A fallen man, I climb out of my fear.
The mind enters itself, and God the mind,
And one is One, free in the tearing wind.

IN EVENING AIR

1

A dark theme keeps me here,
Though summer blazes in the vireo's eye.
Who would be half possessed
By his own nakedness?
Waking's my care —
I'll make a broken music, or I'll die.

2

Ye littles, lie more close!
Make me, O Lord, a last, a simple thing
Time cannot overwhelm.
Once I transcended time:
A bud broke to a rose,
And I rose from a last diminishing.

3

I look down the far light
And I behold the dark side of a tree
Far down a billowing plain,
And when I look again,
It's lost upon the night —
Night I embrace, a dear proximity.

4

I stand by a low fire
Counting the wisps of flame, and I watch how
Light shifts upon the wall.
I bid stillness be still.
I see, in evening air,
How slowly dark comes down on what we do.

Anne Sexton

HER KIND

I have gone out, a possessed witch,
haunting the black air, braver at night;
dreaming evil, I have done my hitch
over the plain houses, light by light:
lonely thing, twelve-fingered, out of mind.
A woman like that is not a woman, quite.
I have been her kind.

I have found the warm caves in the woods,
filled them with skillets, carvings, shelves,
closets, silks, innumerable goods;
fixed the suppers for the worms and the elves:
whining, rearranging the disaligned.
A woman like that is misunderstood.
I have been her kind.

I have ridden in your cart, driver,
waved my nude arms at villages going by,
learning the last bright routes, survivor
where your flames still bite my thigh
and my ribs crack where your wheels wind.
A woman like that is not ashamed to die.
I have been her kind.

WITH MERCY FOR THE GREEDY

*For my friend, Ruth, who urges me to make an
appointment for the Sacrament of Confession*

Concerning your letter in which you ask
me to call a priest and in which you ask
me to wear The Cross that you enclose;
your own cross,
your dog-bitten cross,
no larger than a thumb,
small and wooden, no thorns, this rose —

I pray to its shadow,
that gray place
where it lies on your letter . . . deep, deep.
I detest my sins and I try to believe
in The Cross. I touch its tender hips, its dark jawed face,
its solid neck, its brown sleep.

True. There is
a beautiful Jesus.
He is frozen to his bones like a chunk of beef.
How desperately he wanted to pull his arms in!
How desperately I touch his vertical and horizontal axes!
But I can't. Need is not quite belief.

All morning long
I have worn
your cross, hung with package string around my throat.
It tapped me lightly as a child's heart might,
tapping secondhand, softly waiting to be born.
Ruth, I cherish the letter you wrote.

My friend, my friend, I was born
doing reference work in sin, and born
confessing it. This is what poems are:
with mercy
for the greedy,
they are the tongue's wrangle,
the world's pottage, the rat's star.

TO A FRIEND WHOSE WORK HAS COME TO TRIUMPH

Consider Icarus, pasting those sticky wings on,
testing that strange little tug at his shoulder blade,
and think of that first flawless moment over the lawn
of the labyrinth. Think of the difference it made!
There below are the trees, as awkward as camels;
and here are the shocked starlings pumping past
and think of innocent Icarus who is doing quite well:
larger than a sail, over the fog and the blast
of the plushy ocean, he goes. Admire his wings!

Feel the fire at his neck and see how casually
he glances up and is caught, wondrously tunneling
into that hot eye. Who cares that he fell back to the sea?
See him acclaiming the sun and come plunging down
while his sensible daddy goes straight into town.

THE ABORTION

Somebody who should have been born
is gone.

Just as the earth puckered its mouth,
each bud puffing out from its knot,
I changed my shoes, and then drove south.

Up past the Blue Mountains, where
Pennsylvania humps on endlessly,
wearing, like a crayoned cat, its green hair,

its roads sunken in like a gray washboard;
where, in truth, the ground cracks evilly,
a dark socket from which the coal has poured,

Somebody who should have been born
is gone.

the grass as bristly and stout as chives,
and me wondering when the ground would break,
and me wondering how anything fragile survives;

up in Pennsylvania, I met a little man,
not Rumpelstiltskin, at all, at all . . .
he took the fullness that love began.

Returning north, even the sky grew thin
like a high window looking nowhere.
The road was as flat as a sheet of tin.

Somebody who should have been born
is gone.

Yes, woman, such logic will lead
to loss without death. Or say what you meant,
you coward . . . this baby that I bleed.

MAN AND WIFE

> *To speke of wo*
> *that is in mariage . . .*

We are not lovers.
We do not even know each other.
We look alike
but we have nothing to say.
We are like pigeons . . .
that pair who came to the suburbs
by mistake,
forsaking Boston where they bumped
their small heads against a blind wall,
having worn out the fruit stalls in the North End,
the amethyst windows of Louisburg Square,
the seats on the Common
And the traffic that kept stamping
and stamping.

Now there is green rain for everyone
as common as eyewash.
Now they are together
like strangers in a two-seater outhouse,
eating and squatting together.
They have teeth and knees
but they do not speak.
A soldier is forced to stay with a soldier
because they share the same dirt
and the same blows.

ANNE SEXTON

They are exiles
soiled by the same sweat and the drunkard's dream.
As it is they can only hang on,
their red claws wound like bracelets
around the same limb.
Even their song is not a sure thing.
It is not a language;
it is a kind of breathing.
They are two asthmatics
whose breath sobs in and out
through a small fuzzy pipe.

Like them
we neither talk nor clear our throats.
Oh darling,
we gasp in unison beside our window pane,
drunk on the drunkard's dream.
Like them
we can only hang on.

But they would pierce our heart
if they could only fly the distance.

IN CELEBRATION OF MY UTERUS

Everyone in me is a bird.
I am beating all my wings.
They wanted to cut you out
but they will not.
They said you were immeasurably empty
but you are not.
They said you were sick unto dying
but they were wrong.
You are singing like a school girl.
You are not torn.

Sweet weight,
in celebration of the woman I am
and of the soul of the woman I am
and of the central creature and its delight
I sing for you. I dare to live.

Hello, spirit. Hello, cup.
Fasten, cover. Cover that does contain.
Hello to the soil of the fields.
Welcome, roots.

Each cell has a life.
There is enough here to please a nation.
It is enough that the populace own these goods.

Any person, any commonwealth would say of it,
"It is good this year that we may plant again
and think forward to a harvest.
A blight had been forecast and has been cast out."
Many women are singing together of this:
one is in a shoe factory cursing the machine,
one is at the aquarium tending a seal,
one is dull at the wheel of her Ford,
one is at the toll gate collecting,
one is tying the cord of a calf in Arizona,
one is straddling a cello in Russia,
one is shifting pots on the stove in Egypt,
one is painting her bedroom walls moon color,
one is dying but remembering a breakfast,
one is stretching on her mat in Thailand,
one is wiping the ass of her child,
one is staring out the window of a train
in the middle of Wyoming and one is
anywhere and some are everywhere and all
seem to be singing, although some can not
sing a note.

Sweet weight,
in celebration of the woman I am
let me carry a ten-foot scarf,
let me drum for the nineteen-year-olds,
let me carry bowls for the offering
(if that is my part).

ANNE SEXTON

Let me study the cardiovascular tissue,
let me examine the angular distance of meteors,
let me suck on the stems of flowers
(if that is my part).
Let me make certain tribal figures
(if that is my part).
For this thing the body needs
let me sing
for the supper,
for the kissing,
for the correct
yes.

US

I was wrapped in black
fur and white fur and
you undid me and then
you placed me in gold light
and then you crowned me,
while snow fell outside
the door in diagonal darts.
While a ten-inch snow
came down like stars
in small calcium fragments,
we were in our own bodies
(that room that will bury us)
and you were in my body
(that room that will outlive us)
and at first I rubbed your
feet dry with a towel
because I was your slave
and then you called me princess.
Princess!

Oh then
I stood up in my gold skin
and I beat down the psalms
and I beat down the clothes
and you undid the bridle

and you undid the reins
and I undid the buttons,
the bones, the confusions,
the New England postcards,
the January ten o'clock night,
and we rose up like wheat,
acre after acre of gold,
and we harvested,
we harvested.

THE FURY OF COCKS

There they are
drooping over the breakfast plates,
angel-like,
folding in their sad wing,
animal sad,
and only the night before
there they were
playing the banjo.
Once more the day's light comes
with its immense sun,
its mother trucks,
its engines of amputation.
Whereas last night
the cock knew its way home,
as stiff as a hammer,
battering in with all
its awful power.
That theater.
Today it is tender,
a small bird,
as soft as a baby's hand.
She is the house.
He is the steeple.
When they fuck they are God.
When they break away they are God.
When they snore they are God.
In the morning they butter the toast.

ANNE SEXTON

They don't say much.
They are still God.
All the cocks of the world are God,
blooming, blooming, blooming
into the sweet blood of woman.

ROWING

A story, a story!
(Let it go. Let it come.)
I was stamped out like a Plymouth fender
into this world.
First came the crib
with its glacial bars.
Then dolls
and the devotion to their plastic mouths.
Then there was school,
the little straight rows of chairs,
blotting my name over and over,
but undersea all the time,
a stranger whose elbows wouldn't work.
Then there was life
with its cruel houses
and people who seldom touched —
though touch is all —
but I grew,
like a pig in a trenchcoat I grew,
and then there were many strange apparitions,
the nagging rain, the sun turning into poison
and all of that, saws working through my heart,
but I grew, I grew,
and God was there like an island I had not rowed to,
still ignorant of Him, my arms and my legs worked,
and I grew, I grew,
I wore rubies and bought tomatoes
and now, in my middle age,
about nineteen in the head I'd say,
I am rowing, I am rowing
though the oarlocks stick and are rusty

and the sea blinks and rolls
like a worried eyeball,
but I am rowing, I am rowing,
though the wind pushes me back
and I know that that island will not be perfect,
it will have the flaws of life,
the absurdities of the dinner table,
but there will be a door
and I will open it
and I will get rid of the rat inside of me,
the gnawing pestilential rat.
God will take it with his two hands
and embrace it.

As the African says:
This is my tale which I have told,
if it be sweet, if it be not sweet,
take somewhere else and let some return to me.
This story ends with me still rowing.

TWO HANDS

From the sea came a hand,
ignorant as a penny,
troubled with the salt of its mother,
mute with the silence of the fishes,
quick with the altars of the tides,
and God reached out of His mouth
and called it man.
Up came the other hand
and God called it woman.
The hands applauded.
And this was no sin.
It was as it was meant to be.

I see them roaming the streets:
Levi complaining about his mattress,
Sarah studying a beetle,
Mandrake holding his coffee mug,

ANNE SEXTON

Sally playing the drum at a footballl game,
John closing the eyes of the dying woman,
and some who are in prison,
even the prison of their bodies,
as Christ was prisoned in His body
until the triumph came.

Unwind, hands,
you angel webs,
unwind like the coil of a jumping jack,
cup together and let yourselves fill up with sun
and applaud, world,
applaud.

Charles Simic

POEM

Every morning I forget how it is.
I watch the smoke mount
In great strides above the city.
I belong to no one.

Then, I remember my shoes,
How I have to put them on,
How bending over to tie them up
I will look into the earth.

PASTORAL

I came to a meadow
Where the grass was silence
And the flowers
Words

I saw the blossoms
Were of flesh and blood
And that they tremble and fear
The wind like a knife

So sat I between the word *truth*
And the word *fable*
Took out my empty bowl
And spoon

Asked both about *love*
In the silence
With the night falling
Heard her call my name

Spat in the palms of my hands
To catch stars in them
Like fireflies
And light her way to me

CHARLES SIMIC

DISMANTLING THE SILENCE

Take down its ears first,
Carefully, so they don't spill over.
With a sharp whistle slit its belly open.
If there are ashes in it, close your eyes
And blow them whichever way the wind is pointing.
If there's water, sleeping water,
Bring the root of a flower that hasn't drunk for a month.

When you reach the bones,
And you haven't got a dog with you,
And you haven't got a pine coffin
And a cart pulled by oxen to make them rattle,
Slip them quickly under your skin.
Next time you hunch your shoulders
You'll feel them pressing against your own.

It is now pitch dark.
Slowly and with patience
Search for its heart. You will need
To crawl far into the empty heavens
To hear it beat.

BESTIARY FOR THE FINGERS
OF MY RIGHT HAND

1

Thumb, loose tooth of a horse.
Rooster to his hens.
Horn of a devil. Fat worm
They have attached to my flesh
At the time of my birth.
It takes four to hold him down,
Bend him in half, until the bone
Begins to whimper.

Cut him off. He can take care
Of himself. Take root in the earth,
Or go hunting with wolves.

2

The second points the way.
True way. The path crosses the earth,
The moon and some stars.
Watch, he points further.
He points to himself.

3

The middle one has backache.
Stiff, still unaccustomed to this life;
An old man at birth. It's about something
That he had and lost,
That he looks for within my hand,
The way a dog looks
For fleas
With a sharp tooth.

4

The fourth is mystery.
Sometimes as my hand
Rests on the table
He jumps by himself
As though someone called his name.

After each bone, finger,
I come to him, troubled.

5

Something stirs in the fifth
Something perpetually at the point
Of birth. Weak and submissive,
His touch is gentle.
It weighs a tear.
It takes the mote out of the eye.

WATERMELONS

Green Buddhas
On the fruit stand.
We eat the smile
and spit out the teeth.

TOY FACTORY

My mother works here,
And so does my father.

It's the night shift.
At the assembly line.
They wind toys up
To inspect their springs.

The seven toy members
Of the firing squad
Point their rifles,
And lower them quickly.

The one being shot at
Falls and gets up,
Falls and gets up.
His blindfold is just painted on.

The toy gravediggers
Don't work so well.
Their spades are heavy,
Their spades are much too heavy.

Perhaps that's how
It's supposed to be?

CHARLES SIMIC

CLASSIC BALLROOM DANCES

Grandmothers who wring the necks
Of chickens; old nuns
With names like Theresa, Marianne,
Who pull schoolboys by the ear;

The intricate steps of pickpockets
Working the crowd of the curious
At the scene of an accident; the slow shuffle
Of the evangelist with a sandwich-board;

The hesitation of the early morning customer
Peeking through the window-grille
Of a pawnshop; the weave of a little kid
Who is walking to school with eyes closed;

And the ancient lovers, cheek to cheek,
On the dancefloor of the Union Hall,
Where they also hold charity raffles
On rainy Monday nights of an eternal November.

NORTHERN EXPOSURE

When old women say, it smells of snow,
In a whisper barely audible
Which still rouses the sick man upstairs
So he opens his eyes wide and lets them fill

With the grayness of the remaining daylight.
When old women say, how quiet it is,
And truly today no one came to visit,
While the one they still haven't shaved

Lifts the wristwatch to his ear and listens.
In it, something small, subterranean
And awful in intent, chews rapidly.
When old women say, time to turn on the lights,

And not a single one gets up to do so,
For now there are loops and loose knots around their feet
As if someone is scribbling over them
With a piece of charcoal found in the cold stove.

MY WEARINESS OF EPIC PROPORTIONS

I like it when
Achilles
Gets killed
And even his buddy Patroclus —
And that hothead Hector —
And the whole Greek and Trojan
Jeunesse doree
Is more or less
Expertly slaughtered
So there's finally
Peace and quiet
(The gods having momentarily
Shut up)
One can hear
A bird sing
And a daughter ask her mother
Whether she can go to the well
And of course she can
By that lovely little path
That winds through
The olive orchard

TO HELEN

Tomorrow early I'm going to the doctor
In the blue suit and shirt you ironed.
Tomorrow I'm having my bones photographed
With my heart in its spiked branches.

It will look like a bird's nest in autumn
On a bleak day, one foot into the evening.
The tree is ill-shapen and alone in a field.
It must have been an apple, a crab apple

Tough and sour to make each tooth sore,
So that one goes off regretting, for now
The road's dark and there are new worries,
Fast swerving cars without headlights on,

Unknown drivers asleep at the wheel.
Because it's such a fine bone-chilling night.
Shadowy women are stirring black coffee,
Or they come out on the road to wait,

Wind-twisted and exquisitely blurred
In the wake of these cars that are moving
So fast or so slow, one barely hears them.
They're like clouds, if you hear them, the dark clouds.

AGAINST WHATEVER IT IS THAT'S ENCROACHING

Best of all is to be idle,
And especially on a Thursday,
And to sip wine while studying the light:
The way it ages, yellows, turns ashen
And then hesitates forever
On the threshold of the night
That could be bringing the first frost.

It's good to have a woman around just then,
And two is even better.
Let them whisper to each other
And eye you with a smirk.
Let them roll up their sleeves and unbutton their shirts a bit
As this fine old twilight deserves,

And the small schoolboy
Who has come home to a room almost dark
And now watches wide-eyed
The grownups raise their glasses to him,

The giddy-headed, red-haired woman
With eyes tightly shut,
As if she were about to cry or sing.

A LETTER

Dear philosophers, I get sad when I think.
Is it the same with you?
Just as I'm about to sink my teeth into the noumenon,
Some old girlfriend comes to distract me.
"She's not even alive!" I yell to the skies.

The wintry light made me go that way.
I saw beds covered with identical gray blankets.
I saw grim-looking men holding a naked woman
While they hosed her with cold water.
Was that to calm her nerves, or was it punishment?

I went to visit my friend Bob who said to me:
"We reach the real by overcoming the seduction of images."
I was overjoyed, until I realized
Such abstinence will never be possible for me.
I caught myself looking out the window.

Bob's father was taking their dog for a walk.
He moved with pain; the dog waited for him.
There was no one else in the park,
Only bare trees with an infinity of tragic shapes
To make thinking difficult.

THE BIG MACHINE

The insides of the machine at night
Like a garden of carnivorous plants.
There goes the mad doctor in short pants
Wielding a butterfly net.

Hairpins, shaving mirrors, blown-up condoms
With spikes, or could they be levers,
Pulleys, dangling counterweights
Enacting their shadow-farces and tragedies?

Is it a lady's dainty slipper
They're raising or lowering,
Or the ghost of the machine
Riding an empty swing?

The Monster who can't tell
Plugs himself into an electric outlet
And gathers a spray
Of pig-iron immortelles.

THE BIG WAR

We played war during the war,
Margaret. Toy soldiers were in big demand,
The kind made from clay.
The lead ones they melted into bullets, I suppose.

You never saw anything as beautiful
As those clay regiments! I used to lie on the floor
For hours staring them in the eye.
I remember them staring back at me in wonder.

How strange they must have felt
Standing stiffly at attention
Before a large, incomprehending creature
With a moustache made of milk.

In time they broke, or I broke them on purpose.
There was wire inside their limbs,
Inside their chests, but nothing in the heads!
Margaret, I made sure.

Nothing at all in the heads . . .
Just an arm, now and then, an officer's arm,
Wielding a saber from a crack
In my deaf grandmother's kitchen floor.

HEIGHTS OF FOLLY

O crows circling over my head and cawing!
I admit to being, at times,
Suddenly, and without the slightest warning,
Exceedingly happy.

On a morning otherwise sunless,
Strolling arm in arm
Past some gallows-shaped trees
With my dear Helen,
Who is also a strange bird,

With a feeling of being summoned
Urgently, but by a most gracious invitation
To breakfast on slices of watermelon
In the company of naked gods and goddesses
On a patch of last night's snow.

PARADISE

In a neighborhood once called "Hell's Kitchen"
Where a beggar claimed to be playing Nero's fiddle
While the city burned in mid-summer heat;
Where a lady barber who called herself Cleopatra
Wielded the scissors of fate over my head
Threatening to cut off my ears and nose;
Where a man and a woman went walking naked
In one of the dark side streets at dawn.

I must be dreaming, I told myself.
It was like meeting a couple of sphinxes.
I expected them to have wings, bodies of lions:
Him with his wildly tattooed chest;
Her with her huge, dangling breasts.

It happened so quickly, and so long ago!

CHARLES SIMIC

You know that time just before the day breaks
When one yearns to lie down on cool sheets
In a room with shades drawn?
The hour when the beautiful suicides
Lying side by side in the morgue
Get up and walk out into the first light.

The curtains of cheap hotels flying out of windows
Like sea gulls, but everything else quiet . . .
Steam rising out of the subway gratings . . .
Bodies glistening with sweat . . .
Madness, and you might even say, paradise!

Louis Simpson

TO THE WESTERN WORLD

A siren sang, and Europe turned away
From the high castle and the shepherd's crook.
Three caravels went sailing to Cathay
On the strange ocean, and the captains shook
Their banners out across the Mexique Bay.

And in our early days we did the same.
Remembering our fathers in their wreck
We crossed the sea from Palos where they came
And saw, enormous to the little deck,
A shore in silence waiting for a name.

The treasures of Cathay were never found.
In this America, this wilderness
Where the axe echoes with a lonely sound,
The generations labor to possess
And grave by grave we civilize the ground.

HOT NIGHT ON WATER STREET

A hot midsummer night on Water Street —
The boys in jeans were combing their blond hair,
Watching the girls go by on tired feet;
And an old woman with a witch's stare
Cried "Praise the Lord!" She vanished on a bus
With hissing air brakes, like an incubus.

Three hardware stores, a barbershop, a bar,
A movie playing Westerns — where I went
To see a dream of horses called *The Star.* . . .
Some day, when this uncertain continent
Is marble, and men ask what was the good
We lived by, dust may whisper "Hollywood."

Then back along the river bank on foot
By moonlight. . . . On the West Virginia side
An owlish train began to huff and hoot;
It seemed to know of something that had died.
I didn't linger — sometimes when I travel
I think I'm being followed by the Devil.

At the newsstand in the lobby, a cigar
Was talkative: "Since I've been in this town
I've seen one likely woman, and a car
As she was crossing Main Street knocked her down."
I was a stranger here myself, I said,
And bought the *New York Times*, and went to bed.

IN THE SUBURBS

There's no way out.
You were born to waste your life.
You were born to this middleclass life

As others before you
Were born to walk in procession
To the temple, singing.

WALT WHITMAN AT BEAR MOUNTAIN

"*. . . life which does not give the preference to any other life, of any previous period,
which therefore prefers its own existence . . .*"

— *Ortega y Gasset*

Neither on horseback nor seated,
But like himself, squarely on two feet,
The poet of death and lilacs
Loafs by the footpath. Even the bronze looks alive
Where it is folded like cloth. And he seems friendly.

"Where is the Mississippi panorama
And the girl who played the piano?
Where are you, Walt?
The Open Road goes to the used-car lot.

"Where is the nation you promised?
These houses built of wood sustain
Colossal snows,
And the light above the street is sick to death.

"As for the people — see how they neglect you!
Only a poet pauses to read the inscription."

"I am here," he answered.
"It seems you have found me out.
Yet, did I not warn you that it was Myself
I advertised? Were my words not sufficiently plain?

"I gave no prescriptions,
And those who have taken my moods for prophecies
Mistake the matter."
Then, vastly amused — "Why do you reproach me?
I freely confess I am wholly disreputable.
Yet I am happy, because you have found me out."

A crocodile in wrinkled metal loafing . . .

Then all the realtors,
Pickpockets, salesmen, and the actors performing
Official scenarios,
Turned a deaf ear, for they had contracted
American dreams.

But the man who keeps a store on a lonely road,
And the housewife who knows she's dumb,
And the earth, are relieved.

All that grave weight of America
Cancelled! Like Greece and Rome.
The future in ruins!

The castles, the prisons, the cathedrals
Unbuilding, and roses
Blossoming from the stones that are not there . . .

The clouds are lifting from the high Sierras,
The Bay mists clearing.
And the angel in the gate, the flowering plum,
Dances like Italy, imagining red.

AMERICAN POETRY

Whatever it is, it must have
A stomach that can digest
Rubber, coal, uranium, moons, poems.

Like the shark, it contains a shoe.
It must swim for miles through the desert
Uttering cries that are almost human.

AFTER MIDNIGHT

The dark streets are deserted,
With only a drugstore glowing
Softly, like a sleeping body;

With one white, naked bulb
In the back, that shines
On suicides and abortions.

Who lives in these dark houses?
I am suddenly aware
I might live here myself.

The garage man returns
And puts the change in my hand,
Counting the singles carefully.

LOUIS SIMPSON

LUMINOUS NIGHT

I love the dark race of poets,
And yet there is also happiness.
Happiness . . .

If I can stand it, I can stand anything.
Luminous night, let fall your pearls!
Wind, toss the sodden boughs!

Then let the birch trees shine
Like crystal. Light the boughs!
We can live here, Cristina,

We can live here,
In this house, among these trees,
This world so many have left.

AMERICAN DREAMS

In dreams my life came toward me,
my loves that were slender as gazelles.
But America also dreams. . . .
Dream, you are flying over Russia,
dream, you are falling in Asia.

As I look down the street
on a typical sunny day in California
it is my house that is burning
and my dear ones that lie in the gutter
as the American army enters.

Every day I wake far away
from my life, in a foreign country.
These people are speaking a strange language.
It is strange to me
and strange, I think, even to themselves.

LOUIS SIMPSON

THE SILENT PIANO

We have lived like civilized people.
O ruins, traditions!

And we have seen the barbarians,
breakers of sculpture and glass.

And now we talk of "the inner life,"
and I ask myself, where is it?

Not here, in these streets and houses,
so I think it must be found

in indolence, pure indolence,
an ocean of darkness,

in silence, an arm of the moon,
a hand that enters slowly.

*

I am reminded of a story
Camus tells, of a man in prison camp.

He had carved a piano keyboard
with a nail on a piece of wood.

And sat there playing the piano.
This music was made entirely of silence.

SACRED OBJECTS

I am taking part in a great experiment —
whether writers can live peacefully in the suburbs
and not be bored to death.

LOUIS SIMPSON

As Whitman said, an American muse
installed amid the kitchen ware.
And we have wonderful household appliances . . .
now tell me about the poets.

Where are your children, Lucina?
Since Eliot died and Pound
has become . . . an authority,
chef d'école au lieu d'être tout de go,

I have been listening to the whispers
of U.S. Steel and Anaconda:
'In a little while it will stiffen . . .
blown into the road,

drifting with the foam of chemicals.'

2

The light that shines through the *Leaves*
is clear: 'to form individuals.'

A swamp where the seabirds brood.
When the psyche is still and the soul does nothing,
a Sound, with shining tidal pools and channels.

And the kingdom is within you . . .
the hills and all the streams
running west to the Mississippi.
There the roads are lined with timothy
and the clouds are tangled with the haystacks.

Your loves are a line of birch trees.
When the wind flattens the grass, it
shines, and a butterfly
writes dark lines on the air.

There are your sacred objects,
the wings and gazing eyes
of the life you really have.

3

Where then shall we meet?

Where you left me.

At the drive-in restaurant . . .
the fields on either side covered with stubble,
an odor of gasoline and burning asphalt,
glare on tinted glass, chrome-plated hubcaps and bumpers.

I came out, wiping my hands
on my apron, to take your orders.
Thin hands, streaked with mustard,
give us a hot-dog,
give us a Pepsi-Cola.

Listening to the monotonous grasshoppers
for years I have concentrated on the moment.

And at night when the passing headlights hurl
shadows flitting across the wall,
I sit in a window, combing my hair
day in day out.

THE PEOPLE NEXT DOOR

He isn't a religious man.
So instead of going to church
on Sunday they go to sea.

They cruise up and down,
see the ferry coming from Bridgeport
to Green Harbor, and going back
from Green Harbor to Bridgeport . . .
and all the boats there are.
The occasional silent fisherman . . .
When the kids start to get restless
he heads back to shore.

I hear them returning
worn out and glad to be home.
This is as close to being happy
as a family ever gets.
I envy their content. And yet
I've done that too, and know
that no hobby or activity
distracts one from thinking
forever. Every human being
is an intellectual more or less.

I too was a family man.
It was a phase I had to go through.
I remember tenting in the Sierras,
getting up at dawn to fly cast.

I remember my young son
almost being blown off the jetty
in Lochalsh. Only the suitcase
he was carrying held him down.
The same, at Viareggio,
followed me into the sea
and was almost swept away by the current.

These are the scenes I recall
rather than Christmas and Thanksgiving.
My life as the father of a family
seems to have been a series
of escapes, not to mention illnesses,
confrontations with teachers,
administrators, police.
Flaubert said, "They're in the right,"
looking at a bourgeois family,
and then went back happily
to his dressing gown and pipe.

Yes, I believe in the family . . .
next door. I rejoice
at their incomings and outgoings.
I am present when Betty
goes out on her first date.
I hear about Joey's being chosen

for the team. I survive the takeover
of the business, and the bad scare
at the doctor's.
I laugh with them that laugh
and mourn with them that mourn.

I see their lights, and hear a murmur
of voices, from house to house.

It gives me a strange feeling
to think how far they've come
from some far world to this,
bending their necks to the yoke
of affection.

      And that one day,
with a few simple words
and flowers to keep them company
they'll return once more to the silence
out there, beyond the stars.

RIVERSIDE DRIVE

I have been staring at a sentence
for fifteen minutes. The mind
was not made for social science.

I take my overcoat and go.

Night has fallen on Riverside Drive . . .
the sign for Spry shining
across the Hudson: "Spry for Frying****
for Baking."

I am thinking of Rilke
and "Who if I cried would hear me
among the angelic orders?"

LOUIS SIMPSON

It seems that we are here to say
names like "Spry" and "Riverside Drive" . . .
to carry the names of places
and things with us, into the night

glimmering with stars and constellations.

W. D. Snodgrass

APRIL INVENTORY

The green catalpa tree has turned
All white; the cherry blooms once more.
In one whole year I haven't learned
A blessed thing they pay you for.
The blossoms snow down in my hair;
The trees and I will soon be bare.

The trees have more than I to spare.
The sleek, expensive girls I teach,
Younger and pinker every year,
Bloom gradually out of reach.
The pear tree lets its petals drop
Like dandruff on a tabletop.

The girls have grown so young by now
I have to nudge myself to stare.
This year they smile and mind me how
My teeth are falling with my hair.
In thirty years I may not get
Younger, shrewder, or out of debt.

The tenth time, just a year ago,
I made myself a little list
Of all the things I'd ought to know,
Then told my parents, analyst,
And everyone who's trusted me
I'd be substantial, presently.

I haven't read one book about
A book or memorized one plot.
Or found a mind I did not doubt.
I learned one date. And then forgot.
And one by one the solid scholars
Get the degrees, the jobs, the dollars.

And smile above their starchy collars.
I taught my classes Whitehead's notions;
One lovely girl, a song of Mahler's.
Lacking a source-book or promotions,

I showed one child the colors of
A luna moth and how to love.

I taught myself to name my name,
To bark back, loosen love and crying;
To ease my woman so she came,
To ease an old man who was dying.
I have not learned how often I
Can win, can love, but choose to die.

I have not learned there is a lie
Love shall be blonder, slimmer, younger;
That my equivocating eye
Loves only by my body's hunger;
That I have forces, true to feel,
Or that the lovely world is real.

While scholars speak authority
And wear their ulcers on their sleeves,
My eyes in spectacles shall see
These trees procure and spend their leaves.
There is a value underneath
The gold and silver in my teeth.

Though trees turn bare and girls turn wives,
We shall afford our costly seasons;
There is a gentleness survives
That will outspeak and has its reasons.
There is a loveliness exists,
Preserves us, not for specialists.

from HEART'S NEEDLE

9

I get numb and go in
though the dry ground will not hold
the few dry swirls of snow
and it must not be very cold.
A friend asks how you've been
and I don't know

or see much right to ask.
Or what use it could be to know.
   In three months since you came
the leaves have fallen and the snow;
your pictures pinned above my desk
   seem much the same.

   Somehow I come to find
myself upstairs in the third floor
   museum's halls,
walking to kill my time once more
among the enduring and resigned
   stuffed animals,

   where, through a century's
caprice, displacement and
   known treachery between
its wars, they hear some old command
and in their peaceable kingdoms freeze
   to this still scene,

   Nature Morte. Here
by the door, its guardian,
   the patchwork dodo stands
where you and your stepsister ran
laughing and pointing. Here, last year,
   you pulled my hands

   and had your first, worst quarrel,
so toys were put up on your shelves.
   Here in the first glass cage
the little bobcats arch themselves,
still practicing their snarl
   of constant rage.

   The bison, here, immense,
shoves at his calf, brow to brow,
   and looks it in the eye
to see what is it thinking now.
I forced you to obedience;
   I don't know why.

   Still the lean lioness
beyond them, on her jutting ledge

of shale and desert shrub,
stands watching always at the edge,
stands hard and tanned and envious
    above her cub;

    with horns locked in tall heather,
two great Olympian Elk stand bound,
    fixed in their lasting hate
till hunger brings them both to ground.
Whom equal weakness binds together
    none shall separate.

    Yet separate in the ocean
of broken ice, the white bear reels
    beyond the leathery groups
of scattered, drab Arctic seals
arrested here in violent motion
    like Napoleon's troops.

    Our states have stood so long
At war, shaken with hate and dread,
    they are paralyzed at bay;
once we were out of reach, we said,
we would grow reasonable and strong.
    Some other day.

    Like the cold men of Rome,
we have won costly fields to sow
    in salt, our only seed.
Nothing but injury will grow.
I write you only the bitter poems
    that you can't read.

    Onan who would not breed
a child to take his brother's bread
    and be his brother's birth,
rose up and left his lawful bed,
went out and spilled his seed
    in the cold earth.

    I stand by the unborn,
by putty-colored children curled
    in jars of alcohol,

that waken to no other world,
unchanging where no eye shall mourn.
        I see the caul

        that wrapped a kitten, dead.
I see the branching, doubled throat
    of a two-headed foal;
I see the hydrocephalic goat;
here is the curled and swollen head,
        there, the burst skull;

    skin of a limbless calf;
a horse's foetus, mummified;
    mounted and joined forever,
the Siamese twin dogs that ride
belly to belly, half and half,
        that none shall sever.

    I walk among the growths,
by gangrenous tissue, goitre, cysts,
    by fistulas and cancers,
where the malignancy man loathes
is held suspended and persists.
        And I don't know the answers.

    The window's turning white.
The world moves like a diseased heart
    packed with ice and snow.
Three months now we have been apart
less than a mile. I cannot fight
        or let you go.

THE MOTHER

She stands in the dead center like a star;
They form around her like her satellites
Taking her energies, her heat, light
And massive attraction on their paths, however far.

Born of her own flesh; still, she feels them drawn
Into the outer cold by dark forces;

They are in love with suffering and perversion,
With the community of pain. Thinking them gone,

Out of her reach, she is consoled by evil
In neighbors, children, the world she cannot change,
That lightless universe where they range
Out of the comforts of her disapproval.

If evil did not exist, she would create it
To die in righteousness, her martyrdom
To that sweet dominion they have bolted from.
Then, at last, she can think that she is hated

And is content. Things can decay, break,
Spoil themselves; who cares? She'll gather the debris
With loving tenderness to give them; she
Will weave a labyrinth of waste, wreckage

And hocus-pocus; leave free no fault
Or cornerhole outside those lines of force
Where she and only she can thread a course.
All else in her grasp grows clogged and halts.

Till one by one, the areas of her brain
Switch off and she has filled all empty spaces;
Now she hallucinates in their right places
Their after-images, reversed and faint.

And the drawn strands of love, spun in her mind,
Turn dark and cluttered, precariously hung
With the black shapes of her mates, her sapless young,
Where she moves by habit, hungering and blind.

"AFTER EXPERIENCE TAUGHT ME . . ."

After experience taught me that all the ordinary
Surroundings of social life are futile and vain;

I'm going to show you something very
Ugly: someday, it might save your life.

Seeing that none of the things I feared contain
In themselves anything either good or bad

What if you get caught without a knife;
Nothing — even a loop of piano wire;

Excepting only in the effect they had
Upon my mind, I resolved to inquire

Take the first two fingers of this hand;
Fork them out — kind of a "V for Victory" —

Whether there might be something whose discovery
Would grant me supreme, unending happiness.

And jam them into the eyes of your enemy.
You have to do this hard. Very hard. Then press

No virtue can be thought to have priority
Over this endeavor to preserve one's being.

Both fingers down around the cheekbone
And setting your foot high into the chest

No man can desire to act rightly, to be blessed,
To live rightly, without simultaneously

You must call up every strength you own
And you can rip off the whole facial mask.

Wishing to be, to act, to live. He must ask
First, in other words, to actually exist.

And you, whiner, who wastes your time
Dawdling over the remorseless earth,
What evil, what unspeakable crime
Have you made your life worth?

W. D. SNODGRASS

from THE FÜHRER BUNKER

Eva Braun

— 22 April, 1945.

(Hitler's mistress received no public recognition and often felt badly neglected. Her small revenges included singing American songs, her favorite being "Tea for Two." Having chosen to die with him in the bunker, she appeared quite serene during the last days.)

   Tea for two
And two for tea

             I ought to feel ashamed
Feeling such joy. Behaving like a spoiled child!
So fulfilled. This is a very serious matter.
All of them have come here to die. And they grieve.
I have come here to die. If this is dying,
Why else did I ever live?

                     Me for you
                  And you for me

   We ought never to flaunt our good luck
In the face of anyone less fortunate —
These live fools mourning already
For their own deaths; these dead fools
Who believe they can go on living . . .

And you for me
  Alone.

   Who out of all of them, officers, ministers,
These liars that despise me, these empty
Women that envy me — so they hate me —
Who else of them dares to disobey Him
As I dared? I have defied Him to His face
And He has honored me.

                 We will raise
               A family

They sneer at me — at my worrying about
Frau Goebbels' children, that I make fairytales
For them, that we play at war. Is our war
More lost if I console these poor trapped rabbits?
These children He would not give me . . .

A boy for you
A girl for me

They sneer that I should bring
Fine furniture down this dank hole. Speer
Built this bed for me. Where I have slept
Beside our Chief. Who else should have it?
My furs, my best dress to my little sister —
They would sneer even at this; yet
What else can I give her?

Can't you see
How happy we would be?

Or to the baby
She will bear Fegelein? Lechering dolt!
Well, I have given her her wedding
As if it was my own. And she will have
My diamonds, my watch. The little things you
Count on, things that see you through your
Missing life, the life that stood you up.

Nobody near us
To see us or hear us

I have it all. They are all gone, the others —
The Valkyrie; and the old rich bitch Bechstein;
Geli above all. No, the screaming mobs above all.
They are all gone now; He has left them all.
No one but me and the love-struck secretaries —
Traudl, Daran — who gave up years ago.

No friends or relations
On weekend vacations

That I, above all, am chosen — even I
Must find that strange. I who was always
Disobedient, rebellious — smoked in the dining car,

Wore rouge whenever he said I shouldn't.
When he ordered that poor Chancellor Schussnig
Was to starve, I sent in food.

We won't have it known, dear,
That we own a telephone, dear.

> I who joined the Party, I who took Him
> For my lover just to spite my old stiff father —
> Den Alten Fritz! — and those stupid nuns.
> I ran my teachers crazy, and my mother — I
> Held out even when she stuck my head in water.
> He shall have none but me.

> > *Day will break*
> > *And you will wake*

> We cannot make it through another month;
> We follow the battles now on a subway map.
> Even if the Russians pulled back —
> His hand trembles, the whole left side
> Staggers. His marvellous eyes are failing.
> We go out to the sunlight less each day. We live
> Like flies sucked up in a sweeper bag.

And start to bake
A sugar cake

> He forbade me to leave Berchtesgaden,
> Forbade me to come here. I tricked
> My keepers, stole my own car, my driver Jung.
> He tried to scold me; He was too
> Proud of me. Today He ordered me to leave,
> To go back to the mountain. I refused.
> I have refused to save my own life and He,
> In public, He kissed me on the mouth.

> > *For me to take*
> > *For all the boys to see.*

Once more I have won, won out over Him
Who spoke one word and whole populations vanished.
Until today, in public, we were good friends.
He is mine. No doubt

I did only what He wanted; no doubt
I should resent that. In the face
Of such fulfillment? In the face
Of so much joy?

> *Picture you*
> *Upon my knee;*
> *Tea for two*
> *And two for tea* . . .

Dr. Joseph Goebbels

— 1 May, 1945; 1800 hours.

(The day after Hitler's death, Goebbels and his wife climbed the steps into the garden where both committed suicide.)

Say goodbye to the help, the ranks
Of Stalin-bait. Give too much thanks
To Naumann — Magda's lover: we
Thank him for *all* his loyalty.
Schwaegermann; Rach. After a while
Turn back to them with a sad smile:
We'll save them trouble — no one cares
Just now to carry us upstairs.

Turn away; check your manicure;
Pull on your gloves. Take time; make sure
The hat brim curves though the hat's straight.
Give her your arm. Let the fools wait;
They act like they've someplace to go.
Take the stairs, now. Self-control. Slow.
A slight limp; just enough to see,
Pass on, and infect history.

The rest is silence. Left like sperm
In a stranger's gut, waiting its term,
Each thought, each step lies; the roots spread.
They'll believe in us when we're dead.
When we took "Red Berlin" we found
We always worked best underground.
So; the vile body turns to spirit
That speaks soundlessly. They'll hear it.

from SNOW SONGS

i.

one. now another. one
more. some again; then done.
though others run
down your windshield, when
up ahead a sudden
swirl and squall comes on
like moths, mayflies in a swarm
against your lights, a storm
of small fry, seeds, unknown
species, populations. every one
particular and special; each one
melting, breaking, hurling on
into the blank black. soon,
never to be seen again.
most never seen.
all, gone.

iii.

White out; white out; so
    that the landscape's ledger
        balances again.
On the hill, the white-tailed deer's
    remains are spirited
        away like laundered funds:
flesh, pelt and all
    the inner workings nibbled
        down, salted away inside
the general, unmentionable,
    unseen economy of the woods.
        Bones, like the broken branches,
soften, sink back down
    in ground that sent them
        out to reconnoitre.
Soon this whole, broad
    Stalingrad will be no more
        than scattered fading photographs,

just some ageing soldiers'
    recollections till at last
        all thought dies down to the
perfection of the blank page
    and the lighted
        screen that will flick off.

iv.

The leading colonists of summer,
Carriers of what we called progress,
    Uplift, or flat success,
Have gone south taking their plunder.
    All crucial witnesses

Are safely hushed-up underground
Or live on on the season's scraps.
    Thick snow blots out the maps;
The woods, the air, the memory's found
    Compromised by gaps.

We're left with dwindled and diminished
Hopes, left with those hangers on
    Too listless to get gone,
With long abandoned, half-finished
    Plans, conclusions drawn.

vi.

Now snow lies level
    with the windowsills. Along
the thruway, traffic
    like fresh water flows
between banks ten feet
    above our heads. Still
it sifts down slow
    as infinite, small
skeletons of diatoms drift,
    settling through the salt seas,
falling only inches year
    by year, some 20,000 species,

geometric, crystalline, no
    two shells alike, covering
the sea's floor hundreds
    of feet deep. Now turn
the radio up louder; try to
    catch the local dialect.

vii.

8,000,000 *alleluias* or
lace paper valentines, these
bitsy webs and doilies —
such dear wee scallops
on each twig, a sweet
tiara for each flower. Oh,
vast crochet hooks of the
skies, God's bobbin mills,

tat us this day our peekaboo
bra and scanties; glamorize
the gamey soiled loins of
one more incontinent season;
fall, plastic popcorn, pack
and seal the year up, draw
this dull white coverlet
over the patient's eyes.

viii.

Leaving the snow
    bank, your boot leaves
        a fossil print — an
emptiness remains. Just so,
    across the field you've made
        a trail of absences.
    Still the snow
falls — as a clean sheet smooths
        your shape out of the bed
    you don't go back to.
        You are the missing
    tooth, the one place

at the table, lost
        wax from the casting — though,
    long as they last,
these chicken scratchings hold
        the voice unspoken on
    the finished page as under
        plaster hardening,
a fading face.

Gary Snyder

RIPRAP

Lay down these words
Before your mind like rocks.
           placed solid, by hands
In choice of place, set
Before the body of the mind
           in space and time:
Solidity of bark, leaf, or wall
           riprap of things:
Cobble of milky way,
           straying planets,
These poems, people,
           lost ponies with
Dragging saddles —
           and rocky sure-foot trails.
The worlds like an endless
           four-dimensional
Game of Go.
           ants and pebbles
In the thin loam, each rock a word
           a creek-washed stone
Granite: ingrained
           with torment of fire and weight
Crystal and sediment linked hot
           all change, in thoughts,
As well as things.

MILTON BY FIRELIGHT

"O hell, what do mine eyes
           with grief behold?"
Working with an old
Singlejack miner, who can sense
The vein and cleavage
In the very guts of rock, can
Blast granite, build
Switchbacks that last for years

Under the beat of snow, thaw, mule-hooves.
What use, Milton, a silly story
Of our lost general parents,
   eaters of fruit?

The Indian, the chainsaw boy,
And a string of six mules
Came riding down to camp
Hungry for tomatoes and green apples.
Sleeping in saddle-blankets
Under a bright night-sky
Han River slantwise by morning.
Jays squall
Coffee boils

In ten thousand years the Sierras
Will be dry and dead, home of the scorpion.
Ice-scratched slabs and bent trees.

No paradise, no fall,
Only the weathering land
The wheeling sky,
Man, with his Satan
Scouring the chaos of the mind.
Oh Hell!

Fire down
Too dark to read, miles from a road
The bell-mare clangs in the meadow
That packed dirt for a fill-in
Scrambling through loose rocks
On an old trail
All of a summer's day.

Piute Creek, August 1955

HAY FOR THE HORSES

He had driven half the night
From far down San Joaquin
Through Mariposa, up the

GARY SNYDER

Dangerous mountain roads,
And pulled in at eight a.m.
With his big truckload of hay
      behind the barn.
With winch and ropes and hooks
We stacked the bales up clean
To splintery redwood rafters
High in the dark, flecks of alfalfa
Whirling through shingle-cracks of light,
Itch of haydust in the
      sweaty shirt and shoes.
At lunchtime under Black oak
Out in the hot corral,
— The old mare nosing lunchpails,
Grasshoppers crackling in the weeds —
"I'm sixty-eight" he said,
"I first bucked hay when I was seventeen.
I thought, that day I started,
I sure would hate to do this all my life.
And dammit, that's just what
I've gone and done."

VAPOR TRAILS

Twin streaks twice higher than cumulus,
Precise plane icetracks in the vertical blue
Cloud-flaked light-shot shadow-arcing
Field of all future war, edging off to space.

Young expert U.S. pilots waiting
The day of criss-cross rockets
And white blossoming smoke of bomb,
The air world torn and staggered for these
Specks of brushy land and ant-hill towns —

    I stumble on the cobble rockpath,
Passing through temples,
Watching for two-leaf pine
      — spotting that design.

SONG OF THE TASTE

Eating the living germs of grasses
Eating the ova of large birds

   the fleshy sweetness packed
   around the sperm of swaying trees

The muscles of the flanks and thighs of
      soft-voiced cows
   the bounce in the lamb's leap
   the swish in the ox's tail

Eating roots grown swoll
     inside the soil

Drawing on life of living
   clustered points of light spun
      out of space
hidden in the grape.

Eating each other's seed
      eating
  ah, each other.

Kissing the lover in the mouth of bread:
     lip to lip.

I WENT INTO THE MAVERICK BAR

I went into the Maverick Bar
In Farmington, New Mexico.
And drank double shots of bourbon
         backed with beer.
My long hair was tucked up under a cap
I'd left the earring in the car.

Two cowboys did horseplay
       by the pool tables,

A waitress asked us
               where are you from?
a country-and-western band began to play
"We don't smoke Marijuana in Muskokie"
And with the next song,
               a couple began to dance.

They held each other like in High School dances
               in the fifties;
I recalled when I worked in the woods
               and the bars of Madras, Oregon.
That short-haired joy and roughness —
               America — your stupidity.
I could almost love you again.

We left — onto the freeway shoulders —
               under the tough old stars —
In the shadow of bluffs
               I came back to myself,
To the real work, to
               "What is to be done."

THE BATH

Washing Kai in the sauna,
The kerosene lantern set on a box
    outside the ground-level window,
Lights up the edge of the iron stove and the
    washtub down on the slab
Steaming air and crackle of waterdrops
    brushed by on the pile of rocks on top
He stands in warm water
Soap all over the smooth of his thigh and stomach
    "Gary don't soap my hair!"
    — his eye-sting fear —
    the soapy hand feeling
    through and around the globes and curves of his body
    up in the crotch,
And washing-tickling out the scrotum, little anus,
    his penis curving up and getting hard
    as I pull back skin and try to wash it

GARY SNYDER

Laughing and jumping, flinging arms around,
    I squat all naked too,
                is this our body?

Sweating and panting in the stove-steam hot-stone
    cedar-planking wooden bucket water-splashing
    kerosene lantern-flicker wind-in-the-pines-out
    sierra forest ridges night —
Masa comes in, letting fresh cool air
    sweep down from the door
    a deep sweet breath
And she tips him over gripping neatly, one knee down
    her hair falling hiding one whole side of
    shoulder, breast, and belly,
Washes deftly Kai's head-hair
    as he gets mad and yells —
The body of my lady, the winding valley spine,
    the space between the thighs I reach through,
    cup her curving vulva arch and hold it from behind,
    a soapy tickle   a hand of grail
The gates of Awe
That open back a turning double-mirror world of
    wombs in wombs, in rings,
    that start in music,
                is this our body?

The hidden place of seed
The veins net flow across the ribs, that gathers
    milk and peaks up in a nipple — fits
    our mouth —
The sucking milk from this our body sends through
    jolts of light; the son, the father,
    sharing mother's joy
That brings a softness to the flower of the awesome
    open curling lotus gate I cup and kiss
As Kai laughs at his mother's breast he now is weaned
    from, we
    wash each other,
                this our body

Kai's little scrotum up close to his groin,
    the seed still tucked away, that moved from us to him
In flows that lifted with the same joys forces

as his nursing Masa later,
    playing with her breast,
Or me within her,
Or him emerging,

                        this is our body:

Clean, and rinsed, and sweating more, we stretch
        out on the redwood benches hearts all beating
Quiet to the simmer of the stove,
        the scent of cedar
And then turn over,
        murmuring gossip of the grasses,
        talking firewood,
Wondering how Gen's napping, how to bring him in
        soon wash him too —
These boys who love their mother
        who loves men, who passes on
        her sons to other women;

The cloud across the sky. The windy pines.
        the trickle gurgle in the swampy meadow

    this is our body.

Fire inside and boiling water on the stove
We sigh and slide ourselves down from the benches
        wrap the babies, step outside,

black night & all the stars.

Pour cold water on the back and thighs
Go in the house — stand steaming by the center fire
Kai scampers on the sheepskin
Gen standing hanging on and shouting,

"Bao! bao! bao! bao! bao!"

This is our body. Drawn up crosslegged by the flames
        drinking icy water
        hugging babies, kissing bellies,

Laughing on the Great Earth

Come out from the bath.

GARY SNYDER

AS FOR POETS

As for poets
The Earth Poets
Who write small poems,
Need help from no man.

The Air Poets
Play out the swiftest gales
And sometimes loll in the eddies.
Poem after poem,
Curling back on the same thrust.

At fifty below
Fuel oil won't flow
And propane stays in the tank.
Fire Poets
Burn at absolute zero
Fossil love pumped back up.

The first
Water Poet
Stayed down six years.
He was covered with seaweed.
The life in his poem
Left millions of tiny
Different tracks
Criss-crossing through the mud.

With the Sun and Moon
In his belly,
The Space Poet
Sleeps.
No end to the sky —
But his poems,
Like wild geese,
Fly off the edge.

A Mind Poet
Stays in the house.
The house is empty
And it has no walls.

The poem
Is seen from all sides,
Everywhere,
At once.

SOY SAUCE

for Bruce Boyd and Holly Tornheim

Standing on a stepladder
          up under hot ceiling
tacking on wire net for plaster,
a day's work helping Bruce and Holly on their house,
I catch a sour salt smell and come back
          down the ladder.

"Deer lick it nights" she says,
and shows me the frame of the window she's planing,
clear redwood, but dark, with a smell.
"Scored a broken-up, two-thousand-gallon redwood
soy sauce tank from a company went out of business
down near San Jose."

Out in the yard the staves are stacked:
I lean over, sniff them, ah! it's like the Shinshu miso,
the darker saltier miso paste of the Nagano
uplands, central main island, Japan —
it's like Shinshu pickles!

I see in mind my friend Shimizu Yasushi and me,
one October years ago, trudging through days of snow
crossing the Japan Alps and descending
the last night, to a farmhouse,
taking a late hot bath in the dark — and eating
          a bowl of chill miso radish pickles,
               nothing ever so good!

Back here, hot summer sunshine dusty yard,
          hammer in hand.

But I know how it tastes
      to lick those window frames
    in the dark,
          the deer.

AXE HANDLES

One afternoon the last week in April
Showing Kai how to throw a hatchet
One-half turn and it sticks in a stump.
He recalls the hatchet-head
Without a handle, in the shop
And go gets it, and wants it for his own.
A broken-off axe handle behind the door
Is long enough for a hatchet,
We cut it to length and take it
With the hatchet head
And working hatchet, to the wood block.
There I begin to shape the old handle
With the hatchet, and the phrase
First learned from Ezra Pound
Rings in my ears!
"When making an axe handle
      the pattern is not far off."
And I say this to Kai
"Look: We'll shape the handle
By checking the handle
Of the axe we cut with —"
And he sees. And I hear it again:
It's in Lu Ji's *Wên Fu*, fourth century
A.D. "Essay on Literature" — in the
Preface: "In making the handle
Of an axe
By cutting wood with an axe
The model is indeed near at hand."
My teacher Shih-hsiang Chen
Translated that and taught it years ago
And I see: Pound was an axe,
Chen was an axe, I am an axe

And my son a handle, soon
To be shaping again, model
And tool, craft of culture,
How we go on.

© Barbara Stafford Wilson

William Stafford

AT THE BOMB TESTING SITE

At noon in the desert a panting lizard
waited for history, its elbows tense,
watching the curve of a particular road
as if something might happen.

It was looking at something farther off
than people could see, an important scene
acted in stone for little selves
at the flute end of consequences.

There was just a continent without much on it
under a sky that never cared less.
Ready for a change, the elbows waited.
The hands gripped hard on the desert.

TRAVELING THROUGH THE DARK

Traveling through the dark I found a deer
dead on the edge of the Wilson River road.
It is usually best to roll them into the canyon:
that road is narrow; to swerve might make more dead.

By glow of the tail-light I stumbled back of the car
and stood by the heap, a doe, a recent killing;
she had stiffened already, almost cold.
I dragged her off; she was large in the belly.

My fingers touching her side brought me the reason —
her side was warm; her fawn lay there waiting,
alive, still, never to be born.
Beside that mountain road I hesitated.

The car aimed ahead its lowered parking lights;
under the hood purred the steady engine.
I stood in the glare of the warm exhaust turning red;
around our group I could hear the wilderness listen.

I thought hard for us all — my only swerving —,
then pushed her over the edge into the river.

VOCATION

This dream the world is having about itself
includes a trace on the plains of the Oregon trail,
a groove in the grass my father showed us all
one day while meadowlarks were trying to tell
something better about to happen.

I dreamed the trace to the mountains, over the hills,
and there a girl who belonged wherever she was.
But then my mother called us back to the car:
she was afraid; she always blamed the place,
the time, anything my father planned.

Now both of my parents, the long line through the plain,
the meadowlarks, the sky, the world's whole dream
remain, and I hear him say while I stand between the two,
helpless, both of them part of me:
"Your job is to find what the world is trying to be."

MY FATHER: OCTOBER 1942

He picks up what he thinks is
a road map, and it is
his death: he holds it easily, and
nothing can take it from his firm hand.
The pulse in his thumb on the map
says, "1:19 P.M. next Tuesday, at
this intersection." And an ambulance
begins to throb while his face looks tired.

Any time anyone may pick up something
so right that he can't put it down:
that is the problem for all who travel — they
fatally own whatever is really theirs,

and that is the inner thread, the lock,
what can hold. If it is to be, nothing breaks
it. Millions of observers guess all the
time, but each person, once, can say, "Sure."

Then he's no longer an observer. He isn't right,
or wrong. He just wins or loses.

ACROSS KANSAS

My family slept those level miles
but like a bell rung deep till dawn
I drove down an aisle of sound,
nothing real but in the bell,
past the town where I was born.

Once you cross a land like that
you own your face more: what the light
struck told a self; every rock
denied all the rest of the world.
We stopped at Sharon Springs and ate —

My state still dark, my dream too long to tell.

A FAMILY TURN

All her Kamikaze friends admired my aunt,
their leader, charmed in vinegar,
a woman who could blaze with such white blasts
as Lawrence's that lit Arabia.
Her mean opinions bent her hatpins.

We'd take a ride in her old car
that ripped like Sherman through society:
Main Street's oases sheltered no one
when she pulled up at Thirty-first
and whirled that Ford for another charge.

We swept headlines from under rugs, names
all over town, which I learned her way, by heart,
and blazed with love that burns because it's real.
With a turn that's our family's own,
she'd say, "Our town is not the same" —

Pause — "And it's never been."

AN INTRODUCTION TO SOME POEMS

Look: no one ever promised for sure
that we would sing. We have decided
to moan. In a strange dance that
we don't understand till we do it, we
have to carry on.

Just as in sleep you have to dream
the exact dream to round out your life,
so we have to live that dream into stories
and hold them close at you, close at the
edge we share, to be right.

We find it an awful thing to meet people,
serious or not, who have turned into vacant
effective people, so far lost that they
won't believe their own feelings
enough to follow them out.

The authentic is a line from one thing
along to the next; it interests us.
Strangely, it relates to what works,
but is not quite the same. It never
swerves for revenge,

Or profit, or fame: it holds
together something more than the world,
this line. And we are your wavery
efforts at following it. Are you coming?
Good: now it is time.

WILLIAM STAFFORD

REPORT FROM A FAR PLACE

Making these word things to
step on across the world, I
could call them snowshoes.

They creak, sag, bend, but
hold, over the great deep cold,
and they turn up at the toes.

In war or city or camp
they could save your life;
you can muse them by the fire.

Be careful, though: they
burn, or don't burn, in their own
strange way, when you say them.

THE STICK IN THE FOREST

A stick in the forest that pointed
where the center of the universe is
broke in the wind that started
its exact note of mourning
when Buddha's mother died.

Around us then a new crystal
began to form itself, and men —
awakened by what happened —
held precious whatever breathed:
we are all gestures that the world makes.

"Be, be," Buddha said.

TEMPORARY FACTS

That look you had, Agnes, was a temporary fact.
Probably by now Time has it back.
From spiral nebulae I call it here now.

Through the trance of high school you pass along the hall.
Lockers clang the hours; you pass windows.
A Christmas candle shines on your hair.

On spellbound evenings you call your brother home,
coming toward the streetlight through shadows of the elm.
Shadows touch your mouth when you say a name.

All of these things were temporary facts.
Only for an instant Time gives them back.
In spiral nebulae a shadow goes on.

ASSURANCE

You will never be alone, you hear so deep
a sound when autumn comes. Yellow
pulls across the hills and thrums,
or the silence after lightning before it says
its names — and then the clouds' wide-mouthed
apologies. You were aimed from birth:
you will never be alone. Rain
will come, a gutter filled, an Amazon,
long aisles — you never heard so deep a sound,
moss on rock, and years. You turn your head —
that's what the silence meant: *you're not alone.*
The whole wide world pours down.

ODE TO GARLIC

Sudden, it comes for you
in the cave of yourself where you know
and are lifted by important events.

Say you are dining and it happens:
soaring like an eagle, you are
pierced by a message from the midst of life:

Memory — what holds the days together — touches
your tongue. It is from deep in the earth
and it reaches out kindly, saying, "Hello, Old Friend."

It makes us alike, all offspring of powerful
forces, part of one great embrace of democracy,
united across every boundary.

You walk out generously, giving it back
in a graceful wave, what you've been given.
Like a child again, you breathe on the world, and it shines.

ANSWERERS

There are songs too wide for sound. There are quiet
places where something stopped a long time
ago and the days began to open
their mouths toward nothing but the sky. We live
in place of the many who stir only
if we listen, only because the living
live and call out. I am ready
as all of us are who wake at night:
we become rooms for whatever almost
is. It speaks in us, trying. And even if
only by a note like this, we answer.

THINGS THAT HAPPEN
WHERE THERE AREN'T ANY PEOPLE

It's cold on Lakeside Road
with no one traveling. At its turn
on the hill an old sign sags and
finally goes down. The traveler rain
walks back and forth over its victim
flat on the mud.

You don't have to have any people when
sunlight stands on the rocks or gloom
comes following the great dragged clouds
over a huddle of hills. Plenty of
things happen in deserted places, maybe
dust counting millions of its little worlds
or the slow arrival of deep dark.

And out there in the country a rock has been
waiting to be mentioned for thousands of years.
Every day its shadow leans, crouches,
then walks away eastward in one measured stride
exactly right for its way of being. To reach
for that rock we have the same reasons
that explorers always have for their journeys:
because it is far, because there aren't any people.

THE EARLY ONES

They kept it all level. And low. Even
little stones they swept away. They went on
for miles, a bend at a hill, then a bend
back. Around them birch forest mostly
or openings for lakes, and a few hidden lakes.

They carved on the rocks — these are what stay,
hardly worn at all if sheltered, some
broken and all of them gray, that distant
gray that clouds have, or storms that moan
at the coast. They carved and went away.

Level and low. And the carved things. And one
more thing: when you look around and listen,
the last thing is there. You hear it wait.
Because they were early and quiet, and because
of that last bend, and because of the gray —

There is something left. We'll find it some day.

WILLIAM STAFFORD

NOTICE WHAT THIS POEM IS NOT DOING

The light along the hills in the morning
comes down slowly, naming the trees
white, then coasting the ground for stones to nominate.

Notice what this poem is not doing.

A house, a house, a barn, the old
quarry, where the river shrugs —
how much of this place is yours?

Notice what this poem is not doing.

Every person gone has taken a stone
to hold, and catch the sun. The carving
says, "Not here, but called away."

Notice what this poem is not doing.

The sun, the earth, the sky, all wait.
The crows and redbirds talk. The light
along the hills has come, has found you.

Notice what this poem has not done.

Gerald Stern

LORD, FORGIVE A SPIRIT

So what shall we do about this angel,
growing dizzy every time he climbs a ladder,
crying over his old poems.
I walk out into the garden and there he is,
watering the lilies and studying the digitalis.
He is talking to his own invisible heart;
he is leaking blood.
    The sun shines on him all day long
as he wanders from bush to bush.
His eyes flash with fire, his eyelashes blaze and
his skin shines like brass,
but he trips in the dirt just like any gardener, or grieving poet.
    I watch him walk beside the cactus;
I watch him kneel in front of the wet horsetails;
I touch his lips.
I write all day. I sit beside him all
day long and write the garbled words.
I sit in the sun and fill a whole new book
with scrawls and symbols.
I watch the sky as he talks about the gold leaf
and the half-forgotten ruins; I watch the words
drift from his mouth like clouds.
I watch the colors change from orange to red
to pink as he tries to remember his old words —
his old songs, his first human songs —
lost somewhere in the broken glass and the cinders,
a foot below the soft nails and the hinges.

AT BICKFORD'S

You should understand that I use my body now for everything
whereas formerly I kept it away from higher regions.
My clothes are in a stack over against the orange pine cupboard
and my hair is lying in little piles on the kitchen floor.

I am finally ready for the happiness I spent my youth arguing and fighting
        against.
      Twenty years ago — walking on Broadway —
I crashed into Shaddai and his eagles.
My great specialty was darkness then
and radiant sexual energy.
Now when light drips on me I walk around without tears.
— Before long I am going to live again on four dollars a day
in the little blocks between 96th and 116th.
I am going to follow the thin line of obedience
between George's Restaurant and Salter's Books.
There is just so much feeling left in me for my old ghost
and I will spend it all in one last outburst of charity.
I will give him money; I will listen to his poems;
I will pity his marriage.
— After that I will drift off again to Bickford's
and spend my life in the cracked cups and the corn muffins.
I will lose half my hatred
at the round tables
and let any beliefs that want to overtake me.
On lucky afternoons the sun will break through the thick glass
and rest like a hand on my forehead.
I will sit and read in my chair;
I will wave from my window.

THE CEMETERY OF ORANGE TREES IN CRETE

In Crete the old orange trees are cut back until they are stumps,
with little leaves coming out again from the butchered arms.
They are painted white and stand there in long straight rows
like the white gravestones at Gettysburg and Manassas.
    I first came across them on the bus ride to Omalos
as we began our climb through the empty mountains,
thinking of the beauty and exhaustion that lay ahead.
They are mementos of my journey south, the renewal
of my youth, green leaves growing out of my neck,
my shoulders flowering again with small blossoms,
my body painted white, my hands joining
the other hands on the hill, my white heart remembering
the violence and sorrow that give us our life again.

GERALD STERN

THE WAR AGAINST THE JEWS

Look how peaceful these wooden figures are, going to their death.
How happy they were to go instead of me.
They love to march back and forth under the iron clock.
One tips his hat endlessly to a mother and her three children.
One dries his tears in front of the water fountain.
They bump their heads as they bend down to drink.

Over there a German soldier is blowing his whistle.
He was carved while he still could remember his mother's garden.
How glad he was to go to Poland.
How young he felt in his first pair of boots.

I would give anything to bring them back:
to let them sit again on the polished benches;
to let them see the great glass roof again;
to rush through the noisy crowd screaming
"Stop! It's a dream! It's a dream!
Go back to your shuls. Go back to your mother's garden.
O wooden figures, go back, go back."

THE SHIRT POEM

It is ten years since I have seen these shirts
screaming from their hangers, crying for blood and money.
They shake their empty arms
and grow stiff as they wait for the light to come.
I open the door an inch at a time to let them out
and start candles all over the room to soothe them.
— Gone is sweetness in that closet, gone is the dream
of brotherhood, the affectionate meeting
of thinkers and workers inside a rented hall.
Gone are the folding chairs, gone forever
the sacred locking of elbows under the two flags.

On Sunday night they used to sing for hours
before the speeches. Once the rabbis joined them
and religion and economics were finally combined in exile.
"Death is a defect," they sang, and threw their hats

GERALD STERN

on the floor. "We will save nature from death,"
they shouted, and ended up dancing on the small stage,
the dark crows and the speckled doves finally arm in arm.

They will never come back — in a thousand years;
it is not like bringing a forest back, putting a truckload
of nitrogen in the soil, burning some brush,
planting seedlings, measuring distance —
these are people, whose secret habits we no longer know,
how they tore their bread and what designs they made on the tablecloth,
what they thought about as they stared through the warped glass,
what the melting ice meant to them.

Poor dead ones! Forgive me for the peace I feel as I walk out
to the mailbox. Forgive me for the rich life I lead.
Forgive me for the enormous budget and the bureaucracy and the perma-
    nent army.
When I come home from New York City I stand outside
for twenty minutes and look out at the lights.
Upstairs the shirts are howling and snapping,
marching back and forth in front of the silver radiator.
In a minute I will be up there closing doors
and turning on lamps.
I will take the papers out of my coat pocket
and put them in their slots.
I will think of you with your own papers and your rubber bands.
What is my life if not a substitute for yours,
and my dream a substitute for your dream?
Lord, how it has changed, how we have
made ourselves strange, how embarrassing the words
sound to us, how clumsy and half-hearted we are.

I want to write it down before it's forgotten,
how we lived, what we believed in;
most of all to remember the giants
and how they walked, always with white hair,
always with long white hair hanging down over their collars,
always with red faces, always bowing and listening,
their heads floating as they moved through the small crowd.

Outside the wind is blowing
and the snow is piling up against the pillars.
I could go back in a minute to the synagogue in Beechview
or the Carnegie Library on the North Side.

I could turn and shake hands with the tiny man
sitting beside me and wish him peace.
I could stand in front and watch the stained-glass
window rattle in its frame and the guest speaker
climb into the back seat of his car.

I am writing about the past because there was
still affection left then, and other sorrows;
because I believed my white silk scarf could save me,
and my all-day walks;
because when I opened my window the smell
of snow made me tremble with pleasure;
because I was a head taller than the tiny man sitting next to me;
because I was always the youngest;
because I believed in Shelley;
because I carried my entire memory along with me in the summer;
because I stared at the old men with loving eyes;
because I studied their fallen shoulders and their huge hands;
because I found relief only in my drawings;
because I knew the color and texture of every rug and every chair
and every lampshade in my first house.

Give this to Rabbi Kook who always arrived
with his clothes on fire and stood between the mourners,
singing songs against death in all three languages
at the crowded wall, in the dark sunlight.

And give this to Malatesta who believed in
the perfect world and lived in it as he moved
from country to country, for sixty years, tasting the
bread, tasting the meat, always working,
cursing the Church, cursing the State,
seeing through everything, always seeing the heart
and what it wanted, the beautiful cramped heart.

My shirts are fine. They dance
by themselves along the river
and bleed a little as they fall down on the dirty glass.
If they had knees they would try to
crawl back up the hill and stop the trucks
or march back and forth singing their swamp songs.
They see me coming and fly up to the roof;
they are like prehistoric birds,
half leaping, half sailing by.

GERALD STERN

They scream with cold, they break through the hall window
and knock over baskets and push open doors
until they stand there in place, in back of the neckties,
beside the cold plaster, in the dust
above the abandoned shoes, weeping in silence,
moaning in exhaustion,
getting ready again to live in darkness.

WEEPING AND WAILING

I like the way my little harp makes trees
leap, how putting the metal between my teeth
makes half the animals in my back yard quiver,
how plucking the sweet tongue makes the stars
live together in love and ecstasy.

I bend my face and cock my head. My eyes
are open wide listening to the sound.
My hand goes up and down like a humming bird.
My mouth is opening and closing, I am singing
in harmony, I am weeping and wailing.

ROMANCE

After thirty years
I am still listening to the pipes,
I am still enchanted
with the singing and moaning of the dry boards.

I am lying there night after night
thinking of water.
I am joining palms, or whistling Mozart
and early Yeats.

I am living without savagery,
stretching my body and turning on my left side
for music,
humming to myself and turning on my right side
for words.

THREE HEARTS

A chicken with three hearts, that is a vanished
breed, a day of glory in the corn,
romance against a fence. It was the sunset
just above New Egypt that made me wince,
it was the hay blown up from Lakewood. God
of chance, how much I loved you in those days,
how free I felt and what a joy it was
sitting there with my book, my two knees braced
against the dashboard. How empty it was then,
and how my mind went back. How many hearts
did the chickadee have? How much whistling and singing
was in those fields? How far did I have to go
to disappear in those grasses, to pick those trillium?

R FOR ROSEMARY

I heard a fluttering — just inside the door
of my *casita*; it was inside a bush,
a kind of pine, a kind of blue rosemary,
and since I saw two doves wandering under
my window yesterday and over my stones
I thought there had to be a mourning dove —
or two of them — puffed up and asleep,
living inside that bush, one of them frightened
by my loud steps. But I will know them later
by their sweet smell, whether they stretch their necks
or stick their chests out, getting ready to soar,
for they have made the mistake of living in rosemary
and they are spies for now and carry the stench
of betrayal on them. I could have reached inside
and heard them scream and watched the bushes shudder
with terror, but I let them go. More
and more I do that. Why did I wait so long
to let them have their darkness? I rub the leaves
under my chin and over my wrists. I know
the smell will last. I crawl up under my window
and try my keys. I'll have to pull the blinds
and close the curtains, those doves are so rotten; they are
such eavesdroppers. We listen to each other

through the glass, we preen in our mirrors; their cooing
is absurd, it is the noisy sound
of codex international; I know
the tapping, I know the turning of the head;
and it is odd to watch them stretch a wire
between their beaks and under my windowsill,
then walk off unaffected. I put powder
over my shoes. I know that trick. I called it
blue rosemary because of the flowers, I should have
called it lavender; it was my color
when I was a boy; there were *two* doves; we wandered
from bush to bush; it was a disease of the spine
that took the other one; she was a dove. If I
spend year after year explaining it is because
I was left without her. I have a sprig
of the dried-up plant, the leaves and the flowers have mixed,
the color is greenish-blue, almost an olive;
it has some weight, the woody part is heavy,
it is itself a kind of flattened tree;
it is a bookmark; it is a perfumed wing.

ONE GIFT

If I have one gift, it is rising in the dark
and falling to my death down a vertical stairway.

It is walking with my feet spread out in both directions
and pressing the white plaster with my red fingers.

One time I was paralyzed, my leg disappeared,
and there was mist between my right knee and the floor.

One time I rose to the ceiling. I closed like a knife
after banging my head against the gritty stucco.

Sometimes there is fleece, the sheets are in shreds
and a white face is floating over the window;

sometimes there is blood, my hand is sticky,
the back of my head is wet, my mouth is salty.

Blood is my terror, blood just under the skin,
blood in the toilet, blood on the pillow. I hear

of every disgrace. I shake from fear. I hate
the heart being where it is, a piece of leather

covered with jelly, pressed against the backbone;
I hate the rotten lungs; I feel like a chicken

lying open, there is a speck of liver
above the gall — what pain if I were alive! —

what sadness there is for the spirit! There is the rope
that carries thought, there is love behind

the bladder. Down I go on one knee.
Sometimes I snore; I do that while I am lying.

It is my other gift. I crawl outside
to get at the moon. There is a balcony

over my head. I should be up there moaning.
Sometimes I end up wandering, sometimes sleeping.

Mark Strand

SLEEPING WITH ONE EYE OPEN

Unmoved by what the wind does,
The windows
Are not rattled, nor do the various
Areas
Of the house make their usual racket —
Creak at
The joints, trusses and studs.
Instead,
They are still. And the maples,
Able
At times to raise havoc,
Evoke
Not a sound from their branches'
Clutches.
It's my night to be rattled,
Saddled
With spooks. Even the half-moon
(Half man,
Half dark), on the horizon,
Lies on
Its side casting a fishy light
Which alights
On my floor, lavishly lording
Its morbid
Look over me. Oh, I feel dead,
Folded
Away in my blankets for good, and
Forgotten.
My room is clammy and cold,
Moonhandled
And weird. The shivers
Wash over
Me, shaking my bones, my loose ends
Loosen,
And I lie sleeping with one eye open,
Hoping
That nothing, nothing will happen.

MARK STRAND

OLD PEOPLE ON THE NURSING HOME PORCH

Able at last to stop
And recall the days it took
To get them here, they sit
On the porch in rockers
Letting the faded light
Of afternoon carry them off

I see them moving back
And forth over the dullness
Of the past, covering ground
They did not know was there,
And ending up with nothing
Save what might have been.

And so they sit, gazing
Out between the trees
Until in all that vacant
Wash of sky, the wasted
Vision of each one
Comes down to earth again.

It is too late to travel
Or even find a reason
To make it seem worthwhile.
Already now, the evening
Reaches out to take
The aging world away.

And soon the dark will come,
And these tired elders feel
The need to go indoors
Where each will lie alone
In the deep and sheepless
Pastures of a long sleep.

MARK STRAND

KEEPING THINGS WHOLE

In a field
I am the absence
of field.
This is
always the case.
Wherever I am
I am what is missing.

When I walk
I part the air
and always
the air moves in
to fill the spaces
where my body's been.

We all have reasons
for moving.
I move
to keep things whole.

THE MAILMAN

It is midnight.
He comes up the walk
and knocks at the door.
I rush to greet him.
He stands there weeping,
shaking a letter at me.
He tells me it contains
terrible personal news.
He falls to his knees.
"Forgive me! Forgive me!" he pleads.

I ask him inside.
He wipes his eyes.
His dark blue suit
is like an inkstain
on my crimson couch.

Helpless, nervous, small,
he curls up like a ball
and sleeps while I compose
more letters to myself
in the same vein:

"You shall live
by inflicting pain.
You shall forgive."

EATING POETRY

Ink runs from the corners of my mouth.
There is no happiness like mine.
I have been eating poetry.

The librarian does not believe what she sees.
Her eyes are sad
and she walks with her hands in her dress.

The poems are gone.
The light is dim.
The dogs are on the basement stairs and coming up.

Their eyeballs roll,
their blond legs burn like brush.
The poor librarian begins to stamp her feet and weep.

She does not understand.
When I get on my knees and lick her hand,
she screams.

I am a new man.
I snarl at her and bark.
I romp with joy in the bookish dark.

MARK STRAND

THE ONE SONG

I prefer to sit all day
like a sack in a chair
and to lie all night
like a stone in my bed.

When food comes
I open my mouth.
When sleep comes
I close my eyes.

My body sings
only one song;
the wind turns
gray in my arms.

Flowers bloom.
Flowers die.
More is less.
I long for more.

THE GARDEN

for Robert Penn Warren

It shines in the garden,
in the white foliage of the chestnut tree,
in the brim of my father's hat
as he walks on the gravel.

In the garden suspended in time
my mother sits in a redwood chair;
light fills the sky,
the folds of her dress,
the roses tangled beside her.

And when my father bends
to whisper in her ear,
when they rise to leave
and the swallows dart

and the moon and stars
have drifted off together, it shines.

Even as you lean over this page,
late and alone, it shines; even now
in the moment before it disappears.

SHOOTING WHALES

for Judith and Leon Major

When the shoals of plankton
swarmed into St. Margaret's Bay,
turning the beaches pink,
we saw from our place on the hill
the sperm whales feeding,
fouling the nets
in their play,
and breaching clean
so the humps of their backs
rose over the wide sea meadows.

Day after day
we waited inside
for the rotting plankton to disappear.
The smell stilled even the wind,
and the oxen looked stunned,
pulling hay on the slope
of our hill.
But the plankton kept coming in
and the whales would not go.

That's when the shooting began.
The fishermen got in their boats
and went after the whales,
and my father and uncle
and we children went, too.
The froth of our wake sank fast
in the wind-shaken water.

The whales surfaced close by.
Their foreheads were huge,

the doors of their faces were closed.
Before sounding, they lifted
their flukes into the air
and brought them down hard.
They beat the sea into foam,
and the path that they made
shone after them.

Though I did not see their eyes,
I imagined they were
like the eyes of mourning,
glazed with rheum,
watching us, sweeping along
under the darkening sheets of salt.

When we cut our engine and waited
for the whales to surface again,
the sun was setting,
turning the rock-strewn barrens a gaudy salmon.
A cold wind flailed at our skin.
When finally the sun went down
and it seemed like the whales had gone,
my uncle, no longer afraid,
shot aimlessly into the sky.

Three miles out
in the rolling dark
under the moon's astonished eyes,
our engine would not start
and we headed home in the dinghy.
And my father, hunched over the oars,
brought us in. I watched him,
rapt in his effort, rowing against the tide,
his blond hair glistening with salt.
I saw the slick spillage of moonlight
being blown over his shoulders,
and the sea and spindrift
suddenly silver.

He did not speak the entire way.
At midnight
when I went to bed,
I imagined the whales
moving beneath me,

sliding over the weed-covered hills of the deep;
they knew where I was;
they were luring me
downward and downward
into the murmurous
waters of sleep.

ALWAYS

for Charles Simic

Always so late in the day
in their rumpled clothes, sitting
around a table lit by a single bulb,
the great forgetters were hard at work.
They tilted their heads to one side, closing their eyes.
Then a house disappeared and a man in his yard
with all his flowers in a row.
The moon was next to go.
The great forgetters wrinkled their brows.
Then Florida went and San Francisco
where tugs and barges leave
small gleaming scars across the Bay.
One of the great forgetters struck a match.
Gone were the harps of beaded lights
that vault the rivers of New York.
Another filled his glass
and that was it for crowds at evening
under sulphur yellow streetlamps coming on.
And afterwards Bulgaria was gone, and then Japan.
'Where will it end?' one of them said.
'Such difficult work, pursuing the fate
of everything known,' said another.
'Yes,' said a third, 'down to the last stone,
and only the cold zero of perfection
left for the imagination.'
The great forgetters slouched in their chairs.
Suddenly Asia was gone, and the evening star
and the common sorrows of the sun.
One of them yawned. Another coughed.
The last one gazed at the window:
not a cloud, not a tree,
the blaze of promise everywhere.

MARK STRAND

THE END

Not every man knows what he shall sing at the end,
Watching the pier as the ship sails away, or what it will seem like
When he's held by the sea's roar, motionless, there at the end,
Or what he shall hope for once it is clear that he'll never go back.

When the time has passed to prune the rose or caress the cat, when
The sunset torching the lawn and the full moon icing it down
No longer appear, not every man knows what he'll discover instead.
When the weight of the past leans against nothing, and the sky

Is no more than remembered light, and the stories of cirrus
And cumulus come to a close, and all the birds are suspended in flight,
Not every man knows what is waiting for him, or what he shall sing
When the ship he is on slips into darkness, there at the end.

Lucien Stryk

AWAKENING

Homage to Hakuin, Zen Master, 1685–1768

I

Shoichi brushed the black
on thick.
His circle held a poem
like buds
above a flowering bowl.

Since the moment of my
pointing,
this bowl, an "earth device,"
holds
nothing but the dawn.

II

A freeze last night, the window's
laced ice flowers, a meadow drifting
from the glacier's side. I think of Hakuin:

"Freezing in an icefield, stretched
thousands of miles in all directions,
I was alone, transparent, and could not move."

Legs cramped, mind pointing
like a torch, I cannot see beyond
the frost, out nor in. And do not move.

III

I balance the round stone
    in my palm,
turn it full circle,

slowly, in the late sun,
    spring to now.
Severe compression,

like a troubled head,
    stings my hand.
It falls. A small dust rises.

IV

Beyond the sycamore
dark air moves
westward —

smoke, cloud, something
wanting a name.
Across the window,

my gathered breath,
I trace
a simple word.

V

My daughter gathers shells
where thirty years before
I'd turned them over, marveling.

I take them from her,
make, at her command,
the universe. Hands clasped,

marking the limits of
a world, we watch till sundown
planets whirling in the sand.

VI

Softness everywhere,
snow a smear,
air a gray sack.

Time. Place. Thing.
Felt between
skin and bone, flesh.

VII

I write in the dark again,
rather by dusk-light,
and what I love about

this hour is the way the trees
are taken, one by one,
into the great wash of darkness.

At this hour I am always happy,
ready to be taken myself,
fully aware.

TO A JAPANESE POET

You stood frozen there,
One hand gripping my arm,
In the other your lunchbasket,
And when I turned
To look into your face,
It was like witnessing a birth.

When the poem came,
Your fingers loosened and you
Spoke the dozen words as if
Directing one who'd
Lost his way upon
A mountain path, the night descending.

Finally we went to join
The others, but you were not the same.
All that brilliant autumn day
You avoided me
As if I'd surprised you
In some intimacy, as if my being

Near had suddenly
Cut us off. Later, when I mentioned
A hurt no memory of scarlet leaves
Could ease, you laughed
And said, "Why should you
Have felt badly? We had an enjoyable outing."

THE CANNERY

In summer this town is full of rebels
Come up from Tennessee to shell the peas.

And wetbacks roam the supermarts, making
A Tijuana of the drab main street.

The Swedes and Poles who work at Wurlitzer,
And can't stand music, are all dug in:

Doors are bolted, their pretty children warned,
Where they wait for the autumnal peace.

At night the cannery's like a train,
A runaway, cans flung up like clinkers.

Sometimes on an evening hot as Southland
When even fear won't keep the windows down,

One hears the drawl of Tennessee, the quick
Laugh of Mexico in the empty streets.

SUMMER

My neighbor frets about his lawn,
and he has reasons —
dandelions, crabgrass, a passing dog.

He scowls up at my maple, rake
clogged and trembling,
as its seeds spin down —

not angels, moths, but paratroopers
carried by the wind,
planting barricades along his eaves.

He's on the ladder now, scaring
the nibbling squirrels,
scattering starlings with his water hose.

Thank God his aim is bad
or he'd have drowned
or B-B gunned the lot. Now he

shakes a fist of seeds at me
where I sit poeming
my dandelions, crabgrass and a passing dog.

I like my neighbor, in his way
he cares for me. Look what
I've given him — something to feel superior to.

LETTER TO JEAN-PAUL BAUDOT, AT CHRISTMAS

Friend, on this sunny day, snow sparkling
everywhere, I think of you once more,
how many years ago, a child Resistance

fighter trapped by Nazis in a cave
with fifteen others, left to die, you became
a cannibal. Saved by Americans,

the taste of a dead comrade's flesh foul
in your mouth, you fell onto the snow
of the Haute Savoie and gorged to purge yourself,

somehow to start again. Each winter since
you were reminded, vomiting for days.
Each winter since you told me at the Mabillon,

I see you on the first snow of the year
spreadeagled, face buried in that stench.
I write once more, Jean-Paul, though you don't

answer, because I must: today men do far worse.
Yours in hope of peace, for all of us,
before the coming of another snow.

FARMER

Seasons waiting the miracle,
dawn after dawn framing
the landscape in his eyes:

bound tight as wheat, packed
hard as dirt. Made shrewd
by soil and weather, through

the channel of his bones
shift ways of animals,
their matings twist his dreams.

While night-fields quicken,
shadows slanting right, then left
across the moonlit furrows,

he shelters in the farmhouse
merged with trees, a skin of wood,
as much the earth's as his.

CHERRIES

Because I sit eating cherries
which I did not pick
a girl goes bad under

the elevator tracks, will
never be whole again.
Because I want the full bag,

grasping, twenty-five children
cry for food. Gorging,
I've none to offer. I want

to care, I mean to, but not
yet, a dozen cherries
rattling at the bottom of my bag.

One by one I lift them to
my mouth, slowly break
their skin — twelve nations

bleed. Because I love, because
I need cherries, I
cannot help them. My happiness,

bought cheap, must last forever.

LUCIEN STRYK

EXTERMINATOR

Phone vibrates all winter. The
exterminator cringes —
yet another squeal, demanding

he come fast. He plays at cat
and mouse, stalling them hours,
days. Then pocketing thick

gloves, flashlight, steelwool,
poison, he enters musty corners,
sets dry traps, pours tempting

pellets into little paper boats,
launches them here and there.
As he stuffs holes, he contemplates

the toughness of a world which
outlaws creatures he has learned
to love: starved from frozen

corn-stripped fields, small wonder
they outsmart those who grudge them
a few crumbs, a little warmth. The

exterminator does his job, takes his
money, leaves. In the long run of
things, he knows who will survive.

WATCHING WAR MOVIES

Always the same: watching
World War II movies on TV,
landing barges bursting onto

islands, my skin crawls —
heat, dust — the scorpion
bites again. How I deceived

myself. Certain my role would
not make me killer, my unarmed
body called down fire from

scarred hills. As life took
life, blood coursed into
one stream. I knew one day,

the madness stopped, I'd make
my pilgrimage to temples,
gardens, serene masters of

a Way which pain was bonding.
Atoms fuse, a mushroom cloud,
the movie ends. But I still

stumble under camouflage, near
books of tranquil Buddhas by the
screen. The war goes on and on.

JUGGLER

Someone with skill juggles
three worlds together,
rainbow, miraculous arc.

Something compels a fourth,
widening the circle. Five,
six float in the charged

steep of his mind: soon
others whirl his wrist.
Seven, eight — now he's on

his toes, up, up, rising
with the music of the
spheres. Still unsatisfied,

risks the lot, down on his
knees. He dare not drop one.
Our lives depend on it.

LUCIEN STRYK

BLACK MONDAY

(NYC, October 1987)

After an early morning trek
under a spill of trees
anchored in rock, where sky-
beams blue as chicory outline

palisades along the Hudson's
bank across the way, I take
the A-train down to 42nd Street.
Across the aisle a young man

beats a rhythm with his feet,
mouthing the rap. As we speed
on, faster, even faster goes
his song. Indifferent to eyes

blinking over headlines of the
market crash, faces grim
as bogs, his soul's raw poem
belts out its need from stop

to stop. Doors open, slam and
open. He takes off, jiving
down the platform toward
gray streets of unending sound.

IN OUR TIME

When after the blast
they turned to the poet,
he asked for a handful
of nails. Pounded them
like phrases into old
boards. No bittersweet,
no roses now. He knelt
in silence in the wasted
town — a stain under the
fallout moon. Nails, line
by line, his only song.

Richard Wilbur

ADVICE TO A PROPHET

When you come, as you soon must, to the streets of our city,
Mad-eyed from stating the obvious,
Not proclaiming our fall but begging us
In God's name to have self-pity,

Spare us all word of the weapons, their force and range,
The long numbers that rocket the mind;
Our slow, unreckoning hearts will be left behind,
Unable to fear what is too strange.

Nor shall you scare us with talk of the death of the race.
How should we dream of this place without us? —
The sun mere fire, the leaves untroubled about us,
A stone look on the stone's face?

Speak of the world's own change. Though we cannot conceive
Of an undreamt thing, we know to our cost
How the dreamt cloud crumbles, the vines are blackened by frost,
How the view alters. We could believe,

If you told us so, that the white-tailed deer will slip
Into perfect shade, grown perfectly shy,
The lark avoid the reaches of our eye,
The jack-pine lose its knuckled grip

On the cold ledge, and every torrent burn
As Xanthus once, its gliding trout
Stunned in a twinkling. What should we be without
The dolphin's arc, the dove's return,

These things in which we have seen ourselves and spoken?
Ask us, prophet, how we shall call
Our natures forth when that live tongue is all
Dispelled, that glass obscured or broken

In which we have said the rose of our love and the clean
Horse of our courage, in which beheld
The singing locust of the soul unshelled,
And all we mean or wish to mean.

Ask us, ask us whether with the worldless rose
Our hearts shall fail us; come demanding
Whether there shall be lofty or long standing
When the bronze annals of the oak-tree close.

LOVE CALLS US TO THE THINGS OF THIS WORLD

The eyes open to a cry of pulleys,
And spirited from sleep, the astounded soul
Hangs for a moment bodiless and simple
As false dawn.
     Outside the open window
The morning air is all awash with angels.

Some are in bed-sheets, some are in blouses,
Some are in smocks: but truly there they are.
Now they are rising together in calm swells
Of halcyon feeling, filling whatever they wear
With the deep joy of their impersonal breathing;

Now they are flying in place, conveying
The terrible speed of their omnipresence, moving
And staying like white water; and now of a sudden
They swoon down into so rapt a quiet
That nobody seems to be there.
       The soul shrinks

From all that it is about to remember,
From the punctual rape of every blessèd day,
And cries,
   "Oh, let there be nothing on earth but laundry,
Nothing but rosy hands in the rising steam
And clear dances done in the sight of heaven."

Yet, as the sun acknowledges
With a warm look the world's hunks and colors,
The soul descends once more in bitter love
To accept the waking body, saying now
In a changed voice as the man yawns and rises,

"Bring them down from their ruddy gallows.
Let there be clean linen for the backs of thieves;
Let lovers go fresh and sweet to be undone,
And the heaviest nuns walk in a pure floating
Of dark habits,
           keeping their difficult balance."

ON THE EYES OF AN SS OFFICER

I think of Amundsen, enormously bit
By arch-dark flurries on the ice plateaus,
An amorist of violent virgin snows
At the cold end of the world's spit.

Or a Bombay saint asquat in the market place,
Eyes gone from staring the sun over the sky,
Who still dead-reckons that acetylene eye,
An eclipsed mind in a blind face.

But this one's iced or ashen eyes devise,
Foul purities, in flesh their wilderness,
Their fire; I ask my makeshift God of this
My opulent bric-a-brac earth to damn his eyes.

YEAR'S END

Now winter downs the dying of the year,
And night is all a settlement of snow;
From the soft street the rooms of houses show
A gathered light, a shapen atmosphere,
Like frozen-over lakes whose ice is thin
And still allows some stirring down within.

I've known the wind by water banks to shake
The late leaves down, which frozen where they fell
And held in ice as dancers in a spell

Fluttered all winter long into a lake;
Graved on the dark in gestures of descent,
They seemed their own most perfect monument.

There was perfection in the death of ferns
Which laid their fragile cheeks against the stone
A million years. Great mammoths overthrown
Composedly have made their long sojourns,
Like palaces of patience, in the gray
And changeless lands of ice. And at Pompeii

The little dog lay curled and did not rise
But slept the deeper as the ashes rose
And found the people incomplete, and froze
The random hands, the loose unready eyes
Of men expecting yet another sun
To do the shapely thing they had not done.

These sudden ends of time must give us pause.
We fray into the future, rarely wrought
Save in the tapestries of afterthought.
More time, more time. Barrages of applause
Come muffled from a buried radio.
The New-year bells are wrangling with the snow.

A BAROQUE WALL-FOUNTAIN
IN THE VILLA SCIARRA

for Dore and Adja

Under the bronze crown
Too big for the head of the stone cherub whose feet
A serpent has begun to eat,
Sweet water brims a cockle and braids down

Past spattered mosses, breaks
On the tipped edge of a second shell, and fills
The massive third below. It spills
In threads then from the scalloped rim, and makes

A scrim or summery tent
For a faun-ménage and their familiar goose.
　　Happy in all that ragged, loose
Collapse of water, its effortless descent

　　And flatteries of spray,
The stocky god upholds the shell with ease,
　　Watching, about his shaggy knees,
The goatish innocence of his babes at play;

　　His fauness all the while
Leans forward, slightly, into a clambering mesh
　　Of water-lights, her sparkling flesh
In a saecular ecstasy, her blinded smile

　　Bent on the sand floor
Of the trefoil pool, where ripple-shadows come
　　And go in swift reticulum,
More addling to the eye than wine, and more

　　Interminable to thought
Than pleasure's calculus. Yet since this all
　　Is pleasure, flash, and waterfall,
Must it not be too simple? Are we not

　　More intricately expressed
In the plain fountains that Maderna set
　　Before St. Peter's — the main jet
Struggling aloft until it seems at rest

　　In the act of rising, until
The very wish of water is reversed,
　　That heaviness borne up to burst
In a clear, high, cavorting head, to fill

　　With blaze, and then in gauze
Delays, in a gnatlike shimmering, in a fine
　　Illumined version of itself, decline,
And patter on the stones its own applause?

If that is what men are
Or should be, if those water-saints display
   The pattern of our areté,
What of these showered fauns in their bizarre,

   Spangled, and plunging house?
They are at rest in fulness of desire
   For what is given, they do not tire
Of the smart of the sun, the pleasant water-douse

   And riddled pool below,
Reproving our disgust and our ennui
   With humble insatiety.
Francis, perhaps, who lay in sister snow

   Before the wealthy gate
Freezing and praising, might have seen in this
   No trifle, but a shade of bliss —
That land of tolerable flowers, that state

   As near and far as grass
Where eyes become the sunlight, and the hand
   Is worthy of water: the dreamt land
Toward which all hungers leap, all pleasures pass.

POTATO

for André du Bouchet

An underground grower, blind and a common brown;
Got a misshapen look, it's nudged where it could;
Simple as soil yet crowded as earth with all.

Cut open raw, it looses a cool clean stench,
Mineral acid seeping from pores of prest meal;
It is like breaching a strangely refreshing tomb:

Therein the taste of first stones, the hands of dead slaves,
Waters men drank in the earliest frightful woods,
Flint chips, and peat, and the cinders of buried camps.

RICHARD WILBUR

Scrubbed under faucet water the planet skin
Polishes yellow, but tears to the plain insides;
Parching, the white's blue-hearted like hungry hands.

All of the cold dark kitchens, and war-frozen gray
Evening at window; I remember so many
Peeling potatoes quietly into chipt pails.

"It was potatoes saved us, they kept us alive."
Then they had something to say akin to praise
For the mean earth-apples, too common to cherish or steal.

Times being hard, the Sikh and the Senegalese,
Hobo and Okie, the body of Jesus the Jew,
Vestigial virtues, are eaten; we shall survive.

What has not lost its savor shall hold us up,
And we are praising what saves us, what fills the need.
(Soon there'll be packets again, with Algerian fruits.)

Oh, it will not bear polish, the ancient potato,
Needn't be nourished by Caesars, will blow anywhere,
Hidden by nature, counted-on, stubborn and blind.

You may have noticed the bush that it pushes to air,
Comical-delicate, sometimes with second-rate flowers
Awkward and milky and beautiful only to hunger.

A DUBIOUS NIGHT

A bell diphthonging in an atmosphere
Of shying night air summons some to prayer
Down in the town, two deep lone miles from here,

Yet wallows faint or sudden everywhere,
In every ear, as if the twist wind wrung
Some ten years' tangled echoes from the air.

What kyries it says are mauled among
The queer elisions of the mist and murk,
Of lights and shapes; the senses were unstrung,

Except that one star's synecdochic smirk
Burns steadily to me, that nothing's odd
And firm as ever is the masterwork.

I weary of the confidence of God.

PRAISE IN SUMMER

Obscurely yet most surely called to praise,
As sometimes summer calls us all, I said
The hills are heavens full of branching ways
Where star-nosed moles fly overhead the dead;
I said the trees are mines in air, I said
See how the sparrow burrows in the sky!
And then I wondered why this mad *instead*
Perverts our praise to uncreation, why
Such savor's in this wrenching thing awry.
Does sense so stale that it must needs derange
The world to know it? To a praiseful eye
Should it not be enough of fresh and strange
That trees grow green, and moles can course in clay,
And sparrows sweep the ceiling of our day?

COTTAGE STREET, 1953

Framed in her phoenix fire-screen, Edna Ward
Bends to the tray of Canton, pouring tea
For frightened Mrs. Plath; then, turning toward
The pale, slumped daughter, and my wife, and me,

Asks if we would prefer it weak or strong.
Will we have milk or lemon, she enquires?
The visit seems already strained and long.
Each in his turn, we tell her our desires.

It is my office to exemplify
The published poet in his happiness,

RICHARD WILBUR

Thus cheering Sylvia, who has wished to die;
But half-ashamed, and impotent to bless,

I am a stupid life-guard who has found,
Swept to his shallows by the tide, a girl
Who, far from shore, has been immensely drowned,
And stares through water now with eyes of pearl.

How large is her refusal; and how slight
The genteel chat whereby we recommend
Life, of a summer afternoon, despite
The brewing dusk which hints that it may end.

And Edna Ward shall die in fifteen years,
After her eight-and-eighty summers of
Such grace and courage as permit no tears,
The thin hand reaching out, the last word *love*,

Outliving Sylvia who, condemned to live,
Shall study for a decade, as she must,
To state at last her brilliant negative
In poems free and helpless and unjust.

THE WRITER

In her room at the prow of the house
Where light breaks, and the windows are tossed with linden,
My daughter is writing a story.

I pause in the stairwell, hearing
From her shut door a commotion of typewriter-keys
Like a chain hauled over a gunwale.

Young as she is, the stuff
Of her life is a great cargo, and some of it heavy:
I wish her a lucky passage.

But now it is she who pauses,
As if to reject my thought and its easy figure.
A stillness greatens, in which

The whole house seems to be thinking,
And then she is at it again with a bunched clamor
Of strokes, and again is silent.

I remember the dazed starling
Which was trapped in that very room, two years ago;
How we stole in, lifted a sash

And retreated, not to affright it;
And how for a helpless hour, through the crack of the door,
We watched the sleek, wild, dark

And iridescent creature
Batter against the brilliance, drop like a glove
To the hard floor, or the desk-top,

And wait then, humped and bloody,
For the wits to try it again; and how our spirits
Rose when, suddenly sure,

It lifted off from a chair-back,
Beating a smooth course for the right window
And clearing the sill of the world.

It is always a matter, my darling,
Of life or death, as I had forgotten. I wish
What I wished you before, but harder.

TRANSIT

A woman I have never seen before
Steps from the darkness of her town-house door
At just that crux of time when she is made
So beautiful that she or time must fade.

What use to claim that as she tugs her gloves
A phantom heraldry of all the loves
Blares from the lintel? That the staggered sun
Forgets, in his confusion, how to run?

RICHARD WILBUR

Still, nothing changes as her perfect feet
Click down the walk that issues in the street,
Leaving the stations of her body there
As a whip maps the countries of the air.

C. K. Williams

IT IS THIS WAY WITH MEN

They are pounded into the earth
like nails; move an inch,
they are driven down again.
The earth is sore with them.
It is a spiny fruit
that has lost hope
of being raised and eaten.
It can only ripen and ripen.
And men, they too are wounded.
They too are sifted from their loss
and are without hope. The core
softens. The pure flesh softens
and melts. There are thorns, there
are the dark seeds, and they end.

THEN THE BROTHER OF THE WIND

there's no such thing as death everybody
knows that also
nothing in the world that can batter you
and hang you on a fencepost like a towel

and no such thing as love that stays inside
getting thicker and heavier falling
into the middle one seed
that weighs more than the universe

and no angels either
and even if there were even if we hadn't laughed
the second heart out and made the second brain
have whole wars happening inside it like bacteria

and if they were made out of tin cans like shacks
in rio and rubber tires like crete sandals
and were all the same place rags in ratholes
in harlem rags sticking to burned faces in bengal

we'd still break like motors
and slip out of them anyway like penises
onto the damp thigh
and have to begin over

THEY WARNED HIM THEN THEY THREW HIM AWAY

there's somebody who's dying
to eat god
when the name happens
the juices leap from the bottom of his mouth like waves
he almost falls over with lightheadedness
nobody has ever been this hungry before
you might know people who've never had anything
but teaspoons of rice or shreds
from the shin of an ape well that's nothing
you should know what this person would do
he'd pull handfuls of hair out of his children
and shove them down
he'd squeeze the docile bud in his wife
until it screamed
if you told him god lived in his own penis
he'd bite into it
and tear like a carnivore
this is how men renounce
this is how we obliterate
one morning near the end he'll climb into the fire
and look back at himself
what was dark will be light
what was song will be roaring
and the worst thing is you'll still want this
beyond measure you'll still want this
believe me
you should know this

THE GAS STATION

This is before I'd read Nietzsche. Before Kant or Kierkegaard, even before
    Whitman and Yeats.
I don't think there were three words in my head yet. I knew, perhaps, that
    I should suffer,

I can remember I almost cried for this or for that, nothing special, nothing
  to speak of.
Probably I was mad with grief for the loss of my childhood, but I wouldn't
  have known that.
It's dawn. A gas station. Route twenty-two. I remember exactly: route
  twenty-two curved,
there was a squat, striped concrete divider they'd put in after a plague of
  collisions.
The gas station? Texaco, Esso — I don't know. They were just words
  anyway then, just what their signs said.
I wouldn't have understood the first thing about monopoly or imperialist
  or oppression.
It's dawn. It's so late. Even then, when I was never tired, I'm just holding
  on.
Slumped on my friend's shoulder, I watch the relentless, wordless misery
  of the route twenty-two sky
that seems to be filming my face with a grainy oil I keep trying to rub off
  or in.
Why are we here? Because one of my friends, in the men's room over
  there, has blue balls.
He has to jerk off. I don't know what that means, "blue balls," or why he
  has to do that —
it must be important to have to stop here after this long night, but I don't
  ask.
I'm just trying, I think, to keep my head as empty as I can for as long as
  I can.
One of my other friends is asleep. He's so ugly, his mouth hanging, slack
  and wet.
Another — I'll never see this one again — stares from the window as
  though he were frightened.
Here's what we've done. We were in Times Square, a pimp found us,
  corralled us, led us somewhere,
down a dark street, another dark street, up dark stairs, dark hall, dark
  apartment,
where his whore, his girl or his wife or his mother for all I know dragged
  herself from her sleep,
propped herself on an elbow, gazed into the dark hall and agreed, for two
  dollars each, to take care of us.
Take care of us. Some of the words that come through me now seem to
  stay, to hook in.
My friend in the bathroom is taking so long. The filthy sky must be
  starting to lighten.

It took me a long time, too, with the woman, I mean. Did I mention that
   she, the woman, the whore or mother,
was having her time and all she would deign do was to blow us? Did I
   say that? Deign? Blow?
What a joy, though, the idea was in those days. Blown! What a thing to
   tell the next day.
She only deigned, though, no more. She was like a machine. When I
   lift her back to me now,
there's nothing there but that dark, curly head, working, a machine, up
   and down, and now,
Freud, Marx, Fathers, tell me, what am I, doing this, telling this, on her,
   on myself,
hammering it down, cementing it, sealing it in, but a machine, too! *Why
   am I doing this?*
I still haven't read Augustine. I don't understand Chomsky that well.
   Should I?
My friend at last comes back. Maybe the right words were there all along.
   Complicity. Wonder.
How pure we were then, before Rimbaud, before Blake. *Grace. Love.
   Take care of us. Please.*

TAR

The first morning of Three Mile Island: those first disquieting, uncertain,
   mystifying hours.
All morning a crew of workmen have been tearing the old decrepit roof
   off our building,
and all morning, trying to distract myself, I've been wandering out to
   watch them
as they hack away the leaden layers of asbestos paper and disassemble the
   disintegrating drains.
After half a night of listening to the news, wondering how to know a
   hundred miles downwind
if and when to make a run for it and where, then a coming bolt awake at
   seven
when the roofers we've been waiting for since winter sent their ladders
   shrieking up our wall,
we still know less than nothing: the utility company continues making
   little of the accident,
the slick federal spokesmen still have their evasions in some semblance of
   order.

C. K. WILLIAMS

Surely we suspect now we're being lied to, but in the meantime, there are the roofers,
setting winch-frames, sledging rounds of tar apart, and there I am, on the curb across, gawking.

I never realized what brutal work it is, how matter-of-factly and harrowingly dangerous.
The ladders flex and quiver, things skid from the edge, the materials are bulky and recalcitrant.
When the rusty, antique nails are levered out, their heads pull off; the underroofing crumbles.
Even the battered little furnace, roaring along as patient as a donkey, chokes and clogs,
a dense, malignant smoke shoots up, and someone has to fiddle with a cock, then hammer it,
before the gush and stench will deintensify, the dark, Dantean broth wearily subside.
In its crucible, the stuff looks bland, like licorice, spill it, though, on your boots or coveralls,
it sears, and everything is permeated with it, the furnace gunked with burst and half-burst bubbles,
the men themselves so completely slashed and mucked they seem almost from another realm, like trolls.
When they take their break, they leave their brooms standing at attention in the asphalt pails,
work gloves clinging like Brer Rabbit to the bitten shafts, and they slouch along the precipitous lip,
the enormous sky behind them, the heavy noontime air alive with shimmers and mirages.

Sometime in the afternoon I had to go inside: the advent of our vigil was upon us.
However much we didn't want to, however little we would do about it, we'd understood:
we were going to perish of all this, if not now, then soon, if not soon, then someday.
Someday, some final generation, hysterically aswarm beneath an atmosphere as unrelenting as rock,
would rue us all, anathematize our earthly comforts, curse our surfeits and submissions.
I think I know, though I might rather not, why my roofers stay so clear to me and why the rest,
the terror of that time, the reflexive disbelief and distancing, all we should hold on to, dims so.

C. K. WILLIAMS

I remember the president in his absurd protective booties, looking absolutely unafraid, the fool.
I remember a woman on the front page glaring across the misty Susque-
hanna at those looming stacks.
But, more vividly, the men, silvered with glitter from the shingles, clinging like starlings beneath the eaves.
Even the leftover carats of tar in the gutter, so black they seemed to suck
the light out of the air.
By nightfall kids had come across them: every sidewalk on the block was
scribbled with obscenities and hearts.

FROM MY WINDOW

Spring: the first morning when that one true block of sweet, laminar,
complex scent arrives
from somewhere west and I keep coming to lean on the sill, glorying in
the end of the wretched winter.
The scabby-barked sycamores ringing the empty lot across the way are
budded — I hadn't noticed —
and the thick spikes of the unlikely urban crocuses have already broken
the gritty soil.
Up the street, some surveyors with tripods are waving each other left and
right the way they do.
A girl in a gym suit jogged by a while ago, some kids passed, playing
hooky, I imagine,
and now the paraplegic Vietnam vet who lives in a half-converted warehouse down the block
and the friend who stays with him and seems to help him out come
weaving towards me,
their battered wheelchair lurching uncertainly from one edge of the sidewalk to the other.
I know where they're going — to the "Legion": once, when I was putting
something out, they stopped,
both drunk that time, too, both reeking — it wasn't ten o'clock — and
we chatted for a bit.
I don't know how they stay alive — on benefits most likely. I wonder if
they're lovers?
They don't look it. Right now, in fact, they look a wreck, careening
haphazardly along,
contriving, as they reach beneath me, to dip a wheel from the curb so
that the chair skewers, teeters,

tips, and they both tumble, the one slowly, almost gracefully sliding in stages from his seat,

his expression hardly marking it, the other staggering over him, spinning heavily down,

to lie on the asphalt, his mouth working, his feet shoving weakly and fruitlessly against the curb.

In the storefront office on the corner, Reed and Son, Real Estate, have come to see the show.

Gazing through the golden letters of their name, they're not, at least, thank god, laughing.

Now the buddy, grabbing at a hydrant, gets himself erect and stands there for a moment, panting.

Now he has to lift the other one, who lies utterly still, a forearm shielding his eyes from the sun.

He hauls him partly upright, then hefts him almost all the way into the chair but a dangling foot

catches a support-plate, jerking everything around so that he has to put him down,

set the chair to rights and hoist him again and as he does he jerks the grimy jeans right off him.

No drawers, shrunken, blotchy thighs: under the thick, white coils of belly blubber,

the poor, blunt pud, tiny, terrified, retracted, is almost invisible in the sparse genital hair,

then his friend pulls his pants up, he slumps wholly back as though he were, at last, to be let be,

and the friend leans against the cyclone fence, suddenly staring up at me as though he'd known,

all along, that I was watching and I can't help wondering if he knows that in the winter, too,

I watched, the night he went out to the lot and walked, paced rather, almost ran, for how many hours.

It was snowing, the city in that holy silence, the last we have, when the storm takes hold,

and he was making patterns that I thought at first were circles then realized made a figure eight,

what must have been to him a perfect symmetry but which, from where I was, shivered, bent,

and lay on its side: a warped, unclear infinity, slowly, as the snow came faster, going out.

Over and over again, his head lowered to the task, he slogged the path he'd blazed,

but the race was lost, his prints were filling faster than he made them now and I looked away,

up across the skeletal trees to the tall center city buildings, some, though
    it was midnight,
with all their offices still gleaming, their scarlet warning-beacons signalling
    erratically
against the thickening flakes, their smoldering auras softening portions of
    the dim, milky sky.
In the morning, nothing: every trace of him effaced, all the field pure
    white,
its surface glittering, the dawn, glancing from its glaze, oblique, relentless,
    unadorned.

FIRST DESIRES

It was like listening to the record of a symphony before you knew anything
    at all about the music,
what the instruments might sound like, look like, what portion of the
    orchestra each represented:
there were only volumes and velocities, thickenings and thinnings, the
    winding cries of change
that seemed to touch within you, through your body, to be part of you
    and then apart from you.
And even when you'd learned the grainy timbre of the single violin, the
    ardent arpeggios of the horn,
when you tried again there were still uneases and confusions left, an ache,
    a sense of longing
that held you in chromatic dissonance, droning on beyond the dominant's
    resolve into the tonic,
as though there were a flaw of logic in the structure, or in (you knew it
    was more likely) you.

REPRESSION

More and more lately, as, not even minding the slippages yet, the aches
    and sad softenings,
I settle into my other years, I notice how many of what I once thought
    were evidences of repression,
sexual or otherwise, now seem, in other people anyway, to be varieties of
    dignity, withholding, tact,

and sometimes even in myself, certain patiences I would have once called
    lassitude, indifference,
now seem possibly to be if not the rewards then at least the unsuspected,
    undreamed-of conclusions
to many of the even-then-preposterous self-evolved disciplines, rigors, al-
    most mortifications
I inflicted on myself in my starting-out days, improvement days, days
    when the idea alone of psychic peace,
of intellectual, of emotional quiet, the merest hint, would have meant
    inconceivable capitulation.

THE CRITIC

In the Boston Public Library on Boylston Street, where all the bums come
    in stinking from the cold,
there was one who had a battered loose-leaf book he used to scribble in
    for hours on end.
He wrote with no apparent hesitation, quickly, and with concentration;
    his inspiration was inspiring:
you had to look again to realize that he was writing over words that were
    already there —
blocks of cursive etched into the softened paper, interspersed with poems
    in print he'd pasted in.
I hated to think of the volumes he'd violated to construct his opus, but I
    liked him anyway,
especially the way he'd often reach the end, close his work with weary
    satisfaction, then open again
and start again: page one, chapter one, his blood-rimmed eyes as rapt as
    David's doing psalms.

THE LADDER

God was an accident of language, a quirk of the unconscious mind, but
    unhappily never of my mind.
God had risen from dream, was dream, was a dream I wanted, would do
    much to have, but never had had.
Therefore, or maybe therefore, God became functioned, with want, with
    lack, with need, denial.

Then therefore, maybe therefore, equations: God and death, God and
    war, God injustice, hatred, pain.
Then my only revelation, knowing that if God did speak what He'd say
    would be, *Your heart is dull.*
I let my sophistries and disputations fail: I knew that only in His own fire
    would God be consumed.
God, a sheet of paper scrawled with garbled cipher, flared, then cooled
    to cinder, then the cinder,
pounded by these hammerings, blended with the textures of my — could
    I still say "soul"? — my soul.

WAR

Jed is breathlessly, deliriously happy because he's just been deftly am-
    bushed and gunned down
by his friend Ha Woei as he came charging headlong around the corner
    of some bushes in the *bois.*
He slumps dramatically to the ground, disregarding the damp, black, gritty
    dirt he falls into,
and holds the posture of a dead man, forehead to the earth, arms and legs
    thrown full-length east and west,
until it's time for him to rise and Ha Woei to die, which Ha Woei does
    with vigor and abandon,
flinging himself down, the imaginary rifle catapulted from his hand like
    Capa's Spanish soldier's.
Dinnertime, bath time, bedtime, story time: *bam, bambambam, bam* —
    Akhilleus and Hektor.
Not until the cloak of night falls do they give themselves to the truces and
    forgivenesses of sleep.

THE MODERN

Its skin tough and unpliable as scar, the pulp out of focus, weak, granular,
    powdery, blank,
this tomato I'm eating — wolfing, stuffing down: I'm so hungry — is
    horrible and delicious.
Don't tell me, I know all about it, this travesty-sham; I know it was plucked
    green and unripe,

then was locked in a chamber and gassed so it wouldn't rot till I bought
  it but I don't care:
I was so famished before, I was sucking sweat from my arm and now my
  tomato is glowing inside me.
I muscle the juice through my teeth and the seeds to the roof of my mouth
  and the hard,
scaly scab of where fruit met innocent stem and was torn free I hold on
  my tongue and savor,
a coin, a dot, the end of a sentence, the end of the long improbable
  utterance of the holy and human.

Courtesy of the author

Charles Wright

THE NEW POEM

It will not resemble the sea.
It will not have dirt on its thick hands.
It will not be part of the weather.

It will not reveal its name.
It will not have dreams you can count on.
It will not be photogenic.

It will not attend our sorrow.
It will not console our children.
It will not be able to help us.

BLACKWATER MOUNTAIN

That time of evening, weightless and disparate,
When the loon cries, when the small bass
Jostle the lake's reflections, when
The green of the oak begins
To open its robes to the dark, the green
Of water to offer itself to the flames,
When lily and lily pad
Husband the last light
Which flares like a white disease, then disappears:
This is what I remember. And this:

The slap of the jacklight on the cove;
The freeze-frame of ducks
Below us; your shots; the wounded flop
And skid of one bird to the thick brush;
The moon of your face in the fire's glow;
The cold; the darkness. Young,
Wanting approval, what else could I do?
And did, for two hours, waist-deep in the lake,
The thicket as black as death,
Without success or reprieve, try.

The stars over Blackwater Mountain
Still dangle and flash like hooks, and ducks
Coast on the evening water;
The foliage is like applause.
I stand where we stood before and aim
My flashlight down to the lake. A black duck
Explodes to my right, hangs, and is gone.
He shows me the way to you;
He shows me the way to a different fire
Where you, black moon, warm your hands.

SNOW

If we, as we are, are dust, and dust, as it will, rises,
Then we will rise, and recongregate
In the wind, in the cloud, and be their issue,

Things in a fall in a world of fall, and slip
Through the spiked branches and snapped joints of the evergreens,
White ants, white ants and the little ribs.

EQUATION

I open the phone book, and look for my adolescence.
How easy the past is —
Alphabetized, its picture taken,
It leans in the doorway, it fits in the back pocket.

The crime is invisible,
But it's there. Why else would I feel so guilty?
Why else would that one sorrow still walk through my sleep,
Looking away, dressed in its best suit?

I touch my palm. I touch it again and again.
I leave no fingerprint. I find no white scar.
It must have been something else,
Something enormous, something too big to see.

CHARLES WRIGHT

REUNION

Already one day has detached itself from all the rest up ahead.
It has my photograph in its soft pocket.
It wants to carry my breath into the past in its bag of wind.

I write poems to untie myself, to do penance and disappear
Through the upper right-hand corner of things, to say grace.

APRIL

The plum tree breaks out in bees.
A gull is locked like a ghost in the blue attic of heaven.
The wind goes nattering on,
Gossipy, ill at ease, in the damp room it will air.
I count off the grace and stays
My life has come to, and know I want less —

Divested of everything,
A downfall of light in the pine woods, motes in the rush,
Gold leaf through the undergrowth, and come back
As another name, water
Pooled in the black leaves and holding me there, to be
Released as a glint, as a flash, as a spark . . .

DRIVING THROUGH TENNESSEE

It's strange what the past brings back.
Our parents, for instance, how ardently they still loom
In the brief and flushed
Fleshstones of memory, one foot in front of the next
Even in retrospect, and so unimpeachable.

And towns that we lived in once,
And who we were then, the roads we went back and forth on
Returning ahead of us like rime

In the moonlight's fall, and Jesus returning, and Stephen Martyr
And St. Paul of the Sword . . .

— I am their music,
Mothers and fathers and places we hurried through in the night:
I put my mouth to the dust and sing their song.
Remember us, Galeoto, and whistle our tune, when the time comes,
For charity's sake.

from THREE POEMS FOR THE NEW YEAR

2

How strange it is to awake
Into middle age, Rimbaud left blue and out cold
In the snow,
        the Alps wriggling away to a line
In the near distance,
           someone you don't know
Coming to get your body, revive it, and arrange for the train.

How strange to awake to that,

The windows all fogged with breath,
The landscape outside in a flash,
           and gone like a scarf
On the neck of someone else,
        so white, so immaculate,
The deserts and caravans
Hanging like Christmas birds in the ice-dangled evergreens.

3

All day at the window seat
        looking out, the red knots

Of winter hibiscus deep in the foregreen,
Slick globes of oranges in the next yard,
Many oranges,
        and slow winks in the lemon trees
Down the street, slow winks when the wind blows the leaves back.

The ache for fame is a thick dust and weariness in the heart.
All day with the knuckle of solitude
To gnaw on,
              the turkey buzzards and red-tailed hawk
Lifting and widening concentrically over the field,
Brush-tails of the pepper branches
                        writing invisibly on the sky . . .

The ache for anything is a thick dust in the heart.

CALIFORNIA DREAMING

We are not born yet, and everything's crystal under our feet.
We are not brethren, we are not underlings.
We are another nation,
                living by voices that you will never hear,
Caught in the net of splendor
                    of time-to-come on the earth.
We shine in our distant chambers, we are golden.

———————

Midmorning, and Darvon dustfall off the Pacific
Stuns us to ecstasy,
              October sun
Stuck like a tack on the eastern drift of the sky,
The idea of God on the other,
                body by body
Rinsed in the Sunday prayer-light, draining away
Into the undercoating and slow sparks of the west,
                  which is our solitude and our joy.

———————

I've looked at this ridge of lights for six years now
                    and still don't like it,
Strung out like Good Friday along a cliff
That Easters down to the ocean,
A dark wing with ruffled feathers as far out as Catalina
Fallen from some sky,
                ruffled and laid back by the wind,
Santa Ana that lisps its hot breath
                  on the neck of everything.

———————

What if the soul indeed is outside the body,
                              a little rainfall of light
Moistening our every step, prismatic, apotheosizic?
What if inside the body another shape is waiting to come out,
White as a quilt, loose as a fever,
                              and sways in the easy tides there?
What other anagoge in this life but the self?
What other ladder to Paradise
                    but the smooth handholds of the rib cage?
High in the palm tree the orioles twitter and grieve.
We twitter and grieve, the spider twirls the honey bee,
Who twitters and grieves, around in her net,
                              then draws it by one leg
Up to the fishbone fern leaves inside the pepper tree
                              swaddled in silk
And turns it again and again until it is shining.

————————

Some nights, when the rock-and-roll band next door has quit playing,
And the last helicopter has thwonked back to the Marine base,
And the dark lets all its weight down
                    to within a half inch of the ground,
I sit outside in the gold lamé of the moon
                    as the town sleeps and the country sleeps
Like flung confetti around me,
And wonder just what in the hell I'm doing out here
So many thousands of miles away from what I know best.
And what I know best
                    has nothing to do with Point Conception
And Avalon and the long erasure of ocean
Out there where the landscape ends.
What I know best is a little thing.
It sits on the far side of the simile,
                    the like that's like the like.

————————

Today is sweet stuff on the tongue.
The question of how we should live our lives in this world
Will find no answer from us
                    this morning,
Sunflick, the ocean humping its back
Beneath us, shivering out
                    wave after wave we fall from
And cut through in a white scar of healed waters,

Our wet suits glossed slick as seals,
                         our boards grown sharp as cries.
We rise and fall like the sun.

———————

Ghost of the Muse and her dogsbody
Suspended above the beach, November 25,
Sun like a Valium disc, smog like rust in the trees.
White-hooded and friar-backed,
                    a gull choir eyeballs the wave reach.
Invisibly pistoned, the sea keeps it up,
            plunges and draws back, plunges and draws back,
Yesterday hung like a porcelain cup behind the eyes,
Sonorous valves, insistent extremities,
                    the worm creeping out of the heart . . .

———————

Who are these people we pretend to be,
                    untouched by the setting sun?
They stand less stiffly than we do, and handsomer,
First on the left foot, and then the right.
Just for a moment we see ourselves inside them,
                                        peering out,
And then they go their own way and we go ours,
Back to the window seat above the driveway,
Christmas lights in the pepper tree,
                         black Madonna
Gazing out from the alicanthus.
Chalk eyes downcast, heavy with weeping and bitterness,
Her time has come round again.

———————

Piece by small piece the world falls away from us like spores
From a milkweed pod,
                    and everything we have known,
And everyone we have known,
Is taken away by the wind to forgetfulness,
Somebody always humming,
                    California dreaming . . .

CHARLES WRIGHT

NIGHT JOURNAL

— I think of Issa, a man of few words:
The world of dew
Is the world of dew.
And yet . . .
And yet . . .

— Three words contain
                    all that we know for sure of the next life
Or the last one: Close your eyes.
Everything else is gossip,
                    false mirrors, trick windows
Flashing like Dutch glass
In the undiminishable sun.

— I write it down in visible ink,
Black words that disappear when held up to the light —
I write it down
            not to remember but to forget,
Words like thousands of pieces of shot film
                            exposed to the sun.
I never see anything but the ground.

— Everyone wants to tell his story.
The Chinese say we live in the world of the 10,000 things,
Each of the 10,000 things
                    crying out to us
Precisely nothing,
A silence whose tune we've come to understand,
Words like birthmarks,
                embolic sunsets drying behind the tongue.
If we were as eloquent,
If what we say could spread the good news the way that dogwood does,
Its votive candles
            phosphorous and articulate in the green haze
Of spring, surely something would hear us.

— Even a chip of beauty
                    is beauty intractable in the mind,
Words the color of wind
Moving across the fields there
                        wind-addled and wind-sprung,

Abstracted as water glints,
The fields lion-colored and rope-colored,
As in a picture of Paradise,
                      the bodies languishing over the sky
Trailing their dark identities
That drift off and sieve away to the nothingness
Behind them
             moving across the fields there
As words move, slowly, trailing their dark identities.

— Our words, like blown kisses, are swallowed by ghosts
Along the way,
               their destinations bereft
In a rub of brightness unending:
How distant everything always is,
                   and yet how close,
Music starting to rise like smoke from under the trees.

— Birds sing an atonal row
               unsyncopated
From tree to tree,
          dew chants
Whose songs have no words
              from tree to tree
When night puts her dark lens in,
One on this limb, two others back there.

— Words, like all things, are caught in their finitude.
They start here, they finish here
No matter how high they rise —
                  my judgment is that I know this
And never love anything hard enough
That would stamp me
            and sink me suddenly into bliss.

© Gerard Malanga

James Wright

SAINT JUDAS

When I went out to kill myself, I caught
A pack of hoodlums beating up a man.
Running to spare his suffering, I forgot
My name, my number, how my day began.
How soldiers milled around the garden stone
And sang amusing songs; how all that day
Their javelins measured crowds; how I alone
Bargained the proper coins, and slipped away.

Banished from heaven, I found this victim beaten.
Stripped, kneed, and left to cry. Dropping my rope
Aside, I ran, ignored the uniforms:
Then I remembered bread my flesh had eaten,
The kiss that ate my flesh. Flayed without hope,
I held the man for nothing in my arms.

GOODBYE TO THE POETRY OF CALCIUM

> *Dark cypresses —*
> *The world is uneasily happy:*
> *It will all be forgotten.*
>
> *Theodor Storm*

Mother of roots, you have not seeded
The tall ashes of loneliness
For me. Therefore,
Now I go.
If I knew the name,
Your name, all trellises of vineyards and old fire
Would quicken to shake terribly my
Earth, mother of spiralling searches, terrible
Fable of calcium, girl. I crept this afternoon
In weeds once more,
Casual, daydreaming you might not strike
Me down. Mother of window sills and journeys,
Hallower of scratching hands,

The sight of my blind man makes me want to weep.
Tiller of waves or whatever, woman or man,
Mother of roots or father of diamonds,
Look: I am nothing.
I do not even have ashes to rub into my eyes.

AS I STEP OVER A PUDDLE AT THE END OF WINTER, I THINK OF AN ANCIENT CHINESE GOVERNOR

> *And how can I, born in evil days*
> *And fresh from failure, ask a kindness*
> *of Fate?*
>
> Written A.D. *819*

Po Chu-i, balding old politician,
What's the use?
I think of you,
Uneasily entering the gorges of the Yang-Tze,
When you were being towed up the rapids
Toward some political job or other
In the city of Chungshou.
You made it, I guess,
By dark.

But it is 1960, it is almost spring again,
And the tall rocks of Minneapolis
Build me my own black twilight
Of bamboo ropes and waters.
Where is Yuan Chen, the friend you loved?
Where is the sea, that once solved the whole loneliness
Of the Midwest? Where is Minneapolis? I can see nothing
But the great terrible oak tree darkening with winter.
Did you find the city of isolated men beyond mountains?
Or have you been holding the end of a frayed rope
For a thousand years?

AUTUMN BEGINS IN MARTINS FERRY, OHIO

In the Shreve High football stadium,
I think of Polacks nursing long beers in Tiltonsville,
And gray faces of Negroes in the blast furnace at Benwood,

And the ruptured night watchman of Wheeling Steel,
Dreaming of heroes.

All the proud fathers are ashamed to go home.
Their women cluck like starved pullets,
Dying for love.

Therefore,
Their sons grow suicidally beautiful
At the beginning of October,
And gallop terribly against each other's bodies.

LYING IN A HAMMOCK AT WILLIAM DUFFY'S FARM IN PINE ISLAND, MINNESOTA

Over my head, I see the bronze butterfly,
Asleep on the black trunk,
Blowing like a leaf in green shadow.
Down the ravine behind the empty house,
The cowbells follow one another
Into the distances of the afternoon.
To my right,
In a field of sunlight between two pines,
The droppings of last year's horses
Blaze up into golden stones.
I lean back, as the evening darkens and comes on.
A chicken hawk floats over, looking for home.
I have wasted my life.

THE JEWEL

There is this cave
In the air behind my body
That nobody is going to touch:
A cloister, a silence
Closing around a blossom of fire.
When I stand upright in the wind,
My bones turn to dark emeralds.

FEAR IS WHAT QUICKENS ME

1

Many animals that our fathers killed in America
Had quick eyes.
They stared about wildly,
When the moon went dark.
The new moon falls into the freight yards
Of cities in the south,
But the loss of the moon to the dark hands of Chicago
Does not matter to the deer
In this northern field.

2

What is that tall woman doing
There, in the trees?
I can hear rabbits and mourning doves whispering together
In the dark grass, there
Under the trees.

3

I look about wildly.

A BLESSING

Just off the highway to Rochester, Minnesota,
Twilight bounds softly forth on the grass.
And the eyes of those two Indian ponies
Darken with kindness.
They have come gladly out of the willows
To welcome my friend and me.
We step over the barbed wire into the pasture
Where they have been grazing all day, alone.
They ripple tensely, they can hardly contain their happiness
That we have come.

They bow shyly as wet swans. They love each other.
There is no loneliness like theirs.
At home once more,
They begin munching the young tufts of spring in the darkness.
I would like to hold the slenderer one in my arms,
For she has walked over to me
And nuzzled my left hand.
She is black and white,
Her mane falls wild on her forehead,
And the light breeze moves me to caress her long ear
That is delicate as the skin over a girl's wrist.
Suddenly I realize
That if I stepped out of my body I would break
Into blossom.

IN RESPONSE TO A RUMOR THAT THE OLDEST
WHOREHOUSE IN WHEELING, WEST VIRGINIA,
HAS BEEN CONDEMNED

I will grieve alone,
As I strolled alone, years ago, down along
The Ohio shore.
I hid in the hobo jungle weeds
Upstream from the sewer main,
Pondering, gazing.

I saw, down river,
At Twenty-third and Water Streets
By the vinegar works,
The doors open in early evening.
Swinging their purses, the women
Poured down the long street to the river
And into the river.

I do not know how it was
They could drown every evening.
What time near dawn did they climb up the other shore,
Drying their wings?
For the river at Wheeling, West Virginia,
Has only two shores:
The one in hell, the other
In Bridgeport, Ohio.

And nobody would commit suicide, only
To find beyond death
Bridgeport, Ohio.

A POEM OF TOWERS

I am becoming one
Of the old men.
I wonder about them,
And how they became
So happy. Tonight
The trees in the Carl Schurz
Park by the East River
Had no need of electricity
To light their boughs, for the moon
And my love were enough.
More than enough the garbage
Scow plunging, the front hoof
Of a mule gone so wild through the water,
No need to flee. Who pities
You tonight, white-haired
Lu Yu? Wise and foolish
Both are gone, and my love
Leans on my shoulder precise
As the flute notes
Of the snow, with songs
And poems scattered
Over Shu, over the East River
That loves them and drowns them.

BEAUTIFUL OHIO

Those old Winnebago men
Knew what they were singing.
All summer long and all alone,
I had found a way
To sit on a railroad tie
Above the sewer main.
It spilled a shining waterfall out of a pipe

Somebody had gouged through the slanted earth.
Sixteen thousand and five hundred more or less people
In Martins Ferry, my home, my native country,
Quickened the river
With the speed of light.
And the light caught there
The solid speed of their lives
In the instant of that waterfall.
I know what we call it
Most of the time.
But I have my own song for it,
And sometimes, even today,
I call it beauty.

SAYING DANTE ALOUD

You can feel the muscles and veins rippling in widening and rising circles,
like a bird in flight under your tongue.

A SMALL GROVE IN TORRI DEL BENACO

Outside our window we have a small willow, and a little beyond it a fig
tree, and then a stone shed. Beyond the stone the separate trees suddenly
become a grove: a lemon, a mimosa, an oleander, a pine, one of the tall
slender cypresses that a poet here once called candles of darkness that
ought to be put out in winter, another willow, and a pine.

She stands among them in her flowered green clothes. Her skin is
darker gold than the olives in the morning sun. Two hours ago we got up
and bathed in the lake. It was like swimming in a vein. Everything that
can blossom is blossoming around her now. She is the eye of the grove,
the eye of mimosa and willow. The cypress behind her catches fire.

THE JOURNEY

Anghiari is medieval, a sleeve sloping down
A steep hill, suddenly sweeping out
To the edge of a cliff, and dwindling.
But far up the mountain, behind the town,

We too were swept out, out by the wind,
Alone with the Tuscan grass.

Wind had been blowing across the hills
For days, and everything now was graying gold
With dust, everything we saw, even
Some small children scampering along a road,
Twittering Italian to a small caged bird.
We sat beside them to rest in some brushwood,
And I leaned down to rinse the dust from my face.

I found the spider web there, whose hinges
Reeled heavily and crazily with the dust,
Whole mounds and cemeteries of it, sagging
And scattering shadows among shells and wings.
And then she stepped into the center of air
Slender and fastidious, the golden hair
Of daylight along her shoulders, she poised there,
While ruins crumbled on every side of her.
Free of the dust, as though a moment before
She had stepped inside the earth, to bathe herself.

I gazed, close to her, till at last she stepped
Away in her own good time.

Many men
Have searched all over Tuscany and never found
What I found there, the heart of the light
Itself shelled and leaved, balancing
On filaments themselves falling. The secret
Of this journey is to let the wind
Blow its dust all over your body,
To let it go on blowing, to step lightly, lightly
All the way through your ruins, and not to lose
Any sleep over the dead, who surely
Will bury their own, don't worry.

OHIOAN PASTORAL

On the other side
Of Salt Creek, along the road, the barns topple
And snag among the orange rinds,
Oil cans, cold balloons of lovers.

One barn there
Sags, sags and oozes
Down one side of the copperous gully.
The limp whip of a sumac dangles
Gently against the body of a lost
Bathtub, while high in the flint-cracks
And the wild grimed trees, on the hill,
A buried gas main
Long ago tore a black gutter into the mines.
And now it hisses among the green rings
On fingers in coffins.

LIGHTNING BUGS ASLEEP IN THE AFTERNOON

These long-suffering and affectionate shadows,
These fluttering jewels, are trying to get
Some sleep in a dry shade beneath the cement
Joists of the railroad trestle.

I did not climb up here to find them.
It was only my ordinary solitude
I was following up here this afternoon.
Last evening I sat here with a girl.

It was a dangerous place to be a girl
And young. But she simply folded her silent
Skirt over bare knees, printed with the flowered cotton
Of a meal sack her mother had stitched for her.

Neither of us said anything to speak of.
These affectionate, these fluttering bodies
Signaled to one another under the bridge
While the B&O 40-and-8's rattled away.

Now ordinary and alone in the afternoon,
I find this little circle of insects
Common as soot, clustering on dim stone,
Together with their warm secrets.

I think I am going to leave them folded
And sleeping in their slight gray wings.
I think I am going to climb back down
And open my eyes and shine.

Contemporary American Poetry: The Radical Tradition

American poetry since 1945 may be viewed as the product of the dialectics of generations. A recurrent phenomenon in literary as well as in much human history, the pattern of one generation's revolt against another is familiar — indeed, seemingly always close at hand. That rebellion, however, is usually not so much against the preceding generation's essential beliefs as against its excesses: principle atrophied into prejudice, freshness of thought and sensibility petrified into cliché, discipline forged into tyranny. Moreover, the revolution doesn't always realize a clean break with the immediate or distant past: the blood, the genes remain, camouflaged by a radical facade.

While emphasizing the freshness of contemporary poetry, some poets and critics have argued that it reflects a violent break with the first-generation modernist poetry of T. S. Eliot and Ezra Pound — if not with all tradition. In the introduction to his own important anthology of contemporary American poetry (1962), Donald Hall announced that the orthodoxy of T. S. Eliot and the New Critics had ceased: "In modern art anarchy has proved preferable to the restrictions of a benevolent tyranny." The contemporary artist, Hall wrote, "has acted as if restlessness were a conviction and has destroyed his own past in order to create a future." In *The Poem in Its Skin* (1968), Paul Carroll argued that contemporary poets have attempted "to write poems either alien or hostile to the poem as defined and explored by Eliot and leading writers dominating the scene ten or fifteen years ago." Later Carroll asserted: "This generation of American poets is on the high, happy adventure of creating and innovating a complex of new ways in which to view our common condition — an adventure which in its abundance, freshness, and originality is . . . as interesting as any since the Olympians of 1917."

That the adventure of today's poets has been somewhat anarchic but abundantly fresh is unquestionable. That it has produced poems entirely alien to the earlier modernist poetry is open to a good measure of debate. But the proposition that contemporary American poets have destroyed their own past as poets, for whatever reasons, is simply untenable. Admittedly, T. S. Eliot may have been aesthetically, temperamentally, and constitutionally incapable of writing such poems as Sylvia Plath's "Daddy," Maxine Kumin's "The Excrement Poem," Frank O'Hara's campy poem to Lana Turner, or Marge Piercy's "Barbie Doll." And such New Critics as Allen Tate, John Crowe Ransom, and William Empson, who transformed the experiments of modernist poets into a legislative critical system, would not have known what to make of certain kinds of poems. When confronted by the poems in Robert Lowell's *Life Studies*, Allen Tate reportedly turned to Lowell, his former student — known as Cal to friends — and agonizingly blurted: "But, *Cal*, it's not *poetry!*"

Although the dicta of the New Critics are no longer regarded as sacred commandments by contemporary poets, much of their valid aesthetic substance has been retained — as have some of the older and more profound literary traditions. In *The New Poets* (1967), M. L. Rosenthal convincingly traced the connections by which much of today's poetry may be considered a continuation and expansion of a strong Romantic tradition. Hyatt H. Waggoner (*American Poetry from the Puritans to the Present*, 1968) and more recently Robert Pinsky (*The Situation of Poetry*, 1976) have explored the ways in which the contemporary American poet actively participates in various other traditions, especially the Emersonian tradition. No less important is the continuing presence of the equally profound Puritan and Whitman traditions: they are both still active and vital, influencing the formal and thematic directions of much contemporary poetry. In short, if today's poets have achieved a unique vitality, they have done so by making full (if not always quite so obvious) use of the past — immediate and distant, personal and communal, literary and cultural — while simultaneously contributing new and energizing elements of their own.

The characteristics of the first-generation modernist poem are obviously vital elements in the work of such poets as Richard Wilbur, Robert Lowell, John Berryman, and Stanley Kunitz, who in 1945 were the "younger" poets of the modernist generation and whose sensibilities were shaped by the New Critics. Commenting on his own work in *Poets on Poetry* (1966), Wilbur said: "Most American poets of my generation were taught to admire the English Metaphysical poets of the seventeenth century and such contemporary masters of irony as John Crowe Ransom. We were led by our teachers and by the critics whom we read to feel that the most adequate and convincing poetry is that which accommodates mixed feelings, clashing ideas, and incongruous images. Poetry could not be honest, we thought, unless it began by acknowledging the full discordancy of modern life and consciousness. I still believe that to be a true view of poetry." Written under the tutelage of John Crowe Ransom and Allen Tate, Robert Lowell's early work, in particular, was immediately hailed as a model of what the modernist poem could and should be. And John Berryman's later monumental series, *The Dream Songs*, clearly employs the essential techniques and assumptions of modernist poetry, as does some of the work by younger poets such as Louise Glück and William Matthews.

One of the major differences between modernist and contemporary poetry is that the latter is more intimate and personal — or at least seems to be. The elements of the modernist poem seemed consciously employed toward assuring a certain artistic distance between the poets and their subjects, the poets and their poems. From the purposeful use of persona to the conscious use of unmistakable "literary" tradition, each technique was a formal, emotional, and intellectual device for the poets' objectification of subject, emotion, and medium. The individual personality of the poets, their more intimate experiences and emotions, were not just seemingly absent: indeed, in light of Eliot's misunderstood dictum that poetry was an escape from personality, what are now considered to be the personal elements in poetry were virtually taboo among modernist poets. And in the hands of lesser poets, such an attitude often resulted in a depersonalized and inhuman versification.

As Ralph J. Mills, Jr., has amply demonstrated in his brilliant essay "Creation's Very Self" (reprinted in *Cry of the Human*, 1974), what distinguishes the work of contemporary poets from that of their modernist predecessors is especially the presence and vitality of the personal element. Although possibilities for objectification remain, poetry is no longer considered an escape from personality by contemporary poets but rather a fuller cultivation and use of personality. The personality of the poet is seemingly more central and more vibrant than the poetic device of the persona: "he" or "she" is now frequently replaced by "I." The speaker of the poem and the poet often seem to be one and the same, an indivisible person; the subject of a poem often seems to be the poet's own — at times intimate — experiences, which the poet seemingly does not seek to present as anything other than personal experience. Consequently, the full appreciation of some contemporary poems sometimes seems to hinge on the reader's knowledge of biographical details of the poet's personal and intimate life. For example, Robert Lowell was, in fact, jailed as a conscientious objector — as he says he was in "Memories of West Street and Lepke"; Sylvia Plath did attempt suicide — as she says she did in "Lady Lazarus"; Lucien Stryk and Charles Simic did confront firsthand the extremities of those war experiences they speak of in their poems. With the poet's private self as both subject and speaker of the poem, with the presence and use of the poet's own personality in the poem, the interaction between the work of art and the reader becomes proportionately more intimate: the poet seems to speak more directly to the reader, as if that reader were a confessor, psychiatrist, intimate friend, or lover.

The personalization of poetry has evolved in various other ways. In the work of Robert Bly, James Wright, and W. S. Merwin, for example, a personal poetry occurs as the result of the exploration of and response to the most inner reaches of the poet's self below the rational and conscious levels. Poems grow out of images discovered in the depths of human darkness, as it were, amidst the substrata of preconscious feeling and intuition. The personalization that occurs in Mark Strand's poetry is strangely the result of the extent to which he seems to consciously obliterate all traces of the surface textures of personality, thus offering a personality of absence rather than of presence. Through shifts of emotion, language, and tone all within the same poem, one senses in the work of John Logan the vital interaction among the various facets of an individual personality: the harmonious counterpoint between intellectual irony and corny self-deprecating humor, between religious feeling and vulgarity, between commonplace banality and high lyrical excitement — in short, an integration of the individual parts of a multidimensional personality.

Although they contain moments of private joy and grief, the poems of Allen Ginsberg and Frank O'Hara take another direction: they depend primarily on the self's discovery of the outer world and response to it. In these poems one often senses the poet's self, his personality, being shaped by the "surround" in which he finds himself. The reader hears with O'Hara's ears or touches with Ginsberg's hands. In the poetry of others, the personal element seems to evolve primarily out of the relationship between the poet's private self and the social as well as geographical landscape he inhabits and with which he interacts: the sophisticated suburban landscape of Simpson's poems; the bleak and desolate western landscape of Hugo's poems; both the urban and suburban sources of grief and joy in Gerald Stern's poems; the stark, almost threatening, presence of the city in C. K. Williams's later work; and the range of both emotional and geographical landscape from the hills of Tennessee to Laguna Beach, California, in the work of Charles Wright.

The personalization of American poetry since 1945 is probably most obvious in the work of those poets who have chosen to incorporate in their poems elements of their personal histories — and events in their individual lives usually considered intimate, private, or confidential. Until recently the sexual preferences of some of this century's great poets were among the best-kept secrets in literary history — in large part because they were rightfully considered irrelevant to the poetry. Consequently, Allen Ginsberg's and Robert Duncan's poems about aspects of their homosexuality, Adrienne Rich's open and moving explorations of her lesbianism, and even William Matthews's poem about his penis and peeing off the back of a boat or Rita Dove's tender poem about her and her daughter showing each other their vaginas may be somewhat startling to some readers. Indeed, many Americans still feel threatened by such sexual honesty. It is worth noting, however, that even a poem such as "The Love Song of J. Alfred Prufrock," which does not seem intimate, is probably as much an exploration of T. S. Eliot's feelings of sexual impotency as it is a record of Prufrock's frustrations. In any case, private revelations of personal illness, madness, failure, and self-destruction are some of the recurring subjects in the work of such personal-confessional poets as Lowell, Plath, Sexton, and Snodgrass.

Today's poets, then, have succeeded in making poetry that often resonates as being radically personal; however, under closer scrutiny other factors come into focus to temper the reader's immediate response. Subject and voice paradoxically work toward making even the most intimate poetry less personal than it first seems and result in erecting another kind of persona — the part of the private self that the poet chooses to make public. Because they have been primarily concerned with physical and psychic limitations, the personal-confessional poets have written a poetry that, to a large extent, reveals *only* the deteriorating self speaking in a chosen voice, ranging from the elegiac lament of W. D. Snodgrass to the modulated hysteria of Sylvia Plath. Moreover, in the work of some poets, the requirements of technique and craftsmanship raise further questions about just how personal and immediate a poem can be: by drawing attention to its formal qualities, even the poem ostensibly about the most intimate subject reminds the reader that the poem, any poem, is a fabrication and takes time and calculation to complete. Like any other art, personal poetry is a selective, calculated, and public gesture, a formal utterance for which the poet *selects* not only a language but also a voice, even if they are as approximate to his or her own as the poet can manage.

In his lecture entitled "The Inward Muse," Donald Hall may have been speaking for a number of his contemporaries when he said that while working on his early poems he "could sometimes hear the voice of Mr. Ransom" reminding him of irony and that "it took ten years to get rid of that voice." Nevertheless, irony and paradox continue to be vitally present in the work of today's poets. Confronted by the quality of our common condition, the sensitive and mature human being may not survive without a strong ironic sense: although irony may thwart much genuine emotion, its absence also makes genuine emotion virtually impossible. The uses of irony in contemporary poetry can be seen in the work of two rather different poets, Sylvia Plath and Frank O'Hara. In Sylvia Plath's poetry, the presence of irony serves to temper the intensity of suffering by undercutting the vehement and often near-Gothic imagery and the highly charged emotion. Indeed, many of Plath's more intense poems survive as *poems* specifically because her sharp ironic sense is also at play. For example, "Lady Lazarus" is protected from bathos not only by the ironic sense of humor that views the would-be suicide as "the big strip tease" in a three-ring circus of Nazi-artistic-Christian horrors but also through the intonation and line-break that begin the poem by suggesting that it could be spoken by a rich Jewish woman coming out of a beauty spa.

The irony in Frank O'Hara's poems may be more implicit — a pervasive impetus behind the total poem; nevertheless, it is present and crucial. In the poem to Lana Turner, for example, an ironic sensibility functions in a manner directly opposite to Plath's: it undercuts the humor by suggesting the emptiness — if not the decadence — of the emotion. In other words, in O'Hara's poems one recognizes the peculiar contemporary phenomenon of camp irony.

Because so much contemporary poetry seems so intensely personal, it also generally seems very direct and transparent; but the essential complexity of emotion, the richness of language, and the potential of form — not the least of which is the organic form of free verse — make ambiguity inescapable. On a rather basic level, for example, today's reader cannot avoid the rather obvious *double-entendre* in the opening lines of John Logan's "Love Poem": "Last night you would not come, / and you have been gone so long." John Ashbery's use of wide-open form and broken syntax in a poem like "Leaving the Atocha Station" often commands that the reader invent interpretation. The Proustian quality of James Merrill's later poems offers readers still another kind of complexity of language and texture. Robert Creeley's poems depend largely on structural ambiguity — the emotional and thematic tension between the linear unit and the syntactical unit — for their introverted effect. By eliminating punctuation in many of his poems since *The Moving Target*, W. S. Merwin succeeds in creating additional levels of ambiguity; and John Berryman achieves still another kind of ambiguity through a manipulation of pronouns referring to his schizoid persona.

Because many of today's poets have not been working in traditional poetic form in their pursuit of a more personal poetry, it would be a serious misunderstanding of the very nature of art in general and of poetry in particular if one were to assume that poets have discarded form altogether. In nature and in the world of things made by humans, form is virtually indistinguishable from essence. A tree is a tree, in part, because it has the general shape or form of a tree which differentiates it from that of a bush. A chair is a chair because its shape or form is what it is; there may be several variations of that form, but if one variation goes too far away from the essence of chairness, you have a stool; in the other direction, you have a chaise longue, which is one step removed from a couch or a bed. In poetry the line of demarcation may be somewhat subtle, as in the later poems of Louis Simpson and C. K. Williams, but it is nonetheless actively and recognizably real. While the language of those poems may sound like conversational prose, the energy that shapes the conversational tone is undoubtedly that of poetry and not that of conversation.

Clearly, a number of today's poets have continued to work with traditional forms throughout their career: Richard Wilbur, Carolyn Kizer, Isabella Gardner, and W. D. Snodgrass come to mind. Dissatisfied, unsympathetic, impatient, or simply uncomfortable with traditional form, John Berryman — by contrast — invented an entirely new form for his *Dream Songs*. For his poem sequence *History*, Robert Lowell modified the sonnet form. In "Counting the Mad," Donald Justice adopted and adapted the form of a nursery rhyme, "This Little Piggy Went to Market." In "Three Moves" John Logan made use of a musical structure somewhat like that of Mozart's "Eine Kleine Nachtmusik." And in "Long Island" Marvin Bell used syntactical repetitions and overlaid images as still another means of giving both internal and external shape to the poem.

Nevertheless, the long-standing battle between advocates of free verse and defenders of traditional forms goes on. Of late, in various essays and prefaces to anthologies, defenders of traditional form in poetry have sought to counter the celebration and influence of free verse (or poems in "open forms") found in anthologies like *Naked Poetry* and *New Naked Poetry*, edited by Stephen Berg and Robert Mezey and published in the 1970s. Robert Richman, the editor of *The Direction of Poetry: An Anthology of Rhymed and Metered Verse Written in the English Language Since 1975* (1988), would have us believe that, "After two decades of obscure, linguistically flat poetry, there has been a decisive shift . . . ; narration, characterization, and, perhaps most significantly, musicality are showing new vigor. The musicality is tied to a recent upsurge among poets in the use of metrical language." (Richman excluded certain poets from his anthology because of their "ambivalent attitude toward meter.")

If Richman's position is extreme, the position of his more vigorous critics — such as Ira Sadoff in an essay entitled "Neo-Formalism: A Dangerous Nostalgia," which originally appeared in *American Poetry Review* (1990) — is equally extreme. Sadoff (and others) argue that "neo-formalist" critics like Richman "have a social as well as a linguistic agenda. When they link pseudo-populism (the 'general reader') to regular meter, they disguise their nostalgia for moral and linguistic certainty, for a universal ('everyone agrees') and univocal way of conserving culture. . . . It is also no accident," Sadoff continues, "that at a time in our history when neo-conservatism dominates our social and political life, when the American Empire is shrinking, that the poetic fashion parallels the historical moment: conservative poets want to restore art to the nostalgic ideal of fixed harmonies, of pure beauty and grace, to restore the 'essential moral values' of 'western civilization'. . . ." As is often the case, the truth is perhaps closer to the center than at the opposite ends of ideological postures. Although some poets and critics may believe (in the words of Stanley Kunitz) that "Non-metrical verse has swept the field," Philip Dacey and David Jauss, the editors of *Strong Measures: Contemporary American Poetry in Traditional Forms* (1986), have rightfully argued that free verse, which was once revolutionary, "has long since become the fashion. . . ." Nevertheless, "many poets have continued to write in traditional forms (and) poetry in fixed forms continues to have value and relevance."

One characteristic of the modernist poem that seems less prevalent in contemporary poetry is wit, especially as the word is used to refer to a kind of cerebral-aesthetic humor. A measure of this intellectual wit still can be found in the poems of William Matthews and Carolyn Kizer, and, most obviously, in a poem like Richard Wilbur's "Praise in Summer," in which the genuine and vibrant wit controlling the thrust of the last line paradoxically negates *and* affirms the entire poem's thematic concern. However, much of today's poetry is generally marked by a much broader brand of humor, often a buffoonish or slapstick comedy. In "Pro Femina," Carolyn Kizer obviously relies on a broad, healthy humor to achieve her feminist theme effectively, and in many of her poems Lucille Clifton employs the kind of sharp and wry humor that is recognizably a part of the rich African American tradition of humor; in Clifton's poems, humor is as much an engagement of the physical body as it is a matter of language. In *The Dream Songs*, Berryman consciously uses minstrel comedy, situation comedy, and burlesque techniques, including a kind of verbal double take. In many of his poems, Lawrence Ferlinghetti is the literary Red Skelton of his generation, the innocent clown bumbling through an absurd, though sophisticated, universe where he, as poet and person, is constantly risking absurdity. As Paul Carroll has observed, Ferlinghetti — especially when he reads his poems — sounds like a hip Will Rogers. Moreover, in contemporary poetry comedy often belies the poet's intent; humor verges on hysteria, laughter camouflages horror: Pagliacci facing a firing squad.

The reader of modernist poetry has come to expect allusion as part and parcel of a poem: T. S. Eliot's *The Waste Land* is the archetype of the poem as footnote. However, contemporary poets have consciously avoided the excesses of literary allusion that resulted in a "poetry about poetry." Although most post–World War II poets are university graduates and professional academicians, their poems do not obviously wear their erudition on their sleeves. The reasons are varied and complex. The scarcity of allusion, in part, is the result of the democratization of poetry under the strong influence of Walt Whitman and of William Carlos Williams, both of whom advocated the use of an American language and rhythm. Moreover, because much contemporary poetry is often intensely personal, the poet responds to experience in a visceral rather than in an intellectual fashion. Response is not filtered or controlled by knowledge or formal education, nor is it shaped by a conscious sense of the formal tradition. That this is an age when the individual, the self, is threatened by the dehumanization of a technocratic society and by the overwhelming sense of imminent atomic or ecological annihilation has long been a journalistic cliché — albeit one that has recently been infused with unequaled urgency. The energy we depend on for survival, just as surely as the fetus depends on the mother's blood for survival, is running out. Accidents at the Three Mile Island and Chernobyl nuclear power plants remind us too acutely that our technology is as flawed and dangerous as the human intelligence that produced it. Despite the cliché of annihilation, the phenomenon is all too real and has resulted in the poet's vehement affirmation of the individual self and in an equally intense effort to respond fully to experience as a person and as an artist. This kind of Emersonian self-reliance — with absolute stakes — is an implicit repudiation of Eliot's theory of tradition and the individual talent, perhaps in large part because of the contemporary poet's profound fear of that history, culture, and tradition, which are ultimately responsible for the deterioration of the modern self.

Compared to Eliot and his followers, today's poet is noticeably less concerned with the use of allusion. However, as Susan Sontag has written: "Language is the most impure, the most contaminated, the most exhausted of all materials out of which art is made. . . . It's scarcely possible for the artist to write a word (or render an image or make a gesture) that doesn't remind him of something already achieved." Consequently, because language is contaminated, because history shackles, and because post–World War II poets simply cannot escape their own (and our) ruthless memory, allusion — conscious or not — persists and is found in both expected and unexpected places.

The more obvious examples of allusion can be found in the early work of Lowell, such as "Christmas Eve Under Hooker's Statue"; it can be found in such poems as Snodgrass's "April Inventory," which can be read as a retelling of an academic Prufrock's story, with intermittent references to Shakespeare's seventy-third sonnet, Hopkins's "God's Grandeur," Edward Taylor's "Meditation Six, First Series" — and with echoes of Thoreau and Camus. Ferlinghetti's "I Am Waiting," in spite of his renunciation of "poetry about poetry," relies heavily on obvious and well-known literary phrases. In Ashbery's "Leaving the Atocha Station," Paul Carroll has ferreted out mangled echoes of Pound, Eliot, Hopkins, and others. Certain critics have noted that James Dickey's famous "The Heaven of Animals" is derivative of and perhaps consciously fashioned after Edwin Muir's "The Animals." A number of Louis Simpson's poems rely on the reader's being fully conversant with the work of Walt Whitman.

The burden of language and the grasp of memory result in the contemporary poet's using other kinds of allusion. For example, the presence of Rilke is clearly felt in the concluding line of James Wright's "Lying in a Hammock . . ." The position, tone, and emotional impact of Wright's line, "I have wasted my life," echoes the concluding line of Rilke's "Torso of an Archaic Apollo," which is generally translated as "You must change your life." Rilke's ninth "Duino Elegy" is present in the very title of Maxine Kumin's book, *House, Bridge, Fountain, Gate* — just as it is present in the concluding lines of Richard Hugo's poem "Montgomery Hollow." Moreover, in much of John Ashbery's more recent poetry, there is an even more all-pervasive *frisson* of Rilke's own elusive exploration of states of feeling; a specific poem like "Street Musicians" recalls the kind of vision and perspective found in Rilke's *Das Buch der Bilder* (*The Book of Pictures*) and *Neue Gedichte* (*New Poems*). The imagery, tone, and effect of several of Robert Bly's poems reflect the more intense presence and influence of the Spanish surrealists Neruda and Vallejo. The imaginative and emotional lilt of Cavafy, the Greek master, is occasionally felt in Gerald Stern's poems, just as the influence of the Italian poet Eugenio Montale (whom Wright has translated) is occasionally felt in Charles Wright's poems.

Rather than relying on sometimes obscure literary allusions of the past, today's poet prefers to introduce more personal allusions to specific places, people, and experiences in the poet's personal life: Long Island, Missoula, Pine Island, William Duffy. The contemporary arts, especially the popular arts and popular performers, also become points of reference: movies, folk-rock, jazz, Lana Turner, Joan Baez, Bob Dylan, John Coltrane, and others. Contemporary poetry, then, is very much the poetry of today, requiring from the reader as much full consciousness of the present as of the past, of the banal as of the sublime.

Just as the contemporary poet is more drawn toward existential experience, he or she is also less inclined to use what Eliot understood to be "the mythical method" to organize and present experience. Indeed, except as a subconscious, elemental, and perhaps inevitable ritualistic pattern of human response, myth is virtually absent from the work of most post–1945 poets. However, if the traditional mythic method at this moment in history is not entirely viable, the mythical vision and the need for it remain an active force in contemporary poetry. During the past forty years, American poets seem to have felt an increasing need to be not simply myth users, but myth makers. Even when poets feel the need to use traditional myth, as Carolyn Kizer does in "Semele Recycled" and Rita Dove does in "Bulrush," that need is accompanied by a commensurate need to modify the figures and configurations of the original. Both as persons and as poets, myth makers reflect "the instinct that their work-a-day world is interpenetrated with a super rational or extrarational activity in which they can and do share." If the pattern of such more-than-human activity is not immediately accessible as part of a formalized tradition, then poets must dig it out of the accumulation of their experience and create myths closer to the contemporary experience than those inherited from myth makers of the past. By so doing, contemporary poets are also returning poetry to one of its primal and sacred functions. Along with Carolyn Kizer, they trust that future generations will "concoct a scripture explaining this."

In the poetry of W. D. Snodgrass, a rather clear pattern of extrarational activity emerges, against which the action of the poem takes place and in which the speaker senses inevitable participation. As Snodgrass says in *Heart's Needle*, "We need the landscape to repeat us." This pattern is quite simply Darwin's theory of evolution subsequently transformed into the law of the survival of the fittest. Snodgrass may not be pleased to find himself participating in this brutal dialectic, but he recognizes its energy as one of the major determinants of human activity: in "After Experience . . . ," he juxtaposes the rules of survival spoken softly by the gentle philosopher Spinoza with those shouted by a military instructor. The same concern for survival is also the energy generating "April Inventory," in which those who seem most fit to survive are the "solid scholars" who get "the degrees, the jobs, the dollars." In his more recent cycle of poems, *The Führer Bunker*, Snodgrass has coupled the myth of the survival of the fittest with the drama of Nazi Germany, and he has sought to reconstruct this contemporary myth without subjective or moral comment.

Other poets also have discovered myth in this and other contemporary dramas and figures. For an age of violence, Sylvia Plath has turned away from the ancient mythology found in her earlier poetry, such as the Colossus of Rhodes, and toward more recent history — Hiroshima, Hitler's concentration camps — for the mythic background against which her personal suffering occurs. For an age of media, Frank O'Hara has recognized the mythic dimensions of those "stars" whose personal and public lives determine the rhythm and quality of this civilization just as surely as the fabricated gods of other mythologies. Michael S. Harper has acknowledged much the same role that African American jazz musicians serve in his imagination and no doubt in the imagination of a great many other Americans (William Matthews among them) who have had an intense emotional and aesthetic relationship with those musical artists. In the character of Henry Pussycat, Berryman has erected a myth out of, and for, the suffering, middle-aged, white "human American man." But throughout contemporary poetry, one also senses that the isolated self — the multifaceted and complex "I" — rises above communal, historical, and extrarational events and assumes mythic proportions of its own. Contemporary poets seem determined to accept Wallace Stevens's words at face value and "to make of their fate an instance of all fate." The collective impact of today's poetry, then, seems to say: I am my own myth.

The blood and genes inherited by contemporary poetry, however, are not merely the formal demands of New Criticism but the full tradition of American and British poetry. Muted, modified, transformed — nonetheless, the spirit and energy of this tradition continue as vital forces in today's poetry. And it is not simply an aesthetic heritage, but a complex of formal and thematic stances that constitute the polarities not only of our art but also probably of our psychic and mythic life.

The polarized stances — toward humankind, its history, the substance and quality of its individual and communal life, its art, and its destiny — constituting the mainstream of American poetry are the Puritan tradition and the Whitman tradition. Of course, other less powerful currents also have contributed to the evolution of American poetry. But the life and energy of American poetry, especially in the twentieth century, spring primarily from the tension, balance, and occasional reconciliation between the microcosmic and macrocosmic vision of the Puritan and Whitman traditions. What is vitally important about these two major traditions is specifically that each is a comprehensive vision of and response to the total human and cosmic experience. The significance of such a vision cannot be stressed enough, for it strongly influences (perhaps determines) what a poet sees and how a poet responds — influencing the subjects and the themes of poems — as well as the poet's mode of expression of style — shaping the language, rhythm, structure, and form of poems.

Whether written by Edward Taylor or Robert Lowell, Puritan poetry arises out of the fundamental view of humans as the heirs of the specific history of the fallen Adam. It views humans as essentially corrupt, as seeking the contours of their lives in an equally corrupt universe, and as incapable of personal salvation. Characteristically intellectual and highly personal, seeking the speaker's place in history, this poetry focuses primarily on the individual's spiritual and physical limitations and deterioration. Its structure is usually complex, emblematic, and metaphysical; the texture of its language is intricate. Because contemporary Puritan poets have rejected the possibility of the traditional concept of salvation — the one thread of light that sustained the original Puritan — in large part because the death of God is accepted as a premise of contemporary existence, sin is therefore symbolically replaced by mental and emotional imbalance. Lacking the hope of salvation while still believing in profound personal evil, the more recent Puritan poet is threatened by madness and is tempted to self-destruction, even though the very act of writing poetry is an affirmative one, a saying *no* to any force that would destroy the human spirit. The poetry of Robert Lowell, Sylvia Plath, and Anne Sexton probably best exemplifies the aesthetic and moral dimensions of the Puritan tradition in contemporary American poetry.

The Whitman tradition in contemporary poetry stands in stark contrast to the earlier Puritan tradition. Refusing to submit humans to the bonds of history, sacred or secular, this tradition asserts the holiness of the Adamic self, inside and out, and celebrates the grace of purely human and physical activity in a holy universe. Impatient with and often scornful of intellectualization, it focuses on the unique and separate self and points to the self's limitless potential for transcendence. Open, loose, often the product of emotion rather than of intellect or conspicuous craftsmanship, its language also tends to be more recognizably "American" and earthy. However, if poets in the contemporary Puritan tradition accept the death of God as a premise of existence, so too do poets in the contemporary Whitman tradition accept the rather tragic futility of the original Whitman vision. Thus Whitman's vision and his poems often serve as the basis for lament, and the contemporary poet decries the betrayal of history since Whitman's prophetic songs. Such a sense of betrayal is at the root of Allen Ginsberg's "Howl" and serves as the aesthetic and moral background against which so much of Louis Simpson's and David Ignatow's poetry evolves.

As critics have noted, American poetry also has continued to experience a large measure of internationalization and reflects the presence of other traditions. The influence of the French symbolists persists. Rilke's presence seems to loom larger and larger. Pound's "discovery" of the East can be traced to the next generation: one can observe the influence of Japanese poetry on the work of poets like Gary Snyder, Robert Hass, and, especially, Lucien Stryk; the influence of Chinese poetry on the work of James Wright is also unmistakable. The work of Spanish surrealists has had a profound effect on the work of poets like Philip Levine and Robert Bly. And the fact that Charles Simic spent his formative years in Yugoslavia no doubt molded his imagination. That so many of today's American poets are also active and distinguished translators — as their bibliographies in this book make obvious — has also contributed to the internationalization of contemporary poetry in America.

Clearly, then, the vitality of contemporary American poetry depends in large part on its full participation in and transformation of a rich tradition of poetry. And yet, after having posited this participation, one must also recognize the contemporary poets' real measure of dissatisfaction and restlessness not only with that tradition but also with their specific art and medium — which also accounts for the vitality and diversity of today's poetry.

The poets' restlessness with their medium is largely evident in the number of those who, for various reasons, have changed their styles radically in the course of their careers. These stylistic transformations, in turn, reflect equally radical shifts in the poets' basic assumptions about the nature and function of their art. After having mastered the lyric rooted in the tenets of New Criticism, Robert Lowell discarded the lyric form in favor of a semi-sonnet form, which he subsequently discarded to return once again to the lyric in his last poems. From compact and trippingly anapestic poems dealing with somewhat private experience, James Dickey's poems have grown more expansive, looser, and more public — often charged by a kind of revivalist energy. On the other hand, W. S. Merwin's poems have moved from technical and structural complexity toward an imaginative and emotional density that is almost hermetic. At times savagely personal, some of Merwin's poems seemed to refuse all further human contact. Donald Hall's poems have evolved from a relatively strict formalism to a more expansive, Whitmanesque, and commensurately more human organic form. The poems of Charles Wright, Louise Glück, and C. K. Williams have moved from a certain tight and knotty intensity to a more accessible and serene expansiveness.

Other poets have shown a restlessness with their chosen medium by attempting the techniques of other media. Experiments with the prose poem by such writers as Robert Bly, Robert Hass, Charles Simic, and James Wright are self-evident manifestations of discontent with the limits of more traditional poetic forms. In most of *The Anonymous Lover*, John

Logan sought a closer, more obvious relationship between poetic and musical language. Lawrence Ferlinghetti's poems often explore the possibilities of poetry as a kind of verbal jazz; and some of John Ashbery's poems clearly reflect the influence of action painting. Drawing on Ashbery's experiments in his early work, Gertrude Stein's writing, Charles Olson's theory of projective verse, the French surrealists and dadaists, as well as on the aesthetics of composer John Cage, the "language" poets (not represented in this anthology) have taken language itself as their subject. Breaking down the syntax of normal communication and experimenting with traditional notions of how "meaning" is conveyed, they push T. S. Eliot's "cinematic technique" to its limits in a high-tech, video age. Underlying these stylistic transformations and experiments is not merely an obsession with originality but also a profound need to shape the structures and rhythms — as well as to explore the timbre — of the voice of the individual poet and of the times.

Each age discovers or fabricates one or two all-encompassing metaphors for the quality of human experience that it confronts or seeks. It was T. S. Eliot, of course, who fabricated the first encompassing metaphor for the twentieth century; the waste land was the image of human spiritual and cultural sterility — an image that, after Hiroshima and Nagasaki, proved to be frighteningly precise in its prophetic implications. To date, no single poet seems to have fabricated *the* central metaphor for the quality of our experience since World War II. Rather, this is what seems to have happened: although *The Waste Land* was a powerful *mise en scène* of the modern situation, to a large extent its characters were composite ghosts, unreal men and women in an unreal city. Eliot was describing the human condition, not the individual condition. In other words, Eliot set the scene, but contemporary poets have peopled that waste land, mostly with their individual selves. They have described the deterioration and sterility of the individual self, thereby fabricating a cumulative metaphor for our own age.

The language of this metaphor is as stark, brutal, and familiar as the experience. More often than not, it is the language of experience and emotion — and not "recollected in tranquillity" (Wordsworth). The brutalized self responds neither in pentameters nor in euphemisms — nor, at times, even in metaphor. In the midst of unbearable suffering, Sylvia Plath, as do most of us, utters the most commonplace of clichés. In "Three Moves," at the peak of emotion and frustration, John Logan utters what in polite society would be considered vulgarities — but here transformed into lyrical epiphanies by their contextual power. The emotional and aesthetic impact of Lucille Clifton's poems relies especially on her use of an African American idiom that not only seeks to duplicate the rhythms of the street but is also deeply rooted in African and African American folk songs and tales. In differing ways, today's poets have followed the advice and example of Walt Whitman and of William Carlos Williams, who both sought to democratize the language of poetry; and they agree with George Starbuck's remark: "We've got language we haven't yet used." Above all, it is the language of today's poetry that immediately strikes us as vital, contemporary, and fresh. By making poetry out of the full range of everyday speech — including obscenity, vulgarity, and slang — contemporary poets have returned to poetry a richness of expression and experience that had been absent probably since the Renaissance.

Contemporary poets have managed to reinstate in poetry a directness and honesty toward the human tribe's sexual identity and experience, with all its ramifications. The range is virtually all-encompassing: menstruation, masturbation, lovemaking, adultery, homosexuality, lesbianism, sodomy, abortion. Whether the cause for celebration or lamentation or both, sexuality in today's poetry is neither a programmatic metaphor, a consciously Freudian exploration, nor a pseudomystical Lawrencian Victorianism. Although clearly an essential element of the poet's theme, first and foremost it is an existential human experience, capable of being simultaneously ugly and the source of grace and, as John Berryman suggests, simultaneously lyrical and vulgar: "like the memory of a lovely fuck."

An imagination of commitment that responds directly, honestly, and morally to a broad spectrum of everyday political realities is also one of the distinguishing elements of today's poetry. The political climate has become a crucial arena within which contemporary poets have exercised their talents. This interest in politics reflects the contemporary poets' belief in a poetry *engagé* and thereby returns poetry to one of its long and vital traditions. The political tradition was all but ignored during the first half of the century, especially when the notion of art for art's sake virtually prohibited poetry from being anything but hermetic and when political concern had to be masked with myth, clothed with wit, and moved by indirection. Some reactionary critics still haven't forgiven Archibald MacLeish for his political involvements and concerns. But the contemporary poet agrees with Sartre and Camus that art must be committed if it is to survive. As Ferlinghetti said, "Only the dead are disengaged."

Commitment, however, does not necessitate blatant "headline" poetry. In a statement for *The London Magazine* (1962), Sylvia Plath suggested what an imagination of commitment really implies: "The issues of our time which preoccupy me at the moment are the incalculable genetic effects of fallout and . . . the terrifying, mad, omnipotent marriage of big business and the military in America . . . [But] my poems do not turn out to be about Hiroshima, but about a child forming itself finger by finger in the dark. They are not about the terrors of mass extinction, but about the bleakness of the moon over a yew tree in a neighborhood graveyard."

The imagination of commitment is reflected in at least three obvious, though by no means exclusive, ways in today's poetry. The first includes poems informed by a general and sometimes indirect sociopolitical consciousness. Plath's preoccupation with the "incalculable genetic effects of fallout" is reflected in "Nick and the Candlestick"; addressing her young — perhaps unborn — child, she suggests the end of the world and of the universe in two stanzas that also reflect the scientific quality of her imagination:

> Let the stars
> Plummet to their dark address.
>
> Let the mercuric
> Atoms that cripple drip
> Into the terrible well. . . .

The possible destruction of the world through a nuclear holocaust is also the immediate occasion for Wilbur's "Advice to a Prophet." In "After Experience Taught Me . . . ," Snodgrass suggests not only the inherent horror in any system of ideas or values carried to its logical conclusion but also that terrifying brotherhood of men — the seeming inevitability of the military-industrial-university complex. The extent to which most Americans live their conscious or subconscious lives in the constant threat of nuclear annihilation is eminently clear in Kinnell's "Vapor Trail Reflected in the Frog Pond," in Snyder's "Vapor Trails," in Stafford's "At the Bomb Testing Site," and in C. K. Williams's "Tar." Clearly it is an active sociopolitical consciousness that informs Gwendolyn Brooks's "The Lovers of the Poor," as well as so many of Louis Simpson's and David Ignatow's poems. The manner in which war transmogrifies even children's games into a surrealistic warfare between child and toys is at the heart of Simic's "The Big War." Moreover, a poem like Ginsberg's "Howl" is a full-scale indictment of the quality of American life and the recent history that has contributed to such an experience.

In the second group, specific historical events inform the poets' imaginations. The poems from W. D. Snodgrass's *The Führer Bunker* are obvious examples, since Snodgrass uses specific historical personages and events to reconstruct that Nazi *Götterdämmerung*. Meanwhile, other poets are responding to the Nazi experience in other ways — such as Bell, in "The Extermination of the Jews," and Stern, in "The War Against the Jews" — and to other specific historical events, recalled in Justice's poem "The Assassination" and in Hayden's "Frederick Douglass" and "Night, Death, Mississippi." These are only a few of the poems that suggest the imagination of commitment in contemporary poetry has not been challenged exclusively by the war in Vietnam.

However, Vietnam probably did occasion the largest number of overtly political poems, perhaps more than any other single event since World War I. Of course, World War II had generated poetry about war: Wilbur's "On the Eyes of an SS Officer," Stryk's "Letter to Jean-Paul Baudot, at Christmas," and Jarrell's "The Death of the Ball Turret Gunner" are only a few examples. Despite the fact that many of today's poets were active participants in World War II — or perhaps because they were — that experience did not seem to grip their imaginations as much as the conflict in Vietnam did. The poets' opposition to the war and to the political figures responsible for it was eminently clear — in their poetry as well as in their active political lives. Poems like Bly's "Counting Small-Boned Bodies," Levertov's "The Altars in the Street," and Merwin's "Some Last Questions" reflect a profound moral outrage against this nation's participation in and support of the war in Vietnam, as well as the depth of frustration that the continued involvement in this war generated. At the root of much antiwar poetry, moreover, was not only outrage at the atrocities but also a kind of implicit belief that the war might be stopped with the language of poetry. Thus, in "Wichita Vortex Sutra" (not included in this anthology), Allen Ginsberg wrote: "I lift my voice aloud, / make Mantra of American language now, / I here declare the end of the War!"

Political or moral questions aside, contemporary antiwar poetry does raise important questions — the most obvious of which is where does poetry leave off and propaganda begin? And this question raises the equally important question: can propagandistic poetry be good? (Dryden's "Mac Flecknoe" was an early poem to provoke these questions; more recently, some of the more militant feminist poets, among others, have done so.) Moreover, contemporary antiwar poetry is the result of a peculiar set of circumstances, for, unlike the poetry that emerged out of World War I and World War II, the poetry generated by the war in Vietnam was written by individuals who were noncombatants, most of whom had never been in the embattled country. (One is reminded of the shocking contrast between Wilfred Owen's poems written in the trenches and Rupert Brooke's chauvinistic sonnets written in the comfort of his precious university circle.) Thus the antiwar poetry of the sixties and seventies was based not on the reality of direct experience but on the removed reality of the media: the atrocities were not *witnessed*, they were "viewed." Often this was a poetry not about the victims of war but about the perpetrators of war; not about the blood of war but about the language of war; not about the pity of war but about the policy of war. Nevertheless, if it was imperfect as poetry, as it sometimes was — an increasing number of those poems now strain our willing suspension of aesthetic disbelief — it did testify to the contemporary poets' full and human commitment to the quality of their fellow creatures' lives.

Moreover, if the political climate has become a crucial arena within which today's poets have exercised their talents, so too their work has generated an aesthetic and critical climate in which the imagination of commitment is more fully understood as a vital element in contemporary poetry. An imagination of commitment empowers poems like "Mississippi" by Rita Dove and "The Origin of Cities" by Robert Hass. It is difficult to read much of the poetry of David Ignatow or of Philip Levine without being aware of the strong sociopolitical consciousness the work reflects. The poetry of Denise Levertov continues to reflect a refined revolutionary commitment that was so much a part of the poetry she wrote during the late sixties and early seventies. In many of her recent poems, Adrienne Rich has brought her enviable powers as a poet to bear on the question of sexual identity and sexual politics. The strong, though differing, feminist sensibilities informing the work of Carolyn Kizer and Marge Piercy are clearly a direct response to an identifiable sociopolitical and cultural situation that was all but ignored by generations of poets. In his poetry and prose, Robert Bly has repeatedly sought to come to grips with a fuller reintegration of the feminine and masculine principles, as have Gary Snyder and John Logan. Of course, at the heart of much of Snyder's poetry, and of W. S. Merwin's later poetry, is also a profound concern for this planet's ecological balance. In short, the imagination of commitment is not only a vital element in much of today's poetry but also seems to have become an essential attitude of the reader as well as of the poet.

However, the imagination of commitment also has led to a splintering of contemporary American poetry into various sociological categories: African American poetry, Italian American poetry, Asian American poetry, Native American poetry, protest poetry, feminist poetry, gay poetry, lesbian poetry, African American lesbian poetry, gay Native American poetry, et al. While the result has been to allow the emergence of voices that were previously unheard, and to heighten our consciousness of American poetry's great diversity and richness, it has also led to the introduction of non-aesthetic criteria for the evaluation of poetry. Thus, certain poetry is sometimes published or celebrated, not for its aesthetic achievement *as poetry*, but rather for the extent to which it serves a given sociopolitical objective. And that may well be the most radical departure from tradition that has occurred in American poetry since 1945.

The poets' moral stance toward sociopolitical events is only part of their more inclusive aesthetic, ethical, and spiritual concerns. It is important to note that many poets have been just as much concerned in their poems with the nature of poetry itself as with political phenomena. Indeed, the radical tradition in contemporary poetry and the poetics governing American poetry since 1945 might well be approached simply by a reading of poems that are either explicitly or implicitly about the art of poetry. Ashbery's "Leaving the Atocha Station" may well be an articulation of the need for a revolutionary poetic technique and a new poetic sensibility. Many of Ammons's poems are as much about the nature of poetry as they are ostensibly about natural phenomena. Snyder's "Riprap," Ferlinghetti's "Constantly risking absurdity," Creeley's "The Language," Charles Wright's "The New Poem," Bell's "White Clover," Clifton's humorous "Admonitions," Kunitz's "Single Vision," and many of Duncan's and Olson's poems — these are all statements of contemporary poetics, reflecting the contemporary poets' acute and ongoing concern about the nature of their art. In a less explicit manner, it is conceivable that James Dickey's "The Heaven of Animals," Robert Hayden's "The Night-Blooming Cereus," and Donald Hall's "Ox Cart Man" are as much explorations of the poetic process as they are observations of animals, flowers, and a shrewd old man. If the past few decades have been called an "age of poetry" rather than an "age of criticism" — because poets have only infrequently engaged in the writing of poetic theory in critical essays — they nevertheless have wrestled with the elusive nature of their art in the poems themselves, which may offer a more essential understanding of today's poetics than any analytical essay.

When confronting contemporary American poetry, it is also essential to realize that what may seem to be political issues, what may seem to be linguistic devices, and what may seem to be shockingly intimate experiences of the bedroom are, in fact, profoundly moral and spiritual explorations. Moreover, the issues of the day ought not be imposed on poems in order to reduce them to the equivalent of buzz words or slogans. It is clear, for example, that a poem like Mary Oliver's "The Fish" is not merely a statement of ecological concern any more than Elizabeth Bishop's "The Fish," Maxine Kumin's "The Grace of Geldings in Ripe Pastures," or Randall Jarrell's "The Black Swan" are merely poems about the animals mentioned in the titles. The preponderance of poems about animals in contemporary poetry suggests far more than a mere fascination with fauna, far more than a concern for ecological balance; rather, it suggests a moral and spiritual vision of the animal kingdom as an emblematic, if not always totemic, kingdom. In an age noticeably lacking in angels, saints, and heroes, certain poets seem to be returning to more primal symbols of hierarchy in the natural world.

Meanwhile, the concern of contemporary poets for various aspects of human sexuality is far more important than a seemingly adolescent fascination with bedroom antics or sex and its range of dirty words; indeed, it's more important than sexual politics. In a technocratic age that would obliterate all identity, one's sexuality is at the physical and psychic root of individual identity. Carolyn Kizer's "A Widow in Wintertime" and Isabella Gardner's "The Milkman" explore the profound psychological and emotional consequences of repressed sexuality, while Marge Piercy's "You Ask Why Sometimes I Say Stop" and Louise Glück's "Mock Orange" unearth the polarity of masculine-feminine sexual experience. The celebration of the male torso in Robert Duncan's poem by that name is as essential to the poet's homosexual identity as Anne Sexton's celebration of her uterus is essential to her female identity. Moreover, a poem like Gary Snyder's "The Bath" not only celebrates the glory of the sexual human body but also attempts to redeem that physical glory from this society's more prevalent attitude, described in James Wright's "Autumn Begins in Martins Ferry, Ohio," where "sons grow suicidally beautiful" and therefore "gallop terribly against each other's bodies." The sexual concerns of today's poets thus constitute an attempt to redeem the sexual self in a society that has traditionally suppressed it, distorted it, and indeed transformed it into a weapon.

These same sexual concerns extend far beyond social mores, practices, and weaponry. Since an explicit or implicit belief in the death of God necessarily posits the end of belief in a supernatural life or life force, it simultaneously necessitates a greater understanding of what is ostensibly the most powerful manifestation of the human life force, sexuality. In the past, the spiritual and cultural heritage of the West has been such that the traditional affirmation of the supernatural life force has been at the expense of the natural life force. Indeed, we have no comfortable language for our sexuality except for precise scientific terms or the more graphic language of the street. And so in a language that may sometimes be awkward or fumbling, the contemporary poets' celebration of sexuality may well be equivalent to a celebration of the god within as well as an implicit affirmation of the sexual nature of poetry itself — thereby suggesting a double measure of the sacred. Clearly, the sexual concerns in a poem like James Dickey's "The Sheep Child" extend far beyond the level of the dirty joke, far beyond the matter of sexual politics; they reach into the very heart of the god and of the creator within.

Although none of these poets has publicly proclaimed allegiance to any formal ethical or religious system to date, and although some have been members of the Catholic church, for example, and later quietly left it, one can point to a diversity of profound religious experiences in the work of most contemporary poets. In some of Richard Wilbur's poems — "A Dubious Night," for example — the existence of God is at best irrelevant, at worst a handicap to the discovery of that more profound salvation discovered in purely human activity. For Charles Simic, paradise is "a neighborhood once called 'Hell's Kitchen' . . ." where "the beautiful suicides / Lying side by side in the morgue / Get up and walk out into the first light." The ending of Lawrence Ferlinghetti's "Sometime during eternity" affirms — but implicitly laments — the contemporary theological stance that God is dead; his "I Am Waiting" humorously reveals the poet's quest for and anticipation of salvation. A profound mystical sense is clearly at the heart of Allen Ginsberg's "Wales Visitation," just as it is at the heart of much of Roethke's poetry. In "Mary's Song," Sylvia Plath sees the cycle of Christian salvation reflected in contemporary history's need for sacrificial victims. Moreover, in much of her poetry one senses the ancient mysticism that affirms salvation through suffering: "The fire makes it precious."

To a large extent, most contemporary poets — like many of their modernist predecessors — view traditional, formal, and established religious belief as impossible. Rather, they affirm a personal and vital religious or mystical, spiritual sense. John Berryman is one of the few who uses the traditional Judeo-Christian mythology — complete with God, Saint Peter, and Satan — as a potentially legitimate framework for religious experience. However, the work of John Logan, perhaps one of the most truly religious poets of the generation, is a clearer example of the contemporary poet's movement from a formal and established religious belief to a more personal one. Logan's early work relied primarily on what James Dickey called an "orthodox symbology" and a religious sense. His later work, having shed the formal accouterments of religion, also gained in intensity — tempered by a greater human complexity. The mystery of salvation is seen in its human incarnation. Grace is discovered and given and received specifically through human and incarnate acts.

Politics, sex, and religion in all their complex ramifications — the outdated taboos of so-called civilized society and polite conversation — are only a few of the primary concerns to which today's poets have addressed themselves. They are also only a few of the themes that contribute to the freshness, and especially to the relevance, of contemporary poetry. Alive with the blood and genes of the immediate and distant tradition of poetry, rebelling against all that is petrified and dead in that heritage, and asserting their fierce personal response to all that is demanded of a human being at this moment in history, contemporary American poets repeatedly affirm, with Louis Simpson, that American poetry:

> Whatever it is . . . must have
> A stomach that can digest
> Rubber, coal, uranium, moons, poems. . . .
>
> It must swim for miles through the desert
> Uttering cries that are almost human.

Notes on the Poets

This section offers information on the life and work of the poets in *Contemporary American Poetry*. Each note includes a bibliography broken down by genre. Audiotape and videotape recordings are now included, reflecting the increasingly integral role of technology in our culture and reminding us that poetry was spoken long before it was written.

Because recordings of poetry are not yet as readily available as books, each entry in these selected discographies and videographies includes a code indicating the source of the recording. Those codes are listed here, with the full name and address of the source:

APA: The American Poetry Archive, The Poetry Center, San Francisco State University, 1600 Holloway, San Francisco, CA 94132

BWF: The Brockport Writers Forum, Department of English, State University of New York, College at Brockport, Brockport, NY 14420

LLS: The Lannan Literary Series, The Lannan Foundation, 5401 McConnell Avenue, Los Angeles, CA 90066

NLA: New Letters on the Air, University of Missouri — Kansas City, Kansas City, MO 64110

PBS: PBS Video, 1320 Braddock Place, Alexandria, VA 22314

SA: Spoken Arts Records, P.O. Box 289, New Rochelle, NY 10802

TPV: The Poet's Voice, Harvard University Press, 79 Garden Street, Cambridge, MA 02138

WT: Watershed Tapes, Poet's Audio Center, P.O. Box 50145, Washington, DC 20091

Codes not identified here generally refer to recordings available from The Poet's Audio Center.

A. R. AMMONS (1926)

Born in Whiteville, North Carolina, A. R. Ammons was educated at Wake Forest College and the University of California at Berkeley. From 1952 to 1962, he worked as an executive of a biological glass company; since 1964 he has taught at Cornell University where he is presently Goldwin Smith Professor of Poetry. The recipient of fellowships from the Guggenheim Foundation and the American Academy of Arts and Letters, Ammons also was awarded the National Book Award and the Bollingen Prize in Poetry.

Ammons has been called an American Romantic. So he is — in

more ways than one. To begin with, the surface of his poems bristles and blooms primarily with the flora of the natural world observed by a well-trained and informed sensibility. At times one senses that this poet has observed the ever-shifting vagaries of the natural world with the zeal of a professional bird watcher. At the same time, the world that Ammons perceives seems remarkably devoid of other humans and — perhaps as a consequence — devoid of that darker, painful, and seamier side of human life we've come to expect in the work of contemporary poets. Even when he turns his attention to an urban existence quite removed from nature, as in "The City Limits," or to the possibility of "the explosion or cataclysm," as in "The Eternal City," Ammons has a distinctive capacity for reaffirming the "gold-skeined wings of flies swarming . . . / the coil of shit" and the manner in which even ruinage must "accept into itself . . . all the old / perfect human visions, all the old perfect loves."

At the heart of Ammons's poetry and vision seems to be a profound philosophical belief that the radiant energy at the heart of the natural world — as perceived by the seer-poet — becomes the inward and organic energy of the poem itself, which in turn is transformed from within into an emblematic and musical affirmation of the cosmic energy at the heart of all life. In the presence of this radiance, even "fear lit by the breadth of such calmly turns to praise." And the more we hear Ammons's philosophical music, the more we see those "hues, shadings, rises, flowing bends and blends"; as we move further into the world of Ammons's poetry, the better we can understand his moral and aesthetic conviction: "I understand / and won't give assertion up."

Poetry: *Ommateum, with Doxology* (1955). *Expressions of Sea Level* (1964). *Corsons Inlet* (1965). *Tape for the Turn of the Year* (1965). *Northfield Poems* (1966). *Selected Poems* (1968). *Uplands* (1970). *Briefings: Poems Small and Easy* (1971). *Collected Poems 1951–1971* (1972). *Sphere: The Form of a Motion* (1974). *Diversifications* (1975). *The Snow Poems* (1977). *The Selected Poems 1951–1977* (1977). *Selected Longer Poems* (1980). *A Coast of Trees* (1981). *Worldly Hopes* (1982). *Lake Effect Country* (1983). *Selected Poems: Expanded Edition* (1986). *Sumerian Vistas* (1987). *The Really Short Poems of A. R. Ammons* (1991).

Recordings: AUDIO: *A. R. Ammons* (NLA, 1984).

About: H. Bloom, ed., *A. R. Ammons* (1988). A. Holder, *A. R. Ammons* (1980).

JOHN ASHBERY (1927)

John Ashbery was born in Rochester, New York. A graduate of Harvard and Columbia, he lived in France for many years, and he was executive editor of *Art News* from 1965 to 1972; he currently teaches at Brooklyn College. His many honors include MacArthur and Fulbright fellowships, grants from the Ingram Merrill and Guggenheim foundations, and a National Institute of Arts and Letters award. In 1975 Ashbery's *Self-Portrait in a Convex Mirror* was awarded the Pulitzer Prize, the National Book Award, and the National Book Critics Circle Award.

With the publication of *The Tennis Court Oath*, Ashbery was recognized as one of the most experimental and as, at times, one of the most exasperating poets of his generation: montages of words and unrelated, juxtaposed images threatened the reader to attention, but then these fragments slipped away like verbal hallucinations, leaving the atmosphere charged with an emotional haze. Critics recognized the possible influences of Wallace Stevens, the French symbolists, and New York action painters; however, even the most unorthodox tools of criticism were blunted by this enigmatic poetry whose syntax refused to yield a recognizable sense of development or sustained meaning. While Ashbery's recent poems have become ostensibly more accessible and translucent, most critics continue to be baffled and to venture complex interpretations that, by comparison, make Ashbery's poems sound utterly transparent.

One critic has observed that Ashbery's largest aesthetic principle is the discovery that the world consents, every day, to being shaped into a poem. Ashbery himself has modified this view by asserting that there are no traditional subjects or themes in his poetry: "Most of my poems," he has said in an interview, "are about the experience of experience . . . and the particular experience is of lesser interest to me than the way it filters through to me. I believe this is the way in which it happens with most people, and I'm trying to record a kind of generalized transcript of what's really going on in our minds all day long."

Before the publication of *Three Poems* — long prose poems that may be viewed, at least in part, as an extended statement of poetics — Ashbery offered a somewhat minimal key to his enigmatic poetics when he wrote, "the carnivorous / Way of these lines is to devour their own nature, leaving / Nothing but a bitter impression of absence, which as we know involves presence, but still. / Nevertheless these are fundamental absences, struggling to get up and be off themselves." And the more one reads Ashbery's work, the more it is clear that these "absences" in his poetry — as in the work of Rilke — are the consequences of the innocent eye confronting experience: the lingering pain of loss.

Poetry: *Turandot and Other Poems* (1953). *Some Trees* (1956). *The Tennis Court Oath* (1962). *Rivers and Mountains* (1966). *Sunrise in Suburbia* (1968). *Fragment* (1969). *The New Spirit* (1970). *The Double Dream of Spring* (1970). *Three Poems* (1972). *The Vermont Journal* (1975). *Self-Portrait in a Convex Mirror* (1975). *Houseboat Days* (1977). *As We Know* (1979). *Shadow Train* (1981). *A Wave* (1984). *Selected Poems* (1985). *April Galleons* (1987).

Prose: *A Nest of Ninnies*, a novel, with James Schuyler (1969). *Three Plays* (1978). *Reported Sightings: Art Chronicles 1957–1987*, edited by D. Bergman (1989).

Recordings: AUDIO: *John Ashbery* (NLA, 1968). *John Ashbery* (APA, 1975). *The Spoken Arts Treasury*, Vol. XVII (SA, 1975). *The Songs We Know Best* (WT,

1988). VIDEO: *John Ashbery* (APA, I-1966, II-1973, III-1985). *The Writing of John Ashbery* (BWF, 1972).

About: H. Bloom, ed., *John Ashbery* (1985). D. Lehman, *Beyond Amazement: New Essays on John Ashbery* (1980). D. Shapiro, *John Ashbery: An Introduction to the Poetry* (1979).

MARVIN BELL (1937)

Marvin Bell was born in New York City. He attended Alfred University and Syracuse University; then he received his M.A. from the University of Chicago and his M.F.A. from the University of Iowa. In 1964–1965 he served as a foreign military training officer for the U.S. Army, and since 1965 he has been teaching in the Writer's Workshop at the University of Iowa, where he is Flannery O'Connor Professor of Letters. He also has been Senior Fulbright Scholar to Yugoslavia and to Australia. His book *A Probable Volume of Dreams* was the Academy of American Poets' Lamont Poetry Selection for 1969. He has been nominated for the National Book Award, and been awarded fellowships from the National Endowment for the Arts and the Guggenheim Foundation.

Because Bell is committed to enlarging the experiment of American free verse, the surface quality of his poems can be deceptively laconic. But they amply demonstrate the fact that the "freer" poetry seems to be, the more carefully crafted it is. (Of course, the obverse is equally true: the more carefully crafted a poem is, the freer it seems.) The effectiveness of his seemingly straightforward but somewhat strange love poem "To Dorothy," for example, is highly controlled by Bell's drawing on the centuries-old tradition of love lyrics using gardens and flowers as metaphors for the loved one. The power of "Long Island," on the other hand, depends in part on a careful blending of concentric and intraconnecting images, rhythms, and syntactical repetitions.

On a philosophical level, Bell's subjects include love; desire; the nature of reality, knowledge, and belief; the existential nature of truth and of the human condition; courage; and a pursuit of truths behind appearances that is peculiarly American. Those philosophical subjects, however, are rooted in the day-to-day human experiences of a father and lover, remembering World War II or clover in moonlight, discovering a potter's sponge in a foreign country, and, especially, trying to understand the inner nature of his vocation and his craft and to capture the ecstasy at the heart of metaphor — or the metaphor at the heart of ecstasy.

What is also remarkable about much of Bell's work is that, by fully *doing* what it *says*, a poem is not only "about" the immediate subject at hand but also is its own statement of poetics — just as Robert Frost's "Birches" is as much a poem about the nature of poetic craft as it is a poem about trees. A few other poets of this generation have written poems that are their own statement of poetics: Snyder's "Riprap," Creeley's "The Language," and Dickey's "In the Mountain Tent" come to mind.

However, perhaps no poet has pursued the philosophical and ecstatic dimensions of aesthetics in so many individual poems as rigorously as Bell has. The rewards of that quest have been abundant and rich, as much for his readers as for Bell.

Although it isn't possible to devise a full-fledged system of aesthetics from Bell's poetry (that isn't what poetry does), it is possible to suggest a few of the touchstones that inform Marvin Bell's vibrant vision: a vigorous life of the imagination leads to much the same depth of knowledge as that offered by the pursuit of history, mathematics, and physics and the exploration of unknown frontiers ("Long Island"); commitment to one's art demands the same painful, self-effacing mortification, and loneliness as any other quest for genuine excellence ("Homage to the Runner"); and human beings, born to be makers and lovers, realize that the ultimate source of meaningful loving and making is that ever-endless chain of honorable human labor — "because men and women had sown green grass, / and flowered to my eye in man-made light, / and to some would be as fire in the body / and to others a light in the mind. . . ."

Poetry: *Things We Dreamt We Died For* (1966). *Poems for Nathan and Saul* (1966). *A Probable Volume of Dreams* (1969). *The Escape into You: A Sequence* (1971). *Woo Havoc* (1971). *Residue of Song* (1974). *Stars Which See, Stars Which Do Not See* (1977). *These Green-Going-to-Yellow* (1981). *Segues: A Correspondence in Poetry*, with William Stafford (1983). *Drawn by Stones, by Earth, by Things That Have Been in the Fire* (1984). *Annie-Over*, with William Stafford (1988). *Iris of Creation* (1990).

Prose: *Old Snow Just Melting: Essays and Interviews* (1983).

Recordings: AUDIO: *The Self and the Mulberry Tree: Selected Poems 1956–1976* (WT, 1977). *Marvin Bell* (NLA, I-1981, II-1985).

JOHN BERRYMAN (1914–1972)

John Berryman graduated from Columbia and Clare College (Cambridge). He taught at Brown, Harvard, Princeton, and at the University of Minnesota. A recipient of Rockefeller and Guggenheim fellowships and of a special grant from the National Arts Council, he also won the Pulitzer Prize and the National Book Award. On January 7, 1972, John Berryman committed suicide.

In the course of his career, Berryman wrote not only a distinguished long poem in homage to Anne Bradstreet but also an equally notable sonnet sequence. However, his major work is his sequence of 385 *Dream Songs*, for which he may well be recognized as one of the truly great poets of the century. The scope, depth, daring, and craftsmanship of these poems have caused critics to compare Berryman with Homer, Dante, and Whitman.

The Dream Songs constitute a loose narrative about a multidimensional figure most often called Henry Pussycat. Berryman wrote that

Henry is "an imaginary character (not the poet . . .), a white American in early middle age sometimes in blackface, who has suffered an irreversible loss and talks to himself sometimes in the first person, sometimes in the third, sometimes even in the second; he has a friend, never named, who addresses him as Mr Bones and variants thereof." There are moments in *The Dream Songs* when Henry, Mr Bones, and the poet are barely distinguishable from one another — and are not meant to be distinguishable. Thus Berryman attempts and achieves a linear-multidimensional vision — maneuvered by a dazzling shift of pronouns — which is a verbal equivalent to what Picasso achieved in his cubist period.

Like Odysseus, Henry Pussycat undergoes a fantastic range of experience. He even dies and comes back to life. His emotions shift from incredible panic, horror, and self-pity to sheer joy and self-deprecating slapstick. If Henry gets out of hand, his friend and conscience, his sidekick and minstrel chorus are always there either to cut him down to size or to support him through despair. At the end of his journey, which takes him across spiritual as well as spatial and historical boundaries, Henry, the schizophrenic Odysseus of the atomic age, returns to his wife and child, scarred but bearing that most ancient and essential knowledge: to be human is to suffer.

Poetry: *Poems* (1942). *The Dispossessed* (1948). *Homage to Mistress Bradstreet* (1956). *His Thoughts Made Pockets & The Plane Buckt* (1958). *Short Poems* (1964). *77 Dream Songs* (1967). *His Toy, His Dream, His Rest* (1968). *The Dream Songs* (1969). *Love & Fame* (1970, revised 1972). *Delusions, Etc.* (1972). *Henry's Fate & Other Poems, 1967–1972* (1977). *Collected Poems 1937–1971*, edited by C. Thornbury (1989).

Prose: *Stephen Crane*, a biography (1950). *Recovery*, a novel (1973). *The Freedom of the Poet*, essays and stories (1976). *We Dream of Honour: John Berryman's Letters to His Mother* (1987).

Recordings: AUDIO: *The Spoken Arts Treasury*, Vol. XII (SA, 1975). *John Berryman* (TPV, 1978). VIDEO: *The Poetry of John Berryman* (BWF, 1970).

About: G. A. Arpin, *Master of the Baffled House: The Dream Songs of John Berryman* (1976). S. G. Berndt, *Berryman's Baedeker: The Epigraphs to the Dream Songs* (1976). J. Connaroe, *John Berryman: An Introduction to the Poetry* (1977). B. Gustavsson, *The Soul Under Stress: A Study of the Poetics of John Berryman* (1984). J. Haffenden, *John Berryman: A Critical Commentary* (1980). J. Haffenden, *The Life of John Berryman* (1983). E. M. Halliday, *John Berryman and the Thirties: A Memoir* (1988). M. Harris, ed., *A Tumult for John Berryman: A Homage* (1976). P. Mariani, *Dream Song: The Life of John Berryman* (1989). W. J. Martz, *John Berryman* (1969). H. Thomas, ed., *Berryman's Understanding: Reflections on the Poetry of John Berryman* (1988).

ELIZABETH BISHOP (1911–1979)

A native of Worcester, Massachusetts, Elizabeth Bishop received her formal education at Vassar. She lived in Brazil for the better part of sixteen years but also taught at the University of Washington and at Harvard. She was Consultant in Poetry at the Library of Congress, a chancellor of the Academy of American Poets, and a member of the National Institute of Arts and Letters. Her many other honors include grants from the Guggenheim and Ingram Merrill foundations, the Pulitzer Prize, the National Book Award, and the Order of Rio Branco (Brazil).

Although Bishop was far less prolific than most poets of her generation, she was one of the few poets about whom it could be said that each new book — indeed each new poem — was an "event." One reason may be that she was far less predictable than many of her contemporaries; that is, readers of poetry did not come to expect a particular kind of poem from Bishop the way that they had come to expect a certain kind of poem from Anne Sexton or Robert Lowell.

Another reason why Bishop's poems are rare moments of delight and epiphany stems from her stunning perceptions and reconstruction of the details of physical reality. As Randall Jarrell says in *Poetry and the Age*, "all her poems have written underneath, *I have seen it.*" Whether the matter at hand is the exotic rainbow glow of a tremendous fish or the commonplace sheen of oil in a dingy filling station, Bishop knows that poetry and vision are rooted, first of all, in what Archibald MacLeish has called "the shine of the world." In her better poems, Bishop amply demonstrates that the perception of sensible objects and moral vision, for the poet, may be one and the same experience.

Ralph J. Mills, Jr., has rightfully noted another, more ambitious dimension of Bishop's achievement. In addition to her graceful use of fairly strict forms — and the unmistakable presence of a formalist approach even in the freer verse — Bishop's poems are distinguished by what Mills calls a "total accomplishment of language, technique, music, and imagery working simultaneously, or (in T. S. Eliot's phrase) 'the complete consort dancing together.' "

Poetry: *North and South* (1946). *Poems: North and South — A Cold Spring* (1955). *Questions of Travel* (1965). *Selected Poems* (1967). *The Ballad of the Burglar of Babylon* (1968). *The Complete Poems* (1969/1979). *Geography III* (1976). *The Complete Poems 1927–1979* (1983).

Prose: *The Collected Prose*, edited by R. Giroux (1984).

Translations: *The Diary of Helena Morley* (1957). *Anthology of Contemporary Brazilian Poetry*, editor and translator, with others (1972).

Recording: AUDIO: *The Spoken Arts Treasury*, Vol. X (SA, 1975).

About: H. Bloom, ed., *Elizabeth Bishop* (1985). D. Kalstone, *Becoming a Poet: Elizabeth Bishop with Marianne Moore and Robert Lowell* (1989). L. Schwartz and S. Estess, eds., *Elizabeth Bishop and Her Art* (1982). A. Stevenson, *Elizabeth Bishop* (1966). T. Travisano, *Elizabeth Bishop: Her Artistic Development* (1988).

ROBERT BLY (1923)

Robert Bly lives in rural Minnesota. For the 1975 edition of *Contemporary Poets*, Bly wrote, "I earn my living giving readings at American colleges and universities, and by translating." Fifteen years later, to a large extent, he still does. He graduated from Harvard and — though he hates to admit it — later did graduate work at the University of Iowa Writers' Workshop. The founder of the influential journal *The Fifties* (later *The Sixties, The Seventies, The Eighties,* and *The Nineties*), he has received fellowships from the Fulbright, Guggenheim, and Rockefeller foundations and the National Institute of Arts and Letters, and the National Book Award.

Influenced by the thought of the seventeenth-century German theosophist Jacob Boehme, and the techniques of such twentieth-century Spanish surrealists as Lorca and Neruda, Bly's poems tend to be almost purely phenomenological. Revolting against the rationalism and empiricism of his century, Boehme emphasized an intuitive perception of the outer tangible world of humans and things as a symbol of the corresponding and truer inner spiritual world. The outward man is asleep, Boehme wrote; he is only the husk of the real inner man. Like the American Romantic Transcendentalist Emerson, Boehme insisted that men neither see nor respond to that inner spiritual world: "The wise of this world . . . have shut and locked us up in their art and rationality, so that we have had to see with their eyes."

Bly himself has written that American poetry took a wrong turn, moving in "a destructive motion outward" rather than a "plunge inward, trying for a great (spiritual and imaginative) intensity." In his revolt against Eliot's theory of the "objective correlative" and against Pound's practice in the *Cantos* of "eating up more and more of the outer world, with less and less life at the center," Bly has fashioned his poems after the work of Rilke, Trakl, and twentieth-century Spanish surrealists. In them, he seems to have found a poetics that corresponds to Boehme's mysticism, enabling him to plunge beneath the phenomenology of surfaces and find images and words to suggest the inner reality and spiritual intensity of experience. Moreover, many of Bly's poems continue to be implicit reaffirmations of a statement that appeared on the flyleaf of *The Lion's Tail and Eyes* in which he suggests that his poems come from "the part of the personality which is nourished by notice of things that are growing" and simultaneously that they "resist the Puritan insistence on being busy, the need to think of everything in terms of work."

Poetry: *The Lion's Tail and Eyes: Poems Written Out of Laziness and Silence,* with James Wright and William Duffy (1962). *Silence in the Snowy Fields* (1962). *The Light Around the Body* (1967). *The Morning Glory* (1969; expanded edition, 1975). *The Teeth Mother Naked at Last* (1970). *Jumping Out of Bed* (1973; revised and expanded edition, 1988). *Sleepers Joining Hands* (1973). *Point Reyes Poems* (1974/1989). *Old Man Rubbing His Eyes* (1975). *This Body Is Made of Camphor and Gopherwood* (1977). *This Tree Will Be Here for a Thousand Years* (1979). *The Man in the Black Coat Turns* (1981). *Loving a Woman in Two Worlds* (1985). *Selected Poems* (1986).

Prose: *Leaping Poetry: An Idea with Poems and Translations* (1975). *Talking All Morning: Collected Interviews and Conversations* (1979). *The Eight Stages of Translation* (1983). *A Little Book on the Human Shadow*, edited by W. Booth (1988). *American Poetry: Wildness and Domesticity*, critical essays (1990).

Translations and Versions: POETRY: *Twenty Poems of Georg Trakl*, with J. Wright (1961). *Twenty Poems of César Vallejo*, with J. Knoepfle and J. Wright (1962). *Juan Ramón Jiménez: Forty Poems* (1967). *Late Arrival on Earth: Selected Poems of Gunnar Ekelöf*, with C. Paulston (1967). *Pablo Neruda: Twenty Poems*, with J. Wright (1967). *Tomas Tranströmer: Twenty Poems* (1970). *Neruda and Vallejo: Selected Poems*, with J. Knoepfle and J. Wright (1971). *Night Visions*, poems by Tomas Tranströmer (1971). *Bashō* (1972). *Lorca and Jiménez: Selected Poems* (1973). *Blase de Otero and Miguel Hernandez: Selected Poems* (1974). *Friends, You Drank Some Darkness: Three Swedish Poets: Martinson, Ekelöf and Tranströmer* (1976). *The Kabir Book: 44 of the Ecstatic Poems of Kabir* (1977). *Vicente Alexandre: Twenty Poems*, with L. Hyde (1977). *Rolf Jacobsen: Twenty Poems* (1977). *Rainer Maria Rilke: The Voices* (1977). *I Never Wanted Fame: Ten Poems and Proverbs*, by Antonio Machado (1979). *Mirabai: Six Versions* (1980). *Rumi: Night and Sleep*, with C. Barks (1980). *Canciones*, by Antonio Machado (1980). *Truth Barriers: Poems by Tomas Tranströmer* (1980). *Selected Poems of Rainer Maria Rilke* (1981). *When Grapes Turn to Wine: Versions of Rumi* (1983). *When Alone: Selected Poems of Antonio Machado* (1983).

Anthologies: *A Poetry Reading Against the Vietnam War*, with D. Ray (1960). *Forty Poems Touching on Recent American History* (1966/1970). *The Sea and the Honeycomb: A Book of Tiny Poems* (1966/1971). *News of the Universe: Poems of Twofold Consciousness* (1980).

Recordings: AUDIO: *Robert Bly* (APA, I-1961, II-1967). *For the Stomach: Selected Poems 1974* (WT, 1974). *The Spoken Arts Treasury*, Vol. XVI (SP, 1975). *Robert Bly* (NLA, 1979). *Poetry Reading: An Ancient Tradition* (Dolphin Tapes, 1983). *The Six Powers of Poetry* (Dolphin Tapes, 1983). *Loving a Woman in Two Worlds* (WT, 1985). *Fairy Tales for Men and Women* (WT, 1987). *Men and the Wounds* (Ally Press, 1988). VIDEO: *The Poetry of Robery Bly* (BWF, I-1970, II-1971). *Robert Bly* (APA, I-1983, II-1984). *Moyers: The Power of the Word: "The Simple Acts of Life"* and *"Where the Soul Lives"* (PBS, 1989).

About: W. Davis, *Understanding Robert Bly* (1988). J. Friberg, *Moving Inward: A Study of Robert Bly's Poetry* (1977). R. Jones and K. Daniels, eds., *Of Solitude and Silence: Writings on Robert Bly* (1981). H. Nelson, *Robert Bly: An Introduction to the Poetry* (1984). J. Peseroff, *Robert Bly: When Sleepers Awaken* (1984). R. P. Sugg, *Robert Bly* (1986).

GWENDOLYN BROOKS (1917)

A graduate of Wilson Junior College in Chicago, Gwendolyn Brooks began her professional career in 1941 with Inez Stark Boulton's poetry workshop at the South Side Community Art Center in Chicago. She was awarded two Guggenheim fellowships, a grant from the National Institute of Arts and Letters, and the Pulitzer Prize for her second book of poems. In 1969 Brooks was named Poet Laureate of the State of Illinois, an honor formerly held by Carl Sandburg.

Brooks's poems are often marked by direct and bold social observation and by language that precedes — indeed foreshadows — much of the poetry written by younger African American poets today. Her African American hero's assertion, "I helped to save them . . . / Even if I had to kick their law into their teeth in order to do that for them," might well have been written in the 1960s or 1970s rather than in the 1940s. In those poems addressed specifically to the horror of the African American experience in America, she is also capable of a range of emotions: brutal anger, wry satire, and visionary serenity.

Informed by the spectrum of the African American experience and her own emotional objectivity, some of her poems are also marked by the simplicity, quiet, and gentility of a woman's sensibilities. Yet in a poem like "The Mother," she also demonstrates the kind of fierce emotion that other women poets like Anne Sexton and Adrienne Rich have displayed in more consciously personal or political poems. Gentle or fierce, personal or social, her poems consistently affirm the common denominator of human experience in poetry and in the human community.

Poetry: *A Street in Bronzeville* (1945). *Annie Allen* (1949). *Bronzeville Boys and Girls* (1956). *Selected Poems* (1963). *In the Time of Detachment, In the Time of Cold* (1965). *In the Mecca: Poems* (1968). *Riot* (1969). *The Wall* (nd). *Family Pictures* (1970). *Aloneness* (1971). *Beckonings* (1975). *To Disembark* (1981). *The Near-Johannesburg Boy and Other Poems* (1986). *Blacks* [collected poems], (1987). *Gottschalk and the Grande Tarantelle* (1988).

Prose: *Maud Martha*, a novel (1953). *Report from Part One: An Autobiography* (1972). *The World of Gwendolyn Brooks* (1972). *Primer for Blacks* (1980).

Recordings: AUDIO: *Gwendolyn Brooks Reading Selected Poems* (WT, 1973). *The Spoken Arts Treasury*, Vol. XIII (SA, 1975). *An Interview with Gwendolyn Brooks* (BWF, 1978). *Gwendolyn Brooks* (NLA, I-1984, II-1988, III-1988).

About: G. E. Kent, *A Life of Gwendolyn Brooks* (1989). D. H. Melham, *Gwendolyn Brooks: Poetry and the Heroic Voice* (1987). M. K. Mootry and G. Smith, eds., *A Life Distilled: Gwendolyn Brooks, Her Poetry and Fiction* (1987). H. B. Shaw, *Gwendolyn Brooks* (1980).

LUCILLE CLIFTON (1936)

Lucille Clifton was born in Depew, New York, and educated at the State University of New York at Fredonia and Howard University. Currently teaching at St. Mary's College in Maryland, her other academic appointments have been Elliston Poet at the University of Cincinnati, Jenny Moore Visiting Lecturer in Creative Writing at George Washington University, and Woodrow Wilson Scholar at Fisk University and at Trinity College. Clifton's awards and distinctions as a poet, fiction writer, and screenplay writer include the University of Massachusetts Press's Juniper Prize for poetry, two nominations for the Pulitzer Prize in poetry, an Emmy Award from the American Academy of Television Arts and Sciences, and creative writing fellowships from the National Endowment for the Arts.

Clifton's entire comment on her work in the third edition of *Contemporary Poets* (1980) consists of one brief sentence: "I am a Black woman poet, and I sound like one." And yet, after reading even a short selection of her poems, we quickly realize that Clifton's description of herself does not explain why she is one of the most unique voices of her generation. Of course, like numerous other women writers, she explores the dimensions of her sexual identity and her role as daughter, as mother, as lover, as woman; like many other African American poets (men and women), she too addresses herself to the quality of the African American experience in America, just as she too makes full use of the African American idiom. But no other poet of her generation (regardless of gender or race) *sounds* quite like Clifton. Why that is, however, is rather difficult to identify in the standard language of literary criticism.

Clifton's subjects and themes run the gamut of human experience. She laments the loss of an aborted child, and she celebrates her own mature body and sexuality with wonderful verve. She admonishes children to "come home from the movies" and face the responsibilities of everyday life, but she also recalls the pain and terror of her own growth into adult responsibility. She engages in social criticism and in criticism of individual human beings, but she also affirms "the bond of live things everywhere." She feels religious doubts, but she is nonetheless a profoundly religious spirit whose sensibility encompasses both the Judeo-Christian tradition and a primal sense of spiritualism and magic. Despite the high seriousness of many of her poems, she also obviously revels in a vibrant sense of humor that she directs not only at others, but also at herself and her craft. She can poke gentle fun at herself because "she is a poet / she don't have no sense," but after the joy and celebration, after the anguish and despair, after the doubt and struggle to believe, she also can assert, "I am left with plain hands and / nothing to give you but poems."

One of the striking characteristics of Clifton's poems is their distilled brevity. Like Emily Dickinson, Clifton rarely offers any but the most essential elaborations on experience. However, for a clue to the sound of Clifton's poems, we have to turn elsewhere: African American spirituals and secular folksongs; the rich history of rhythm and blues; the rhythms and sounds of an African American fundamentalist revival meeting and of magical incantations; the phrasing and timing of classic African American humorists; an utterly physical sense of language (somehow we can *see* how these poems incorporate a range of bodily movements); a belief in the power of idiom to give voice to the human heart as much by transcending individual race and culture as by affirming it; a belief in the language of poetry, not as a threat of further social and human alienation but as a bridge of reconciliation; a belief in the power of song and in the impotency of slogans; a belief in tongues.

Poetry: *Good Times* (1969). *Good News About the Earth* (1972). *An Ordinary Woman* (1974). *Two-Headed Woman* (1980). *Good Woman: Poems and a Memoir 1969–1980* (1987). *Next: New Poems* (1987). *Quilting: Poems 1987–1990* (1991).

Prose: *Generations of Americans: A Memoir* (1976).

Recordings: AUDIO: *The Place for Keeping* (WT, 1979). *Lucille Clifton* (NLA, 1989). VIDEO: *The Poetry of Lucille Clifton* (BWF, 1987). *Lucille Clifton* (LLS, 1989). *Moyers: The Power of the Word:* "Where the Soul Lives" (PBS, 1989).

ROBERT CREELEY (1926)

A New Englander by birth and sensibility, Robert Creeley was born in Arlington, Massachusetts, and was educated at Harvard, Black Mountain College, and the University of New Mexico. He has traveled widely and has taught at the University of New Mexico and at Black Mountain College where he also edited the influential journal *Black Mountain Review*. He is currently David Gray Professor of Poetry and Letters at the State University of New York at Buffalo.

Generally associated with the "Projectivists" and poets of the Black Mountain School, Creeley nevertheless is a Puritan at heart — Emily Dickinson's cool, hip, one-eyed, and unvirginal nephew. Like all good Puritans, Creeley is "hung up": "I think I grow tensions / like flowers . . ." ("The Flower"). Pain is central to his work — a sharp, stinging pain evoked in such images as "I can / feel my eye breaking" ("The Window"). In other poems, such as "Moment" and "On Vacation," a Puritan sensibility surfaces more explicitly, as it does in the very structure and substance of collections such as *A Day Book* and *Hello* — sustained attempts at recording and discovering the "meaning" of diurnal events, an implicit quest for signs of salvation, especially love. "I love you. / Do you love me. / What to say / when you see me" ("A Form of Women") might be a summary of one of Creeley's central concerns.

No critical essay or explanatory statement reveals Creeley's poetics as precisely as his own poems, especially "The Language" and "The Window." In the former, he states simply, "Locate *I* . . ."; in the latter, he writes, "Position is where you / put it, where it is . . ." The position of the *I* — as locus, as viewer, and as speaker — largely determines the form and the direction of the poem. The position of words on the page results from the location of this *I*, who, by arranging the poem as it is, speaks not only in grammatical units but also in linear units. In other words, Creeley's poems evolve on both a sequential grammatical level and on a cumulative linear level, with each individual line reaffirming or modifying the sense of the sentence and of the poem. And such contrapuntal tension in the very structure of Creeley's poems — perhaps more than the sparse, occasionally hesistant language — reflects the contemporary struggle with those forces that would make us all inarticulate.

Poetry: *Le Fou* (1952). *The Kind of Act of* (1953). *The Immoral Proposition* (1953). *All That Is Lovely in Men* (1955). *A Form of Women* (1959). *For Love: Poems 1950–1960* (1962). *Words* (1967). *The Charm: Early and Uncollected Poems* (1967/1969). *The Finger*, with Bobbie Creeley (1968). *Pieces* (1968). *St. Martin's*, with Bobbie Creeley (1971). *1–2–3–4–5–6–7–8–9–0*, with Arthur Okamura (1971). *A Day Book* (1972). *Thirty Things*, with Bobbie Creeley (1974). *Away*, with Bobbie Creeley (1976). *Presences*, with Marisol (1976). *Selected Poems* (1976). *Hello: A Journal* (1978). *Later* (1979). *The Collected Poems of Robert Creeley 1945–1975* (1983). *Mirrors* (1983). *Memory Gardens* (1986). *The Company* (1988). *Windows* (1990). *Selected Poems* (1991).

Prose: ESSAYS AND CRITICISM: *A Quick Graph: Collected Notes and Essays* (1970). *Contexts of Poetry: Interviews 1961–1971*, edited by D. M. Allen (1973). *Was That a Real Poem & Other Essays*, edited by D. M. Allen (1979). *Charles Olson & Robert Creeley: The Complete Correspondence*, edited by G. F. Butterick (1983). *Collected Essays* (1989). *Autobiography* (1990). FICTION: *The Island* (1963). *The Gold Diggers and Other Stories* (1965). *Mabel: A Story* (1976). *The Collected Prose of Robert Creeley* (1984).

Recordings: AUDIO: *Robert Creeley* (APA, I-1956, II-1959, III-1962, IV-1966, V-1970, VI-1971). *Robert Creeley Reading at the New York Poetry Center* (WT, 1966). *The Spoken Arts Treasury*, Vol. XVI (SA, 1975). *Robert Creeley* (NLA, I-1981, II-1988). VIDEO: *Robert Creeley* (APA, I-1965, II-1973, III-1978). *The Poetry of Robert Creeley* (BWF, I-1970, II-1973). *Robert Creeley* (LLS, 1990).

About: C. Edelberg, *Robert Creeley's Poetry: A Critical Introduction* (1978). A. Ford, *Robert Creeley* (1978). A. Mandel, *Measures: Robert Creeley's Poetry* (1974). *Dorn, and Robert Duncan* (1981). R. A. Sheffler, *The Development of Robert Creeley's Poetry* (1971). W. Tallman, *Three Essays on Robert Creeley* (1973). C. F. Terrell, ed., *Robert Creeley: The Poet's Workshop* (1984). J. Wilson, ed., *Robert Creeley's Life and Work: A Sense of Increment* (1987).

JAMES DICKEY (1923)

James Dickey received his bachelor's and master's degrees from Vanderbilt University. He was a night fighter pilot during both World War II and the Korean War; as a civilian, he has worked as an advertising executive in Atlanta and New York; and he has taught at a variety of colleges and universities, including the University of South Carolina where he is presently poet-in-residence. In 1966 Dickey received the National Book Award for poetry and was appointed Consultant in Poetry at the Library of Congress.

One of the less ostensibly "academic" poets of his generation, Dickey's poems are often disarmingly frank in subject matter and in "moral tone." He has refused to assume those moral postures often expected of today's poets: during Vietnam, he did not write antiwar poetry but rather, as in "The Firebombing," he confronted his own understanding of and sympathy with the pilot whose mission was to drop napalm on enemy villages without the luxury of questioning the morality of such an act. In several other poems, he has explored varieties of sexual experiences, including implicit and explicit sexual encounters between humans and animals, as in "The Sheep Child."

Dickey's poems are marked by an exuberant language and by a primal energy, passion, and ritual. Probing the most elemental in humankind, his poems often trace a human's mythic subconscious and paradoxical evolution to a primitive level where humans and animals become companions and mates in the same irrational but holy species. Moreover, at the heart of Dickey's vision poetry is the tongue articulating the consciousness of all creation on this planet, from the mute stone up the earthly chain of being to humankind. And in this way, his poems often recall Whitman's poetry and vision.

Simultaneously, many of Dickey's poems are also marked by a Southern Puritanism similar to that found in the work of William Faulkner and Flannery O'Connor. His characters are grotesque — physically and spiritually wounded. They are violent creatures; their brutal sexuality is immersed in pain and death. And they move about in a world churning with violence and profound evil that is as much inherent in the human condition as it is man-made. Dickey's vision, then, includes the polarities of light and grace, darkness and sin. The total impact of his poems is often the drama of Adam, shimmering with primal light, awakening to guilt, and finding it magical.

Poetry: *Into the Stone and Other Poems*, in *Poets of Today VII* (1960). *Drowning with Others* (1962). *Helmets* (1964). *Buckdancer's Choice* (1965). *Poems 1957–1967* (1967). *The Eye-Beaters, Blood, Victory, Madness, Buckhead and Mercy* (1970). *Exchanges* (1971). *The Zodiac* (1976). *The Strength of Fields*, for the inauguration of Jimmy Carter (1977). *Veteran Birth: The Gadfly Poems 1947–1949* (1978). *The Enemy from Eden* (1978). *The Strength of Fields* (1979). *The Early Motion: Drowning with Others and Helmets* (1981). *Falling, May Day Sermon, and Other Poems* (1981). *Puella* (1982). *The Central Motion: Poems 1968–1979* (1983). *The Eagle's Mile* (1990).

Prose: ESSAYS AND CRITICISM: *The Suspect in Poetry* (1964). *Babel to Byzantium: Poets & Poetry Now* (1968). *Self-Interviews*, edited by B. and J. Reiss (1970/ 1984). *Sorties: Journals and New Essays* (1971). FICTION AND OTHER PROSE: *Deliverance* (1970). *Jericho: The South Beheld*, with paintings by Hubert Shuptrine (1974). *God's Images*, with photographs by Marvin Hayes (1974). *In Pursuit of the Grey Soul* (1979). *Wayfarer* (1980). *The Poet Turns on Himself* (1982). *Night Hurdling* (1983). *Alnilam* (1988).

Recordings: AUDIO: *James Dickey: Selected Poems* (SA, 1967). *James Dickey Reads His Poetry and Prose* (CD, nd). *The Poems of James Dickey* (SA, nd). *The Spoken Arts Treasury*, Vol. XV (SA, 1975). *James Dickey* (NLA, 1987). VIDEO: *The Writing of James Dickey* (BWF, 1970).

About: R. Baughman, *The Voiced Connections of James Dickey* (1990). N. Bowers, *James Dickey: The Poet as Pitchman* (1985). R. J. Calhoun, ed., *James Dickey: The Expansive Imagination* (1973). R. J. Calhoun and R. W. Hill, *James Dickey* (1973). P. de la Fuente, ed., *James Dickey: Splintered Light* (1979). L. Lieberman, *The Achievement of James Dickey* (1968). B. Weigle and T. R. Hummer, *The Imagination as Glory: Essays on the Poetry of James Dickey* (1984).

RITA DOVE (1952)

Rita Dove was born in Akron, Ohio. She received a B.A. from Miami University, studied modern European literature at the University of Tübingen, and received an M.F.A. from the University of Iowa. A professor of English at the University of Virginia, Dove's literary honors include grants and fellowships from the National Endowment for the Arts, the Guggenheim Foundation, the Academy of American Poets, and the General Electric Foundation. In 1987 she was awarded the Pulitzer Prize for poetry.

Many of Dove's poems are deeply rooted in moments of intimate personal experience: a child marvels at the power of language; an adolescent girl fantasizes the arrival of a dreamed-of lover; a young mother teaches her daughter the truth and mystery of her vagina. And many of her poems — most notably the book-length sequence, *Thomas and Beulah* — find their source in extended family history.

Unlike such predecessors as Sylvia Plath and W. D. Snodgrass, Dove is not a personal-confessional poet. No doubt there is suffering and anguish in her poems, often revealed in haunting surreal images (as in "Adolescence III," where the appearance of the father strikes at the heart like the appearance of the ghost of Hamlet's father: "He carries his tears in a bowl, / And blood hangs in the pine-soaked air."); but there is no sense of personal evil to confess or to exorcise. Rather, Dove is what might be called a "fictive" poet, in whose work autobiography and family history are transformed into a lyrical fiction, into a larger drama in which the reader participates. This communal drama does not borrow from established myth for its resonance; instead, it strives to become archetype, to be its own myth.

Even when she uses traditional myth, Dove seems compelled to retell it from her own perspective — Moses (as a child) in the bulrush rehearsing his striking a stone for water in the desert; the terrifying rediscovery of the garden of Eden in Mississippi — thereby implicitly reaffirming her assertion that "each god is empty / without us. . . ." But whether focusing on personal experience, family history, or communal archetype, Dove's poems not only erect verbal silos — "the ribs of the modern world" — at the heart of the American myth, they are also carefully structured circles of images, layers of metaphors that re-create an epiphanal moment irrevocably sculpted in words.

Poetry: *Ten Poems* (1977). *The Yellow House on the Corner* (1980). *Museum* (1983). *Thomas and Beulah* (1986). *Grace Notes* (1989).

Prose: *Fifth Sunday*, short stories (1985). *Through the Ivory Gate*, a novel (1991).

Recordings: AUDIO: *Rita Dove* (NLA, 1985). VIDEO: *The Poetry of Rita Dove* (BWF, 1985). *Thomas and Beulah* (Video Press, 1989). *Six Pages on Rita Dove* (University of Akron, 1989).

ALAN DUGAN (1923)

Born in Brooklyn and a graduate of Mexico City College, Alan Dugan's first book of poems won the Yale Series of Younger Poets award, the Pulitzer Prize, and the National Book Award. He subsequently received the Shelley Memorial Award from the Poetry Society of America and an Award in Literature from the American Academy and Institute of Arts and Letters.

Although Dugan's most effective poems can be humorous, lyrical, or cerebral, his work also can be tough, brutal, and "ugly." For William J. Martz's *The Distinctive Voice* (1966), Dugan wrote about his voice as a poet: "I am trying to say what is hardest to say; that is, words wrung out of intense experience and not constructed." Moreover, as Richard Howard has observed, in Dugan's poetry one senses that "the act of writing poetry is, precisely, an invocation of destruction, a luring of language to its wreck. . . . He is too honest . . . for the consolation of some visionary transcendence of language. . . ."

In many of his poems, Dugan talks about the least public of experiences in a language still generally considered the least public — perhaps "unpoetic." Moreover, he refuses to burden his subject and language with any obviously stated mystical, magical, or "great social" impact. He tells it "like it is" and, rather than being offensive — as one might vaguely and uneasily wish they were — his poems emerge as the product of a fierce and fully American honesty and of a craftsmanship generating words that burn through all pretense like acid.

Poetry: *Poems* (1961). *Poems 2* (1963). *Poems 3* (1967). *Collected Poems* (1969). *Poems 4* (1974). *Sequence* (1976). *New and Collected Poems 1961–1983* [includes *Poems 5*] (1983). *Poems 6* (1989).

ROBERT DUNCAN (1919–1988)

A native of California, Robert Duncan was educated at the University of California, Berkeley. He traveled extensively, taught at San Francisco State, the University of British Columbia, and at Black Mountain College with Charles Olson, and served as editor of *The Experimental Review* and *The Berkeley Miscellany*. His awards include the Harriet Monroe Memorial Prize, two grants from the National Endowment for the Arts, a Guggenheim Fellowship, and the National Poetry Award.

In *The Truth & Life of Myth*, Duncan wrote, "The meaning and intent of what it is to be a man and, among men, to be a poet, I owe to the working of myth in my spirit, both the increment and associations gathered in my continuing study of mythological lore and my own apprehension of what my life is at work here." And in his statement reprinted in Donald Allen's anthology, *The New American Poetry* (1960), Duncan stated that "every moment of life is an attempt to come to life. Poetry is a 'participation,' a oneness." It is "the very life of the soul: the body's dreaming that it can dream. And perish into its own imagination." A poem, according to Duncan, is "a ritual referring to divine orders."

If not so much through his seemingly anachronistic use of classical and medieval mythology, then surely in his fundamental attitude toward his art, Duncan attempts to return poetry to its most profound roots in the rituals of the divine orders. Erudite, orphic, at times homoerotic (long before sexual preference was a political and aesthetic issue), lyrical, and often profoundly religious, Duncan's poems gather a momentum that is more, much more, than the "passages of moonlight upon the floor." Rather, they are human clues to what might conceivably be "the meaning of the music of the spheres."

Poetry: *Heavenly City, Earthly City* (1947). *Poems 1948–1949* (1950). *Medieval Scenes* (1950). *The Song of the Border Guard* (1952). *Caesar's Gate: Poems 1949–1950* (1955). *Letters: Poems 1953–1956* (1958). *Selected Poems* (1959). *The Opening of the Field* (1960). *Roots and Branches* (1964). *Writing, Writing: A New Composition Book of Madison 1953, Stein Imitations* (1964). *Wine* (1964). *Uprising* (1965). *A Book of Resemblances: Poems 1950–1953* (1966). *Of the War: Passages 22–27* (1966). *The Years as Catches: First Poems 1939–1946* (1966). *Fragments of a Disordered Devotion* (1966). *Boob* (1966). *Epilogos* (1967). *The Cat and the Blackbird* (1967). *Christmas Present, Christmas Presence!* (1967). *Bending the Bow* (1968). *My Mother Would Be a Falconress* (1968). *Names of People* (1968). *The First Decade: Selected Poems 1940–1950* (1968). *Derivations: Selected Poems 1950–1956* (1968). *Play Time, Pseudo Stein* (1969). *Achilles' Song* (1969). *Poetic Disturbances* (1970). *Bringing It Up from the Dark* (1970). *Tribunals: Passages 31–35* (1970). *In Memoriam Wallace Stevens* (1972). *The Truth and Life of Myrtle* (1972). *An Ode and Arcadia*, with Jack Spicer (1974). *Dante* (1974). *The Venice Poem* (1975). *Groundwork: Before the War* (1984). *Groundwork II: In the Dark* (1987).

Prose: *The Artist's View* (1952). *Faust Foutou: Act One of Four Acts: A Comic Mask* (1958). *Faust Foutou: An Entertainment in Four Parts*, drama (1960). *On Poetry* (1964). *As Testimony: The Poem and the Scence* (1964). *The Sweetness and Greatness of Dante's "Divine Comedy," 1265–1965* (1965). *Medea at Kolchis: The Maiden Head*, drama (1965). *Six Prose Pieces* (1966). *The Truth and Life of Myth: An Essay in Essential Autobiography* (1968). *Notes on Grossinger's "Solar Journal: Oecological Sections"* (1970). *An Interview with George Bowering and Robert Hogg, April 19, 1969* (1971). *Fictive Certainties: Five Essays in Essential Autobiography* (1979). *Towards an Open Universe* (1982).

Recordings: AUDIO: *Robert Duncan* (APA, I-1959 [i–ii], II-1963, III-1972, IV-1977). VIDEO: *Robert Duncan* (APA, I-1965, II-1973, III-1974, IV-1978, V-1984).

About: M. A. Andrews, *Robert Duncan* (1987). R. Bertholf and W. Reid, eds., *Robert Duncan: Scales of the Marvellous* (1979). G. Bowering and R. Hogg, *Robert Duncan: An Interview* (1971). E. Faas, *Young Robert Duncan: A Portrait of the Poet as Homosexual in Society* (1983). W. Tallman, *Godawful Streets of Man* (1976).

LAWRENCE FERLINGHETTI (1919)

Born in Yonkers, New York, Lawrence Ferlinghetti received an A.B. from the University of North Carolina, an M.A. from Columbia, and a Doctorat de l'Université from the Sorbonne. He was a lieutenant-commander in the Naval Reserve during World War II and worked for *Time* magazine in the 1940s. He was cofounder of City Lights Books in 1952 and has been both owner and editor-in-chief since 1953. He is also generally recognized as having been one of the leading figures of what is known as the San Francisco Renaissance and the Beat Generation.

In a "Note on Poetry in San Francisco" (1955), Ferlinghetti wrote, "the kind of poetry which has been making the most noise here . . . is what should be called street poetry. For it amounts to getting the poet out of the inner esthetic sanctum where he has too long been contemplating his complicated navel. It amounts to getting poetry back into the street where it once was, out of the classroom, out of the speech department, and — in fact — off the printed page. The printed word has made poetry so silent." As a more recent poem, "Uses of Poetry," clearly indicates, Ferlinghetti hasn't changed his mind about what poetry should do and be in forty years.

Ferlinghetti's own poems, often conceived as "oral messages," are designed primarily for their oral impact and often share the characteristics of popular songs. In fact, Ferlinghetti's experiments with poetry and jazz in the early 1960s may well have foreshadowed the later successful fusion of music and lyrics by such popular poets as Bob Dylan. Intended to be understood by the ear, not primarily by the eye, Ferlinghetti's poems often lack the density and complexity of the printed poem. For the same reason, they often depend on the literary cliché, which serves much the same function as the formula in ancient oral poetry. And yet many of his poems — which, ironically, have survived more on the printed page than on the sidewalks — are also replete with classic literary and cultural allusions.

Like Hart Crane, Ferlinghetti sees the poet as "a charleychaplin man," and with a measure of self-directed irony that Crane never could quite muster, he admits that the poet is "constantly risking absurdity." Thus in his poems, while engaging in slapstick and often corny humor aimed at sociocultural evils and absurdities, he pokes fun at the world and at himself, seeks moments of tenderness, sometimes succumbs to sentimentality, and occasionally discovers moments of terror.

Poetry: *Pictures of the Gone World* (1955). *A Coney Island of the Mind* (1958). *Tentative Description of a Dinner Given to Promote the Impeachment of President Eisenhower* (1958). *One Thousand Fearful Words for Fidel Castro* (1961). *Berlin* (1961). *Starting from San Francisco* (1961; revised edition, 1967). *Where Is Vietnam?* (1965). *The Secret Meaning of Things* (1969). *Tyrannus Nix?* (1969). *Back Roads to Far Places* (1971). *Open Eye, Open Heart* (1973). *Who Are We Now?* (1976). *Northwest Ecolog* (1978). *Landscapes of Living & Dying* (1979). *Endless Life: Selected Poems* (1981). *The Populist Manifesto* (1981). *Over All the Obscene Boundaries: European Poems and Transitions* (1984). *Wild Dreams of a New Beginning* (1988). *A Wild Soft Laughter* (in press).

Prose & Drawings: FICTION: *Her* (1960). *Leaves of Life: Fifty Drawings from the Model* (1983). *Love in the Days of Rage* (1989). DRAMA: *Unfair Arguments with Existence* (1963). *Routines* (1964). OTHER: *Dear Ferlinghetti / Dear Jack: The Spicer–Ferlinghetti Correspondence* (1962). *The Mexican Night: Travel Journal* (1970).

Translations: POETRY: *Selections from Paroles*, by Jacques Prevert (1958). *Dogalypse*, by Andrei Voznesensky (1972).

Recordings: AUDIO: *Lawrence Ferlinghetti* (APA, I-1956, II-1958, III-1961). *The Spoken Arts Treasury*, Vol. XVI (SA, 1975). *Into the Deeper Pools* (WT, 1984). *Lawrence Ferlinghetti* (NLA, 1988). VIDEO: *Lawrence Ferlinghetti* (APA, I-1965, II-1976). *The Writing of Lawrence Ferlinghetti* (BWF, 1973).

About: N. Cherkovski, *Ferlinghetti: A Biography* (1979). B. Silpsky, *Ferlinghetti: The Artist in His Time* (1990). L. Smith, *Lawrence Ferlinghetti: Poet-at-Large* (1983).

ISABELLA GARDNER (1915–1981)

A native of Newton, Massachusetts, a great-niece of Isabella Stewart Gardner (who bequeathed a museum to the city of Boston), and a cousin of Robert Lowell, Isabella Gardner insisted that she had received a minimal formal education. In fact, she attended the Foxcroft School, the Leighton Rollins School of Acting, and the Embassy School of Acting in London. She was a professional actress for several years and served as associate editor of *Poetry* while Karl Shapiro was editor. The last book Gardner published in her lifetime, *That Was Then: New and Selected Poems*, was nominated for the 1980 American Book Award for poetry, and in 1981 Gardner was selected as the first recipient of the New York State Walt Whitman Citation of Merit for Poetry.

Having suffered a self-imposed silence during the last fifteen years of her life, Gardner published only four, relatively short, books of poetry during her life. And yet, what a remarkable artistic legacy she bequeathed to contemporary American poetry, no doubt because of her total commitment to her art as its own end. For example, despite the painfully dramatic events in her personal life — divorce, the disappearance and presumed death of her son, the institutionalization of her daughter — Gardner consistently eschewed the potential sensationalism of confessional poetry and the potential political stridency of some feminist poetry. In "The Fellowship with Essence," the afterword she wrote for *That Was Then*, Gardner said, "I don't believe the poet should write with a cudgel, a lance or a crystal ball. A poet is no wiser nor more compassionate than anyone else; yet I feel that the poet is focused on a particularized participation in the most minute or enormous instants, as well as in incidents of hourly existence."

Ralph J. Mills, Jr., has rightly noted that Gardner's own participation in the minute and enormous incidents of hourly existence resulted in a poetry characterized by an intense musical quality. That music, in turn, is the result of the richness of her language (reminiscent of that found in the work of Dylan Thomas, Edith Sitwell, and Gerard Manley Hopkins), coupled with her own innate rhythmic sense. Many of Gardner's poems, such as "The Widow's Yard" and "The Milkman," also reflect an acute precision of psychosexual observation such as that found in the work of Emily Dickinson. Her best poems are also perfectly crafted gems whose sharply focused brilliance leaves us breathless. Short lyrics like "Lines to a Sea-Green Lover" are masterpieces of that genre, and the concluding stanzas of "Lines to a Sea-Green Lover" and "Letter from Slough Pond" achieve much the same kind of intense emotional catharsis found in this classic little poem of the sixteenth century, "Western wind, when will thou blow, / The small rain down can rain? / Christ, if my love were in my arms, / And I in my bed again!"

That many of Isabella Gardner's better poems are concerned with various dimensions of love is no accident. In "The Fellowship with Essence" she asserted, "If there is a theme with which I am particularly concerned, it is the contemporary failure of love. I don't mean romantic love or sexual passion, but the love which is the specific and particular recognition of one human being by another — the responses by eye and voice and touch of two solitudes. The democracy of universal vulnerability."

Poetry: *Birthdays from the Ocean* (1955). *The Looking Glass: New Poems* (1961). *West of Childhood: Poems 1960–1965* (1965). *That Was Then: New and Selected Poems* (1980). *Isabella Gardner: The Collected Poems* (1990).

Recording: AUDIO: *Isabella Gardner* (NLA, 1981).

ALLEN GINSBERG (1926)

Born in Newark, New Jersey, Allen Ginsberg attended Columbia University and was dismissed, but returned later to receive his B.A. in 1948. A leader of the Beat Movement and the San Francisco Renaissance, in 1954 he married Peter Orlovsky. He is the recipient of grants from the Guggenheim Foundation, the National Endowment for the Arts, and the National Institute of Arts and Letters, of which he is a member. In 1974, with Adrienne Rich, he was cowinner of the National Book Award.

In his poem "Ego Confession," Ginsberg asserts, "I want to be known as the most brilliant man in America . . . . / I want to be the spectacle of Poesy triumphant over trickery of the world . . ." Poet, guru, world traveler, prophet, and visionary Uncle Sam of the Flower-Acid-Rock Generation, Ginsberg may well be the planet's most renowned poet. And if Ginsberg's notoriety as a sociocultural *enfant terrible* has obscured his power as a poet, he is nevertheless recognized by his contemporaries as one of the most influential post-1945 poets. His first major poem, "Howl," is a milestone, perhaps as significant a poem and document for his generation as "The Waste Land" was for Eliot's. It is conceivable that Ginsberg's entire work may eventually achieve the stature of *Leaves of Grass*.

At once intimate and prophetic, hilarious and terrifying, profoundly religious and, at times, commensurately outrageous, Ginsberg's poetry encompasses a myriad of experiences, ranges over the full spectrum of human life on this planet, and — like the poetry of Whitman — is a combination of incredible power and drivel. Clearly, in technique, scope, and intent, Whitman is Ginsberg's model and mentor; like him, Ginsberg is attempting to re-create not only the world but also the full dimensions of a human's physical and spiritual odyssey through a given moment in history — with the crucial difference that Whitman's poems were hefty songs and Ginsberg's are often reverberating lamentations.

Part of Ginsberg's impact results from his prophetic stance as a man and as a poet, sustained by the vital spirit of William Blake and the prophets of the Old Testament. A modern-day Isaiah, whose public personality often betrays the depth and range of his erudition, Ginsberg is the public conscience of the nation — if not of the species — lamenting the imponderable evil humankind has perpetrated against life. But like Isaiah, Blake, and Whitman, he is also moved by a profound belief in the holiness of life and by a vision of a new Jerusalem, a new world.

Poetry: *Howl and Other Poems* (1956). *Empty Mirror: Early Poems* (1961). *Kaddish and Other Poems* (1961). *Reality Sandwiches* (1963). *T.V. Baby Poems* (1967/1968). *Airplane Dreams: Compositions from Journals* (1968/1969). *Ankor-Wat* (1968). *Planet News, 1961–1967* (1968). *Bixby Canyon Ocean Path Word Breeze* (1972). *The Gates of Wrath: Rhymed Poems, 1948–1952* (1972). *The Fall of America: Poems of These States, 1965–1971* (1973). *Iron Horse* (1973). *First Blues* (1975). *Sad Dust Glories* (1975). *Mind Breaths: Poems 1972–1977* (1978). *Poems All Over the Place, Mostly 'Seventies* (1978). *Mostly Sitting Haiku* (1979). *Plutonium Ode: Poems 1977–1980* (1982). *Collected Poems: 1947–1980* (1984). *White Shroud: Poems 1980–1985* (1986).

Prose: *The Yage Letters*, with William Burroughs (1963). *Indian Journals* (1970). *Improvised Poetics*, edited by M. Robinson (1971). *Gay Sunshine Interview* (1974). *Allen Verbatim: Lectures on Poetry, Politics, Consciousness*, edited by G. Ball (1974). *The Visions of the Great Rememberer* (1974). *Chicago Trial Testimony* (1975). *To Eberhart from Ginsberg: A Letter About Howl 1956* (1976). *As Ever: The Collected Correspondence of Allen Ginsberg & Neal Cassady*, edited by B. Gifford (1977). *Journals: Early Fifties Early Sixties*, edited by G. Ball (1977). *Composed on the Tongue*, edited by D. Allen (1980). *Straight Hearts Delight: Love Poems and Selected Letters 1974–1980*, with Peter Orlovsky, edited by W. Layland (1980). *Howl, Original Draft Facsimile, Fully Annotated*, edited by B. Miles (1986). *Your Reason and Blake's System* (1988).

Recordings: AUDIO: *Allen Ginsberg: "Howl" and Other Poems* (APA, 1956). *Allen Ginsberg* (APA, 1959). *The Spoken Arts Treasury*, Vol. XVI (SA, 1975). *Allen Ginsberg* (NLA, 1988). *Allen Ginsberg: The Lion for Real* (Island Records, 1989). *"Howl" and Other Poems* (Fantasy, 1959). VIDEO: *Allen Ginsberg* (APA, I-1965, II-1974, III-1978). *The Poetry of Allen Ginsberg* (BWF, I-1970, II-1973). *Allen Ginsberg* (LLS, 1989).

About: M. Barry, *Ginsberg: A Biography* (1989). J. W. E. Ehrlich, *Howl of the Censor* (1956). L. Hyde, ed., *On the Poetry of Allen Ginsberg* (1984). J. Kramer, *Allen Ginsberg in America* (1969). T. F. Merrill, *Allen Ginsberg* (1969). P. Portuges, *The Visionary Poetics of Allen Ginsberg* (1979).

LOUISE GLÜCK (1943)

Born in New York City and raised on Long Island, Louise Glück attended Sarah Lawrence College and Columbia University, where she studied with Stanley Kunitz. She has taught at many colleges and universities, including Goddard College, the University of California at Los Angeles, and Williams College. She has received fellowships from the National Endowment for the Arts and the Guggenheim and Rockefeller foundations, an award from the American Academy and Institute of Arts and Letters, and the National Book Critics Circle Award.

"I have always been too at ease with extremes," writes Louise Glück. Whether those extremes are life and death, love and pain, possession and release, or illusion and reality, it is from the tension between them that many of her most moving poems draw their force. But because of her skill with the striking image, the canny tonal shift, and the poetic line, the weight of her themes never overwhelms the poem. Whether writing in her early dense, near-surrealistic mode ("Fish bones walked the waves off Hatteras") or in the looser, more conversational style of her later work ("I have a friend who still believes in heaven") she controls the rhythm of the poetic line the way a skilled rider handles the reins, alternately tightening and loosening to keep the desired momentum.

Though aspects of autobiography are present in Glück's poems, they rarely serve an expiational purpose. Rather, her self-scrutiny is linked to a wider search for meaning and value, and above all for what it means to be human. It is that exploration of human existence — the "hard loss" of birth, the "thrust and ache" of male/female relations — that may account for the frequent presence in her poems of ancient Greek characters, themes, and images. Taking to heart the Sophoclean edict that "Man is the measure of all things," she seems to forswear both a specifically Christian redemption and a generically spiritual transcendence. In "Celestial Music," a friend who believes in God tells her to look up: "When I look up, nothing. / Only clouds, snow, a white business in the trees."

If the gods long ago "sank down to human shape with longing" — if there is no supernatural world — Glück's poetry seems all the more urgent on the question of what makes us human. Achilles, part god and part man, is "a victim / of the part that loved, / the part that was mortal." That is the common denominator in her poetry: to be human is to love, to long, to suffer, and to know you will die. Not that Glück would seem to want it otherwise, for "There is always something to be made of pain."

Poetry: *Firstborn* (1968/1981). *The House on Marshland* (1975). *Descending Figure* (1980). *The Triumph of Achilles* (1985). *Ararat* (1990).

Recordings: VIDEO: *Louise Glück* (APA, 1976). *Louis Glück* (LLS, 1989).

DONALD HALL (1928)

Born in New Haven, Connecticut, Donald Hall is a graduate of Harvard and Oxford. In a way, he is also a "graduate" of the University of Michigan, where he taught for several years before returning to his family's farm in New Hampshire, where he now lives and writes. In 1954, his book *Exiles and Marriages* was the Academy of American Poets' Lamont Poetry Selection. His other literary awards include the Lenore Marshall Prize, the National Book Critics Circle Award, and appointment as Poet Laureate of New Hampshire.

Hall's many other accomplishments include monographs on Marianne Moore and Henry Moore and such noted textbooks as *Writing Well* and *To Read Literature*. He also has edited many anthologies, including *Contemporary American Poetry* (1962), the introduction to which offers a vital point of contention for the essay "The Radical Tradition" (see page 651 of this book).

In a variety of statements — and especially in his dazzling essay "Goatfoot, Milktongue, Twinbird: The Psychic Origins of Poetic Form" — Hall has repeatedly affirmed that the essential beauty of poetry lies in the sensual body of the poem — the sheer physical pleasure that a poem offers. That physical pleasure, Hall observes, "reaches us through our mouths (Milktongue) . . . in the muscles of our legs (Goatfoot) . . . in the resolution of dance and noise (Twinbird)." Hall's quest for the sensual body of his own poems was originally in more traditional forms; later, his poems became less formal, more expansive, and more sensual — without losing the control and discipline learned in the atelier of formalism.

Moreover, Hall's quest for the sensual body of poetry hasn't been the aesthete's pursuit of pleasure found in the notions of Walter Pater or in the work of some of Hall's own contemporaries. For Hall knows all too well: "Milktongue also remembers hunger, and the cry without answer. Goatfoot remembers falling, and the ache that bent the night. Twinbird remembers the loss of the brother, so long he believed in abandonment forever." At the heart of Hall's own poetry are the ever-present ache and modulated cry of abandonment, of grief over loss that is also at the heart of human experience.

More recently the sense of loss in Hall's poems has been complemented and perhaps surpassed by a large measure of a joyous reconciliation with personal history, a discovery of the redemptive power inherent in all cycles of existence. Thus twenty-five years after the grandfather's body has slid into the ground like snow melting on the roof of the saphouse, his grandchildren dip their fingers in the maple syrup the dead man preserved in his cellar. Thus Hall himself can exclaim, "Oh, this delicious falling into the arms of leaves, / into the soft laps of leaves! . . . / Now I leap and fall, exultant, recovering / from death, on account of death, in accord with the dead . . ." And thus he evokes still another ancient image of the sensual pleasure of poetry in the myth of Philomel, magically transformed into a nightingale whose torn tongue makes song, makes music, out of grief.

Poetry: *(Poems)* (1952). *Exile* (1952). *To the Loud Wind and Other Poems* (1955). *Exiles and Marriages* (1955). *The Dark Houses* (1958). *A Roof of Tiger Lilies* (1964). *The Alligator Bride: Poems New and Selected* (1969). *The Yellow Room: Love Poems* (1971). *The Town of Hill* (1975). *Kicking the Leaves* (1978). *The Toy Bone* (1979). *The Happy Man* (1986). *The Bone Ring* (1987). *The One Day: A Poem in Three Parts* (1988). *Old and New Poems, 1947–1990* (1990).

Prose: FICTION: *The Ideal Bakery* (1987). CRITICISM: *Goatfoot Milktongue Twin-bird: Interviews, Essays, and Notes on Poetry 1970–76* (1978). *To Keep Moving: Essays 1959–69* (1980). *Claims for Poetry*, editor (1982). *The Weather for Poetry: Essays, Reviews, and Notes on Poetry 1977–81* (1983). *Poetry and Ambition: Essays 1982–1988* (1990). MEMOIRS AND OTHER: *String Too Short To Be Saved: Childhood Reminiscences* (1961/1979). *Dock Ellis in the Country of Baseball* (1976). *Remembering Poets: Reminiscences and Opinions* (1978). *Fathers Playing Catch with Sons: Essays on Sports* (1985). *Seasons at Eagle Pond* (1987). *Daylilies at Eagle Pond* (1990). *Here at Eagle Pond* (1990).

Recordings: AUDIO: *The Spoken Arts Treasury*, Vol. XVII (SA, 1975). *Names of Horses* (WT, 1985). *Donald Hall* (NLA, 1987). VIDEO: *The Poetry of Donald Hall* (BWF, 1982). *Donald Hall* (APA, I-1976, II-1986).

About: L. Rector, *The Day I Was Older: A Collection of Poems, Photos, Essays, Reviews on Donald Hall* (1989).

MICHAEL S. HARPER (1938)

Michael S. Harper was born in Brooklyn and educated at California State University at Los Angeles and the University of Iowa. In 1978 he was also a postdoctoral fellow at the Center for Advanced Study at the University of Illinois. He has taught at Lewis and Clark College, Reed College, Harvard, and Yale. In 1979 he was Elliston Poet and Distinguished Professor at the University of Cincinnati and Benedict Distinguished Professor at Carleton College. Since 1970 he has taught at Brown University, where he is the I. J. Kapstein Professor of English. In addition to fellowships from the Guggenheim Foundation and the National Endowment for the Arts, Harper's awards include the Black Academy of Arts and Letters Award, the Melville Cane Award from the Poetry Society of America, and a National Institute of Arts and Letters grant.

The titles of Michael Harper's books are genuine flags of his substantive and sustained concerns. Many of his poems are indeed "images of kin": the woman to whom he is married, their living children, their children who died as infants, his own parents and grandparents. But in Harper's poems kinship also expands in time and space to include historical figures, ranging from Frederick Douglass to Martin Luther King and Malcolm X, as well as members of the artistic community, jazz musicians such as John Coltrane, Charlie Parker, Bessie Smith, and Billie Holiday and writers such as Richard Wright and, especially among his contemporaries, Robert Hayden.

Moreover, the focus of Harper's concern is a powerful sense of kinship as shared history. Such a vision, then, begins by asserting that "history is your own heartbeat," but it necessarily expands in ever-widening circles of kinship, generated by the pulse that is at the heart of the human family. Full and active participation in those human bonds, Harper knows, may often result in considerable pain and anguish, for to be fully human often necessitates recognizing the nightmare of our condition and accepting its necessary consequence: "nightmare begins responsibility."

Harper is also one of the poets of his generation whose poetry and sensibility has been as influenced by the work and presence of the classic American jazz musicians. In his poems they assume the dimensions and implications of larger figures from ancient myths. But they are more than just mythical presences, for in their work Harper has searched for and learned what he calls "the cadence of street talk in the inner ear of the great musicians, the great blues singers." And as Ralph J. Mills, Jr., has noted, Harper's poetry is infused with "a complex jazz of sudden leaps, silences, long rides." No less important, Harper reflects that rich tradition of making music out of fundamental human suffering, whether it be personal, racial, or historical. The conscious transmutation of suffering into song is at once an assertion of our humanity and an affirmation of our freedom. But in one of his essays Harper also tells the story of how John Coltrane tried to find an especially soft reed that would alleviate his pain as he played his horn in search of a particular tone. Coltrane eventually gave up looking for such a reed, regardless of how painful it was for him to make music. "There was no easy way to get that sound," Harper concludes: "play through the pain to *a love supreme*" — the phrase that appears most frequently in Harper's work. No wonder Michael Harper's poems are such "healing songs."

Poetry: *Dear John, Dear Coltrane* (1970). *History Is Your Own Heartbeat* (1971). *Photographs: Negatives: History as Apple Tree* (1972). *Song: I Want a Witness* (1972). *Debridement* (1973). *Nightmare Begins Responsibility* (1974). *Images of Kin: New and Selected Poems* (1977). *Healing Song for the Inner Ear* (1984). *Spiritual Warfare* (1984). *Rhode Island: Eight Poems* (1985).

Recordings: AUDIO: *Michael Harper* (APA, 1969). *Michael Harper* (NLA, 1980). *Here Where Coltrane Is* (WT, 1984). VIDEO: *The Poetry of Michael Harper* (BWF, 1985).

ROBERT HASS (1941)

Born in San Francisco and raised in San Rafael, California, Robert Hass received a B.A. from St. Mary's College and a Ph.D. from Stanford University. He has taught at the State University of New York at Buffalo, St. Mary's College, and, since 1989, at the University of California at Berkeley. The recipient of a Guggenheim Fellowship, Hass also won the Yale Series of Younger Poets award, an award from the American Institute and Academy of Arts and Letters, the National Book Critics Circle Award for criticism, and is the recipient of a distinguished John D. and Catherine T. MacArthur Fellowship.

Representing the second generation of poets since 1945, Hass is both heir to and active participant in the restlessness and eclectic spirit of contemporary American poetry.   In his early work there is the unmistakable and vibrant influence of the previous generation of poets who helped shape the aesthetics of the late sixties and early seventies.   In many poems the Chinese and Japanese aesthetics that so influenced Gary Snyder are present.   By contrast, the imagery, tone, structure, and especially closure of a poem like "The Failure of Buffalo to Levitate" vividly call to mind Robert Bly's and Louis Simpson's earlier experiments in north-American neo-surrealism.   A poem like "Bookbuying in the Tenderloin," meanwhile, reflects the aesthetic and thematic sensibilities of poets such as Robert Lowell and John Logan: the deterioration of Judeo-Christian spiritual values, commensurate with commerce in sex, and the deterioration of sexual mores and values, foreshadows the death of western civilization — expressed in rhymed, occasional couplets: "The sky glowers. My God, it is a test, / this riding out the dying of the West."

Peculiar to Hass's poetry is the obsession with the relationship between language and the physical world — between word and thing.   This tension, never fully resolved, is explored both explicitly ("a word is elegy to what it signifies") and implicitly through the joy Hass takes in simply naming things ("Tall Buttercup. Wild Vetch"; "*silver* or *moonlight* or *wet grass*").   If the body, the flesh is "this sickness of this age" and if "The dead with their black lips are heaped / on one another, intimate as lovers" are images central to Hass's early poems, so too is the belief in "the magic of names and poems" and in the vision that "our words are clear / and our movements give off light."   And it is a sustained belief in such magic that enables Hass in later poems — most of them written in long, lyrical lines — to wrestle with "All the new thinking . . . about loss," to affirm "moments when the body is as numinous as words, days that are the good flesh continuing" and to celebrate the physical, sensual, and transcendent pleasures of this world (not the least of which is food): "Such tenderness, these afternoons and evenings, / saying *blackberry, blackberry, blackberry.*"

Poetry: *Field Guide* (1973). *Praise* (1979). *Human Wishes* (1989).

Prose: *Twentieth Century Pleasures: Prose on Poetry*, essays (1984).

Translations: *The Separate Notebooks*, poems by Czeslaw Milosz, with R. Gorcynski and R. Pinsky (1984). *Unattainable Earth*, poems by Czeslaw Milosz, with the author (1986). *Collected Poems*, by Czeslaw Milosz, with the author and others (1989).

Recordings: AUDIO: *A Story About the Body* (WT, 1986). VIDEO: *Robert Hass* (APA, I-1979, II-1984).

ROBERT HAYDEN (1913–1980)

A native of Detroit, Robert Hayden received a B.A. from Wayne State University and an M.A. from the University of Michigan.   He taught at

Fisk, Louisville, and Washington, and he was professor of English at the University of Michigan.   He was a staff member of the Breadloaf Writers Conference, and from 1976 to 1978 he served as Consultant in Poetry at the Library of Congress.   His honors and awards included a Rosenwald Fellowship, a Ford Foundation grant, and the First World Festival of Negro Arts Prize for Poetry, Dakar, Senegal, in 1966.

From the publication of his first book in 1940, Hayden's poetry consistently reflected a sensibility informed by a vital awareness of and participation in the broad spectrum of the African American experience.   He explored dimensions of his own childhood and personal life; he focused on central historical and cultural figures and events; and he re-created such immeasurable horrors as an African American man's castration at the hands of the Ku Klux Klan.   No less important, while eschewing political rhetoric, he recognized that much the same moral poison infected the air of both Selma and Saigon, that the ashes in the pits at Dachau resulted from a fire not unlike that which burned on lawns in innumerable American towns.

Hayden's moral vision is all the more powerful because his work reveals that he is equally conscious of the broader aesthetic traditions in the art of poetry and of the obvious — but often overlooked — fact that the wellsprings of poetry run more deeply and serendipitously than even the most active pools of political or racial experience.   The impact of a poem like "Monet's 'Waterlilies'" emerges out of the fact that Hayden's vision is rooted specifically in such a seemingly apolitical and nonmoral work of art.   The depths of horror in "Night, Death, Mississippi" are intensified by the delicate and exquisite lyrical qualities of "The Night-Blooming Cereus."

In short, whether writing about Frederick Douglass or Rilke or a diver, Robert Hayden's poems are themselves vibrant "lives grown out of his life, the lives / fleshing his dream of *the beautiful, needful thing."*

Poetry: *Heart-Shape in the Dust* (1940).   *The Lion and the Archer*, with Myron O'Higgins (1948).   *Figures of Time: Poems* (1955).   *A Ballad of Remembrance* (1962).   *Selected Poems* (1966).   *Words in the Mourning Time* (1970).   *The Night-Blooming Cereus* (1975).   *Angle of Ascent: New and Selected Poems* (1975).   *American Journal* (1978/1982).   *Robert Hayden: Collected Poems* (1985).

Prose: *The Collected Prose of Robert Hayden* (1984).

Recordings: VIDEO: *The Poetry of Robert Hayden* (BWF, 1975).

About: J. Hatcher, *From the Auroral Darkness: The Life and Poetry of Robert Hayden* (1984).   P. Williams, *Robert Hayden: A Critical Analysis of His Poetry* (1987).

RICHARD HUGO (1923–1982)

Richard Hugo was born in Seattle and educated at the University of Washington.   He was a bombardier in the U.S. Army Air Corps during World

War II and subsequently worked for the Boeing Company for twelve years. From 1964 to 1982 he was a member of the English Department at the University of Montana (Missoula), where he was professor of English and director of the creative writing program. From 1977 to 1982 he also served as the editor of the Yale Series of Younger Poets. His awards include the Theodore Roethke Memorial Poetry Prize and fellowships from the Rockefeller and Guggenheim foundations.

Perhaps more than the work of any other poet of his generation, Hugo's poetry is rooted in and mines a specific, identifiable landscape — the American Far West. However, Hugo's landscape isn't the breathtaking panorama of a Grand Canyon or spectacular hills and plains against a blazing sunset of romantic American western movies. The landscape in his poetry is suggested in Hugo's comment: "Usually I find a poem is triggered by something, a small town or an abandoned house, that I feel others would ignore." Thus the geographic, human, and moral landscape in Hugo's poems is a bleak and threatening panorama in which one finds those small, dry, and blistered towns where all life and human constructs decay too soon — and where perhaps nothing dies soon enough.

If, like Wallace Stevens, Hugo understands the extent to which "the soil is man's intelligence," he nevertheless does not succumb to easy fatalism. In poems whose language and texture assert their own organic shapes and rhythms, as if in defiance of the odds of lunar dust, Hugo affirms the things of this earth and of his poetic landscape. Just as Rilke could assert, "Maybe we're here only to say: *house*, / *bridge, well, gate, jug, olive tree, window* — / at most, *pillar, tower* . . . but to say them, remember, / oh, to say them in a way that the things themselves / never dreamed of existing so intensely," so Hugo can assert, "To live good, keep your life and the scene. / Cow, brook, hay; these are names of coins."

"A part of the West belongs to Hugo," William Stafford has written. "By telling over and over again its places and people, he reclaims it from the very bleakness he confronts; and it all begins to loom as a great intense abode that we can't neglect, that we can't bear to let go." Thus Richard Hugo's intense love of the things of *his* earth keeps them and us alive at a level of intensity and joy we could not know without the melancholy and redemptive beauty of his poems.

Poetry: *A Run of Jacks* (1961). *Five Poets of the Pacific Northwest*, with Kenneth Hanson, Carolyn Kizer, William Stafford, and David Wagoner (1964). *Death of the Kapowsin Tavern* (1985). *Good Luck in Cracked Italian* (1969). *The Lady in Kicking Horse Reservoir* (1973). *Rain Five Days and I Love It* (1975). *What Thou Lovest Well, Remains American* (1975). *Duwamish Head* (1976). *31 Letters and 13 Dreams* (1977). *Road Ends at Tahola* (1978). *Selected Poems* (1979). *White Center* (1980). *The Right Madness of Skye* (1980). *Making Certain It Goes On: The Collected Poems of Richard Hugo* (1983). *Sea Lanes Out* (1983).

Prose: *The Triggering Town: Lectures and Essays on Poetry and Writing* (1979). *Death and the Good Life*, a novel (1981). *The Real West Marginal Way: A Poet's Autobiography* (1986).

Recordings: AUDIO: *No Bells to Believe* (WT, 1979). *Richard Hugo* (NLA, 1980). VIDEO: *Richard Hugo* (APA, 1974). *The Poetry of Richard Hugo* (BWF, 1974).

About: M. S. Allen, *We Are Called Human: The Poetry of Richard Hugo* (1982). J. Myers, ed., *A Trout in the Milk: A Composite Portrait of Richard Hugo* (1982). *The Devil's Millhopper: A Memorial to Richard Hugo* (1983).

DAVID IGNATOW (1914)

A native of Brooklyn, David Ignatow has worked as a salesman, public relations writer, shipyard handyman, and treasurer and president of a bindery firm. He has taught at the New School for Social Research, Vassar, and Columbia and subsequently as poet-in-residence at York College. In addition to awards from the National Institute of Arts and Letters and the National Endowment for the Arts he has received fellowships from the Rockefeller and Guggenheim foundations. In 1975 he was awarded the Bollingen Prize in Poetry.

An avowed disciple of William Carlos Williams, who focuses primarily on the urban experience, Ignatow has written in his *Notebooks* that his role is to remind other poets — and, by implication, all readers of poetry — that "there is a world outside, the more decisive world that yet must be treated tragically by us in the highest intensity and sensuousness, though while it ignores us we must not run off into separate worlds of our own." Admitting that he is "antipoetic," he affirms that experience must be looked at and accepted just as it is and that "nothing should be taken for more than it says to you on its surface."

Ranging from comedy, through rage, to tragedy — and addressing himself to both his personal experiences as well as to our communal life — Ignatow constantly attempts to see life as it really is, without illusion or self-deception of any kind. And in so doing, he views himself as being at the opposite pole of Whitman's affirmative optimism. "My idea of being a moral leader," he writes, "is to point out the terrible deficiencies in man. Whitman spent his life boosting the good side. My life will be spent pointing out the bad." But he adds a most crucial phrase: if he is intent on pointing to human deficiencies, he says that he will do so "from the standpoint of forgiveness and peace."

In his book-length sequence, *Shadowing the Ground*, Ignatow brought the same tragic sense of human existence to bear on aging and death — but with humor and unmatched serenity. By so doing he became the first poet of his generation, as Yeats did, to mine a new mother-lode of gorgeous and lively poetry in old age and the prospect of death. A singular and powerful voice in contemporary poetry, eschewing all current modes of language to be himself first of all, David Ignatow's poetry is marked by a certain nontheatrical directness and is also charged with a unique strength of spirit, humanity, and wisdom.

Poetry: *Poems* (1948). *The Gentle Weight Lifter* (1955). *Say Pardon* (1962). *Figures of the Human* (1964). *Rescue the Dead* (1968). *Poems 1934–1969* (1970). *Facing the Tree: New Poems* (1975). *Selected Poems*, chosen by R. Bly (1975). *The Animal in the Bush: Poems on Poetry*, edited by P. Carey (1978). *Tread the Dark: New Poems* (1978). *Sunlight: A Sequence for My Daughter* (1979). *Whisper to the Earth* (1981). *Leaving the Door Open* (1984). *New and Collected Poems: 1970–1985* (1986). *Despite the Plainness of the Day: Love Poems* (1990). *Shadowing the Ground* (1991).

Prose: *The Notebooks of David Ignatow*, edited by R. J. Mills, Jr. (1983). *Open Between Us: Essays, Reviews, and Interviews*, edited by R. J. Mills, Jr. (1980). *The One in Many: A Poet's Memoirs* (1988).

Recordings: AUDIO: *The Spoken Arts Treasury*, Vol. III (SA, 1975). *David Ignatow* (NLA, 1979). VIDEO: *The Poetry of David Ignatow* (BWF, 1973). *David Ignatow* (APA, nd).

RANDALL JARRELL (1914–1965)

Randall Jarrell was born in Nashville and educated at Vanderbilt University, where he received degrees in psychology and English. He served as a control tower operator in the U.S. Army Air Corps during World War II. Before and after the war, he taught at several colleges and universities, including Sarah Lawrence, Kenyon, the University of North Carolina, and Princeton. In addition, he was literary editor for *The Nation* and poetry critic for the *Partisan Review* and *Yale Review*. In 1956 he was appointed Consultant in Poetry at the Library of Congress and was elected a member of the National Institute of Arts and Letters and a chancellor of the Academy of American Poets. His many awards included fellowships from the Guggenheim and Ingram Merrill foundations, a grant from the National Institute of Arts and Letters, and the National Book Award.

Heralded for his translations, his criticism, and his poetry, Jarrell seemed destined to be one of his generation's authentic men of letters before his untimely and enigmatic death. However, a measure of controversy continues to hound Jarrell's reputation as a poet. Some would argue that he was too much of a formalist, and yet a poem like "The Black Swan" certainly compares well to other formal poems written by someone like Richard Wilbur, while simultaneously calling to mind a coupling of Yeats's romantic and mythic concerns. Others would argue that too many of his poems succumbed to an excessive conversational and prosaic style, and yet Jarrell's successful nonformalist poems seem to presage the structural and lyrical quality of Robert Lowell's later work, especially the poems in *Day by Day*.

At the heart of Jarrell's vision as a poet is an intense, Rilkean pursuit of transformation, if not transcendence. Jarrell was obsessed by the need to discover the possibility of *more* in the world around him and especially in himself. Like the speaker in "The Woman at the Washington Zoo," Jarrell repeatedly insists, "You know what I was, / You see what I am:

change me, change me!" But the magnificent snow-leopard is "the heart of heartlessness"; the soul of the European emigrant to the new world "finds Europe waiting for it over every sea"; the ball turret gunner who dies for his country and topples from the sky like a modern-day Icarus isn't immortalized; rather, his body is washed out of the turret with a hose. In short, "nothing comes from nothing . . . / Pain comes from the darkness / And we call it wisdom. It is pain." Given such evidence, no wonder Robert Lowell said that Jarrell was "the most heart-breaking . . . poet of his generation."

Poetry: *Five Young American Poets*, with others (1940). *Blood for a Stranger* (1942). *Little Friend, Little Friend* (1945). *Losses* (1948). *The Seven-League Crutches* (1951). *Selected Poems* (1955). *The Woman at the Washington Zoo: Poems and Translations* (1960). *Selected Poems* (1964). *The Lost World: New Poems* (1965). *The Complete Poems* (1969). *Selected Poems*, edited by W. H. Pritchard (1990).

Prose: FICTION: *Pictures from an Institution: A Comedy* (1954). CRITICISM: *Poetry and the Age* (1953). *Poetry, Critics, and Readers* (1959). *A Sad Heart at the Supermarket: Essays and Fables* (1962). *The Third Book of Criticism* (1969). *Kipling, Auden & Co.* (1980). OTHER: *Randall Jarrell's Letters: An Autobiographical and Literary Selection*, edited by M. Jarrell (1985).

Translations: VERSE DRAMA: *Goethe's Faust: Part One* (1974). FICTION: *The Ghetto and the Jews of Rome*, by Ferdinand Gregorovius; with Moses Hadas (1948). *The Rabbit Catcher and Other Fairy Tales of Ludwig Bechstein* (1962). *The Golden Bird and Other Fairy Tales by the Brothers Grimm* (1962). *Snow White and the Seven Dwarfs: A Tale from the Brothers Grimm* (1972). *The Juniper Tree and Other Tales by the Brothers Grimm* (1973).

Recordings: AUDIO: *Randall Jarrell* (APA, 1956). *Randall Jarrell Reading at the New York Poetry Center* (WT, 1963). *The Spoken Arts Treasury of 100 Modern American Poets Reading Their Poems*, Vol. XII (SA, 1975). *Randall Jarrell* (TPV, 1978).

About: C. M. Adams, *Randall Jarrell* (1958). C. H. Beck, *Worlds and Lives: The Poetry of Randall Jarrell* (1983). J. A. Bryant, Jr., *Understanding Randall Jarrell* (1986). S. Ferguson, *The Poetry of Randall Jarrell* (1971). S. Ferguson, ed., *Critical Essays on Randall Jarrell* (1983). H. Hagenbuchle, *The Black Goddess: A Study of the Archetypical Feminine in the Poetry of Randall Jarrell* (1975). R. Lowell, P. Taylor, and R. P. Warren, eds., *Randall Jarrell 1914–1965* (1967). Sr. B. Quinn, *Randall Jarrell* (1980). M. L. Rosenthal, *Randall Jarrell* (1972).

DONALD JUSTICE (1925)

Donald Justice was born in Miami, Florida. He attended the University of Miami, the University of North Carolina at Chapel Hill, Stanford University, and the University of Iowa. He has taught at the University of Missouri, Syracuse University, the University of California, and the University of Iowa. He is currently professor of English at the University of Florida at Gainesville. Since his book *The Summer Anniversaries* was the Academy of American Poets' Lamont Poetry Selection for 1959, Justice also has been the recipient of grants, awards, and fellowships from the Ford and Guggenheim foundations, the National Endowment for the Arts, and the National Institute of Arts and Letters. In 1980 he was awarded the Pulitzer Prize for his *Selected Poems.*

Many of Justice's poems generate much the same kind of emotional center and aura as Edward Hopper's well-known paintings (such as *Nighthawks*): the figures, landscapes, the dramatic situations reflect the depth of loneliness, the isolation, and the spiritual desolation at the heart of twentieth-century experience. Any number of these people or situations could suddenly turn up in our own nightmares or in our living rooms. However, while Hopper achieves his effects by means of bold colors, thick strokes, and stark contrasts, the surface texture of Justice's poems is far more delicate and subtle — the restrained turn of a phrase (as in "Men at Forty"), the carefully controlled but haunting repetition of a line (as in "Bus Stop").

Given a list of some of Justice's subjects — loneliness, isolation, madness, despair, terror — he might be wrongfully associated with some of the personal-confessional poets. His poems, however, do not suggest any of the verbal or emotional sensationalism that occasionally may be ascribed to some of those other poets. Rightfully celebrated for his formal qualities, as a craftsman, Justice is a master of sparse elegance, with none of the pejorative connotations that may be clustered around those words. Justice's poems are not the result of emotional or technical self-indulgence; rather, they are moving because of his consummate linguistic, tonal, and formal exactitude.

If Justice's commitment to the "well-made poem" suggests his formal schooling among the New Critics, he is also one of the obvious emotional-spiritual heirs of T. S. Eliot — that is, the vision found in Eliot's earlier poems, before his conversion to Christianity. Like the work of other poets of his generation, Justice's poems flesh out in more intimate and sustained detail the figures and states of being that Eliot only sketched in poems like "The Love Song of J. Alfred Prufrock," "Preludes," and "The Waste Land." What further distinguishes Justice's work is not only his unrelieved sense of loss ("Everything going away in the night again and again"), but also his profound acceptance of (*not* resignation to) the human condition as he finds it. But if Donald Justice's poems are elegies of loss, they are also unswerving and powerful affirmations that to be human is to make poetry of "the boredom, and the horror, and the glory."

Poetry: *The Summer Anniversaries* (1960). *A Local Storm* (1963). *Four Poets,* with others (1963). *Night Light* (1967). *Sixteen Poems* (1970). *From a Notebook* (1972). *Departures* (1973). *Selected Poems* (1979). *The Sunset Maker: Poems/ Stories/A Memoir* (1987).

Prose: *Platonic Scripts,* essays (1984).

Translations: *The Man Closing Up,* poems by Guillevic (1973).

Recordings: AUDIO: *Donald Justice* (NLA, I-1980, II-1984, III-1989). *Childhood and Other Poems* (WT, 1983). VIDEO: *The Poetry of Donald Justice* (BWF, 1970).

GALWAY KINNELL (1927)

Galway Kinnell received an A.B. from Princeton and an M.A. from the University of Rochester. He was a Fulbright Fellow in Paris, served in the U.S. Navy and as a field worker for the Congress of Racial Equality, and has traveled widely in the Middle East and Europe. Kinnell has taught at the universities of Grenoble and Nice (France), California (at Irvine), and Pittsburgh, as well as at Sarah Lawrence and New York University. He has received the Brandeis University Creative Arts Award, fellowships from the Rockefeller, MacArthur, and Guggenheim foundations, an award from the National Institute of Arts and Letters, and the Pulitzer Prize.

Kinnell's earlier poems were both traditionally formal and informed by a traditional Christian sensibility. However, while retaining an essentially religious and sacramental dimension, his later work — as he has said in an interview — has become an increasing "struggle against the desire for heaven," as well as a movement away from competent poetry that risks being ornamental and toward a freer verse that takes more risks and in which "there is the chance of finding that great thing you might be after, of finding glory."

Confronted by a constant threat of extinction, in his poetry Kinnell accepts all forms of death as part of the rhythm that produces life, but he is capable of witnessing even the most elemental energy as an affirmation of life. Perhaps human life is a participation in the ultimate madness of a universe flinging itself into emptiness; the image of fire often reappearing in his poems may not be the flame of the phoenix. Thus Kinnell insists that for man, "as he goes up in flames, his own work / is / to open himself, to *be* / the flames."

In their language and substance, Kinnell's poems achieve that rhythm and solemnity often found in a shaman's chant. And yet his poems are also intensely personal, reflecting an attempt to strip away personality, to go deeper into the self "until," he says, "you're just a person. If you could keep going deeper and deeper, you'd finally not be a person either; you'd be an animal; and if you kept going deeper and deeper, you'd be a blade of grass or ultimately perhaps a stone. And if a stone could read, [poetry] would speak for it." For Kinnell, then, poetry is primal experience and myth, the most elemental kind of prayer, or a "paradigm of what people might wish to say in addressing the cosmos."

Poetry: *What a Kingdom It Was* (1960). *Flower Herding on Mount Monadnock* (1964). *Body Rags* (1968). *First Poems: 1946–54* (1970). *The Book of Nightmares* (1971). *The Avenue Bearing the Initial of Christ into the New World: Poems 1946–64* (1974). *Mortal Acts, Mortal Words* (1980). *Selected Poems* (1982). *The Past* (1985). *When One Has Lived a Long Time Alone* (1990).

Prose: *Black Light,* novel (1966; revised edition, 1981). *Walking Down the Stairs: Selections from Interviews* (1978).

Translations: POETRY: *The Poems of François Villon* (1965; revised version, 1977; new edition, 1982). *On the Motion and Immobility of Douve,* by Yves Bonnefoy (1968). *Lackawanna Elegy,* by Yvan Goll (1970). *Early Poems 1947–1959,* by Yvan Goll; with R. Pevear (1990). FICTION: *Bitter Victory,* by René Hardy (1965).

Recordings: AUDIO: *Galway Kinnell* (APA, I-1965, II-1971). *The Poetry and Voice of Galway Kinnell* (Caedmon, 1975). *The Spoken Arts Treasury* (SA, 1975). *Galway Kinnell* (NLA, 1982). VIDEO: *The Poetry of Galway Kinnell* (BWF, I-1969, II-1971, [i–ii], 1982). *Galway Kinnell* (APA, I-1974, II-1981). *Galway Kinnell* (LLS, 1989). *Moyers: The Power of the Word: "The Simple Acts of Life"* (PBS, 1989).

About: H. Nelson, ed., *On the Poetry of Galway Kinnell: The Wages of Dying* (1987). L. Zimmerman, *Intricate and Simple Things: The Poetry of Galway Kinnell* (1987).

CAROLYN KIZER (1925)

Born in Spokane, Washington, Carolyn Kizer graduated from Sarah Lawrence College and was a fellow of the Chinese government in comparative literature at Columbia University, followed by a year of study in Nationalist China. The founder of the quarterly *Poetry Northwest,* in 1964–1965 she was a Specialist in Literature for the U.S. State Department in Pakistan, and from 1966 to 1970 she served as the first director of the Literature Program for the newly established National Endowment for the Arts. Since 1970 she has been professor, visiting professor, or poet-in-residence at universities throughout the United States. She currently lives in Berkeley, California.

With the publication of her first book-length collection of poems Carolyn Kizer staked out the diverse technical and thematic territories of her art. Whether she is working with free verse, with more formal verse, or with combinations of free verse and occasional slant rhymes, Kizer's poetry is always remarkable for its consummate grace and control. (She is one member of her generation who continues to explore the possibilities and power of strict form.) The intellectual credibility and emotional impact of her poems are further enhanced by her unique intellectual wit and hearty, often stinging, sense of humor. Indeed, Kizer was one of the first poets to approach feminist subjects and themes with a measure of healthy humor and sophisticated wit, which are an integral part of her sensibility rather than merely the device of poetic irony.

Kizer's concern for the cause of feminism has been at the heart of her poetry from the very start of her career — for the most fundamental of reasons: ". . . we are the custodians of the world's best-kept secret: / Merely the private lives of one-half of humanity." And it's important to note that the composition of "Pro Femina" dates back to the mid-1950s, before feminism was an issue of general consciousness. But Kizer's interest isn't limited to feminism as a sociopolitical cause; rather, what generally rivets her attention is the quality of representative women's diurnal experiences. "The Blessing," for example, is an exploration of the relationships of three generations of women. Similar in its subject matter to Isabella Gardner's "The Widow's Yard," Kizer's "A Widow in Wintertime" is a portrait of repressed sexuality, disciplined loneliness, and "metaphysic famines."

However, Kizer doesn't limit herself to the "famines" of experience either, for also at the heart of her poetry is her vision of the profound patterns of physical and metaphysical life: change, transformation, and transubstantiation in nature and in the spirit, for good or ill; birth, death, and rebirth of love, the self, the soul, as in "Semele Recycled," where "the inner parts remember . . . / the comfortable odor of dung, the animal incense, / and passion, its bloody labor, / its birth and rebirth and decay." In short, without sacrificing their feminist edge, Kizer's poems are powerful, myth-making hymns in celebration of "we who invented dying / And the whole alchemy of resurrection."

Poetry: *Poems* (1959). *The Ungrateful Garden* (1961). *Five Poets of the Pacific Northwest*, with Kenneth Hanson, Richard Hugo, and William Stafford; edited by R. Skelton (1964). *Knock Upon Silence* (1965/1966). *Midnight Was My Cry: New and Selected Poems* (1971). *Mermaids in the Basement: Poems for Women* (1984). *Yin: New Poems* (1984). *The Nearness of You* (1986).

Translations: *Carrying Over: Poems from the Chinese, Urdu, Macedonian, Yiddish, and French African* (1988). *A Splintered Mirror: Contemporary Chinese Poets*, with D. Finkel (1990).

Recordings: AUDIO: *Carolyn Kizer* (APA, I-1959, II-1967). *An Ear to the Earth* (WT, 1977). *Carolyn Kizer* (NLA, I-1982, II-1985). VIDEO: *The Poetry of Carolyn Kizer* (BWF, I-1974, II-1982). *Carolyn Kizer* (APA, I-1973, II-1973, III-1979).

About: D. Rigsbee, ed., *An Answering Music: On the Poetry of Carolyn Kizer* (1990).

MAXINE KUMIN (1925)

Born in Philadelphia, Maxine Kumin received both a bachelor's and a master's degree from Radcliffe. The author of some twenty books for children (three of which she wrote with Anne Sexton), Kumin has served as a consultant for the Central Atlantic Regional Educational Laboratory and the Board of Coordinated Educational Services (Nassau County, New York). She also has taught at Tufts, the University of Massachusetts, Centre College (Kentucky), and at Princeton. An officer of the Radcliffe Institute's Society of Fellows and former chairperson of the Literature Panel of the National Endowment for the Arts, Kumin was awarded the Pulitzer Prize in 1973.

One of Kumin's critics has faulted her work for often being "the poetry of a special world, unmistakably upper middle-class, comfortable, urbane, safe in its place at the center of things." To suggest that such arenas of experience may not be legitimate or "worthy" concerns of poetry in this century and country is nonsense, of course. Besides, when Eliot posited his dictum, "Redeem the time," he didn't specify that it had to be an urban and industrial time fraught with its unique sets of psychic and physical terrors. Moreover, if Kumin's poetry does focus on the middle-class experience, like Louis Simpson she too is "taking part in a great experiment — / whether writers can live peacefully in the suburbs / and not be bored to death."

Kumin's personal experiment as a poet also has an edge of intensity that goes considerably beyond mere survival of boredom. Because of her powerful sense of observation and her masterful handling of technique, the objects and experiences of suburban life in Kumin's poetry assume a greater hum and buzz of emblematic implication of the direction of the human soul.

Consequently, the ordinary task of ridding one's garden of woodchucks suggests a greater kind of historical extermination. Beneath the ostensible safety of suburban life lies the nightmare of a cleansing fire all inhabitants must pass through. No less important, one senses in Kumin's poetry a conscious urgency to discover in the natural world not only emblems of endurance, survival, and continuity but also momentary symbols of that more human longing for the possibility of transcendence. With remark-able grace and wit, the poems of Maxine Kumin do indeed redeem the personal and communal time and space in which she lives, in which most of us measure the worth of our lives.

Poetry: *Halfway* (1961). *The Privilege* (1965). *The Nightmare Factory* (1970). *Up Country* (1972). *House, Bridge, Fountain, Gate* (1975). *The Retrieval System* (1978). *Our Ground Time Here Will Be Brief: New and Selected Poems* (1982). *Closing the Ring* (1984). *The Long Approach* (1985). *Nurture: Poems* (1989). *Looking for Luck* (1991).

Prose: ESSAYS: *To Make a Prairie: Essays on Poets, Poetry, and Country Living* (1979). *In Deep: Country Essays* (1988). FICTION: *Through Dooms of Love* (1965). *The Passions of Uxport* (1968). *The Abduction* (1971). *The Designated Heir* (1974). *Why Can't We Live Together Like Civilized Human Beings?* (1982).

Recordings: AUDIO: *Progress Report* (WT, 1976). *Maxine Kumin* (NLA, I-1980, II-1987). VIDEO: *Maxine Kumin* (APA, I-1974, II-1984). *The Poetry of Maxine Kumin* (BWF, 1976).

STANLEY KUNITZ (1905)

Born in Worcester, Massachusetts, and educated at Harvard, Stanley Ku-nitz has taught at Bennington, Brandeis, Columbia, and Yale. He also has been a Cultural Exchange Scholar in the Soviet Union and Poland. From 1969 to 1976, he was editor of the Yale Series of Younger Poets; from 1974 to 1976, he served as Consultant in Poetry at the Library of Congress. The recipient of grants from the Guggenheim and Ford foundations, the Academy of American Poets, and the National Institute of Arts and Letters, he was also awarded the Pulitzer Prize in 1959 and elected a chancellor of the Academy of American Poets in 1970.

In addition to his moving translations of the poetry of Anna Akhmatova, Kunitz has been a major contributor to the many collections of translations of the poetry of Andrei Voznesensky and Yevgeny Yevtushenko that have appeared in this country. Moreover, since 1931, he has been one of the editors of eight major dictionaries of literary biographies.

After the publication of *The Testing-Tree* in 1971, Stanely Kunitz wrote, "I am no more reconciled than I ever was to the world's wrongs and the injustice of time." Among the wrongs and injustices present in Kunitz's poetry are the memories of a painful childhood that seemingly cannot be redeemed or reshaped; inevitable participation in the outrageous scientific and technological violence against the human spirit; and — despite the moments of beauty's hope — the inescapable promise of "a dusty finger on my lip."

Throughout his career, Kunitz's measure of emotional and moral energy has been further intensified by his equally passionate reverence for and use of form. In his poems, more than in the work of most poets of his generation, one senses that any experience or vision — regardless of how intense it might have been in itself — has consistently been forged by the white heat of a metaphysical sensibility. Thus Kunitz's poems have a physical presence and quality that are verbal equivalents of graceful sculptures forged out of the toughest metal — just as the works of certain contemporary metalsmiths are intricate sculptures of iron and steel that seem to be leaping toward pure sound.

Poetry: *Intellectual Things* (1930). *Passport to the War: A Selection of Poems* (1944). *Selected Poems 1928–1958* (1958). *The Testing-Tree: Poems* (1971). *The Lincoln Relics: A Poem* (1979). *The Poems of Stanley Kunitz 1928–1978* (1979). *The Wellfleet Whale and Companion Poems* (1983). *Next-to-Last Things: New Poems and Essays* (1985).

Prose: *A Kind of Order, a Kind of Folly: Essays and Conversations* (1975). *The Art of Poetry: Interviews with Stanley Kunitz* (1989).

Translations: *Poems of Akhmatova*, with M. Hayward (1973).

Recordings: AUDIO: *Stanley Kunitz* (APA, I-1956, II-1960). *The Spoken Arts Treasury* (SA, 1975). *The Only Dance* (WT, 1984). VIDEO: *The Poetry of Stanley Kunitz* (BWF, 1974). *Stanley Kunitz* (APA, 1975). *Moyers: The Power of the Word: "Dancing on the Edge of the Road"* (PBS, 1989).

About: M. Henault, *Stanley Kunitz* (1980). G. Orr, *Stanley Kunitz: An Introduction to the Poetry* (1985).

DENISE LEVERTOV (1923)

Born in Essex, England, Denise Levertov was privately educated, served as a nurse during World War II, and emigrated to the United States in

1948. She has taught at Vassar, Drew, City College of New York, MIT, and at Tufts University. A scholar at the Radcliffe Institute for Independent Study, Levertov also has received the Morton Dauwen Zabel Award, a fellowship from the Guggenheim Foundation, an award from the National Institute of Arts and Letters, and a distinguished Senior Fellowship from the National Endowment for the Arts.

Influenced by William Carlos Williams and the Black Mountain School — or simply their natural aesthetic compatriot — Denise Levertov's poems are nevertheless charged by an unmistakably distinctive voice, capable of ranging from a tough to a tender lyricism that is proportionately intense. Her poems are not simply spoken by a woman; they fully explore and — with assurance, pleasure, or grief — celebrate the multifaceted experience of the contemporary woman. By so doing, they invite all of us into a celebration of the full range of human experience.

In an early interview Levertov said, "I believe in writing about what lies under the hand, in a sense. . . . Not necessarily in the visual world — the external world — it can be an inner experience — but it must be something true." And in one of her poems Levertov writes, "The best work is made / from hard, strong materials, / obstinately precise. . . ." Her own poems repeatedly assert that the most obstinate and hard materials — even in that kind of natural lyrical poem she has mastered — are not onyx and steel, but rather the small, at times elusive, materials of daily human life.

An antiwar poem such as "The Altars in the Street" affirms the inestimable power of the simple but sacred human gesture over "the frenzy of weapons, their impudent power." But so much of her work also reminds us that each new poem is that difficult and laborious Jacob's ladder between the facts of the diurnal and the bid for the eternal; each poem carves the physical details and quality of our daily communal experience in the unyielding onyx and steel of a cosmic history that would obliterate us.

Poetry: *The Double Image* (1946). *Here and Now* (1957). *Overland to the Islands* (1958). *With Eyes at the Back of Our Heads* (1959). *The Jacob's Ladder* (1961). *O Taste and See: New Poems* (1964). *The Sorrow Dance* (1967). *A Tree Telling of Orpheus* (1968). *Embroideries* (1969). *Relearning the Alphabet* (1970). *To Stay Alive* (1971). *Footprints* (1972). *The Freeing of the Dust* (1975). *Life in the Forest* (1978). *Collected Earlier Poems 1940–1960* (1979). *Candles in Babylon* (1982). *Denise Levertov: Poems 1960–1967* (1983). *Oblique Prayers* (1984). *Breathing the Water* (1971). *Denise Levertov: Poems 1968–1972* (1987). *A Door in the Hive* (1989).

Prose: *The Poet in the World*, essays (1973). *Light Up the Cave*, essays (1981).

Translations: *In Praise of Krishna: Songs from the Bengali*, with E. R. Dimmock, Jr. (1968). *Selected Poems of Guillevic* (1969). *Black Iris*, poems by Jean Joubert (1988).

Recordings: AUDIO: *Denise Levertov* (APA, I-1958, [i–ii], II-1961). *The Spoken Arts Treasury* (SA, 1975). *Denise Levertov* (NLA, 1983). *The Acolyte* (WT, 1985). VIDEO: *The Poetry of Denise Levertov* (BWF, 1970).

About: H. Marten, *Understanding Denise Levertov* (1988). L. W. Wagner, *Denise Levertov* (1967). W. Slaughter, *The Imagination's Tongue: Denise Levertov's Poetics* (1981). L. W. Wagner, ed., *Denise Levertov: In Her Own Province* (1979).

PHILIP LEVINE (1928)

Philip Levine was born in Detroit. He received a B.A. and an M.A. from Wayne State University and an M.F.A. from the University of Iowa. Subsequently, he held a fellowship in poetry at Stanford University. Since 1958 he has taught at California State University, Fresno. He has received grants from the National Endowment for the Arts, the National Institute of Arts and Letters, and the Guggenheim Foundation.

Critics can't seem to agree on what Levine's central theme is. One says it's a "rogue's gallery" of drunks, draft-dodgers, boxers, Hell's Angels, midgets, poor neighbors." Another asserts that his themes include "Hiroshima, the torture of Algerian prisoners, soldiers in eye-to-eye combat, generalized and brutal bigotry . . . man's cruelty to man." Still another critic argues that Levine's "fields of exploration" include "experiences which manifest themselves in irrational, dreamlike, fantastic or visionary forms." In fact, all these observations are true, for what is consistently striking about Levine's poetry is precisely his wide range of themes.

Levine himself has written, "I try to pay homage to the people who taught me my life was a holy thing, who convinced me that my formal education was a lie. . . . These people, both Black and white, were mainly rural people, and the horror of the modern world was clearer to them than to me, and the beauty and value of the world was something they knew in a way I did not, first hand." No less important in his poetry is the vital role of Levine's own sense of place — especially the bleak, dirty, and threatening industrial cityscape of Levine's childhood in Detroit; more recently one notes references to Levine's own personal life and background, especially members of his family.

Equally striking — although not immediately noticeable to the more casual reader — is Levine's mastery of a range of forms, from the most ostensible manipulation of tighter forms, through the freer lyric, to the more surrealistic and incantatory poems. Levine displays a seemingly contradictory range of emotional, moral, and often profoundly religious responses to the horror and beauty in the world around him — and inside us all.

Reading the body of Levine's work, one senses a fiercely honest exploration of the totality of a complex human life and a particular personality moving about the crucial arenas of our common experience. One also senses a complex, intense, and disciplined sensibility's response — in pity and in condemnation, in anger and in awe, in lamentation and in song — to the conflicting phenomena of contemporary life that offer us these choices: to sit on the father's shoulders and awaken in another world, to pray to become all we'll never be, or to offer ourselves as sacrificial animals in the slaughterhouse of a blasphemous industrial liturgy of annihilation. Philip Levine's answer to the last alternative continues to be a resounding "No. Not this pig."

Poetry: *On the Edge* (1963). *Silent in America: Vivas for Those Who Failed* (1965). *Not This Pig* (1968). *Five Detroits* (1970). *Pili's Wall* (1971). *Red Dust* (1971). *They Feed They Lion* (1972). *1933* (1974). *The Names of the Lost* (1976). *Ashes: Poems Old and New* (1979). *7 Years from Somewhere* (1979). *One for the Rose* (1981). *Selected Poems* (1984). *Sweet Will* (1985). *A Walk with Tom Jefferson* (1988). *What Works* (1991).

Prose: *Don't Ask*, essays (1981).

Translations: *Tarumba: The Selected Poems of Jaime Sabines*, with E. Trejo (1979). *Off the Map: The Selected Poems of Gloria Fuertes*, with A. Long (1984).

Recordings: AUDIO: *Philip Levine* (APA, I-1958, II-1962, III-1970). *The Poetry and Voice of Philip Levine* (Caedmon, 1975). *Hear Me, Poems* (WT, 1977). *Philip Levine* (NLA, 1986). VIDEO: *Philip Levine* (APA, I-1974, II-1983). *Philip Levine* (LLS, 1989).

About: C. Buckley, ed., *On the Poetry of Philip Levine* (1990).

JOHN LOGAN (1923–1987)

Born in Red Oak, Iowa, John Logan received a B.A. in zoology from Coe College, an M.A. in English from the University of Iowa, and did graduate work in philosophy at Georgetown, Notre Dame, and Berkeley. He taught at Notre Dame, San Francisco State, the University of Hawaii, and the State University of New York at Buffalo. Logan served as poetry editor for *The Nation*; he also founded and, with Aaron Siskind, edited *Choice* — a magazine of poetry and photography. He was the recipient of a Rockefeller grant, a Morton Dauwen Zabel Award from the National Institute of Arts and Letters, a Guggenheim Fellowship, a fellowship from the National Endowment for the Arts, and the Lenore Marshall Poetry Prize.

Perhaps because he began his career as a scientist, Logan's poems are constructed out of the most minute details observed from the world around him. Such lines as "I let the rain / move its audible little hands / gently on my skin" suggest the sensuousness of his language in response to the physical world. He lingers on things and the words for things, delighting in their sound and texture. In Logan's poetry, suffering neither negates the fact of beauty nor the possibility of celebration. Pain and guilt do not negate the alternatives of joy and grace. His poems repeatedly affirm that "there is a freshness / nothing can destroy in us / not even we ourselves."

Logan's work is distinguished from that of most personal-confessional poets by its lack of any self-flagellation. He spares us the leprous details of individual incidents of failure, deterioration, and guilt. If he asks his readers to be confessors, as he openly does in "Three Moves," he doesn't seek absolution for any given act or general Manichean sense of sin. Rather, he offers an exchange of that more human and grace-giving embrace of an accepting forgiveness of the guilt that is in each of us. And thus each of us readers becomes, as it were, Logan's anonymous lover.

The full organic development and structure of his poems, as well as the careful orchestration of tone, further distinguish Logan's work. At his best, his poems are utterly personal and natural, determined neither by structural, thematic, nor tonal formula. His poems succeed in sounding as natural as breathing; they begin simply and grow in intensity out of their own emotional necessity, as the breath of a man in battle or in love. Through a harmonious counterpoint of tones that reflect the varied inner strains of a total personality, these poems rise to — and are themselves — epiphanies. Rich mosaics of an integrated personality's experience of the human, illuminations of that range of music rising from the total self, the poems of John Logan are at once "unpredictable as grace" and "a ballet for the ear."

Poetry: *Cycle for Mother Cabrini* (1955; revised edition 1971). *Ghosts of the Heart* (1960). *Spring of the Thief: Poems 1960–1962* (1963). *The Thrity-three Ring Circus* (1964). *The Zig-Zag Walk: Poems 1963–1968* (1969). *The Anonymous Lover* (1973). *Poem in Progress* (1975). *John Logan / Poems / Aaron Siskind / Photographs* (1976). *The Bridge of Change: Poems 1974–1979* (1980). *Only the Dreamer Can Change the Dream: Selected Poems* (1981). *The Transformation: Poems January to March 1981* (1983). *John Logan: The Collected Poems* (1989). *The Poem as Relic*, [uncollected poems], edited by M. Basinski (1989).

Prose: *The House That Jack Built; or, A Portrait of the Artist as a Sad Sensualist* (1974; revised edition 1984). *A Ballet for the Ear: Interviews, Essays, and Reviews*, edited by A. Poulin, Jr. (1983). *John Logan: The Collected Fiction* (1991).

Recordings: AUDIO: *John Logan* (APA, I-1963, II-1966 [i–ii], III-1971, IV-1972). *Only the Dreamer Can Change the Dream* (WT, 1978). *John Logan* (NLA, 1981). VIDEO: *The Poetry of John Logan* (BWF, I-1970, II-1971). *John Logan* (APA, 1980).

About: M. Waters, ed., *Dissolve to Island: On the Poetry of John Logan* (1984).

ROBERT LOWELL (1917–1977)

Born in Boston in 1917, Robert Lowell attended Harvard and graduated from Kenyon College in 1940. A conscientious objector during World War II, he spent several months in prison. During his career, he taught at various universities, including Harvard, the University of Iowa, and Boston University; in 1947–48, he served as Consultant in Poetry at the Library of Congress. His many awards included the Pulitzer Prize, the National Book Award, the Bollingen Poetry Translation Award, the Copernicus Award, and the National Book Critics Circle Award (posthumously).

Lowell's career seems to have evolved in three stages. His early poems, written under the tutelage of John Crowe Ransom and Allen Tate, were intricately wrought and complex, clearly reflecting the dictates of the New Criticism. Emerging out of a Christian spiritual tradition, an English poetic tradition influenced by the French symbolists, and a New England historical and ethical tradition, they were poems written by a young man whose sensibilities and talent began to mature at a time when T. S. Eliot was an overpowering presence in American poetry.

In *Life Studies* — perhaps his most brilliant and significant book, and the result of an encounter with W. D. Snodgrass — Lowell implicitly renounced many of the New Critics' formal demands and Eliot's cultural and spiritual vision. These poems were less consciously wrought and extremely intimate. As M. L. Rosenthal has observed, the orchestration of *Life Studies* traced the deterioration of Western civilization, the U.S. republic, Lowell's own family, and his very self. In the powerful concluding poem, "Skunk Hour," Lowell asserted, "The season's ill . . . / My mind's not right." And in this cultural and personal wasteland, he found no kingfisher, no Christ diving in fire.

"I am tired. Everyone's tired of my turmoil," Lowell wrote in *For the Union Dead*, and this realization marked the start of a third phase in his career. The poems grew more serenely formal, less intricate, and surely less hysterical. In *Near the Ocean*, he turned to muted couplets; his *Notebook* and *History*, though tracing intimate aspects of his life, were sonnet sequences. Although their central theme of the desolation and deterioration of humans and their world remained, Lowell was able to view that drama with a measure of objectivity, distance, and — at times — a detachment that bordered on ennui. In his last book, *Day by Day*, Lowell returned once again to the lyrical and personal modes; however, despite the intimacy of subject matter, the poems continued to be marked by a kind of intellectual detachment.

Poetry: *Land of Unlikeness* (1944). *Lord Weary's Castle* (1946). *The Mills of the Kavanaughs* (1951). *Life Studies* (1959). *Imitations* (1961). *For the Union Dead* (1964). *The Old Glory*, verse drama (1965; expanded edition 1968). *Near the Ocean* (1967). *Notebook 1967–1968* (1969). *Notebook* (augmented edition, 1970). *For Lizzie and Harriet* (1973). *History* (1973). *The Dolphin* (1973). *Selected Poems* (1976). *Day by Day* (1977).

Prose: *Robert Lowell: Interviews and Memoirs*, edited by J. Myers (1987).

Translations: POETRY: *The Voyage and Other Versions of Poems by Baudelaire* (1968). VERSE DRAMA: *Phaedra*, by Racine (1961). *Prometheus*, by Aeschylus (1969). *The Oresteia of Aeschylus* (1979).

Recordings: AUDIO: *Robert Lowell* (APA, I-1957, II-1966 [i–ii]). *The Spoken Arts Treasury*, Vol. XIII (SA, 1975). *Robert Lowell Reads His Poetry* (Caedmon/ PAC, 1976). *Robert Lowell* (NLA, 1980). *Robert Lowell* (TPV, 1978).

About: S. Axelrod and H. Deese, eds., *Robert Lowell: Essays on the Poetry* (1988). V. B. Bell, *Robert Lowell: Nihilist as Hero* (1983). P. Cooper, *The Autobiographical Myth of Robert Lowell* (1970). P. Cosgrave, *The Public Poetry* *of Robert Lowell* (1970). J. Crick, *Robert Lowell* (1974). R. J. Fein, *Robert Lowell* (1970). P. Hobsbaum, *A Reader's Guide to Robert Lowell* (1988). D. Kalstone, *Becoming a Poet: Elizabeth Bishop with Marianne Moore and Robert Lowell* (1989). M. London and R. Boyers, eds., *Robert Lowell: A Portrait of the Artist in His Time* (1970). W. J. Martz, *The Achievement of Robert Lowell* (1966). J. Mazzaro, *The Poetic Themes of Robert Lowell* (1965). J. Mazzaro, ed., *Profile of Robert Lowell* (1971). J. Meyers, *Manic Power: Robert Lowell and His Circle* (1987). T. Parkinson, ed., *Robert Lowell: A Collection of Critical Essays* (1968). M. Perloff, *The Poetic Art of Robert Lowell* (1973). B. Raffel, *Robert Lowell* (1981). M. Rudman, *Robert Lowell: An Introduction to the Poetry* (1984). H. B. Staples, *Robert Lowell: The First Twenty Years* (1962). K. Wallingford, *Robert Lowell's Language of the Self* (1988). A. Williamson, *Pity the Monsters: The Political Poetry of Robert Lowell* (1974). S. Yenser, *Circle to Circle: The Poetry of Robert Lowell* (1975).

WILLIAM MATTHEWS (1942)

Born in Cincinnati, Ohio, William Matthews is a graduate of Yale University and the University of North Carolina at Chapel Hill. He began his teaching career at Wells College and subsequently taught at the University of Colorado, the University of Washington, Columbia University, and City College of New York, where he is a professor of English. Cofounding editor of Lillabulero Press and its magazine from 1966–1974 and a member of the New Poets Editorial Board for Wesleyan University Press, Matthews has received grants and fellowships from the National Endowment for the Arts and the Guggenheim and Ingram Merrill foundations.

The fertile turmoil of the radical tradition in contemporary American poetry is fully alive in William Matthews's poems. Like the work of other poets whose first books appeared in the late 1960s and early 1970s, his early poems reflect both a direct and indirect involvement in the continuing aesthetic ferment of the time. In such poems as "The Search Party," he openly wrestles with the aesthetics of the new critics — symbol, irony, and the detached impersonality of the artist. Meanwhile, the structural texture of the imagery and metaphor in poems like "Swimming off Cape Hatteras" and "Good Night" ("I dream that the earth beneath the house / is an old ship . . . / drifting in new waters") reflect the experiments with the neo-surrealist deep image inaugurated by the generation of Robert Bly and James Wright.

Matthews's range of subjects and themes is as broad and challenging as the aesthetic and cultural strands that shape his work. But whether the ostensible subject is baseball, jazz, onions, or the search for a lost child, a Matthews poem is always "about" much more. In "Masterful," a poem on baseball, the meeting of bat and ball is a "violent tryst," and the wrists "spend themselves." In "Blues for John Coltrane . . . ," death is "leaping up the saxophone / with its wet kiss." "Pissing off the Back of the Boat in the Nivernais Canal" begins as a funny take on the drunken poet's penis, but draws the reader into a meditation on the relationship between penis and tongue as they concern sex and the artistic process (themes explored in William Irwin Thompson's brilliant 1982 study, *The Time Falling Bodies Take to Light*); it is a poem about flesh and the imagination, and, ultimately, it is a poem about poetry itself.

If "Pissing off the Back of a Boat" affirms the inseparability of desire and linguistic creation in Matthews's poetry, it also signals his abiding search for profundity within humor and lightness at the core of the profound. Indeed, his poems consistently seek to unite perceived dualities. "Each emotion lusts for its opposite," Matthews writes. Thus (as in "The Search Party") there is truth at the heart of fiction; excellence uncoils with a "sweet ferocity"; and, despite "death's old sweet song . . . / [a] relentless joy infests the blues all day."

Poetry: *Ruining the New Road* (1970). *Sleek for the Long Flight* (1972). *Sticks and Stones* (1975). *Rising and Falling* (1979). *Flood* (1982). *A Happy Childhood* (1984). *Foreseeable Futures* (1987). *Blues If You Want* (1989).

Prose: *Curiosities*, essays (1989).

Translations: *A World Rich in Anniversaries*, prose poems by Jean Follain, with M. Feeney (1979).

Recordings: AUDIO: *Days Beyond Recall* (WT, 1984). VIDEO: *The Poetry of William Matthews* (BWF, 1974). *William Matthews* (APA, 1981). *William Matthews and Linda Pastan* (BWF, 1987).

JAMES MERRILL (1926)

James Merrill was born in New York City. A son of Charles Merrill, the founder of the Wall Street brokerage firm Merrill Lynch, he attended Lawrenceville School, served in the U.S. Army, and graduated from Amherst College in 1947. Merrill's awards include the Bollingen Prize in Poetry, the Pulitzer Prize, and the National Book Award. He was elected a member of the National Institute of Arts and Letters in 1971, and later elected a chancellor of the Academy of American Poets. In 1990, Merrill was the first recipient of the Rebekah Johnson Bobbitt National Prize for Poetry awarded by the Library of Congress. Unlike most of his contemporaries, Merrill has not sought a professional teaching career. He generally divides his time between Florida and Connecticut.

Most critics would agree that James Merrill's poetry has consistently reflected the influence of New Criticism and that his mentor is more likely W. H. Auden than William Carlos Williams. Indeed, in Merrill's long trilogy *The Changing Light at Sandover* Auden's spirit is Merrill's "guide." Clearly, Merrill is a masterful formalist whose manipulation of metrics and of sound — especially end rhymes — reveals the range of startling and subtle nuances in language in much the same way as Rothko unveils the nuances of color in painting. Even in what seem to be more personal poems, one is never quite sure whether the speaker is Merrill or a persona.

Most of his poems are marked by a tone edged with a measure of ironic detachment that, in some literary circles — where irony is blasphemy and guts rule — might be considered indicative of high, albeit elegant, decadence.

When so many poets of his generation lead their readers into the bedlam of their tortured souls and the bedrooms of their monstrous marriages — and, indeed, into their very own and much-used beds — one emerges from the surroundings of Merrill's poetry with the heady sense of having lingered in a rather rarified atmosphere. (Indeed, as a son of Charles Merrill, the cofounder of the Merrill Lynch stock brokerage house, James Merrill was born into enormous wealth and privilege.) This is the physical, moral, and aesthetic world as perceived by Proust rather than by Baudelaire, by Henry James rather than by Walt Whitman. This is the world where, in Merrill's words, "Light into the olive entered / And was oil," an arena of human experience where it does seem that "the world beneath the world is brightening."

And yet, despite the seeming orderliness of his poems, Merrill's Weltanschauung and aesthetic often lead him — and us — to the very edge of chaos. Merrill's persona in "Laboratory Poem" knows that the heart must climb "through violence into exquisite disciplines." And whatever entrances into immortality that art may offer, it leaves us *and* the artist with that unnerving realization that "the life it asks of us is a dog's life." Thus, if poetry, if speech "is but a mouth pressed / Lightly and humbly against the angel's hand," in a Rilkean attempt to impress the angel with the things of this world, it's distinctly possible that this very angel "does not want even these few lines written." In short, in a society where "Art, Public Spirit / Ignorance, Economics, Love of Self / Hatred of Self" are earnestly dedicated to "*sparing* us the worst" and just as earnestly *inspire* the worst, Merrill's poems stand on the edge of chaos, radiant attempts to survive its meanings — and our own.

Poetry: *The Black Swan* (1946). *First Poems* (1951). *The Country of a Thousand Years of Peace and Other Poems* (1959; revised edition, 1970). *Water Street* (1962). *Nights and Days* (1966). *The Fire Screen* (1969). *Braving the Elements* (1972). *The Yellow Pages* (1974). *Divine Comedies* (1976). *Mirabell: Book of Numbers* (1978). *Scripts for a Pageant* (1980). *From the First Nine: Poems 1946–1976* (1982). *The Changing Light at Sandover* (1982). *Late Settings* (1985). *The Inner Room* (1988).

Prose: FICTION: *The Seraglio* (1957). *The (Diblos) Notebook* (1965). ESSAYS: *Recitative: Prose*, edited and with an introduction by J. D. McClatchy (1986).

Recordings: AUDIO: *The Spoken Arts Treasury*, Vol. XVI (1975). *Reflected Houses* (WT, 1986). VIDEO: *James Merrill* (APA, 1956).

About: C. Berger and D. Lehman, eds., *Merrill: Studies in Criticism* (1982). R. Labrie, *James Merrill* (1982). J. Moffett, *James Merrill: An Introduction to the Poetry* (1984). S. Yenser, *The Consuming Myth: The Work of James Merrill* (1987).

W. S. MERWIN (1927)

W. S. Merwin was born in New York City and educated at Princeton. He was tutor to Robert Graves's son for a year, but — unlike most of his contemporaries — he has not had a teaching career. Since 1951 he has devoted most of his time to writing, to giving poetry readings, and to translating French, Spanish, Latin, Portuguese, Greek, Chinese, and Japanese writers. He has lived in the United States, England, Mexico, southern France, and currently resides in Hawaii. In addition to the Pulitzer Prize and the Shelley Memorial Award, he has received grants from the National Endowment for the Arts, the Rockefeller Foundation, the Academy of American Poets, the National Institute of Arts and Letters, and the Arts Council of Great Britain.

One of the most prolific poets and translators of his generation, Merwin is among those contemporary poets (others include James Wright and John Logan) whose talents were originally shaped by New Criticism and whose style underwent a radical change in the course of his career. His early poems were elegant, controlled, symmetrical, and often concerned with myth and archetype. However, the appearance of *The Drunk in the Furnace* suggested a dissatisfaction with old techniques: his forms were looser; his language appeared less contrived and closer to the spoken word. Like other poets of the period, he turned to family history and individual human suffering in search of larger, more immediate patterns of human experience.

Merwin's most radical departure — and most exciting style — appeared still later in *The Moving Target*. Open and terse, these surrealistic poems — and most of the poems that Merwin has published since — are controlled not as much by a craftsman's delicate hand as by a powerful imagination. And they rise out of the depths of a more personal, sometimes enigmatic necessity. Merwin's aesthetics are clear in the statement that he wrote for *Naked Poetry* (edited by Stephen Berg and Robert Mezey): "In an age when time and technique encroach hourly, or appear to, on the source itself of poetry, it seems as though what is needed for any particular nebulous hope that may become a poem is not a manipulable, more or less predictably recurring pattern, but an unduplicatable resonance, something that would be like an echo except that it is repeating no sound. Something that always belonged to it: its sense and its conformation before it entered words."

Throughout his career, one of Merwin's dominant concerns has been death — or perhaps more specifically, extinction. The journey motif that critics have recognized in Merwin's poetry is emblematic of all life's motion toward death. However, in later poems, this concern doesn't necessarily focus on any sudden or cataclysmic end of life — although many of his later poems are clearly laments for the destruction of our ecology and, thus, our society and culture. Rather, it is more manifest in powerful and menacing shadows surrounding frail light, in sound struggling against the tyranny of silence, in the slow but seemingly inevitable transformation of all organic life into inert matter. And if Merwin agrees with Berryman that the individual has undertaken the biggest job of all — *son fin* — Merwin has also erected a powerful emblem of his vision in his poetic prose piece, "Tergvinder's Stone." In the presence of a mysterious, almost mystical stone in the middle of his living room and his life, Merwin's central character kneels in the darkness of the stone, converses with the stone, and even in the silence of the stone "knows that it is peace."

Poetry: *A Mask for Janus* (1952). *The Dancing Bears* (1954). *Green with Beasts* (1956). *The Drunk in the Furnace* (1960). *The Moving Target* (1963). *The Lice* (1967). *Animae: Poems* (1969). *The Carrier of Ladders* (1970). *Writings to an Unfinished Accompaniment* (1973). *The First Four Books of Poems* (1975). *The Compass Flower* (1977). *Finding the Islands* (1982). *Opening the Hand* (1983). *Selected Poems* (1988). *The Rain in the Trees* (1988).

Prose: FICTION: *A New Right Arm* (1969). *The Miner's Pale Children* (1970). *Houses and Travellers* (1977). AUTOBIOGRAPHY: *Unframed Originals* (1982). ESSAYS: *Regions of Memory: Uncollected Prose 1949–1982*, edited by E. Folsom and C. Nelson (1987).

Translations: POETRY: *The Poem of the Cid* (1959). *Spanish Ballads* (1961). *The Song of Roland* (1963). *Selected Translations 1948–1968* (1968). *Transparence of the World*, poems by Jean Follain (1969). *Voices*, poems by Antonio Porchia (1969/1988). *Twenty Love Poems and a Song of Despair*, by Pablo Neruda (1969). *Chinese Figures: Second Series* (1971). *Japanese Figures* (1971). *Asian Figures* (1973). *Selected Poems of Osip Mandelstam*, with C. Brown (1974). *Vertical Poetry*, by Roberto Juarroz (1977/1988). *Selected Translations 1968–1978* (1979). *The Peacock's Egg: Love Poems from Ancient India*, with J. M. Masson (1981). *From the Spanish Morning* (1985). *Sun at Midnight*, poems by Muso Soseki (1989). PROSE: *The Satires of Perseus* (1960). *The Life of Lazarillo de Tormes: His Fortunes and Adversities* (1962). *Products of the Perfected Civilization*, by Sebastian Chamfort (1969). DRAMA: *Iphigenia at Aulis*, by Euripides; with G. E. Dimmock, Jr. (1977). *Four French Plays* (1985).

Recordings: AUDIO: *The Poetry and Voice of W. S. Merwin* (Caedmon, 1971). *W. S. Merwin* (APA, I-1961, II-1964). VIDEO: *The Poetry of W. S. Merwin* (BWF, 1971). *W. S. Merwin* (APA, I-1979, II-1983). *W. S. Merwin* (LLS, 1989).

About: C. Davis, *W. S. Merwin* (1981). M. Christhilf, *W. S. Merwin, The Mythmaker* (1986). C. Nelson and E. Folsom, ed., *W. S. Merwin: Essays on the Poetry* (1987).

FRANK O'HARA (1926–1966)

Before his untimely, accidental death on Fire Island, Frank O'Hara was associate curator and then curator of the international program at the Museum of Modern Art in New York and an editorial associate for *Art News*. Born in Baltimore, O'Hara was educated at the New England Conservatory of Music, Harvard, and the University of Michigan. He collaborated in various projects involving poetry and the visual arts, and in 1956 was awarded a Ford Fellowship for drama.

Before the publication of his *Collected Poems* (and the companion volume, *Poems Retrieved*), O'Hara was almost a closet poet, the product and hero of a pop-camp imagination whose seeming antipoems were often light and chatty, marked by a spontaneity, exuberance, and wit that were characteristic of his contemporaries in the visual arts. His most memorable poems, like the paintings of Oldenburg and Warhol, focused on the all-too-obvious things of our urban and suburban world: hamburgers, malts, cigarettes, instant coffee. Looming above that world were its own godly artifacts: Lichtenstein's suprahuman heroes of the comic strips and Warhol's movie stars. Their mythic proportions were — and continue to be — the dimensions of contemporary human fantasies and dreams of redemption. Moreover, in O'Hara's poems there is the stinging, if somewhat hysterical, crackle of a melancholy comment on the absurdity of such hollow rites.

It now seems clear that O'Hara's scope and power as a poet extend far beyond the circumscribed world of a merely campy and gay subculture. One leaves the body of O'Hara's poetry — and his sense of what constitutes the identifiable substance and quality of our communal experience — with a verbal-emotional equivalent of Kandinsky's acute perception of "the particular spiritual perfume of the triangle." One also leaves the existential world of O'Hara's poems with a fuller understanding of the truth of Cocteau's rejection of history: "*J'ai une très mauvaise mémoire de l'avenir.*"

Poetry: *A City Winter and Other Poems* (1952). *Meditations in an Emergency* (1957). *Hartigan and Rivers with O'Hara: An Exhibition of Pictures, with Poems* (1959). *Second Avenue* (1960). *Odes* (1960). *Lunch Poems* (1964). *Love Poems: Tentative Title* (1965). *In Memory of My Feelings: A Selection of Poems*, edited by B. Berkson (1967). *Odes* (1969). *The Collected Poems of Frank O'Hara*, edited by D. Allen (1971). *The Selected Poems of Frank O'Hara*, edited by D. Allen (1974). *Hymns of St. Bridget*, with Bill Berkson (1974). *Early Poems 1946–1951*, edited by D. Allen (1976). *Poems Retrieved*, edited by D. Allen (1977).

Prose: *Jackson Pollack* (1959). *A Frank O'Hara Miscellany* (1974). *Art Chronicles 1954–1966* (1975). *Standing Still and Walking in New York*, notes and essays, edited by D. Allen (1975). *Early Writing*, edited by D. Allen (1977). *Selected Plays* (1978).

Recordings: AUDIO: *Frank O'Hara* (APA, 1964). VIDEO: *Frank O'Hara* (APA, 1966).

About: B. Berkson, ed., *Homage to Frank O'Hara* (1988). J. Elledge, ed., *Frank O'Hara: To Be True to a City* (1989). M. Perloff, *Frank O'Hara: Poet Among Painters* (1968).

MARY OLIVER (1935)

Born in Cleveland and educated at Ohio State University and Vassar College, Mary Oliver has been visiting professor in creative writing and poet-in-residence at Case Western Reserve. She is also a member of the writing staff at the Fine Arts Work Center in Provincetown, Massachusetts, where she lives. Her awards include the Achievement Award from the American Academy and Institute of Arts and Letters, a Guggenheim Fellowship, the Alice Fay di Castagnola Award from the Poetry Society of America, and a creative writing fellowship from the Literature Program of the National Endowment for the Arts. In 1984 she was awarded the Pulitzer Prize.

To read Oliver's poems is to immerse oneself in a world of intense physical sensation made doubly acute by the emotional transformation that Oliver achieves while registering the impact of the physical world on the world of her feelings: the "icy kick" of water, "the small kingdoms" of birds and insects breathing in the dark, the fish at spawning time following "the fragrance spilling / from her old birth pond," "the crows, plump / As black rocks in the cold trees" in winter. Reminiscent of the poetry of Theodore Roethke, James Wright, and Emily Dickinson in the precise observations of the things of this world, Oliver's poems have a physical impact like "the dark thorns of the wild grapes / on the unsuspecting tongue."

Although somewhat ambiguous, that image of pleasure and pain is also central to Oliver's hard-earned vision profoundly accepting an essential tension between the polarities that define the boundaries of all experience — whether in the physical world, in the realm of human relationships, or in the self. There is great pleasure and beauty and joy in the poems of Mary Oliver; but there is also a commensurate (though muted) measure of pain resulting from the recognition of one's full awareness of those elements of the natural and human world that transport and transform us, giving us a glimpse of eternity, perhaps, or of some kind of immortality — a recognition that also gives us a fuller awareness of the world's, and of our own, mortality.

The acceptance of the hard truths of mortal existence is at the heart and boundaries of Oliver's poems. If thrown into the water and told to sink or swim, what we learn isn't necessarily how to swim, but "How to put off, one by one, / Dreams and pity, love and grace, — / How to survive in any place." Art in itself is no escape. While the beauty of music may be a "lick of flame" that transports and transforms the audience, for the artist it is only a momentary stay against a dreary and petty reality, against "the duties of flesh and home," perhaps against "the knife at the throat," and in fact, against that very "death in the metronome." "To live in this world," Oliver reminds us, requires three measures of acceptance: "to love what is mortal; / to hold it / against your bones knowing / your own life depends on it; / and, when the time comes to let it go, / to let it go." If life, love, and work do not negate our mortality, then our acceptance of it may allow us to view our daily deaths as repeated vanishings "into something better." In Mary Oliver's poems, such acceptance is epiphany.

Poetry: *No Voyage and Other Poems* (1965). *The River Styx, Ohio and Other Poems* (1972). *The Night Traveler* (1978). *Sleeping in the Forest* (1979). *Twelve Moons* (1979). *American Primitive* (1983). *Dreamwork* (1986). *House of Light* (1990).

Recording: VIDEO: *The Poetry of Mary Oliver* (BWF, 1981).

CHARLES OLSON (1910–1970)

Charles Olson was born in Worcester, Massachusetts, and educated at Wesleyan, Yale, and Harvard, where he received his doctorate. From 1951 to 1956, he was an instructor and rector at Black Mountain College in North Carolina where he worked with other artists and writers such as Robert Creeley and Merce Cunningham. He taught at Harvard, the State University of New York at Buffalo, and other universities. The recipient of two Guggenheim fellowships, he also received a grant from the Gren Foundation to study Mayan hieroglyphics. During much of his life, he resided in Gloucester, Massachusetts, the setting for many of his *Maximus Poems*.

    Clearly the most substantial theoretician and one of the most influential of the postmodernist poets, Olson's criticism and speculations concerning the nature and structure of verse have become the basis for what is generally known as the Projectivist School in contemporary poetry. Olson's celebrated essay, "Projective Verse," originally published in 1950, articulates some of his basic attitudes toward poetry and remains one of the central documents of the "revolution" that took place in American poetry after 1945.

    Complex and often refusing to yield specific meaning, "Projective Verse" is no easy essay to summarize; but some of its central ideas are worth noting. Olson's premise is that if poetry "is to be of *essential* use," it must "catch up and put into itself certain laws and possibilities of the breath, of the breathing of the man who writes, as well as of his listenings." And he posits "open" or "field composition" as an alternative to non-Projective verse with its inherited line, its stanzas, and its overall traditional form. According to Olson, field or open composition includes (1) *kinetics:* "A poem is energy transferred from where the poet got it . . . by way of the poem itself to . . . the reader"; (2) *principle:* "Form is never more than an extension of content" (as rephrased by Robert Creeley); and (3) *process:* "One perception must immediately and directly lead to a further perception." Although various poets have cited Olson as their mentor, it may well be that he is the only genuine practitioner of his own theories.

    Charles Olson's major work is his long series of *Maximus Poems*, the first ten of which were originally published in 1953. As various critics have noted, one of the characteristics of this series is Olson's delicate and all-encompassing sense of place — the vibrant details of an ever-changing landscape. But equally present are Olson's sweeping sense of history and his vast range of knowledge, which have caused some critics to compare the *Maximus Poems* to Pound's *Cantos*. From an entirely different point of view, Olson's central character in the *Maximus Poems* also might be compared with Henry Pussycat in John Berryman's *Dream Songs*.

Poetry: *Y & X* (1948). *In Cold Hell, in Thicket* (1953/1967). *The Maximus Poems 1–10* (1953). *The Maximus Poems 11–22* (1956). *O'Ryan 2 4 6 8 10* (1958). *The Maximus Poems* (1960). *The Distances: Poems* (1960). *O'Ryan 1 2 3 4 5 6 7 8 9 10* (1965). *West* (1966). *The Maximus Poems IV, V, VI* (1968). *Archeologist of Morning: The Collected Poems Outside the Maximus Series* (1971). *The Maximus Poems, Volume Three*, edited by C. Boer and C. Butterick (1975). *Spearmint and Rosemary* (1975). *Some Early Poems* (1978). *The Maximus Poems*, edited by G. F. Butterick (1983). *The Collected Poems of Charles Olson*, edited by G. F. Butterick (1988). *Nothing But Poetry: Supplementary Poems*, edited by G. F. Butterick (1989).

Prose: CRITICISM AND OTHER PROSE: *Call Me Ishmael: A Study of Melville* (1947/1967). *Projective Verse* (1959). *Procioception* (1965). *The Human Universe and Other Essays*, edited by D. Allen (1967). *Selected Writings of Charles Olson*, edited by R. Creeley (1967). *Causal Mythology* (1969). *The Special View of History*, edited by A. Charters (1970). *Additional Prose: A Bibliography on America, Procioception, and Other Notes and Essays*, edited by G. F. Butterick (1974). *The Post Office: A Memoir of His Father* (1974). *Charles Olson & Ezra Pound: An Encounter at St. Elizabeth's*, edited by C. Seelye (1975). *The Fiery Hunt and Other Plays* (1977). LECTURES AND INTERVIEWS: *Charles Olson Reading at Berkeley*, transcribed by Z. Brown (1966). *Poetry & Truth: The Beloit Lectures and Poems*, transcribed and edited by G. F. Butterick (1971). *Muthologos: The Collected Lectures & Interviews*, Vol. 1, edited by G. F. Butterick (1978). *Muthologos: The Collected Lectures & Interviews*, Vol. 2, edited by G. F. Butterick (1979). CORRESPONDENCE: *The Mayan Letters*, edited by R. Creeley (1953/1968). *Letters for Origin 1950–1956*, edited by A. Glover (1970/1988). *Charles Olson and Robert Creeley: The Complete Correspondence*, Vols. 1–6, edited by G. F. Butterick (1980–1985).

Recordings: AUDIO: *Charles Olson* (APA, I-1963, II-nd). VIDEO: *Charles Olson* (APA, 1966).

About: C. Boer, *Charles Olson in Connecticut* (1975). G. F. Butterick, *Guide to the Maximus Poems of Charles Olson* (1978). D. Byrd, *Charles Olson's Maximus* (1980). J. Cech, *Charles Olson and Edward Dahlberg: A Portrait of Friendship* (1982). A. Charters, *Olson/Melville: A Study in Affinity* (1968). A. Charters, *Charles Olson: The Special View of History* (1970). P. Christensen, *Charles Olson: Call Him Ishmael* (1978). C. Corman, *Projectile, Percussive, Prospective* (1982). E. Dorn, *What I See in the Maximus Poems* (1960). T. Merrill, *The Poetry of Charles Olson: A Primer* (1982). P. Sherman, *Olson's Push: Origin, Black Mountain and Recent American Poetry* (1978). C. Stein, *The Secret of the Black Chrysanthemum: The Poetic Cosmology of Charles Olson and His Use of the Writing of C. G. Jung* (1987). R. Von Hallberg, *Charles Olson: The Scholar's Work* (1978).

MARGE PIERCY (1936)

Marge Piercy was born in Detroit, Michigan. She received an A.B. from the University of Michigan and an M.A. from Northwestern University. One of the few writers of her generation to eschew a full-time university affiliation, Piercy nevertheless has given readings and conducted workshops in well over a hundred colleges and universities throughout the country. Periodically, she also has been visiting professor or poet-in-residence at such institutions as the University of Kansas and the Fine Arts Work Center (in Provincetown, Massachusetts), and she has held the Butler Chair of Letters at the State University of New York at Buffalo. Her awards include two Borestone Mountain Poetry Awards, a fellowship from the Literature Program of the National Endowment for the Arts, and the Literature Award from the (Massachusetts) Governor's Commission on the Status of Women.

That Piercy works primarily with organic form, rather than with stricter and external traditional forms, is certainly no accident and perhaps not entirely a matter of conscious choice, either; rather, it is more probably the result of aesthetic necessity growing out of a deeply rooted philosophical vision. Thus, the form (and sometimes even the shape) of Piercy's successful poems is recognizably informed by their subject matter and theme. For example, on the surface "A Work of Artifice" is about the way in which the limbs of the traditional Japanese bonzai tree are repeatedly pruned so that a full-grown bonzai is only nine inches high (rather than achieving its natural height of eighty feet); the form and effectiveness of this poem also result in part from the manner in which the lines, syntax, and tone are appropriately "clipped."

The subjects of many of Piercy's poems are objects and experiences in the natural world, as well as love, sex, and day-to-day human relationships. A central theme in her work is the powerful tension between one's inner identity and the force of outer (personal, social, and cultural) pressures. Such is the age-old tension between essence and existence as the determining factors of all life. And if one's essence is the primary determination of identity and growth, then the parameters within which one develops that identity and nurtures that growth are severely limited.

Piercy is especially concerned with the extent to which the sexual identity and individual personality of a woman in contemporary society is in conflict with those outer forces attempting to determine who and what she is. Of course, that dichotomy is at the heart of the feminist vision; but Piercy's work also attempts to reconcile even more powerful philosophical conflicts over whether *meaning* or *purpose* is the ultimate goal of human existence and activity. (Perhaps it is worth noting that in our culture the conflict between meaning and purpose is also at the root of the conflict between the sciences and the humanities.) In her poems Piercy repeatedly affirms the necessity for the self to be in conflict with those outer forces intent on shaping it into something other than it is or wants to be. However, while recognizing the symbiotic relationship between the self and nature, in a variety of ways she also discovers the means to reaffirm the need for both meaning *and* purpose. In short, her poems repeatedly assert that the genuine meaning of the self and of all natural and human creation is "to be of use." She reminds us that Greek amphoras and Hopi vases are beautiful objects now kept in museums, "but you know they were made to be used. / The pitcher cries for water to carry / and a person for work that is real." Immersing herself and her readers in the physical substance and metaphysical serenity of such a reconciliation, Piercy also can periodically offer moments of enlightened discovery: "You are learning to live in circles / as well as straight lines."

Poetry: *Breaking Camp* (1968). *Hard Loving* (1969). *A Work of Artifice* (1970). *4-Telling*, with B. Hershon, E. Jarrett, and D. Lourie (1971). *When the Drought Broke* (1971). *To Be of Use* (1973). *Living in the Open* (1976). *The Twelve-Spoked Wheel Flashing* (1978). *The Moon Is Always Female* (1980). *Circles on the Water: Selected Poems* (1982). *Stone, Paper, Knife* (1983). *My Mother's Body* (1985). *Available Light* (1988).

Prose: FICTION: *Going Down Fast* (1969). *Dance the Eagle to Sleep* (1970). *Small Changes* (1973). *Woman on the Edge of Time* (1976). *The High Cost of Living* (1978). *Vida* (1979). *Braided Lives* (1983). *Fly Away Home* (1984). *Gone to Soldiers* (1987). *Summer People* (1989). CRITICISM: *Parti-Colored Blocks for a Quilt* (1983). DRAMA: *The Last White Class*, with I. Wood (1979).

Recordings: AUDIO: *At the Core: Selected Poems* (WT, 1976). VIDEO: *The Writing of Marge Piercy* (BWF, 1975).

SYLVIA PLATH (1932–1963)

A native of Boston and a graduate of Smith College, in 1955 Sylvia Plath won a Fulbright Scholarship to Newnham College, Cambridge. While in England, she met and married the British poet Ted Hughes. After she taught for a year at Smith (1957–58), the couple returned to England where in 1960 she published her first book of poems and subsequently completed her novel, *The Bell Jar*. On February 11, 1963, Sylvia Plath committed suicide.

A friend of Anne Sexton and student of Robert Lowell, Sylvia Plath wrote poems that were intended to sound and to feel brutally personal, almost unbearably painful. Her poems are not merely *about* acute mental and emotional suffering; their very structure — the controlled flow of images, the insistent appositives — draws the reader fully into that suffering. Indeed, her later poems are so well crafted that some critics have argued, wrong-headedly, that she seemed engaged in "a murderous art" — that after writing such frighteningly honest and painfully personal poems, her suicide was virtually inevitable. As a *critical premise*, such an argument is utter nonsense, its absurdity manifestly clear when transferred to another artist and to his or her work. If Plath virtually had no choice but to commit suicide after writing the poems in *Ariel*, then what inevitable choice did Melville have after writing *Moby Dick*?

What makes Plath interesting as a poet is not primarily her ostensible subject matter and tone; rather, the success of the poems depends largely on her precision of observation, imagination, and language — as well as on the mastery of her craftsmanship. For example, the onion simile in "Cut" not only accurately describes the swirls of a thumb print but also serves as the entire poem's controlling metaphor. Moreover, in such poems as "Cut" and "Lady Lazarus," or even in a celebrated poem such as "Daddy," there is also a strong measure of wit and humor — albeit black — often conveyed through resuscitated clichés that manage to rescue the poems from pathos.

On more than one occasion, Plath insisted that even the most personal poetry cannot be merely a *cri de coeur*; it must be informed by and participate in a greater historical drama. Her own poems participate fully in the vibrant Puritan tradition, not only through her preoccupation with evil (which is utterly distinct from personal suffering) but also through her metaphysical and emblematic technique. They also occur against a constant historical drama, especially the contemporary phenomenon of Nazi Germany out of which she fabricates a modern myth. In short, the pain, the suffering, the fine edge of madness — all are ultimately crafted and controlled by the poet's reasoned and careful hand flashing a measure of genius.

Poetry: *The Colossus* (1962). *Uncollected Poems* (1965). *Ariel* (1966). *Crossing the Water: Transitional Poems* (1971). *Crystal Gazer and Other Poems* (1971). *Lyonesse: Poems* (1971). *Winter Trees* (1972). *The Collected Poems of Sylvia Plath*, edited by T. Hughes (1981). *Stings*, original drafts of the poem in facsimile with an essay by S. R. Van Dyne (1982).

Prose: *The Bell Jar,* novel (published under pseudonym of Victoria Lucas, 1963; published under the name of Sylvia Plath, 1971). *Letters Home,* edited by A. Plath (1975). *Johnny Panic and the Bible of Dreams: Short Stories, Prose, and Diary Excerpts,* edited by T. Hughes (1979). *The Journals of Sylvia Plath*, edited by T. Hughes and F. McCullough (1982).

Recordings: AUDIO: *The Spoken Arts Treasury*, Vol. XVIII (SA, 1975). *Sylvia Plath Reading Her Poetry* (CD, 1976). *Sylvia Plath* (TPV, 1978). *Sylvia Plath* (WT, 1980).

About: E. Aird, *Sylvia Plath: Her Life and Work* (1973). S. G. Axelrod, *Sylvia Plath: The Wound and the Cure of Words* (1990). S. Bassnet, *Women Writers: Sylvia Plath* (1987). M. L. Broe, *Protean Poetics: The Poetry of Sylvia Plath* (1980). L. K. Bundtzen, *Plath's Incarnations: Woman and the Creative Process* (1983). E. Butscher, *Sylvia Plath: Method and Madness* (1976). E. Butscher, ed., *Sylvia Plath: The Woman and Her Work* (1977). D. Holbrook, *Sylvia Plath: Poetry and Existence* (1976). J. Inness, *The Bell Jar Notes* (1984). J. Kroll, *Chapters in a Mythology: The Poetry of Sylvia Plath* (1976). G. Lane, ed., *Sylvia Plath: New Views on the Poetry* (1979). C. Newman, ed., *The Art of Sylvia Plath* (1971). J. Rosenblatt, *Sylvia Plath: The Poetry of Initiation* (1979). N. H. Steiner, *A Closer Look at Ariel: A Memory of Sylvia Plath* (1973). A. Stevenson, *Bitter Fame: A Life of Sylvia Plath* (1989). M. D. Uroff, *Sylvia Plath and Ted Hughes* (1979). L. Wagner, ed., *Critical Essays on Sylvia Plath* (1984). L. Wagner, *Sylvia Plath: A Biography* (1987).

ADRIENNE RICH (1929)

Adrienne Rich's first book of poems won the Yale Series of Younger Poets award while she was completing her undergraduate studies at Radcliffe. She has taught at Brandeis, Swarthmore, Columbia, Harvard, Rutgers, and City College of New York. Rich's many honors include awards from the American Institute of Arts and Letters, the Guggenheim and Ingram Merrill foundations, and a commission from the Bollingen Foundation for the translation of Dutch poetry. In 1974 Rich and Allen Ginsberg were cowinners of the National Book Award for poetry. Rich rejected her share as a personal award, but in a statement written by herself and the two other women nominated that year, she accepted the award in the name of all women.

Adrienne Rich has described her poems written since the late 1970s as "a coming-home to the darkest and richest source of my poetry: sex, sexuality, sexual wounds, sexual identity, sexual politics: many names for pieces of one whole. I feel [this poetry] continues the work I've been trying to do — breaking down the artificial barriers between private and public, between Vietnam and the lovers' bed, between the deepest images we carry out of our dreams and the most daylight events 'out in the world.' This is the intention and longing behind everything I write."

Sexual identity and its profound political implications are indeed among the substantial sources of Rich's more recent work, especially in her courageous and beautiful sequence of love poems addressed to another woman — a theme that reappears in *The Dream of a Common Language*. Moreover, even as she speaks about and for women, her poetry is informed by a vigorous intelligence that transcends any unilateral sense of sexuality and politics; her poetry reaches beyond the limited periphery of any "movement" to become at once a profoundly personal statement forged into a powerful description of our common condition.

If some of Rich's poems can be read as a "diving into the wreck," it is crucial to realize that her purpose is not only "to see the damage that was done" but also to catch a glimpse of "the treasures that prevail." Like the astronomer in "Planetarium," she is "a woman trying to translate pulsations / into images," not only for their own sake, not only for her own sake, but "for the relief of the body / and the reconstruction of the mind." Meanwhile, having found the courage to utter, "I choose to love   this time   for once / with all my intelligence," she also can assert and demonstrate *"a whole new poetry beginning here."*

Poetry: A Change of World (1951). The Diamond Cutters (1955). Snapshots of a Daughter-in-Law: Poems 1954–1962 (1963; revised edition, 1967). Necessities of Life: Poems 1962–1965 (1966). Leaflets: Poems 1965–1968 (1969). The Will to Change: Poems 1968–1970 (1971). Diving into the Wreck: Poems 1971–1972 (1973). Poems: Selected and New, 1950–1974 (1975). Twenty-One Love Poems (1976). The Dream of a Common Language: Poems 1974–1977 (1978). A Wild Patience Has Taken Me This Far: Poems 1978–1981 (1981). Sources (1983). The Fact of a Doorframe: Poems Selected and New 1950–1984 (1985). Your Native Land, Your Life (1986). Time's Power: Poems 1985–1988 (1989).

Prose: *Of Woman Born: Motherhood as Experience and Institution* (1976). *On Lies, Secrets and Silence: Selected Prose 1966–1978* (1979). *Compulsory Heterosexuality and Lesbian Experience* (1982). *Women and Honor: Some Notes on Lying* (1982). *Blood, Bread, and Poetry: Selected Prose 1979–1985* (1986).

Recordings: AUDIO: *The Spoken Arts Treasury*, Vol. XVII (SA, 1975). *Planetarium: A Retrospective 1950–1980* (WT, 1986). *Tracking the Contradictions: Poems 1981–1985* (WT, 1986). VIDEO: *The Poetry of Adrienne Rich* (BWF, 1973). *Adrienne Rich* (APA, I-1974, II-1982, III-1988).

About: B. C. Gelpi and A. Gelpi, eds., *Adrienne Rich's Poetry*, poems by A. Rich and essays on the poetry (1975). J. R. Cooper, *Reading Adrienne Rich: Reviews and Re-Visions 1951–1981* (1984). C. Keyes, *The Aesthetics of Power: The Poetry of Adrienne Rich* (1986). W. Martin, *An American Triptych: Anne Bradstreet, Emily Dickinson and Adrienne Rich* (1983).

THEODORE ROETHKE (1908–1963)

Theodore Roethke was born in Saginaw, Michigan. The son of a florist, he received a bachelor's and a master's degree from the University of Michigan. He taught at Lafayette College (where he was also tennis coach and director of public relations), Michigan State, and Bennington. He also taught at the University of Washington where, after fifteen years of teaching and having received every major literary award in this country, he was eventually appointed poet-in-residence in 1962. Roethke's awards included two Guggenheim Foundation fellowships, the Pulitzer Prize, the National Book Award twice, and the Bollingen Prize in Poetry.

In his notebooks, Roethke repeatedly insisted on — and demonstrated with incredible brilliance — the crucial need for the poet to *look*, to be a good reporter, and to record even the most minute details of the physical world. His poems reflect not only attention to but also reverence for the glory and terror of the physical world: "Hair on a narrow wrist bone." But Roethke also insisted that it is not enough just to look and report; the poet also must learn: "It's the poet's business to be more, not less, than a man."

The range of Roethke's poems amply demonstrates his own dictum. In addition to his often masterful control of form, his poems are marked by a precise observation of natural phenomena and include a gentle, lilting humor or ironic eroticism, a quiet horror in the face of an inevitable annihilation, and a contrapuntal tension between existential despair and the hope for transcendence. If throughout much of his life Roethke was a man who walked the void, his poems are finally a prayer and an affirmation that, although the "dark comes down on what we do," the human spirit finally cannot be overwhelmed by time.

Poetry: *Open House* (1941). *The Lost Son and Other Poems* (1948). *Praise to the End!* (1951). *The Waking: Poems 1933–1953* (1953). *Words for the Wind: The Collected Verse of Theodore Roethke* (1958). *Sequence, Sometimes Metaphysical* (1963). *The Far Field* (1964). *The Collected Poems of Theodore Roethke* (1966).

Prose: *On the Poet and His Craft: Selected Prose of Theodore Roethke*, edited by R. J. Mills, Jr. (1965). *Selected Letters of Theodore Roethke*, edited by R. J. Mills, Jr. (1968). *Straw for the Fire: From the Notebooks of Theodore Roethke*, selected and arranged by D. Wagoner (1972).

Recordings: AUDIO: *Theodore Roethke* (APA, I-1954, II-1959). *The Spoken Arts Treasury*, Vol. IX (SA, 1975). *Theodore Roethke Reads His Poetry* (CD, nd). *Theodore Roethke* (TPV, 1978).

About: R. Blessing, *Roethke's Dynamism: Vision and Technique* (1974). H. Bloom, ed., *Theodore Roethke* (1987). N. Bowers, *Theodore Roethke: The Journey from I to Otherwise* (1983). N. Chaney, *Theodore Roethke: The Poetics of Wonder* (1982). A. T. Foster, *Theodore Roethke's Meditative Sequences: Contemplation and the Creative Process* (1985). W. Heyen, ed., *Profile of Theodore Roethke* (1970). G. Lane, *A Concordance to the Poems of Theodore Roethke* (1972). K. Malkoff, *Theodore Roethke: An Introduction to the Poetry* (1971). R. J. Mills, Jr., *Theodore Roethke* (1963). J. Parini, *Theodore Roethke: An American Romantic* (1979). N. A. Scott, *The Wild Prayer of Longing: Poetry and the Sacred* (1971). A. Seager, *The Glass House: The Life of Theodore Roethke* (1968). A. Stein, ed., *Theodore Roethke: Essays on the Poetry* (1965). R. Sullivan, *Theodore Roethke: The Garden Master* (1974). H. Williams, *"The Edge Is What I Have": Theodore Roethke and After* (1976). G. Wolf, *Theodore Roethke* (1981).

ANNE SEXTON (1928–1974)

Anne Sexton was born in Newton, Massachusetts. According to the short autobiographical note she wrote for *A Controversy of Poets* (1965), Anne Sexton received "no visible education." However, with Sylvia Plath and George Starbuck, she did attend seminars by Robert Lowell at Boston University; she participated in a summer seminar taught by W. D. Snodgrass at Antioch College; and she was a scholar at the Radcliffe Institute. In addition to her several books of poetry, she wrote three children's books with Maxine Kumin. Her many awards included fellowships from the American Academy of Arts and Letters, the Radcliffe Institute, and the Ford Foundation; she was awarded the Pulitzer Prize; and was elected a fellow of the Royal Society of Literature in London. On October 4, 1974, Anne Sexton committed suicide.

Possibly the most famous of the personal-confessional poets, Anne Sexton also probably confessed to more than any of her contemporaries, re-creating experiences with unabashed, almost embarrassing honesty. Indeed, it is also probable that she "confessed" to a number of events that she simply invented. In "With Mercy for the Greedy" she wrote, "I was born / doing reference work in sin, and born / confessing it." Like other confessional Puritans, she did just that. But in various interviews, she also insisted that poetry is as much fabrication as it is confession — that even the most brutal truth is shaped by imagination's energy and the artisan's hand. Moreover, doing research in sin, by necessity, must involve a commensurate search for grace, for God. That combination, for Sexton, was absolute — and as risky as a poker game.

When it wasn't yet fashionable for women to write poems about being a woman, Sexton wrote them — openly, unashamedly, and without resorting to political rhetoric. She knew all along that the victimized woman is "misunderstood" and "not a woman, quite." But, like Hester Prynne, the first liberated woman in American literature, Sexton also knew that a relationship between a man and woman could make them gods. And she knew that she could be the ultimate survivor: "A woman like that is not ashamed to die."

Like Sylvia Plath and John Berryman, Anne Sexton chose the moment of her death. But before doing so — as Maxine Kumin has reported — she found the signs of grace and hope spelled out on her typewriter keys. Sexton knew full well that, regardless of how painful it might seem, each poem is an affirmation and celebration of life — as is all poetry.

Poetry: *To Bedlam and Part Way Back* (1960). *All My Pretty Ones* (1962). *Live or Die* (1966). *Love Poems* (1969). *Transformations* (1971). *The Book of Folly* (1972). *The Death Notebooks* (1974). *The Awful Rowing Toward God* (1975). *45 Mercy Street*, edited by L. G. Sexton (1976). *Words for Dr. Y: Uncollected Poems with Three Stories*, edited by L. G. Sexton (1978). *Anne Sexton: The Complete Poems*, edited by L. G. Sexton, with a foreword by M. Kumin (1981). *Selected Poems of Anne Sexton*, edited with an introduction by D. W. Middlebrook and D. H. George (1988).

Prose: *Anne Sexton: A Self-Portrait in Letters*, edited by L. G. Sexton and L. Ames (1977). *No Evil Star: Selected Essays, Interviews, Prose*, edited by S. E. Colburn (1985).

Recordings: AUDIO: *Anne Sexton Reading at the New York Poetry Center* (WT, 1964). *Anne Sexton*, interview with critics (WT, 1964). *Anne Sexton Reads Her Poetry* (CD, 1973). *The Spoken Arts Treasury*, Vol. XVII (SA, 1975). VIDEO: *Anne Sexton* (APA, 1966). *The Poetry of Anne Sexton* (BWF, 1973).

About: S. E. Colburn, ed., *Anne Sexton: Telling the Tale* (1988). D. H. George, *Oedipus Anne: The Poetry of Anne Sexton* (1987). D. H. George, ed., *Sexton: Selected Criticism* (1988). J. D. McClatchy, ed., *Anne Sexton: The Artist and Her Critics* (1978).

CHARLES SIMIC (1938)

Charles Simic was born in Belgrade, Yugoslavia, raised in Paris, Chicago, and New York City, and received a B.A. from New York University. He has worked as a bookkeeper, accountant, house painter, and shirt salesman; he served in the U.S. Army from 1961 to 1963; and he has taught at California State University at Hayward. Since 1973 he has been teaching at the University of New Hampshire. He has received several PEN Translation Awards, fellowships from the National Endowment for the Arts and the Guggenheim and Ingram Merrill foundations, and the Pulitzer Prize for Poetry.

Charles Simic has described himself as "a realist *and* a surrealist, always drawn between the two." Thus, for some readers, reading Simic's poetry for the first time may be a little like walking into a landscape designed by Salvador Dali ("a meadow / Where the grass was silence / And the flowers / Words") and populated by Hieronymous Bosch ("Grandmothers who wring the necks / Of chickens; old nuns . . . / Who pull schoolboys by the ear"). This rare combination may be partly accounted for by Simic's childhood and early adolescence in wartime Yugoslavia — where, in his own words, "Hitler and Stalin fought over my soul, my destiny. . . ." and his essential imagination was shaped — and by his education in the United States, where he learned the first literature he knew, American literature. Whatever the reasons, clearly this is not the realism of high seriousness found in the poetry of someone like Robert Lowell; neither is it the kind of stark and dark surrealism found in the work of poets like Mark Strand. Rather, throughout Simic's poetry, even in scenes that are emotionally devastating, there are almost always threads of humor, ranging from ironic, sophisticated wit to cunning peasant wit.

Moreover, in Simic's world, where old women sniff the air for snow and silence is some enormous animal to be dismantled, the real and the surreal coexist and have value primarily as image and substance and not as idea and abstraction. In "A Letter," a friend insists, " 'We reach the real by overcoming the seduction of images.' " Simic answers, "Such abstinence will never be possible for me," because "trees with an infinity of tragic shapes / . . . make thinking difficult." Perhaps that accounts for the seemingly total absence of the pursuit of transcendence in his work. For Simic, "paradise" is "Hell's Kitchen"; and salvation, as it were, is "To breakfast on slices of watermelon / In the company of naked gods and goddesses / on a patch of last night's snow."

Simic's persistent humor (which may suggest a sense of the absurdity of human existence, as in Beckett's play, *Waiting for Godot*) and the absence of traditional transcendence (which might suggest the commensurate absence of spirituality) do not preclude a profound moral commitment. In "The Big Machine," he laments the consequences of industrial technology. "The insides of the machine at night / [are] Like a garden of carnivorous plants"; in "The Toy Factory," some dolls are members of a firing squad and "The one being shot at / Falls and gets up, / Falls and gets up," in a perpetual cycle of destruction — much as in the human world. And in "A Letter," Simic writes, "I saw grim-looking men holding a naked woman / While they hosed her with cold water" in the wintry light. The images — often lingering from his childhood — speak for themselves; there is no need for Simic to explain.

The great themes of literature are all present in Charles Simic's work, but they are incarnate in the images of the simple and the small. It is the drama of a life found in a bit of thread; it is the sudden discovery of a poem not when the poet looks up at the sky, but when he bends over to tie his shoes and looks into the earth. It is to stare steadily into the small pieces of this fractured world, "So that briefly, in that one spell, / Your heartache hushes at the beauty of it."

Poetry: *What the Grass Says* (1967). *Somewhere Among Us a Stone Is Taking Notes* (1969). *Dismantling the Silence* (1971). *White* (1972). *Return to a Place Lit by a Glass of Milk* (1974). *Charon's Cosmology* (1977). *Classic Ballroom Dances* (1980). *Austerities* (1982). *Weather Forecast for Utopia and Vicinity* (1983). *Selected Poems 1963–1983* (1985). *Unending Blues* (1986). *The World Doesn't End* (1989). *Selected Poems 1963–1983* (revised and expanded edition, 1990). *The Book of Gods and Devils* (1990).

Prose: *The Uncertain Certainty*, essays (1985). *Wonderful Words, Silent Truth*, essays (1990).

Translations: POETRY: *Fire Gardens*, by Ivan V. Lalić, with C. W. Truesdale (1970). *The Little Box*, by Vasko Popa (1970). *Four Modern Yugoslav Poets* (1970). *Homage to the Lame Wolf*, by Vasko Popa (1979; expanded edition, 1987). *Atlantis*, by Salvko Mihalić, with P. Kastmiler (1987). *Selected Poems of Tomaž Šalamun* (1987). *Roll Call of Mirrors*, selected poems of Ivan V. Lalić (1987). *Some Other Wine and Light*, by Aleksandar Ristović (1989).

Recordings: AUDIO: *Charles Simic* (APA, 1971). *School for Dark Thoughts* (WT, 1978). *Charles Simic* (NAL, 1983). VIDEO: *Charles Simic* (APA, 1986).

LOUIS SIMPSON (1923)

Educated at Murro College (Jamaica, West Indies) and at Columbia, where he received his doctorate, Louis Simpson has taught at Columbia, the University of California at Berkeley and at the State University of New York at Stony Brook. With Donald Hall and Robert Pack, he edited the celebrated anthology *New Poets of England and America* (1957) and he is the author and editor of the textbook *An Introduction to Poetry* (1968). He has received the Rome Fellowship of the American Academy of Arts and Letters, a *Hudson Review* Fellowship, a Guggenheim Foundation fellowship, and the Pulitzer Prize.

Like many other poets of his generation, Simpson began his poetic career as a formalist and gradually worked toward a verse in which content primarily determines form. In the process, his own language has become increasingly natural and closer to the colloquial idiom of American speech — a language "closely related to the language in which men actually think and speak." At the same time, both his language and his view of the American experience — the root source of much of his poetry — have retained an educated and literate edge that inform his poems with a fully conscious sense of history and tradition.

Reading Simpson's poetry, one might be reminded of Robert Frost's famous aphorism about his lover's-quarrel with the world. No less a lover, Simpson's quarrel is more specifically with America. It is an ongoing struggle to come to grips with the pathetic or tragic failure of the American dream and myth — especially as announced by Whitman. "Where are you, Walt? / The Open Road goes to the used-car lot," he says in "Walt Whitman at Bear Mountain." The open road also leads to the suburbs where, it seems, "You were born to waste your life." Simpson's grief is further intensified by his realization that the American dream has been perverted into a weapon capable of destroying not only supposed enemies but also America itself, which has become a foreign country where people speak a language that is strange even to themselves. "And yet there is also happiness. / Happiness . . ." A discovery of a music, even if it is "made entirely of silence."

Poetry: *The Arrivistes: Poems 1940–1949* (1949). *Good News of Death and Other Poems,* in *Poets of Today II,* with Norma Faber and Robert Pack (1955). *A Dream of Governors* (1959). *At the End of the Open Road* (1963). *Selected Poems* (1965). *Adventures of the Letter I* (1971). *Searching for the Ox* (1976). *Armidale* (1980). *Caviare at the Funeral* (1980). *The Best Hour of the Night* (1983). *People Live Here: Selected Poems 1949–1983* (1983). *Collected Poems* (1988). *In the Room We Share* (1990).

Prose: *James Hogg: A Critical Study* (1962). *Riverside Drive,* a novel (1962). *North of Jamaica,* autobiography (1972). *Three on the Tower: The Lives and Works of Ezra Pound, T. S. Eliot and William Carlos Williams* (1975). *A Revolution in Taste: Studies of Dylan Thomas, Allen Ginsberg, Sylvia Plath and Robert Lowell* (1978). *A Company of Poets* (1981). *The Character of the Poet* (1986). *Selected Prose,* autobiography, fiction, literary criticism (1989).

Recordings: AUDIO: *Louis Simpson* (APA, I-1960, II-1965). *The Spoken Arts Treasury,* Vol. XV (SA, 1975). *Louis Simpson* (NLA, 1983). *Physical Universe* (WT, 1985). VIDEO: *The Poetry of Louis Simpson* (BWF, 1974, 1984). *Louis Simpson* (APA, 1978).

About: H. Lazer, ed., *On Louis Simpson: Depths Beyond Happiness* (1988). R. Moran, *Louis Simpson* (1972). W. Roberson, *Louis Simpson: A Reference Guide* (1982).

W. D. SNODGRASS (1926)

Born in Wilkinsburg, Pennsylvania, and educated at Geneva College and at the University of Iowa, W. D. Snodgrass has taught at the University of Rochester, Wayne State, Syracuse, and Old Dominion; he is currently a professor of English at the University of Delaware. He has received fellowships from the Guggenheim and Ingram Merrill foundations, the Academy of American Poets, the National Institute of Arts and Letters, and the National Endowment for the Arts. His first book of poems won the Pulitzer Prize in 1960.

Until the late 1970s, Snodgrass was known primarily as a personal-confessional poet; indeed, he, rather than Robert Lowell, was probably responsible for the emergence of that mode of poetry in the late 1950s and early 1960s. Unlike Lowell, Plath, and Sexton, Snodgrass made poetry not out of madness and sensationally violent suffering but rather out of the daily neuroses and everyday failures of a man — a husband, father, and teacher. Snodgrass also saw such domestic suffering as occurring against a backdrop of a more universal suffering inherent in the whole of human experience. In *Heart's Needle,* he stated *and* demonstrated,

"We need the landscape to repeat us." Snodgrass also shared that fundamental concern of his generation announced by Albert Camus: "There is but one truly serious philosophical problem, and that is suicide." In "April Inventory," he wrote, "I have not learned how often I / Can win, can love, but choose to die."

Although noted for their candor, Snodgrass's early poems were also controlled by an unmistakable sense of irony, directed by a highly literate imagination shaped by the New Critics, and organized by a consciously formal craftsmanship. Consequently, Snodgrass achieves a good measure of distance between himself as subject and himself as poem; thus the speaker of a "personal" Snodgrass poem often sounds more like a personal-confessional "persona."

In any case, little in Snodgrass's early poetry foreshadowed the appearance of *The Führer Bunker*. A cycle of dramatic monologues, these poems are spoken by leading figures of the Nazi regime during the last days of the Third Reich — including Albert Speer, Martin Bormann, Joseph Goebbels, Magda Goebbels, Eva Braun, and Adolf Hitler. Displaying an even more powerful range of dazzling craftsmanship in *The Führer Bunker* — which unfolds like a modern-day *Inferno* — Snodgrass zeros in on the historical and moral landscape that modern humankind seems intent or fated to repeat. The power and the horror of this cycle do not depend on what Snodgrass has to say about the historical figures and events *per se*; he knows all too well that there is little that can be said. Rather, the emotional and moral impact of this cycle — that promises to be one of the truly great achievements of post-1945 poetry in the U.S. — emerges out of the fact that, like the dark and suffering creatures Dante encountered in hell, the personages in this Nazi *Götterdämmerung* are not the monsters we have met in the history books. They are all too recognizable, all too human.

Poetry: *Heart's Needle* (1959). *After Experience* (1968). *Remains* (under pseudonym of S. S. Gardons, 1970; revised edition under the name of W. D. Snodgrass, with a foreword by A. Poulin, Jr., 1985). *The Führer Bunker: A Cycle of Poems in Progress* (1977). *If Birds Build with Your Hair* (1979). *The Boy Made of Meat* (1983). *A Locked House* (1986). *Selected Poems: 1957–1987* (1987). *W. D.'s Midnight Carnival*, in collaboration with the painter DeLoss McGraw (1988). *The Death of Cock Robin*, in collaboration with the painter DeLoss McGraw (1989).

Prose: *In Radical Pursuit: Critical Essays and Lectures* (1975).

Translations: *Gallows Songs*, poems by Christian Morgenstern, translated with L. Segal (1967). *Six Troubadour Songs* (1977). *Traditional Hungarian Songs* (1978). *Six Minnesinger Songs* (1983). *Antonio Vivaldi: The Four Seasons* (1984). *Star and Other Poems*, by Mihai Eminescu (1990).

Recordings: AUDIO: *W. D. Snodgrass* (APA, 1962). *The Spoken Arts Treasury*, Vol. XV (SA, 1975). *Calling from the Woods' Edge* (WT, 1985). VIDEO: *The Poetry of W. D. Snodgrass* (BWF, I-1968, II-1975).

About: P. Gaston, *W. D. Snodgrass* (1978).

GARY SNYDER (1930)

Born in San Francisco, Gary Snyder received a bachelor's degree in literature and anthropology from Reed College. He did further study in languages at Berkeley and later studied Zen Buddhism in a monastery in
Kyoto, Japan. He has worked as a seaman, logger, and forester, and he
has taught at Berkeley. The recipient of a Bollingen Foundation grant
for Buddhist Studies, a grant from the National Institute of Arts and
Letters, and a Guggenheim Foundation fellowship, he was awarded the
Pulitzer Prize in 1975.

In *Six San Francisco Poets* (1969), David Kherdian quotes Snyder as
saying, "As much as the books I've read, the jobs I've had have been
significant in shaping me. My sense of body and language and the knowledge that intelligence and insight, sensitivity, awareness, and brilliance
are not limited to educated people, or anything like it." Many of Snyder's
poems are direct and simple, marked by an elemental reverence for life
and salvaging poetry from the most basic human experience.

The simplicity, however, is not simplistic, for it reflects the profound
influence of Zen on Snyder's sensibility and thought. As Snyder has said,
"A poet faces two directions: one is the world of people and language and
society, and the other is the nonhuman, nonverbal world, which is nature
as nature is itself; and the world of human nature — the inner world, as
it is itself, before language, before custom, before culture. There's no
words in that realm."

Snyder's response to both the inner and outer worlds has resulted in
the quest for a primitive identification with nature and a contemporary
concern for the ecological consequences of progress and civilization. "As
a poet," Snyder has said, "I hold the most archaic values on earth. They
go back to the late Paleolithic: the fertility of the soil, the magic of animals,
the power-vision in solitude, the terrifying initiation and rebirth, the love
and ecstasy of the dance, the common work of the tribe. I try to hold
history and wilderness in mind, that my poems may approach the true
measure of things and stand against the unbalance and ignorance of our
times."

Among the "archaic values" that Snyder has attempted to erect
"against the unbalance and ignorance of our times" are a vital and sacred
reintegration of human sexuality and a full celebration of the whole sexual
self. Few poets of his generation have celebrated heterosexual love as
vividly as Snyder has. Fewer poets have dared explore the precarious
sensual and sexual dimensions of such a simple habit as eating, as Snyder
has in "Song of the Taste." And Snyder's "The Bath" marks the first
time that any American poet perhaps since Whitman has celebrated the
pleasurable glory of the male and female bodies with such unabashed and
reverential joy.

Poetry: *Riprap* (1959/1990). *Myths and Texts* (1960/1978). *Riprap and Cold
Mountain Poems* (1965). *Six Sections from Mountains and Rivers Without End*
(1965). *Three Worlds. Three Realms. Six Roads* (1966). *A Range of Poems*

(1966). *The Back Country* (1968). *The Blue Sky* (1969). *Regarding Wave* (1970). *Manzanita* (1972). *Fudo Trilogy* (1973). *Turtle Island* (1974). *Axe Handles* (1983). *Left Out in the Rain: Poems 1947–1984* (1986).

Prose: ESSAYS AND INTERVIEWS: *Earth House Hold: Technical Notes and Queries to Fellow Dharma Revolutionaries* (1969). *The Old Ways* (1977). *He Who Hunted Birds in His Father's Village: Dimensions of a Haida Myth* (1979). *The Real Work: Interviews & Talks 1964–1979*, edited by S. McLean (1980). *Good Wild Sacred* (1984). *A Passage Through India* (1984). *The Practice of the Wild* (1990).

Recordings: AUDIO: *Gary Snyder* (APA, I-1964, II-1969, III-1974). *Gary Snyder* (APA, 1977). *This Is Our Body* (WT, 1989). VIDEO: *Gary Snyder* (APA, I-1965, II-1976, III-1977, IV-1977). *The Poetry of Gary Snyder* (BWF, 1972). *Gary Snyder* (LLS, I-II-1989).

About: B. Almon, *Gary Snyder* (1979). H. McCord, *Some Notes to Gary Snyder's Myths & Texts* (1971). C. Molesworth, *Gary Snyder's Vision: Poetry and the Real Work* (1983). B. Steuding, *Gary Snyder* (1976).

WILLIAM STAFFORD (1914)

William Stafford received his B.A. and M.A. from the University of Kansas and his Ph.D. from the University of Iowa, where he was also a member of the Writers' Workshop. A conscientious objector during World War II and active in pacifist organizations, he has taught at Manchester College, San Jose State College, and Lewis and Clark College, where he is presently professor emeritus. From 1970 to 1971, he was Consultant in Poetry at the Library of Congress. In addition to a fellowship from the Guggenheim Foundation, a grant from the National Endowment for the Arts, the Shelley Memorial Award, and the Melville Cane Award, he also has received the National Book Award.

In a statement for William J. Martz's *The Distinctive Voice* (1966), William Stafford wrote, "When you make a poem you merely speak or write the language of every day, capturing as many bonuses as possible and economizing on the losses; that is, you come awake to what always goes on in the language, and you use it to the limit of your ability and your power of attention at the moment." Part of what is truly distinctive about Stafford's poetry is his sustained ability to make each poem sound as though it were, in fact, the language of everyday. But it's clear that his power as a poet arises equally out of his ability to capture an extraordinary number of bonuses — the intensity of feeling that daily speech cannot maintain. By so doing, he achieves what he considers to be the meaningful opportunity in the social process of language: "to become more aware of what being alive means."

To a large extent, this awareness also may be the primary thematic focus of Stafford's work: "Your job is to find out what the world is trying to be," he writes in his poem "Vocation." Thus his poetry reflects his attempt not only to capture the possibilities of everyday language but also to maintain "the worth of local things": the plains and small towns of the midwestern and western landscape, the often overlooked experiences of everyday life, and his relationship with his family. Stafford's is also a highly personal poetry, but one which is neither self-torturing nor confessional; rather, it is calm and gentle while remaining honest and firm. Moreover, while neither ostensibly religious nor trailing remnants of the kind of Puritanism inherent in the work of many of his contemporaries, Stafford's poems — as Richard Howard notes in *Alone with America* (1980) — occur within a *paysage moralisé* and are informed by an equally powerful moral vision.

Poetry: *West of Your City* (1961). *Traveling Through the Dark* (1961). *Five Poets of the Pacific Northwest*, with Kenneth Hanson, Richard Hugo, Carolyn Kizer, and David Wagoner; edited by R. Skelton (1964). *The Rescued Year* (1966). *Eleven Untitled Poems* (1968). *Weather* (1969). *Allegiances* (1970). *Temporary Facts* (1970). *In the Clock of Reason* (1973). *Someday, Maybe* (1973). *That Other Alone, Poems* (1973). *Going Places* (1974). *North by West* (1975). *Braided Apart* (1976). *Late, Passing Prairie Farm* (1976). *Stories That Could Be True: New and Collected Poems* (1977). *The Design on the Oriole* (1977). *All About Light* (1978). *Tuft by Puff* (1978). *Smoke's Way* (1978). *Tuned in Late One Night* (1978). *Two About Music* (1978). *A Meeting with Disma Tumminello and William Stafford*, poems by William Stafford, photographs of Disma Tumminello's sculptures (1978). *The Quiet of the Land* (1979). *Around You, Your House & A Catechism* (1979). *Things That Happen Where There Aren't Any People* (1980). *Wyoming Circuit* (1980). *Sometimes a Legend: Puget Sound Country* (1981). *A Glass Face in the Rain* (1982). *Segues: A Conversation in Poetry*, with Marvin Bell (1983). *Smoke's Way: Poems from Limited Editions 1968–1981* (1983). *Roving Across Fields: A Conversation and Uncollected Poems 1942–1982* (1983). *Stories and Storms and Strangers* (1984). *Listening Deep* (1984). *Wyoming* (1985). *Brother Wind* (1986). *An Oregon Message* (1987). *You and Some Other Character* (1987). *Annie Over*, with Marvin Bell (1988). *Fin, Feather, Fur* (1989). *How to Hold Your Arms When It Rains* (1990). *Passwords* (1991).

Prose: *Down in My Heart*, a memoir (1947/1971/1985). *The Achievement of Brother Antoninus* (1967). *Leftovers, a Care Package: Two Lectures* (1973). *Writing the Australian Crawl: Views of the Writer's Vocation* (1978). *You Must Revise Your Life*, essays (1986).

Recordings: AUDIO: *William Stafford* (APA, I-1959, II-1962, III-1967, IV-1973). *William Stafford* (NLA, I-1983, II-1984). *Troubleshooting* (WT/PAC, 1984). VIDEO: *The Poetry of William Stafford* (BWF, I-1969, II-1974). *William Stafford* (APA, 1980). *Moyers: The Power of the Word: "The Simple Acts of Life"* (PBS, 1989).

About: J. Holden, *The Mark to Turn: A Reading of William Stafford's Poetry* (1976). J. Kitchen, *Understanding William Stafford* (1988). T. Koonts and T. Tammaro, eds., *The View from the Top of the Mountain* (1981).

GERALD STERN (1925)

Born in Pittsburgh, Gerald Stern was educated at the University of Pittsburgh and Columbia University. He served in the U.S. Army Air Corps in 1949 and subsequently traveled widely in Europe, where he also tutored and taught high school English. In this country he has taught at various colleges and universities, including Sarah Lawrence, Somerset County College, Temple University, the University of Pittsburgh, and the University of Iowa. Stern's book *Lucky Life* was the Academy of American Poets' Lamont Poetry selection for 1977. He has also been the recipient of the Poetry Society of America's Melville Cane Award, a fellowship from the Guggenheim Foundation, and two creative writing grants from the National Endowment for the Arts.

Compared with many of today's poets, who publish their first books when they are in their early twenties, Gerald Stern came to poetry relatively late in life; he was forty-six when his first book was published. The wait, the years of seeming silence, the apprenticeship proved to be worthwhile, for Stern has grown into a unique presence in contemporary poetry.

Reading Stern's poems and being moved by the persuasive rhythms of their exhilaration or by the resonating cadences of their sorrow, one may exclaim quite spontaneously, "Wonderful! Wonderful!" (At their best, Stern's poems warrant a *physical* response.) But the specific reasons for the poems' effectiveness or for our response may not be identified quite so spontaneously. Clearly, the cultural and literary "influences" are all there: the biblical prophets and psalmists, William Blake and Walt Whitman, Allen Ginsberg and Frank O'Hara. Those influences, however, are more like translucent flags or crystalline signals, rather than prescriptive aesthetic or moral imperatives. Enigmatically, Stern seems to combine Ginsberg's visionary moral stance and O'Hara's chatty urban sophistication, but in the process sounds entirely unique. In an interview published in *American Poetry Review* in early 1984, Stern offered a more personal explanation for his voice: "Everything depends on your signature, your breath, your person. Maybe your rhythm. Your peculiarity, your uniqueness. Your crankiness. That thumb print of yours."

Perhaps the seeming enigma lies more deeply in the expansiveness of Stern's imagination, for he is a poet whose work not only includes, but also attempts to reconcile, the emotional, moral, and existential polarities of experience into a more integrally human whole. Thus his poems encompass the urban experience as much as the rural experience; Cavafy's Alexandria as much as O'Hara's Bickford's; Dionysian joy as much as Judaic anguish. The poem "The Cemetery of Orange Trees in Crete" begins on a level of straightforward realism and suddenly blooms into a lovely surrealistic lyric, while the poem "Weeping and Wailing" begins with an Orphic figure making the trees, animals, and stars dance, moves progressively inward, and suddenly shifts from "I am singing / in harmony" to "I am weeping and wailing." In the same interview, Stern said, "Poets are witnesses, living proof of the uniqueness of the individual soul, of the unforgivable sadness of its perishing, of its immortality. . . . The more living the poet, the more unbearable the death; the greater the poem, the more it ransoms." To that end this poet understands the essential need for the reconciliation of polarities: "stretching my body and turning on my left side / for music, / humming to myself and turning on my right side / for words."

Poetry: *The Pineys* (1971). *The Name of Beasts and Other Poems* (1972). *Rejoicings* (1973; reprinted as *Rejoicings: Poems 1966–1972*, 1984). *Lucky Life* (1977). *The Red Coal* (1981). *Paradise Poems* (1984). *Lovesick* (1987). *Two Long Poems* (1990). *Leaving Another Kingdom: Selected Poems* (1990).

Recordings: AUDIO: *Gerald Stern* (NLA, 1983). *The Rotten Angel* (WT, 1988). VIDEO: *Gerald Stern* (APA, 1979). *The Poetry of Gerald Stern* (BWF, 1982).

MARK STRAND (1934)

Mark Strand was born of American parents in Summerside, Prince Edward Island, Canada. He holds degrees from Antioch College, Yale University, and the University of Iowa, and he was a Fulbright Fellow at the University of Florence. Strand has taught at Iowa, Columbia, Yale, Brooklyn, Princeton, Brandeis, Wesleyan, and the University of Utah. He has received grants and fellowships from the MacArthur, Ingram Merrill, Guggenheim, and Rockefeller foundations, as well as from the National Endowment for the Arts. His prizes include the Edgar Allan Poe Prize, the National Institute of Arts and Letters award, and the fellowship of the Academy of American Poets. In 1981 Mark Strand was elected a member of the American Academy and Institute of Arts and Letters, and in 1990 he was appointed Poet Laureate Consultant in Poetry to the Library of Congress.

The development and impact of Mark Strand's poems, like those of Elizabeth Bishop, depend in large part on the straightforward technique of reportage: a seemingly simple presentation of surface facts. What differentiates Strand's poetry from that of others who employ this technique, however, is that Strand doesn't report only the factual images of the perceived physical world, but especially the figures, contours, and dramatic configurations of dreams and of nonconscious states — what Jung termed the archetypal symbols of the collective unconscious. Even when they address themselves to recognizable figures and situations of the tangible world, Strand's poems continue to generate an aura of the dream world.

Strand's work is further differentiated — not only from other poets who use the technique of reportage but also from those who, like Robert Bly, use the unconscious as a source of imagery — by the measure of irony that suffuses so many of his poems. Given the dramatic situation of a Strand poem, the speaker seems to bring a very conscious intelligence to bear on his reporting; that conscious intelligence directs the development of the action and choreographs the emotional impact of the images, thereby harnessing the full surge of the subconscious — occasionally with an edge of humor. Thus, one of Strand's unique characteristics is that many of his poems reflect a controlling sensibility that might be termed ironic surrealism.

Another characteristic that is almost entirely unique to the poetry of Mark Strand is the extent to which the personality of the speaker of his poems seems to be the result of a conscious obliteration of all traces of the surface texture of personality. In other words, these poems offer us a personality of absence rather than of presence. This personality suggests, "Wherever I am / I am what is missing." But such absence — the fact of absence, the threat of absence, the longing for absence — is also one of Strand's central themes. And so there's a startling but also wonderful irony at work when Strand asserts, "More is less. / I long for more." Should some readers fault Strand's poems for the personality of its speakers and theme of absence, it is important to note Strand's own realization that, confronted by such absence, it is possible to see "the blaze of promise everywhere."

Poetry: *Sleeping with One Eye Open* (1964). *Reasons for Moving* (1968). *Darker* (1970). *The Sargentville Notebook* (1973). *The Story of Our Lives* (1973). *The Late Hour* (1978). *Elegy for My Father* (1973). *Selected Poems* (1980/1990). *The Continuous Life* (1990).

Prose: *The Monument*, poetic prose (1978). *Mr. & Mrs. Baby*, fiction (1985).

Translations: POETRY: *18 Poems from the Quechua* (1971). *The Owl's Insomnia: Selected Poems of Rafael Alberti* (1973). *Souvenir of the Ancient World*, by Carlos Drummond de Andrade (1976). *The Selected Poems of Carlos Drummond de Andrade* (1983). PROSE: *Texas*, by Jorge Luis Borges (1975).

Recordings: AUDIO: *The Untelling* (WT, 1972). *The Spoken Arts Treasury*, Vol. XVIII (SA, 1975). VIDEO: *The Poetry of Mark Strand* (BWF, 1972).

About: D. Kirby, *Mark Strand and the Poet's Place in Contemporary Culture* (1990).

LUCIEN STRYK (1924)

Raised in Chicago, Lucien Stryk was educated at Indiana University, the University of London, the Sorbonne (Paris), and the University of Iowa. He has taught at Niigata and Yamaguchi universities in Japan, and he has been a Fulbright Lecturer and Researcher in Iran and in Japan. Since 1958 he has taught at Northern Illinois University (DeKalb), where he is professor of English and Asian literatures. Stryk's many grants and awards for his poetry, translations, and study of East Asian philosophy and literature include a National Endowment for the Arts poetry fellowship, the Islands and Continents Translation Award, a National Translation Center grant, fellowships from the Rockefeller and Ford foundations, and a National Institute of Arts and Letters award.

One of the admirable qualities of Stryk's poetry is his recognizable range and diversity of subjects. Since he spent much of his career as a scholar of East Asian thought and translator of Japanese poetry, it is natural that that experience is also the focus of some of his poems, such as "Awakening" and "To a Japanese Poet." However, he is just as emotionally and temperamentally comfortable writing about the effect of migrant workers in a small town, the petty conflicts of suburbia, and the yearly extermination of field mice. In the poem "Letter to Jean-Paul Baudot, at Christmas," Stryk confronts, accepts, and forgives the inhumanities of war's greater conflicts, just as in "Cherries" he recognizes and accepts his own far more distant, though no less real, capacity for participation in the cycles of human annihilation.

Clearly, there is a dark edge to many of Stryk's poems; but that dark assumes a more human opacity, because it is countered by at least a proportionate measure of epiphany — a result of the aesthetic-moral vision informing Stryk's poetry. "A man's poems should reveal the full range of his life, and hide nothing except the art behind them," Stryk wrote in his essay "Making Poems" (in *American Poets in 1976*). One of the ways to "hide" that art, he suggests, paraphrasing the Chinese Zen master Hui-neng, is to engage in "pure seeing — not to look *at* things, but *as* things" — which, in Western aesthetics, is similar to Keats's "negative capability." It is also a necessary corollary to Stryk's own pursuit of a seemingly unadorned and simple poetry that "reveals . . . a quality of life . . . [and] takes on a moral grandeur."

The moral grandeur of Lucien Stryk's poetry emerges specifically from his ability to reveal, to accept, and to forgive (not in any Judeo-Christian sense of guilt) even the darker edges of human experience, because to do so is to awaken to, and to be fully aware of, our own most profound humanity. If that is akin to Whitman's assertion "Nothing human is alien to me," it also reflects the capacity to know that "near / books of tranquil Buddhas by the / screen. The war goes on and on"; to know "who will survive"; to know the possibility that "the book may jostle just a / bit, the paper bear a poem"; to know "Our lives depend on it"; to know that at this hour "the trees / are taken, one by one, / into the great wash of darkness" — and yet, to know, too, the epiphanac serenity that "At this hour I am always happy, / ready to be taken myself, / fully aware."

Poetry: *Taproot* (1953). *The Trespasser* (1956). *Notes for a Guidebook* (1965). *The Pit and Other Poems* (1969). *Awakening* (1973). *Selected Poems* (1976). *The Duckpond* (1978). *Zen Poems* (1980). *Cherries* (1983). *Willows* (1983). *Collected Poems 1953–1983* (1984). *Bells of Lombardy* (1986). *Of Pen and Ink and Paper Scraps* (1989).

Translations: *Zen: Poems, Prayers, Sermons, Anecdotes, Interviews*, with T. Ikemoto (1965). *Afterimages: Zen Poems of Shinkichi Takahashi*, with T. Ikemoto (1971). *Twelve Death Poems of the Chinese Zen Masters* (1973). *Zen Poems of China and Japan: The Crane's Bill*, with T. Ikemoto and T. Takayama (1973/1981). *Three Zen Poems after Shinkichi Takahashi* (1976). *The Duckweed Way: Haiku of Issa* (1977). *Haiku of the Japanese Masters*, with T. Ikemoto (1977). *The Penguin Book of Zen Poetry*, with T. Ikemoto (1977/1981). *On Love and*

Barley: Haiku of Basho, with T. Ikemoto (1985). *Triumph of the Sparrow: Zen Poems of Shinkichi Takahashi*, with T. Ikemoto (1986). *The Dumpling Field: Haiku of Issa* (1991).

Recordings: AUDIO: *Lucien Stryk* (NLA, 1984). VIDEO: *The Poetry of Lucien Stryk* (BWF, I-1971, II-1976, III-1984).

RICHARD WILBUR (1921)

A graduate of Amherst and Harvard, Richard Wilbur has taught at Harvard, Wellesley, and Wesleyan where he was an editor of the Wesleyan University Press poetry series; he is currently professor of English at Smith College. In addition to having served as Poet Laureate Consultant in Poetry to the Library of Congress, he has been awarded Guggenheim and Ford Foundation fellowships, the Prix de Rome, the Pulitzer Prize, and the National Book Award.

In addition to his stunning poetry and translations, Wilbur's work includes an operetta, *Candide* (with Lillian Hellman, 1957); poetry for children, *Loudmouse* (1963) and *Opposites* (1973); and editions of the poems of Keats, Poe, and Shakespeare.

Among poets whose sensibilities were shaped by the New Critics, Wilbur continues to be the consummate artist. His poetry is marked by grace, wit, and a kind of masterful craftsmanship equaled by few of his contemporaries. In his statement for John Ciardi's *Mid-Century American Poets* (1950), Wilbur affirmed the poet's need for form, for "artistry," saying that "limitation makes for power: the strength of the genie comes of his being confined in a bottle." Elsewhere he has stated that the poet must move "to attempt a maximum range" and to do so "without apparent strain." At his best, Wilbur's mastery of language and form is not merely without strain — it is dazzling and breathtaking.

The precision of sensuous detail and the verbal entrechats in Wilbur's poems are formal affirmations of his profound humanism, his belief in humankind's potential natural grace in this "world of sensible objects." In an era when many other poets have loitered around the deterioration of social, psychic, and personal fabrics and have proclaimed us and our world absurd, Wilbur has consistently sought for "a reconciliation between joy and pleasure, between acceptance and transcendence" — often against strenuous odds. And he has succeeded. By so doing, his poems have found and continue to offer the possibility of human beauty and grace.

Poetry: *The Beautiful Changes and Other Poems* (1947). *Ceremony and Other Poems* (1950). *Things of This World: Poems* (1956). *Advice to a Prophet and Other Poems* (1961). *The Poems of Richard Wilbur* (1963). *Walking to Sleep: New Poems and Translations* (1969). *The Mind-Reader: New Poems* (1976). *Opposites: Poems and Drawings* (1979). *Seven Poems* (1981). *New and Collected Poems* (1988).

Prose: *Responses: Prose Pieces 1953–1976*, essays (1976).

Translations: POETRY: *The Whale and Other Uncollected Translations* (1982).   VERSE DRAMA: *The Misanthrope,* by Molière (1955).   *Tartuffe,* by Molière (1963).   *The School for Wives,* by Molière (1971).   *The Learned Ladies,* by Molière (1978).   *Andromache,* by Racine (1982).   *Four Comedies,* by Molière (1982).

Recordings: AUDIO: *Richard Wilbur* (APA, 1956).   *Richard Wilbur Translating* (APA, 1956).   *The Spoken Arts Treasury,* Vol. XIV (1975).   *The Poems of Richard Wilbur* (SA, nd).   *Richard Wilbur Reading His Poetry* (CD, nd).   VIDEO: *The Poetry of Richard Wilbur* (BWF, 1969).   *Richard Wilbur* (APA, 1966).   *Richard Wilbur* (LLS, 1990).

About: P. F. Cummings, *Richard Wilbur: A Critical Essay* (1971).   D. L. Hill, *Richard Wilbur* (1967).   W. Salinger, ed., *Richard Wilbur's Creation* (1983).

C. K. WILLIAMS (1936)

Born in Newark, New Jersey, and educated at Bucknell University and the University of Pennsylvania, C. K. Williams has spanned a wide range of activities during his professional career.   He established a program of poetry-therapy for emotionally disturbed patients at the Institute of the Pennsylvania Hospital in Philadelphia, where he was also a group therapist in the treatment of disturbed adolescents.   He has been an editor and ghostwriter of articles, booklets, and speeches in the fields of psychiatry and architecture.   And he has taught creative writing at Drexel University, the University of California at Irvine, Boston University, Columbia University, and George Mason University.   Williams has been awarded a Guggenheim Fellowship, the *Paris Review*'s Bernard F. Connor Prize, and the National Book Critics' Circle Award for poetry.

Reading the poems of C. K. Williams, we are quickly struck by how much pain and grief are harbored in their stark lines.   Perhaps no other postwar poet in the U.S. has confronted so unswervingly and relentlessly the levels and dimensions of anguish as the fulcrum of human experience. Moreover, unlike many of his contemporaries, Williams has explored human suffering without the seeming intellectual comfort of a formal philosophical system such as existentialism (W. D. Snodgrass), without even a precarious solace of faith or of a theological framework (John Berryman), and certainly without the emotional-aesthetic buffer of a strong ironic sense in the service of sustained artifice (Sylvia Plath). Whether confronting inner states of psychic pain in earlier poems or more external constructs of human anguish in later poems, Williams's poetry has as its heart the fundamental and essentially unconsoled vision announced in "It Is This Way with Men": "They are pounded into the earth / like nails; move an inch, / they are driven down again. / The earth is sore with them."

The anguish of our common condition, in an age that threatens annihilation on all sides, also seems to have rendered Williams commensurately unsympathetic to the kinds of artifices we have come to expect from poetry. Thus, in his earlier poems he seemed intent on stripping language down to its most essential syntax and then stripping it even further of most signs of syntax's own formal artifice. Consider the intense aesthetic and syntactical starkness of these lines: "if you told him god lived in his own penis / he'd bite into it / and tear like a carnivore / this is how men renounce / this is how we obliterate. . . ." Clearly, the visual aesthetic equivalent of such lines would be found more in Käthe Kollwitz's hauntingly sparse but blunt depictions of pain than in the more complex, inventive, and often witty depictions by Hieronymous Bosch.

In his fifth book, *Tar*, Williams introduced a long tonal line that may well be unique in postwar American poetry. Williams's lines may look like Ginsberg's, but they are not marked by the incantatory quality in many of Ginsberg's poems. And while their tone is very conversational, like many of Simpson's recent poems, Williams's tone isn't marked by the crackling terseness found in Simpson's. Approaching the quality of a highly refined, sparse prose, Williams's new tonal lines continue to accommodate his dark vision but also enable him to be more experientially, intellectually, and aesthetically expansive, allowing the reader to participate in the poet's own thought processes. These new poems also reflect a maturation of Williams's vision: the pain, the anguish, the annihilation are still present and unconsoled, but that vision is also counterpointed by the recognition of the possibility of beauty in scenes such as "all the field pure white, / its surface glittering, the dawn, glancing from its glaze, oblique, relentless, unadorned."

Poetry: *A Day for Anne Frank* (1968). *Lies* (1969). *I Am the Bitter Name* (1972). *With Ignorance* (1977). *Tar* (1983). *Flesh and Blood* (1988). *Poems 1963–1983* (1988).

Translations: POETRY: *The Lark. The Thrush. The Starling*, by Issa (1983). VERSE DRAMA: *Women of Trachis*, by Sophocles; with G. Dickerson (1978). *The Bacchae*, by Euripides (1990).

Recordings: AUDIO: *Tar & Other Poems* (WT/PAC, 1985). VIDEO: *The Poetry of C. K. Williams* (BWF, 1974). *C. K. Williams* (APA, 1981).

CHARLES WRIGHT (1935)

Born in Pickwick Dam, Tennessee, Charles Wright was educated at Davidson College, the University of Iowa, and the University of Rome, where he was a Fulbright Fellow. From 1957 to 1961 he served in the U.S. Army Intelligence Service, and since 1966 he has been teaching at various universities, including the University of Padua (Italy), where he was a Fulbright Lecturer, as well as Iowa, Princeton, Columbia, the University of California at Irvine, and the University of Virginia in Charlottesville. Wright's grants, awards, and prizes include fellowships from the National Endowment for the Arts and the Guggenheim and Ingram Merrill foundations; the Edgar Allan Poe Award of the Academy of American Poets; a grant from the American Academy and Institute of Arts and Letters; and the PEN Translation Prize. In 1983 Wright also was cowinner of the American Book Award for poetry.

If Charles Wright's "The New Poem" were read as a statement of his poetics (in the way that Marvin Bell's "White Clover" or Robert Creeley's "The Window" may be read), we might rightfully conclude that Wright's sense of poetics — and the implicit broader vision from which it might issue — is desolate to the brink of barbarism. For the "new poem" would have nothing to do with the physical world, would reflect no characteristic inherent in the art of poetry, and would address no human concerns. It's no wonder that in 1979 one critic asserted that Wright's poetry struggles to render the connections between his life and his poems "tenuous, often invisible" and characterized Wright's poems as being "unanchored to inci-dent," thus "resisting description" and "defying exposition."

In light of Wright's full body of poetry, however, "The New Poem" is more rightly read as a statement of antipoetics, perhaps even as a parody of a certain modish aesthetic. That is, it is a poem suggesting what Wright hopes his own poems will *not* be, a nine-commandment tablet listing what poetry in general ought *not* to do, and, indeed, perhaps a kind of oxymoron repudiating the view in some literary circles that finds quality and worth in poetry that is seemingly not rooted in any recogniz-able human reality.

Because they are carefully, delicately crafted, and because, as other critics have noted, they often rely more on links of the imagination than on narrative and other surface connections, some of Wright's poems may seem less immediately accessible than the work of other poets. However, on closer examination it is clear that the range of Wright's concerns is fully rooted in the range of recognizable and shared human experience. His work includes poems of place energized by the spirit of that place, whether it is Blackwater Mountain in Tennessee or Laguna Beach, Cali-fornia; it includes poems emerging out of childhood, adolescent, and mature experience and the states of emotional feeling inherent in those stages of human development; and it includes poems of the natural, physi-cal world with its splendors and horrors.

What is also striking about the work of Charles Wright is its strong and consistent religious nature; Wright is one of the few poets of his generation who continues to wrestle openly with the traditional values (if not the working tenets) of the Judeo-Christian tradition and to use the symbols, saints, and metaphors of that tradition as an integral part of his sensibility and vocabulary. The poem "Snow" uses as its launching point the biblical phrase "Dust thou art, and unto dust shalt thou return"; "Equation," in part, is an exploration of guilt *as guilt*, rather than as a symptom of neurosis; and the poems *Three Poems for the New Year* and "California Dreaming," whose very tone resonates with biblical rhythms and whose language incorporates traditional religious phrases and con-cepts, are profound explorations of the possibility of a tradition-oriented spirituality within the boundaries and texture of contemporary experience. What if, in his quest for transcendence, Wright recognizes that "The ache for anything is a thick dust in the heart," that transcendence may be no more than being "Released as a glint, as a flash, as a spark," and that the "other ladder to Paradise / [is] but the smooth handholds of the rib cage"? Of the people and places in his world, past and present, he asserts, "I am their music"; of his music, he ventures, "I write poems to untie myself, to do penance and disappear / Through the upper right-hand corner of things, to say grace."

Poetry: *The Voyage* (1963). *6 Poems* (1965). *The Dream Animal* (1968). *Private Madrigals* (1969). *The Grave of the Right Hand* (1970). *The Venice Notebook* (1971). *Backwater* (1973). *Hard Freight* (1973). *Bloodlines* (1975). *China Trace* (1977). *Colophons* (1977). *The Southern Cross* (1981). *Country Music: Selected Early Poems* (1982). *The Other Side of the River* (1984). *Zone Journals* (1988). *The World of the Ten Thousand Things: Poems 1980–1990* (1990).

Prose: *Halflife: Improvisations and Interviews* (1988).

Translations: *The Storm and Other Poems,* by Eugenio Montale (1978). *The Motets,* poems by Eugenio Montale (1981). *Orphic Songs,* poems by Dino Campana (1984).

Recordings: AUDIO: *The Tongue Is a White Water* (WT, 1985). VIDEO: Charles Wright (APA, 1980). *The Poetry of Charles Wright* (BWF, 1986).

JAMES WRIGHT (1927–1980)

James Wright was born in the steel town of Martin's Ferry, Ohio — a place he subsequently transformed into a literary landmark in the contemporary imagination. He received his B.A. from Kenyon College, his M.A. and Ph.D. from the University of Washington, and attended the University of Vienna as a Fulbright Scholar. The recipient of several awards for poetry — including the Pulitzer Prize — he taught at Macalester College, the University of Minnesota, and Hunter College.

Like many other poets of his generation, James Wright's style underwent significant changes in the course of his career. With the publication of his first book, Wright stated that he "wanted to make [his] poems say something humanly important" and pointed to Robert Frost and E. A. Robinson as his models. Thus his early poems, such as "Saint Judas," are often concerned with his response to the life and suffering of others. After his second book, however, he asserted, "Whatever I write from now on will be entirely different."

According to Robert Bly, Wright's decision was largely the result of his having read — and translated — the work of the German poet Georg Trakl, a contemporary of Rilke. "In Trakl," Bly writes, "a series of images makes a series of events. Because these events appear out of their 'natural' order, without the connection we have learned to expect from reading newspapers, doors silently open to unused parts of the brain." In Wright's poems such as "The Jewel," "Lying in a Hammock . . . ," and "A Blessing" — generally written between 1960 and 1970 — the doors open to startling images, strange but emotionally precise. More personal than his earlier poems, these discover in his own subconscious and imagination the secret pools of human fear and joy. Moreover, the poems themselves seem to evolve quietly through layers of images until they surface with the quick thrust of a striking final image and epiphany.

In poems written after the publication of his *Collected Poems* in 1971, Wright sought a vital integration of his earlier concern with others — "those old Winnebago men" — and the image of epiphany — "the instant in the waterfall." The results enable us to join Wright in his assertion: "I know what we call it / Most of the time. / But I have my own song for it, / And sometimes, even today, / I call it beauty."

Poetry: *The Green Wall* (1957). *Saint Judas* (1959). *The Lion's Tail and Eyes: Poems Written Out of Laziness and Silence*, with Robert Bly and William Duffy (1962). *The Branch Will Not Break* (1963). *Shall We Gather at the River* (1968). *Collected Poems* (1971). *Two Citizens* (1973). *Moments of the Italian Summer* (1976). *To a Blossoming Pear Tree* (1977). *Leave It to the Sunlight*, edited by A. Wright (1981). *A Reply to Matthew Arnold*, edited by A. Wright (1981). *This Journey*, edited by A. Wright (1981). *The Shape of Light*, edited by A. Wright (1986). *Above the River: The Complete Poems*, edited by A. Wright (1990).

Prose: *Collected Prose*, essays, edited by A. Wright (1982). *The Delicacy and Strength of Lace*, letters between James Wright and Leslie Marmon Silko, edited by A. Wright (1985). *A Secret Field: Selections from the Final Journals*, edited by A. Wright (1985). *Against the Exile*, letters to Wayne Burns, edited by J. R. Doheny (1985).

Translations: *Twenty Poems of Georg Trakl*, with R. Bly (1961). *Twenty Poems of César Vallejo*, with R. Bly (1962). *The Rider on the White Horse: Selected Short Fiction of Theodor Storm* (1964). *Pablo Neruda: Twenty Poems*, with R. Bly (1967). *Poems by Hermann Hesse* (1970). *Neruda and Vallejo: Selected Poems*, with R. Bly and J. Knoepfle (1971). *Wandering: Notes and Sketches by Hermann Hesse*, with F. Wright (1972).

Recordings: AUDIO: *James Wright* (APA, I-1965, II-1968). *The Spoken Arts Treasury*, Vol. XVII (SA, 1975). *The Poetry and Voice of James Wright* (CD, 1977). VIDEO: *The Poetry of James Wright* (BWF, 1970).

About: M. Cuddihy, ed., *Ironwood 10: James Wright: A Special Issue* (1977). D. C. Dougherty, *James Wright* (1987). F. Graziano and P. Stitt, eds., *James Wright: A Profile* (1988). F. Graziano and P. Stitt, eds., *James Wright: The Heart of the Light* (1990). D. Smith, ed., *The Pure Clear Word: Essays on the Poetry of James Wright* (1983). K. Stein, *James Wright: The Poetry of a Grown Man* (1989).

Criticism: A Selected Bibliography

Most of the following books and pamphlets contain substantial discussions of the work of individual poets, especially those represented in this book; some also include critical essays or statements of poetics by these poets. A few books in this bibliography, however, are primarily concerned with poetry in the U.S. before 1945; still others focus on various aspects of the art of poetry in the twentieth century.

Advanced students of poetry will want to turn to book-length bibliographies devoted to individual poets, as well as to such standard bibliographical sources as *Contemporary Poets* (St. Martin's Press); *Contemporary Authors* (Gale Research Company); the annual bibliographies published in *PMLA*, *American Literature*, and *Journal of Modern Literature*; the regular bibliographies in *Twentieth Century Literature*; and *Contemporary Literary Criticism* (Gale Research Company), an annual volume of critical excerpts. Of course, many of the books listed here also include their own individual bibliographies.

Lastly, readers should be aware that several of the earlier, seminal books of criticism devoted to post-1945 U.S. poetry are now out of print and available only in larger libraries.

D. M. Allen and W. Tallman, eds., *The Poetics of the New American Poetry* (1973).

C. Altieri, *Enlarging the Temple: New Directions in American Poetry During the 1960's* (1979).

C. Altieri, *Painterly Abstraction in Modernist American Poetry: Infinite Incantations of Ourselves* (1990).

H. A. Baker, Jr., *Afro-American Poets* (1988).

J. D. Bellamy, ed., *American Poetry Observed: Poets on Their Work* (1984).

R. Berke, *Bounds Out of Bounds: A Compass for Recent American and British Poetry* (1981).

M. K. Blasing, *American Poetry: The Rhetoric of Its Forms* (1988).

H. Bloom, *The Anxiety of Influence: A Theory of Poetry* (1973).

H. Bloom, *A Map of Misreading* (1975).

R. Bly, *American Poetry: Wildness and Domesticity* (1990).

R. Boyers, ed., *Excursions: Selected Literary Essays* (1977).

J. E. B. Breslin, *From Modern to Contemporary: American Poetry 1945–1965* (1984).

N. Bunge, ed., *Finding the Words: Interviews with Writers Who Teach* (1984).

G. Cambon, *Recent American Poetry* (1962).

P. Carroll, *The Poem in Its Skin* (1968).

S. Charters, *Some Poems/Poets: Poets and Poetry* (1971).

C. Clausen, *The Place of Poetry: Two Centuries of an Art in Crisis* (1981).

J. Clausen, *A Movement of Poets: Thoughts on Poetry & Feminism* (1983).

M. Davidson, *The San Francisco Renaissance: Poetics and Community at Mid-Century* (1989).

M. Duberman, *Black Mountain: An Experiment in Community* (1972).

I. Ehrenpreis, *American Poetry* (1965).

E. Faas, ed., *Towards a New American Poetics: Essays and Interviews* (1978).

R. Frank and H. Sayre, eds., *The Line in Postmodern Poetry* (1989).

S. Fredman, *Poet's Prose: The Crisis in American Verse* (1983).

S. Friebert and D. Young, eds., *A Field Guide to Contemporary Poetry and Poetics* (1980).

T. Gardner, *Discovering Ourselves in Whitman: The Contemporary American Long Poem* (1988).

A. Gayle, *The Black Aesthetic* (1971).

A. Gelpi, *A Coherent Splendor: The American Poetic Renaissance 1910–1950* (1987).

P. Goodman, *Speaking and Language: A Defense of Poetry* (1971).

J. Gould, *Modern American Women Poets* (1984).

J. Grahn, *The Highest Apple: Sappho and the Lesbian Poetic Tradition* (1985).

D. Hall, ed., *Claims for Poetry* (1982).

M. Harris and K. Aguero, eds., *A Gift of Tongues: Critical Challenges in Contemporary Poetry* (1988).

R. Hass, *Twentieth Century Pleasures* (1984).

S. Henderson, ed., *Understanding the New Black Poetry: Black Speech and Black Music as Poetic Reference* (1973).

W. Heyen, ed., *American Poets in 1976* (1975).

J. Holden, *The Rhetoric of the Contemporary Lyric* (1980).

R. Howard, *Alone with America: Essays on the Art of Poetry in the United States Since 1950* (1969; enlarged edition, 1980).

E. B. Hungerford, *Poets in Progress: Critical Prefaces to Thirteen Modern American Poets* (1967).

R. Jackson, *Acts of Mind: Conversations with Contemporary Poets* (1983).

R. Jackson, *The Dismantling of Time in Contemporary Poetry* (1988).

D. Kalstone, *Five Temperaments: Elizabeth Bishop, Robert Lowell, James Merrill, Adrienne Rich, John Ashbery* (1977).

L. Keller, *Remaking It New: Contemporary Poetry and the Modern Feminist* (1989).

D. Kherdian, *Six San Francisco Poets* (1969).

R. Kostelanetz, *The Old Poetries and the New* (1981).

R. Kostelanetz, ed., *On Contemporary Literature* (1964).

G. Kuzma, ed., *A Book of Rereadings in Recent American Poetry* (1980).

H. Lazer, *What Is a Poet?* (1987).

D. Lehman, ed., *Ecstatic Occasions, Expedient Forms: Sixty-Five Leading Contemporary Poets Select and Comment on Their Poems* (1988).

G. Lensing and R. Moran, *Four Poets and the Emotive Imagination: Robert Bly, James Wright, Louis Simpson and William Stafford* (1976).

L. Lieberman, *Unassigned Frequencies: American Poetry in Review* (1977).

H. R. Madhubuti (Don L. Lee), *Dynamite Voices* (1971).

K. Malkoff, *Crowell's Handbook of Contemporary American Poetry: A Critical Handbook of American Poetry Since 1940* (1973).

K. Malkoff, *Escape from the Self* (1977).

P. Mariani, *A Useable Past: Essays on Modern and Contemporary Poetry* (1984).

R. K. Martin, *The Homosexual Tradition in American Poetry* (1979).

J. Mazzaro, ed., *Modern American Poetry: Essays in Criticism* (1970).

J. Mazzaro, *Postmodern American Poetry* (1980).

J. D. McClatchy, *White Paper: On Contemporary American Poetry* (1987).

D. Meltzer, *The San Francisco Poets* (1971).

J. F. Mersmann, *Out of the Vietnam Vortex: A Study of Poets and Poetry Against the War* (1974).

D. M. Middlebrook and M. Yalom, eds., *Coming to Light: American Women Poets in the Twentieth Century* (1985).

B. Miller, ed., *Black American Poets Between Worlds 1940–1960* (1987).

R. J. Mills, Jr., *Creation's Very Self: On the Personal Element in Recent American Poetry* (1969).

R. J. Mills, Jr., *Cry of the Human: Essays on Contemporary American Poetry* (1974).

C. Molesworth, *The Fierce Embrace: A Study of Contemporary American Poetry* (1979).

C. Nelson, *Our Last First Poets: Vision and History in Contemporary American Poetry* (1984).

H. Nemerov, ed., *Poets on Poetry* (1961).

H. Nemerov, *Reflections on Poetry & Poets* (1972).

A. Oberg, *Modern American Lyric* (1978).

D. Ossman, *The Sullen Art: Interviews by David Ossman with Modern American Poets* (1963).

A. Ostriker, *Stealing the Language: The Emergence of Women's Poetry in America* (1986).

A. Ostroff, ed., *The Contemporary Poet as Artist and Critic* (1964).

G. Owen, ed., *Modern American Poetry: Essays in Criticism* (1972).

W. Packard, ed., *The Craft of Poetry: Interviews from the New York Quarterly* (1974).

T. Parkinson, ed., *A Casebook on the Beat* (1961).

T. Parkinson, *Poets, Poems, Movements* (1988).

S. Paul, *The Lost America of Love: Rereading Robert Creeley, Edward Dorn, and Robert Duncan* (1981).

R. Peters, *The Great American Poetry Bake-Off* (1979).

R. Peters, *The Great American Poetry Bake-Off, Second Series* (1982).

R. Philips, *The Confessional Poets* (1973).

R. H. Pierce, *The Continuity of American Poetry* (1973).

R. Pinsky, *The Situation of Poetry: Contemporary Poetry and Its Traditions* (1977).

G. Plimpton, *Poets at Work* (1989).

W. Prunty, *Fallen from the Symboled World: Precedents for the New Formalism* (1990).

K. Rexroth, *American Poetry in the Twentieth Century* (1973).

S. Rodman, *Tongues of Fallen Angels*, interviews (1984).

M. L. Rosenthal, *The Modern Poetic Sequence: The Genius of Modern Poetry* (1983).

M. L. Rosenthal, *The Modern Poets: A Critical Introduction* (1962).

M. L. Rosenthal, *The New Poets: American and British Poetry Since World War II* (1967).

M. L. Rosenthal, *Poetry and the Common Life* (1974; revised edition, 1984).

M. L. Rosenthal, *The Poet's Art* (1989).

R. B. Shaw, ed., *American Poetry Since 1960: Some Critical Perspectives* (1974).

M. Sienicka, *The Making of a New American Poem: Some Tendencies in the Post–World War II American Poetry* (1972).

E. Simpson, *Poets in Their Youth: A Memoir* (1982).

L. Simpson, *A Revolution in Taste: Studies of Dylan Thomas, Allen Ginsberg, Robert Lowell and Sylvia Plath* (1978).

D. Smith, *Local Assays: On Contemporary American Poetry* (1985).

T. Steele, *Missing Measures: Modern Poetry and the Revolt Against Meter* (1990).

S. Stepanchev, *American Poetry Since 1945: A Critical Survey* (1965).

J. Sternberg, ed., *The Writer on Her Work* (1980).

P. Stitt, *The World's Hieroglyphic Beauty: Five American Poets* (1987).

G. Thurley, *The American Moment: American Poetry in the Mid-Century* (1977).

C. Tomlinson, *Some Americans: A Personal Record* (1981).

L. P. Turco, *Visions and Revisions in American Poetry* (1986).

H. Vendler, *The Music of What Happens: Poems, Poets, Critics* (1989).

H. Vendler, *Part of Nature, Part of Us* (1980).

J. Vinson, ed., *Contemporary Poets* (1985).

R. Von Hallberg, *American Poetry and Culture: 1945–1980* (1988).

H. H. Waggoner, *American Poetry from the Puritans to the Present* (1968; revised edition, 1984).

A. Williamson, *Introspection and Contemporary Poetry* (1984).

Writers at Work: The Paris Review *Interviews* (First Series, 1958; Second Series, 1963; Third Series, 1967; Fourth Series, 1976; Fifth Series, 1981).

A Note on the Editor

A. Poulin, Jr., was born of immigrant Québecois parents in Lisbon, Maine, in 1938. He received a B.A. from St. Francis College, an M.A. from Loyola University (Chicago), and an M.F.A. from the University of Iowa; he also did postgraduate work at the State University of New York at Buffalo. He has taught for the European Division of the University of Maryland, at the University of New Hampshire, and at St. Francis College, where he was chairman of the Division of Humanities and assistant to the president for curriculum planning and development. Since 1971 Poulin has been on the faculty at the State University of New York, College at Brockport, where he is professor of English and Faculty Exchange Scholar. In 1980 he was Visiting Fulbright Lecturer in Contemporary American Poetry at the universities of Athens and Thessaloniki in Greece.

Poulin also has been Director of the Brockport Writers Forum and has recorded videotaped interviews with more than twenty contemporary poets, including John Ashbery, Robert Bly, Robert Creeley, Lawrence Ferlinghetti, Allen Ginsberg, Robert Hayden, David Ignatow, Galway Kinnell, Carolyn Kizer, Stanley Kunitz, John Logan, William Matthews, Adrienne Rich, Anne Sexton, Louis Simpson, Gary Snyder, William Stafford, and Mark Strand — some of the poets represented in *Contemporary American Poetry.*

A poet, translator, and editor, Poulin has written the following books and chapbooks of poetry: *In Advent* (1972), *Catawba: Omens, Prayers & Songs* (1977), *The Widow's Taboo; Poems After the Catawba* (1977), *The Nameless Garden* (1978), *The Slaughter of Pigs* (1981), *A Nest of Sonnets* (1986), *A Momentary Order* (1987), and *Cave Dwellers* (1991). His books of translations include *Poems* by the Québecois poet, Anne Hébert (1980) and *Anne Hébert: Selected Poems* (1986), *Duino Elegies and The Sonnets to Orpheus* by Rainer Maria Rilke (1977), and six collections of French poems by Rilke: *Saltimbanques* (1978), *The Roses & The Windows* (1979), *The Astonishment of Origins* (1982), *Orchards* (1982), *The Migration of Powers* (1984), and *The Complete French Poems of Rainer Maria Rilke* (1986). Besides having edited the five editions of *Contemporary American Poetry* (1971, 1975, 1980, 1985, 1991), Poulin has also edited *A Ballet for the Ear: Interviews, Essays, and Reviews* by John Logan (1983) and with David A. DeTurk coedited *The American Folk Scene: Dimensions of the Folksong Revival* (1967).

For his poetry and translations, Poulin has received both a creative writing fellowship and translator's grant from the National Endowment for the Arts, as well as a poetry fellowship from the New York Foundation for the Arts, two translation awards from Columbia University's Translation Center, a Faculty Enrichment Programme grant for research and translation from the Embassy of Canada, and several fellowships and grants-in-aid from the Research Foundation of the State University of New York. In 1989 Poulin was awarded an honorary Doctorate of Humane Letters by the University of New England.

In addition to teaching and writing, Poulin is founding editor and publisher of BOA Editions, Ltd., a nonprofit organization devoted to the publication of poetry and of poetry in translations. He also has served as a member of the State University of New York's University–Wide Committee on the Arts and as a member of the Literature Panel of the New York State Council on the Arts, and he was founding executive director of the New York State Literary Center.

A. Poulin, Jr. currently resides in Brockport, New York, with his wife, the metalsmith and jeweler B. H. Poulin.

Acknowledgments

A. R. Ammons: "Apologia Pro Vita Sua," "He Held Radical Light," "Working with Tools," "The Unifying Principle," "Cut the Grass," "The City Limits," and "The Eternal City" are reprinted from *Collected Poems, 1951–1971*, by A. R. Ammons. Copyright © 1972 by A. R. Ammons. "White Dwarf," "Distraction," and "Breaking Out" are reprinted from *A Coast of Trees*, Poems by A. R. Ammons. Copyright © 1981 by A. R. Ammons. "Extrication" and "Volitions" are reprinted from *Worldly Hopes*, Poems by A. R. Ammons. Copyright © 1982 by A. R. Ammons. "Chiseled Clouds" and "Loft" are reprinted from *Sumerian Vistas*, Poems by A. R. Ammons. Copyright © 1987 by A. R. Ammons. All by permission of W. W. Norton & Company, Inc.

John Ashbery: "'They Dream Only of America'" and "Leaving the Atocha Station" from *The Tennis Court Oath* by John Ashbery. Copyright © 1962 by John Ashbery. Reprinted by Wesleyan University Press by permission of University Press of New England. "Some Trees," "As You Came from the Holy Land," "Street Musicians," and "Paradoxes and Oxymorons" from *Selected Poems* by John Ashbery. Copyright © 1985 by John Ashbery. Reprinted by permission of the publisher, Viking Penguin, a division of Penguin Books USA Inc. "Posture of Unease," "One Coat of Paint," and "Vetiver" from *April Galleons* by John Ashbery. Copyright © 1984, 1985, 1986, 1987 by John Ashbery. Reprinted by permission of the publisher, Viking Penguin, a division of Penguin Books USA Inc. "Definition of Blue" from *The Double Dream of Spring*. Copyright © 1966, 1967, 1968, 1969, 1970 by John Ashbery. Reprinted by permission of Georges Borchardt Inc. and the author.

Marvin Bell: "To Dorothy." Reprinted with permission of Atheneum Publishers, an imprint of Macmillan Publishing Company, from *Stars Which See, Stars Which Do Not See* by Marvin Bell. Copyright © 1977 by Marvin Bell. "Long Island." Reprinted with permission of Atheneum Publishers, an imprint of Macmillan Publishing Company, from *New and Selected Poems* by Marvin Bell. Copyright © 1987 by Marvin Bell. "The Extermination of the Jews" from *A Probable Volume of Dreams*; "Homage to the Runner" from *The Escape into You: A Sequence*; "During the War" and "The Last Thing I Say" from *These Green-Going-to-Yellow*; "White Clover," "They," and "Drawn by Stones, by Earth, by Things That Have Been in the Fire" from *Drawn by Stones, by Earth, by Things That Have Been in the Fire*; copyright 1969, 1971, 1981, 1984, 1990 by Marvin Bell; reprinted with the permission of Marvin Bell. "How He Grew Up" and "If I Had One Thing to Say" from *Iris of Creation* copyright © 1990 by Marvin Bell, published by Copper Canyon Press. Copyright © 1990 by Marvin Bell. "Ending with a Line from Lear" copyright © 1990 by Marvin Bell. Originally published by *The Atlantic Monthly* and reprinted with the permission of Marvin Bell.

John Berryman: Excerpt from "Eleven Addresses to the Lord," "The Song of the Tortured Girl," and "Henry's Understanding" from *Collected Poems, 1937–1971* by John Berryman. Copyright © 1989 by Kate Donahue Berryman. #1, #4, #8, #9, #13, #14, #29, #45, #46, #55, #230, #384 from *The Dream Songs* by John Berryman. Reprinted by permission of Farrar, Straus and Giroux, Inc.

Elizabeth Bishop: "The Man-Moth," "The Fish," "The Armadillo," "In the Waiting Room," "The Moose," "One Art," and "North Haven" from *The Complete Poems, 1927–1979* by Elizabeth Bishop. Copyright © 1936, 1940, 1957, 1968, 1971, 1972, 1976, 1978 by Elizabeth Bishop. Copyright © 1979, 1983 by Alice Helen Methfessel. Reprinted by permission of Farrar, Straus and Giroux, Inc.

Robert Bly: "A Man Writes to Part of Himself" and "Opening the Door of a Barn I Thought Was Empty on New Year's Eve" copyright © 1962, 1975 by Robert Bly; reprinted from *Selected Poems*, as published by Harper & Row, Publishers, 1986, with the permission of Robert Bly. "After Long Busyness" copyright © 1973 by Robert Bly. Reprinted from *Jumping Out of Bed*, as published by White Pine Press, 1988, with the permission of Robert Bly. "Looking into a Tide Pool" copyright © 1973 by Robert Bly. Reprinted from *The Morning Glory*, as published by Kayak Books, with the permission of Robert Bly. "Surprised by Evening," "Waking from Sleep," "Poem in Three Parts," "Snowfall in the Afternoon," "In a Train," "Driving to Town Late to Mail a Letter," and "Watering the Horse" copyright © 1962 by Robert Bly. Reprinted from *Silence in the Snowy Fields*, as published by Wesleyan University Press, with permission from Robert Bly. "For My Son Noah, Ten Years Old" from *The Man in the Black Coat Turns* by Robert Bly, copyright © 1981 by Robert Bly.

ACKNOWLEDGMENTS

Used by permission of Doubleday, a division of Bantam Doubleday Dell Publishing Group, Inc. "At Midocean" and "In Rainy September" from *Loving a Woman in Two Worlds* by Robert Bly, copyright © 1985 by Robert Bly. Used by permission of Doubleday, a division of Bantam Doubleday Dell Publishing Group, Inc. "Counting Small-Boned Bodies." Copyright © 1967 by Robert Bly. "Looking into a Face." Copyright © 1965 by Robert Bly. "The Hermit." Copyright © 1967 by Robert Bly. From *The Light around the Body* by Robert Bly. Reprinted by permission of HarperCollins Publishers. "Shack Poem." Copyright © 1971 by Robert Bly. From *Sleepers Joining Hands* by Robert Bly. Reprinted by permission of HarperCollins Publishers. "Insect Heads." Copyright © 1979 by Robert Bly. "Passing an Orchard by Train." Copyright © 1979 by Robert Bly. "Driving My Parents Home at Christmas." Copyright © 1979 by Robert Bly. From *This Tree Will Be Here for a Thousand Years* by Robert Bly. Reprinted by permission of HarperCollins Publishers.

Gwendolyn Brooks: "The Near-Johannesburg Boy," "Tornado at Talladega," "Telephone Conversations," and "To the Young Who Want to Die" copyright © 1988 by Gwendolyn Brooks Blakely. Reprinted from *The Near-Johannesburg Boy*, as published by The David Company, Chicago, with the permission of Gwendolyn Brooks Blakely. From *A Street in Bronzeville*: "the mother," "a song in the front yard," "of De Witt Williams on his way to Lincoln Cemetery"; "The Lovers of the Poor," "We Real Cool," "An Aspect of Love, Alive in the Ice and Fire," "To Don at Salaam," and "To Black Women" copyright © 1945, 1949, 1953, 1960, 1963, 1968, 1969, 1970, 1971, 1975, 1981, 1987 by Gwendolyn Brooks Blakely. Reprinted from *Blacks*, as published by The David Company, Chicago, with the permission of Gwendolyn Brooks Blakely.

Lucille Clifton: "[here is another bone]" and "the lost woman" copyright © 1987 by Lucille Clifton. Reprinted from *Next: New Poems* by Lucille Clifton with the permission of BOA Editions, Ltd., 92 Park Ave., Brockport, NY 14420. "admonitions," "miss rosie," "[if i stand in my window]," "the lost baby poem," "god's mood," "roots," "[come home from the movies]," "to a dark moses," "she understands me," "cutting greens," "[at last we killed the roaches]," "breaklight," and "the carver" copyright © 1987 by Lucille Clifton. Reprinted from *Good Woman: Poems and a Memoir 1969–1980* with the permission of BOA Editions, Ltd., 92 Park Ave., Brockport, NY 14420. "homage to my hips," "[there is a girl inside]," "forgiving my father," "speaking of loss," and "i once knew a man" from *two-headed woman* by Lucille Clifton. Copyright © 1980 by The University of Massachusetts Press. Reprinted by permission of Curtis Brown Ltd. "adam thinking," "eve thinking," and "lucifer understanding" by Lucille Clifton. Copyright © 1991 by Lucille Clifton. Reprinted by permission of Curtis Brown Ltd.

Robert Creeley: "I Know a Man," "The Business," "A Form of Women," "The Flower," "The Rain," "The Memory," "A Wicker Basket," "The Rescue," "The Language," "The Window," "Moment," and "On Vacation" from *Collected Poems of Robert Creeley, 1945–1975* by Robert Creeley. Copyright © 1983 The Regents of the University of California. Reprinted by permission of the University of California Press. "First Rain" and "Mother's Voice." Robert Creeley: *Mirrors*. Copyright © 1983 by Robert Creeley. "Lost." Robert Creeley: *Memory Gardens*. Copyright © 1986 by Robert Creeley. "First Love." Robert Creeley: *Windows*. Copyright © 1990 by Robert Creeley. Reprinted by permission of New Directions Publishing Corporation.

James Dickey: "The Heaven of Animals," "The Performance," "The Hospital Window," "In the Mountain Tent," "Sled Burial, Dream Ceremony," "The Sheep Child," "Adultery," "Deer Among Cattle." Reprinted from *Poems 1957–1967*. Copyright © 1967 by James Dickey. Wesleyan University Press by permission of University Press of New England. "Purgation." Reprinted from *The Eagle's Mile*. Copyright © 1990 by James Dickey. By Wesleyan University Press by permission of University Press of New England. "False Youth: Autumn: Clothes of the Age" from *The Strength of Fields* by James Dickey, copyright © 1979 by James Dickey. Used by permission of Doubleday, a division of Bantam Doubleday Dell Publishing Group, Inc.

Rita Dove: "Reading Hölderlin on the Patio with the Aid of a Dictionary," "In the Bulrush," and "A Father out Walking on the Lawn" copyright © 1983 by Rita Dove. Reprinted from *Museum*, as published by Carnegie Mellon University Press, with the permission of Rita Dove. "Variation on Pain," "Compendium," "Daystar," "Sunday Greens," and "Company" copyright © 1986 by Rita Dove. Reprinted from *Thomas and Beulah*, as published by Carnegie Mellon University Press, with the permission of Rita Dove. "'Teach Us to Number Our Days'," "Adolescence — III," "Nexus," and "Then Came Flowers" copyright © 1980 by Rita Dove. Reprinted from *The Yellow House on the Corner*, as published by Carnegie Mellon University Press, with the permission of Rita Dove. "Mississippi," "Silos," "The Breathing, the Endless News," "After Reading *Mickey in the Night Kitchen* for the Third Time Before Bed," and "The Island Women of Paris" reprinted from *Grace Notes*, Poems by Rita Dove, by permission of W. W. Norton & Company, Inc. Copyright © 1989 by Rita Dove.

Alan Dugan: "Surviving the Hurricane," copyright © 1989 by Alan Dugan. From *Poems 6*, first published by The Ecco Press in 1989. Reprinted by permission. "Love Song: I and Thou," "Tribute to Kafka for Someone Taken," "General Prothalamion for Wartimes," "To a Red-Headed Do-Good Waitress," "For Masturbation," "Fabrication of Ancestors," "Poem," "Elegy for a Puritan Conscience," "Prayer," "On Leaving Town," "Untitled Poem," "On Finding the Tree of Life," and "Last Statement for a Last Oracle" copyright © 1961, 1962, 1968, 1972, 1973, 1974, 1983 by Alan Dugan. From *New and Collected Poems, 1961–1983*, first published by The Ecco Press in 1983. Reprinted by permission. "Closing Time at the Second Avenue Deli" copyright © 1990 by Alan Dugan. Originally published by the *Harvard Book Review* and reprinted with the permission of Alan Dugan.

Robert Duncan: "Often I Am Permitted . . .," "Poetry, a Natural Thing," and "Ingmar Bergman's *Seventh Seal*." Robert Duncan: *The Opening of the Field*. Copyright © 1960 by Robert Duncan. "Such is the Sickness . . .," "Bending the Bow," "My Mother Would Be a Falconress," and "The Torso (Passages 18)." Robert Duncan: *Bending the Bow*. Copyright © 1968 by Robert Duncan. "The Work," from "Dante Etudes." Robert Duncan: *Groundwork*. Copyright © 1984 by Robert Duncan. All reprinted by permission of New Directions Publishing Corporation.

Lawrence Ferlinghetti: "Constantly risking absurdity," "Sometime during eternity," "The pennycandy store beyond the El," and "I Am Waiting." Lawrence Ferlinghetti: *A Coney Island of the Mind*. Copyright © 1958 by Lawrence Ferlinghetti. "Monet's Lillies Shuddering" and "Making Love in Poetry." Lawrence Ferlinghetti: *Over All the Obscene Boundaries*. Copyright © 1984 by Lawrence Ferlinghetti. All reprinted by permission of New Directions Publishing Corporation. "Ascending over Ohio" and "Uses of Poetry" copyright © 1990 by Lawrence Ferlinghetti. Reprinted with the permission of Lawrence Ferlinghetti.

Isabella Gardner: "Summers Ago," "Lines to a Seagreen Lover," "In the Museum," "The Widow's Yard," "The Milkman," "Letter from Slough Pond," "Part of the Darkness," "On Looking in the Looking Glass," "The Accomplices," "This Neighborhood," "That Was Then." Copyright © 1990 by Isabella Gardner. Reprinted from *Isabella Gardner: The Collected Poems* by Isabella Gardner with the permission of BOA Editions, Ltd., 92 Park Ave., Brockport, NY 14420.

Allen Ginsberg: "Howl" copyright © 1955 by Allen Ginsberg. "America" copyright © 1956, 1959 by Allen Ginsberg. "Love Poem on Theme by Whitman" copyright © 1978 by Allen Ginsberg. "Psalm III" copyright © 1978 by Allen Ginsberg. "Wales Visitation" copyright © 1968 by Allen Ginsberg. "On Neal's Ashes" copyright © 1968 by Allen Ginsberg. "Fourth Floor, Dawn, Up All Night Writing Letters" copyright © 1980 by Allen Ginsberg. "Ode to Failure" copyright © 1980 by Allen Ginsberg. From *The Collected Poems: 1947–1980* by Allen Ginsberg. Reprinted by permission of HarperCollins Publishers.

Louise Glück: "Celestial Music" and "The Untrustworthy Speaker" copyright © 1990 by Louise Glück. From *Ararat*, first published by The Ecco Press in 1990. Reprinted by permission. "Hyacinth," "Mock Orange," and "The Triumph of Achilles" copyright © 1985 by Louise Glück. From *The Triumph of Achilles*, first published by The Ecco Press. Reprinted by permission. "The Drowned Children," "The Garden," "Palais des Arts," "Thanksgiving," and "The Mirror" copyright © 1976, 1977, 1978, 1979, 1980 by Louise Glück. From *Descending Figure*, first published by the Ecco Press in 1980. Reprinted by permission. "Messengers" and "Love Poem" copyright © 1971, 1972, 1973, 1974, 1975 by Louise Glück. From *The House on Marshland*, first published by The Ecco Press in 1975. Reprinted by permission. "Cottonmouth Country" copyright © 1968 by Louise Glück. From *Firstborn*, first published by The Ecco Press in 1983. Reprinted by permission.

Donald Hall: "Christmas Eve in Whitneyville," "Maple Syrup," "Kicking the Leaves," "Ox Cart Man," "Great Day in the Cows' House"; "The Pond," "The Day," and "The

ACKNOWLEDGMENTS

Cup," excerpts from "The Day I Was Older"; all from *Old and New Poems* by Donald Hall. Copyright © 1990 by Donald Hall. Reprinted by permission of Houghton Mifflin Company.

Michael S. Harper: "Healing Song," "Grandfather," "Nightmare Begins Responsibility," and "Here Where Coltrane Is" from *Images of Kin: New and Selected Poems* by Michael S. Harper, reprinted by permission of The University of Illinois Press. Copyright © 1977 by The University of Illinois Press. "The Borning Room" and "Song: I Want a Witness" reprinted from *Song: I Want a Witness*, by Michael S. Harper, by permission of the University of Pittsburgh Press. © 1972 by Michael S. Harper. "Motel Room" and "Protégé: 1962" copyright © 1990 by Michael S. Harper. Reprinted with the permission of Michael S. Harper. "Black Study" and "New Season" copyright © 1970 by Michael S. Harper. Reprinted from *Dear John, Dear Coltrane*, as published by The University of Pittsburgh Press, with permission from Michael S. Harper.

Robert Hass: "Bookbuying in the Tenderloin," "Letter," and "The Failure of Buffalo to Levitate" from *Field Guide* by Robert Hass. Copyright © 1973 by Robert Hass. Reprinted by permission of The Yale University Press. "Meditation at Lagunitas," "Like Three Fair Branches from One Root Deriv'd," "The Pure Ones," "The Origin of Cities," and "Picking Blackberries with a Friend Who Has Been Reading Jacques Lacan" copyright © 1974, 1975, 1976, 1977, 1978, 1979 by Robert Hass. From *Praise*, first published by The Ecco Press in 1979. Reprinted by permission. "Late Spring," "Spring Drawing 2," "A Story About the Body," and "Privilege of Being" copyright © 1989 by Robert Hass. From *Human Wishes*, first published by The Ecco Press in 1989. Reprinted by permission.

Robert Hayden: "Frederick Douglass," "'From the Corpse Woodpiles, from the Ashes'," "Those Winter Sundays," "The Prisoners," "Night, Death, Mississippi," "Monet's 'Waterlilies'," "Soledad," "The Night-Blooming Cereus," and "The Tattooed Man" are reprinted from *Collected Poems of Robert Hayden*, Edited by Frederick Glaysher, by permission of Liveright Publishing Corporation. Copyright © 1985 by Erma Hayden.

Richard Hugo: "Death of the Kapowsin Tavern," "G.I. Graves in Tuscany," "Degrees of Gray in Philipsburg," "Montgomery Hollow," "Montana Ranch Abandoned," "The House on 15th S.W.," "Farmer, Dying," "The Hilltop," "Here, but Unable to Answer," and "Distances" reprinted from *Making Certain It Goes On: The Collected Poems of Richard Hugo*, by permission of W. W. Norton & Company, Inc. Copyright © 1984 by The Estate of Richard Hugo.

David Ignatow: "Communion," "Sunday at the State Hospital," "My Place," "Epitaph," "The Bagel," "Rescue the Dead," "Against the Evidence," "First Coffin Poem," and "Waiting Inside" from *Poems 1934–1969*. Copyright © 1970 by David Ignatow. "1 (The world is so difficult)," "7 (This is the solution)," "9 (Old men spend their days)," "25 (Here I am)," "33 (White-haired, I walk)," "38 (I would be buried)," "42 (We are an aging couple)," "43 (I don't know)," "47 (We are here)," "55 (How lonely it is)," "59 (I just know)," "61 (About death)," "66 (Ignatow is dying)," and "67 (I live with my contradictions)," excerpts from *Shadowing the Ground*. Copyright © 1991 by David Ignatow. All reprinted by Wesleyan University Press by permission of University Press of New England.

Randall Jarrell: "The Black Swan," "To the New World," "90 North," "The Snow-Leopard," "The Death of the Ball Turret Gunner," "Eighth Air Force," "A Camp in the Prussian Forest," and "The Player Piano" from *The Complete Poems* by Randall Jarrell. Copyright © 1941, 1945, 1946, 1947, 1951, 1967, renewal copyright © 1968, 1969, 1972, 1973 by Mrs. Randall Jarrell. Reprinted by permission of Farrar, Straus and Giroux, Inc. "The Woman at the Washington Zoo" by Randall Jarrell. From *The Woman at the Washington Zoo*, copyright © 1960 by Randall Jarrell.

Donald Justice: "Landscape with Little Figures," "Counting the Mad," and "Variations for Two Pianos" from *The Summer Anniversaries*, Rev. ed. Copyright © 1981 by Donald Justice. "Men at Forty," "The Missing Person," "Bus Stop," and "Hands" from *Night Light*. Copyright © 1967 by Donald Justice. All reprinted by Wesleyan University Press by permission of University Press of New England. "Children Walking Home from School through Good Neighborhood" reprinted with permission of Atheneum Publishers, an imprint of Macmillan Publishing Company, from *The Sunset Maker* by Donald Justice. Copyright © 1987 by Donald Justice. "Poem (This poem is not addressed)," "Variations on a Text by Vallejo," "Presences," "Sonatina in Yellow," and "Two Small Vices Beginning with the Letter 'L'" copyright © 1979/1990 by Donald Justice. Reprinted from *Selected*

Poems, as published by Atheneum Publishers, with the permission of Donald Justice. "Dance Lessons of the Thirties" copyright © 1990 by Donald Justice. Originally published by *The New Criterion* and reprinted with the permission of Donald Justice.

Galway Kinnell: "On Frozen Fields" from *Flower Herding on Mount Monadnock* by Galway Kinnell. Copyright © 1964 by Galway Kinnell. "Under the Maud Moon" from *The Book of Nightmares* by Galway Kinnell. Copyright © 1971 by Galway Kinnell. "First Song" from *What a Kingdom It Was* by Galway Kinnell. Copyright © 1960 by Galway Kinnell. "Vapor Trail Reflected in the Frog Pond," "The Bear," "Last Songs," and "Saint Francis and the Sow" from *Body Rags* by Galway Kinnell. Copyright © 1965, 1966 by Galway Kinnell. All reprinted by permission of Houghton Mifflin Co. "When One Has Lived a Long Time Alone," #'s 3, 4, 8, 10, 11. From *When One Has Lived a Long Time Alone* by Galway Kinnell. Copyright © 1990 by Galway Kinnell. Reprinted by permission of Alfred A. Knopf, Inc.

Carolyn Kizer: "Three (I will speak about women)" from "Pro Femina," "A Widow in Wintertime," "I (Daughter-my-mother)" and "III (Daughter, you lived)" from "The Blessing," and "Bitch," all from *Mermaids in the Basement*, by Carolyn Kizer. Copyright © 1984 by Carolyn Kizer. "The Ungrateful Garden" from *The Nearness of You*, by Carolyn Kizer. Copyright © 1986 by Carolyn Kizer. All reprinted by permission of the Copper Canyon Press. "The Copulating Gods," "Semele Recycled," "Afternoon Happiness" copyright © 1984 by Carolyn Kizer. Reprinted from *Yin* by Carolyn Kizer with the permission of BOA Editions, Ltd., 92 Park Ave., Brockport, NY 14420.

Maxine Kumin: "Morning Swim," "Stones," "Woodchucks," "How It Is," "The Longing To Be Saved," "The Excrement Poem," "The Grace of Geldings in Ripe Pastures," "In the Pea Patch," and "Family Reunion" from *Our Ground Time Here Will Be Brief* by Maxine Kumin. Copyright © 1965, 1971, 1972, 1975, 1976, 1978, 1979, 1981 by Viking. "Nurture" and "In the Park" from *Nurture* by Maxine Kumin. Copyright © 1989 by Maxine Kumin. All reprinted by permission of Viking Penguin, a division of Penguin Books USA, Inc.

Stanley Kunitz: "The Wellfleet Whale" and "The Abduction" from *Next-to-Last Things* by Stanley Kunitz. Copyright © 1985 by Stanley Kunitz. Used by permission of Atlantic Monthly Press. "Single Vision," "Father and Son," "End of Summer," "The War Against the Trees," "Indian Summer at Land's End," "The Artist," "The Portrait," "The Unquiet Ones," and "The Knot" from *The Poems of Stanley Kunitz 1928–1978* by Stanley Kunitz. Copyright © 1930, 1944, 1958, 1971, 1973, 1974, 1978, 1979 by Stanley Kunitz. By permission of Little, Brown and Company.

Denise Levertov: "The Jacob's Ladder," "Hypocrite Women," "A Psalm Praising the Hair of Man's Body," "The Wings," and "The Altars in the Street." Denise Levertov: *Poems 1960–1967*. Copyright © 1961, 1964, 1966 by Denise Levertov Goodman. "The Poem Unwritten." Denise Levertov: *Poems 1968–1972*. Copyright © 1970 by Denise Levertov Goodman. "Ways of Conquest." Denise Levertov Goodman: *The Freeing of the Dust*. Copyright © 1975 by Denise Levertov. "Wedding-Ring." Denise Levertov: *Life in the Forest*. Copyright © 1975 by Denise Levertov. "Passage." Denise Levertov: *Oblique Prayers*. Copyright © 1984 by Denise Levertov. "The Well" and "Standoff." Denise Levertov: *Breathing the Water*. Copyright © 1987 by Denise Levertov. "Intimation," "The Blind Man's House . . .," and "Where Is the Angel?" Denise Levertov: *A Door in the Hive*. Copyright © 1989 by Denise Levertov. All reprinted with the permission of New Directions Publishing Corporation. "Stele" copyright © 1990 by Denise Levertov. Reprinted with the permission of Denise Levertov.

Philip Levine: "Starlight." Reprinted with permission of Atheneum Publishers, an imprint of Macmillan Publishing Company, from *Ashes* by Philip Levine. Copyright © 1979 by Philip Levine. "The House." Reprinted with permission of Atheneum Publishers, an imprint of Macmillan Publishing Company, from *Sweet Will* by Philip Levine. Copyright © 1985 by Philip Levine. "Coming Home" from *They Feed They Lion*; "You Can Have It" and "Let Me Begin Again" from *7 Years from Somewhere* copyright © 1972, 1979, 1990 by Philip Levine; reprinted with the permission of Philip Levine. "Among Children" copyright © 1990 by Philip Levine. Originally published by *The Atlantic Monthly* and reprinted with the permission of Philip Levine. "What Work Is" copyright © 1990 by Philip Levine. Originally published by *The New Yorker* and reprinted with the permission of Philip Levine.

"Animals Are Passing from Our Lives" and "To a Child Trapped in a Barber Shop." Reprinted from *Not This Pig*. Copyright © 1967 by Philip Levine. Wesleyan University Press by permission of University Press of New England.

John Logan: "To a Young Poet Who Fled" and "Spring of the Thief" copyright © 1955, 1960, 1961, 1962, 1963, 1964, 1965, 1966, 1967, 1968, 1969, 1970, 1973, 1981 by John Logan. From *Only the Dreamer Can Change the Dream*, first published by The Ecco Press in 1981. Reprinted by permission. "Three Moves," "Suzanne," "Love Poem," "Second Prelude . . .," "Poem for My Brother," "Avocado," "Happening on Aegina," "Believe It," and "The Gift" copyright © 1989 by the John Logan Literary Estate. Reprinted from *John Logan: The Collected Poems* with the permission of BOA Editions, Ltd., 92 Park Ave., Brockport, NY 14420.

Robert Lowell: "Memories of West Street and Lepke," "Man and Wife," "'To Speak of Woe That Is in Marriage'," "Skunk Hour," "Eye and Tooth," and "History" from *Selected Poems* by Robert Lowell. Copyright © 1956, 1959, 1960, 1961, 1962, 1963, 1964, 1965, 1967, 1968, 1969, 1970, 1973, 1976 by Robert Lowell. Excerpt from "Homecoming" and "Epilogue" from *Day by Day* by Robert Lowell. Copyright © 1975, 1976, 1977 by Robert Lowell. All reprinted by permission of Farrar, Straus and Giroux, Inc. "Colloquy in Black Rock" and "Christmas Eve Under Hooker's Statue" from LORD WEARY'S CASTLE, copyright © 1946 and renewed 1974 by Robert Lowell, reprinted by permission of Harcourt Brace Jovanovich, Inc.

William Matthews: "Pissing off the Back of the Boat into the Nivernais Canal." From *Flood* by William Matthews. Copyright © 1981 by William Matthews. First appeared in *Seattle Review*. "Masterful." From *A Happy Childhood* by William Matthews. Copyright © 1983 by William Matthews. First appeared in *Moose*. Both reprinted with the permission of Little, Brown and Company. "The Search Party," "Blues for John Coltrane, Dead at 41," "Swimming off Cape Hatteras," and "Good Night" copyright © 1970 by William Matthews. Reprinted from *Ruining the New Road* with the permission of William Matthews. "Puberty" and "Blue Notes" from *Foreseeable Futures* by William Matthews. Copyright © 1987 by William Matthews. "Smoke Gets in Your Eyes," "Onions," and "Mood Indigo" from *Blues If You Want* by William Matthews. Copyright © 1989 by William Matthews. All reprinted by permission of Houghton Mifflin Co.

James Merrill: "Angel," reprinted from *Water Street* by James Merrill. Copyright © 1960 by James Merrill. Originally appeared in *Poetry*. "After Greece," reprinted from *Water Street* by James Merrill. Copyright © 1960 by James Merrill. Originally appeared in *The New Yorker*. "A Dedication" reprinted from *The Country of a Thousand Years of Peace* by James Merrill. Copyright © 1970 by James Merrill. "The Octopus" and "Laboratory Poem" both reprinted from *The Country of a Thousand Years of Peace* by James Merrill. Copyright © 1970 by James Merrill. Both originally appeared in *Poetry*. "Charles on Fire," reprinted from *Nights and Days* by James Merrill. Copyright © 1966 by James Merrill. "Up and Down, #2: The Emerald" and "The Victor Dog" reprinted from *Braving the Elements* by James Merrill. Copyright © 1972 by James Merrill. "Up and Down #2: The Emerald" originally appeared in *The New Yorker*. All reprinted with permission of Atheneum Publishers, an imprint of Macmillan Publishing Company. "Waterspout." From *The Inner Room* by James Merrill. Copyright © 1988 by James Merrill. Reprinted by permission of Alfred A. Knopf, Inc.

W. S. Merwin: "The Drunk in the Furnace" from *The First Four Books of Poems* © 1956, 1975 by W. S. Merwin. "Dead Hand," "Air," and "We Continue" from *The Moving Target* © 1960, 1967 by W. S. Merwin. "Some Last Questions," "December Night," and "For the Anniversary of My Death" from *The Lice* © 1963, 1984 by W. S. Merwin. "Tergvinder's Stone" from *The Miner's Pale Children* © 1969, 1970 by W. S. Merwin. "Do Not Die" and "Animula" from *The Carrier of Ladders* © 1967, 1980 by W. S. Merwin. "A Door" from *Writing to an Unfinished Accompaniment* © 1969, 1980 by W. S. Merwin. "Son," "A Family," and "The Black Jewel" from *Opening the Hand* © 1983, 1984 by W. S. Merwin. All reprinted by permission of Georges Borchardt Inc. and the author. "To the Insects," "After the Alphabets," "Chord," "Losing a Language," and "Witness." From *The Rain in the Trees* by W. S. Merwin. Copyright © 1988 by W. S. Merwin. Reprinted by permission of Alfred A. Knopf, Inc.

Frank O'Hara: "Autobiographia Literaria" copyright © 1967 by Maureen Granville-Smith, Administratrix of the Estate of Frank O'Hara. "Poem (All the mirrors)" copyright ©

1970 by Maureen Granville-Smith, Administratrix of the Estate of Frank O'Hara. "To My Dead Father" copyright © 1971 by Maureen Granville-Smith, Administratrix of the Estate of Frank O'Hara. "To John Ashbery" copyright © 1971 by Maureen Granville-Smith, Administratrix of the Estate of Frank O'Hara. "Why I Am Not a Painter" copyright © 1958 by Maureen Granville-Smith, Administratrix of the Estate of Frank O'Hara. Reprinted from *The Collected Poems of Frank O'Hara*, by permission of Alfred A. Knopf, Inc. "Poem (the eager note)" and "Meditations in an Emergency" from *Meditations in an Emergency* by Frank O'Hara. Copyright © 1957 by Frank O'Hara. Reprinted by permission of Grove Weidenfeld. "The Day Lady Died," "Steps," "Yesterday Down at the Canal," and "Poem (Lana Turner has collapsed)" from *Lunch Poems* by Frank O'Hara. Copyright © 1964 by Frank O'Hara. Reprinted by permission of City Lights Books.

Mary Oliver: "The Kitten," "Tasting the Wild Grapes," "An Old Whorehouse," and "In Blackwater Woods." From *American Primitive* by Mary Oliver. Copyright © 1978, 1979, 1980, 1981, 1982, 1983 by Mary Oliver. "The Kitten" first appeared in *American Scholar*, "Tasting the Wild Grapes" first appeared in *Western Humanities Review*, "An Old Whorehouse" first appeared in *Three Rivers Poetry Journal*, and "In Blackwater Woods" first appeared in *Yankee*. By permission of Little, Brown and Company. "Sleeping in the Forest," "The Fish," "Music Lessons," and "The Black Walnut Tree." From *Twelve Moons* by Mary Oliver. Copyright © 1972, 1973, 1974, 1976, 1977, 1978, 1979 by Mary Oliver. "Sleeping in the Forest," "Music Lessons," and "The Black Walnut Tree" first appeared in *The Ohio Review*. By permission of Little, Brown and Company. "Singapore" from *House of Light* by Mary Oliver. Copyright © 1990 by Mary Oliver. Reprinted by permission of Beacon Press and Mary Oliver. "A Visitor," from *Dreamwork* by Mary Oliver. Copyright © 1986 by Mary Oliver. Used by permission of Atlantic Monthly Press. "The Swimming Lesson" from *No Voyage and Other Poems* by Mary Oliver, published by Houghton Mifflin Co. Copyright © 1965 by Mary Oliver. Used by permission of the author.

Charles Olson: "Maximus, to Himself," "I, Maximus of Gloucester, to You," "The Librarian," "Maximus to Gloucester, Letter 27 [Withheld]," "A Later Note on Letter #15," and "Moonset, Gloucester, December 1, 1957, 1:58 AM" from *Collected Poetry of Charles Olson* by Charles Olson. Copyright © 1987 Estate of Charles Olson (previously published poetry), © University of Connecticut (previously unpublished).

Marge Piercy: "The Skyscrapers of the Financial District Dance with Gasman." Reprinted from *Breaking Camp*. Copyright © 1968 by Marge Piercy. "The Friend." Reprinted from *Hard Loving*. Copyright © 1969 by Marge Piercy. Both reprinted by Wesleyan University Press by permission of University Press of New England. "Touch Tones" and "My Mother's Body." From *My Mother's Body* by Marge Piercy. Copyright © 1985 by Marge Piercy. "A Work of Artifice," "Barbie Doll," "To Be of Use," "You Ask Why Sometimes I Say Stop," and "Digging In." From *Circles on the Water* by Marge Piercy. Copyright © 1982 by Marge Piercy. All reprinted by permission of Alfred A. Knopf, Inc.

Sylvia Plath: "Daddy," "Mary's Song," "Lady Lazarus," "Cut," "Ariel," "Winter Trees," "Crossing the Water," "Witch Burning," and "Brasília" by Sylvia Plath from *The Collected Poems of Sylvia Plath*. Copyright © 1960, 1965, 1971, and 1981 by the Estate of Sylvia Plath. "Nick and the Candlestick" by Sylvia Plath from *The Collected Poems of Sylvia Plath*. Copyright © 1966 by Ted Hughes, copyright © 1981 by the Estate of Sylvia Plath. All reprinted by permission of HarperCollins Publishers Inc. "The Colossus." Copyright © 1961 by Sylvia Plath. Reprinted from *The Colossus and Other Poems* by Sylvia Plath, by permission of Alfred A. Knopf, Inc.

Adrienne Rich: "For a Friend in Travail" copyright © 1990 by Adrienne Rich. Reprinted with the permission of Adrienne Rich. "Aunt Jennifer's Tigers," "Planetarium," "Diving into the Wreck," "Splittings"; "Twenty-One Love Poems: I, II, XII, XXI," "Integrity," and "North American Time" are reprinted from *The Fact of a Doorframe: Poems Selected and New, 1950–1984*, by permission of W. W. Norton & Company, Inc. Copyright © 1984 by Adrienne Rich. Copyright © 1975, 1978 by W. W. Norton & Company, Inc. Copyright © 1981 by Adrienne Rich. "For an Occupant" is reprinted from *Your Native Land, Your Life*, Poems by Adrienne Rich, by permission of W. W. Norton & Company, Inc. Copyright © 1986 by Adrienne Rich. Part 5 of "Turning" is reprinted from *Time's Power, Poems 1985–1988*, by Adrienne Rich, by permission of W. W. Norton & Company, Inc. Copyright © 1989 by Adrienne Rich.

Theodore Roethke: "The Premonition," copyright © 1941 by Theodore Roethke.

"Cuttings (later)," copyright © 1948 by Theodore Roethke. "In Evening Air," copyright © 1960 by Beatrice Roethke, Administratrix of the Estate of Theodore Roethke. "In a Dark Time," copyright © 1960 by Beatrice Roethke, Administratrix of the Estate of Theodore Roethke. "Meditation at Oyster River," copyright © 1960 by Beatrice Roethke, Administratrix of the Estate of Theodore Roethke. "Elegy for Jane," copyright © 1950 by Theodore Roethke. "The Waking," copyright © 1953 by Theodore Roethke. "I Knew a Woman," copyright © 1954 by Theodore Roethke. "Forcing House," copyright © 1946 by Theodore Roethke. "Weed Puller," copyright © 1946 by Editorial Publications, Inc. "My Papa's Waltz," copyright © 1942 by Hearst Magazines, Inc. From *The Collected Poems of Theodore Roethke.* All used by permission of Doubleday, a division of Bantam Doubleday Dell Publishing Group, Inc.

Anne Sexton: "Us" and "In Celebration of My Uterus" from *Love Poems* by Anne Sexton. Copyright © 1967, 1968, 1969 by Anne Sexton. "The Fury of Cocks" from *The Death Notebooks* by Anne Sexton. Copyright © 1974 by Anne Sexton. "With Mercy for the Greedy," "To a Friend Whose Work Has Come to Triumph," and "The Abortion" from *All My Pretty Ones* by Anne Sexton. "Her Kind" from *To Bedlam and Part Way Back* by Anne Sexton. Copyright © 1960 by Anne Sexton. "Man and Wife" from *Live or Die* by Anne Sexton. Copyright © 1966 by Anne Sexton. "Rowing" and "Two Hands" from *The Awful Rowing Toward God* by Anne Sexton. Copyright © 1975 by Loring Conant, Jr., Executor of the Estate of Anne Sexton. All reprinted by permission of Houghton Mifflin Co.

Charles Simic: "Pastoral" copyright © 1971 by Charles Simic. "Dismantling the Silence" copyright © 1971 by Charles Simic. "Bestiary for the Fingers of My Right Hand" copyright © 1971 by Charles Simic. "Poem (Every morning)" copyright © 1971 by Charles Simic. "Watermelons" copyright © 1974 by Charles Simic. "Toy Factory" copyright © 1980 by Charles Simic. "Classic Ballroom Dances" copyright © 1980 by Charles Simic. "Northern Exposure" copyright © 1982 by Charles Simic. "My Weariness of Epic Proportions" copyright © 1982 by Charles Simic. From *Selected Poems 1963–1983* (Revised and Expanded) copyright © 1990 by Charles Simic. All reprinted with the permission of George Braziller, Inc. "A Letter," "The Big Machine," "The Big War," "Heights of Folly," and "Paradise" from THE BOOK OF GODS AND DEVILS, copyright © 1990 by Charles Simic, reprinted by permission of Harcourt Brace Jovanovich, Inc. "To Helen" and "Against Whatever it is That's Encroaching" from UNENDING BLUES, copyright © 1986 by Charles Simic, reprinted by permission of Harcourt Brace Jovanovich, Inc.

Louis Simpson: "Luminous Night," "After Midnight," "American Dreams," "The Silent Piano," and "Sacred Objects" copyright © 1983 by Louis Simpson. Reprinted from *People Live Here: Selected Poems 1949–1983* by Louis Simpson with the permission of BOA Editions, Ltd., 92 Park Ave., Brockport, NY 14420. "To the Western World" and "Hot Night on Water Street." Reprinted from *A Dream of Governors.* Copyright © 1959 by Louis Simpson. Wesleyan University Press by permission of University Press of New England. "American Poetry," "In the Suburbs," and "Walt Whitman at Bear Mountain." Reprinted from *At the End of the Open Road.* Copyright © 1963 by Louis Simpson. Wesleyan University Press by permission of University Press of New England. "Riverside Drive" and "The People Next Door" reprinted from *In the Room We Share* by Louis Simpson. Copyright © 1990 by Paragon House Publishers. By permission of Paragon House Publishers.

W. D. Snodgrass: "April Inventory," "9 (I get numb)," from "Heart's Needle," and "'After Experience Taught Me . . .'," from *Selected Poems.* Copyright © 1987 by W. D. Snodgrass. Reprinted with the permission of Soho Press. "The Mother," copyright © 1977 by W. D. Snodgrass. Reprinted from *Remains* by W. D. Snodgrass. "Eva Braun [22 April, 1944]," "Dr. Joseph Goebbels [1 May, 1945; 1800 hours]," copyright © 1977 by W. D. Snodgrass. Reprinted from *The Führer Bunker: A Cycle of Poems in Progress* by W. D. Snodgrass. All with the permission of BOA Editions, Ltd., 92 Park Ave., Brockport, NY 14420. Selections from "Snow Songs" copyright © 1990 by W. D. Snodgrass. Originally published in the *Kenyon Review.* Reprinted with permission of W. D. Snodgrass.

Gary Snyder: "Vapor Trails." Gary Snyder: *The Back Country.* Copyright © 1968 by Gary Snyder. "Song of the Taste." Gary Snyder: *Regarding Wave.* Copyright © 1968 by Gary Snyder. First Printed in *Poetry.* "I Went into the Maverick Bar," "The Bath," and "As for Poets." Gary Snyder: *Turtle Island.* Copyright © 1974 by Gary Snyder. All reprinted by permission of New Directions Publishing Corporation. "Hay for the Horses," "Riprap," and "Milton by Firelight." Excerpted from *Riprap and Cold Mountain Poems*, copyright © 1965 by Gary Snyder. Published by North Point Press and reprinted by permission. "Axe Handles" and "Soy Sauce." Excerpted from *Axe Handles*, copyright © 1983 by Gary Snyder. Published by North Point Press and reprinted by permission.

William Stafford: "At the Bomb Testing Site," "Travelling Through the Dark," "Vocation," "My Father: October 1942," "Across Kansas," "A Family Turn," "An Introduction to Some Poems," "Report from a Far Place," and "The Stick in the Forest" copyright © 1977 by William Stafford. Reprinted from *Stories That Could Be True: New and Collected Poems* with permission of William Stafford. "Answerers," "The Early Ones," "Things That Happen Where There Aren't Any People," "Notice What This Poem Is Not Doing," copyright © 1980 by William Stafford. Reprinted from *Things That Happen Where There Aren't Any People* by William Stafford with the permission of BOA Editions, Ltd., 92 Park Ave., Brockport, NY 14420. "Temporary Facts" and "Assurance," from *Smoke's Way: Poems from Limited Editions 1968–1981* (Graywolf Press, 1983). Reprinted with the permission of Graywolf Press, St. Paul, Minnesota. "Ode to Garlic" from *An Oregon Message* by William Stafford. Copyright © 1987 by William Stafford. Reprinted by permission of Harper & Row, Publishers.

Gerald Stern: "At Bickford's," "The Cemetery of Orange Trees in Crete," "The Shirt Poem," "Weeping and Wailing," and "Romance" from *Leaving Another Kingdom — Selected Poems* by Gerald Stern. Copyright © 1990 by Gerald Stern. Reprinted by permission of HarperCollins Publishers Inc. "R for Rosemary," "One Gift," "Three Hearts" copyright © 1990 Gerald Stern. Reprinted with the permission of Gerald Stern. "Lord, Forgive a Spirit," and "The War Against the Jews" copyright © 1981 by Gerald Stern. Reprinted from *Red Coal*, as published by Houghton Mifflin Company, with the permission of Gerald Stern.

Mark Strand: "Sleeping with One Eye Open," "Old People on the Nursing Home Porch," "Keeping Things Whole," "The Mailman," "Eating Poetry," "The One Song," "The Garden," "Shooting Whales." From *Selected Poems* by Mark Strand. Copyright © 1979, 1980 by Mark Strand. Reprinted by permission of Alfred A. Knopf, Inc. "The End." From *The Continuous Life* by Mark Strand. Copyright © 1990 by Mark Strand. Reprinted by permission of Alfred A. Knopf, Inc. "Always" copyright © 1983 by Mark Strand. Reprinted from the broadside published by Palaemon Press, with the permission of Mark Strand.

Lucien Stryk: "Awakening," "To a Japanese Poet," "The Cannery," "Summer," "Letter to Jean-Paul Baudot," "Farmer," "Cherries," "Exterminator," "Watching War Movies," "Juggler," and "In Our Time" from *Collected Poems 1953–1983* by Lucien Stryk. "Black Monday" from *Of Pen and Ink and Paper Scraps* by Lucien Stryk. Reprinted with the permission of The Ohio University Press/Swallow Press, Athens, OH.

Richard Wilbur: "Transit" from NEW AND COLLECTED POEMS, copyright © 1988 by Richard Wilbur, reprinted by permission of Harcourt Brace Jovanovich, Inc. "Cottage Street, 1953" and "The Writer" from THE MIND-READER: NEW POEMS, copyright © 1976 by Richard Wilbur, reprinted by permission of Harcourt Brace Jovanovich, Inc. "A Baroque Wall-Fountain in the Villa Sciarra" and "Love Calls Us to the Things of This World" from THINGS OF THIS WORLD, copyright © 1956 and renewed 1984 by Richard Wilbur, reprinted by permission of Harcourt Brace Jovanovich, Inc. "On the Eyes of an SS Officer," "Potato," "A Dubious Night," and "Praise in Summer" from THE BEAUTIFUL CHANGES AND OTHER POEMS, copyright © 1947 and renewed 1975 by Richard Wilbur, reprinted by permission of Harcourt Brace Jovanovich, Inc. "Year's End" from CEREMONY AND OTHER POEMS, copyright © 1950 and renewed 1978 by Richard Wilbur, reprinted by permission of Harcourt Brace Jovanovich, Inc. "Advice to a Prophet" from ADVICE TO A PROPHET AND OTHER POEMS, copyright © 1961 and renewed 1989 by Richard Wilbur, reprinted by permission of Harcourt Brace Jovanovich, Inc.

C. K. Williams: "It Is This Way with Men," "Then the Brother of the Wind," "They Warned Him Then They Threw Him Away," "From My Window," "The Gas Station," and "Tar" from *Poems 1963–1983* by C. K. Williams. Copyright © 1969, 1971, 1977, 1983, 1988 by C. K. Williams. "First Desires," "Repression," "The Critic," "The Ladder," "War," and "The Modern" from *Flesh and Blood* by C. K. Williams. Copyright © 1987 by C. K. Williams. Reprinted by permission of Farrar, Straus and Giroux, Inc.

ACKNOWLEDGMENTS

Charles Wright: "The New Poem," "Blackwater Mountain," "Snow," "Equation," "Reunion," "April." Reprinted from *Country Music: Selected Early Poems.* Copyright © 1982 by Charles Wright. Wesleyan University Press by permission of University Press of New England. Excerpt from "Three Poems for the New Year," "Driving Through Tennessee," "California Dreaming," and "Night Journal" from *The World of the Ten Thousand Things* by Charles Wright. Copyright © 1990 by Charles Wright. Reprinted by permission of Farrar, Straus and Giroux, Inc.

James Wright: "A Poem of Towers" and "Beautiful Ohio" from *Above the River* by James Wright. Copyright © 1990 by Anne Wright. Reprinted by permission of Farrar, Straus and Giroux, Inc. "A Blessing," "As I Step Over a Puddle . . .," "Autumn Begins in Martins Ferry, Ohio," "Fear is What Quickens Me," "In Response to a Rumor . . .," "The Jewel," "Lying in a Hammock . . .," "Saint Judas," "Goodbye to the Poetry of Calcium," "Saying Dante Aloud," and "A Small Grove in Torri del Benaco." Reprinted from *Above the River: The Complete Poems.* Copyright © 1990 by Anne Wright. Introduction © 1990 by Donald Hall. Wesleyan University Press by permission of University Press of New England. "Ohioan Pastoral," "Lightning Bugs Asleep in the Afternoon," and "The Journey." From *This Journey* by James Wright. Copyright © 1977, 1978, 1979, 1980, 1981, 1982 by Anne Wright. Reprinted by permission of Random House, Inc.

To the Student

Will you take the time to write your reactions to *Contemporary American Poetry*? Your comments will help us to plan future editions of the work. Please fill out the questionnaire and mail it to:

Marketing Services
College Division
Houghton Mifflin Company
One Beacon Street
Boston, MA 02108

1. Please give the name and number of the course for which you used this textbook. Indicate whether the course is one or two semesters.

   _____

   Name of your college or university

   _____

   Which year did you take the course?
   ____ Freshman ____ Sophomore ____ Junior ____ Senior

2. Please check the name of each poet below whose works you read for the course.

__ Ammons	__ Gardner	__ Kunitz	__ Roethke
__ Ashbery	__ Ginsberg	__ Levertov	__ Sexton
__ Bell	__ Glück	__ Levine	__ Simic
__ Berryman	__ Hall	__ Logan	__ Simpson
__ Bishop	__ Harper	__ Lowell	__ Snodgrass
__ Bly	__ Hass	__ Matthews	__ Snyder
__ Brooks	__ Hayden	__ Merrill	__ Stafford
__ Clifton	__ Hugo	__ Merwin	__ Stern
__ Creeley	__ Ignatow	__ O'Hara	__ Strand
__ Dickey	__ Jarrell	__ Oliver	__ Stryk
__ Dove	__ Justice	__ Olson	__ Wilbur
__ Dugan	__ Kinnell	__ Piercy	__ Williams
__ Duncan	__ Kizer	__ Plath	__ C. Wright
__ Ferlinghetti	__ Kumin	__ Rich	__ J. Wright

3. Of the poets you read, please list the five or so who made the strongest impression on you. _____

   _____

4. Of the poets you read, please list any whose works you feel you did not understand or appreciate. _____

   _____

5. When you studied a given poet, did you read all of his or her works in the anthology?   __ Usually   __ Sometimes   __ Rarely

6. Did your course include poets who are not represented in this text-book? __ Yes __ No   If you read additional poets, please list as many as you can recall. _____

_____

7. Do you plan to keep this textbook for your own library?
__ Yes   __ No

8. How much did you use the Notes on the Poets at the back of the book?
__ Very often __ Often __ Occasionally __ Rarely __ Never

9. Did you read the essay about contemporary poetry at the back of the book?   __ Yes __ No   If yes; please comment on its usefulness. _____

_____

10. Did you use the selected bibliography of critical works?
__ Yes   __ No

11. Please make any additional comments that you care to about the anthology.

_____

_____

_____

_____

_____

_____

_____

_____

_____

_____

_____

_____

Thank you for your help.